An Investment in the Future

Charles Schwab the great industrialist and entrepreneur said, "We are all sales-people every day of our lives, selling our ideas and enthusiasm to those with whom we come in contact." As authors, we suggest that you retain this book for future reference. Periodic review of the ideas in this text will help you daily in areas such as:

- interviewing for new jobs in the future
- understanding and training salespeople who work for you or with you
- selling new ideas to senior management, co-workers, or employees you might be supervising
- selling products or services that you represent as a salesperson

We wish you much success and happiness in applying your knowledge of personal selling.

Gerald L. Manning   *Barry L. Reece*

Selling Today

BUILDING QUALITY PARTNERSHIPS

SEVENTH EDITION

Selling Today

BUILDING QUALITY PARTNERSHIPS

GERALD L. MANNING
DES MOINES AREA COMMUNITY COLLEGE

BARRY L. REECE
VIRGINIA POLYTECHNIC INSTITUTE AND STATE UNIVERSITY

Prentice Hall
Upper Saddle River, New Jersey 07458

Senior Acquisitions Editor: Donald J. Hull
Assistant Editor: John Larkin
Editorial Assistant: Jim Campbell
VicePresident/Editorial Director: James Boyd
Director of Development: Steve Deitmer
Marketing Manager: John Chillingworth
Production Editor: Aileen Mason
Managing Editor: Dee Josephson
Associate Managing Editor: Linda DeLorenzo
Manufacturing Supervisor: Arnold Vila
Manufacturing Manager: Vincent Scelta
Design Manager: Pat Smythe
Interior Design: Siren Design
Cover Design: Pat Smythe
Composition: Progressive Publishing Alternatives
Cover Illustration: Salem Krieger
Photo Research: Melinda Alexander

Credits and acknowledgments for materials borrowed from other sources and reproduced, with permission, in this textbook appear on pages 507–508.

Copyright © 1998, 1995, 1992 by Prentice-Hall, Inc.
A Simon & Schuster Company
Upper Saddle River, New Jersey 07458

Library of Congress Cataloging-in-Publication Data

Manning, Gerald L.
    Selling today : building quality partnerships / Gerald L. Manning,
Barry L. Reece.—7th ed.
        p.   cm.
    Includes bibliographical references and index.
    ISBN 0-13-613837-3
    1. Selling.   I. Reece, Barry L.   II. Title.
HF5438.25.M35   1997
658.85—dc21   97-11434
                                                                        CIP

Prentice-Hall International (UK) Limited, London
Prentice-Hall of Australia Pty. Limited, Sydney
Prentice-Hall Canada, Inc., Toronto
Prentice-Hall Hispanoamericana, S.A., Mexico
Prentice-Hall of India Private Limited, New Delhi
Prentice-Hall of Japan, Inc., Tokyo
Simon & Schuster Asia Pte. Ltd., Singapore
Editora Prentice-Hall do Brasil, Ltda., Rio de Janeiro

Printed in the United States of America

10 9 8 7 6 5 4 3 2 1

WE WISH TO DEDICATE THIS BOOK TO
OUR WIVES WHOSE PATIENCE AND SUPPORT
MAKE OUR WORK POSSIBLE.

BETH HALL MANNING
AND
VERA MARIE REECE

BRIEF CONTENTS

CONTENTS

Part II

Developing a Relationship Strategy

4. ETHICS: THE FOUNDATION FOR RELATIONSHIPS IN SELLING   72

Part III

Developing a Product Strategy

5. ACQUIRING PRODUCT INFORMATION   92

Part IV

Developing a Customer Strategy

Part V

Developing a Presentation Strategy

14. SERVICING THE SALE — 316

Part VI

Management of Self and Others

15. MANAGEMENT OF SELF: THE KEY TO GREATER SALES PRODUCTIVITY — 340

16. COMMUNICATION STYLES: MANAGING THE RELATIONSHIP PROCESS   362

PREFACE

Personal selling continues to be a field of study characterized by two contrasting themes. Salespeople who achieve long-term success are well grounded in the fundamentals of personal selling. The ability to accurately identify the customer's needs and to prescribe the appropriate solution provides one example of a timeless fundamental. On the other hand, salespeople must be prepared to adopt new practices in response to ever-changing market conditions. Many of today's sales are very complex and are characterized by an intense flow of information and contacts with several people who can influence the purchase decision. Success in dealing with a complex sale may require greater mastery of relationship-building skills and the application of modern sales automation technology. The seventh edition of *Selling Today: Building Quality Partnerships* provides balanced treatment of both of these major themes.

Previous editions of *Selling Today* have chronicled the evolution of consultative selling, strategic selling, partnering, value-added selling, sales force automation, and other major developments in personal selling. This edition provides new material on each of these important concepts. *Selling Today* is a practical text that includes a large number of real-world examples obtained from a range of progressive organizations (large and small) such as Baxter Healthcare, Hyatt Regency Hotels, Nordstrom, IBM, Cadalyst Resources, and Xerox Corporation.

SPECIAL ACKNOWLEDGMENTS

Selling Today has been the recipient of many accolades over the years. Two of the most important honors will be of interest to current and potential adopters. *Selling Today* was selected by Intelecom for use in its telecourse entitled, *The Sales Connection*. An esteemed panel of business and academic professionals spent over 2 years developing this important new college course. *Selling Today* was also selected by Certified Marketing Services, Inc. (CMSI) for use with the first international program for sales certification. The International Organization for Standardization (ISO) authorized CMSI to develop and administer this important new program. The major objective of this certification program is to increase the standard of excellence in the field of personal selling.

IMPROVEMENTS IN THE SEVENTH EDITION

The seventh edition of *Selling Today: Building Quality Partnerships* reflects suggestions from current adopters and reviewers, interviews with salespeople and sales managers, and a thorough review of the current literature on personal selling. Several important improvements appear in this edition and in the teaching/learning package. The most significant changes include:

1. Expanded coverage of ethics in personal selling. This edition provides a three-dimensional approach to the study of ethical decision making. One dimension is a chapter on ethics (Chapter 4) titled "Ethics: The Foundation for Relationships in Selling." Chapter 4 provides a contemporary examination of ethical considerations in selling. This chapter, formerly Chapter 17, has been positioned closer to the front of the text. The second dimension involves the discussion of ethical issues in selected chapters throughout the text. The authors believe that ethics in selling is so important that it cannot be covered in a single chapter. The third dimension is an exciting business game entitled, *Gray Issues—Ethical Decision Making in Personal Selling.* Participation in this game provides students with an introduction to a range of real-life ethical dilemmas. It stimulates in-depth thinking about the ethical consequences of their decisions and actions. Students play the game to learn without having to play for keeps.

2. The seventh edition keeps the reader in touch with what is happening in the real world with "Internet Exercises" provided at the end of each chapter. These exercises provide students with an opportunity to acquire additional information on such topics as career opportunities in selling, sales training, sales automation, ethical issues in selling, developing prospect lists and many other topics. "Internet Exercises" give students a greater appreciation for the Internet as a source of additional information on topics presented in each chapter.

3. Expanded coverage of value-added selling strategies. In today's new age of boundless competition, salespeople need to know how to add value to the products they sell. Value-added benefits often provide the competitive edge needed to close the sale. The salesperson is usually in the best position to discover what adds value (in the mind of the customer) and then determine ways to add this value. Expanded coverage of value-added selling strategies throughout the text is a significant improvement in the seventh edition.

4. A set of 100 color transparencies is available for use by adopters of the seventh edition of *Selling Today.* The transparency program includes figures, graphs, and key concepts featured in the text. These acetates, with approximately 70 additional slides, will also be available on PowerPoint 4.0. The disk is designed to allow you to present the transparency to your class electronically.

5. With this new edition, we introduce the *Selling Today* home page. This site contains useful information for professors and students, as well as information formerly on disk for ACT! The Professional Contact Management System. Move selling into the information age by going to http://www.selling-today.com.

ORGANIZATION OF THIS BOOK

The material in *Selling Today* is organized around the four pillars of personal selling: relationship strategy, product strategy, customer strategy, and presentation strategy. The two chapters that make up Part I set the stage for an in-depth study of the four strategies. The first chapter describes the evolution of personal selling from 1950 to the present and introduces the four strategies. The second chapter gives students an opportunity to explore specific career opportunities in the four major employment areas: service, retail, wholesale, and manufacturing. Career-minded students will also find the first appendix, "Finding Employment: A Personalized Marketing Approach," very helpful.

Research indicates that high-performance salespeople are better able to build and maintain relationships than are moderate performers. Part II, "Developing a Relationship Strategy," focuses on several important person-to-person relationship-building practices that contribute to success in personal selling. Chapter 4, a new addition to Part II, examines the influence ethics on relationships between customers and salespeople.

Part III, "Developing a Product Strategy," examines the importance of complete and accurate product, company, and competitive knowledge in personal selling. A well-informed salesperson is in a strong position to apply the fundamentals of consultative selling.

Part IV, "Developing a Customer Strategy," presents information on why and how customers buy and explains how to identify prospects. With increased knowledge of the customer, salespeople are in a better position to achieve their sales goals.

The concept of a salesperson as advisor, consultant, and partner to buyers is stressed in Part V, "Developing a Presentation Strategy." The traditional sales presentation that emphasizes closing as the primary objective of personal selling is abandoned in favor of three types of need-satisfaction presentations. As in the sixth edition, the salesperson is viewed as a counselor and consultant. Part VI includes three chapters: "Management of Self: The Key to Greater Sales Productivity," "Communication Styles: Managing the Relationship Process," and "Management of the Sales Force."

LEARNING TOOLS THAT ENHANCE INSTRUCTION

The seventh edition of *Selling Today* includes several learning tools that will aid both teaching and learning.

1. Six challenging video case problems are provided. Each video case problem (10–13 minutes in length) is introduced in the text. These introductions take the form of an opening vignette provided at the beginning of selected chapters. Once students view the video, they study additional case information at the end of the chapter and then prepare answers to thought-provoking questions. The video introduces the student to salespeople employed by real companies. Video case problems are provided for Chapters 1, 3, 5, 7, 9, and 12.

2. An optional role play/simulation provides students with a realistic opportunity to apply major concepts presented in selected chapters. All materials needed for both salesperson and customer roles are provided in this easy-to-use exercise. Easy-to-follow instructions are provided in the text at the end of Chapters 1, 5, 9, 10, 11, 12, 13, and 14. These instructions refer to assignments in Appendix 3. The role play/simulation provides a

bridge between classroom instruction and the real world of personal selling.

3. Each chapter features two insights that focus on the themes "Building Quality Partnerships," and "Building Partnerships in a Diverse World." These insights explore current real-world examples of what the student is learning throughout the text. This feature gives students a contemporary look at personal selling. Each chapter includes the following special features that aid the teaching and learning process:

- A list of learning objectives to help the student focus on the important concepts.
- A summary that provides a brief review of the most important ideas presented.
- A list of key terms that follows the chapter summary.
- A set of review questions that reinforce the student's understanding of the major concepts presented in the chapter.
- A series of application exercises that will provide the reader with an opportunity to apply concepts and practices presented. Each chapter includes one "Internet Exercise."
- A case problem that permits the reader to analyze and interpret actual selling situations. Each case problem is based on a real-life situation.

4. The expansion of information and exercises on sales force automation (SFA) and the opportunity to use an actual SFA program are offered. The trend toward greater use of technology to improve personal selling practices will continue in the years ahead. In response to this important trend the seventh edition features 12 "Building Relationships Through Technology" insights. Each insight explains how salespeople use sales automation to improve quality in the selling process. Optional SFA application exercises are also included in this edition. These interactive exercises give students the opportunity to use the highly acclaimed ACT! software program developed by Symantec, a leader in the field of sales force automation.

See the *Selling-Today* home page at http://www.selling-today.com. The student can use the *Selling-Today* home page to access the ACT! Contact Management System that features a prospect database and other information to be used by students as they make a range of decisions regarding qualifying prospects, approaching prospects, the sales presentation, demonstration, negotiation, closing, and servicing the sale. Students can print prospect profiles, sales letters, and telephone contact lists; conduct key word searches to find important references in the database; and do many other things. Simple single-stroke instructions are provided that enable students to experience the many advances in sales automation. SFA is effectively explained in *ACT! Contact Management System*, a commercially developed two-part video available to qualified adopters.

INTELECOM TELECOURSE

The seventh edition of *Selling Today*, as noted previously, has been selected by Intelecom for use in its video course entitled, "The Sales Connection." A growing number of colleges and universities are embracing distance learning, so this telecourse will likely enjoy continued popularity in the academic community.

SUPPLEMENTS AVAILABLE WITH THE TEXTBOOK

A complete supplements package is available to adopters including a new set of transparency masters with acetates that is available with the seventh edition and 100 color acetates available to adopters. New to this edition is the interactive power point presentation software with over 170 slides covering key concepts presented in the text. Also included in this package is a complete Instructors Resource Manual that contains:

➢ Detailed presentation outlines

➢ Answers to review questions

➢ Copies to be printed for students, and a trainer's guide for the "gray issues" selling ethics game

➢ Suggested responses to learning activities

➢ Copies of printouts for Sales Automation Exercises

➢ Detailed instructions for using the video case problems

➢ A complete trainers guide for using the role play and simulation

➢ A role-playing video tape supplement carefully keyed to learning activities in the text.

A completely revised author-developed test bank that includes over 1,000 questions is available, as is a computerized test bank, Prentice Hall Custom Test.

Prentice Hall Test Manager 2.0: This powerful computerized testing package is available for DOS-based computers in either 3.5-in. or 5.25-in. format. It offers full mouse support, complete question editing, random test generation, graphics and printing capabilities. Toll free technical support is offered to all users, and the Test Manager is free. You may contact your local rep or call our Faculty Support Services department at **1-800-333-7945.** Please identify the main text author, title, and disk size. Some test item files are also available on Macintosh.

For those instructors without access to a computer, we offer the popular **Prentice Hall Telephone Testing Service.** It is simple, fast, and efficient. Simply pick the questions you would like on your test from this bank and call our College Media department at **1-800-842-2958;** outside the United States call 1-201-592-3263. Identify the main text and test questions you would like, as well as any special instructions. We will create the test (or multiple versions, if you wish) and send you a master copy for duplication within 48 hours. Free to adopters for life of text use.

ACKNOWLEDGMENTS

Many people have made contributions to *Selling Today: Building Quality Partnerships*. We are very grateful to Jack W. Linge, who contributed significantly to the development of the sales force automation case study, which is an important addition to this textbook. We would also like to provide special recognition to Russell P. Moorehead for his creative development of the power point presentation, transparencies and to Darvish Shadravah for his creative work as our Web master. Throughout the years the text has been improved as a result of numerous helpful comments and recommendations. We extend special appreciation to the following persons.

Robert Bochrath
Gateway Technical Institute

Jim Boespflug
Arapahoe Community College

Jerry Boles
Western Kentucky University

Jim Boles
Georgia State University

Duane Brickner
South Mountain Community College

Don Brumlow
St. Johns College

Murray Brunton
Central Ohio Technical College

William R. Christensen
Community College of Denver (North Campus)

Larry Davis
Youngstown State University

Lynn Dawson
Louisiana Technical University—Ruston

Dayle Dietz
North Dakota State School of Science

Wendal Ferguson
Richland College

Dean Flowers
Waukesha County Technical College

Donald Hackett
Wichita State University

Jon Hawes
The University of Akron

Ken Hodge, Marketing Manager
Nordson

Norm Humble
Kirkwood Community College

Richard Jones
Marshall University

Katy Kemp
Middle Tennessee State University

Wesley Koch
Illinois Central College

Stephen Koernig
University of Illinois—Chicago

R. Dale Lounsburg
Emporia State College

George H. Lucas, Jr.
Texas A & M University

Alice Lupinacci
University of Texas at Arlington

Leslie E. Martin
University of Wisconsin, Whitewater

Jack Maroun
Herkimer County Community College

Tammy McCullough
Eastern Michigan University

Bob McMahon
Appalachian State University

Darrel Millard
Kirkwood Community College

Ron Milliaman
Western Kentucky University

Irene Mittlemark
Kingsborough Community College

Rita Mix
Our Lady of the Lake University—Dallas

Mark Mulder
Grand Rapids Junior College

Gordon Myron
Util. Inc.

John Odell
Marketing Catalysts

James Randall
Georgia Southern University

Stan Salzman
American River College

Donald T. Sedik
William Rainey Harper College

Robert E. Smiley
Indiana State University, Terra Houte

C. Phillip Smith
*John C. Calhoun, State Community
College, Alabama*

Robert Thompson
Indiana State University

Rae Verity
Southern Alberta Institute of Technology

Curtis W. Youngman
Salt Lake Community College

Donald A. Zimmerman
University of Akron

Finally, we thank the people on the book team at Prentice Hall in New Jersey: Don Hull, Aileen Mason, John Larkin, Jim Campbell, John Chillingworth, Pat Smythe, and Arnold Vila.

ABOUT THE AUTHORS

Dr. Barry L. Reece, Professor
Virginia Polytechnic Institute and State University

Dr. Reece has devoted more than 25 years to teaching, research, consulting, and the development of training programs in the areas of sales, supervision, human relations, and management. He has conducted over 600 seminars and workshops for public and private sector organizations. He has written several textbooks and articles in the areas of sales, supervision, and management. Dr. Reece was named "Trainer of the Year" by the Valleys of Virginia Chapter of the American Society for Training and Development and was awarded the "Excellence in Teaching Award" by the College of Human Resources and Education at Virginia Polytechnic Institute and State University.

Mr. Gerald L. Manning, Chair
Marketing/Management Department Des Moines Area Community College

Mr. Manning has served as a chair of the Marketing/Management Department since 1967. In addition to his teaching and administrative duties, he is actively involved as a consultant and trainer to numerous national sales and marketing firms. Mr. Manning also serves as a consultant to several companies that provide computer aided design and sales automation services, and firms that produce and distribute sales training materials. He appears regularly as a speaker at national conferences. Mr. Manning has received the "Outstanding Instructor of the Year" award given annually by his college.

Keeping Current in a Changing World

Throughout the past decade, Professors Manning and Reece have relied on three strategies to keep current in the dynamic field of personal selling. First, both are actively involved in sales training and consulting. Frequent interaction with salespeople and sales managers provides valuable insights regarding contemporary issues and developments in the field of personal selling. A second major strategy involves extensive research and development activities. The major focus of these activities has been factors that contribute to high-performance salespeople. The third major strategy involves completion of training and development programs offered by America's most respected sales training companies. Professors Manning and Reece have completed seminars and workshops offered by Learning International, Wilson Learning Corporation, Forum Corporation, Franklin Quest, and several other companies.

Selling Today

BUILDING QUALITY PARTNERSHIPS

Part I

Developing a Personal Selling Philosophy

The two chapters that make up Part I explain the important role of personal selling in organizations, in economic systems, in social reform movements, and most importantly in the personal lives of the millions of men and women enjoying rewarding sales-oriented careers in the new global marketplace.

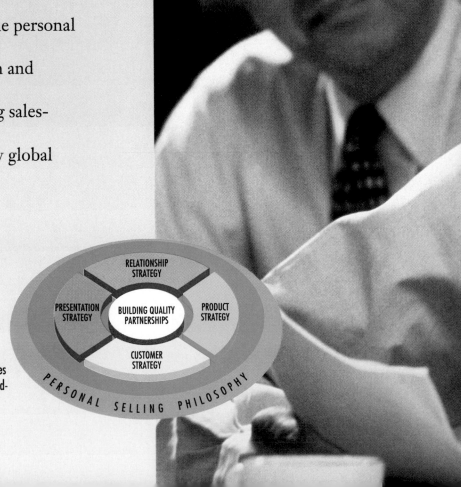

Every employee at Federal Express must be sales oriented and each manager must be an outstanding individual salesperson.

FEDERAL EXPRESS

CHAPTER 1

Personal Selling and the Marketing Concept

LEARNING OBJECTIVES

When you finish reading this chapter, you should be able to

1. Describe the contributions of personal selling to the global economy

2. Define personal selling and discuss personal selling as an extension of the marketing concept

3. Describe the evolution of consultative-style selling from the marketing era to the present

4. Define strategic selling and name the four broad strategic areas in the strategic/consultative selling model

5. Describe the evolution of partnering and discuss how it relates to the quality improvement process

6. Describe the personal benefits that can be derived from developing the skill of selling

Body Glove International, a leading manufacturer of wet suits for a variety of water sports, had a humble beginning. Bill and Randy Meistrell, founders of the company, were active in surfing and scuba diving in the early 1950s when good quality wet suits were hard to find. They decided to turn this problem into an opportunity and developed their own wet suit design.

The first suits were sold at a small dive shop in Redondo Beach, California. Today Body Glove International is a multimillion dollar global company with a reputation for quality products and quality service. According to Randy Meistrell, executive vice president, it is a company that relies on a well-trained sales force to enhance sales and service.[1]

Personal Selling—A Positive Influence on Our Global Economy

Zak Mandour is a foot soldier in the economic battle to win the hearts of consumers who are willing to spend from $40,000 to $70,000 for a luxury automobile. His battle station is Jaguar of Ottawa, a Jaguar dealer located in Ottawa, Canada.[2] Like other Jaguar sales representatives in Canada, Germany, France, and the United States, he has plenty of competition from BMW, Lexus, and Mercedes-Benz. Also, Cadillac would like to achieve a stronger presence in the international market. Like many other salespeople today, Zak recognizes that global competition brings both challenges and opportunities.

Throughout the past several decades the global economy has evolved from one of excess demand to one of excess supply. Many industries do not operate at full capacity. Unless we can find buyers for the world's goods and services, the health of our global economy will suffer.

A one-world market exists for products ranging from consulting services to computers. Global companies that build, buy, and sell across borders have, in many cases, been rewarded with increased sales. Colgate-Palmolive Company provides a good example of a company that maintains a sales staff in several international markets. The company reaps over 60 percent of its total sales from outside the United States and Canada.[3] Market-oriented economies depend heavily on promotional activities. The vigorous promotion of sales has become the hallmark of developed nations.

Personal selling, sometimes described as *micromarketing* in action, also stimulates the growth and development of business firms across North America. It can be argued that in an age when markets are becoming increasingly fragmented, the personalized approach used in personal selling will become more important. This is true in the case of those companies serving markets charac-

BUILDING RELATIONSHIPS IN A DIVERSE WORLD

PERSONAL SELLING IN CHINA

When Arthur Miller went to China to direct his award winning play *Death of a Salesman* he was warned that the Chinese would probably not be familiar with the major theme of the play. The China experts said, "The Chinese are never going to understand. They don't know what a salesman is." Miller discovered that they know very well what a salesperson is, but they were prohibited from engaging in personal selling. Now, just a few years later, every little town and village has some kind of privately owned factory; and, whether they're making pottery or shirts, they've got a sales force out on the road seeking customers.

Some marketers said the Chinese are too poor to form a major international market. Procter and Gamble didn't agree with this viewpoint. Several years ago Procter and Gamble began selling Tide laundry detergent, Head & Shoulders shampoo, and other products in China. To gain entry into local retail stores, Procter and Gamble hired and trained a large number of salespeople who presented the American products with enthusiasm. Today, Procter and Gamble is the largest daily-use–consumer-products company in China.

Motorola is betting that China will emerge as the world's largest consumer of electronic products—everything from microwave ovens to telephones to PCs and TVs. Motorola has invested $1.2 billion in a variety of Chinese ventures.[a]

The Jaguar XK8. Salespeople like Zak Mandour recognize that global competion brings both challenges and opportunities.

terized by high-value customized goods and services with relatively long and complex decision-making processes.[4]

There are millions of salespeople employed throughout the world. Because neither income nor profit results until a sale is made, firms are heavily dependent on salespeople to keep orders coming.

Personal Selling—A Definition and a Philosophy

Personal selling involves person-to-person communication with a prospect. It is a process of developing customer relationships, discovering customer needs, matching the appropriate products with these needs, and communicating benefits through informing, reminding, or persuading. The term **product** should be broadly interpreted to encompass services, ideas, and issues. Increasingly, personal selling is viewed as an important form of customer service. In an ideal situation the salesperson diagnoses the customer's needs and custom fits the product to meet these needs.

Preparation for a career in personal selling begins with the development of a personal philosophy or set of beliefs that provides guidance. To some degree this philosophy is like the rudder that steers a ship. Without a rudder the ship's direction is unpredictable. Without a personal philosophy the salesperson's behavior is also unpredictable.

The development of a **personal selling philosophy** involves three things: adopt the marketing concept, value personal selling, and assume the role of a problem solver or partner in helping customers make buying decisions (Fig. 1.1). These three prescriptions for success in personal selling are presented here as part of the Strategic/Consultative Selling Model. This model will be expanded in future chapters to include additional strategic steps in the selling process.

Strategic/Consultative Selling Model	
Strategic step	Prescription
DEVELOP A PERSONAL SELLING PHILOSOPHY	☐ ADOPT MARKETING CONCEPT ☐ VALUE PERSONAL SELLING ☐ BECOME A PROBLEM SOLVER/PARTNER

FIGURE 1.1 Today, salespeople use a strategic plan based on a personal philosophy that emphasizes adopting the marketing concept, valuing personal selling, and becoming a problem solver/partner.

Personal Selling as an Extension of the Marketing Concept

A careful examination of personal selling practices during the past 40 years reveals some positive developments. We have seen the evolution of personal selling from an era that emphasized *pushing or peddling products* to an era that emphasizes *partnering*. Throughout this period we have seen the emergence of new thinking patterns concerning every aspect of sales and sales management. Salespeople today are no longer the flamboyant product "pitchmen" of the past. Instead they are increasingly becoming diagnosticians of customers' needs and problems. A growing number of salespeople recognize that the quality of the partnerships they create is as important as the quality of the products they sell.

THE ULTIMATE PURPOSE OF BUSINESS

The ultimate purpose of every business should be to satisfy the customer. As Peter Drucker observed, "The customers define the business." Thomas Stewart, *Fortune* editor, agrees:

> . . . *an economy cannot be described by adding up how many tons of rebar it makes, how many passenger-miles of air travel it logs, how much wood its woodchucks chuck per hour. All these count (and we count them), but in the final analysis what matters is how well an economy satisfies its customers' needs and wants.*[5]

As you might expect, business firms vary in terms of how strongly they embrace customer-driven marketing. Some firms have adopted this philosophy only in recent years.

EVOLUTION OF THE MARKETING CONCEPT

What is the **marketing concept?** When a business firm moves from a product orientation to a consumer orientation, we say it has adopted the marketing concept. This concept springs from the belief that the firm should dedicate all of its policies, planning, and operation to the satisfaction of the customer.

The marketing era in the United States began in the 1950s (Table 1.1). J. B. McKitterick, a General Electric executive, is credited with making one of the earliest formal statements indicating corporate interest in the marketing concept. In a paper written in 1957 he observed that the principal marketing function of a company is to determine what the customer wants and then develop the appropriate product or service. This view contrasted with the prevail-

The foundation for the marketing concept is a belief that a firm should dedicate all of its policies, planning, and operations to the satisfaction of the customer.

ing practice of that period, which was to develop products and then build customer interest in those products.

The foundation for the marketing concept is a business philosophy that leaves no doubt in the mind of every employee that customer satisfaction is of primary importance. All energies are directed toward satisfying the customer. Many business leaders believe that excellent customer service is the most important reason for growth and customer confidence.

Business firms vary in terms of how strongly they support the marketing concept. Some firms have gone the extra mile to satisfy the needs and wants of their customers:

> Nordstrom, a Seattle-based department store chain, has turned exacting standards of customer service into a billion-dollar annual business. A major key to Nordstrom's success is the quality of the sales staff. They are well trained and encouraged to do almost anything within reason to satisfy customers. Recently Nordstrom received the highest American Customer Satisfaction Index score in the department store category.[6]

> IBM has recovered from a long period of depressed sales by returning to its roots. Once again the company is paying close attention to customer needs and figuring out how to satisfy them. IBM is trying harder to get close to the customer and become a trusted partner.

> Frito-Lay, one of the largest U.S. manufacturers of snack foods, has adopted a "service to sales" approach to doing business. Every effort is made to provide needed support services for the company's 12,800-member sales force to meet the needs of retailers. Frito-Lay was one of the first companies to give its salespeople handheld computers to transmit sales data back to headquarters.[7]

TABLE 1.1 EVOLUTION OF PERSONAL SELLING (1950 TO PRESENT)

SALES AND MARKETING EMPHASIS	TIME PERIOD	IMPORTANT EVENTS	SELLING EMPHASIS
Marketing Era Begins *Organizations determine needs and wants of target markets and adapt themselves to delivering desired satisfaction. Product orientation is replaced by a customer orientation.*	*Middle 1950s*	• *J. B. McKitterick, General Electric executive, presents a paper in 1957 on applications of the marketing concept.* • *John Naisbitt cites 1956–1957 as the beginning of the information age.*	• *More organizations recognize that the salesperson is in a position to collect product, market, and service information regarding the buyer's needs.*
Consultative Selling Era *Salespeople are becoming diagnosticians of customers' needs as well as consultants offering well-considered recommendations. Mass markets are breaking into target markets.*	*Late 1960s to early 1970s*	• *In the late 1960s Wilson Learning Corporation developed a sales training course entitled "Counselor Selling."* • *In 1973 Mack Hanan writes* Consultative Selling.	• *Buyer needs are identified through two-way communication.* • *Information giving and negotiation tactics replace manipulation.*
Strategic Selling Era *The evolution of a more complex selling environment and greater emphasis on market niches creates the need for greater structure and more emphasis on planning.*	*Early 1980s*	• Strategic Selling *is written by Robert Miller and Stephen Heiman in 1985.* • *Learning International, The Forum Corporation, and Wilson Learning Corporation develop sales training courses that emphasize strategic selling.*	• *Strategy is given as much attention as selling tactics.* • *Product positioning is given more attention.*
Partnering Era *Salespeople are encouraged to think of everything they say or do in the context of their long-term, high quality partnership with individual customers. Sales force automation provides specific customer information.*	*1990 to the present*	• *Tom Peters, Larry Wilson and others popularize the "Lifetime" customer concept.* • *American Media, Inc. produces a training film entitled "Partnering: The Heart of Selling Today."*	• *Customer supplants the product as the driving force in sales.* • *Greater emphasis on total quality relationships that result in repeat business and referrals.*

Nordstrom views personal selling as an important dimension of their marketing program. This company also realizes the value of relationships in creating repeat business.

MARKETING CONCEPT YIELDS MARKETING MIX

Once the marketing concept becomes an integral part of a firm's philosophy, its management seeks to develop a network of marketing activities that will maximize customer service and ensure profitability. The combination of elements making up a program based on the marketing concept is known as the **marketing mix** (Fig. 1.2). According to Jerome McCarthy, these elements are product, promotion, place, and price.[8] For a marketing program to achieve the desired results, each function must be executed effectively.

One of the four P's, promotion, can be further subdivided into advertising, public relations, sales promotion, and personal selling. When a company

FIGURE 1.2   Each of the elements that make up the marketing mix must be executed effectively for a marketing program to achieve the desired results.

Product	Place
Price	Promotion

adopts the marketing concept, it must determine how some combination of these elements can result in maximum customer satisfaction.

THE EXPANDING ROLE OF PERSONAL SELLING

Every marketer must decide how much time and money to invest in each of the four areas of the marketing mix. The decision must be objective; no one can afford to invest money in a marketing strategy that does not provide continuing customer satisfaction. *Personal selling is the major promotional method used in American business—whether measured by people employed, by total expenditures, or by expenses as a percentage of sales.*[9] Firms make large investments in personal selling in response to several major trends: products and services are becoming increasingly sophisticated and complex; competition has greatly increased in most product areas; and demand for quality, value, and service by customers has risen sharply. In response to these trends, personal selling has evolved to a new level of professionalism. Personal selling has evolved through three distinct developmental periods: the consultative selling era, the strategic selling era, and the partnering era. We will examine each of these developments.

Evolution of Consultative-Style Selling

Consultative-style selling, which emerged in the late 1960s and early 1970s, is an extension of the marketing concept (see Table 1.1). This approach emphasizes need identification, which is achieved through effective communication between the salesperson and the customer. The salesperson establishes two-way communication by asking appropriate questions and listening carefully to the customer's responses. The salesperson assumes the role of consultant and offers well-considered recommendations. Negotiation replaces manipulation as the salesperson sets the stage for a long-term partnership. Salespeople who have adopted the consultative style of selling possess a keen ability to listen, define the customer's problem, and offer one or more solutions.[10]

Wilson Learning Corporation developed one of the first sales training courses that featured consultative-style selling concepts. In the late 1960s the company began offering "Counselor Selling," a course that emphasized need identification by use of effective two-way communications. In 1973 Mark Hanan authored the first book on consultative selling. In *Consultative Selling* (which emphasized industrial selling) he encouraged salespeople to research the client's operation, analyze trends within the client's industry, and in general become an expert problem solver.

Service, retail, manufacturing, and wholesale firms that embrace the marketing concept have already adopted or are currently adopting consultative-style selling practices. The major features of consultative-style selling are as follows:

1. The customer is seen as a *person to be served*, not a prospect to be sold. Consultative salespeople believe their function is to help the buyer make an intelligent decision. They use a four-step process that includes need discovery, selection of the product, a need-satisfaction presentation, and servicing the sale (Fig. 1.3). These customer-centered strategies will be fully developed and explained in Chapters 9 to 14.

FIGURE 1.3 The Consultative Sales Presentation Guide. This comtemporary presentation guide emphasizes the customer as a person to be served.

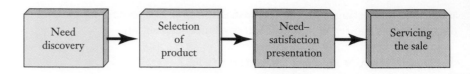

Need discovery → Selection of product → Need–satisfaction presentation → Servicing the sale

2. The consultative salesperson, unlike the peddler of an earlier era, does not try to overpower the customer with a high-pressure sales presentation. Instead the buyer's needs are identified through *two-way* communication. The salesperson asks the potential buyer questions in an attempt to learn as much as possible about the person's needs and perceptions. Eileen Tertocha, an award-winning real estate salesperson employed by Skipper Morrison Realtors in Atlanta, describes her role in meeting the needs of her customers:

   My purpose is to help families escape the trauma of relocating to a new city. It's such a joy to see their faces light up when you've found the right home for them. I don't sell houses, I sell a way of life. To do that, I take all the needs of my customers into consideration.[11]

3. Consultative selling emphasizes *information giving and negotiation rather than manipulation*. This approach leads to a more trusting relationship between buyer and seller. Customers want help in making the best decision possible. Helping the buyer make an informed and intelligent buying decision adds value to the product. The *value-added* approach enhances the worth of your product so that it will be worth more to customers.

4. Consultative selling emphasizes *service* after the sale. Theodore Levitt, author-consultant, recognizes that the relationship between a seller and a buyer seldom ends when a sale is made. In an increasing number of transactions the relationship actually intensifies because the customer has higher expectations after the sale. The personalized service provided after the sale may include making credit arrangements, supervising product delivery and installation, servicing warranties, and following up on complaints. The

In Consultative-style selling, negotiation replaces manipulation as the salesperson sets the stage for a long-term relationship.

proper handling of these postsale activities builds a long-term partnership between the customer and the salesperson. The salesperson personifies the corporation in the customer's eyes and is the visible, genuine demonstrator of how the company feels about its customers.[12]

At first glance, it may appear that consultative-style selling practices can be easily mastered. The truth is, consultative selling is a complex process that puts great demands on sales personnel.[13] This approach to personal selling requires an understanding of concepts and principles borrowed from the fields of psychology, communications, and sociology. It takes a great deal of personal commitment and self-discipline to become a sales consultant/advisor.

THE ENHANCEMENT OF CONSULTATIVE SELLING

Throughout the past 30 years consultative selling has evolved into a more mature and more focused approach to meeting the customer's needs. With each passing year we have learned more about high-performance salespeople who use this approach; and this information has been incorporated into many sales training programs, training videos, and books devoted to personal selling.

The early consultative sales training programs emphasized the development of face-to-face selling skills. These skills continue to be important today, but they must be enhanced with strategic planning and a strong commitment to building partnerships. Today salespeople are encountering better educated and more demanding customers who are asking harder questions and seeking more precise solutions to their buying problems. Time is a precious commodity for most of today's customers. They want to partner with a salesperson who is well organized, well informed, and able to use strategic thinking to meet their complex needs. The remainder of this chapter will be devoted to an introduction of strategic selling and partnering.

Evolution of Strategic Selling

Strategic selling began receiving considerable attention during the 1980s (see Table 1.1). It was during this period that we witnessed the beginning of several trends that resulted in a more complex selling environment. These trends, which include increased competition, broader and more diverse product lines, more decision makers involved in major purchases, and greater demand for specific, custom-made solutions, will continue to influence personal selling and sales training in the future.

As companies face increased levels of complexity in the marketplace, they must give more attention to strategic planning. The strategic planning done by salespeople is often influenced by the information included in the company's strategic market plan. A **strategic market plan** takes into consideration all of the major functional areas of the business that must be coordinated, such as production, marketing, finance, and personnel.[14] Almost every aspect of the plan directly or indirectly influences the sale of products.

The strategic market plan should be a guide for a strategic selling plan. This plan includes strategies that you use to position yourself with the customer before the sales call even begins.[15] The authors of *Strategic Selling* point out that there is a difference between a *tactic* and a *strategy*. **Tactics** are techniques, practices, or methods you use when you are face to face with a customer. Examples are the use of questions to identify needs, presentation skills, and various types of closes. These and other tactics will be discussed in Chapters 9 to 14.

A **strategy,** on the other hand, is a prerequisite to tactical success. If you develop the correct strategies, you are more likely to make your sales presentation to the right person, at the right time, in a manner most likely to achieve positive results.

A selling strategy is a carefully conceived plan that is needed to accomplish a sales objective. Let's assume you are a sales representative employed by a food service distributor (wholesaler) and you call on full-service restaurants. A strategy might include careful analysis of restaurant menus prior to sales calls. Menu analysis helps you determine what products the restaurant needs to prepare the items served to customers.[16] With this information you can select the most appropriate selling tactic (method), which might be to present samples of food and beverage items the restaurant is currently not buying from you.

Strategic planning sets the stage for a higher quality form of consultative selling that is more structured, more focused, and more efficient. The result of this planning is better time allocation, more precise problem solving, and a greater chance that there will be a good match between your product or service and the customer's needs.

In the 1980s strategic selling achieved a new level of importance. Andrew Parsons, director of consumer marketing for McKinsey and Company, notes that in the current selling environment salespeople must choose from a sophisticated range of alternatives. He points out in general terms that personal selling has moved from "a game of checkers to a game of chess." For many salespeople, strategic planning is not an option, but the key to survival.

Today's customer wants a quality product and a quality relationship. Salespeople who build partnering style relationships will be rewarded with repeat business and referrals.

THE STRATEGIC/CONSULTATIVE SELLING MODEL

When you study an advanced approach to personal selling that combines strategic planning, consultative selling practices, and partnering principles, you experience a mental exercise that is similar to solving a jigsaw puzzle. You are given many pieces of information that must ultimately form a complete picture. Putting the parts together isn't nearly as difficult if you can see the total picture at the beginning. Therefore a single model has been developed to serve as a source of reference throughout the entire text. Figure 1.4 shows this model.

The Strategic/Consultative Selling Model features five steps, and each step is based on three prescriptions. The first step involves the development of a personal selling philosophy. Each of the other steps relates to a broad strategic area of personal selling. Each makes an important and unique contribution to the selling/buying process. A brief introduction to each strategic area is presented here.

DEVELOPING A RELATIONSHIP STRATEGY

Success in selling depends heavily on the salesperson's ability to develop, manage, and enhance interpersonal relations with the customer. People seldom buy products or services from someone they dislike or distrust. Harvey B. Mackay, chief executive officer of Mackay Envelope Corporation, says, "People don't care how much you know until they know how much you care." Most customers are more apt to openly discuss their needs and wants with a salesperson with whom they feel comfortable.

A **relationship strategy** is a well-thought-out plan for establishing, building, and maintaining quality relationships. This type of plan is essential for success in today's marketplace, which is characterized by vigorous competition, look-alike products, and customer loyalty dependent on quality relationships as well as quality products. The relationship strategy must encompass every aspect of selling from the first contact with a prospect to servicing the sale once this prospect becomes an established customer. The primary goal of the relationship strategy is to create rapport, trust, and mutual respect, which will ensure a long-term partnership. To establish this type of relationship, salespeople must adopt a double-win philosophy (that is, if the customer wins, I win); project a professional image; and maintain high ethical standards (see Fig. 1.4). These topics will be discussed in detail in Chapters 3 and 4.

Some people think that the concept of *relationships* is too soft and too emotional for a business application; these people think that it's too difficult to think about relationships in strategic terms. In fact this is not the case at all. Every salesperson can formulate a strategic plan that will build and enhance relationships.

DEVELOPING A PRODUCT STRATEGY

Products and services represent problem-solving tools. The **product strategy** is a plan that helps salespeople make correct decisions concerning the selection and positioning of products to meet identified customer needs. The development of a product strategy begins with a thorough study of one's product (see

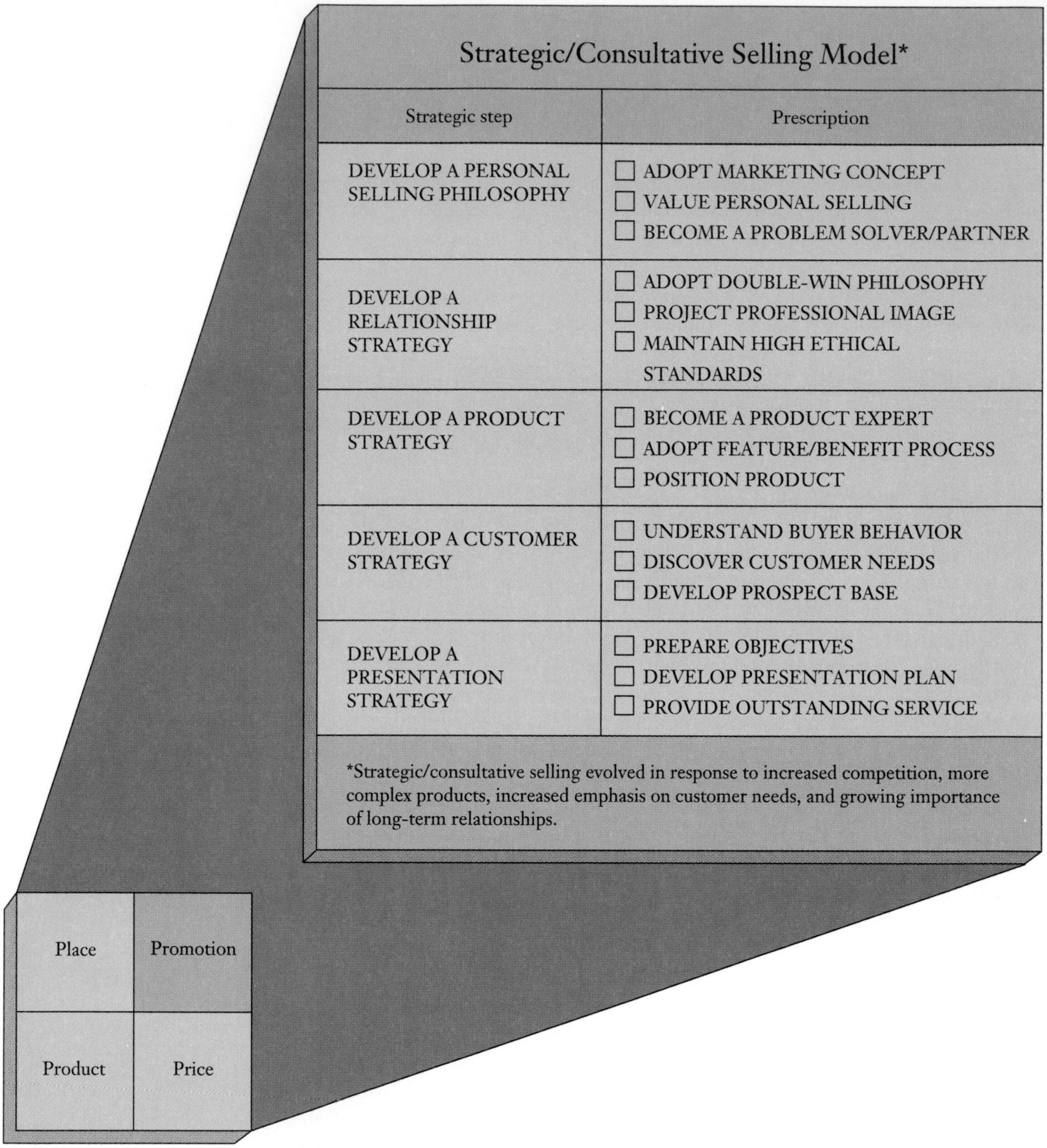

Strategic/Consultative Selling Model*

Strategic step	Prescription
DEVELOP A PERSONAL SELLING PHILOSOPHY	☐ ADOPT MARKETING CONCEPT ☐ VALUE PERSONAL SELLING ☐ BECOME A PROBLEM SOLVER/PARTNER
DEVELOP A RELATIONSHIP STRATEGY	☐ ADOPT DOUBLE-WIN PHILOSOPHY ☐ PROJECT PROFESSIONAL IMAGE ☐ MAINTAIN HIGH ETHICAL STANDARDS
DEVELOP A PRODUCT STRATEGY	☐ BECOME A PRODUCT EXPERT ☐ ADOPT FEATURE/BENEFIT PROCESS ☐ POSITION PRODUCT
DEVELOP A CUSTOMER STRATEGY	☐ UNDERSTAND BUYER BEHAVIOR ☐ DISCOVER CUSTOMER NEEDS ☐ DEVELOP PROSPECT BASE
DEVELOP A PRESENTATION STRATEGY	☐ PREPARE OBJECTIVES ☐ DEVELOP PRESENTATION PLAN ☐ PROVIDE OUTSTANDING SERVICE

*Strategic/consultative selling evolved in response to increased competition, more complex products, increased emphasis on customer needs, and growing importance of long-term relationships.

Place	Promotion
Product	Price

FIGURE 1.4   The Strategic/Consultative Selling Model is an extension of the marketing concept.

Fig. 1.4) using a feature-benefit analysis approach. Product features such as technical superiority, reliability, fashionableness, design integrity, or guaranteed availability should be converted to benefits that will appeal to the customer. Today's high-performance salespeople strive to become product experts. Chapter 5 focuses on company, product, and competition knowledge needed by salespeople.

BUILDING QUALITY PARTNERSHIPS

ADDING VALUE IN COMMODITY SALES

Selling a commodity requires talent and perseverance. We use the term *commodity* to describe products that are nearly identical or appear to be the same in the consumer's mind. A good example of a commodity is the business envelope. There are 235 envelope companies in America according to Harvey Mackay, president of Mackay Envelope Corporation. He says that the best way to increase market share in this competitive industry is to use a form of personal selling that adds value to look-alike products. In his best selling book *Swim with the Sharks* he offers some advice to salespeople who sell commodities. He suggests using a service-oriented approach to personal selling to give the product or service a measure of uniqueness in the eyes of the customer. Mackay says that knowing as much as possible about your customer gives you the information needed to build a personal and a business relationship. This information will help you personalize and customize your sales presentation.

Mutual funds have become a modern day commodity. Investors can now choose from over 7,600 different mutual funds. People who sell funds need to add value to their product with enhanced service.[b]

A well-conceived product strategy also requires that decisions be made concerning product positioning. The positioning of a product refers to the decisions, activities, and communications that establish and maintain a firm's intended product concept in the customer's mind. The goal of salespeople at a Mercedes-Benz dealership, for example, is to create the perception that their automobiles are the best in the high-performance luxury category and the company will stand behind its products with an excellent customer service program. The brokers at Paine Webber Incorporated strive to create the perception that they are well-informed consultants and that the company is able to service its accounts to maximize customer satisfaction. The positioning of products and other product-related sales strategies is the major focus of Chapter 6.

The development of a product strategy often requires thoughtful decision making. Today's more knowledgeable customers seek a cluster of satisfactions that arise from the product itself, from the manufacturer or distributor of the product, and from the salesperson. The "new" product that customers are buying today is the sum total of the satisfactions that emerge from all three sources. The cluster of satisfactions concept will be discussed in more detail in Chapter 6. The three prescriptions for the product strategy are: become a product expert, adopt feature-benefit process, and position product.

DEVELOPING A CUSTOMER STRATEGY

Customers have become increasingly sophisticated in their buying strategies. More and more, they have come to expect value added products and services and long-term commitments.[17] Selling to today's customer starts with getting on the customers' agenda and carefully identifying their needs, wants, and buying conditions.

A **customer strategy** is a carefully conceived plan that will result in maximum responsiveness to the customer's needs. This strategy is based on the fact that success in personal selling depends, in no small measure, on the salesperson's ability to learn as much as possible about the prospect.[18] It involves the collection and analysis of specific information on each customer. When developing a customer strategy, the salesperson should: develop a broad understanding of buying behaviors, discover individual customer needs, and build a strong prospect base (see Fig. 1.4). The first two parts of the customer strategy will be introduced in Chapter 7. Suggestions regarding ways to build a solid prospect base will be discussed in Chapter 8.

Many of the most progressive companies in the United States have well-established customer strategies. Baxter Healthcare, a company based in Deerfield, Illinois, provides a good example of a marketer who has adopted a unique customer strategy.

Baxter's salespeople are encouraged to continuously collect information from those who use their products, or prospective customers in the medical field, and then use this information to refine existing products or develop new products (Fig. 1.5). The collection and analysis of information results in better management of orders and deliveries. Baxter is helping many hospitals make progress toward just-in-time supply management.[19]

DEVELOPING A PRESENTATION STRATEGY

Typical salespeople spend less than half of their time in actual face-to-face selling situations. However, the sales presentation is a critical part of the selling process. The **presentation strategy** is a well-developed plan that includes preparing the sales presentation objectives, preparing a presentation plan that is needed to meet these objectives, and renewing one's commitment to provide outstanding customer service (see Fig. 1.4).

The presentation strategy usually involves developing one or more objectives for each sales call. For example, a salesperson might update personal information about the customer, provide information on a new product, and close a sale during one sales call. Multiple-objective sales presentations, which are becoming more common, will be discussed in Chapter 9.

Presale presentation plans give salespeople the opportunity to consider those activities that will take place during the sales presentation. For example, a salesperson might preplan a demonstration of product features to use when meeting with the customer. Presale planning ensures that salespeople will be well organized during the sales presentation and prepared to offer outstanding service.

FIGURE 1.5 The Baxter's customer strategy loop illustrates how salespeople obtain information on ways to better serve their customer.

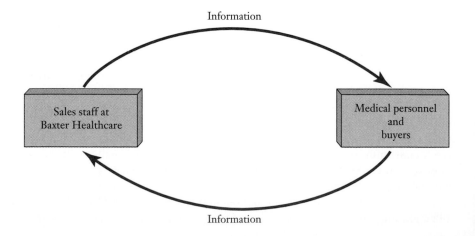

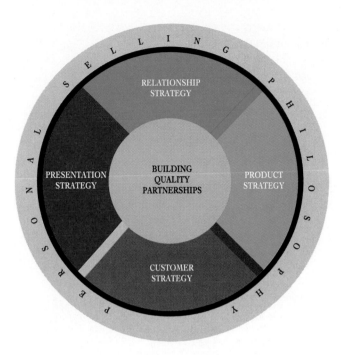

INTERRELATIONSHIP OF BASIC STRATEGIES

The major strategies that form the Strategic/Consultative Selling Model are by no means independent. The relationship, product, and customer strategies all influence development of the presentation strategy (Fig. 1.6). For example, one relationship-building practice might be developed for use during the initial face-to-face meeting with the customer and another for possible use during the negotiation of buyer resistance. Another relationship-building method might be developed for use after the sale is closed. The discovery of customer needs (part of the customer strategy) will greatly influence planning for the sales presentation.

The Evolution of Partnering

In the early 1990s we witnessed the demise of the product solution in many major industries. A growing number of customers began buying relationships, not products. This trend is the result of a situation where the products of one company in an industry are becoming nearly identical to those of the competition. When a given industry (service, retail, wholesale, or manufacturing) is dominated by look-alike products, the product strategy becomes less important than the relationship strategy.

The term **relationship selling,** popularized over the past several years, recognizes the growing importance of relationships in selling. Salespeople who have adopted relationship selling work hard to build and nourish long-term partnerships. They rely on a personal, customized approach to each customer.[20] This approach stands in stark contrast to the more traditional *transaction-oriented* selling.

Today's customer wants a quality product *and* a quality relationship. Salespeople willing to abandon short-term thinking and invest the time and energy

Uncle Ben's understands the evolution of selling from "peddling to partnering." The company wants to help distributors establish partnerships and increase customer satisfaction.

A strong partnership begins with effective two-way communication between the salesperson and the customer.

needed to develop a high-quality, long-term relationship with customers will be strongly rewarded. A strong partnership serves as a barrier to competing salespeople who want to sell to your accounts. Salespeople who are able to build partnerships enjoy more repeat business and referrals. Keeping existing customers happy makes a great deal of sense from an economic point of view. Many experts in the field of sales and marketing agree with Steve Arbeit, president of Decision Based Resources, who said, "It costs five times more to get a new customer than to keep an existing one."[21]

Partnering requires that salespeople continuously search for ways to add quality to their selling relationships. The salespeople at Mackay Envelope Corporation achieve this goal by making sure they know more about their customers than the competitors. Salespeople who work for Xerox Corporation are responding to a sales orientation that emphasizes postsale service. Bonuses are based on a formula that includes not just sales, but customer satisfaction as well.[22]

PARTNERING IS ENHANCED WITH HIGH ETHICAL STANDARDS

In the field of selling there are certain pressures which can influence the ethical conduct of salespeople, and poor ethical decisions can weaken or destroy partnerships. To illustrate, let us assume a competitor makes exaggerated claims about a product. Do you counteract by promising more than your product can deliver? What action do you take when there is a time management problem and you must choose between servicing past sales and making new sales? What if a superior urges you to use a strategy that you consider unethical? These and other pressures must be dealt with every day.

Although pressures exist in every selling position, most salespeople are able to draw the line between ethical and unethical behavior. This is especially true

Hillshire Farm & Kahn's Salutes LABATT Food Service

Partners in providing premium quality center of the plate meals.

Center Piece Bacon

Hillshire Farm
Smoked Sausage

Hearthstone Ham

For more details or for a
product cutting contact

Hillshire Farm & Kahn's Foodservice
Marketing at 1-800-543-4465
Ask for Mail Box #999

Hillshire Farms and Kahns' Foodservice invite institutional customers to call an 800 number for sales and marketing assistance. Company sales representatives explain the benefits of building a partnership.

BUILDING RELATIONSHIPS THROUGH TECHNOLOGY

THE **ACT!** COMPUTER SOFTWARE PROGRAM

In Appendix 2, in the back of the text you will find information on ACT!, the number-one computer software program for sales representatives. The information presented can be used immediately for a general overview of how computers can help sales representatives in their daily work. Also, at various points in the text, Building Relationships through Technology boxes will suggest specific files for you to open, so you can become conversant with the program. Information on equipment you need to use ACT!, how to access the program, and the files that are included in the ACT! program, is found in Appendix 2, p. 415.

More and more sales representatives use computers in the field as part of their daily work. As computers have become lighter and more compact,

they can now be used in the car, on the airplane, and even while the salesperson is waiting to see a customer. They also enable the salesperson to do much of his or her paperwork—submitting orders, writing letters, mailing query cards, and other tasks—in less time. Many salespeople have computers that can be tied in to the company's computers, so orders can be submitted instantly or customer queries can be received instantly. Some computers now have keypads on which one can write with a stylus, and the computer learns to "read" the individual's handwriting! As computers become smaller and more powerful, they become more and more important as a tool to enable the salesperson to keep in touch with the customer, provide faster service, and create customized solutions for particular situations.

of those who have taken a long-range view of sales work that emphasizes building partnerships. These people know that the best way to ensure repeat business is to deal honestly and fairly with every customer.

Although Chapter 4 is devoted entirely to ethical considerations in personal selling, it should be noted that ethics is a major theme of the text. The topic of ethics has been interwoven throughout several chapters. The authors believe that ethical decisions must be made every day in the life of a salesperson, so this important topic cannot be covered in a single chapter.

PARTNERING IS ENHANCED WITH SALES AUTOMATION

Many companies are using some form of sales automation to enhance partnerships with customers. **Sales automation** is the term used to describe those technologies used to improve communications in a sales organization and improve customer responsiveness. Some of the most common technologies used by salespeople are personal computers, electronic mail (E-mail), cellular phones, and pagers.[23] Quick access to information enhances customer service and reduces communication problems.

Benefits from Developing the Skill of Selling

Personal selling skills permeate almost everything we do. Robert Louis Stevenson once said, "Everybody lives by selling something." He recognized that people are constantly involved in selling their ideas, their beliefs, and themselves to other people. Organizations that once considered salespeople unnecessary are now implementing well-developed personal selling strategies. Banks, accounting firms, and even hospitals are today involved in selling their services.

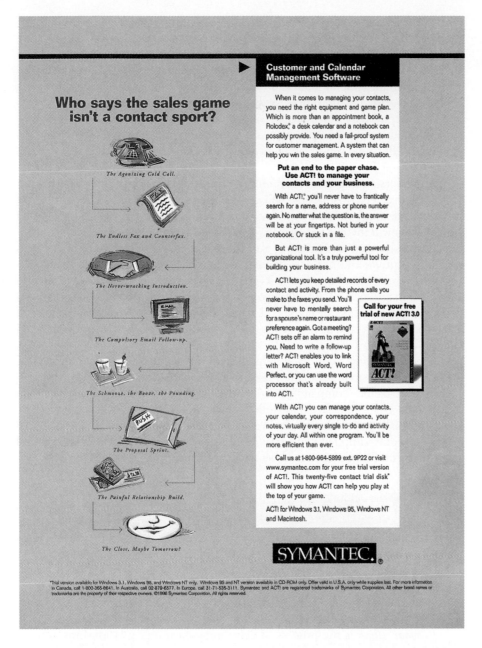

The award winning ACT! Contact management software is backed up by a money back guarantee. Salespeople are increasingly using various forms of technology to build strong partnerships with their customers.

The *skills of selling* have taken on new meaning in a nation shifting rapidly from industrial production to providing services and information. John Naisbitt, author of *Megatrends* and *Megatrends 2000*, notes we are in an information economy and people who can transfer information effectively will be rewarded

Almost everything people want in their lives requires convincing someone else to help provide it. It might be money, goods, services, friendship, security, or wider acceptance of a cherished belief. When we want something, we must convince others that they ought to give it to us, sell it to us, help us make it, or help us keep it. This means we must make a case and sell our point of view.[c]

SALES TIPS

with financial and career success. The skill of selling enables one person to effectively transfer ideas to another.

Personal selling is an important auxiliary activity in many professional fields. Financial planning consultants, property managers, human resource development managers, lawyers, and many others have discovered the importance of personal selling skills. These skills are also needed by small business owners and managers. Many new business owners have discovered that no matter how sophisticated your marketing plan, nothing really happens until someone sells something. Personal selling as an auxiliary activity will be discussed in more detail in Chapter 2.

An understanding of the art and science of personal selling can be helpful in the job market. Most people will change jobs several times. To get a job with any organization, you must be able to convince an employer that you are worth hiring. This will involve persuasion.

Leadership and management also involve personal selling skills. Most successful executives and business owners are busy selling to their customers, employees, vendors, and suppliers. They are selling not only products but also ideas and inspiration. C. D. Peterson, successful business owner, sees personal selling as the master skill. He says that personal selling is often "your only edge over competitors, and it can easily mean the difference between success and failure."[24]

Personal selling skills have helped many people achieve career success. A surprising number of company presidents began their careers in sales. When Sears Roebuck and Company celebrated its 100th birthday, Edward A. Brennan was named chairman. Brennan joined Sears in 1956 as a salesperson in the men's furnishings department. Wesley Cantrell, president of Lanier, still stresses product simplicity and friendliness to the customer, concepts he found to be important when he started his sales career with the company.

SUMMARY

As the global economy has shifted from one of excess demand to one of excess supply, competition has increased, both within the United States and from foreign competitors. However, many new markets are opening up in Latin America, Africa, Eastern Europe and Russia, and the East including China. Vigorous sales promotion, including personal selling, will be key factors in stimulating global demand for products.

Personal selling is the process of developing customer relationships, discovering customer needs, matching the appropriate products with those needs, and communicating benefits through informing, reminding, or persuading. (A *product* can be a service, idea, issue, or thing.) The *marketing concept* is the belief that a firm should dedicate all of its policies, planning, and operation to the satisfaction of the customer; personal selling, similarly, regards customer satisfaction as of primary importance.

The *marketing era* that began in the United States in the 1950s looked first at customer needs and wants, and then created goods and services to meet those needs and wants. (Previously the emphasis had been on creating products and then building customer interest in those products.) *Consultative-style selling* emerged in the late 1960s and early 1970s as an approach that emphasizes identification of customer needs through effective communication between the salesperson and the customer. *Strategic selling* evolved in the 1980s and involves the preparation of a carefully conceived plan to accomplish sales objectives. In the 1990s, the development of *partnership selling* involves providing customers with a quality product *and* a quality, long-term relationship.

Strategic selling is based on a company's *strategic market plan*, which takes into consideration the coordination of all of the major functional areas of the business—production, marketing, finance, and personnel. The four broad strategic areas in the strategic/consultative selling model (after development of a personal selling philosophy) are developing a relationship strategy, developing a product strategy, developing a customer strategy, and developing a presentation strategy.

Partnering is the creation of long-term relationships with customers, which requires salespeople to continuously search for ways to add quality to their selling relationships. The quality improvement process reinforces partnering through the firm's search for ways to provide a higher quality, lower cost product, and the salesperson's attempt to continuously improve the quality of customer service.

Personal benefits that come from developing the skill of selling include greater marketability of one's skills, development of one's leadership and management potential, and success in one's career. Personal selling is an important auxiliary activity in many professional fields.

Ethical considerations are particularly important in the field of personal selling because the salesperson represents his company to the buyer. The salesperson may encounter pressures to "bend" principles of honesty or straightforwardness, so it is necessary to consider and develop ethical principles that will be the guidelines for one's entire career.

➤ KEY TERMS

Personal Selling	*Strategy*
Product	*Relationship Strategy*
Personal Selling Philosophy	*Product Strategy*
Marketing Concept	*Customer Strategy*
Marketing Mix	*Presentation Strategy*
Consultative-Style Selling	*Relationship Selling*
Strategic Market Plan	*Sales Automation*
Tactics	

➤ REVIEW QUESTIONS

1. Explain how personal selling can help solve the problem of excess global supply.
2. According to the Strategic/Consultative Selling Model (Fig. 1.1), what are the three prescriptions for developing a successful personal selling philosophy?
3. Why is peddling or "pushing products" inconsistent with the marketing concept?
4. What is consultative selling? Give examples.
5. Diagram and label the four-step Consultative Sales Presentation Guide.

6. List and briefly explain the four broad strategic areas that make up the selling process.

7. Briefly describe the evolution of partnering. Discuss the forces that contributed to this approach to selling.

8. Read the Building Quality Partnerships boxed insight on p. 15 and then discuss ways to add value when selling a commodity.

9. List the personal benefits to be derived from developing personal selling skills.

10. Explain why the ethical conduct of salespeople has become so important today.

➤ APPLICATION EXERCISES

1. Assume that you are an experienced professional salesperson. A professor who teaches at a nearby university has asked you to speak to a consumer economics class about the social and economic benefits of personal selling. Make an outline of what you will say.

2. A friend of yours has invented a unique and useful new product. This friend, an engineer by profession, understands little about marketing and selling this new product. She does understand, however, that "nothing happens until somebody sells something." She has asked you to describe the general factors that need to be considered when you market a product. Prepare an answer to her question.

3. Sharon Alverez has been teaching college biology courses. Recently, she was offered a position selling pharmaceutical products. This position requires that she call on doctors and pharmacists to explain her product line. Describe the similarities and the differences between her two positions.

4. To learn more about the sales training programs currently offered by Learning International, Wilson Learning Corporation, Dale Carnegie & Associates, and Zig Ziglar Corporation, search the internet and review the offerings.

➤ CASE PROBLEM

This chapter opened with an introduction to Body Glove International, a global company that manufactures a quality line of wet suits for persons who like water sports. Many of the consumers who are involved in water skiing, scuba diving, surfing, or jet skiing purchase Body Glove products because they represent both quality and value. The company was started in 1953 by Bill and Randy Meistrell, two persons who shared a passion for surfing and diving. The first suits were custom made for customers who responded to ads placed in local publications. As sales increased the Meistrell brothers developed a small manufacturing facility and began distributing their products through retail stores on the West Coast. Soon Body Glove became a national company and later an international company. The success of Body Glove can be traced to several factors:

➤ A company philosophy that is based on the belief that you never sacrifice quality. A product that is comfortable and well made attracts the customer who is willing to spend a little more to get the best product.

➤ A belief that success in sales and marketing is achieved by staying close to the customer. At Body Glove, a well-trained sales force makes regular visits to retailers who handle their products. Kurt Rios, vice president of sales at Body Glove, wants every salesperson to build a strong partnership with each retail customer. Of course, the company also attempts to learn as much as possible about the wants and needs of the ultimate consumer who buys their product at the retail level.

➤ Maintain a well-trained sales force who develop new customers and provide service to establish customers. The salespeople who work for Body Glove not only possess a high degree of product knowledge, they are prepared to help the retailer make decisions in the areas of pricing, advertising, display, and inventory control. They know how to help the retailer stimulate demand for Body Glove products. These salespeople are in a unique position to collect product, market, and service information regarding the buyers' needs. Recently most of the commission salespeople were converted to a straight salary compensation plan. Randy Meistrell, executive vice president of Body Glove, feels the salespeople will give more attention to customer service if they are not focusing so much attention on making a commission.

➤ Investment in a first class customer service center. The people at Body Glove believe that excellent customer service adds value to the product. Celeste Barouty, sales office manager, makes sure that all orders are carefully processed. With the aid of modern computers, Celeste can check on the status of any order. She and her staff can also process special orders quickly. The customer service staff and the salespeople work together to build the strongest possible partnership with the customer.

QUESTIONS

1. Does it appear that the management team at Body Glove International and members of the sales force have adopted the three prescriptions of a personal selling philosophy? (See Strategic/Consultative Selling Model.) Explain your answer.

2. What are the characteristics of the product strategy adopted by Body Glove International? How will this strategy contribute to the company's long-term success?

3. How would you describe the customer strategy developed by Body Glove International? How does this strategy contribute to long-term success?

4. The company officers have made a decision to convert salespeople from a commission plan to a straight salary plan. Do you think this was a good decision? Explain.

5. Does it appear that Body Glove has adopted the four broad strategic areas that are part of the Strategic/Consultative Selling Model? Explain.

PARTNERSHIP SELLING: A ROLE PLAY/SIMULATION (see Appendix 3, p. 421)

[If your instructor has chosen to use the *Partnering Role Play/Simulation* exercise that accompanies this text, these boxes will alert you to your *Role Play/Simulation* assignments. Your instructor will also provide you with needed information.]

Preview the role play simulation materials in Appendix 3. These materials are produced by the Park Inn International Hotel and Convention Center, and you will be using them in your role as a new sales trainee (and, at times, as the customer) for the hotel and its convention services.

The role play exercises will begin in Chapter 5, as you begin to create your product strategy. However, in anticipation of the role play, you can begin to imagine yourself in the role of an actual salesperson. Start to think about how you will develop your personal selling philosophy. What are some ethical guidelines that you may wish to adopt for yourself? (Ethics is also the subject of Chapter 4, Ethics—The Foundation for Relationships in Selling.) What skills will you need to develop to become a partner with your prospective customers?

The Park Inn has implemented a Quality Improvement process. How will this affect your role as a sales representative?

Career Opportunities in Selling Today

LEARNING OBJECTIVES

When you finish reading this chapter, you should be able to

1. Discuss the rewarding aspects of personal selling careers

2. Describe the opportunities for women and minorities in the field of personal selling

3. Discuss the characteristics of selling positions in four major employment settings: service, retailing, wholesaling, and manufacturing

4. Identify emerging career opportunities in personal selling

5. Discuss personal selling as an auxiliary activity

6. Identify the four major sources of sales training

For many years Catherine Leonard was a teacher helping students. Today she is a salesperson helping customers. The decision to make a career transition began to take shape while she was working on a Ph.D. in apparel merchandising. She began to question whether a career in college teaching would provide the financial stability and job security she desired. Soon after completing the Ph.D. she obtained a sales position with Freudenberg Nonwovens, a textile supplier serving such customers as Levi Strauss and Liz Claiborne. She pursued a sales career with Freudenberg because the company rewards professional development and integrity.[1]

Careers in Personal Selling

According to the Bureau of Labor Statistics there are 14.8 million sales jobs in America.[2] In addition, the number of sales positions is increasing in most industrialized countries. A close examination of these positions reveals that there is no single "selling" occupation. Our labor force includes hundreds of different selling careers and chances are there are positions that match your interests, talents, and ambitions. The diversity within selling will become apparent as you study the career options discussed in this chapter.

A professional selling position encompasses a wide range of tasks (Fig. 2.1), and therefore salespeople must possess a variety of skills. A salesperson representing Federal Express (FedEX) will make numerous sales calls each day in an attempt to establish new accounts and provide service to established accounts. There are a wide range of potential customers who can use FedEX delivery services. A salesperson working for a Caterpillar construction equipment dealer may make only two or three sales calls per day. The products offered by the dealer are expensive and are not purchased frequently.

Just as selling occupations differ, so do the titles by which salespeople are known. Their titles reflect, in part, the variety of duties they perform. A survey of current job announcements indicates that fewer and fewer companies are us-

FIGURE 2.1 How Salespeople Spend Their Time During an Average 46.5-Hour Workweek (Source: Dartnell Sales Force Compensation Survey)

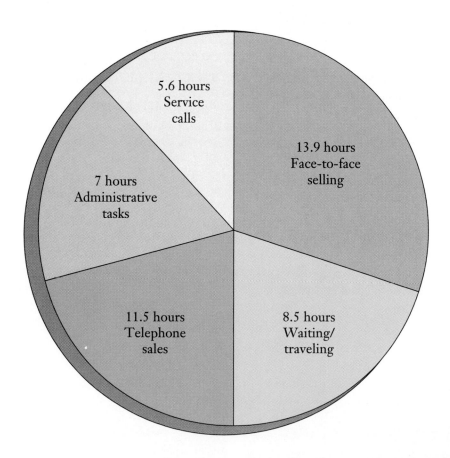

ing the word *salesmen* to refer to the people they employ to sell their products. Instead they are using such titles as these:

Account Executive	Sales Consultant
Account Representative	Senior Account Representative
Sales Account Manager	Sales Associate
Sales Coordinator	Marketing Representative
District Representative	Territory Sales Manager

Salespeople who call on supermarkets make eight to ten calls during a single day.

REWARDING ASPECTS OF SELLING CAREERS

Martin Shafiroff is one of the top stockbrokers of the 8,800 who sell for Smith-Barney. On an average day he closes over $3 million worth of business. During a ten-year period Shafiroff earned sales commissions in excess of $50 million.[3] He enjoys serving as an investment counselor for a large group of loyal customers. From a personal and economic standpoint, selling can be a rewarding career. Careers in selling offer financial rewards, recognition, security, and opportunities for advancement to a degree that is unique, compared with other occupations.

ABOVE-AVERAGE INCOME

Most studies dealing with incomes in the business community indicate that salespeople earn significantly higher incomes than other workers. Some salespeople actually earn more than their sales managers and other executives within the organization. This high level of compensation (whether from base salary, bonus, or incentives) is justified for good performance.[4] Over a period of nearly three decades Dartnell Corporation, a publisher of sales training materials, has conducted surveys to determine the compensation earned by salespeople. Definitions for each sales position category and the compensation (salary plus incentives) earned by each type of salesperson follow. This information appeared in the 1996–1997 compensation report.

Entry level sales representative An **entry level sales representative** has acquired knowledge of the company's products, services, policies, and successful sales techniques. Average total compensation is $39,800.

Intermediate sales representative An **intermediate sales representative** (mid-level salesperson) is a salesperson who has broad knowledge of the company's products and services and sells in a specifically assigned territory. He or she maintains contact with established customers and develops new prospects. Average total compensation is $50,700.

Senior sales representative A **senior sales representative** is a salesperson at the highest nonsupervisory level of selling responsibility. He is completely familiar with the company's products, services, and policies; usually has years of experience; and is assigned to major accounts and territories. Average total compensation is $68,300.

The amount earned by salespeople is clearly tied to their selling skill and the amount of effort put forth. Unlike many other workers, salespeople are rewarded financially when they give extra effort. This effort is often triggered by commissions, bonuses, incentives, and other rewards.

ABOVE-AVERAGE PSYCHIC INCOME

Two major psychological needs common to all people are recognition and security. **Psychic income,** which consists of factors that provide psychological rewards, helps satisfy these important needs and motivates us to achieve higher levels of performance. The need for recognition will be examined here; the need for security will be discussed later in this chapter.

Several years ago a study was conducted to determine what people wanted most from their jobs. Several hundred employees from a wide range of occupational areas participated in the study. They were asked to rank a total of ten morale-building factors—job characteristics that would make work more pleasant and rewarding. The list included such items as "good working conditions," "work that keeps you interested," and "money." The number one choice was "full appreciation for work done." In selling, recognition will come more frequently and with greater intensity than in most other occupations. Because selling contributes so visibly to the success of most business firms, the accomplishments of sales personnel will seldom go unrecognized.

OPPORTUNITY FOR ADVANCEMENT

Each year, thousands of openings appear in the ranks of supervision and management. Because salespeople work in positions of high visibility, they are in an excellent position to be chosen for advancement to positions of greater responsibility. The presidents of many of today's companies began their marketing careers in the ranks of the sales force.

Of course, not all salespeople can become presidents of large corporations, but in the middle-management ranks there are numerous interesting and high-paying positions in which experience in selling is a prime requisite for advancement. Sales experience is usually a prerequisite for such positions as branch sales manager, regional sales manager, product sales manager, retail department or store manager, general sales manager, director of marketing, and vice president of sales and marketing. For more information on careers in sales management see Chapter 17.

JOB SECURITY

We mentioned earlier that the need for security is a strong psychological force in our lives. Most people want to achieve some measure of security in their work. Selling is one of those occupations that usually provides job security during both good and bad times. An increasing number of companies are reducing the size of their labor force, and this trend will continue. Workers who contribute directly to the value of the enterprise through research, product development, manufacturing, and sales are most likely to avoid these layoffs. It is also worth noting that salespeople tend to receive the greatest amount of formal training in an organization.[5] Effective training contributes to one's preparation for advancement.

OPPORTUNITIES FOR WOMEN

Prodded by a growing awareness that gender is not a barrier to success in selling, business firms are recruiting qualified women in growing numbers. The percentage of women in the sales force has more than tripled in the past twelve years. Although women are relative newcomers to industrial sales, they have enjoyed expanded career opportunities in such areas as real estate, insurance, advertising services, investments, and travel services. A growing number of women are turning to sales employment, so many in fact that some observers describe personal selling as the fastest growing career for women. Women are also discovering that sales experience is often essential for reaching the upper levels of management.[6]

OPPORTUNITIES FOR MINORITIES

From a historical perspective the field of selling has not provided equal opportunity to minorities. In the past it was not easy for a member of a minority group to obtain a sales position. Today the picture has changed, and many firms are actively recruiting employees from minority groups. Although state and federal equal opportunity legislation can be credited, in part, for bringing about changes in hiring practices, many firms now view the recruitment and training of minority employees as simply good business. Minority salespeople have become top producers in many organizations.

The 1990s have brought a strong shift away from discriminating against people who are different and toward **valuing diversity.** To value diversity means that an organization intends to make full use of the talents, experiences, and perspectives of all employees at all levels within that organization.[7]

Opportunities for minorities exist in a variety of selling careers.

BUILDING RELATIONSHIPS IN A DIVERSE WORLD

OPPORTUNITIES AND CHALLENGES FOR WOMEN IN SALES

In a world that is beginning to value diversity we are seeing growth in employment opportunities for women in sales. Research conducted by Catalyst, a nonprofit organization working with business to effect change for women, indicates that line experience such as sales is advantageous, if not essential, for promotions to upper levels of management. How does success in sales set the stage for advancement? One major reason is that sales success is measured primarily by objective criteria such as sales volume, development of new accounts, and specific contributions to the organization's profitability. Successful salespeople quickly achieve high visibility within the firm.

Paula Morgan, vice-president of sales and marketing for the Schering division of Schering-Plough, found sales to be the key to advancement. She chose a career in pharmaceutical sales because it was financially rewarding and she realized she

would be rewarded for performance. Gwen Wooten joined the Xerox Corporation sales team because she knew the company would provide her with outstanding sales training. Today Wooten is district sales manager for the Washington, DC metropolitan area.

Although a pay gap between men and women exists in the field of sales, it is relatively small. Women earn a median 92 cents for every dollar earned by men. This compares favorably with the 70 cents on the dollar earned by women working full time in the work force as a whole. Despite the favorable career opportunities for women in sales, they do face some special challenges according to studies conducted by Catalyst. The biggest problem cited by female sales representatives was working in a male-dominated work environment. Women said that they experienced more difficulty with their male colleagues than with their male customers.[a]

Diane Elder, sales representative for the Hotel Roanoke and Conference Center, loves her work and loves her family. As a telecommuter, she can achieve her sales goals and still spend quality time everyday with her children. "All my life I wanted to be the one to take my kids to school and pick them up," says Diane. Supported by modern technology, she is able to keep in touch with the hotel staff and her customers. With the flip of a switch she can check her two electronic mailboxes, review any new voice-mail messages on her telephone, and log into the hotel's automated booking network. Prior to becoming a telecommuter, Diane worked out of an office at the hotel. Since moving into her home office she has reduced her commute from an hour to 30 seconds, and she no longer struggles with "guilty mom syndrome."

This philosophical shift should open doors for our growing population of minorities.

Employment Settings in Selling Today

Careers in the field of selling may be classified in several ways. One of the broadest differentiations is based on whether the product is a tangible or an intangible. Tangibles are physical goods such as furniture, homes, and data processing equipment. Intangibles are nonphysical products or services such as stocks and bonds, insurance, and consulting services. This chapter will classify selling careers according to employer. We will explore the following four major employment settings and identify some of the unique characteristics of each:

Selling a service

Selling for a retailer

Selling for a wholesaler

Selling for a manufacturer

We will also explain how financial planners, interior designers, accountants, lawyers, business consultants, and many other professionals use personal selling skills in their daily work. As noted in Chapter 1, personal selling is an important auxiliary activity that supports the efforts of a great number of professionals who work in the public and private sector. In addition, we will discuss the growing practice of assigning selling duties to employees who have customer service responsibilities.

SELLING A SERVICE

What do Ernst & Young, AT&T, Marriott Hotels, UPS, Mayflower Transit, and ADT Security Systems have in common? Each of these companies is selling services. In recent years the number of consumer and business dollars spent on services in our society has steadily increased. Customers feel the need for assistance from a knowledgeable salesperson when making purchases in such areas as insurance, real estate, vacation planning, business security, and advertising.

Brian Stutzman is typical of the many salespeople who sell services. As an account executive for Lucent Technologies, he sells telecommunications services to organizations. He recently sold an $800,000 telephone system to the Colorado Springs public schools. After a careful study of the school district's communication needs, he recommended a system that was custom designed to meet the schools needs.[8]

We will look briefly at some of the career opportunities in the service field.

Financial services At the present time there are 2.9 million sales jobs in the securities and financial services field, and employment is expected to increase at least 35 percent by the year 2005.[9] Banks, brokerage firms, and other businesses are branching out, selling a broader range of financial planning and investment services. Demand for financial services has increased, in part, because of growing interest in retirement savings.

Radio and television Revenue from advertising supports the radio and television broadcasting industry. Every station must employ a force of salespeople whose job is to call on current and prospective advertisers. Each client's needs are unique, and meeting them makes the work of a media sales representative interesting. Additionally there is a creative side to media sales, for members of the sales staff often help develop commercials.

Newspaper advertising There are approximately 1700 daily and over 6000 weekly newspapers in this country. Each newspaper is supported by both local and national advertisers and must sell advertising space to stay in business.

Hotel, Motel, and Convention Center salespeople play a key role in attracting meetings. They are often rewarded with repeat business and referrals.

Many business firms rely heavily on media sales personnel for help in developing effective advertising campaigns.

Hotel, motel, and convention center services Each year, thousands of seminars, conferences, and business meetings are held throughout the United States. Most of these events are hosted by hotels, motels, or convention centers. By diversifying their markets and upscaling their services these marketers are catering to business clients in many new and exciting ways. The salespeople employed by these firms play an important role in attracting meetings. They sell room space, food, beverages, and other services needed for a successful meeting. (See the job description of a Convention Center Salesperson on p. 428 of Appendix 3.)

Real estate Buying a home is a monumental undertaking. It is usually the single largest expenditure in the average consumer's lifetime. The purchase of commercial property by individual investors or business firms is also a major economic decision. Therefore the people who sell real estate assume an important responsibility. The career opportunities for well-trained real estate salespeople will always exist.

Insurance Selling insurance has always been one of the most rewarding careers in sales. Common forms of insurance sold include fire, liability, life, health, automobile, casualty, and homeowners. There are two broad groups of insurance salespeople. One group is employed by major companies such as Allstate, Prudential, Travelers, State Farm, and Mutual of Omaha. The second group is made up of independent insurance agents who serve as representatives for a number of various companies. The typical independent agency will offer a broad line of personal and business insurance services.

Banking The banking industry is very competitive today. Most banks have a sales promotion program, and personal selling is one of their key strategies. An increasing number of bank officers and customer service representatives are involved in personal selling activities. They develop new accounts and service established accounts. Bank personnel are completing sales training courses in record numbers these days.

Business services The heavy volume of business mergers and corporate downsizing has increased demand for business services provided by outside contractors. Some of the business services purchased today are computer programming, training, printing, credit reporting, payroll, and recruiting. Sales positions in the business services field are expected to increase by at least 50 percent by the year 2005.[10]

The list of careers involving the sales of services is much longer. We have not explored the expanding fields of home and business security, travel and recreation, pest control, and transportation. As the demand for services increases, so will the employment opportunities for salespeople.

SELLING FOR A RETAILER

Harolds, a multimillion dollar clothing store in Houston, Texas, has been growing more than 10 percent a year. This progressive retailer sells top-of-the-line men's and women's apparel to a group of discriminating customers who understand the difference between price and value. The success of Harolds is due in large part to an expert staff of full-time career salespeople who know their customers by name and are knowledgeable regarding clothing. Customers are willing to pay full price because they value the quality products and assistance offered by Harolds.[11]

The **retail salesperson** usually engages in full-time professional selling and is paid well for her contributions to the business. Products sold at the retail level range from exotic foreign automobiles to fine furniture. Here is a partial list of retail products that usually require a high degree of personal selling:

Automobiles	Recreational Vehicles
Musical Instruments	Television and Radio Receivers
Photographic Equipment	Furniture/Decorating Supplies
Fashion Apparel	Tires and Related Accessories
Major Appliances	Microcomputers

Success in personal selling at the retail level requires different kinds and amounts of training. A person employed in a retail jewelry store may need to complete the American Gem Society certificate program to be fully prepared to assist the customer in making a purchase. A salesperson who sells or leases aircraft may need a pilot's license to conduct a product demonstration.

SELLING FOR A WHOLESALER

Jerry Upchurch is a field representative for Super Valu, a wholesaler of grocery products. Jerry's career in food marketing began when he obtained a part-time job in a supermarket while attending high school. He worked his way up to assistant store manager, a position he held for two years. Later he was promoted to store manager with the Kroger chain. With a background in food retailing, Jerry was able to obtain a sales job with Super Valu. His title is retail counselor, a name that reflects the type of consultative selling he does.

Jerry Upchurch is one of more than a million wholesale salespeople who are employed in the United States. Wholesalers play an important role in making channels of distribution efficient. A full-service wholesaler offers a wide variety of services to their customers, including maintaining inventories, gathering and interpreting market information, extending credit, distributing goods, and providing promotional activities.[12] Wholesalers employ two kinds of salespeople: "inside" and "outside."

INSIDE SALESPERSON

The **inside salesperson** relies almost totally on telephone orders and follows a strict timetable of customer contact. Because of the escalating cost of personal selling, selling by telephone is growing in popularity.[13] This selling method has become so popular that some companies are taking their salespeople off the road and bringing them back to headquarters, where they are retrained to sell by telephone. Ellett Brothers, a South Carolina-based wholesale firm specializing in the sale of guns and shooting supplies, uses inside sales personnel exclusively. This company employs 125 inside salespeople who average a total of

4,400 calls a day and generate in excess of $50 million in sales each year. Chilton Ellett, president of the company, reports that new employees complete a ten-week training program before they begin contacting customers.

OUTSIDE SALESPERSON

The duties of an **outside salesperson** vary from one wholesale firm to another. Some specialize in a single area such as electronics or small appliances, while others sell a wide range of product lines. The typical outside salesperson must have knowledge of many products and be able to serve as a consultant to the customer. For example, a sales representative for a pharmaceutical wholesaler calling on retail stores will need to be familiar with advertising and display techniques, store layout, and other merchandising strategies. Most important, this person must be completely familiar with the customer's operation.

SELLING FOR A MANUFACTURER

Although Donna Crowell is a member of the Hewlett-Packard sales force, she spends much of her time at Texas Instruments. Texas Instruments makes software that runs on Hewlett-Packard hardware. Hewlett-Packard stands to sell more if Texas Instruments recommends its hardware. Thus Crowell spends a lot of time making sure there is a good relationship between the two large companies. She says, "It's more than traditional selling. I'm really a business relationship manager." [14]

Manufacturers employ salespeople in many different capacities. Three of the most common titles—field salesperson, sales engineer, and detail salesperson—are described here.

FIELD SALESPERSON

A **field salesperson** usually handles well-established products. This type of selling usually does not require a high degree of technical knowledge. A person selling standard office equipment would be classified as a field salesperson.

SALES ENGINEER

A **sales engineer** must have detailed and precise technical knowledge and the ability to discuss the technical aspects of his products. Expertise in identifying, analyzing, and solving customer problems is of critical importance. A sales engineer may be responsible for introducing a new product that represents a breakthrough in technology and must be prepared to answer a wide range of highly technical questions with conviction.

DETAIL SALESPERSON

The primary goal of a **detail salesperson** is to develop goodwill and stimulate demand for the manufacturer's products. This person is usually not compensated on the basis of the orders obtained, but receives recognition for increasing the sale of goods indirectly. The detail salesperson calls on wholesale, retail, and other customers to help improve their marketing. In a typical day this salesperson may help train a sales staff or offer advice to a firm that is planning an advertising campaign. Detail salespeople also collect valuable information

Sales engineers must have detailed and precise technical knowledge.

BUILDING QUALITY PARTNERSHIPS

BOTH ART AND SCIENCE

Is personal selling an art or a science? This question has been debated at length by professionals in the field of sales and marketing, but the issue has not been fully resolved. To get at the heart of this matter, we first need to define these two terms. A *science* is usually thought of as systematized knowledge that can be attained through study or research. There is a body of knowledge regarding personal selling that has been reported in numerous books and articles. Much of this knowledge is based on in-depth research. *Art* has been defined as skill in performance acquired by experience, study, or training.

Selling actually combines elements of both art and science. Support for this position can be found in *Profiles in Customer Loyalty*, an industry-by-industry examination of buyer-seller relationships conducted by Learning International. This study indicates that salespeople need to possess several types of knowledge: knowledge of business and economic trends, product knowledge, and knowledge of the competition, to name just a few areas. All of this

knowledge is described as *business experience* by authors of the Learning International study. The other important category described in this study is *image*. When a prospect has contact with a client, this person will form certain perceptions of the salesperson and the company he represents. The image projected by the salesperson greatly influences these perceptions. To illustrate, let us assume that two salespeople possess the same business expertise, but one is able to effectively communicate pride in his products, respect for his company, and genuine concern for the customer's welfare. The other salesperson is unable to communicate the same information effectively. This salesperson has not yet mastered the art of selling.

Many sales training programs focus on development of the art of selling. One of the most common training techniques used is the role play. A well-planned role play gives the trainee realistic experiences that are similar to actual on-the-job experiences.[b]

regarding customer acceptance of products. They must be able to offer sound advice in such diverse areas as credit policies, pricing, display, store layout, and storage. The detail salesperson is sometimes referred to as a missionary salesperson.

PERSONAL SELLING AS AN AUXILIARY ACTIVITY

The accounting firm Ernst & Young sets aside several days each year to train its professional staff in personal selling. The National Law Firm Marketing Association recently featured Neil Rackham, author of *Spin Selling*, as keynote speaker at its national conference. Faced with increased competition and more cost-conscious customers, a growing number of law, accounting, engineering, and architectural firms are discovering the merits of personal selling as an auxiliary activity.[15] Providers of financial planning services, training, property management, landscape design, and health care services are also discovering that personal selling can be used to obtain and keep new customers.

While many professional service firms are trying to train their employees to sell, others have been hiring professional salespeople to assist or team up with their service professionals. A common approach is to use a team selling approach that involves a salesperson and a service professional who has received training in the area of team selling.[16]

A growing number of professionals such as architects, accountants, and interior designers have discovered that personal selling is a very important "auxiliary" activity.

Another trend developing in America is the assignment of selling duties to employees who have customer service responsibilities. In many cases it makes sense to prepare customer contact personnel to sell products and services. The following companies have adopted this approach:

Item: Western Kansas Xpress (WKX), a highly successful freight company based in Wichita, Kansas, encourages all of its drivers to carry business cards to distribute to potential customers. Every employee is expected to discover needs and sell WKX services.[17]

Item: Tampa-based Fort Brooke Bank discovered that tellers had many opportunities to sell the bank's services. Seventeen tellers attended a series of selling seminars where they learned how to identify customer needs and suggest specific bank services. The selling strategy has been successful at this community bank.[18]

Item: George's at the Cove Restaurant, a successful eatery located in La-Jolla, California, provides its waiters and waitresses with the training needed to sell special entrees, wines, and desserts. The service staff are encouraged to suggest appropriate food and beverage items and carry business cards that can be given to customers.

As noted in Chapter 1, many small business owners rely on personal selling to build their business. James Koch, chief executive officer of the Boston Beer Company (brewer of the popular Samuel Adams beer), makes a strong case for personal selling. Like most new companies, his started with no customers. To get established, he assumed the role of salesperson and set a goal of establishing one new account each week. He recalls the ecstasy he felt when he closed his first sale:

When I got home that evening, the vision in my head was that it's really selling that drives most businesses; the direct interface between the product and customer; the crucial feedback loop. And if more CEOs had to go out and sell their products, day in and day out, they'd pay a lot more attention to what they were making.[19]

Today, James Koch's company is very successful. Like so many other business owners he discovered that no matter how sophisticated your marketing plan, nothing really happens until somebody sells something.

Learning to Sell

"Are salespeople made or are they born?" This classic question seems to imply that some people are born with certain qualities that give them a special advantage in the selling field. This is not true. The principles of selling can be learned and applied by people whose personal characteristics are quite different.

In the past few decades, sales training has expanded on four fronts. These four sources of training are corporate-sponsored training, training provided by commercial vendors, certification studies, and courses provided by colleges and universities.

Hundreds of business organizations, such as Xerox Corporation, IBM, Maytag, Western Electric, and Zenith, have established or expanded training

BUILDING RELATIONSHIPS THROUGH TECHNOLOGY

ACT!, APPREHENSION, EXPERIMENTATION, AND AUTOMATION

 Salespeople, when first introduced to automation, are often apprehensive about using computers and software to enhance their customer contacts and relationships. However, research on salespeople who have converted from pens and typewriters reveals a high degree of acceptance. Many comment that they don't know how they got along so long without automation.

The demonstration software with this book, ACT!, is a robust software program. A person inexperienced with computer use can approach the keyboard with no concern about damaging the software. An individual can feel free to experiment with the one key-based menu choices just to "see what happens." This program is also very responsive, which encourages new users to test its capabilities. Experimentation with this sample software will give people a feel for the potential power of using technology to enhance a sales career.

Help Screens. Potential users new to ACT! are encouraged to experiment with the various menu choices available in the ACT! demo. Each choice has an accompanying Help Screen (F1) to provide guidance and explanations. Although it is difficult to damage the program itself, sample data, such as the notes, can be lost (deleted). Because the user will be prompted (asked) to confirm before data is permanently altered or deleted, these messages should be studied before responding. (See Sales Automation Application Exercise on p. 44 for more information.)

programs. These large corporations spend millions of dollars each year to develop their salespeople. *Training* magazine, which conducts annual analysis of employer-provided training in U.S. organizations, indicates that salespeople are among the most intensively trained employee groups.

The programs designed by firms specializing in the development of sales personnel are a second source of sales training. Some of the most popular courses are offered by Wilson Learning Corporation, the Forum Corporation, Dale Carnegie & Associates, Learning International, and Zig Ziglar Corporation. At the present time, there are approximately 700 sales training courses offered by vendors.[20] These training programs have proved to be a good investment for many business firms.

The trend toward increased professionalism in personal selling has been the stimulus for a third type of training and education initiative. Many salespeople are returning to the classroom to earn certification in a sales or sales related area. In the pharmaceutical industry many salespeople earn the Certified Medical Representative (CMR) designation.[21] The National Automobile Dealers Association sponsors the Code of Conduct Certification program for automotive sales representatives.[22] Both of these certification programs require extensive study of modules and completion of rigorous examinations. The International Organization for Standardization (ISO) authorized Certified Marketing Services, Inc. to launch the first international program for marketing and sales certification. The CMSI program grants certification to those individuals who have reached certain achievement levels during their careers, as attested by their experience and personal references. Recipients must also complete an authorized training program and pass a comprehensive monitored examination. The major objective of this certification program is to increase the standard of excellence in the field of personal selling.[23]

The fourth source of sales training is the personal selling course offered by colleges and universities throughout America. A large majority of the nation's undergraduate business schools offer this course, and it is attracting more interest among business majors. Some two- and four-year colleges have developed extensive education programs for students interested in a sales career. Cardinal Stritch College offers a Sales Certificate Program that includes a five-course sequence. Weber State University located at Ogden, Utah offers a bachelor of science degree in technical sales. The University of Akron and the University of Memphis offer undergraduate majors in sales and sales management.

TOWARD GREATER PROFESSIONALISM

Personal selling is definitely moving in the direction of greater professional commitment. Broadly speaking, a professional is someone whose work requires a high level of training and skill. Professionals do not stop with a basic educa-

You've improved product quality, invested in new technology, even lowered your prices...

So why is the competition gaining on you?

A critical element may be missing from your competitive strategy—a focus on your relationships with your customers.

In a world of parity products and services, the quality of your customer relationships may be the only thing that can set you apart.

The key question: How do you ensure that your sales and service people have the skills they need to build and maintain lasting partnerships with your customers?

The very survival of your company depends on the answer to that question. And we can help you.

We're Learning International, the world's leading training company dedicated to strengthening clients' sales and service performance. For more than 30 years, we've been helping the world's most successful organizations to outdistance the competition.

We provide market-tested training programs for both sales and service professionals. Training that will help you leverage every point of customer contact to your advantage.

Training that will help your people develop the skills needed to win new business — and build customer loyalty.

Training that will help you not only achieve a competitive advantage, but sustain it. In a word, training that gets results.

If you'd like to know more about what Learning International can do for you, or to obtain a copy of our white paper on the new buyer-seller relationships, *Profiles in Customer Loyalty*, call or write today.

Learning International
225 High Ridge Road
Stamford, CT 06905
1-800-456-9390,
extension 85

Learning
INTERNATIONAL

Circle No. 120 on Reader Service Card

Sales and customer service training programs such as those offered by Learning International are very popular. This type of training is viewed as a good investment by firms that want to establish a long-term relationship with the customer.

tion; salespeople are spending more and more time in continuing education perfecting their skills. Integrity is another characteristic of a professional. There is no universal code of ethics for salespeople, but there is a definite trend toward the adoption of higher standards of ethical conduct.

SUMMARY

Selling careers offer many rewards not found in other occupations. Income, both monetary and psychic, is above average, and there are many opportunities for advancement. Salespeople enjoy job security, mobility, and independence. Opportunities in selling for members of minority groups and for women are growing. In addition, selling is very interesting work, because a salesperson is constantly in contact with people. The redundant adage "No two people are alike" reminds us that sales work will never be dull or routine.

The text described each of the four major career options in the field of personal selling. We have provided a brief introduction to the variety of employment opportunities in service, retail, wholesale, and manufacturer's sales. Keep in mind that each category features a wide range of selling positions, which vary in terms of educational requirements, earning potential, and type of customer served. The discussion and examples should help you see which kind of sales career best suits your talents and interests.

We explained how many professionals use selling skills in their daily work. Personal selling skills are also used by a growing number of customer contact personnel.

➤ KEY TERMS

Entry Level Sales Representative	*Inside Salesperson*
Intermediate Sales Representative	*Outside Salesperson*
Senior Sales Representative	*Field Salesperson*
Psychic Income	*Sales Engineer*
Valuing Diversity	*Detail Salesperson*
Retail Salesperson	

➤ REVIEW QUESTIONS

1. List and describe the four employment settings for people who are considering a selling career.
2. Explain the meaning of *psychic income*.
3. Explain why personal selling is an important auxiliary activity in such professional fields as accounting, financial planning, convention planning, and landscape design.
4. What future is there in selling for women and minorities?
5. Develop a list of retail products that require a high degree of personal selling.
6. Some salespeople have an opportunity to earn certification in a sales or sales related area. How can a salesperson benefit from certification?

7. Describe the two types of wholesale salespeople.

8. List three titles commonly used to describe manufacturing salespeople. Describe the duties of each.

9. Develop a list of eight selling career opportunities in the service field.

10. List and briefly describe the four major sources of sales training.

➤ APPLICATION EXERCISES

1. Examine a magazine or newspaper ad for a new product or service that you have never seen before. Evaluate its chances for receiving wide customer acceptance. Will this product require a large amount of personal selling effort? What types of salespeople (service, manufacturing, wholesale, or retail) will be involved in selling this product?

2. For each of the following job classifications, list the name of at least one person you know in that field:

   a. Full-time retail salesperson
   b. Full-time wholesale salesperson
   c. Full-time manufacturer's salesperson
   d. Full-time person who sells a service

Interview one of the people you have listed, asking the following questions concerning her duties and responsibilities:

   a. What is your immediate supervisor's title?
   b. What would be a general description of your position?
   c. What specific duties and responsibilities do you have?
   d. What is the compensation plan and salary range for a position like yours?

Write a job description from this information.

3. Shelly Jones, a vice president and partner in the Chicago office of the consulting firm Korn/Ferry International, has looked into the future and he sees some new challenges for salespeople. He recently shared the following predictions with *Selling* magazine:

   a. Salespeople will spend more time extending the range of applications or finding new markets for the products they sell.
   b. The selling function will be less pitching your product and more integrating your product into the business equation of your client. Understanding the business environment in which your client operates will be critical.
   c. In the future you will have to be a financial engineer for your client. You need to understand how your client makes money and be able to explain how your product or service contributes to profitable operation of the client's firm.

Interview a salesperson who is involved in business-to-business selling (a manufacturer's representative, for example) and determine if this person agrees with the views of Shelly Jones.

4. There are many information sources on selling careers and career opportunities on the internet. *Search the Internet for information on selling careers.*

WWW

Use one of the search engines (AltaVista is one option) to find career information on a pharmaceutical representative, a field sales engineer, and a retail salesperson.

➤ SALES AUTOMATION APPLICATION EXERCISE

ACT! APPREHENSION EXPERIMENTATION AND AUTOMATED SALES REPORTS

Listed next are three applications of the ACT! software that are frequently used by salespeople. Access the ACT! software by following the instructions in Appendix 2, and examine the following functions:

Calendar. Descriptions of the use of certain keys and key combinations are available by pressing Shift and F1 at the same time. This Help Screen tells you that you may access a calendar at any time in the program by pressing function key F4.

Calculator. A calculator will pop up if you press the Shift and F4 keys at the same time.

Report. The Help Screens can guide you through producing a report with ACT! Select Report at the main menu and press F1. A Help Screen will appear with information about the various reports that are available. You may page through this Help Screen by pressing the PgDn key. The Escape (Esc) key will remove the Help Screen so that you may continue.

Prepare a report that shows the contacts in this database and their phone numbers. Select Report on the Main Menu and Phone from the Report Menu. At each of the next two windows, press Enter for the report to print, and in the next window select A for all contacts.

➤ CASE PROBLEM

Ronald McMains is twenty-three years old and works for Metropolitan Financial Bank in the information services department. He was employed part time while attending college and decided to accept a full-time position after graduation.

The position in information services offers an opportunity to learn a great deal about banking, a secure income, a good insurance and retirement program, two weeks vacation a year, and fifteen days of sick leave a year if needed. There will also be opportunities to move into supervision within the next couple of years, since the company is expanding rapidly.

Ron has been thinking about changing jobs and has been described by his friends as an opportunist—a person who seeks out opportunities and takes advantage of them. He sees himself the same way and someday hopes to earn well above the average income.

Ron has been interviewing for several positions. One company has offered him a position that involves calling on potential dealers for a new line of fiberglass boats. The manufacturer has a patent on an improved fiberglassing technique that is setting new standards for boat strength. The boat has proved to be a success and has sold extraordinarily well in the five territories that the company has already opened. Letters are coming from dealers all over the country expressing an interest in taking on a dealership. The company has decided to open up new territories in the southern half of Wisconsin and northern half of Illinois. The latter is the territory they have offered to Ron.

The specific responsibilities of the position include calling on marinas and boat dealers in the territory and setting up the better ones as distributors of the new line of boats. Ron would evaluate each potential distributorship and would select and appoint the new distributors. The company's excellent training program would teach Ron how to help each new dealer set up a promotional program to sell the boats.

The company has offered Ron a commission program that includes a "draw against commission" form of compensation. In this type of program a drawing account enables the salesperson to receive a set amount either weekly or monthly that is later subtracted from earned commissions. Ron's draw would equal his present salary, including his overtime pay. Ron's commissions would be based on the number of boats his dealers sold. The company expects this territory to be one of the best; and if Ron is successful, his income could be well into the $40,000 to $50,000 range within the second year, if not sooner.

Ron would have to relocate about 100 miles from where he now lives. The company has offered relocation expenses of $2,500 to cover the cost of the move. Ron realizes he would be away from home on the average of one night a week, and this poses no problems. The company will cover all of Ron's travel and lodging expenses and will provide him with a new car.

QUESTIONS

1. List the pros and cons of this job opportunity.

2. On the basis of the information given, should Ron accept the new job? Why or why not?

Part II

Developing a Relationship Strategy

High-performance salespeople are generally better able to build and maintain relationships than moderate performers. Part II focuses on the person-to-person–relationship-building strategies that are the foundation for personal development and relationships with customers that result in repeat business and referrals.

The manner in which high-performance salespeople establish, build, and maintain relationships is a key ingredient of success.

Dr. William M. DeMarco and Dr. Michael D. Maginn
Sales Competency Research Report

RELATIONSHIP STRATEGY

PRESENTATION STRATEGY

BUILDING QUALITY PARTNERSHIPS

PRODUCT STRATEGY

CUSTOMER STRATEGY

PERSONAL SELLING PHILOSOPHY

Factors Influencing the Relationship-Building Process

LEARNING OBJECTIVES

When you finish reading this chapter, you should be able to

1. Explain the importance of developing a relationship strategy

2. Define partnering and describe the partnering relationship

3. List the four key groups with which the salesperson needs to develop relationship strategies

4. Discuss how self-image forms the foundation for building long-term selling relationships

5. Describe the importance of a double-win relationship

6. Identify and describe the major nonverbal factors that shape our sales image

7. Define surface language and discuss appropriate dress for sales calls

8. Discuss how voice quality and good manners can affect relationships

9. Describe conversational strategies that help us establish relationships

10. Explain how to establish a self-improvement plan based on personal development strategies

The salespeople who work for Fred Sands Realtors understand the importance of developing relationship strategies. This successful company, with offices throughout the United States and in many parts of the world, strives to build a long-term partnership with each customer. Sandra Khadra, vice president of marketing at Fred Sands Realtors, encourages salespeople to begin building rapport during the first contact. She teaches salespeople the basics of creating a professional image and stresses the importance of empathy with the customer. She knows that when you sincerely care about the welfare of the customer, you add value to the sale.[1]

Helping people buy a home requires a multitude of skills. You must assume the roles of financial adviser, educator, and counselor.[2] Above all, you must listen closely to everything that prospects say in order to accurately identify their wants and needs.

Developing a Relationship Strategy

To develop and apply the wide range of interpersonal skills needed in today's complex sales environment can be challenging. Daniel Goleman, author of the best-selling book *Emotional Intelligence*, notes that there are many forms of intelligence that influence our actions throughout life. One of these, **interpersonal intelligence,** is the ability to discern and respond appropriately to the moods, motivations, temperaments, and desires of other people. Successful teachers, salespeople, clinicians, politicians, and religious leaders are likely to have a high level of interpersonal intelligence.[3] The good news is that interpersonal intelligence can be enhanced with a variety of self-development activities. We discuss many of these activities in this chapter.

Personal selling involves three major relationship challenges. The first major challenge is building new relationships.[4] Salespeople who can quickly build rapport with new prospects have a much greater chance of achieving success in personal selling. Needless to say, building new relationships starts with the communication of positive impressions during the initial contact. The second major challenge is transforming relationships from the personal level to the business level. Once rapport is established, the salesperson is in a stronger position to begin the need identification process. The third major challenge is management of relationships. Dr. Charles Parker—noted consultant and sales trainer—says, "In order to achieve a high level of success salespeople have to manage a multitude of different relationships."[5] Salespeople must develop relationship management strategies that focus on four key groups. These groups are discussed later in this chapter.

Ongoing development of a relationship strategy should be the goal of every salesperson; customers tend to buy from people they like and trust, so we must learn how to establish and build relationships.[6] In this chapter we introduce the double-win philosophy and discuss the importance of projecting a professional image. Chapter 4 focuses on the importance of maintaining high ethical standards in order to build long-term relationships with the customer

Partnering is a strategically developed, high-quality, long-term relationship that focuses on solving the customer's buying problem. Partnering involves establishing, reestablishing and maintaining relationships with customers.

FIGURE 3.1 Every salesperson should have an ongoing goal of developing a relationship strategy that adds value to the sale.

Strategic/Consultative Selling Model	
Strategic step	Prescription
DEVELOP A PERSONAL SELLING PHILOSOPHY	☑ ADOPT MARKETING CONCEPT ☑ VALUE PERSONAL SELLING ☑ BECOME A PROBLEM SOLVER/PARTNER
DEVELOP A RELATIONSHIP STRATEGY	☐ ADOPT DOUBLE-WIN PHILOSOPHY ☐ PROJECT PROFESSIONAL IMAGE ☐ MAINTAIN HIGH ETHICAL STANDARDS

(Fig. 3.1). Chapter 16 explains how an understanding of communication styles can help us better manage the relationship process.

RELATIONSHIPS ADD VALUE

Denis Waitley, in his newest book *Empires of the Mind*, describes recent developments in the business community. He says, "Yesterday value was extra. Today value is everything."[7] Customers have become more sophisticated and more demanding in their buying strategies. They have come to expect partnering, and selling strategies that add value to the purchase. Consequently, salespeople need to become more sophisticated in their selling strategies. Learning International, Wilson Learning Corporation, Dale Carnegie & Associates, Zig Ziglar Corporation, and the Forum Corporation offer sales training that stresses a style of selling that favors a close, trusting, long-term relationship over the quick sell. A representative of Forum noted, "The philosophy is to serve the customer as a consultant, not as a peddler."

The manner in which salespeople establish, build, and maintain relationships is no longer an incidental aspect of personal selling; it is a key to success. A satisfied customer will recommend you to many other prospects, and a disgruntled customer can be counted on to complain about you to numerous prospects.[8]

The salesperson who is honest, accountable, and sincerely concerned about the customer's welfare brings added value to the sale. These characteristics give the salesperson a competitive advantage—an advantage that is becoming increasingly important in a world of "look-alike" products and similar prices.

PARTNERING—THE HIGHEST-QUALITY SELLING RELATIONSHIP

Salespeople today are encouraged to think of everything they say or do in the context of their relationship with the customer. They should constantly strive to build a long-term partnership. In a marketplace characterized by increased levels of competition and greater product complexity, we see the need to adopt a relationship strategy that emphasizes the "lifetime" customer. High-quality relationships result in repeat business and those important referrals. A growing number of salespeople recognize that the quality of partnerships they create is as important as the quality of the products they sell. Today's customer wants a quality product *and* a quality relationship. One example of this trend is the J. D. Power and Associates Automotive Studies research. The Initial Quality Study conducted by this marketing information firm measures the number and type of problems experienced by new car owners. The Sales Satisfaction Study, also conducted by J. D. Power, examines factors that impact on sales satisfaction such as treatment by auto sales representatives and customer experience when the auto was delivered.[9]

Partnering can be defined as a strategically developed, high-quality, long-term relationship that focuses on solving the customer's buying problem.[10] This definition is used in the sales training video entitled "Partnering—The Heart of Selling Today," which was produced by American Media. Some traditional sales training programs emphasized the importance of creating a good first impression and then "pushing" your product. Partnering emphasizes building a strong relationship during every aspect of the sale and working hard to maintain a quality relationship with the customer after the sale.

In the film *Selling in the 90s* Larry Wilson identifies partnering as one of the most important strategic thought processes needed by salespeople. He points out that the salesperson who is selling a "one-shot" solution cannot compete against the one who has developed and nurtured a long-term, mutually beneficial partnership. Wilson believes there are three keys to a partnering relationship:

➤ The relationship is built on shared values. If your client feels that you both share the same ideas and values, it goes a long way toward creating a powerful relationship.

➤ Everyone needs to clearly understand the purpose of the partnership and be committed to the vision. Both the salesperson and the client must agree on what they are trying to do together.

➤ The role of the salesperson must move from selling to supporting. The salesperson in a partnership is actively concerned with the growth, health, and satisfaction of the company to which she is selling.[11]

Salespeople willing to abandon short-term thinking and invest the time and energy needed to develop a high-quality, long-term relationship with customers will be rewarded with greater earnings and the satisfaction of working with repeat customers. Sales resulting from referrals will also increase.

BUILDING RELATIONSHIPS THROUGH TECHNOLOGY

ACT! LETTERS MADE EASY

Letters to customers can be used to establish, reestablish, and maintain relationships. Many salespeople now use word processing software to prepare their correspondence. Most contact management software, such as the ACT! demo, includes such word processing capabilities and adds a new dimension—ease of use. Busy salespeople can use this software to quickly dash off letters, such as the kinds that may have been previously deferred due to time constraints: appointment confirmations, information verification, company or product news, or brief personal notes. (See Sales Automation Application Exercise on p. 70 for more information.)

RELATIONSHIP STRATEGIES FOCUS ON FOUR KEY GROUPS

Establishing and maintaining a partnering-type relationship internally as well as with the customers is a vital aspect of selling. High-performance sales personnel build strong relationships with four groups (Fig. 3.2):

1. *Customers.* As noted previously, a major key to success in selling is the ability to establish working relationships with customers in which mutual support, trust, and goals are nurtured over time. Salespeople who build effective relationships with the customer and provide a valuable service are usually high performers.

   John Franco, former president of Learning International, says that in some cases the salesperson must move beyond the role of trusted consultant to gain full acceptance by the customer. He says that in today's highly competitive business climate the salesperson needs to be perceived as someone who is working on the customer's team as a member of the customer's organization.[12]

2. *Secondary decision makers.* High-performance salespeople understand the importance of building relationships with the people who work with customers. In many selling situations the first person the salesperson meets is a receptionist, secretary, or assistant to the primary decision maker. These persons can often facilitate a meeting with the prospect. Also, the prospect may involve other people in making the buying decision. For example, the decision to buy a new copy machine may be made by a team of persons including the buyer and persons who will actually use the machine.

3. *Company support staff.* The maintenance of relationships internally is a vital aspect of selling. Support staff may include persons working in the areas of market research, product service, credit, training, or shipping. Influencing these people to change their priorities, interrupt their schedules, accept new responsibilities, or fulfill any other request for special attention is a major part of the salesperson's job. Most sales personnel will readily admit that their productivity depends on the contributions of these people.

4. *Management personnel.* Sales personnel usually work under the direct supervision of a sales manager, department head, or some other member of the

FIGURE 3.2 An effective relationship strategy helps high-performing salespeople to build and maintain win-win relationships with a wide range of key groups.

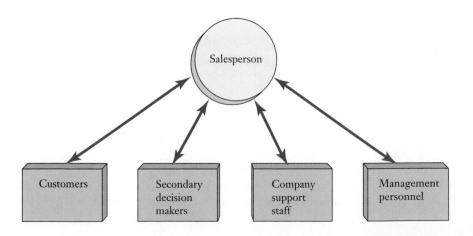

A SELLING PARTNER

P **PREPARES STRATEGICALLY** for a long-term, high-quality relationship that solves customer's problems

A **ASKS QUESTIONS** to get on the customer's agenda

R **RESTATES CUSTOMER NEEDS** with confirmation questions

T **TEAMS** with support people to custom-fit solutions

N **NEGOTIATES DOUBLE-WIN SOLUTIONS** with joint decision making

E **EXCEEDS CUSTOMER EXPECTATIONS** whenever possible

R **REEXAMINES** the ongoing quality of the relationship frequently

firm's management team. Maintaining a good relationship with this person is important.

Developing Thought Processes That Enhance Your Relationship Strategy

Folklore has created the myth of the "born" salesperson—a dynamic, outgoing, highly assertive individual. Experience has taught us that many other factors determine sales success. Key among these factors are a positive self-image and the ability to relate to others in effective and productive ways. With the aid of knowledge drawn from the behavioral sciences we can develop the relationship strategies needed in a wide range of selling situations.

SELF-IMAGE — AN IMPORTANT DIMENSION OF THE RELATIONSHIP STRATEGY

Self-image is shaped by the ideas, attitudes, feelings, and other thoughts you have about yourself that influence the way you relate to others. Psychologists have found that once we form a thought process about ourselves, it serves to edit all incoming information and influence our actions. Let us consider a salesperson who has come to believe that he cannot build strong relationships with high-level decision makers. Once this mental picture, or self-image, has been formed, it is unlikely that this salesperson will be able to influence high-level executives in a sales situation. Essentially, this person is programmed to relate to low-level decision makers. There is no anticipation of improvement, so the negative self-image becomes a self-fulfilling prophecy. You simply cannot succeed at something unless you think you are going to succeed at it.

SELF-IMAGE AND SUCCESS

Self-image is a powerful thought process influencing the direction of our lives. It can set the limits of our accomplishments, defining what we can and cannot do. Realizing the power of self-image is an important breakthrough in our understanding of the factors that influence us.

A pioneer in the area of self-image psychology was the late Dr. Maxwell Maltz, author of *Psycho-Cybernetics* and other books devoted to this topic. We

SIX QUALITIES OF A PROFESSIONAL SALESPERSON

1. Image
Dress, grooming, inflection, posture, personality, and style are all important.

2. Attitude
Develop a sincere respect for your customer.

3. Knowledge
Go deeper than product knowledge to gain an understanding of the history and direction of the industry, and how it relates to the rest of the world.

4. Sensitivity
Be aware of and react to your customer's needs.

5. Enthusiasm
If your customer senses you are sold on the product, she is more likely to buy from you.

6. Maturity
Be able to handle disappointments and setbacks.[a]

are indebted to him for two important discoveries that help us understand better the "why" of human behavior:

1. *Feelings and behavior are consistent with the self-image.* The individual who feels like a "failure" will likely find some way to fail. There is a definite relationship between self-image and accomplishments at work. Generally speaking, the more positive your self-image, the greater your prospects for achieving success, because a positive self-image helps generate the energy needed to get things done.

2. *The self-image can be changed.* Numerous case histories show that you are never too young or too old to change your self-image and thereby achieve new accomplishments.[13]

A positive self-image (high self-esteem) is an important prerequisite to success in selling. According to a study conducted by Sentry Insurance, high self-esteem mixed with candor are the vital ingredients in the makeup of top salespeople.[14]

How can you develop a more positive self-image? How can you get rid of self-destructive ways of thinking? Bringing your present self-image out into the open is the first step in understanding who you are, what you can do, and where you are going. Improving your self-image will not happen overnight, but it can happen. A few practical approaches are summarized here.

1. *Focus on the future and stop being overly concerned with past mistakes or failures.* We should learn from past errors, but we should not be immobilized by them.

BUILDING RELATIONSHIPS IN A DIVERSE WORLD

BUSINESS ETIQUETTE FOSTERS QUALITY RELATIONSHIPS

A diverse workforce often creates new challenges for those who want to practice good manners. To illustrate, what do you do if a client comes into your office in a wheelchair? Do you rise? A man and a woman of equal corporate status walk down an office corridor and arrive at a door. If the woman reaches the door first, should the man move ahead to open it for her?

Changing technology also creates questions in the mind of the person who wants to avoid a violation of the rules of good etiquette. Should you switch on speaker phones without letting the caller know that others are present in the room and listening? Should you leave personal messages on voice mail if several others have access to the messages?

Most business firms want to make sure their employees can correctly answer these questions. Ann Humphries, a representative of Eticon, an etiquette consulting firm in Columbia, South Carolina explains why good manners is receiving so much attention today: "Quality is increasingly a central concept in corporations, and good manners are a central part of delivering on the quality promise." This attitude has prompted many companies to offer business-etiquette training courses. Those who cannot attend a seminar are turning to books such as *Letitia Baldrige's Complete Guide to Executive Manners* by Letitia Baldrige, *Miss Manners' Guide for the Turn-of-the-Millennium* by Judith Martin, and *Business Etiquette in Brief* by Ann Marie Sabath.

Tips on business etiquette may be as close as your daily newspaper. More than a decade ago, Judith Martin started writing a column called "Miss Manners." To her surprise, the column has become extremely popular throughout the United States. Today, more than 250 newspapers carry the column. Judith Martin points out that learning and practicing good manners is a great investment of your time. "In a society as ridden as ours with expensive status symbols, where every purchase is considered a social statement, there is no easier or cheaper way to distinguish oneself than by the practice of gentle manners.[b]

2. *Develop expertise in selected areas.* By developing "expert power" you not only improve your self-image but also increase the value of your contributions to your employer and your customers. Many salespeople are returning to the classroom to study computer technology, active listening, public speaking, and other topics.

3. *Learn to develop a positive mental attitude.* To develop a more positive outlook, read books and listen to audio tapes that describe ways to develop a positive mental attitude. Consider materials developed by Denis Waitley, Stephen Covey, Brian Tracy, Dale Carnegie, and Zig Ziglar.

4. *Set and achieve goals.* Our self-image improves as we set and achieve goals. The secret to goal setting is simple: Establish clearly defined goals; write them down; and then dwell on them with words, mental pictures, and your emotions.[15] Salespeople have many opportunities to set and achieve goals in their daily work.

THE DOUBLE-WIN

Denis Waitley—consultant, national speaker, and author of several books—provides us with a brief and simple definition of the term **double-win:** "If I help you win, I win, too."[16] Both the customer and the salesperson come out of

This salesperson's clothing and facial expression project a professional image. A pleasant smile and eye contact convey friendliness to the customer.

the sale feeling a sense of satisfaction. The salesperson not only obtains the order, but sets the stage for a long-term relationship, repeat business, and future referrals. Here is how one author described this "win-win" approach:

> *You both come out of the sale feeling satisfied, knowing that neither of you has taken advantage of the other and that both of you have profited, personally and professionally, from the transaction. In the simplest terms, you know you have a win-win sales encounter when both you and the buyer come out of it feeling positive.*[17]

The double-win strategy is based on such irrefutable logic that it is difficult to understand why any other approach would be used. However, some salespeople still have not accepted the merits of the win-win approach. They have adopted a win-lose approach, which means that the salesperson wins at the buyer's expense. When a salesperson sells a product that is not the best solution to the buyer's problem, the win-lose strategy has been used.

We can adopt the win-win attitude that is one of the principles of partnering-style selling. The starting point to development of a double-win philosophy is to compare the behaviors of persons who have adopted the win-lose approach with the behaviors of persons who have adopted the win-win approach (Fig. 3.3).

CHARACTER AND INTEGRITY

Your character and integrity strongly influence your relationships with others. **Character** is composed of your personal standards of behavior, including your honesty, integrity, and moral fiber.[18] Your character is based on your internal values and the resulting judgments you make about what is right and what is wrong. When your behavior is in tune with your professed standards and values—when you practice what you believe in—you have integrity. In a world of

Win-lose people

- See a problem in every solution

- Fix the blame

- Let life happen to them

- Live in the past

- Make promises they never keep

Win-win people

- Help others solve their problem

- Fix what caused the problem

- Make life a joyous happening for others and themselves

- Learn from the past, live in the present, and set goals for the future

- Make commitments to themselves and to others and keep them both

FIGURE 3.3   The starting point to developing a double-win philosophy is to compare behaviors of win-lose salespeople with those of salespeople who have adopted the win-win approach. (Adapted from a list of losers, winners, and double winners in *The Double Win* by Denis Waitley.)

uncertainty and rapid change, integrity has become a valuable character trait. Salespeople with integrity can be trusted to do what they say they will do. One way to achieve trustworthiness in personal selling is to avoid deceiving or misleading the customer. More will be said about this topic in Chapter 4, which examines the ethical conduct of salespeople.

Nonverbal Strategies That Improve Relationships

The first contact between a salesperson and a prospect is important. During the first few minutes—or seconds in some cases—the prospect forms a judgment about whether the salesperson is worth getting to know better. Kathryn Volin, president of Communication Concepts International, says that it is very difficult to rebound from a poor first impression. Further, she states that it can take several additional meetings to change a negative first impression.[19]

The image projected by the salesperson can create a positive or a negative first impression. Every salesperson projects an image to prospective customers, and this image influences how a customer feels about the sales representative.

The image you project is the sum total of many verbal and nonverbal factors. The quality of your voice, the clothing you wear, your posture, your manners, your communication style represent some of the factors that contribute to the formation of your image. We discuss body language, surface language, voice quality and manners in this chapter. Communication style is examined in Chapter 16.

THE EFFECT OF BODY LANGUAGE ON RELATIONSHIPS

Body language is a form of nonverbal communication that has been defined as *messages without words* and *silent messages*. For example, a purchasing agent who continually glances at his watch is communicating a concern for time without using the spoken word. A salesperson who leans forward in her chair while

A pleasant smile sends a positive nonverbal message to the customer.

talking to a customer (as opposed to slouching) is more likely to communicate a feeling of concern to this person.

Research indicates that when two people communicate, nonverbal messages convey much more impact than verbal messages. Words play a surprisingly small part in the communication process. Studies indicate that in a typical two-person conversation, only about 7 percent of our understanding comes from words spoken by the other person. About 38 percent of our understanding comes from what we hear. Does the other person sound sincere, credible, and knowledgeable? Every spoken message has a vocal element, coming not from *what* we say, but from *how* we say it. The voice communicates in many ways: through its tone, volume, and speed of delivery. A salesperson wishing to communicate enthusiasm needs to use a voice that is charged with energy.

About 55 percent of the meaning we attach to communication efforts by others is based on what we see or feel (Fig. 3.4). A positive message can be communicated to a customer with a smile, a firm handshake, good eye contact, and professional appearance.[20]

Nonverbal messages can reinforce or contradict the spoken word. When your verbal message and body language are consistent, they give others the impression that you can be trusted and that what you say reflects what you truly believe. When there is a discrepancy between your verbal and nonverbal messages, you are less apt to be trusted.[21]

FIGURE 3.4 When someone else is speaking, your understanding of what is said depends heavily on what you see or feel. (Source: Moravian Study of Nonverbal Communication.)

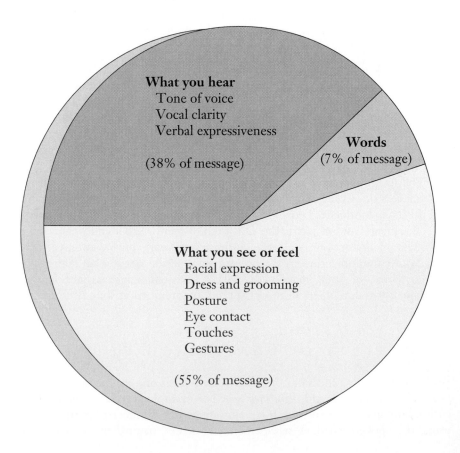

What you hear
Tone of voice
Vocal clarity
Verbal expressiveness

(38% of message)

Words
(7% of message)

What you see or feel
Facial expression
Dress and grooming
Posture
Eye contact
Touches
Gestures

(55% of message)

ENTRANCE AND CARRIAGE

As noted earlier, the first impression we make is very important. The moment a salesperson walks into a client's office, the client begins making judgments. Susan Bixler, author of *The Professional Image* and *Professional Presence*, makes this comment:

> *All of us make entrances throughout our business day as we enter offices, conference rooms, or meeting halls. And every time we do, someone is watching us, appraising us, sizing us up, and gauging our appearance, even our intelligence, often within the space of a few seconds.*[22]

Bixler says that the key to making a successful entrance is simply believing—and projecting—that you have a reason to be there and have something important to offer the client. You can communicate confidence with a strong stride, good posture, and a friendly smile. A confident manner communicates to the client the message, "This meeting will be beneficial to you."

SHAKING HANDS

An inadequate handshake is like dandruff: no one will mention it, but everyone will notice it. An effective handshake establishes a business relationship, signals active participation, and gives a message of confidence and goodwill.[23]

In the field of selling the handshake is usually the *first* and frequently the *only* physical contact one makes during a sales call. The handshake can commu-

The best time to present your name is during the handshake.

nicate warmth, genuine concern for the prospect, and an image of strength. It can also communicate aloofness, indifference, and weakness to the customer. The message we communicate with a handshake will be determined by a combination of five factors:

1. *Eye contact during handshake.* Eyes transmit more information than any other part of the body, so maintaining eye contact throughout the handshaking process is important when two people greet each other.

2. *Degree of firmness.* Generally speaking, a firm handshake will communicate a caring attitude, while a weak grip (the dead-fish handshake) communicates indifference.

3. *Depth of interlock.* A full, deep grip will communicate friendship to the other person.

4. *Duration of grip.* There are no specific guidelines to tell us what the ideal duration of a grip should be. However, by extending the duration of the handshake we can often communicate a greater degree of interest and concern for the other person. Do not pump up and down more than once or twice.

5. *Degree of dryness of hands.* A moist palm not only is uncomfortable to handle but also can communicate the impression that you are quite nervous. Some people have a physiological problem that causes clammy hands and should keep a handkerchief within reach to remove excess moisture. A clammy hand is likely to repel most customers.[24]

The best time to present your name is during the handshake. When you introduce yourself, state your name clearly and then listen carefully to be certain you hear the customer's name. To ensure that you will remember the customer's name, repeat it. In some cases you will need to check to be sure you are pronouncing it properly.[25]

FACIAL EXPRESSIONS

If you want to identify the inner feelings of another person, watch facial expressions closely. A frown or a smile will communicate a great deal. Janet G. Elsea, author of *The Four-Minute Sell*, states:

> *After overall appearance, your face is the most visible part of you. Facial expressions are the cue most people rely on in initial interactions; they are the "teleprompter" by which others read your mood and personality.*[26]

We have all encountered a "look of surprise" or a "look that could kill." Most of our observations are quite accurate. If we are able to assess the inner emotions of a customer, we can be sure that the customer is doing the same to us, drawing conclusions based on our facial expressions (Fig. 3.5).

The customer is continuously looking for congruency between our words and actions. Our facial expressions provide the best test for the customer. If you have genuine enthusiasm for your product, this feeling will register as part of your facial expression. If you lack commitment, your attitude will be evident to the customer. One of the most important facial expressions is the smile. A pleasant smile at the appropriate time will convey friendliness. Intermittent smiles trigger positive emotions within you, and these emotions are transferred

Confidence   Boredom   Evaluation

to the person at whom you are smiling. When you smile at someone, you usually get a smile in return.[27]

THE EFFECT OF SURFACE LANGUAGE ON RELATIONSHIPS

We form opinions about people on the basis of both facts and assumptions.
Many of the assumptions we develop concerning other people are based on
what Dr. Leonard Zunin describes as *surface language*.[28] **Surface language** is
defined as a pattern of immediate impressions conveyed by appearance. The
clothing we wear, the length and style of our hair, the fragrances we use, and
the jewelry we display all combine to make a statement about us to others—a
statement of primary importance to anyone involved in selling.

According to many writers familiar with the concept of surface language,
clothing is particularly important. John T. Molloy, author of *Dress for Success*,
New Dress for Success, and other books, was one of the first to acknowledge pub-
licly the link between dress and the image we project to others. He is credited
with introducing the term *wardrobe engineering*, a concept that was later refined
by William Thourlby, Jacqueline Thompson, Emily Cho, Susan Bixler, and
other noted image consultants. **Wardrobe engineering** combines the elements
of psychology, fashion, sociology, and art into clothing selection. The position
taken by Molloy and others is that clothing can evoke a predictable response.[29]

We all have certain views, or **unconscious expectations,** concerning
appropriate dress. In sales work we should try to anticipate the expectations
of our clientele. The clothing worn by salespeople does make a difference
in terms of customer acceptance because it communicates powerful messages. The clothing we wear can influence our credibility and likability. Martin
Siewert, a member of the business development team for Axiom Management
Consulting, has adopted a flexible approach to dress. His company's policy favors an informal dress code, so he usually wears casual clothing at work unless
he is meeting with a client. When he calls on customers, most of whom are
Fortune 500 companies, he wears a suit and tie. "I want to show that I respect
their culture," he says.[30]

Most image consultants agree that there is no single "dress for success"
look. The appropriate wardrobe will vary from one city or region to another
and from company to company. However, there are some general guidelines

Body language, surface language, voice quality, and manners shape much of the image we project to others.

that we should follow in selecting clothing for sales work. Three key words should govern our decisions: simplicity, appropriateness, and quality.

SIMPLICITY

The color of clothing, as well as design, will communicate a message to the customer. Some colors are showy and convey an air of casualness. In a business setting we want to be taken seriously, so flashy colors should usually be avoided.

Simplicity of dress is reflected in white or light blue shirts for men and white, cream, blue and pale pink blouses for women. These colors are in style season after season within the business community. For men and women, suits in navy blue or gray are appropriate in a wide range of selling situations.

APPROPRIATENESS

Selecting appropriate clothing for sales work can be a challenge. We must carefully consider the clients we serve and decide what will be acceptable to them. In some areas of business the basic suit with tie is rigidly prescribed for men. Insurance, banking, and legal firms provide three examples. In these settings, women would be appropriately dressed in a gray or blue-skirted suit.

QUALITY

The quality of our wardrobe will also influence the image we project to customers. A salesperson's wardrobe should be regarded as an investment, with each item carefully selected to look and fit well. Susan Bixler says, "If you want respect, you have to dress as well as or better than your industry standards."[31]

How you feel about your personal appearance has a direct bearing on how you project yourself to others. We simply feel better when our clothing looks good, fits comfortably, and is appropriate for the task at hand. Improve the way you look outside, and you will improve the way you feel inside.[32]

THE EFFECT OF VOICE QUALITY ON RELATIONSHIPS

As noted previously, voice quality contributes about 38 percent of the meaning attached to spoken messages. On the telephone, voice quality is even more important because the other person cannot see your facial expressions, hand gestures, and other body movements. You cannot trade in your current voice for a new one. However, you can make your voice more pleasing to others. How? Here are two suggestions.

1. *Do not talk too fast or too slowly.* Rapid speech often causes customers to become defensive. They raise psychological barriers because a "rapid-fire monologue" is associated with high-pressure sales methods. Many salespeople could improve their verbal presentation by talking more slowly. The slower presentation allows others to follow, and it allows the speaker time to think ahead—to consider the situation and make judgments. Another good tip is to vary the speed of your speech, leaving spaces between thoughts. Crowding too many thoughts together may confuse the listener.[33]

2. *Avoid a speech pattern that is dull and colorless.* Bert Decker, a communications consultant, says that it is important to vary the tone of your voice.[34] The worst kind of voice has no color and no feeling. Enthusiasm is a critical element of an effective sales presentation. It is also contagious. Your enthusiasm for the product will be transmitted to the customer. Vary your tone of voice to add color and vitality to what you say.

With today's affordable video camcorders you can easily find out how you look and sound. To evaluate the quality of your voice, tape it while talking to another person. Play back the tape, and rate yourself in the previously described areas.

THE EFFECT OF MANNERS ON YOUR RELATIONSHIPS

A study of manners (or etiquette) reveals a number of ways to establish and maintain relationships. Some of today's renewed interest in manners may have been stimulated by the writings of Letitia Baldrige, author of *Letitia Baldrige's Complete Guide to Executive Manners*, and the views expressed by Judith Martin who writes the "Miss Manners" column that appears in over 250 newspapers. It is the view of these two experts that good manners are cost effective.

Good manners are a passport to friendship, respect, and long-term partnerships. They are just as important in a business setting as in a social setting. With practice, anyone can have good manners without appearing to be "stiff" and at the same time win the respect and admiration of those served. Space does not permit a complete review of this topic, but we cover some of the rules of etiquette that are especially important to salespeople.

1. *Avoid the temptation to address a new prospect by first name.* In a business setting, too much familiarity too quickly can cause irritation.
2. *Avoid offensive comments or stories.* Never assume that the customer's value system is the same as your own. Rough language and off-color stories can do irreparable damage to your image.
3. *Do not express personal views on political or religious issues.* There is seldom a "safe" position to take in these areas, so it is better to avoid these topics altogether.
4. *When you invite a customer to lunch, do not discuss business before the meal is ordered unless the client initiates the subject.* Keep in mind that business luncheons and dinners serve different purposes in different cultures. In Japan, for example, the evening meal is viewed as a time to socialize and strengthen friendships.[35]

It has been said that good manners make other people feel better. This is true because good manners require that we place the other person's comfort ahead of our own. One of the best ways to develop rapport with a customer is to avoid behavior that might be offensive to that person.

Conversational Strategies That Enhance Relationships

The foundation for a long-term relationship with the customer is frequently a "get acquainted" type conversation that takes place before any discussion of business matters. Within a few minutes it is possible to reduce the relationship tension that is so common when two people meet for the first time. This informal visit with the customer provides the salesperson with an opportunity to apply three of Dale Carnegie's guidelines for building strong relationships:

➤ Become genuinely interested in other people.
➤ Be a good listener. Encourage others to talk about themselves.
➤ Talk in terms of the other person's interest.[36]

In a relaxed and friendly atmosphere, the customer is more apt to open up and share information that will help the salesperson determine customer needs. A casual conversation is frequently the first step in developing a trusting relationship.

The length of this conversation will depend on your sense of the prospect's reaction to your greeting, how busy the prospect appears to be, and your awareness of topics of mutual interest. In developing conversation the following three areas should be considered.

COMMENTS ON HERE AND NOW OBSERVATIONS

Observant salespeople are aware of the things going on around them. These observations can be as general as unusual trends in the weather or as specific as noticing unique artifacts in the prospect's office.

COMPLIMENTS

When you offer a *sincere* compliment to your prospect, you are saying, "Something about you is special." Most people react positively to compliments because they appeal to the need for self-esteem. Your admiration should not be expressed, however, in phony superlatives that will seem transparent. The prospect may suspect ulterior motives, which are unwelcome.

Observant salespeople are aware of the things going on around them. EMBARC offers computer-based wireless information technology.

SEARCH FOR MUTUAL ACQUAINTANCES OR INTERESTS

A frequent mode for establishing social contact with a new prospect is to find friends or interests you have in common. If you know someone with the same name as your prospect, it may be appropriate to ask whether your friend is any relation. Anything you observe in the prospect's office or home might suggest an interest that you and your prospect share. Such topics of conversation appeal to your prospect's social needs.

Remember that your objectives are to establish and maintain a good relationship with your prospect. Avoid overwhelming your prospect with too many questions, giving unsolicited advice, or pursuing a topic that does not interest your prospect.

Strategies for Self-Improvement

Orson Welles, one of the most highly respected actors in this country, once said, "Every actor is very busy getting better or getting worse." To a large extent, salespeople are also "very busy getting better or getting worse." To improve, salespeople must develop an ongoing program for self-improvement. It is important to keep in mind that all improvement is self-initiated. Each of us controls the switch that allows personal growth and development to take place.

At the beginning of this chapter we introduced the concept of interpersonal intelligence. We noted that this form of intelligence can be increased with the aid of self-development activities. Would you like to develop a more positive self-image? Improve your ability to develop double-win relationships? Develop effective nonverbal communication skills? Improve your speaking voice? These relationship-building strategies can be achieved if you are willing to follow these steps:

Step one: set goals Goal setting, as noted previously, is an important element of any self-improvement plan. The goal-setting process requires that you be clear about what you want to accomplish. If your goal is too general or vague, progress toward achieving that goal will be difficult to observe. An important step in the goal-setting process is to put the goal in writing.[37]

Step two: visualization To make your goals a reality, engage in visualization. Forming a mental picture of yourself succeeding in goal attainment will actually affect your behavior. Mary Lou Retton and many other Olympic stars have used visualization. She described her preparation for the gymnastics event this way:

> When I visualized myself going through a beam routine, I didn't imagine myself falling. I visualized myself on the beam—perfect. Always picture it perfect.[38]

You can work the same "mental magic" in goal setting by visualizing yourself as the person you want to be. For example, spend time developing mental pictures of successful experiences with prospective or established customers.

This salesperson has set a fitness goal. Physical fitness can be an important part of a self-improvement program.

JAMES HANSBERGER'S LIFETIME PLAN

Early in his career as a stockbroker, James Hansberger decided to prepare himself to handle the financial investments of well-paid executives and professionals in the fields of medicine and law. To prepare for this new role, Hansberger started a self-improvement program. He spent long hours studying tax law, investment strategies, and other information related to financial investments. He also decided to change his appearance. Hansberger took up jogging and tennis to get rid of extra weight. (He was 30 pounds overweight at the time.) He adopted a crisp, conservative style of dress. His goal was to look and act like his clients. The plan worked! Throughout a seven-year period he earned more than $1 million in commissions each year. Hansberger's self-improvement plan has been described in his book *Nice Guys Finish Rich*. This marathon-running Smith-Barney senior vice president also shares his ideas on "life planning" at many national conferences and conventions.

The end result of most successful self-improvement plans is increased self-esteem. A high level of self-esteem can set the stage for improved interpersonal relations. An individual with healthy self-esteem realizes the value of other people and the role they play in his success.[d]

Step three: monitor your self-talk Shad Helmstetter, author of *What You Say When You Talk to Yourself*, defines **self-talk** as "a way to override our past negative programming by erasing or replacing it with conscious, positive new directions."[39] It is an effective way to get rid of barriers to goal achievement. Helmstetter suggests that we develop specific positive self-talk statements and repeat them often to keep ourselves on target in terms of goal attainment.

Step four: recognize your progress When you see yourself making progress toward a goal, or achieving a goal, reward yourself. This type of reinforcement is vital when you are trying to change a behavior. There is nothing wrong with taking pride in your accomplishments.

Self-improvement efforts can result in new abilities or powers, and they give us the motivation to utilize more fully the talents we already have. As a result, our potential for success is greater.

SUMMARY

The manner in which salespeople establish, build, and maintain relationships is a major key to success in personal selling. The key relationships in selling include management personnel, company support staff, secondary decision makers, and customers.

The concept of *partnering* was defined and discussed in detail. Partnering emphasizes building a strong relationship during every aspect of the sale and working hard to maintain a quality relationship with the customer after the sale.

An understanding of the psychology of human behavior provides a foundation for developing relationship strategies. In this chapter we discussed the link between *self-image* and success in selling. Self-imposed fears can prevent salespeople from achieving success.

We have described several factors that influence the image you project to customers. The image others have of us is shaped to a great extent by nonverbal communication. We may choose the right words to persuade a customer to place an order, but aversive factors communicated by our clothing, handshake, facial expression, tone of voice, and general manner may prejudice the customer against us and our product or service.

There are few absolute standards for defining aversive factors. Beyond obvious things like slovenly dress and rude manners you must develop your own awareness of geographic and social factors, as well as your knowledge of particular customers, to know what might be considered aversive.

We also discussed the importance of self-improvement. A four-step–self-improvement plan was described.

➤ KEY TERMS

Partnering	*Surface Language*
Self-Image	*Wardrobe Engineering*
Double-Win	*Unconscious Expectations*
Body Language	*Interpersonal Intelligence*
Character	*Self-Talk*

➤ REVIEW QUESTIONS

1. List the three prescriptions that serve as the foundation for development of a relationship strategy.

2. How important are establishing, building, and maintaining relationships in the selling process? List the four groups of people with whom sales personnel must be able to work effectively.

3. Define the term *partnering*. Why has the building of partnerships become more important today?

4. Defend the statement, "Successful relationships depend on a positive self-image."

5. Describe the double-win or win-win approach to selling.

6. How is our self-image formed? Why is a positive self-image so important in personal selling?

7. Describe the meaning of the term **interpersonal intelligence.**

8. Identify three conversational methods that can be used to establish relationships.

9. List and describe each step in the four-step–self-improvement plan.

10. The boxed insert on page 63 features a quote by Jonathan Swift. Do you agree or disagree with his statement? Explain.

➤ APPLICATION EXERCISES

1. Select four salespeople you know and ask them if they have a relationship strategy for working with customers, management personnel, secondary decision makers, and company support staff.

2. The partnering style of selling has been emphasized in Chapters 1 and 3. To gain more insight into the popularity of this concept, use one of the search engines suitable for the Internet to key in the words "partnering+ selling." Notice the large number of documents related to this query. Click on and examine several of these documents to learn more about this approach to selling.

3. Complete the following etiquette quiz. Your instructor will provide you with answers so you can check your responses.

   a. On what side should you wear your name tag?

   b. Is it appropriate to drink beer from a bottle at a reception?

   c. When introducing a female salesperson to a male prospect, whose name should be spoken first?

   d. At the table, when should you place your napkin in your lap?

   e. Is it ever proper to comb, smooth, or touch your hair while seated at a restaurant table?

4. Move quickly through the following list of traits. Use a check mark beside those that fit your self-image. Use an *X* to mark those that do not fit. If you are unsure, indicate with a question mark.

_____ I like myself.	_____ People like to be around me.
_____ People trust me.	_____ I trust myself.
_____ I usually say the right thing.	_____ I often do the wrong thing.
_____ I dislike myself.	_____ People avoid me.
_____ I waste time.	_____ I enjoy work.
_____ I put up a good front.	_____ I control myself.
_____ I use my talents.	_____ I enjoy nature.
_____ I feel hemmed in.	_____ I am dependent on others for ideas.
_____ I use time well.	
_____ I enjoy people.	_____ I am involved in solving community problems.
_____ I usually say the wrong thing.	_____ I do not use my talents fully.
_____ I am discouraged about life.	_____ I do not like myself.
_____ I have not developed my talents.	_____ I do not like to be around people.

Now look at the pattern of your self-assessment.

   a. Is there a pattern?

   b. Is there a winner or loser pattern?

   c. What traits would you like to change? (List them.)

   d. Pick the trait you would like to change the most, and prepare a plan to achieve this change.

5. It has been pointed out in this chapter that clothing communicates strong messages. In this exercise you will become more aware of whether or not your clothes communicate the messages you want them to communicate.

a. Make a chart like the one that follows:

Item of clothing being analyzed	What I want my clothes to say about me to others	What others think my clothing says

b. In the first column, list the clothing you are now wearing (for example, dress slacks, dress shoes, and sweater; athletic shoes, jeans, and T-shirt; or suit, tie, and dress shoes).
c. In the middle column, describe the message you would like the clothes you have chosen to say. For example, "I want to be comfortable," "I want people to notice me," or "I want people to understand how proper and organized I am."
d. Have somebody else fill in the third column by describing what your clothes do say about you.
e. Compare the two columns. Do your clothes communicate what you want them to? Do the same exercise for social dress, casual dress, business attire, and hairstyle.

➤ SALES AUTOMATION APPLICATION EXERCISE

ACT! LETTERS MADE EASY

The ACT! software demonstrates how some contact management programs are designed to be used by people in a hurry or without extensive typing skills. Menu choices can be made by typing only one letter. This means that a procedure, such as preparing and printing correspondence, can be reduced to this simple sequence of keys: WLEHiF10P DS Enter Enter DY. On your screen will appear the brief letter "Hi." With your printer connected you can print this same letter by typing WLEHiF10PD Enter Enter ND.

Access the ACT! software following the instructions in Appendix 2. Using the same sequence of keys above for *printing* a letter, prepare a brief letter to Brad Able confirming an appointment to meet at his office next Thursday at 9:00 A.M. to discuss his training needs. (The keys "Hi" should be deleted from the preceding sequence and replaced by the letter you will prepare.) Your letter should feature the double-win approach discussed in Chapter 3.

➤ CASE PROBLEM

When people buy or sell a home, they hold their realtor to high standards. After all, for most people the home purchase represents the largest single investment they will make throughout their lifetime. The salespeople employed by

Fred Sands Realtors, introduced at the beginning of this chapter, understand the magnitude of the home purchase or home sale experience. They know that the customers are anxious to partner with someone who can be trusted to look after their best interests.

When new salespeople join the Fred Sands Realtors' sales force, they usually come under the tutelage of Sandra Khadra, vice president of marketing. She helps salespeople form a professional image that will appeal to the type of clientele served by the company. She knows that there is a direct link between the image projected by the salespeople and the success of the company. When working with salespeople, she emphasizes the following points:

➤ Customers notice even the little things such as the quality of stationery, note paper, and business cards. If the business card features a photo of the salesperson, the person should be looking straight ahead, not away from the camera. This pose permits the salesperson to make eye contact with the customer.

➤ Salespeople at Fred Sands Realtors must be able to build rapport with a variety of personality types. Some customers are quiet, reserved, and somewhat guarded when expressing their views. Others are more impulsive and express their views openly. Salespeople are encouraged to alter their communication style to increase the comfort level of the customer. Sandra Khadra encourages salespeople to mirror the behavior of the prospect to the greatest extent possible. She says that it is always important to gauge how your communication style impacts on the prospect. A positive attitude is another important aspect of the relationship-building process at Fred Sands Realtors.

➤ In some cases salespeople at Fred Sands Realtors must communicate across language and cultural barriers. Foreign-born clients are becoming more common, and this means that salespeople must gain a greater understanding and respect for cultural diversity. To impose our way of doing business on every prospect is shortsighted.

➤ Sandra Khadra suggests finding out what customers value. What is the most important aspect of the home purchase or home sale? Most customers will not open up and share important information until they trust the salesperson.

QUESTIONS

1. Does it appear that Fred Sands Realtors supports the three prescriptions that serve as a foundation of the relationship strategy? (See Strategic/Consultative Selling Model.) Explain your answer.

2. Why should real estate salespeople spend time developing a relationship strategy? What might be some long-term benefits of this strategy?

3. Is it ever appropriate to touch your client other than a handshake? Explain your answer.

4. What are some benefits to the salesperson who can mirror the behavior of the prospect?

5. What are some precautions to take when preparing a meeting with a foreign-born prospect?

Ethics: The Foundation for Relationships in Selling

Herbert Schulte, a veteran Prudential Insurance sales representative serving a small Illinois community, was forced to make a difficult ethical decision. His sales manager gave him a list of his middle-aged customers and sales literature that described a Prudential life insurance policy as nursing home coverage. He contends that his manager was implicitly recommending an insurance-industry practice called "churning." With this practice, agents pressure customers to use built-up cash value in an old policy to buy a new, more expensive one. In some cases information is withheld so customers fail to understand the negative aspects of the buying decision. Mr. Schulte realized that the sales approach recommended by his sales manager would require that he mislead his established customers. He refused to go along with the plan.[1] Mr. Schulte was one of hundreds of Prudential sales representatives encouraged to use misleading sales practices. Recently Prudential promised to reform its sales practices and pay a $35 million fine for unethical activities. Additional money from Prudential, in excess of $400 million, will provide restitution to abused policyholders. The company has purchased full-page newspaper ads to apologize for the "intolerable" deceptive sales practices.[2] The Prudential scandal provides a powerful example of a sales culture gone bad.

Making Ethical Decisions

Making ethical decisions is a daily reality in the field of personal selling. In every selling situation, salespeople must judge the rightness or wrongness of their actions. As in any other professional field there is the constant temptation to compromise personal standards of conduct to achieve economic goals.

Today, we recognize that character and integrity strongly influence relationships in personal selling. As noted in the previous chapter, character is composed of your personal standards of behavior, including your honesty and integrity. Your character is based on your internal values and the resulting judgments you make about what is right and what is wrong. The ethical decisions you make reflect your character strength.

We are indebted to Stephen Covey, author of *The 7 Habits of Highly Effective People*, for helping us better understand the relationship between character strength and success in personal selling. In his best-selling book, Covey says there are basic principles that must be integrated into our character.[3] One example is to always do what you say you are going to do. Fulfilling your commitments builds trust, and trust is the most important precondition of partnering. Throughout this chapter you will become acquainted with several factors that strengthen character.

The ability to build and maintain long-term relationships is based on character strength. Covey notes that outward attitudes and behaviors such as making favorable first impressions or being a good listener do very little good in the long run *unless* they are based on solid principles governing human effectiveness. These principles include such virtues as honesty, integrity, service, and fairness.

ETHICS DEFINED

James O'Toole, author of *Vanguard Management*, said, "No company has ever gotten into financial trouble because they adhered to ethical principles."[4] On the other hand, many of America's largest corporations—Hertz Corporation, Rockwell International, Chrysler Corporation, and Metropolitan Life Insurance Company, to name a few—have gotten into financial trouble by ignoring ethical principles.

In concise terms, *ethics* is the rules of conduct that reflect the moral principles and standards of the community. Kickbacks and payoffs may be acceptable practices in one part of the world yet may be viewed as unethical practices elsewhere. Exaggerated or inaccurate sales claims may be acceptable at one company, but forbidden at another company. Ethics can also be viewed as a person's adherence to accepted principles of honesty and fairness.

There is no one uniform code of ethics for all salespeople. However, a large number of business organizations, professional associations, and commissions have established a written code of conduct for their employees. Mark Twain once wrote, "To be good is noble. To tell people how to be good is even nobler, and much less trouble." Many corporate leaders have decided that it is time to put their views on ethics in writing. More than 90 percent of the Fortune 1,000 companies have written codes of ethics.[5] A written code, highly publicized throughout the company and enforced without exception, can be a powerful force in preventing unethical behavior. It provides protection for both the salesperson and the company.

BUILDING QUALITY PARTNERSHIPS

GREATEST CAPITALIST IN HISTORY?

Thomas J. Watson, Jr., former president of IBM, has been described by *Fortune* magazine as "the greatest capitalist in history." When he retired as IBM's chief executive officer, the company was worth $36 billion more than when he took office fifteen years before. Like virtually every other IBM executive he started in sales. From salesperson to president of the company he was guided by three principles:

- Give the individual full consideration.
- Spend a lot of time making customers happy.
- Go the last mile to do the right thing.

Not only did he encourage employees to do the right thing, but also he demanded a high level of integrity. When people broke the rules, they were fired.

Watson understood that without integrity, no company could enjoy long-term success. For salespeople, integrity is the primary sales tool, according to Jeffrey Davidson, noted sales consultant. Integrity means you maintain your values steadfastly and focus on what you believe is right.[a]

Companies like Marion Merrell Dow, Inc. have published documents like this one to make it clear to employees, customers, vendors, etc. what the company's core values are regarding ethics.

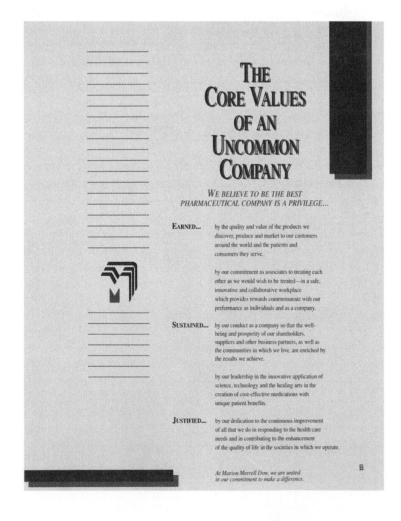

THE CORE VALUES OF AN UNCOMMON COMPANY

WE BELIEVE TO BE THE BEST PHARMACEUTICAL COMPANY IS A PRIVILEGE...

EARNED... by the quality and value of the products we discover, produce and market to our customers around the world and the patients and consumers they serve.

by our commitment as associates to treating each other as we would wish to be treated—in a safe, innovative and collaborative workplace which provides rewards commensurate with our performance as individuals and as a company.

SUSTAINED... by our conduct as a company so that the well-being and prosperity of our shareholders, suppliers and other business partners, as well as the communities in which we live, are enriched by the results we achieve.

by our leadership in the innovative application of science, technology and the healing arts in the creation of cost-effective medications with unique patient benefits.

JUSTIFIED... by our dedication to the continuous improvement of all that we do in responding to the health care needs and in contributing to the enhancement of the quality of life in the societies in which we operate.

At Marion Merrell Dow, we are united in our commitment to make a difference.

55

Marion Laboratories, Incorporated, a company based in Kansas City, Missouri, has published a document entitled, "Marion's Foundation for an Uncommon Company." The first line focuses on relationships with customers, suppliers, and associates: "We should treat others as we would be treated—with dignity, respect, integrity, and honesty."[6] Raychem Corporation, located in California, tells new employees, "We insist that fairness and integrity permeate all decisions we make concerning our people, our products, and our customers."[7] The management team at Rolm Corporation, maker of computerized telephone exchanges, says that its employees' responsibilities include "being honest."[8] One of the operating principles at Lotus Development Corporation is "Insist on integrity."[9]

ETHICS — AN HISTORICAL PERSPECTIVE

For centuries the principal guideline for dealing with merchants was **caveat emptor,** which means, "Let the buyer beware." This meant that a buyer was expected to look the product over carefully. Once the transaction was concluded, the business relationship ended for all practical purposes. The buyer could not make any claims against the seller at some later date.

With the passing of time the caveat emptor philosophy of doing business fell into disfavor. This change resulted from two major forces. First, business leaders discovered that honest business dealings established a foundation for a long-term relationship with customers. Honesty is a trait needed by salespeople because firms are giving greater emphasis to building trust with the customer.[10]

The second force is consumer activism. Buyers have become more knowledgeable and more politically active. They demand high-quality products and honest business dealings. Consumer activists often lobby for new laws that restrict certain types of business practices.

A close examination of the history of ethics and ethical behavior reveals two interesting facts. The first is that it is difficult to define fundamental ethical principles to cover every business practice. What is considered wrong by one person or firm may be considered right by another. In the final analysis, each business firm must establish its own ethical standards. The second finding is that people are continually in the process of negotiating ethical norms. Situations keep changing, and we find it necessary to establish new standards. For example, is it wrong to view good legal advice as being compatible with good ethical advice in today's highly competitive market place?[11] If a good customer is sexually harassing a salesperson, and this behavior is reported to the sales manager, what action should the manager take? The issue of third-party harassment is often not covered in written policies on sexual harassment.[12] You supervise salespeople who travel a great deal. You discover that it is possible to obtain major airfare price reductions by requiring salespeople to stay over on Saturday. Should you require them to spend weekends away from family members?

Factors Influencing the Ethics of Salespeople

In the field of personal selling the temptation to maximize short-term gains by some type of unethical conduct is always present. Salespeople are especially vulnerable to moral corruption because they are subject to many temptations. Here are a few examples:

The competition is using exaggerated claims to increase the sale of its product. Should you counteract this action by using exaggerated claims of your own to build a stronger case for your product?

You have visited the buyer twice, and each time the person displayed a great deal of interest in your product. During the last visit the buyer hinted that the order might be signed if you could provide a small gift. Your company has a long-standing policy that gifts are not to be given under any circumstances. What do you do?

Your sales manager is under great pressure to increase sales. At a recent meeting of the entire sales staff this person said, "We have to beat the competition no matter what it takes!" Will this emotional appeal change your way of dealing with customers?

During a recent business trip you met an old friend and decided to have dinner together. At the end of the meal you paid for the entire bill and left a generous tip. Do you now put these non-business-related expenses on your expense account?

You are selling financial services for a bank and have developed a long list of satisfied customers. You are offered a similar position with a competing bank. If you accept the position, should you attempt to take your good customers with you?

These are the types of temptations that arise frequently in the field of selling. How do salespeople respond? Some ignore company policy, cast aside personal standards of conduct, and yield to the pressure. However, a surprising number of salespeople are able to resist. They are aided by a series of factors that help them distinguish right from wrong. Figure 4.1 outlines the positive forces that

FIGURE 4.1 Factors Determining Ethical Behavior of Salespeople

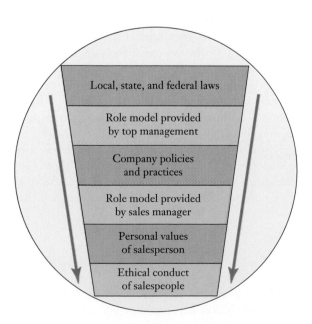

Local, state, and federal laws

Role model provided by top management

Company policies and practices

Role model provided by sales manager

Personal values of salesperson

Ethical conduct of salespeople

help them deal honestly and openly with prospects at all times. We will discuss each of these factors.

LOCAL, STATE, AND FEDERAL LAWS

In the field of selling there are both legal standards and ethical standards. An ethical standard is an outgrowth of society's customs and attitudes. A legal standard is enforced by statute. Throughout the past decade there has been a noticeable increase in government controls and penalties for wrongdoings. Business ethics got the attention of top management in 1991 when new federal sentencing guidelines went into effect. They provided increased fines for corporations that commit illegal acts and jail sentences for officers found to be responsible for the unlawful practice.[13]

Today, nearly all sales activities are subject to regulation. Some of the most common federal laws deal with price competition, credit reporting, debt collection practices, motor vehicle safety, and land sales disclosure. Of course there are also numerous state and local laws that affect personal selling.

THE UNIFORM COMMERCIAL CODE

The Uniform Commercial Code (UCC) and its predecessor, the Uniform Sales Act, are the major laws influencing sales throughout America. Several areas featured in the UCC focus directly on the seller-buyer relationship. Here are some of the primary areas:

1. *Definition of a sale.* The code defines the legal dimensions of a sale. It clearly states that salespeople have the authority to legally obligate the company they represent.

2. *Warranties and guarantees.* The code distinguishes between express warranties and implied warranties. Express warranties are those that are described by the express language of the seller. Implied warranties are the obligations imposed by law on the seller that are not assumed in express language.

3. *Salesperson and reseller.* In many cases the salesperson has resellers as customers or prospects. Salespeople must be aware of their employers' obligations to the reseller.

4. *Financing of sales.* Often salespeople work for firms that are directly involved in financing products or services, or in arranging such financing from outside sources. A salesperson needs to be familiar with the legal aspects of these credit arrangements.

5. *Product consignment.* In some cases, goods are delivered to the buyer, but title remains with the seller. This type of transaction can become complicated if the goods have a limited life span. Depreciation may occur with the passing of time. Salespeople should be familiar with the company's rights in cases where goods are sold on consignment.

The UCC is a legal guide to a wide range of transactions between the seller and the buyer. This law has been adopted throughout the United States and therefore has implications for most salespeople.

BUILDING RELATIONSHIPS IN A DIVERSE WORLD

GIFTS VERSUS BRIBES

One of the most common questions asked by North Americans wanting to do business in China is, "Can I do business without bribery?" Ronnie Chan, chairman of Hang Lung Development Group, a large Hong Kong property company, says that the answer to this question is yes. He says that there are many honest people in China and it is not necessary to make deals with dishonest people. However, avoiding bribery will not be easy, according to most China experts. China's highly regulated economy gives government officials many opportunities to seek payments for special favors. If you make the first payment, expect continued demands for money. The person accepting the first payment will quickly view you as his personal source of cash.

There is another reason you should not pay bribes. U.S. law prohibits such payments. Does the law permit giving gifts or doing special favors for a public official or customer? The answer is yes, but be careful. If you are asked to make donations to local agencies, then try to decide if this activity is legal under U.S. law. The U.S. Commerce Department offers free advice regarding such matters.[b]

COOLING-OFF LAWS

A majority of the states have passed legislation that establishes a cooling-off period, during which the consumer may void a contract to purchase goods or services. Although the provisions of these laws vary from state to state, their primary purpose is to give customers an opportunity to reconsider a buying decision made under a salesperson's persuasive influence. Many laws are designed to deal specifically with sales made in the consumer's home.

In addition to state laws the Federal Trade Commission (FTC) has adopted a trade regulation rule, which deals directly with sales practices. A cooling-off period for door-to-door sales is part of this legislation. To illustrate the application of this rule, assume that an encyclopedia salesperson visits the home of a prospect and obtains an order. The FTC rule specifies that the salesperson must give the buyer a printed description of the notice of cancellation. The notice of cancellation reminds the buyer that she can cancel the transaction, without any penalty or obligation, within three business days of the purchase date.

ETHICS BEYOND THE LETTER OF THE LAW

Too often people confuse ethical standards with legal standards. They believe that if you are not breaking the law, then you are acting in an ethical manner.[14] A salesperson's ethical sense must extend beyond the legal definition of what is right and wrong. To view ethics only in terms of what is legally proper encourages the question, "What can I get by with?" A salesperson must develop a personal code of ethics that extends beyond the letter of the law.

TOP MANAGEMENT AS ROLE MODEL

Ben Edwards, chairman of A. G. Edwards, the seventh-largest stockbroker in the nation, says that following the golden rule is still the best way to achieve success in business. This attitude has had a positive influence on the company's 7,400 employees. He encourages employees who are faced with an ethical conflict to ask themselves, "Is it right?"[15] By contrast, Prudential Insurance Company of America's management failed, in many instances, to adequately investi-

Every leader serves as a role model. The organization's moral tone is usually established by management personnel.

gate and discipline agents who used deceptive sales practices.[16] This failure to take action sent a powerful message to members of the Prudential sales force.

Ethical standards tend to filter down from the top of an organization. Employees look to company leaders for guidance. Chester Barnard, former president of New Jersey Bell, has stated that a leader's role is to harness the social forces in the organization, to shape and guide values. He describes good managers as value shapers concerned with the organization's informal social properties.[17] The organization's moral tone, as established by management personnel, is the most important single determinant of employee ethics. Today, top management must provide the best possible role model in the area of ethical behavior. People at the top must realize that actions speak louder than words. They will be judged by what they do, not by what they say.

Behavior is strongly influenced by modeling, or learning by imitation. "Don't do as I do, do as I say" is recognition of the fact that people sometimes learn more from imitation than we would like.[c]

From Robert Mager, Developing Attitude toward Learning

**SALES
TIPS**

COMPANY POLICIES AND PRACTICES

Company policies and practices can have a major impact on the ethical conduct of salespeople. Two researchers at the University of Pennsylvania surveyed over 400 industrial salespeople who were asked to make decisions concerning fourteen scenarios that posed ethical dilemmas. The findings indicate that company policies can have a significant influence on employees who are faced with ethical conflicts.[18]

As noted previously, many business organizations have found it necessary to develop a series of written policies that deal with ethical problem areas. Developing policy statements forces a firm to "take a stand" on various business practices. Distinguishing right from wrong can be a healthy activity for any organization. The outcome is a more clear-cut philosophy of how to conduct business transactions. These policies give direction to all employees. Some companies are also conducting seminars and workshops to help their employees better understand the firm's ethical orientation.

SHARING CONFIDENTIAL INFORMATION

Personal selling, by its very nature, promotes close working relationships. Customers often turn to salespeople for advice. They disclose confidential information freely to someone they trust. It is important that salespeople preserve the confidentiality of information they receive.

It is not unusual for a customer to disclose information that may be of great value to a competitor. This might include development of new products, plans to expand into new markets, or anticipated changes in personnel. A salesperson may be tempted to share confidential information with a representative of a competing firm. This breach of confidence might be seen as a means of gaining favor. In most cases this action will backfire. The person who receives the confidential information will quickly lose respect for the salesperson. A gossipy salesperson will seldom develop a trusting relationship with another business associate.

RECIPROCITY

Reciprocity is a mutual exchange of benefits, as when a firm buys products from its own customers. Some business firms actually maintain a policy of reciprocity. For example, the manufacturer of commercial sheets and blankets may purchase hotel services from firms that use its products.

Is there anything wrong with the "you scratch my back and I'll scratch yours" approach to doing business? The answer is sometimes yes. In some cases the use of reciprocity borders on commercial blackmail. Salespeople have been known to approach firms that supply their company and encourage them to buy out of obligation. The firm may be forced to buy products of questionable quality at excessive prices.

A business relationship based on reciprocity often has drawbacks. There is the ever-present temptation to take such customers for granted. A customer who buys out of obligation may take a backseat to customers who were won in the open market.

DILBERT *reprinted by permission of United Feature Syndicate, Inc.*

BRIBERY

Several years ago Xerox Corporation developed a fifteen-page ethical code that says: "We're honest with our customers. No deals, no bribes, no secrets, no fooling around with prices. A kickback in any form kicks anybody out. Anybody."[19] Many companies have developed specific policies that condemn the use of payoffs.

In some cases a bribe is wrong from a legal standpoint. In almost all cases the bribe is wrong from an ethical point of view. However, bribery does exist, and a salesperson must be prepared to cope with it. It helps to have a well-established company policy to use as a reference point.

GIFT GIVING

Gift giving is a widespread practice in America. However, some companies do maintain a "no gift" policy. Many companies report that their policy is either no gifts or nothing of real value. At Hewlett-Packard, advertising novelties, favors, or entertainment may be given to customers and suppliers under certain conditions: They are consistent with accepted business practice; they are of limited value and cannot be construed as a bribe or payoff; they do not violate any law, government regulation, or generally accepted ethical standards; and public disclosure of the facts will not embarrass the company.[20]

Many businesses have firm policies to deal with ethical problem areas, such as gift giving.

There are some gray areas that separate a gift from a bribe. Most people agree that a token of insignificant price, such as a pen imprinted with a company logo or a desk calendar, is appropriate. These types of gifts are meant to foster goodwill. A bribe, on the other hand, is an attempt to influence the person receiving the gift.[21]

Are there right and wrong ways to handle gift giving? The answer is yes. The following guidelines will be helpful to any salesperson who is considering giving gifts to customers:

1. Do not give gifts before doing business with a customer. Do not use the gift as a substitute for effective selling methods.

2. Never convey the impression you are "buying" the customer's business with gifts. When this happens, the gift becomes nothing more than a bribe.

3. When gift giving is done correctly, the customer will clearly view it as symbolic of your appreciation—a "no strings attached" goodwill gesture.

4. Be sure the gift is not a violation of the policies of your firm or of your customer's firm. Some firms will not allow employees to accept gifts at all. Other firms place a dollar limit on a gift's value.

In summary, if you have second thoughts about giving a gift, do not do it. When you are sure some token is appropriate, keep it simple and thoughtful.[22]

ENTERTAINMENT

Entertainment is a widespread practice in the field of selling and may be viewed as a bribe by some people. The line dividing gifts, bribes, and entertainment is often quite arbitrary.

Salespeople must frequently decide how to handle entertaining. A few industries see entertainment as the key to obtaining new accounts. This is especially true when competing products are nearly identical. A good example is the cardboard box industry. These products vary little in price and quality. To win an account may involve knowing whom to entertain and how to entertain.

Entertainment is a highly individualized process. One prospect might enjoy a professional football game, while another would be impressed most by a quiet meal at a good restaurant. The key is to get to know your prospect's preferences. How does the person spend leisure time? How much time can the person spare for entertainment? You will need to answer these and other questions before you invest time and money on entertainment.

BUSINESS DEFAMATION

Salespeople frequently compare their product's qualities and characteristics with those of a competitor during the sales presentation. If such comparisons are inaccurate, are misleading, or slander a company's business reputation, such conduct is illegal.[23] Competitors have sued hundreds of companies and manufacturer's representatives for making slanderous statements while selling.

What constitutes business defamation? Steven M. Sack, coauthor of *The Salesperson's Legal Guide*, provides the following examples:

1. *Business slander.* This arises when an unfair and untrue oral statement is made about a competitor. The statement becomes actionable when it is communicated to a third party and can be interpreted as damaging the competitor's business reputation or the personal reputation of an individual in that business.

2. *Business libel.* This may be incurred when an unfair and untrue statement is made about a competitor in writing. The statement becomes actionable when it is communicated to a third party and can be interpreted as damaging the company.

3. *Product disparagement.* This occurs when false or deceptive comparisons or distorted claims are made concerning a competitor's product, services, or property.[24]

The effectiveness of company policies as a deterrent to unethical behavior will depend on two factors. The first is the firm's attitude toward employees who violate these policies. If violations are routinely ignored, the policy's effect will soon be eroded. Second, policies that influence personal selling need the support of the entire sales staff. Salespeople should have some voice in policy decisions; they are more apt to support policies they have helped develop.

THE SALES MANAGER AS ROLE MODEL

The salesperson's actions often mirror the sales manager's behavior and expectations. This is not surprising when you consider the relationship between salespeople and their supervisors. They look to their supervisors for guidance and direction. The sales manager is generally the company's closest point of contact with the sales staff. This person is usually viewed as the chief spokesman for top management.

Sales managers generally provide new salespeople with their first orientation to company operations. They are responsible for interpreting company policy. On a continuing basis the sales manager monitors the salesperson's work and provides important feedback regarding conduct. If a salesperson violates company policy, it is usually the sales manager who is responsible for administering reprimands. If the moral fiber of a sales force begins to break down, the sales manager must shoulder a great deal of responsibility.

Sales managers influence the ethical behavior of salespeople by virtue of what they say and what they do. From time to time, managers must review their expectations of ethical behavior. Salespeople are under continuous pressure to abandon their personal standards to achieve sales goals. Values such as integrity and honesty must receive ongoing support from the sales manager.

The sales manager's behavior must be consistent with a stated philosophy. Actions do speak louder than words; any inconsistency between words and deeds is likely to have a negative influence on the attitude of the sales staff.

THE SALESPERSON'S PERSONAL VALUES

Ann Kilpatrick, a sales representative in the transportation industry, encountered something unexpected when entertaining a potential client. The client said, "Let's go to Johnny's." She was not familiar with Johnny's, but on arrival discovered it was a raunchy bar. Kilpatrick related that she sat there for five minutes and then said, "This is not what I was expecting. This is a sleazy place. Let's go somewhere else where we can talk." She was not willing to compromise her personal values to win a new account.[25]

Values represent the ultimate reasons people have for acting as they do. Values are important because they determine the choices we make every day. Sidney Simon, noted author in the field of values clarification, has said, "There's no place to hide from your values. Everything you do reflects them." Values serve as a foundation for our attitudes, and our attitudes serve as a foundation for our behavior (Fig. 4.2). We do not adopt or discard values quickly. In fact, the development of values is a lifelong process. It is not something that is completed by early adulthood. Throughout life we are constantly making decisions, and our value system aids us in this process.

Although we live by a value system, this system is not always clear to us. One outcome of education and training is frequently the clarification of one's values. Life experiences also help people clarify their values.

Values can serve as a deterrent to unethical behavior in a selling situation. They help to establish our own personal standards concerning what is right and what is wrong. Some salespeople discover a values conflict between themselves and the employer. Some of the salespeople at Prudential Insurance Company of America were asked to engage in deceptive sales practices, and they rebelled. If you view your employer's instructions or influence as improper, you have three choices (see page 84):

PROFITS DO NOT COME FIRST

I guess my religious beliefs did have one important impact on my approach to business—in terms of the ethics and principles I live by. I've always had the attitude that profits don't come first. They can never come first. People have to come first—customers and employees. The funny thing is, if you treat people right, the profits always follow.[d]

William H. Wilson, founder, Pioneer/Eclipse Corporation

FIGURE 4.2 The Relationship of Values, Attitudes, and Behavior

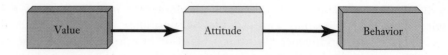

1. Ignore the influence of your values, and engage in unethical behavior. The end result will likely be a loss of job satisfaction and a feeling of guilt.

2. Voice strong opposition to the practice that is in conflict with your value system. Take a stand, and state your beliefs. An anonymous author once said, "Following the path of least resistance is what makes men and rivers crooked." Your objective is to influence decisions made by your superiors.

3. Refuse to compromise your values, and be prepared to deal with the consequences. If you refuse to compromise your values, you can face yourself in the mirror every morning. This may mean leaving the job. It may also mean that you will be fired.

Salespeople face ethical problems and decisions every day. In this respect they are no different from the doctor, the lawyer, the teacher, or any other professional. Ideally, they will make decisions on the basis of the values they hold. Furthermore, one hopes that these values will not be in conflict with the ethical standards of the profession they represent.

Toward a Personal Code of Ethics

Many people considering a career in selling are troubled by the thought that they may be pressured into compromising their personal standards of right and wrong. These fears may be justified. The authors of *The Ethical Edge*, a book that examines organizations that have faced moral crises, contend that business firms have given too little thought to the issue of helping employees to function ethically within organizations.[26] Many salespeople wonder if their own ethical philosophy can survive in the business world. These are some of their questions:

"Will I be forced to abandon my own ethical beliefs?"

"Can good business and good ethics coexist?"

"Are there still business firms that value adherence to high ethical standards?"

"Is honesty still a valued personal trait in the business community?"

It is becoming more difficult to provide a concise yes or no answer to these questions. Times are changing, and it is getting harder and harder to tell the "good guys" from the "bad guys." We read about the unethical use of gifts and bribes by corporate officials. Investigations of the Medicaid program turn up overbilling and other unethical behaviors by doctors, pharmacists, and nursing home operators. Reports from colleges and universities indicate that cheating is becoming more common. Even some of our most respected political leaders have been guilty of tax fraud, accepting illegal campaign contributions, and accepting payments for questionable favors. We are tempted to ask, "Is everybody doing it?"

Our society is currently doing a great deal of soul-searching. Many people want to see a firming of ethical standards. Many leaders are keenly aware that unethical behavior threatens the moral fabric of our free enterprise system. If the business community cannot police itself, more and more people will be looking to government for solutions to the problem. One fact we have learned from history is that we cannot legislate morality.

In the field of athletic competition the participants rely heavily on a written set of rules. The referee or umpire is ever present to detect rule violations and assess a penalty. In the field of personal selling there is no universal code of ethics. However, some general guidelines can serve as a foundation for a personal code of business ethics.

1. *Use an honest approach.* Some salespeople get off to a bad start by using a deceptive approach. One outdated practice is to seek an appointment but avoid stating the purpose of a visit. Some salespeople try to avoid creating the impression that they are selling anything. In nine cases out of ten this practice will backfire once the prospects find out they have been deceived. Doc Porter, vice president of Scandia Trading, said: "The best advice I ever received is to be honest with yourself, with your employer, and with your customers. If you are truthful and direct in your sales responsibilities, you can't help but give the fullest measure of yourself to your assignment, to the product or service that you sell, and, finally, to the needs of your customers."[27]

2. *Put your customer's interest first.* In selling we should always concentrate on the prospect's needs. One of the basic rules of sales success is to help yourself by finding ways to help others. When you find a way to help a prospect solve a problem, save money, or improve business, you will not only close a sale but also assure your customer's future interest in working with you.

3. *Avoid misleading sales claims.* Accuracy and truth should be the basis of all sales claims. Do not stretch the truth or exaggerate. This is not only unethical, but illegal. Stick to the facts, especially when you are emphasizing specific points. Avoid making statements or claims unless you have proof. Do

Salespeople must avoid misleading sales claims. To stretch the truth is not only unethical, but illegal.

not withhold important facts even if they are detrimental to your product. Paul Ekman, author of *Telling Lies*, says that withholding important information is one of the primary ways of lying.[28] A complete and informative sales presentation includes more than just positive facts. In many selling situations the customer needs to be aware of your product's limitations.

4. *Avoid attacking competitors.* Some salespeople mistakenly believe that the most effective way to deal with competition is to attack it. This is almost never an acceptable practice. Such behavior not only is unethical but also is likely to lose respect for you and your company.

5. *Avoid misuses of company resources.* When you mention crime, many people think of the elderly man mugged on the way to the grocery store or the service station attendant robbed at gunpoint. There is another type of crime, however, that is having a serious impact on American business. Many otherwise law-abiding people are stealing from their employers.

   One possible misuse of company resources involves manipulating expense accounts. Most salespeople are reimbursed for legitimate sales-related expenses such as meals, lodging, travel expense, and, in many cases, entertainment expense. There is always the temptation to inflate the expense account for personal gain. There is one broad guideline by which to judge the legitimacy of a business expense: The expenditure must be justifiable in terms of benefit to the company.

6. *Practice honesty after the sale.* A salesperson's ethical standards are often put to the test after the sale. Salespeople are judged by the thoroughness of postsale follow-up. Customers should be contacted after the sale to determine if they are completely satisfied. If problems exist, they should be handled in a way that builds customer goodwill and long-term partnerships.

SUMMARY

At the beginning of this chapter we defined *ethics* as the rules of conduct that reflect the character and the sentiment of the community. Ethics help us establish standards of honesty, loyalty, and fairness. We have noted that ethics are not legally constituted guidelines. To consider only what is legally right and wrong limits our perception of morality. Laws alone will not bring a halt to unethical selling practices.

Salespeople can benefit from the stabilizing influence of good role models. Although top management personnel are usually far removed from day-to-day selling activities, they can have a major impact on salespeople's conduct. Dishonesty at the top of an organization causes an erosion of ethical standards at the lower echelons. Sales managers provide another important role model.

They interpret company policies and help establish guidelines for acceptable and unacceptable selling practices.

Company policies and practices can have a strong influence on the ethical conduct of salespeople. These policies often help salespeople cope with ethical conflicts.

Finally, salespeople must establish their own standards of personal conduct. They must decide how best to serve their company and build strong partnerships with their customers. The pressure to compromise one's ethical standards surfaces almost daily. The temptation to take the easy road to achieve short-term gains is always present. The primary deterrent is a strong sense of right and wrong.

We strongly support the premise, "Bad ethics is bad business and unethical sales practices will ultimately destroy relationships with customers." Anyone who relies on unethical sales practices cannot survive in the selling field very long. These practices undermine the company's reputation and ultimately reduce profits.

➤ KEY TERMS

Ethics
Caveat Emptor
Reciprocity

➤ REVIEW QUESTIONS

1. What is the definition of *ethics?*
2. What does *caveat emptor* mean? What are the two forces that have lessened the impact of this philosophy?
3. A close examination of the history of ethics and ethical behavior reveals two interesting facts. What are they?
4. What five factors help influence salespeople's ethical conduct?
5. What is the Uniform Commercial Code? Why is it needed?
6. What five primary areas in the Uniform Commercial Code focus directly on the relationship between the salesperson and the buyer?
7. Robert Mager (see Sales Tips Box on p. 79) says that we are strongly influenced by modeling, or learning by imitation. What are the implications of his view for sales managers?
8. A good company policy on ethics will cover six major areas. What are they?
9. Is it ever appropriate to give gifts to customers? Explain.
10. List the six guidelines used as a foundation of a self-imposed code of business ethics.

➤ APPLICATION EXERCISES

1. You find that you have significantly overcharged one of your clients. The error was discovered when you received his check. It is unlikely that the customer or your company will become aware of the overcharge. Because

of this error, the company realized a high net profit on the sale. Your commissions are based on this profit. What, if anything, will you do about the overcharge?

2. Members of the National Candy Brokers Association are sales representatives for producers and importers of candy. These members have adopted a code of ethics to guide the development of marketing relationships with both their suppliers and their customers. Examine their code of ethics by accessing their Web address at http:/www.candynet.com/ncbacode.htm.

3. You work for a supplier of medical equipment. Your sales manager informs you that he wants you to capture a certain hospital account. He also tells you to put on your expense account anything it costs to secure the firm as a client. When you ask him to be more specific, he tells you to use your own judgment. Up to this time you have never questioned your sales manager's personal code of ethics. Make a list of the items you feel can be legitimately charged to the company on your expense account.

4. For some time your strongest competitor has been making untrue derogatory statements about your product and about you as a salesperson. You know for a fact that her product is not as good as yours. Yet hers has a higher price. Several of your best customers have confronted you with these charges. Describe how you plan to answer them.

➤ CASE PROBLEM

Melody Peterson was being trained by Laura Stapleton, an older, more experienced salesperson. Laura, who used high-pressure selling methods, had been in the territory for thirteen months and was being transferred. The sales manager assigned Laura and Melody to work together for two weeks. Melody was then to take over the territory on her own.

Laura would enter a store's perfume department, start her sales talk, and then begin to fill out the order without bothering to make a detailed check of the department's inventory. When buyers objected to the size of the order, Laura would promise more counter samples for customers. If that did not work, she would promise show cards for window and counter displays. If she still could not get authorization for the order, she would promise additional cooperative advertising support. Laura would lead buyers to believe they were getting a special deal because of the promotional materials that she was supplying.

Melody finally asked the senior salesperson, "How are you going to get all that promotional material okayed by the district sales manager?"

Laura replied, "I'm not. I only promised it. I never intended to send them the stuff. If they are foolish enough to believe all that, they deserve to be stuck. Besides, chances are good they won't even remember I promised those materials."

This kind of selling did not fit in with Melody's code of ethics. She could see that she was going to have to do something immediately to reconcile the situation. Melody felt that successful selling was built on mutual trust and respect; that this approach provided a foundation for forming an ongoing partnership with the customer. The ongoing partnership arrangement, she felt, should result in satisfaction for the ultimate consumer, profit for the dealer, profit for Melody's company, and good commissions for Melody.

Melody is scheduled to take over the territory on Monday morning.

QUESTIONS

1. What is your opinion of Laura Stapleton's selling practices?

2. Do the "cooling-off" laws apply to this transaction? Explain.

3. What should Melody do about all the promises that have been made?

Part III

Developing a Product Strategy

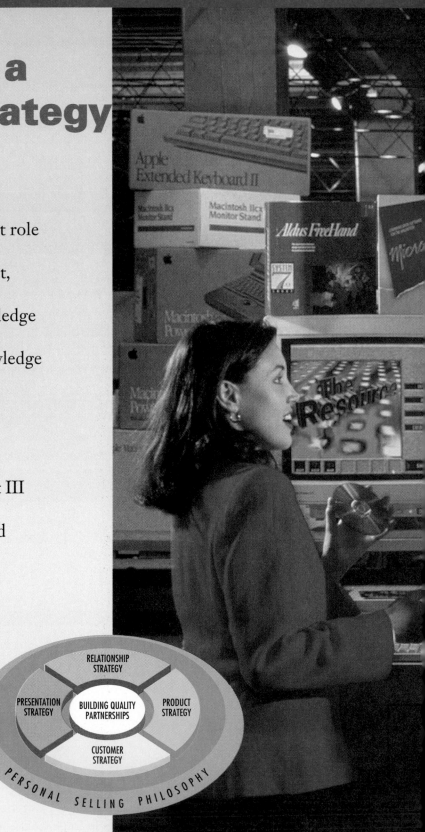

Part III examines the important role of complete and accurate product, company, and competitive knowledge in personal selling. Lack of knowledge in these areas will impair the salesperson's ability to achieve maximum customer service. Part III also describes several value added selling strategies.

Service is not a competitive edge, it is *the* competitive edge. People do not buy just things, they also buy expectations. One expectation is that the item they buy will produce the benefits the seller promised. Another is that if it doesn't, the seller will make good on the promise.

KARL ALBRIGHT AND RON ZEMKE
SERVICE AMERICA: DOING
BUSINESS IN THE NEW ECONOMY

5

Acquiring Product Information

Bobbi Meredith has a lot in common with many members of today's sales force. First, she is selling a service, not a tangible product. She works with corporate clients who use some form of telecommunications to market their goods and services. Second, she is working for a small business firm. After 14 years with AT&T, a giant in the communications field, she took a sales position with Lo/Ad Communications, a small telecommunications service bureau. Most of the prospects Bobbi calls on know that the telephone can be used to enhance sales and customer service, but they need help understanding the specific applications of technology to sales and marketing. Bobbi is viewed by most clients as a consultant who can configure a customized product solution that will enhance their marketing efforts. Her biggest challenge is researching the customer's marketing goals and specific promotional needs, and then preparing a product solution tailored to the customer's needs. The key to success for Bobbi Meredith, and many other salespeople, is the development of a successful product strategy.[1]

Developing a Product Strategy

Determining the right product and right price for the customer may be the most difficult part of a salesperson's job. When the products you are selling need to be custom configured for each client, the task becomes even more challenging.[2] Salespeople need a product strategy that is focused on maximum customer satisfaction.

As noted in Chapter 1, a product strategy helps salespeople make correct decisions concerning the selection and positioning of products to meet identified customer needs. The **product strategy** is a well-conceived plan that emphasizes becoming a product expert, adopting the feature/benefit process, and positioning the product (Fig. 5.1). Positioning the product refers to the decisions, activities, and communications that establish and maintain a firm's intended product concept in the customer's mind. Product positioning is discussed in detail in Chapter 6.

THE EXPLOSION OF PRODUCT OPTIONS

The domestic and global markets are overflowing with a vast array of goods and services. In some industries the number of new products introduced each year is mind-boggling. Consider these examples:

➤ Each year grocery stores introduce more than 10,000 new items.[3] If you are a salesperson employed by a major food wholesaler such as Fleming Companies, Incorporated or Super Value Stores, Incorporated, you face a real challenge when introducing a new product.

➤ Many companies develop and introduce new products to generate additional revenues. A good example is Rubbermaid, the Wooster, Ohio-based rubber and plastics company. Rubbermaid introduces, on the average, one new product every day of the year.[4]

Strategic/Consultative Selling Model	
Strategic step	Prescription
DEVELOP A PERSONAL SELLING PHILOSOPHY	☑ ADOPT MARKETING CONCEPT ☑ VALUE PERSONAL SELLING ☑ BECOME A PROBLEM SOLVER/PARTNER
DEVELOP A RELATIONSHIP STRATEGY	☑ ADOPT DOUBLE-WIN PHILOSOPHY ☑ PROJECT PROFESSIONAL IMAGE ☑ MAINTAIN HIGH ETHICAL STANDARDS
DEVELOP A PRODUCT STRATEGY	☐ BECOME A PRODUCT EXPERT ☐ ADOPT FEATURE-BENEFIT PROCESS ☐ POSITION PRODUCT

FIGURE 5.1 Developing a product strategy enables the salesperson to custom fit products or services to the customer's needs.

➤ We have seen an explosion of new products in the securities and financial services field. In one segment, mutual funds, customers can choose from over 7,600 products.[5]

For the customer, this much variety creates a "good news—bad news" situation. The good news is that almost all buyers have a choice when it comes to purchasing a product or service. People like to compare various options. The bad news is that so many choices often complicate the buying process.

John Naisbitt, author of *Megatrends* and *Megatrends 2000*, says that we are drowning in information, but we are starved for knowledge.[6] To put it another way, people are suffering from consequences of an "information overload." Salespeople must do more than supply the customer with large amounts of information. They must provide the buyer with the specific knowledge needed to make the best possible buying decision. One of the most important roles of the salesperson is to simplify the customer's study of the product choices. Later in this chapter we discuss how product features (information) can add value when converted into specific benefits (knowledge) that can help the buyer make an intelligent buying decision.

PRODUCT KNOWLEDGE ADDS VALUE

Company-sponsored sales training programs are giving increased emphasis to product knowledge because it can give a sales force a competitive advantage. Salespeople who can add value are in a strong position to close sales even when they do not have a price advantage. When sales started to decline at Digital Equipment Corporation, management discovered that many of their salespeople did not know enough about the products they sell. The products were excellent, but salespeople were often not able to prescribe the best product to meet the customer's computing requirements.[7] To solve this problem, Digital increased product knowledge training.

Product knowledge training is an on going activity in the life of a salesperson.

PRODUCT KNOWLEDGE INCREASES SALES

Chris Keith, sales and marketing coordinator for Affiliated Paper Companies, Incorporated, recalls with a smile a recent training exercise he completed. As an enrollee in the National Paper Trade Association (NPTA) Product Training Series he was instructed to go into local restaurant restrooms and pick up toilet paper samples. He would bring the paper back to the classroom and attempt to identify the manufacturer and the product features. Why should a management level employee engage in basic product knowledge training? Affiliated Paper Companies, like many other companies, has discovered that a wide range of employees, at various levels of responsibility, can benefit from increased product knowledge. With more product knowledge, Keith will be in a stronger position to work with customers. One new initiative being considered is the increase of sales through the suggestion of related products. NPTA believes that customer service representatives can also benefit from completion of the product training series. These employees have frequent contact with customers and therefore need to be familiar with the products sold by the company.[a]

This chapter is divided into five major sections. The first two sections examine the kinds of product information and company information required by the salesperson. The third section describes the type of information about the competition that is helpful to salespeople. Sources of information are covered in the fourth section, and the fifth section describes how product features can be translated into buyer benefits.

Becoming a Product Expert

Steve Hawelli, president of Wordhampton Incorporated, an Easthampton, New York firm, believes that a good salesperson is a product expert. He gives this advice to his staff: "Constantly increase your product knowledge. Educate and train yourself to be a professional resource and not just a salesperson."[8] Ideally, a salesperson will possess product knowledge that meets and exceeds customer expectations. This section reviews some of the most common product information categories: (1) product development and quality improvement processes, (2) product configuration, (3) performance data and specifications, (4) maintenance and care, and (5) price and delivery. Each is important as a potential source of knowledge concerning the product or service.

PRODUCT DEVELOPMENT AND QUALITY IMPROVEMENT PROCESSES

Companies spend large amounts of money in the development of their products. In **product development** the original idea for a product or service is tested, modified, and retested several times before it is offered to the customer. Each of the modifications is made with the thought of improving the product. Salespeople should be familiar with product development history. Often this information will set the stage for stronger sales appeals.

MBNA America, issuer of the Gold Card, conducted extensive research to develop a credit card that would compete favorably with similar cards offered by competing companies. The company determined that consumers valued emergency cash assistance, supplemental auto rental insurance, and several

SALES TIPS

Tom Peters says that manufacturing processes can become a "primary marketing tool in the firm's arsenal."[9] He points out that such things as superior quality, innovation, and responsiveness to orders from customers can be traced to the manufacturing and operations area of the company. The manufacturing process for similar products will sometimes vary greatly from one company to another. Peters says that when you have a competitive advantage in the factory, you should schedule plant tours for customers on a regular basis.

other services that ultimately became part of the Gold Card package. MBNA America also discovered that prompt and efficient customer service was very important to card holders.[10]

Quality improvement continues to be an important long-term business strategy for most successful companies.[11] Salespeople need to identify quality improvement processes that provide a competitive advantage and be prepared to discuss this information during the sales presentation. Motorola, Ritz-Carlton Hotels, and Xerox provide examples of companies that have won awards for

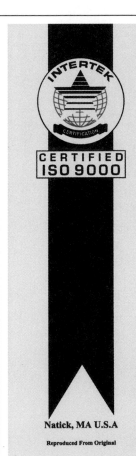

CERTIFICATE OF APPROVAL

This is to Certify that the Quality Management System of:

RYKO Manufacturing Co. Inc.
11600 N.W. 54th Avenue, Grimes, IA
has been assessed and approved by INTERTEK Services Corporation against the following quality assurance standards:

ISO 9001, BS EN 9001, and ANSI/ASQC Q9001-1994

The Quality Management System is applicable to:

The design, development, manufacture, installation and servicing of equipment and systems for the motor vehicle washing industry.

The approval is subject to the company maintaining its system to the required standards, which will be monitored by INTERTEK Services Corporation.

Approval Certificate No. 97-747
Initial Certification Date: *February 28, 1997*
Issue Date: *February 28, 1997*
Expiration Date: *February 28, 2000*

Natick, MA U.S.A
Reproduced From Original

Director, Systems Registration

Accredited by the Dutch Council for Accreditation for certification and registration activities.

Many international and some domestic companies will not purchase a company's *products* unless they have this highly respected ISO certification. As noted in Chapter 2, new ISO certification is now available for sales and marketing personnel.

implementing important quality controls. **Quality control,** which involves measuring products and services against established standards, is one dimension of the typical quality improvement process. At MBNA America, card holders who call cannot be put on hold for more than 21 seconds and requests for credit line increases are processed within 60 minutes or less.[12] At Pfizer's U.S. Pharmaceutical Group, extensive training for salespeople represents an important quality control. Sales representatives must demonstrate their ability to present product information to physicians accurately and effectively.[13]

PRODUCT CONFIGURATION

The challenge facing many salespeople today is deciding which product applications, or combination of applications, to recommend to the customer. If the customer has complex buying needs, then the salesperson may have to bring together many parts of the company's product mix to develop a custom-fitted solution. The product selection process is often referred to as **product configuration.** Salespeople representing Cadalyst Resources, a Des Moines-based computer supplier, develop customer solutions that combine computer hardware, software, installation, and training. After a careful needs assessment, the Cadalyst sales representative prepares a proposal that illustrates how the different parts of the company's product mix come together to solve the customer's problem. In most situations the cost of the proposal is offset by added value to the customer. The process of determining whether or not the proposal adds value is often called **quantifying the solution.** When the purchase represents a major buying decision, such as the purchase of a new computer system, quantifying the solution is important. One way to quantify the solution is to conduct a cost-benefit analysis to determine the actual cost of the purchase and savings the buyer can anticipate from the investment (Table 5.1).

PERFORMANCE DATA AND SPECIFICATIONS

Most potential buyers are interested in performance data and specifications. Here are some typical questions that might be raised by prospects.

"What is the frequency response for this stereo loudspeaker?"

"What is the anticipated rate of return on this mutual fund?"

"What is the energy consumption rating for this appliance?"

"Are all your hotel and conference center rooms accessible to persons with physical disabilities?"

A salesperson must be prepared to answer these types of questions. Performance data are especially critical in cases in which the customer is attempting to compare the merits of one product with another.

In many fields today there are testing programs that provide comparative data concerning various products. For example, the Association of Home Appliance Manufacturers (AHAM) sponsors a program to verify the performance of household refrigerators and freezers. An independent testing laboratory verifies the total refrigerated volume and total shelf area of household refrigerators and freezers. The AHAM certification seal is affixed to each model of a product certified under this program.

TABLE 5.1

Quantifying the solution often involves a carefully prepared cost-benefit analysis. This example compares the higher priced Phoenix semitruck trailer with the lower priced FB model, which is a competing product.

COST SAVINGS OF THE PHOENIX VERSUS FB MODEL FOR A TEN-YEAR PERIOD (ALL PRICES ARE APPROXIMATE)

	Cost Savings
• *Stainless steel bulkhead (savings on sandblasting and painting)*	$ 425.00
• *Stainless steel rear door frame (savings on painting)*	425.00
• *Air ride suspension (better fuel mileage, longer tire life, longer brake life)*	3,750.00
• *Hardwood or aluminum scuff (savings from freight damages and replacement of scuff)*	1,000.00
• *LED lights (lasts longer; approximate savings: $50 per year × ten years)*	500.00
• *Light protectors (save $50 per year on replacement × ten years)*	500.00
• *Threshold plate (saves damage to entry of trailer)*	200.00
• *Internal rail reinforcement (saves damage to lower rail and back panels)*	500.00
• *Stainless steel screws for light attachment (savings on replacement cost)*	200.00
• *Domestic oak premium floor—1⅜ (should last ten years under normal conditions)*	1,000.00
• *Doors—aluminum inner and outer skin, outside white finish, inside mill finish, fastened by five aluminum hinges (savings over life of trailer)*	750.00
• *Five-year warranty in addition to standard warranty covers bulkhead rust, LED lights, floor, scuff liner, glad hands, rear frame, mud flap assembly, and threshold plate (Phoenix provides a higher trade-in value)*	1,500.00
Total approximate savings of Phoenix over ten-year period (All the preceding is standard equipment on a Phoenix; this trailer will sell for $23,500; an FB standard trailer would sell for $19,500)	$10,750.00
Less additional initial cost of Phoenix over FB standard	4,000.00
Overall cost savings of Phoenix over FB trailer	$ 6,750.00

MAINTENANCE AND CARE

Prospects often want information concerning maintenance and care requirements for the products they purchase. The salesperson who can quickly and accurately provide this information will have the edge. Proper maintenance will usually extend the life of the product, so this information should be provided at the time of the sale.

PRICE AND DELIVERY

Potential buyers expect salespeople to be well versed in price and delivery policies on their products. The professional salesperson should also have similar information for competing products. Price objections represent one of the most common barriers to closing the sale.

Guest Quarters adds value to their business meeting facilities with personalized service and attention to every detail.

The complexity of price information will vary from one selling situation to another. In some cases the price is the same for all suppliers, and discounting is not a common practice. In other situations the price will depend on the size of the purchase, payment plan, delivery method, and other factors. The salesperson must be able to price each part of the product configuration. Some salespeople must also be prepared to discuss leasing options. The salesperson who cannot compute and supply price information quickly and accurately is at a serious disadvantage. In Chapter 6 we discuss how to position products according to price.

Know Your Company

A growing number of companies are recognizing that sales personnel are often the firm's closest point of contact with the customer, and therefore they need to be well informed. Often the customer's mental image of the organization is formed entirely through contact with a sales representative. In the eyes of the customer the salesperson is the company.

The decision to purchase a product or service will often depend on the prospect's feeling about the company. We should never underestimate information about the company itself as a strong appeal that can be used during the sales presentation. This is especially true in situations in which products are similar. Life insurance, for example, can be purchased from a large number of firms at nearly identical rates. Companies such as Prudential, Mutual of Omaha, and Hartford spend millions of dollars each year to build a positive image in the minds of consumers. In reality, the customer is buying trust in the reputation of the company and the salesperson.[14]

Some companies such as Campbell Soup, AT&T, and American Express have what might be called "brand power."[15] These companies, and the products offered to consumers, are quite well known. However, if you are selling loudspeakers made by Klipsch or financial services offered by JMC Financial Corporation, you may find it necessary to spend considerable time providing information about the company. These companies are not well known to many consumers.

Acquiring knowledge about your company is an important step toward developing complete product knowledge. In this section we examine the types of information needed in most selling situations.

COMPANY CULTURE AND ORGANIZATION

Many salespeople take special pride in the history of the company they work for. At Procter and Gamble (P & G), a company founded in 1837, employees note with pride that the hallmark of this highly successful firm is brands that enjoy market dominance. The authors of *The 100 Best Companies to Work for in America* note, "If a P & G brand does not hold down first place in its market, it's close to the top."[16] Pride can also develop in much younger companies such as Patagonia, a company that makes high-quality sports and outdoor equipment and clothing. Patagonia has hired many expert kayakers, skiers, climbers, and fishermen who help develop and test the company's products.[17]

Every organization has its own unique culture. **Organizational culture** is a collection of beliefs, behaviors, and work patterns held in common by people employed by a specific firm. Most organizations over a period of time tend to take on distinct norms and practices. At the Forum Corporation, a major provider of sales training, employees are guided by the "Forum Code." This code communicates the values that are held to be important by this company.

Many prospects will use the past performance of a company to evaluate the quality of the current product offering. If the company has enjoyed success in the past, there is good reason to believe that the future will be bright. At least, this is the way most prospects view an organization. We should be prepared to appeal to this type of prospect logic. Many successful salespeople have learned how to translate the organization's past performance into buying appeals.

Every company has its own unique organizational structure. To deal effectively with the needs of customers you must become familiar with all key personnel and departments. The organization chart provides a graphic portrait of the organizational structure. It outlines the basic relationships between key personnel and departments. Beyond this basic information you should be familiar with the authority and responsibility assigned to people who work in sales-support jobs.

Most companies have grouped activities to form several departments. The general focus of the department might be shipping, credit and collections, or customer service. Sales personnel should be familiar with any department that

At The Forum Corporation, salespeople are guided by a code that communicates values held to be important by the company.

FORUM CODE

Responsibility:

I will take responsibility for my own actions.

Esteem:

I will build esteem in myself, the company, and the client franchise.

Stay Healthy:

I will insist on maintaining and improving my own physical and mental health and will encourage others to do the same.

Planning and Executing:

I will develop, execute, and stick to a realistic plan.

Empathy:

I will anticipate the impact that decisions and actions have on others. I will put myself in the other person's shoes.

Confront:

I will confront differences honestly, quickly, and directly with the person involved.

Trust:

I will listen with respect. I will keep my commitments. I will be open and honest. I will not say what I do not mean.

At The Forum Corporation employees are guided by a code that communicates values held to be important by this company. *(Used courtesy of The Forum Corporation.)*

This salesperson uses a cellular phone to communicate effectively with the company and the customer.

has direct influence on sales. To give salespeople a better understanding of support services, some companies are using cross-training. This might involve giving salespeople firsthand experience in delivery, credit, or service departments.[18] Some companies have developed sales teams that include people from support departments.

COMPANY SUPPORT FOR PRODUCT

"Service after the Sale" is the theme of many marketing programs. Companies with this philosophy keep in touch with customers to determine if they are satisfied. For example, Olin Mathieson, a major chemical corporation, regularly checks with customers to get their reaction to services and keep real needs in perspective. Jagemann Stamping Company, a tool-and-die firm in Manitowoc, Wisconsin, often uses a sales team made up of a salesperson, an engineer, and line workers. Line workers can often answer the technical questions raised by a customer. Whenever there is a problem or defect, a small group of line workers is sent out with either a salesperson or an engineer to investigate. This involvement raises the worker's commitment to the customer.[19]

Product service procedures are an important facet of any product support program. These are the maintenance and repair activities that help ensure customer satisfaction after the sale. Many products sold today are quite complex and must be serviced by a highly skilled technician. Customers do not have the option of repairing the item themselves. Knowing this, they naturally seek assurances that the company will be prepared to provide adequate service after the sale.

BUILDING RELATIONSHIPS IN A DIVERSE WORLD

WORLD-CLASS QUALITY AT RITZ-CARLTON

A small minority of American travelers find the $150 to $250 per night room rate at a Ritz-Carlton hotel to be a real bargain. They know that most luxury hotels of Ritz-Carlton's caliber charge much more. The twenty-seven Ritz-Carlton hotels are world renowned for service and quality. The company operates twenty-five business and resort hotels in the United States, two in Australia, and one in Mexico. It also has nine international sales offices and employs 11,500 people. The company received the Malcolm Baldrige National Quality Award, the first given to a hospitality organization.

Ritz-Carlton hotels are characterized by distinctive facilities, highly personalized services, and exceptional food and beverages. The company credits its success to innovative human resource strategies and a high level of professionalism in dealing with customers. Although many hotel companies have rigorous training programs, the Ritz-Carlton Company is in a class by itself according to

M. L. Smith, professor of hospitality marketing at the University of Nevada's College of Hotel Administration. He says, "They have figured out what guests want in a hotel, and they have learned how to exceed their expectations."

Carefully selected employees (many complete three interviews) start their career with a two-day orientation. During this period the new employees get acquainted with the company motto: "Ladies and gentlemen serving ladies and gentlemen." The two-day orientation is followed by 100 additional hours of training. At each level of the company—from corporate leaders to the sales staff and employees in individual work areas—teams are charged with setting objectives and devising action plans.

The salespeople who represent Ritz-Carlton convention and meeting services know they are selling a first-class service. They also know that the product they sell will likely become even better.[b]

CUSTOMER EDUCATION AND TRAINING

A growing number of companies see ongoing customer education and training as a vital part of the company's sales and service effort. Xerox Corporation believes that educated customers are successful customers. The company offers a variety of customized courses to customers who want to improve their marketing, technical, and managerial skills. These courses are offered at the International Center for Training and Management Development in Leesburg, Virginia.[20] Some companies set up special plant tours for their customers. One manufacturer, who takes a great deal of pride in his plant, said, "Apart from our agents, our strongest sales tool is our plant. If we can get customers to visit us, we'll get the business."[21] The most successful plant tours are well planned and customized for the customer.

Know Your Competition

Acquiring knowledge of your competition is another important step toward developing complete product knowledge. Salespeople who have knowledge of their competitor's strengths and weaknesses are better able to understand their own position, and adjust their selling strategy accordingly.[22] Prospects often raise specific questions concerning competing firms. If we cannot provide answers or if our answers are vague, the sale may be lost.

Xerox Corporation believes that education contributes to the success of their customers. Many of the Xerox courses are offered at the International Center for Training and Management Development pictured here.

YOUR ATTITUDE TOWARD YOUR COMPETITION

Regardless of how impressive your product is, the customer will naturally seek information about similar products sold by other companies. Therefore, you must acquire facts about competing products before the sales presentation. Once armed with this information, you are more confident in your ability to handle questions about the competition.

The attitude you display toward your competition is of the utmost importance. Every salesperson should develop a set of basic beliefs about the best way of dealing with competing products. Here are a few helpful guidelines:

1. In most cases, do not refer to the competition during the sales presentation. This will shift the focus of attention to competing products, which is usually not desirable. Always respond to direct questions, but do not initiate the topic.

2. Never discuss the competition unless you have all your facts straight. Your credibility will suffer if you make inaccurate statements. If you do not know the answer to a specific question, simply say, "I do not know." It is also best to avoid generalizations about the competition.

3. Avoid criticizing the competition. You may be called on to make direct comparisons between your product and competing products. In these situations, stick to the facts and avoid emotional comments about apparent or real weaknesses. Prospects tend to become suspicious of salespeople who initiate strong criticism of the competition.

Customers appreciate an accurate, fair, and honest presentation of the facts. They generally resent highly critical remarks about the competition. Avoid mudslinging at all costs. Fairness is a virtue that people greatly admire.

THE VALUE OF COMPARISONS

Requests to compare the features of competing products are quite common in the business community, especially among professional buyers. Many companies now make detailed comparisons among competing products and share this information with the sales staff. These comparisons provide members of the sales staff with specific information to use during sales presentations. Every salesperson should search for features that provide a competitive advantage. Information about your competition may be available on the World Wide Web.

BECOME AN INDUSTRY EXPERT

Lee Boyan, sales consultant, suggests that salespeople become experts in an appropriate niche of an industry or a group of industries.[23] If the sales force includes several persons, each might assume responsibility for a specific area. One member of an office equipment sales team might, for example, concentrate on the banking industry. This person would read the appropriate trade journals and become active in professional associations that serve bankers' needs.

Salespeople should closely examine the sources of information about their products and the industries where these products are used.

Sources of Product Information

There are several sources of product information available to salespeople. Some of the most common include: (1) product literature developed by the company, (2) sales training meetings, (3) plant tours, (4) internal sales and sales support members, (5) customers, (6) the product, (7) the Internet, and (8) publications.

PRODUCT LITERATURE

Most companies prepare literature that provides a detailed description of their product. This material is usually quite informative, and salespeople should review it carefully. If the company markets a number of products, a sales catalog is usually developed. To save salespeople time, many companies give them computer software that provides a constantly updated, on-line product catalog.[24] Advertisements, promotional brochures, and audio cassettes can also be a valuable source of product information.

SALES TRAINING MEETINGS

As noted previously, company sponsored sales training programs frequently focus on product knowledge. Learning International conducted a nationwide survey to determine which sales training topics are viewed as most important. The

BUILDING RELATIONSHIPS THROUGH TECHNOLOGY

FAST START

New salespeople can be overwhelmed by the amount of information they need to master. Information, for example, about the company and its processes, products, and customers. Companies can now make learning easier with information technology. Information about the company and its processes can be stored on network servers and CD-ROM disks. Computer-based training (CBT) permits new employees to learn at their own pace about products, their specifications, features, benefits, uses, and selling points.

Companies can deliver to new salespeople a rich body of customer information through the strong commitment to the use of contact management software. The salesperson who carefully records her business and relationship contacts with customers and prospects will, over time, accumulate a valuable store of information. A new salesperson taking over these accounts can quickly "come up to speed" with these people and their needs. (See the Sales Automation Application Exercise on p. 114 for more information.)

respondents said that training should stress product knowledge over any other area. The sales and marketing executives who participated in the study tended to view product knowledge training as a basic element of any sales training program.

New technology is providing long-distance learning opportunities for many salespeople. Ford Motor Company recently developed a national interactive distance learning network called Fordstar. Salespeople can sit in a room at their home dealerships and learn via satellite from headquarters in Dearborn, Michigan.[25]

PLANT TOURS

Many companies believe that salespeople should visit the manufacturing plant and see the production process firsthand. Such tours not only provide valuable product information but also increase the salesperson's enthusiasm for the product. A new salesperson may spend several days at the plant getting acquainted with the production process. Experienced personnel within the organization can also benefit from plant tours. Joseph Vadala, a sales representative at the Pioneer Centres auto dealership in San Diego, gained a new respect for the durability of the Range Rover sport-utility vehicle when he visited the manufacturing plant in England. During the plant tour he had the opportunity to observe the actual testing of the Range Rover vehicles under extremely demanding conditions.[26]

INTERNAL SALES AND SALES SUPPORT TEAM MEMBERS

Amir Moussavian, senior vice president of sales at Giga Trend, Incorporated, believes professional salespeople learn from each other. He credits the success of his company to building a team knowledgeable about computer technology. Giga Trend's salespeople are not reluctant to communicate their interests and share talents because commissions are pooled. The pooled commissions provide an incentive to help each other and learn from each other.[27] Team selling

SELLING
FRESH BAKED PRODUCTS FROM
FROZEN DOUGHS
IS ALMOST AS EASY AS

LISTENING
TO THIS TAPE.

BAKERY BASICS

8 MIN   A SIDE

HOT TIPS – COOL PROFITS

If you think frozen doughs are a difficult sell, we'd like to put your mind at ease. In just eight minutes, our *free cassette* will teach you all you need to know about the simplicity of handling Rich's® Frozen Doughs. You'll learn about the major sales opportunities that await by taking business from local bakeries and the benefits your customers will gain from selling baked-on-premise products.

It's easy listening. It's easy baking. It's easy selling. So call us toll free at 1-800-659-5251.

RICH'S Bakery

Rich Products Corporation, Food Service Division, 1150 Niagara Street, Buffalo, New York 14213 U.S.A.

CIRCLE 137 FOR MORE INFORMATION

Distributor salespeople for Rich's Bakery are provided a free audio cassette that features tips on how to sell their product.

Surveys indicate that product knowledge training should be a basic element of any sales training program.

has become more popular, in part, because many complex sales require the expertise of several sales and sales support personnel.

CUSTOMERS
Persons who actually use the product can be an important source of information. They have observed its performance under actual working conditions and can provide an objective assessment of the product's strengths and weaknesses. Some companies collect testimonials from satisfied customers and make this persuasive information available to the sales staff.

THE PRODUCT
The product itself should not be overlooked as a source of valuable information. Salespeople should closely examine and, if possible, use each item they sell to become familiar with its features. Investigation, use, and careful evaluation of the product will provide a salesperson with additional confidence.

THE INTERNET
Many companies are using the Internet to showcase the features and benefits of their products. The Internet is also an excellent source of technical reports on various products. Some salespeople turn to the Internet to access information concerning competing products.

PUBLICATIONS
Trade and technical publications such as *Supermarket Business* and *Advertising Age* provide valuable product information. Popular magazines and the business section of the newspaper also offer salespeople considerable information about their products and their competition. A number of publications such as *Consumer Reports* test products extensively and report the findings in nontechnical language for the benefit of consumers. These reports are a valuable source of information.

A WORD OF CAUTION
Is it possible to be overly prepared? Can salespeople know too much about the products and services they sell? The answer to both questions is generally no. Communication problems can arise, however, if the salesperson does not accurately gauge the prospect's level of understanding. There is always the danger that a knowledgeable salesperson will overwhelm the potential buyer with facts and figures. This problem can be avoided when salespeople adopt the feature-benefit strategy.

Adding Value with a Feature-Benefit Strategy
Charles Revson, founder of the Revlon Company, once said, "In the factory we make cosmetics. In the store we sell hope." Throughout this chapter we stress the importance of acquiring information on the features of your product, company, and competition. Now it is important to point out that all successful sales presentations translate product features into buyer benefits. The "hope" that Charles Revson mentioned is a good example of a buyer benefit. It is only when a product feature is converted to a buyer benefit that it makes an impact on the customer. People do not buy features; they buy benefits.

DOONESBURY   **by Garry Trudeau**

DISTINGUISH BETWEEN FEATURES AND BENEFITS

To be sure we understand the difference between a product feature and a benefit, let us define these two terms.

A **product feature** is anything that can be felt, seen, or measured. A feature answers the question, "What is it?" Features include such things as craftsmanship, durability, design, and economy of operation. In most cases these are technical facts about the product. They reveal how the product was developed and manufactured. Product features are often found in the literature provided by the manufacturer.

A **product benefit** is whatever provides the consumer with personal advantage or gain. It answers the question, "How will I benefit from owning or using the product?" If you mention to a prospect that a certain tire has a four-ply rating, you are talking about a product feature. If you go on to point out that this tire will provide greater safety, last longer, and improve gas mileage, you are pointing out benefits.

Syscom Incorporated, based in Catonville, Maryland, sells training administration systems for use by training department administrators. One of its software products, TMS/WIN, can be used to manage a wide range of training department functions. One feature is self-service registration for employees who want to enroll in workshops or seminars. The benefit is a flexible registration procedure that does not require the involvement of a department staff member. The TMS/WIN program also provides electronic mail interface with trainees. The benefit is improved communication with trainees before and after the scheduled training program. These and other features of TMS/WIN software become more appealing once they are converted to benefits the customer can fully appreciate.

We are indebted to Elmer Wheeler, noted sales training authority, for perfecting the concept of buyer benefits. He emphasized that there are always important reasons why people buy any product. They do not purchase the product for its own sake. In one of his many presentations on selling he said, "Don't sell the steak—sell the sizzle." This was his way of saying we should emphasize the real reasons why customers will buy our product. They are rarely interested in facts or technical data alone unless this information promises benefits.

USE BRIDGE STATEMENTS

We know that people buy benefits, not features. One of the best ways to present benefits is to use a bridge statement. A **bridge statement** is a transitional phrase that connects a statement of features with a statement of benefits. This method permits customers to connect the features of your product to the benefits they will receive. A sales representative of Fleming Companies, Incorporated might use bridge statements to introduce a new snack food.

Many forms of product knowledge and sales support tools are available to distributor salespeople.

"This product is nationally advertised, *which means* you will benefit from more presold customers."

"You will experience faster turnover and increased profits *because* the first order includes an attractive display rack."

Some companies prefer to state the benefit first and the feature second. When this occurs, the bridge statement may be a word such as "because."

IDENTIFY FEATURES AND BENEFITS

A careful analysis of the product will help identify both product features and buyer benefits. Once all the important features are identified, arrange them in logical order. Then write beside each feature the most important benefit the customer will derive from that feature. Finally, prepare a series of bridge statements to connect the appropriate features and benefits. Using this three-step approach, a hotel selling conference and convention services, and a manufacturer selling electric motors used to power mining equipment developed feature-benefit worksheets (Tables 5.2 and 5.3). Notice how each feature is translated into a benefit that would be important to someone purchasing these products and services. Table 5.2 reminds us that company features can be converted to benefits. Product analysis helps you decide what information to include in the sales presentation. It helps pinpoint reasons for buying the product or service. Features are backed by benefits with which the prospect can identify.

TABLE 5.2

Salespeople employed by a hotel can enhance the sales presentation by converting features to benefits.

FEATURE	BENEFIT
Facilities	
The hotel conference rooms were recently redecorated.	*Which means all your meetings will be held in rooms that are attractive as well as comfortable.*
All of our guest rooms were completely re-decorated during the past six months and many were designated as nonsmoking rooms.	*Which means your people will find the rooms clean and attractive. In addition, they can select a smoking or nonsmoking room.*
Food Services	
We offer four different banquet entrees prepared by Ricardo Guido who was recently selected Executive Chef-of-the-Year by the National Restaurant Association.	*Which means your conference will be enhanced by delicious meals served by a well-trained staff.*
Our hotel offers twenty-four-hour room service.	*Which means your people can order food or beverage at their convenience.*

TABLE 5.3

Here we see company features translated into customer benefits.

FEATURE	BENEFIT
Our company has . . .	**Which means to you . . .**
1. *The best selection of motors in the area*	• *Choice of the best models to interface with with your current equipment*
	• *Equipment will operate more efficiently*
2. *Certified service technicians*	• *Well-qualified service personnel keep your equipment in top running condition*
	• *Less downtime and higher profits*

FEATURE-BENEFIT APPROACH COMPLEMENTS CONSULTATIVE-STYLE SELLING

Identifying product features and then converting these features to buyer benefits is an integral part of consultative-style selling. The salesperson should approach the customer with complete knowledge of the product or service. With the aid of questions the customer's buying needs are identified. Once the needs are known, the salesperson should discuss the features and benefits that specifically apply to that person. In this way the sales presentation is individualized for each customer. Everyone likes to be treated as an individual. A sales presentation tailored to individual customers communicates the message, "You are important and I want you to be a satisfied customer."

SUMMARY

A salesperson whose product knowledge is complete and accurate is better able to satisfy customers. This is without doubt the most important justification for becoming totally familiar with the products you sell. It is simply not possible to provide maximum assistance to potential customers without this information. Additional advantages to be gained from knowing your product include greater self-confidence, increased enthusiasm, improved ability to overcome objections, and development of stronger selling appeals.

A complete understanding of your company will also yield many personal and professional benefits. The most important benefit, of course, is your ability to serve your customer most effectively. In many selling situations, customers inquire about the company's business practices. They want to know things about support personnel, product development, credit procedures, warranty plans, and product service after the sale. When salespeople are able to provide the necessary company information, they gain respect. They also close more sales.

This chapter also stresses knowing your competition. It pays to study other companies that sell similar products to determine whether they have competitive advantages or disadvantages.

Salespeople gather information from many sources. Company literature and sales training meetings are among the most important. Other sources include factory tours, customers, competition, publications, and actual experience with the product itself.

In the sales presentation your knowledge of the product's features and your company's strengths must be presented in terms of the resulting benefits to the buyer. The information and benefits you emphasize will depend on your assessment of the prospect's needs and motivation.

➤ KEY TERMS

Product Development	*Organizational Culture*
Quality Control	*Product Feature*
Product Configuration	*Product Benefit*
Quantifying the Solution	*Bridge Statement*

➤ REVIEW QUESTIONS

1. Provide a brief description of the term *product strategy.*

2. Some sales managers state, "Training given to sales personnel should stress product knowledge over any other area." List three reasons that support this view.

3. What is *product configuration?* Provide an example of how this practice is used in the sale of commercial stereo equipment.

4. Review the Forum Code on p. 101 and then identify the two items that you believe contribute the most to a salesperson's career success.

5. Define the term *organizational culture*. How might this company information enhance a sales presentation?

6. Basic beliefs underlie the salesperson's method of handling competition. What are three guidelines a salesperson should follow in developing basic beliefs in this area?

7. Explain what the customer's expectations are concerning the salesperson's attitude toward competition.

8. Do buyers ever expect salespeople to present features of competing products? Explain.

9. What are the most common sources of product information?

10. Distinguish between *product features* and *buyer benefits.*

➤ APPLICATION EXERCISES

1. Secure, if possible, a copy of a customer-oriented product sales bulletin that has been prepared by a manufacturer. Many dealers receive such selling tools. Study this information carefully; then develop a features-benefits analysis sheet.

2. Today many companies are listing their features and benefits on the Internet. This enables their present and prospective customers to access this in-

formation. Using a search engine for this information, key in the words "featurebenefits." Notice the large number of documents matching this query. Click on to a familiar company name and review the information provided.

3. Select a product you are familiar with and know a great deal about. (This may be something you recently shopped for and purchased, such as a compact disc player or an automobile.) Under each of the categories listed, fill in the required information about the product.

   a. Where did you buy the product? Why?
   b. Did product design influence your decision?
   c. How and where was the product manufactured?
   d. What different applications or uses are there for the product?
   e. How does the product perform? Are there any data on the product's performance? What are they?
   f. What kinds of maintenance and care does the product require? How often?
   g. Could you sell the product you have written about in terms *a* through *f*? Why or why not?

> ## SALES AUTOMATION APPLICATION EXERCISE

ACT! SORTING BY ACCOUNT CODE

Access the ACT! software following the instructions in Appendix 2. Examine the Contact Screens. One of the Contact Screen fields is labeled ACCOUNT CODE. This field has been used to identify the primary application of the products offered by the selling organization. Review the ACCOUNT CODE entry for each contact and report on what three niches of the computer-aided design industry a salesperson might wish to serve as an "industry expert."

> ## CASE PROBLEM

Bobbi Meredith, introduced at the beginning of this chapter, recently identified a company that seems to be an excellent prospect for the telecommunications services offered by Lo/Ad Communications. The Cart Works manages several freestanding retail booths (often called kiosks) that operate in shopping malls. Many of the newer malls have incorporated kiosks to create the busy and happy atmosphere of an open marketplace. The design of the kiosk will vary from a stationary booth to a moveable cart. A typical kiosk will offer a specialized product line such as greeting cards, inexpensive jewelry, T-shirts, sunglasses, candy, or snacks. A small number of kiosks can add a new dimension to the shopping atmosphere.

The Cart Works is currently seeking new entrepreneurs who want to operate a kiosk in a shopping mall. The company offers training and help in selecting a high-traffic location in the mall. Once a location is selected, members of The Cart Works staff decide what products are most likely to be popular at that location.

During the first call Bobbi learned that The Cart Works wants to expand its business to include several western states. The company is searching for an effective way to reach well-qualified entrepreneurs who will be interested in operating a small business. The prospective entrepreneur will be given a package of material that explains the advantages of operating a kiosk. When Bobbi makes her second call on The Cart Works, she will need to configure a product solution and make a specific proposal. She is considering two options:

Option one: Publicize a toll-free 800 number that is used to receive incoming calls generated by newspaper advertisements and direct mail. Callers will be given a brief introduction to The Cart Works' business opportunity and sent a package of materials.

Option two: Publicize a 900 number to encourage incoming calls. The caller will pay a small fee (50 cents per minute) for the call. The 900 number will be publicized in newspaper advertisements and direct mail. Callers will be given an introduction to The Cart Works concept and sent a package of materials.

A competing firm, Triangle Communications, has also called on The Cart Works and is preparing a proposal. The Triangle proposal involves the use of radio announcements to generate interest in this business opportunity. The radio commercials will encourage interested persons to attend an information meeting at a local hotel. A representative of The Cart Works will conduct the meeting. Persons who attend the meeting will be given a package of materials that explain this business opportunity.

QUESTIONS

1. Explain how Bobbi will use the three prescriptions for a product selling strategy in preparing and presenting her product solutions.

2. What are the major customer benefits of option one that was developed by Bobbi Meredith? Option two?

3. What are the major customer benefits of the proposal developed by Triangle Communications?

4. In addition to the actual product strategy developed by Bobbi Meredith, how important will company information (history, mission, past performance, product support, etc.) be in closing the sale?

5. Should Bobbi Meredith spend time learning about the competition? Explain. What should be her attitude toward the competition?

6. Is Bobbi Meredith's sales career one where becoming an industry expert would be important? Explain.

PARTNERSHIP SELLING: A ROLE PLAY/SIMULATION (see Appendix 3, p.421)

PART I: Developing a Product Strategy

Read Employment Memorandum 1 on p. 425, which introduces you to your new training position with the Hotel Convention Center. You should also study the product strategy materials that follow the memo to become familiar with the company, product, and competitive knowledge you will need in your new position.

Read the Customer Service/Sales Memorandum, on p. 446 and complete the three part customer/service assignment provided by your sales manager. In item 1, you are to complete a feature-benefit worksheet; in item 2, you are to configure a price/product sales proposal; and in item 3 you are to write a sales cover letter for the sales proposal. Note that the information presented in the price/product sales proposal will consist of product facts/features, and the information presented in your sales cover letter should present specific benefit statements. These three forms should all be custom fitted to meet your customer—B. H. Rivera's—specific needs. All the product information you will need is in the product strategy materials provided as enclosures and attachments to Employment Memorandum 1, on p. 447.

Developing Product-Selling Strategies

Sometimes a promising new product enters the marketplace with high hopes, but initial sales are disappointing. This was the case when the Ricoh MV715 was first introduced. The MV715 was a multifunctional office product that gives users the capability to fax, copy, and print from one station. Potential customers were skeptical that a single product could take the place of several others. Ricoh Corporation decided to interview customers who had purchased the MV715 to determine how they used the product and if it had made their offices more efficient. After careful analysis of interviews with 200 buyers, it discovered that salespeople had not adjusted their selling style to fit the new product. They had failed to position the product so that it appealed to buyers.[1]

Achieving Product Differentiation in Personal Selling

One of the basic tenets of sales and marketing is the principle of product differentiation. The competitors in virtually all industries are moving toward differentiating themselves on the basis of quality, price, convenience, economy, or some other factor. Unless a firm can create a niche for its particular product in the marketplace, it will have a difficult time attracting customers.[2] Salespeople, who are on the front line of many marketing efforts, assume an important role in the product differentiation process.

Many of the fastest-growing companies are creating strong positions in specific market segments. Three examples are described here:

Item: Cleveland-based Meridian Travel designed and initiated an education program that helps business customers learn how to spend their travel dollars efficiently. Cyndie Bender, founder and CEO of Meridian, explains that her accounts receive a detailed quarterly report that provides an analysis of their travel expenditures. These user-friendly reports make it easy for the customer to determine ways to reduce unnecessary travel expenses. Some of these reports spell out how a client can spend less with her company, and the result is sometimes lost sales. However, this service helps build customer loyalty, goodwill, and in some cases additional business for Meridian sales representatives.[3]

Item: Nordstrom, a department store chain based in Portland, Oregon, has achieved success by meeting the needs of consumers seeking upscale merchandise and a shopping experience that includes the personal touch. Nordstrom offers an in-depth selection of quality merchandise and outstanding customer service. Each store stocks fashion goods that reflect the lifestyles of customers in the surrounding area. Well-trained salespeople keep records on their customers' sizes and preferences so that they can let customers know when an item arrives at the store that may be of interest to them. The result of this individualized approach is strong customer loyalty and repeat business.[4]

Item: Walden Paddlers, located in Acton, Massachusetts, is a successful new company with one product and one employee. Within one year the company was able to design, produce, and market a technically sophisticated kayak fashioned from recycled plastic. Paul Farrow, founder of the company, launched the new product by forming strategic partnerships with a designer, a manufacturer, a banker, an accountant, and other key persons. The decision to produce and sell a new type of kayak was made after a careful study of the market. Farrow decided to produce a kayak that would retail for $390 (positioned at the low end of the market) and would be easy to maneuver in the water. He decided that a kayak made of recycled plastic would have appeal in the watersport market in which environmental awareness is important to

Paul Farrow, founder of Walden Paddlers, created a niche market for his kayak by making it out of recycled plastic, designing it for ease of maneuverability, and giving it an attractive price. He used these product features to position this product in a competitive market.

buyers. As soon as the first kayaks were manufactured, Farrow started making sales calls to retail and wholesale firms that specialize in outdoor products. Within a few weeks he was able to line up several dealers for his product.[5]

Notice that all these businesses are selling their products and services in highly competitive markets. Also, each is attempting to achieve product and service differentiation.

Redefining the Product

Ted Levitt, former editor of the *Harvard Business Review*, says that products are problem-solving tools. People buy products if they fulfill a problem-solving need. Today's better-educated and more demanding customers are seeking a *cluster of satisfactions*. **Satisfactions** arise from the product itself, from the company that makes or distributes the product, and from the salesperson who sells and services the product.[6] Figure 6.1 provides a description of a three-dimensional *Product Selling Model*.

To illustrate how the cluster of satisfactions concept works in a business setting, let us examine a complex buying decision. King Soopers, a major grocery retailer in Colorado, maintains its own in-house, full-service advertising department. As part of a plan to update the department, the staff decided to purchase a computer system that could be used to develop high-quality–camera-ready copy and graphics for print ads.

The buying decisions at King Soopers were complex because the product, in various configurations, was available from several computer manufacturers. In addition, many distributors sold the same equipment. Of course, different

FIGURE 6.1 Product Selling Model. The product strategy should include a cluster of satisfactions that meet the needs of today's better educated and more demanding customers. Drawing from this cluster, the salesperson can custom fit presentations to meet a wide range of needs.

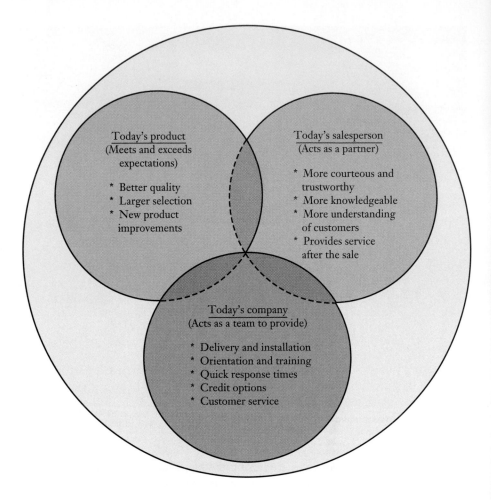

distributors presented different proposals. Here are some of the questions the staff had to answer before making a buying decision:

Questions Related to the Product

What product is best for our type of operation?

Does the product have a good reputation for quality?

Given the cost of this product, will King Soopers receive a good return on investment?

Questions Related to the Company

Does this company provide the most advanced technology?

What is the company's reputation for manufacturing quality products?

What is the company's reputation for standing behind the products it sells?

Questions Related to the Salesperson

Does this salesperson possess the knowledge and experience needed to recommend the right product?

Can this salesperson be trusted?

Will this salesperson provide support services after the sale?

The purchase of a service may be no less complicated. Let us assume that you are planning a retirement banquet for the president of your company. The location of the banquet would likely depend on the type of food and beverage service available at hotels and restaurants in your community. This would be the *product* decision. The qualifications of the food and beverage salesperson or sales manager would also influence your buying decision because this is the person who describes the food, beverage, and meeting room options and works with you after the buying decision. You must be convinced that this person has the experience and skills necessary to do the job.[7] In the final analysis you would make a buying decision that is based on a cluster of satisfactions.

Sales representatives for the New England Company are encouraged to look beyond the customer's immediate basic needs to build a long-term partnership.

Positioning as a Product-Selling Strategy

The term **product positioning** refers to the decisions, activities, and communications that are directed toward trying to create and maintain a firm's intended product concept in the customer's mind. A product's "position" is the customer's concept of the product's attributes relative to the concept of competing products.[8] The goal of Mercedes-Benz salespeople, for example, has always been to create the perception that their automobiles are the best in the high-performance luxury category.

Product positioning is a concept that applies to both new and existing products. Given the dynamics of most markets, it may be necessary to reposition products several times in their life cycle[9] because even a solid, popular product can lose market position quickly. Salespeople have assumed an important and expanding role in positioning products. To succeed in our overcommunicated society, marketers must use a more direct and personalized form of communication with customers. Advertising directed toward a mass market will often fail to position a complex product.

Many years ago, Alvin Toffler used the term *future shock* to describe the stress and disorientation that people experience when they are subjected to a great deal of change in a short period of time. Many customers are experiencing a form of future shock as they try to cope with complex buying decisions. The proliferation of products has turned buying into a decision-making nightmare for many buyers. The factors of competing claims of manufacturers, and the specialties and subspecialties have produced an information glut.[10] People who must make buying decisions hunger for the opportunity to talk to well-prepared salespeople who can reduce the confusion they face.

Throughout the remainder of this chapter we discuss specific ways to use various product-positioning strategies. We explain how salespeople can (1) position new and emerging products versus well-established products, (2) position products with price strategies, and (3) position products with value-added strategies.

POSITIONING NEW AND EMERGING PRODUCTS VERSUS MATURE AND WELL-ESTABLISHED PRODUCTS

In many ways, products are like human beings. They are born, grow up, mature, and grow old. In marketing this process is known as the **product life cycle.** The product life cycle includes the stages a product goes through from the time it is first introduced to the market until it is discontinued. As the product moves through its cycle, the strategies relating to competition, promotion, pricing, and other factors must be evaluated and possibly changed. The nature and extent of each stage in the product life cycle are determined by several factors, including:

1. The product's perceived advantage over available substitutes
2. The product's benefits and the importance of the needs it fulfills
3. Competitive activity, including pricing, substitute product development and improvement, and effectiveness of competing advertising and promotion
4. Changes in technology, fashion, or demographics[11]

As we attempt to develop a product-selling strategy, we must consider where the product is positioned in terms of the life cycle. The sales strategy used to sell a new and emerging product will be much different from the strategy used to sell a mature, well-established product (Fig. 6.2).

SELLING NEW AND EMERGING PRODUCTS

The first domestic microwave oven, produced by the Tappan Company, entered the market in 1952 and retailed for $1,295. The first compact disc players sold for more than $1,000. Needless to say, price resistance was a major barrier to market penetration. Once these products became mature, well-established products, prices dropped.

Price is just one factor to consider when you are selling a new product such as the Ricoh MV715. A product that is both new and innovative will often require the efforts of a highly motivated salesperson who has received intensive sales and technical training.[12] Selling strategies used during the new and emerging stage (see Fig. 6.2) are designed to develop a new level of expectation, change habits, and in some cases establish a new standard of quality. The goal is to build desire for the product. When Apple introduced home computers, the initial sales efforts focused on product features and uses of computers in the home.

SELLING MATURE AND WELL-ESTABLISHED PRODUCTS

Mature and well-established products are usually characterized by intense competition as new brands enter the market. At this point, customers accept the products, and they are aware of competing products. With new and emerging products, salespeople may initially have little or no competition and may dominate the market, however, this condition may not last long.

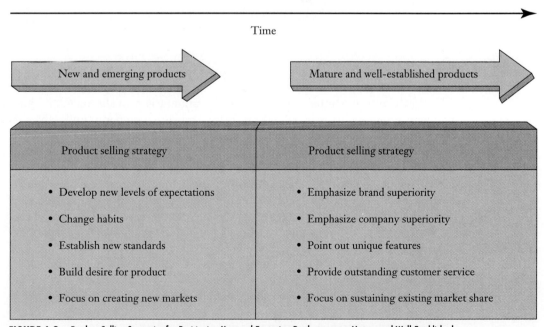

FIGURE 6.2   Product-Selling Strategies for Positioning New and Emerging Products versus Mature and Well-Established Products

In the mature touch-free car-wash market, Ryko's salespeople use a product-selling strategy that focuses on "highest quality." This sales sheet provides important sales support.

Northwestern Mutual Life Insurance continuously provides its 6,000 independent sales agents with new products. Yet the company finds that its new products are quickly copied by competing insurance companies. When competing products enter the market, Northwestern sales agents must adopt new strategies. One positioning strategy is to emphasize the company's 130 years of superior service to policyholders. Agents often describe Northwestern as the "supportive" company that gives a high priority to service after the sale.[13] The objective is to create in the customer's mind the perception that Northwestern is a solid company with a long history of good service to policyholders.

The relationship strategy is often critical in selling mature and well-established products. To maintain market share and ward off competitors, many salespeople work hard to maintain a strong relationship with the customer. At Northwestern, salespeople have found that good service after the sale is one of the best selling strategies because it builds customer loyalty.

POSITIONING PRODUCTS WITH A PRICE STRATEGY

Price, promotion, product, and place are the four elements that make up the marketing mix. Pricing decisions must be made at each stage of the product life cycle. Therefore, setting the price can be a complex process. The first step in establishing price is to determine the firm's pricing objectives. Some firms set their prices to maximize their profits. They aim for a price as high as possible without causing a disproportionate reduction in unit sales. Other firms set a market share objective. Management may decide that the strategic advantage of an increased market share outweighs a temporary reduction in profits.

Pricing strategies often reflect the product's position in the product life cycle. When compact disc players were in the new and emerging stage, customers who wanted this innovative equipment were willing to accept the $1,000 per unit price tag.

SELLING TACTICS THAT EMPHASIZE LOW PRICE

Some marketers have established a positioning plan that emphasizes low price. These companies maintain a basic strategy that focuses on meeting competition. If the firm has meeting competition as its pricing goal, it makes every effort to charge prices that are identical or close to those of the competition. Once this positioning strategy has been adopted, the sales force is given several price tactics to use. Salespeople can alter (lower) the base price through the use

---

BUILDING QUALITY PARTNERSHIPS

HOW DO CUSTOMERS JUDGE SERVICE QUALITY?

In the growing service industry there is intense price competition. From a distance one gets the impression that every buyer decision hinges on price alone. However, a closer examination of service purchases indicates that service quality is an important factor when it comes to developing a long-term relationship with customers.

How do customers judge service quality? Researchers at Texas A&M University have discovered valuable insights about customer perceptions of service quality. They surveyed hundreds of customers in a variety of service industries and discovered that five service-quality dimensions emerged:

1. Tangibles: These are things the customers can see such as the appearance of personnel and equipment.
2. Reliability: This is the ability to perform the desired service dependably, accurately, and consistently.
3. Responsiveness: This is the willingness of sales and customer service personnel to provide prompt service and help customers.
4. Assurance: This includes the employees' knowledge, courtesy, and ability to convey trust and confidence.
5. Empathy: This means the provision of caring, individualized attention to customers.

Customers apparently judge the quality of each service transaction in terms of these five quality dimensions. Companies need to review these service-quality dimensions and make sure that each area measures up to the customers expectations. Salespeople should recognize that these dimensions have the potential to add value to the services they sell.[a]

of discounts and allowances. Discounts and allowances can take a variety of forms. A few of the more common ones follow:

Quantity discount. The **quantity discount** allows the buyer a lower price for purchasing in multiple units or above a specified dollar amount.

Time-period pricing. With **time-period pricing** the salesperson adjusts the price up or down during specific times to spur or acknowledge changes in demand.[14] Off-season travel and lodging prices provide an example.

Promotional allowances. A **promotional allowance** is a price reduction given to a customer who participates in an advertising or a sales support program. Many salespeople give supermarkets promotional allowances for advertising or displaying a manufacturer's products.

These examples represent only a small sample of the many discounts and allowances salespeople use to compete on the basis of price. Price discounting is a competitive tool available to large numbers of salespeople. Excessive focus on low prices and generous discounts, however, can have a negative impact on profits.

CONSEQUENCES OF USING LOW-PRICE TACTICS

Pricing is a critical factor in the sale of many products and services. In markets where competition is extremely strong, setting a product's price may be a firm's most complicated and important decision.

The authors of *The Discipline of Market Leaders* encourage business firms to pick one of three disciplines—best price, best product, or best service—and then do whatever is necessary to outdistance the competition. However, the authors caution us not to ignore the other two disciplines: "You design your business to excel in one direction, but you also have to strive to hit the minimum in the others."[15] The first Yugo automobiles sold in America were advertised at $3,990, but product quality turned off many prospective buyers.

To many salespeople the price-quality relationship is an important factor in selling price. If customers lack other cues to a product's quality, they may judge it by its price. For a growing number of customers, long-term value is more important than short-term savings that result from low prices. A broad-based desire for high quality and "value" as opposed to the lowest possible price suggests that price alone is an inadequate competitive tool.[16]

For many buyers, service after the sale is a critical factor. In some cases, low-price tactics mean less service. If low price results in fewer services after the sale or a reduction in the quality of service, some customers will be less likely to buy the product. More and more customers today are looking for long-term partnerships with salespeople who are committed to providing excellent service after the sale.

POSITIONING YOUR PRODUCT WITH A VALUE-ADDED STRATEGY

Many successful companies have adopted a **strategic market plan** that emphasizes value-added strategies. One of these companies, Frito-Lay, adds value to its products by maintaining a restock program that provides the retailer with an adequate inventory of fresh potato chips and pretzels at all times. Frito-Lay's

12,800 salespeople are well trained and highly motivated. With the aid of hand-held computers to improve inventory control, they give the retailer a level of service that adds value to the product.[17]

When Raytheon Company began selling IBM computer clones, salespeople emphasized the lower price and similarities in the products. However, price discounting alone proved insufficient when competing with a well-established brand name. Once the salespeople began to emphasize the differences in the products, especially features that improved the efficiency of users, sales improved. In the buyers mind, productivity, more than price, added value to the Raytheon computers.[18]

The goal of Mercedes-Benz sales representatives is to create the perception that their automobiles are the best in the high-performance luxury category.

Customers who visit a Nordstrom department store are introduced to a value-added shopping experience. Each department offers a wide selection of top-quality products, and shoppers are waited on by well-trained salespeople who are courteous and knowledgeable. Flowers in the dressing rooms and music from a grand piano on the main floor enhance shopping at the store. Nordstrom spends heavily to "overstaff" the sales floor so customers do not have to wait for assistance.

In recent years we have seen the introduction of many value-added products and services that meet the needs of a well-defined market niche. Mercedes-Benz added value to its automobile by providing Roadside Assistance, a program that lets car owners telephone specially trained Mercedes mechanics when they have problems. Although only a small number of Mercedes owners use the service (fewer than 2 percent), it has proved to be an appealing sales feature. Volvo, BMW, Jaguar, Cadillac, and other luxury car makers have developed competing programs.[19]

VALUE ADDED—A NEW CHALLENGE FOR SALESPEOPLE

Many progressive marketers have adopted the **value-added concept.** This concept means that companies add value to their product with one or more intangibles such as better-trained salespeople, increased levels of courtesy, more dependable product deliveries, better service after the sale, and innovations that truly improve the product's value in the eyes of the customer. In today's highly competitive marketplace these value-added benefits give the company a competitive edge.

Nordstrom department stores provide a value-added shopping experience. Well trained salespeople and increased levels of courtesy improve the product's value in the eyes of the customer.

Salespeople are usually in the best position to explain the features and benefits that add value to a product or service. At Frito-Lay, for example, salespeople can easily explain the benefits of their efficient restock program. At Meridian Travel, introduced at the beginning of this chapter, the travel counselor can describe the benefits of the quarterly travel report given to customers. The salesperson can discover what adds value (in the mind of the customer) and then determine ways to add this value. Adding value starts with building a knowledge base. Dan Kosch, president of a Connecticut-based sales consulting and training company says, "Show customers that you understand their business, their concerns, and what they hope to accomplish."[20] This knowledge will help you direct the customers attention from price to value.

In some cases the salesperson can add value by doing something extra for the customer. For example, the salesperson might offer to help a customer identify ways to make his business more efficient. Suggestions that result in improved cash flow, more effective use of equipment, or expansion of the customer base will certainly be appreciated. This assistance will add value to the relationship between the salesperson and the customer.

Total Product Concept

To understand fully the importance of the value-added concept in selling, and how to apply it in a variety of selling situations, it helps to visualize every product as being four dimensional. The total product is made up of four "possible" products: the generic product, the expected product, the value-added product, and the potential product[21] (Fig. 6.3).

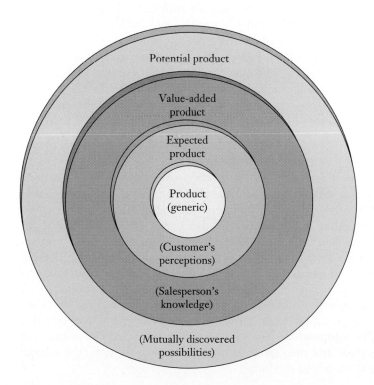

FIGURE 6.3   The Total Product Concept. An understanding of the four "possible" products is helpful when the salesperson develops a presentation for specific types of customers.

Hyatt Regency has adopted a value-added product strategy that emphasizes a high level of personalized service.

GENERIC PRODUCT

The **generic product** is the basic, substantive product you are selling. Generic product describes only the product category, for example, life insurance, rental cars, or microwave ovens. Every Hyatt Regency hotel offers guest rooms, one or more full-service restaurants, meeting rooms, guest parking, and other basic services. For Mayflower Transit, a company that provides moving services, the generic product is the truck and trailer that move the customer's household items. At the generic level, Nordstrom provides categories of goods traditional to an upscale specialty clothing retailer.[22] The generic products at a bank are money that can be loaned to customers and basic checking account services.

The capability of delivering a generic product simply gives the marketer the right to play in the game, to compete in the marketplace.[23] Generic products, even the lowest priced ones, usually cannot compete with products that are "expected" by the customer.

EXPECTED PRODUCT

Every customer has minimal purchase expectations that exceed the generic product itself.[24] Hyatt Regency must offer not only a comfortable guest room, but also a clean one. Some customers expect a "super" clean room. Mayflower must provide a clean, well-maintained moving van *and* a well-trained crew. The **expected product** is everything that represents the customer's minimal expectations. The customer at a Nordstrom store will *expect* current fashions and well-informed salespeople.

The minimal purchase conditions vary among customers, so the salesperson must acquire information concerning the expected product that exists in the customer's mind. Every customer will perceive the product in individualized terms, which a salesperson cannot anticipate. To say that every customer is unique might seem trite, but when salespeople fully accept this fundamental of personal selling, they are better prepared to apply the value-added concept.

When the customer expects more than the generic product, the generic product can be sold *only* if those expectations are met.[25] To determine each customer's expectations requires the salesperson to make observations, conduct background checks, ask questions, and listen to what the customer is saying. We are attempting to discover both feelings and facts.

VALUE-ADDED PRODUCT

The **value-added product** exists when salespeople offer customers more than they expect. When you check into the Hyatt Regency Crown Center in Kansas City, Missouri, you are given a card that says, "Call 50 for a response to any concern within five minutes." If the hotel service staff keeps this promise, guests are likely receiving something they did not expect. Nordstrom spends heavily to overstaff the sales floor by traditional standards. The company also overspends to ensure the availability of more sizes and colors than usual.[26] This upscale retailer is attempting to add value by exceeding customer expectations.

As competition intensifies, and as products and prices become more similar, companies must work harder to distinguish themselves and their products from the competition. They must increase their efforts to find out what customers need and then satisfy those needs. In most cases, the salesperson delivers the value-added product.[27]

How can a salesperson create a value-added product or service? Larry Wilson, noted author and sales consultant, says that adding value means *always* working outside your job description to exceed customer expectations.[28] Salespeople who have adopted the value-added philosophy routinely meet clients' expectations and then do things that exceed those expectations.

The value-added product strategy will vary from one situation to another. Eileen Tertocha, a sales representative with Skipper Morrison Realtors, has developed a unique value-added strategy for new home owners:

> *I give my customers first-class treatment on moving day, including plenty to eat for both the family and the movers. Then, on a regular day-to-day basis, I check to see if everything is going okay or if they need any help from me or anyone else.*[29]

Eileen Tertocha's goal is to make moving as easy as possible. She goes beyond the customer's expectations to take care of a variety of details.

One of the most powerful value-added strategies is personalized service. This **interpersonal value** is win-win relationship building with the customer (as described in Chapter 3) that results from keeping that person's best interests always at the forefront. Salespeople who take the time to get acquainted with the customer's specific needs are able to recommend custom-made solutions instead of generic solutions. Once salespeople can provide a custom-made solution, customers are more apt to view them as partners. Many customers view long-term partnerships with salespeople as a value-added benefit.

POTENTIAL PRODUCT

After the value-added product has been developed, the salesperson should begin to conceptualize the **potential product.** The potential product refers to what may remain to be done, that is, what is possible.[30] As the level of competition increases, especially in the case of mature products, salespeople must look into the future and explore new possibilities.

In the highly competitive food services industry, restaurant owners like to do business with a distribution sales representative (DSR) who wants to help

BUILDING RELATIONSHIPS IN A DIVERSE WORLD

A JAPANESE PLANT ADDS VALUE THROUGH TECHNOLOGY

For many companies the ability to deliver customized products and services is the key to profitability. Many banks, upscale clothing stores, training program developers, and vendors of computer services view customization as a value-added concept. Many manufacturers are also developing customized products. A Japanese manufacturer, the National Bicycle Industrial Company, has applied this value-added concept to the selling of bicycles. It builds one-of-a-kind models by using a flexible manufacturing method. This small company can produce any of 11,231,862 variations of 18 models of racing, road, and mountain bikes in 199 color patterns. Customers visit their local Panasonic bicycle store where salespeople measure them on a special frame and then send the specifications to the factory. At the plant an operator punches the specifications into a Digital Equipment minicomputer (CAD system), which creates a blueprint. The finished bikes sell for $545 to $3,200. As with many value-added marketing efforts, everyone seems to be a winner. Company profits are high, workers are proud, and customers take pride in their customized machines.[c]

General Mills is emphasizing a value-added strategy by supplying independent distributor salespeople with training materials and programs.

make the business profitable. The DSR who assumes this role becomes a true partner and looks beyond the customer's immediate and basic needs. The potential product might consist of a careful study of the restaurant's current menu and appropriate recommendations to the owner. To deliver the potential product, a salesperson must discover and satisfy new customer needs, which requires imagination and creativity.

Steelcase Incorporated, a leading manufacturer of office furniture, recently developed the Personal Harbor Workspaces. The product is designed to be clustered around common work areas that invite teamwork and collaboration. These circular workstations offer buyers a twenty-first century version of the traditional office cubicle. The podlike workstation is such a departure from conventional office design that customers were initially unable to comprehend its potential. Salespeople quickly learned that a traditional product-oriented presentation would not work. Meetings between Steelcase salespeople and customers involved discussions of concepts such as team building, organizational communication, and employee interaction. Steelcase developed "advanced solution teams" that adopted a true consultative role. These teams meet with people in the organization who are more interested in the potential of the Personal Harbor Workspaces than its price.[31]

The potential product is more likely to be developed by salespeople who are close to their customers. Many high-performing salespeople explore product possibilities with their customers on a regular basis. Potential products are often mutually discovered during these exchanges.

MOVING BEYOND THE EXPECTED PRODUCT

The total product concept reminds us that every product and service is four dimensional. Therefore, salespeople are presented with a wide range of possibilities for the products they sell. Once all the possibilities are identified, the stage is set for development of value-added and potential products.

Bayer Medical Services Systems, a Columbus, Ohio medical products supplier, sells a variety of disposable medical supplies. The primary market for these products is the long-term health care industry. Disposable medical supplies can be considered *generic* products. There are other competing suppliers who can offer similar products at nearly identical prices. Disposable medical supplies that meet industry standards, that are priced competitively, and are delivered in a timely manner can be described as *expected* products. A few years ago Bayer began offering customers a *value-added* product. It emerged when a customer requested a product to help monitor her Bayer product inventory more efficiently. After careful study of the customer's needs, Bayer developed an ancillary bar-coded program called Accubar. This technology is similar to the bar code systems used by supermarkets to control their stock. Today the fully developed Accubar system can be viewed as a *potential* product. Bayer sales representatives introduce the system as part of their sales presentations. They point out the Accubar system will help the customer increase revenue control and keep costs down.[32]

By moving beyond the expected product, salespeople build customer loyalty, repeat business, and referrals. In addition, there is less chance that the customer will request or demand price cuts. The added value received tends to discourage such requests.

PREPARING WRITTEN PROPOSALS

Written proposals are frequently part of the sales process. It is only natural that some buyers will want the proposed solution put in writing. *Written proposals* can be defined as a specific plan of action based on the facts, assumptions, and supporting documentation included in the sales presentation.[33] A well-written proposal can set you apart from the competition and increase your chances of closing the sale. It offers the buyer reassurance that you will deliver what has been promised. Written proposals vary in terms of format and content, but most effective proposals include the following parts:

Budget and overview Tell the prospect the cost of the solution you have prescribed. Be specific as you describe the product or service to be provided and specify the price.

Objective The objective should be expressed in terms of benefits. A tangible objective might be to "reduce payroll expense by 10 percent." An intangible objective might be stated as "increased business security offered by a company with a reputation for dependability." Focus on benefits that relate directly to the customers need.

Strategy Briefly describe how you will meet your objective. How will you fulfill the obligations you have described in your proposal? In some cases this section of your proposal includes specific language: "Your account will be assigned to Susan Murray, our senior lease representative."

Schedule Establish a time frame for meeting your objective. This might involve the specification of shipping or installation dates.

Rationale With a mixture of logic and emotion present your rationale for taking action now. Once again, the emphasis should be on benefits, not features.[34]

   The proposal should be printed on quality paper and free of any errors in spelling, grammar, or punctuation. Before completing the proposal, review the content one more time to be sure you have addressed all of the customer's concerns. The customer should be able to quickly determine if the proposed solution meets his needs.

SUMMARY

A growing number of companies are developing strong positions in specialized markets. To accomplish this goal requires more attention to strategic planning. The strategic market plan can be a guide for strategic planning by the salesperson.

   We noted that today's better-educated customers are often seeking a cluster of satisfactions. They seek satisfactions that arise from the product itself, from the company that makes or distributes the product, and from the salesperson who sells and services the product.

   Product positioning was described as the decisions and activities directed toward the attempt to create and maintain a firm's intended product concept in the customer's mind. We introduced the major product-positioning strategies available to salespeople: a price strategy and a value-added strategy.

Part of this chapter was devoted to the total product concept. The total product is made up of four possible products. This range of possibilities includes the generic product, the expected product, the value-added product, and the potential product.

The final section of this chapter was devoted to preparation of *written proposals*. A five-part proposal format was discussed.

➤ KEY TERMS

Satisfactions	*Value-Added Concept*
Product Positioning	*Generic Product*
Product Life Cycle	*Expected Product*
Quantity Discount	*Value-Added Product*
Time-Period Pricing	*Interpersonal Value*
Promotional Allowance	*Potential Product*
Strategic Market Plan	*Written Proposals*

➤ REVIEW QUESTIONS

1. Why has product differentiation become so important in sales and marketing?
2. According to Ted Levitt, what is the definition of a product? What satisfactions do customers want?
3. Explain what is meant by *positioning* as a product-selling strategy.
4. Why have salespeople assumed an important role in positioning products? How does the concept of *future shock* relate to product positioning?
5. List three pricing tactics a salesperson with a low-price strategy can use to achieve a high closing rate.
6. What are the possible consequences a salesperson might experience when using low-price tactics?
7. Read the Sales Tips box on page 128. Do you agree with Regis McKenna's view that intangible factors are very important? Explain your answer.
8. What are some of the common ways salespeople add value to the products they sell?
9. What are the four possible products that make up the *total product* concept?
10. List and describe the five parts of a complete written proposal.

➤ APPLICATION EXERCISES

1. Secure catalogs from two competing industrial supply firms or two competing direct mail catalog companies. Assume one of the represented businesses is your employer. After studying the catalogs, make a comparative analysis of your company's competitive advantages.
2. The Hyatt Regency hotel chain illustrates the total product concept in this chapter. Research value-added information on the Hyatt Regency Waikiki

by locating the Hawaii Web address http://www.hawaii-hotels.com. Click on Aahu Hotels and examine information presented on the Hyatt Regency Waikiki.

3. Interview the manager of a local supermarket that sells a large assortment of national brands such as Nabisco, Kellogg's, and Del Monte. Ask this person what kinds of appeals are used by sales representatives of national brand products when they request more shelf space. Determine how frequently they offer trade or advertising allowances.

4. Call a local financial services representative specializing in stock, bond, or equity fund transactions. Ask what percentage of clients rely on the information given to make complex decisions on their investments. Also ask this person if customers feel that advice in custom fitting investment programs adds value to their decision making. Find out whether financial products are getting more or less complex and what effect this will have on providing value-added service in the future.

➤ CASE PROBLEM

Many of the most profitable companies have discovered that there are "riches in market niches." They have developed products and services that meet the needs of a well-defined or newly created market. Steelcase Incorporated, a leading source of information and expertise on work effectiveness, has been working hard to develop products that meet the needs of people who do most of their work in an office environment. The company motto is, "The office environment company." One of its newest products is the Personal Harbor Workplaces, a self-contained, fully equipped and totally private podlike workstation. Steelcase sales literature describes the product as ideal for companies that are tired of waiting for the future:

> *They were developed to support the individual within a highly collaborative team environment, and they work best when clustered around common work areas equipped with mobile tables, carts, benches, screens, and other Steelcase Activity Products. These "commons" are meant to be flexible spaces that enhance communication and facilitate interaction.*

Steelcase realized that selling this advanced product would not be easy, so a decision was made to develop an advanced sales team to presell the Personal Harbor before its major introduction. Once the team started making sales calls, it became evident that a traditional product-oriented sales presentation would not work. The Personal Harbor was a departure from conventional office design, so many customers were perplexed. Sue Sacks, a team member, said, "People acted like we had fallen from Mars." Team members soon realized that to explain the features and benefits of the product they had to begin studying new organizational developments such as team-oriented work forces and corporate reengineering. The advanced sales team was renamed advanced solutions team. Sales calls put more emphasis on learning about the customers problems and identification of possible solutions. Members of the team viewed themselves as consultants who were in a position to discuss solutions to complex business problems.

The consultative approach soon began to pay off in sales. One customer, a hospital, was preparing to build a new office building and needed workstations for 400 employees. The hospital had formed a committee to make decisions concerning the purchase of office equipment. After an initial meeting between the Steelcase sales team and the hospital committee, a visit to the Steelcase headquarters in Grand Rapids, Michigan was arranged. The hospital committee members were able to tour the plant and meet with selected Steelcase experts. With knowledge of the hospital's goals and directions, Sue Sacks was able to arrange meetings with Steelcase technical personnel who could answer specific questions. The hospital ultimately placed an order worth more than a million dollars.

QUESTIONS

1. To fulfill a problem-solving need, salespeople must often be prepared to communicate effectively with customers who are seeking a cluster of satisfaction (see Fig. 6.1). Is it likely that a customer who is considering the Personal Harbor Workspaces will seek information concerning all three dimensions of the Product Selling Model? Explain your answer.

2. What product-selling strategies are most effective when selling a new and emerging product such as the Personal Harbor Workspaces?

3. Sue Sacks and other members of her sales team discovered that a traditional product-oriented presentation would not work when selling the Personal Harbor Workspaces. Success came only after the team adopted the consultative style of selling. Why was the product-oriented presentation ineffective?

4. Sue Sacks and other members of the advanced team found that the consultative approach resulted in meetings with people higher in the customer's organization. "We get to call on a higher level of buyer," she said. Also, the team was more likely to position the product with a value-added strategy rather than a price strategy. In what ways did the advanced solutions team add value to their product? Why was less emphasis placed on price during meetings with the customer?

Part IV

Developing a Customer Strategy

With increased knowledge of the customer the salesperson is in a better position to achieve sales goals. This part presents information on understanding buyer behavior, discovering individual customer needs, and developing a prospect base.

One of the two sustainable strategic advantages in the new global marketplace is an obsession with customers. Customers, not markets.
TOM PETERS
THRIVING ON CHAOS

139

Understanding Buyer Behavior

LEARNING OBJECTIVES

When you finish reading this chapter, you should be able to

1. Discuss the meaning of a customer strategy

2. Understand the complex nature of customer behavior

3. Discuss the social and psychological influences that shape customer buying decisions

4. Discuss the power of perception in shaping buying behavior

5. Distinguish between emotional and rational buying motives

6. Distinguish between patronage and product buying motives

7. Explain three commonly accepted theories that explain how people arrive at a buying decision

8. Describe three ways to discover individual customer buying motives

A *Business Week* cover story described the new product battleground as "a scene of awful carnage."[1] Each year companies launch a large number of new products, but many fail to meet sales expectations. A new product must satisfy a customer's needs, but identifying these needs can be difficult. No one understands this challenge better then Kim Fernandez, director of natural food sales for Alta Dena Certified Dairy. She sells a wide range of natural dairy foods to wholesalers and retailers. Almost all her products are displayed in the dairy department. In a typical supermarket, the dairy department accounts for about 9 percent of sales. Kim Fernandez is responsible for servicing existing accounts and obtaining new accounts. She is also responsible for introducing new products.[2] This is a challenging part of her work in view of the fact that 800 to 900 new dairy products are introduced each year. The proliferation of new items is an attempt to satisfy more consumer needs.

Developing a Customer Strategy

The greatest challenge to salespeople today is to improve responsiveness to customers. In fact, a growing number of sales professionals believe the customer has supplanted the product as the driving force in sales today.[3] As noted by Larry Wilson, "The products of one company in an industry are becoming more and more similar to those of the competition."[4] The salesperson can distinguish between similar products and services and help the customer to perceive important differences.

ADDING VALUE WITH A CUSTOMER STRATEGY

A **customer strategy** is a carefully conceived plan that will result in maximum customer responsiveness. One major dimension of this strategy is to achieve a better understanding of the customer's buying needs and motives. When salespeople take time to discover these needs and motives, they are in a much better position to offer customers a value-added solution to their buying problem.

Every salesperson who wants to develop repeat business should figure out a way to collect and systematize customer information. As part of the customer strategy, many salespeople use some type of customer profile. The authors of *Reengineering the Corporation* discuss the importance of collecting information about the unique and particular needs of each customer:

> *Customers—consumers and corporations alike—demand products and services designed for their unique and particular needs. There is no longer any such notion as* the *customer; there is only* this *customer, the one with who a seller is dealing at the moment and who now has the capacity to indulge his or her own personal tastes.[5]*

The first prescription for developing a customer strategy focuses on buyer behavior (Fig. 7.1). Every salesperson needs a general understanding of why and how people buy, which is the topic of this chapter. The second prescription emphasizes the discovery of individual customer needs. The third prescription for developing a customer strategy emphasizes building a strong prospect base, which is discussed in Chapter 8.

The Complex Nature of Customer Behavior

The forces that motivate customers can be complex. Arch McGill, former vice president of IBM, reminds us that individual customers perceive the product in their own terms, and that these terms may be "unique, idiosyncratic, human, emotional, end-of-the-day, irrational, erratic terms."[6] Different people doing the same thing (for example, purchasing a personal computer) may have different needs that motivate them, and each person may have several motives for a single action.

The proliferation of market research studies, public opinion polls, surveys, and reports of "averages" makes it easy to fall into the trap of thinking of the customer as a number. The customer is a person, not a statistic. As noted previously, to gain an understanding of what motivates a customer to buy a certain product or service requires an understanding of forces that influence why people buy and knowledge of how customers make most of their buying decisions.

FIGURE 7.1 The greatest challenge to salespeople today is to improve responsiveness to customers. Understanding why and how customers buy and knowing who prospects are form the foundation blocks for the salesperson to develop a highly responsive customer strategy.

Strategic/Consultative Selling Model	
Strategic step	Prescription
DEVELOP A PERSONAL SELLING PHILOSOPHY	☑ ADOPT MARKETING CONCEPT ☑ VALUE PERSONAL SELLING ☑ BECOME A PROBLEM SOLVER/PARTNER
DEVELOP A RELATIONSHIP STRATEGY	☑ ADOPT DOUBLE-WIN PHILOSOPHY ☑ PROJECT PROFESSIONAL IMAGE ☑ MAINTAIN HIGH ETHICAL STANDARDS
DEVELOP A PRODUCT STRATEGY	☑ BECOME A PRODUCT EXPERT ☑ ADOPT FEATURE-BENEFIT PROCESS ☑ POSITION PRODUCT
DEVELOP A CUSTOMER STRATEGY	☐ UNDERSTAND BUYER BEHAVIOR ☐ DISCOVER CUSTOMER NEEDS ☐ DEVELOP PROSPECT BASE

Forces Influencing Buying Decisions

Figure 7.2 illustrates the many forces that influence buying decisions. Notice that psychological and physiological needs, combined with social influences, shape customer perceptions and buying motives. As we explain each part of the model, a better understanding of buyer behavior will emerge.

Customers are motivated by complex forces. With the aid of questions, we can discover some of the forces influencing a buying decision.

BUILDING QUALITY PARTNERSHIPS

MOVE UP TO AN OLDSMOBILE

When John Rock was put in charge of the Oldsmobile division of General Motors, he could not help but reflect on a less complicated period when his father operated a Chevrolet/Oldsmobile dealership in South Dakota. In the 1950s the decision to buy an Oldsmobile was less complex. John Rock explains that an Oldsmobile represented a sense of step-up value:

> Oldsmobile had a clear, defined role. If you had a good crop year, you went to an Olds instead of a Chevy. It was the natural progression, no cloudiness in the focus or the role in those days.

Throughout the mid-to-late eighties the Oldsmobile line of cars was popular with sales of a million units a year. When Rock took over the division, sales for the previous year had dropped to 400,000 cars. One major reason for the sales decline was a serious transmission reliability problem that surfaced in the 1980s. Many customers had transmission problems and could not always get enough help from their dealer or the manufacturer. John Rock said, "The bottom line is we broke the promise to an awful lot of people."

Today Oldsmobile executives are spending time trying to figure out ways to bring business back to the company. They plan to emphasize a "nonproduct" strategy. The objective is to upgrade product quality and service at the dealer level to better satisfy current customers and encourage them to buy another Oldsmobile. The plan is to "Saturn-ize" the division. Saturn car owners rate the convenience of ownership and the quality of the ownership experience very high. They want Oldsmobile owners to feel the same way about their cars. The hope is that many Saturn owners will choose Oldsmobile when they decide to trade up.[a]

MASLOW'S HIERARCHY OF NEEDS

To gain insights into customer behavior motivated by both physiological and psychological needs, it is helpful to study the popular hierarchy of needs developed by Abraham Maslow. According to Maslow, basic human needs are arranged in a hierarchy according to their strength.

PHYSIOLOGICAL NEEDS

Physiological needs, sometimes called primary needs, include the needs of food, water, sleep, and shelter. Maslow placed our physiological needs at the bottom of the pyramid. He believed that these basic needs tend to be strong in the minds of most people. As these more basic needs (hunger, thirst, shelter, etc.) are satisfied, a person seeks to satisfy the higher needs. Efforts to satisfy the higher needs must be postponed until the basic physical needs are met.

Maslow describes people as wanting animals who strive to satisfy higher needs after lower needs have been satisfied. People will satisfy their needs systematically, in most cases, starting with the most basic and moving up the ladder.

SECURITY NEEDS

After physiological needs have been satisfied, the next need level that tends to dominate is safety and security. **Security needs** represent our desire to be free from danger and uncertainty. The desire to satisfy the need for safety and security will often motivate people to purchase such items as medical and life insurance or a security alarm for the home or business. The buyer who voices a

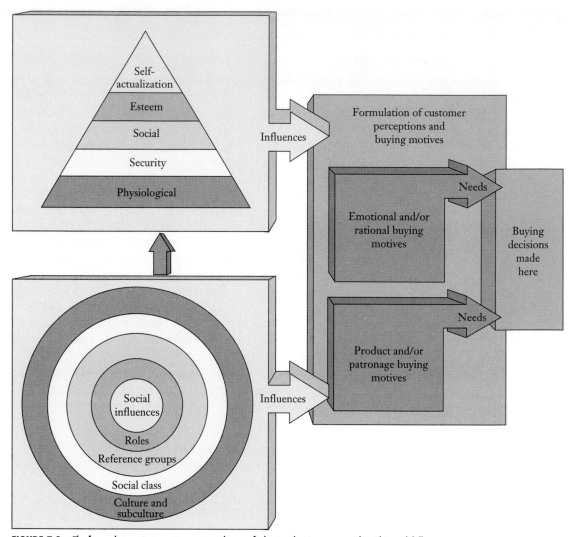

FIGURE 7.2 The forces that motivate customers to make specific buying decisions are complex. This model illustrates the many factors that influence buyer behavior. It can serve the salesperson as a guide for developing a highly responsive customer strategy.

strong desire to have products delivered on time and undamaged may be motivated by security needs. For a banking customer the security need might surface as a desire for accessibility, timely hours of operation, or localized access to service.[7] Needless to say, working with a competent, trusted salesperson gives the customer a feeling of security.

SOCIAL NEEDS
Social needs, or the need to belong, reflect our desire for identification with a group and approval from others. These needs help explain our continuing search for friendship, companionship, and long-term business relationships. This "need to belong" is more than just an urge—it is a fundamental human need.[8] This level of Maslow's hierarchy of needs helps us understand why many

customers want to be treated as partners. They desire an accessible, two-way relationship.

ESTEEM NEEDS

Esteem needs appear at the fourth level of Maslow's need priority model. Esteem needs reflect our desire to feel worthy in the eyes of others. We seek a sense of personal worth and adequacy, a feeling of competence. In simple terms, we want to feel that we are important. When Debra Tarleton, a resident of Charlotte, North Carolina, turned her retirement savings over to a securities broker, she expected to be an involved partner in the investment process. When a year passed without her hearing from the broker, it became apparent he did not value her input. The broker could have easily granted Tarleton prestige and stature by giving her regular reports on her investment and opportunities for input.[9]

SELF-ACTUALIZATION NEEDS

Dr. Maslow defined the term **self-actualization** as a need for self-fulfillment, a full tapping of one's potential. It is the need to "be all that you can be," to have mastery over things you are doing. One goal of consultative selling is to help the customer experience self-actualization in terms of the relationship with the salesperson. The self-actualized customer relationship is a true partnership. The salesperson is continuously updating customer information and providing value-added services. After a bad experience with her first broker, Debra Tarleton experienced a feeling of self-actualization when she turned her investment portfolio over to Lorraine Fiorillo, a Prudential Securities financial planner. Fiorillo helped her set up an individual retirement account and a self-employment pension plan for her business.[10]

The need to earn other people's admiration can be a strong motivating force. (*Drawing by Richter;* © *1977* The New Yorker Magazine, Inc.)

"What do I do? I drive a Maserati."

The five-level need priority model developed by Maslow is somewhat artificial in certain instances. At times several of our needs are interacting together within us. However, the model does provide salespeople with a practical way of understanding which need is most likely to dominate customer behavior in certain situations. One highly successful salesperson uses several questions to clarify which needs will likely influence the purchase decision. Once he has identified the most important needs, he attempts to relate the needs to the appropriate levels of the hierarchy. He often finds that one of the levels has the strongest influence.[11]

SOCIAL INFLUENCES THAT SHAPE CUSTOMER BEHAVIOR

As noted earlier, the people around us also influence our buying decisions. These **social influences** can be grouped into four major areas: (1) role influences, (2) reference groups, (3) social class, and (4) culture and subculture[12] (Fig. 7.3). Salespeople who understand these roles and influences can develop the type of insight customers view as being valuable.

ROLE INFLUENCE

Throughout our lives we occupy positions within groups, organizations, and institutions. Closely associated with each position is a **role:** a set of characteristics and expected social behaviors based on the expectations of others. All the roles we assume (student, member of the school board, or position held at

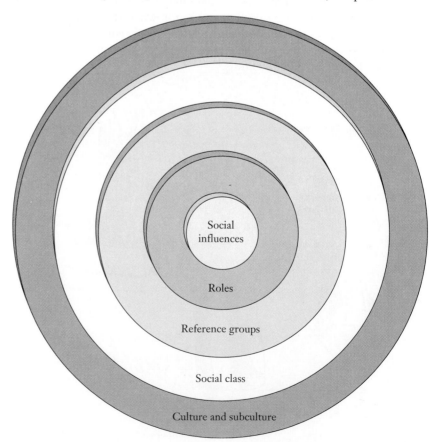

FIGURE 7.3   To gain additional insights into customers' motivations, it is helpful to study the social influences that affect buying decisions.

Social influences

Roles

Reference groups

Social class

Culture and subculture

work) influence not only our general behavior but also our buying behavior. In today's society, for example, a woman may assume the role of mother at home and purchasing manager at work. In the manager's role she may feel the need to develop a conservative wardrobe or purchase several books on leadership.

REFERENCE GROUP INFLUENCE

A **reference group** consists of people who have well-established interpersonal communications and tend to influence the values, attitudes, and behaviors of one another. The reference group may act as a point of comparison and a source of information for the individual member. For example, a fraternity or sorority may serve as a reference group for a college student. In the business community, a chapter of the American Society for Training and Development, or Sales and Marketing Executives International may provide a reference group for its members. As members of a reference group we often observe other people in the group to establish our own norms, and these norms become a guide for our purchasing activity. Of course, the degree to which a reference group influences a buying decision will depend on the strength of the individual's involvement with the group and the degree of susceptibility to reference group influence.

SOCIAL CLASS INFLUENCE

A **social class** consists of people who are similar in occupational prestige, values, lifestyles, interests, and behaviors.[13] The criteria used to rank people according to social class vary from one society to another. In some societies, land ownership allows entry into a higher social class. In other societies, education is a major key to achieving upper-class status. The neighborhood we live in and the type, value, and condition of our home also represent class indicators. To some degree, individuals within social classes have similar attitudes, values, and possessions.

How many social classes are there? There is no clear answer to that question, but sociologists usually employ between three and six categories. At one extreme is the upper class, which usually consists of "old money" people who possess inherited wealth. They buy large homes, obtain degrees from prestigious institutions, travel extensively, and tend to buy quality products. At the other extreme is the lower class, which is characterized by persons with little formal education and considerably less income. Marketers often focus attention on a specific social class. Metropolitan Life Insurance Company, a large provider of life insurance to the middle class, recently announced it is targeting more affluent customers for new business. Met Life has assigned 300 salespeople to sell policies to individuals earning $150,000 to $200,000 annually.[14]

CULTURAL INFLUENCE

Culture can be defined as the arts, beliefs, institutions, transmitted behavior patterns, and thoughts of a community or population. In a general sense, culture is everything around us that is made by human beings. A professor at Dartmouth College said, "Culture is what we see and hear so often that we call it reality. Out of culture comes behavior."[15] We maintain and transmit our culture chiefly through language. Culture has considerable influence on buying behavior. Today, culture is getting more attention because of the rapid increases

Sales force automation. Goldmine Software Corporation offers an automated system for quick access to information on why your customer buys.

BUILDING RELATIONSHIPS THROUGH TECHNOLOGY

MANAGING MULTIPLE CONTACTS WITH ACT!

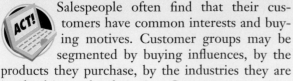

Salespeople often find that their customers have common interests and buying motives. Customer groups may be segmented by buying influences, by the products they purchase, by the industries they are involved in, or by their size. Contact management software can enable the salesperson to easily "mass produce" information that is custom fitted to the needs of people in a specific group. Each owner of a product may receive a telephone call, personalized letter, or report that describes the benefits of a new accessory available from the salesperson. (See the Sales Automation Application Exercise on p. 163 for more information.)

in immigrant groups. As cultural diversity increases, companies must reexamine their sales and marketing strategies.

Within many cultures there are groups whose members share ideals and beliefs that differ from those held by the wider society of which they are a part. We call such a group a **subculture.**[16] Among the many U.S. subcultures are the teenage, elderly, and Native American subcultures. Members of a subculture may have stronger preferences for certain types of foods, clothing, and furniture.

Perception — How Customer Needs Are Formed

Perception is the process whereby we receive stimuli (information) through our five senses and then assign meaning to them.[17] Our perception is shaped by social influences as well as the psychological and physiological conditions within us (see Fig. 7.2). Perception determines what is seen and felt; therefore it influences our buying behavior.

We tend to screen out or modify stimuli, a process known as *selective perception*, for two reasons. First, we cannot possibly be conscious of all inputs at one time. Just the commercial messages we see and hear each day are enough to cause sensory overload. Second, we are conditioned by our social and cultural background, and our physical and psychological needs, to use selectivity.

Buyers may screen out or modify information presented by a salesperson if it conflicts with their previously learned attitudes or beliefs. The prospect who is convinced that "I will never be able to master the personal computer" is apt to use selective perception when the salesperson begins discussing user-friendly features. Salespeople who can anticipate this problem of selective perception should acquire as much background information as possible before meeting with the prospect. During the first meeting with the customer, the salesperson should make every effort to build a strong relationship so the person opens up and freely discusses personal perceptions.

The image projected by Pentium, a processor from Intel, has considerable impact on buyer behavior.

Cartoon by Peter Steiner. Reprinted from AARP News Bulletin *with permission.*

" THESE MAY BE MY 'GOLDEN YEARS,' MR. MILLIGAN. BUT I PREFER THAT THEY BE FUEL INJECTED. "

People involved in sales and marketing need to review their own perceptions periodically to see if they are accurate. For many years, marketers have mistakenly stereotyped older Americans as crotchety grandparents living on a modest fixed income. The truth is that many senior citizens are in the middle to high income bracket and see themselves as ten to fifteen years younger than their chronological years.[18]

Buying Motives

Every buying decision has a motive behind it. A **buying motive** can be thought of as an aroused need, drive, or desire. It acts as a force that stimulates behavior intended to satisfy that aroused need. Our perceptions influence or shape this behavior. An understanding of buying motives provides the salesperson with the reasons why customers buy.

As you might expect, some buying decisions are influenced by more than one buying motive. The buyer of catering services may want food of exceptional quality served quickly so all her guests can eat together. This customer may also be quite price conscious. In this situation the caterer should attempt to discover the *dominant buying motive* (DBM). The DBM will have the greatest influence on the buying decision.[19] If the customer is anxious to make a good impression on guests who have discriminating food tastes, then food quality may be the dominant buying motive.

Successful salespeople have adopted a product strategy that involves discovery of the buying motives that will influence the purchase decision. In Chapter 10 we describe a need identification process that can be used to discover the customer's buying motives.

EMOTIONAL VERSUS RATIONAL BUYING MOTIVES

A careful study of buyer behavior reveals that people make buying decisions based on both emotional and rational buying motives. An **emotional buying motive** is one that prompts the prospect to act because of an appeal to some

10 WAYS TO BIGGER SALES, EXPANDED MARKETS AND HIGHER GROSS PROFIT.

THE BRAND NAME THAT OPENS DOORS

1. Sell the name your customers know and trust for quality, value and performance, the brand they use in their own homes. Reynolds brand opens doors to new accounts and bigger sales.

2. Show your customers the extent of the Reynolds Foodservice line, over 800 products to meet their marketing, foodservice and packaging needs. Competitive pricing and money-saving promotions boost your sales and profits.

INVENTORY SAVINGS

3. Spend less to sell more. Stock the full Reynolds Foodservice line, and eliminate the capital expense of unnecessary product duplication.

4. Cut down on paperwork and ordering time. You make one phone call, place one order for all your foil, film, container and packaging products.

PERSONALIZED SERVICE

5. Count on experienced customer service representatives who understand your needs and your customers' needs. Your rep places orders, answers questions and expedites delivery.

6. Call your toll-free 800 number for direct access to your customer service rep. You talk to the same rep every time you call.

FAST TURN-AROUND

7. Depend on fast turn-around. Our centrally located distribution centers are fully stocked with Reynolds Foodservice products. That means your order — all of it — gets to you quickly, usually within five days.

8. Take advantage of mixed load ordering at full load savings. Order limited quantities on some products, extended quantities on others and get full pallet savings.

DSR MARKET SUPPORT

9. Use your Reynolds Foodservice sales representative, your full-time partner, for more than product knowledge. Our sales reps ride with DSRs on sales calls, do new product demonstrations, full-line and new market presentations — whatever you need to satisfy your customers.

10. Rely on consistent communications to your customers. Strong-selling national advertising in the leading foodservice and supermarket publications keeps your customers informed. Attractive sales brochures help you close sales and make bigger sales.

....

Call your Reynolds Foodservice sales representative or 1-800-446-3020 today. Increase your sales — and profits — with Reynolds Foodservice products.

Reynolds. Because Quality and Service Count. REYNOLDS FOODSERVICE PACKAGING

Rational buying motives are the target of this Reynolds advertisement. These motives can be satisfied by Reynolds products, its sales representatives, and its customer service personnel.

---

sentiment or passion. Emotional reasons for buying products often stem more from the heart than from the head. Some purchases are made to satisfy a wish for pleasure, comfort, or social approval. Emotions are powerful and often serve as the foundation of the dominant buying motive. A **rational buying motive** usually appeals to the prospect's reason or better judgment. Some common rational buying motives would include profit potential, quality of service, and availability of technical assistance.

EMOTIONAL BUYING MOTIVES

A surprising number of purchases are guided by emotional buying motives. This is why many firms use emotional appeals. Even technology firms sometimes rely on these appeals. Cascade Communications Corporation, maker of Internet traffic switches, promises, "Technology that reaches right into our lives." GTE, the giant telecommunications firm, says, "We're working to help make your life easier." Ads for Gulfstream business jets explain how the planes can save executives time and also describe the roomy interiors that offer comfort to the passengers.

Doing business in America, or anyplace else in the world, is never purely a rational or logical process. In many cases buying decisions result from a meeting of the hearts as well as a meeting of the minds.[20] In a world filled with look-alike products, emotional factors can have considerable influence. If two vendors have nearly identical products, then the influence of the vendors' salespeople becomes more important. The salesperson who is able to connect at a personal level will have the advantage.

Phil Kline, a noted sales trainer, says that salespeople should make every effort to discover the emotions that influence buying decisions. The salesperson who is able to satisfy the customers emotional buying motives is performing an important service.[21]

RATIONAL BUYING MOTIVES

A purchase based on rational buying motives is generally the result of an objective review of available information. The buyer closely examines product or service information with an attitude that is relatively free of emotion. Professional buyers or purchasing agents are most likely to be motivated by rational buying motives such as on-time delivery, financial gain, competent installation, saving of time, increased profits, or durability.

The buyers who work for Wal-Mart, the largest and most profitable retailer in the world, are tough, aggressive, and focused. They want to do business with salespeople who are well prepared and know how their product will complement the product mix in Wal-Mart stores. Bob Gehm, a vice president for West Point Stevens, makes frequent calls on Wal-Mart buyers. He says, "They expect you to give them the best price, the best value, and the best service."[22]

In the face of increased competition, professional buyers such as those employed by Wal-Mart will want to partner with salespeople who can respond to their rational buying motives. This is especially true in the fields of manufac-

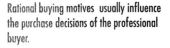

Rational buying motives usually influence the purchase decisions of the professional buyer.

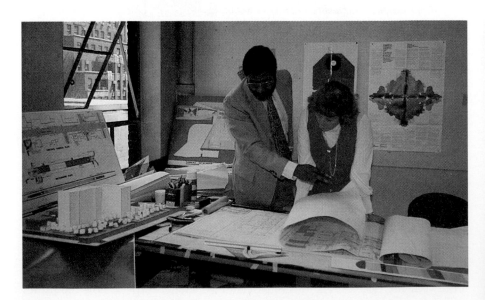

turing and processing, where salespeople are expected to offer powerful insights into helping firms make things better, faster, and cheaper.[23]

PATRONAGE VERSUS PRODUCT BUYING MOTIVES

Another way to help explain buyer behavior is to distinguish between patronage and product buying motives. Patronage buying motives and product buying motives are learned reasons for buying. These buying motives are important because they can stimulate repeat business and referrals.

PATRONAGE BUYING MOTIVES

A **patronage buying motive** is one that causes the prospect to buy products from one particular business. The prospect has usually had prior direct or indirect contact with the business and has judged this contact to be beneficial. In those situations where there is little or no appreciable difference between two products, patronage motives can be highly important. At a time when look-

Now, what can Hewlett-Packard do for you?

Please check for the information you want:

☐ I want increased computing power for less cost.
☐ I want true multi-vendor connectivity.
☐ I want easier access to information.
☐ I want better service and support.

Name

Title

Company name

Street

City

State   Zip Code

MAIL TO: HEWLETT-PACKARD, Inquiries Manager, 19310 Pruneridge Ave., Dept. 740G, Cupertino, CA 95014

Or Call 1 800 752-0900, Dept. 740G

HEWLETT® PACKARD

This advertisement helps Hewlett-Packard generate a prospect data base for the sales force. It also helps the company discover the prospect's buying motives.

alike products are very common, these motives take on a new degree of importance. Some typical patronage buying motives are described as follows.

Superior service As noted earlier in this text, superior service adds value to the product. In many cases the value-added product builds customer loyalty.

Selection Some firms make every effort to carry a complete selection of products. The prospect is usually quite certain that the item needed will be available.

Competence of sales representatives There is no doubt that the salesperson is in a unique position to develop a loyal customer following. A salesperson who knows the product and is willing to give "something extra" to the customer is an asset to any firm.

This ad is designed to attract the attention of customers who understand the advantage of strong brands.

Superior design can be the key to writing orders in the 1990s according to Robert Hayes, Harvard professor.

PRODUCT BUYING MOTIVES

A **product buying motive** is one that leads a prospect to purchase one product in preference to another. Interestingly enough, this decision is sometimes made without direct comparison between competing products. The buyer simply feels that one product is superior to another.

There are numerous buying motives that trigger prospects to select one product over another.

Brand preference Many marketers seek to develop brand loyalty. Maytag, Mercedes-Benz, and United Van Lines serve as examples of companies that have developed a strong brand preference.

Quality preference J. D. Power, founder of J. D. Power and Associates, says, "We define quality as what the customer wants."[24] Today's customer is likely to have high-quality standards.

Price preference Most prospects are price conscious to some degree. If a product has a price advantage over the competition and quality has not been sacrificed, it will probably enjoy success in the marketplace.

Design or engineering preference Robert Hayes, a Harvard Business School professor, says that after years of ferocious competition based on price and quality, many companies are betting that superior product design will be the key to winning customers in the 1990s. If this predication is true, salespeople will need to give this buying motive more attention in the years ahead.[25]

How Customers Make Buying Decisions

Several commonly accepted theories explain how people arrive at a buying decision. Three of the most popular theories are described here. One traditional point of view holds that the salesperson closes the sale by guiding the prospect through five mental processes. We refer to this approach as the **buyer action theory.** A second traditional theory is based on the assumption that a final buying decision is possible only after the prospect has answered five logical questions. This is called the **buyer resolution theory.** Both of these theories thrived during the past forty years when the main focus was on the product. The third explanation of how people buy is "prospect" oriented and is called the **need-satisfaction theory.** This newest approach to the selling-buying process gives maximum attention to a highly responsive customer strategy that ensures satisfaction of prospect needs. It has been adopted by successful marketers who realize the benefits associated with long-term partnerships.

THE BUYER ACTION THEORY

From a traditional point of view there are five mental steps that lead to a buying decision: (1) attention, (2) interest, (3) desire, (4) conviction, and (5) action. The salesperson's role is to guide the prospect through each step.[26] These five steps have application in advertising, public relations, publicity, and sales promotion as well as personal selling.

Attention There is no hope of selling a product unless you first get the prospect's attention. In some cases this is not an easy task. A potential buyer may be preoccupied with a variety of concerns and may view your presence as an intrusion. The salesperson can do a number of things to attract and hold a potential buyer's attention. These are discussed in a later chapter.

Interest The second step in the buying process is development of interest in the product. A salesperson must determine the best way to convert attention to interest. The manner in which this is done will vary, of course. In some selling situations the prospect's interest might be sparked by a product demonstration. In another situation the salesperson may use a series of stimulating questions to create interest.

Desire Desire moves us to possess something or to experience something that we perceive as enjoyable or satisfying. It can be a compelling factor in life. We can all recall instances when the desire within us became almost overwhelming. This desire may have been kindled by the sounds of a high-quality stereo system or by knowledge that a new computer will improve your productivity.

Conviction At the conviction stage the prospect has decided the product is a genuine value, with features that justify its price. Competing products have been ruled out. The salesperson has removed doubt from the buyer's mind. At this stage, the prospect can rationalize the purchase to himself and others.

Action Once the buyer makes the first four decisions, the stage is set to close the sale. Sometimes the fifth decision is made quickly and effortlessly. In other cases the prospect shows signs of procrastination. In some cases a small amount of pressure applied at the right time will motivate buyer action. Several persuasive techniques available to the salesperson will be discussed later in this textbook.

Pros and cons of the buyer action theory This approach to selling is most common in situations where product features and benefits are easily understood by the prospect, the product is not expensive, and the purchase does not require multiple decision makers. It is frequently used to sell clothing, jewelry, household appliances, and other consumer goods. This approach is usually not effective in those selling situations that involve complex products and multiple decision makers.

BUYER RESOLUTION THEORY

The buyer resolution theory (sometimes referred to as the 5-Ws theory) also recognizes that selling is a mental process. This view of the selling-buying process recognizes that a purchase will be made only after the prospect has made five buying decisions involving specific, affirmative responses to the following questions:

1. Why should I buy? (need)
2. What should I buy? (product)
3. Where should I buy? (source)
4. What is a fair price? (price)
5. When should I buy? (time)

WHY SHOULD I BUY?

Realistically, it is sometimes difficult to provide prospects with an answer to this question. In many cases salespeople fail in their attempt to help customers become aware of a need. Thus large numbers of potential customers are not sufficiently persuaded to purchase products that will provide them with genuine buyer benefits. Many businesses are operating with inefficient and outdated equipment. A majority of Americans classified as "head of household" have too little insurance. Also, millions of Americans fail to get enough exercise.

WHAT SHOULD I BUY?

If a prospect agrees that a need does exist, then you are ready to address the second buying decision. You must convince the prospect that the product being offered will satisfy the need. In most cases the buyer can choose from several competing products.

WHERE SHOULD I BUY?

As products become more complex, consumers are giving more attention to "source" decisions. In a major metropolitan area the person who wants to buy a Xerox Document Work Center 250 or a competing product will be able to choose from several sources. As we noted in Chapter 5, company features such as certified service technicians or a complete parts inventory may permit a company to enjoy a competitive advantage.

WHAT IS A FAIR PRICE?

Today's better-educated and better-informed consumers are searching for the right balance between price and value (benefits). They are better able to detect prices that are not competitive or do not correspond in their minds with the

The buyer resolution theory recognizes that a purchase will be made only after the five "w" questions have been answered in the mind of the prospect.

product's value. Salespeople who represent higher priced products and services such as Patek Philippe watches (prices start at $6,000), Oxford suits (prices start at $1,000), or meeting and banquet space at Loews Resort (upscale facility near Tucson) must be prepared to explain the product features that justify the higher price.

WHEN SHOULD I BUY?

A sale cannot be closed until a customer has decided when to buy. In some selling situations the customer will want to postpone the purchase because of reluctance to part with the money. The desire to postpone the purchase might also exist because the customer cannot see any immediate advantage to purchasing the product now.

PROS AND CONS OF THE BUYER RESOLUTION THEORY

The buyer resolution theory recognizes that a purchase will be made only after the prospect has made all five buying decisions. The omission of any of these decisions results in no sale. One strength of this sales approach is that it focuses the salesperson's attention on five important factors that the customer is likely to consider before making a purchase. This approach helps structure the information-gathering process. Answers to these five questions provide valuable insights about the customer's buying strategy. One important limitation of this theory is that it is usually not possible to anticipate which of the five buying decisions will be most difficult for the prospect to make. Therefore, a "canned" or highly inflexible sales presentation would not be appropriate. Also, there is no established sequence in which prospects make these decisions. A decision concerning price may be made before the source decision is made. These limitations remind us that a sales presentation must be flexible enough to accommodate a variety of selling situations.

NEED-SATISFACTION THEORY

The need-satisfaction theory is the foundation of consultative-style selling, which was described in Chapter 1. This buying process theory is based on the assumption that buying decisions are made to satisfy needs. The role of the professional salesperson is to identify these needs and then recommend a product or service that will satisfy them.

The consultative selling approach, coupled with strategic planning, sets the stage for long-term partnerships that result in repeat business and referrals. Put another way, strategic planning gives us the opportunity to maximize the benefits of consultative selling. As noted earlier, salespeople who develop correct strategies are more likely to make sales presentations to the right person, at the right time, and in a manner most likely to achieve positive results.

The need-satisfaction theory encompasses the concept that salespeople should conduct a systematic assessment of the prospect's situation. This usually involves a series of carefully worded questions to obtain the customer's point of view. These questions lead the customer to talk more freely and help the salesperson pinpoint the customer's needs. Each customer should be thought of as a separate target market, with the salesperson trying to adapt to each one's needs.

BUILDING RELATIONSHIPS IN A DIVERSE WORLD

KEEPING PACE WITH A CHANGING CUSTOMER BASE

No other country on earth is as multiracial and multicultural as the United States of America. This diversity presents marketers with major opportunities and major challenges. Marlene L. Rossman, author of *Multicultural Marketing*, says, "While many companies have fought over slices of the tiny yuppie market, the mature market, the senior market, the woman's market, and the other slow-growth markets, they have ignored the ethnic market, the fastest-growing and most profitable market of them all." Several demographic trends indicate that America will be characterized by even more diversity in the years ahead. In the 1980s, 8.7 million people immigrated to America. The U.S. Census Bureau indicates that even more immigrants will enter America in the 1990s. Minority populations now make up one quarter of our total population. Projections indicate that minorities will comprise the U.S. majority in the year 2067. Marketers must recognize that members of ethnic groups are today less inclined to transform their ethnic identity into an American identity. Hispanics, for example, have fueled the rapid growth of Latin music. In California, builders are taking time to study the traditions, beliefs, and customs of the growing Asian population; and home builders in the Atlanta area are attempting to learn more about the African American home buyers. As we approach the year 2000, it is important to learn how to sell to the new demographics.[b]

The need-satisfaction approach to selling is based on a series of basic beliefs about the professional salesperson's role. These beliefs help us develop our own personal philosophy of selling, which serves as our "conscience" in selling situations. The key basic beliefs that serve as foundation stones for the need-satisfaction theory follow.

1. Communication exists between the buyer and the seller throughout the sales presentation. *Two-way communication will provide for a mutual exchange of ideas and perceptions.*

2. Systematic inquiry is necessary to establish a customer's unique need for the product. A lengthy discussion of the product or service is postponed until the salesperson becomes well acquainted with the prospect. In almost every selling situation, information supplied by the customer is essential. We must keep in mind the trend toward *demassification*, a term coined by Alvin Toffler. The mass market is disappearing because a growing number of customers need custom solutions.[27]

3. Salespersons take a *two-way advocacy* position, representing the interests of their company and of their clients with equal dignity and skill.[28] High-performance salespeople bring to the sales task a genuine sensitivity for the customer's needs.

4. In some selling situations the salesperson will reach the conclusion that the product does not provide the best solution (or the entire solution) to the customer's problem. For instance, people who sell elaborate computer systems sometimes help shape a client's entire strategic business plan. These salespeople will naturally use some of their own "solutions" (their companies' products). However, they may incorporate other people's solutions as well, including their competitors' products.[29]

5. Every effort should be made to develop a *long-term relationship with the customer*. Today, customers want a partner, someone who shares the same goals. Emphasis should be given to developing the type of presentation that builds rapport and garners repeat business.

Most customers feel less stress in the presence of a salesperson who has adopted the need-satisfaction philosophy of selling. The buying process is more relaxed and less threatening. They become genuine participants in the selling-buying process and begin to view the salesperson as a partner.

A growing number of firms such as Nordstrom, Xerox, and Marriott use some variation of consultative selling. This approach works effectively in all types of selling situations. It does not matter whether you are selling financial securities, computer systems, or training programs. It does not matter whether you are focusing on the needs of an individual or working on a strategic plan with the divisional vice president of a corporation. You can still apply consultative selling skills. You are engaging in progressive levels of complexity, not a fundamentally different approach.[30]

Figure 7.4 provides a comparison of the need-satisfaction theory with the buyer action and buyer resolution theories. The benefits of the need-satisfaction theory to the buyer and the seller are obvious.

Discovering Individual Customer Buying Motives

Buyer behavior is forever changing as people assume new roles, adopt new reference groups, and experience an increase or decrease in income. This is the reason salespeople need to develop a "customer" orientation rather than a "market" orientation. What is the difference? In the words of Tom Peters and Nancy Austin, "Markets do not buy products, customers do."[31]

A customer orientation can give a salesperson a tremendous competitive advantage in the marketplace. All it takes is the right mind-set. It means recognizing that customer A may well buy or not buy your product for different reasons from those of customer B. We can improve our customer strategy by keeping in mind one simple truth: People do not think and act the same. When we ask appropriate questions, listen to the responses, and make observations, we can often discover the customer's unique buying motives.

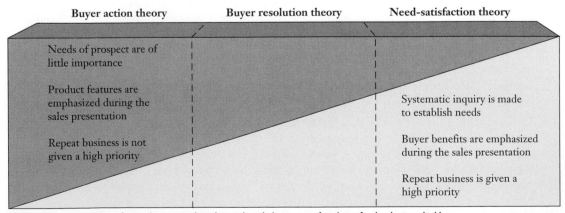

FIGURE 7.4 The need-satisfaction theory provides salespeople with the strongest foundation for developing a highly responsive customer strategy.

QUESTIONS

Salespeople should think of themselves as nondirective counselors. They should use questions to get prospects talking about themselves and their buying needs. As prospects open up, the salesperson is given a golden opportunity to discover their wants, needs, and perceptions. The questioning process is examined in detail in Chapter 10.

LISTENING

It has been said, "We cannot learn when we are talking." This point seems of particular importance as we attempt to get acquainted with prospects. By asking questions and then pausing to let the prospect talk we can obtain a better understanding of the forces that are shaping buyer behavior. If you let people talk and listen carefully, they will actually tell you how to sell them.

OBSERVATION

As noted in Chapter 3, we should be as observant as possible before and during the sales presentation. Before meeting with a prospect, look at the physical surroundings and try to identify clues that will tell you more about the prospect. Read the customer's trade journals. During the presentation, observe the prospect's facial expression and body movements. Emotions are often communicated by nonverbal behavior.

As buyers become better educated and more sophisticated, it will become more critical than ever to gain an understanding of why people buy. Sales personnel must individualize each sales presentation to discover the most dominant buying motives. The most effective ways to discover individual customer buying motives and needs are discussed in Chapter 10.

SUMMARY

The importance of developing a *customer strategy* was introduced in this chapter. This type of planning is necessary to ensure maximum customer responsiveness. The complex nature of customer behavior was also discussed. We noted that buyer behavior is influenced in part by both physical and psychological needs. Maslow's popular model ranks these needs. It shows that the strongest, most basic physiological needs take precedence over the higher level needs. There are also a number of influences that shape our psychological needs to various degrees. Buyer behavior is influenced by the roles we assume: reference groups, social class, and culture.

Perception was defined as the process whereby we receive stimuli through our five senses and then assign meaning to them. Our perception is shaped by social influences as well as the psychological and physiological conditions within us.

We discussed *emotional and rational buying motives*. Emotional buying motives prompt the prospect to act because of an appeal to some sentiment or passion. Rational buying motives tend to appeal to the prospect's reasoning power or better judgment.

We also compared patronage and product *buying motives*. Patronage buying motives grow out of a strong relationship that has developed between the customer and the supplier. When competing products are quite similar, patronage motives can be very important. Product buying motives are usually in evidence when a prospect purchases one product in preference to another.

This chapter also presented several theories that explain the buying process. Three of the most popular theories are the *buyer action theory*, the *buyer resolution theory*, and the *need-satisfaction theory*. The discovery of *buying motives* was also discussed.

➤ KEY TERMS

Customer Strategy
Physiological Needs
Security Needs
Social Needs
Esteem Needs
Self-Actualization
Social Influences
Reference Group
Social Class
Culture
Subculture

Perception
Dominant Buying Motive
Buying Motive
Emotional Buying Motive
Rational Buying Motive
Patronage Buying Motive
Product Buying Motive
Buyer Action Theory
Buyer Resolution Theory
Need-Satisfaction Theory

➤ REVIEW QUESTIONS

1. According to the Strategic/Consultative Selling Model, what are the three prescriptions for the development of a successful customer strategy?
2. Explain how Maslow's hierarchy of needs affects buyer behavior.
3. Describe the four social influences that affect buyer behavior.
4. What is meant by the term *perception?*
5. Distinguish between emotional and rational buying motives.
6. List three commonly accepted theories that explain how people arrive at a buying decision.
7. What are the steps in the buyer action theory? To what other sales promotion methods does this theory apply?
8. List the five basic beliefs that serve as a foundation for the need-satisfaction theory.
9. List and describe three methods salespeople use to discover buying motives.
10. J. D. Power, founder of J. D. Power and Associates, says, "We define quality as what the customer wants." Do you agree or disagree with his observations? Explain your answer.

➤ APPLICATION EXERCISES

1. Select several advertisements from a trade magazine. Analyze each one, and determine what rational buying motives the advertiser is appealing to. Do any of these advertisements appeal to emotional buying motives?
2. Select a magazine that is aimed at a particular consumer group, for example, *Architectural Digest, Redbook,* or *Better Homes and Gardens.* Study the advertisements and determine what buying motives they appeal to.

3. The J. D. Power and Associates company is referenced in the product buying motives section of this chapter. This company is now providing information on customer buying satisfaction and buying habits on the Internet. Locate them at http://www.jdpower.com. Click on "research and consulting" and examine their customer satisfaction reports.

➤ **S A L E S   A U T O M A T I O N
A P P L I C A T I O N   E X E R C I S E**

ACT! MANAGING MULTIPLE CONTACTS

Access the ACT! software following the instructions in Appendix 2. Schedule *telephone calls* to the first three contacts in the database. Follow your calls with a *letter* to each contact, prepare a *report* that shows who you are to call, and then erase the calls that you scheduled.

Scheduling Group Telephone Calls.   Starting with the first profile, Able Profit Machines, Inc., displayed on the screen, enter the following (menu choices) letters: S C D Tab Tab 1 A N PgDn S C D 1 1 Tab Tab 1 A N PgDn S C D 1 1 1 Tab Tab 1 AN. Now press L W and you will see the three calls listed on this display of your "Week at a Glance." Use the arrow keys to position the cursor over the day that shows the scheduled calls, and press Enter to see more details. Another press of the Enter key will take you to the first of the profiles for which you have scheduled calls.

Groups and Form Letters.   Notice that at the lower right, this profile is displayed as 1 of 3. This means that you have selected a group that consists of those you will call tomorrow. Now prepare a letter to this group by typing: W L E I'll call tomorrow, F10 P F Enter Enter D Y. You will notice that the same form letter was prepared for all three contacts in this group.

Groups and Reports.   Prepare a report that lists the scheduled calls to this group. At a contact screen (Main Menu), press R T S and your scheduled calls, meetings, and To Dos will be displayed. Press Enter as many times as needed to return to the contact screen. Confirm that your printer is connected and, to produce a "hard copy" report, press R T Enter Enter.

Changing Your Schedule.   To remove the scheduled calls, press the Home key to return to the first of the three profiles, Able Profit Machines, Inc. Press C C E Y and the Able call will be erased and the next contact will be displayed. Typing C C E Y again will remove the call from this contact and display the last of the three. Press C C E Y and all scheduled calls will have been removed.

➤ **C A S E   P R O B L E M**

Kim Fernandez, director of natural food sales for Alta Dena Certified Dairy, takes a great deal of pride in her efforts to win new customers for her line of natural dairy foods. As a sales representative for this national company (introduced at the beginning of this chapter) she is in a key position to meet the needs of a growing number of health conscious consumers.

Like most professional salespeople, Kim Fernandez is continuously developing new accounts, servicing existing accounts, and introducing new products. When she calls on a large regional grocery wholesaler, such as Fleming Companies, closing the sale can be challenging. Wholesalers do not want to inventory products that do not appeal to the retail supermarkets they serve. Wholesalers want to buy products from companies that maintain the highest quality production standards and provide outstanding service after the sale. Wholesalers also want to buy products at the lowest possible prices. The retail supermarkets (chain operated and independent) that Kim Fernandez calls on are no less demanding. They operate in a competitive environment and must offer products at the lowest possible price.

The motto, "Give the consumers what they want," could easily be adopted by the typical American supermarket. A typical store features from 10,000 to 12,000 items. Some large supermarkets feature over 20,000 different items. Thousands of new products are introduced each year, so buyers must make many difficult purchase decisions. Supermarket dairy departments have been revitalized in recent years by the growth of new items. Each year from 800 to 900 new dairy products are introduced. When Alta Dena Certified Dairy introduces a new product, the sales force must work hard to win acceptance.

Kim's product line includes yogurt, butter, cottage cheese, milk, ice cream, cheese, and many other dairy products. The company makes every effort to offer only products that are of the highest quality and made with all natural ingredients. The Alta Dena research and development laboratory is constantly searching for ways to improve existing products and develop new ones. Customers are often involved in the product development process. They are given samples and encouraged to give their impressions. The Alta Dena product development staff, along with the sales staff, work hard to determine the customers' wants and needs. Kim often takes samples of new products to supermarkets and involves the dairy department staff in a taste test. When Kim meets with a prospect, she asks several questions to determine the person's needs and buying motives. She realizes that in some cases several motives may influence the purchase decision. She also knows that buying behavior is influenced by perception, so she must probe to find out what prospects are really thinking. The prospect who believes that natural dairy products have a short shelf life may be reluctant to carry her line of products. If this perception is uncovered, then Kim knows how to respond to it.

Kim views education as a major sales tool. She often explains the quality controls used at Alta Dena plants and even invites customers to participate in plant tours. She talks about the "contented cows" that make up the Alta Dena dairy herd. She knows that education can add value to her products. Kim also knows that a long-term partnership with the customer is based on attention to details. She checks on deliveries and makes sure all complaints are handled quickly and courteously.

QUESTIONS

1. Does it appear that Kim Fernandez has built her customer strategy on the three prescriptions featured in the Strategic/Consultative Selling Model? Explain.

2. What aspects of the need-satisfaction theory has Kim Fernandez incorporated into her approach to customers? Explain.

3. As a buyer for a large supermarket chain, would you be most influenced by rational or emotional buying motives? Explain.

4. What steps has Kim Fernandez taken to build a long-term partnership with her customers?

Developing a Prospect Base

Graig Phillips, a sales representative for International Dehydrated Foods, has found a "no hassle" method of maintaining contact with over 500 people with whom he works. He is using ACT! contact software developed by Symantec Corporation. He can now maintain a detailed profile of every customer and customer support personnel. With a single key stroke on his laptop computer he can bring up detailed information on each contact. Customer service has been improved because the ACT! software reminds him when it is time to make a follow-up call. The ACT! software also makes it easy to network with other members of the sales force and his sales manager.[1]

Prospecting—An Introduction

Gerhard Gschwandtner, editor of *Selling Power*, says, "The main purpose of a salesperson is not to make sales, but to create customers."[2] Identifying potential customers is an important aspect of the customer strategy. In the terminology of personal selling this process is called **prospecting.** A potential customer, or **prospect,** is someone who has three basic qualifications. First, the person must have a need for the product or service. Many companies attempt to identify a target market that includes those prospects who qualify on the basis of need. Second, the individual must be able to afford the purchase. An important fundamental of consultative-style selling is that people should not be persuaded to buy products they cannot afford. Third, the person must be authorized to purchase the product. Finding prospects who can make the purchase is not as easy as it sounds. In many situations the salesperson must make the sales presentation to multiple decision makers. One of these decision makers might be the technical expert who wants an answer to the question: "Does the product meet the company's specifications?" Another decision maker may be the person who will actually use the product. The employee who will use the forklift truck you are selling may be involved in the purchase decision. Of course, there is often a "purse-string" decision maker who has the ultimate authority to release funds for the purchase.[3]

The goal of prospecting is to build a **prospect base** made up of current customers and potential customers. Many successful companies find that current customers account for a large percentage of their sales. Every effort is made to keep these clients satisfied because they provide the repeat business that is necessary to maintain profitability.

THE IMPORTANCE OF PROSPECTING

Every salesperson must cope with customer attrition, that is, the inevitable loss of customers over a period of time, which can be attributed to a variety of causes. Unless new prospects are found to replace lost customers, a salesperson will eventually face a reduction in income and possible loss of employment.

To better understand the significance of prospecting, let us examine a few common causes of customer attrition.

1. The customer may move to a new location outside the salesperson's territory. The American population is very mobile. This cause of attrition is especially common in the retail and service areas.

2. A firm may go out of business or merge with another company. In some areas of business the failure rate is quite high. In recent years, we have witnessed a record number of mergers which have caused massive changes in purchasing plans.

3. A loyal buyer or purchasing agent may leave the position because of promotion, retirement, resignation, or serious illness. The replacement may prefer to buy from someone else. Warren Rodgers, president of Computer Specialists Incorporated, a computer service business in Monroeville, Pennsylvania, learned this lesson the hard way. When a key contact person with a major customer died suddenly, it took almost a year to build a new

relationship with the client company. Rodgers said, "We realized that we should have been paying a lot more attention to other people in the company—people we might have to do business with in the future."[4]

Some studies reveal that the average company loses 15 to 20 percent of its customers every year. Depending on the type of selling, this figure might be higher or lower. It becomes clear that many customers are lost for reasons beyond the salesperson's control. If salespeople want to keep their earnings at a stable level, they will need to develop new customers.

Joe Girard, popular sales trainer, uses the "Ferris wheel" concept to illustrate the relationship between prospecting and the loss of customers due to the attrition factors described earlier. As people get off the Ferris wheel, the operator fills their seats one at a time, moves the wheel a little, and continues this process until all the original riders have left the wheel and new ones come aboard (Fig. 8.1). In reality, of course, established customers do not come and go this fast. With the passing of time, however, many customers will be replaced.

Prospecting Requires Planning

Prospecting should be viewed as a systematic process of locating potential customers. Some prospecting efforts can be easily integrated into a regular sales call. Progressive marketers are doing three things to improve the quality of the prospecting effort:

1. Increase the number of people who board the Ferris wheel. You want to see a continuous number of potential prospects board the Ferris wheel because they are the source of sales opportunities. If the number of potential prospects declines sharply, the number of sales closed will also decline.

2. Improve the quality of the prospects who board the Ferris wheel. Companies that have adopted the quality improvement process concept view this phase of prospecting as critical. They have established quality standards that ensure a steady supply of prospects with high profit potential.[5]

3. Shorten the sales cycle by quickly determining which of the new prospects are *qualified* prospects—qualified as to need, ability to pay, and authority to purchase the product. During the qualifying process, you should also weed out prospects that have little or no potential. Gerhard Gschwandtner says, "Time is the ultimate scorekeeper in the game of selling." He points out that many salespeople do not meet their sales goals because they do not quickly qualify new prospects.[6] Later in this chapter we examine qualifying practices and discuss how to shorten the sales cycle with sales automation methods.

In most selling situations, prospecting begins with a study of the market for your product or service. When Pitney Bowes first developed the desktop postage meter, the company conducted a careful study of the market. At first glance, equipment of this nature seemed well suited only to a large business firm. With additional market analysis the company identified many additional customers who could benefit from purchasing the product. Many small business firms use this product today.

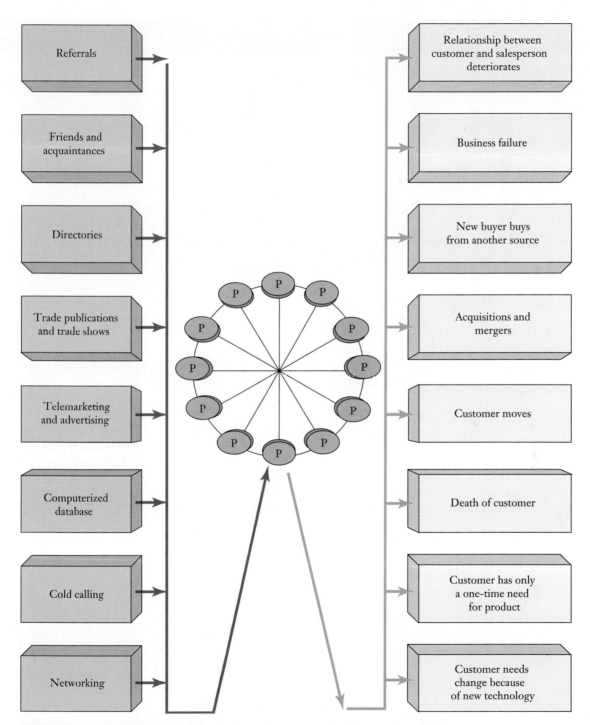

FIGURE 8.1 The "Ferris wheel" concept, which is aimed at supplying an ongoing list of prospects, is part of world sales record holder Joe Girard's customer strategy.

BUILDING RELATIONSHIPS THROUGH TECHNOLOGY

USING THE SAME SOFTWARE AS AT&T

A sales force automation (SFA) program implemented by AT&T resulted in major increases in productivity and improved customer service. The first stage of the automation project involved 11,000 desktop computers and the popular ACT! software program now marketed by Symantec Corporation. This combination of hardware and software resulted in an immediate 15 to 20 percent improvement in productivity. AT&T salespeople gained easier and quicker access to account information such as the prospect's name, title, company, secretary's name, and notes concerning the account. This information can be reviewed prior to calling or visiting the customer, thus ensuring a more personalized contact. Through SFA, salespeople gain a competitive edge in relating to their customer's needs and interests.

You will enjoy the opportunity to use a demonstration version of the same software now in use by AT&T. The Sales Automation Case Study at the end of this chapter (and Chapters 9 to 14 on presentation strategy) guides you through the development of a prospect base using the ACT! demonstration contact management software. ACT! is the industry leader in contact management programs. Just as an AT&T salesperson, you are assigned a number (twenty) of accounts and given individual and company information about each account's contact person in the demo software database. Your participation in the sales automation case studies will give you exciting hands-on strategic selling experience using modern sales technology. Not only will you be using the same software being used by thousands of salespeople but also you will be working with data that are derived from actual selling challenges. (See Sales Automation Case Study on p. 187 for more information.)[a]

PRODUCT AND CUSTOMER ANALYSIS

As noted in Chapter 5, product analysis is an important aspect of developing your product strategy. This analysis gives direction to the search for new customers. In addition to product analysis, salespeople should carefully study the customers who are currently buying the product. Lynden Air Freight, a freight-forwarding company based in Seattle, Washington, uses its current customer base to develop a prospect profile. A careful analysis of top national accounts is used to build a profile of the ideal prospect. The analysis includes an examination of such factors as margin per account, margin per shipment, average shipment size, and several other factors.[7]

Sources of Prospects

Every salesperson must develop a prospecting system suited to a particular selling situation. There are several sources of prospects, and each should be carefully examined.

Referrals

Friends and family members

Directories

Trade publications

Trade shows

Telemarketing

Direct response advertising

The DMI marketing information system

1. Description of the horizontal display
2. Range of the horizontal display
3. Horizontal row totals
4. Vertical column totals
5. State totals
6. SIC Code numbers
7. Description of SIC Code industries

```
JOD 2138                            XYZ CORPORATION - SAMPLE REPORT              PAGE 7
COUNT BY PRIMARY                    D M I M A R K E T P R O F I L E              DATE
910  6  DESCRIPTION              →  RANGE BY EMPLOYEES HERE
                                                                        NOT
STATE    61      NM              0-9 10-19 20-49 50-99 100-499 500-999 1000+ SHOWN   TOTAL
•  2271   WOVEN CARPETS, RUGS      1                                                    1
•  5097   FURNITURE, HOME FURNG    9    2                                        1     12
   5311   DEPARTMENT STORES        5   13    8    3      7                       3     39
   5712   FURNITURE STORES       129   10    5           1                       9    153
•  5713   FLOOR COVERG STORES     27    5    1                                   3     36
•  61     NM                     171   30   14    3      8                      15    241
   STATE
••  2271
   2272  63      NY
•  2279   WOVEN CARPETS, RUGS     14    4    6    1      3               1        8     37
•  5097   TUFTED CARPETS, RUGS     5    4    1                                   4     14
•  5311   CARPETS, RUGS NEC        5    2                                               7
•  5712
•  5713   FURNITURE, HOME FURNG  768  167  105           4                     233  1,304
•  63     DEPARTMENT STORES      199   33   53          72      16     13      245    696
   STATE  FURNITURE STORES     1,964  224   73           4                     402  1,689
•         FLOOR COVERG STORES    876   59   20           1                     132  1,088
••        NY                   3,831  493  258  114     84      17     14    1,024  5,835
   65     NC
          WOVEN CARPETS, RUGS      6    2    1    1      3                        1     14
          TUFTED CARPETS, RUGS     5         1                                   1
                                                        2                      24
```

Computerized product analysis reports such as this one from Dun & Bradstreet help salespeople to locate prospects as part of a customer strategy.

Web site

Computerized database

Cold calling

Networking

Educational seminars

Prospecting by nonsales employees

REFERRALS

The use of referrals as a prospecting approach has been used successfully in a wide range of selling situations. A **referral** is a prospect who has been recommended by a current customer or by someone who is familiar with the product. Satisfied customers, business acquaintances, and even prospects who do not buy, can often recommend the names of persons who might benefit from owning the product. Research in the field of personal selling indicates that it takes much less time to sell a qualified, referred lead than it does to sell a nonqualified, nonreferred lead.[8] Endless chain referrals, and referral letters and cards represent two variations of this prospecting tactic.

BUILDING QUALITY PARTNERSHIPS

MAINTAINING PARTNERSHIPS

Maintaining partnerships requires a great deal of extra effort these days. The competition is continuously searching for ways to sell to your customers. One effective way to keep customers is to develop a good customer profile. Analyze your customer base to clarify the types of companies that do business with your firm. Determine the reasons why they buy from you. Look at your company through your customer's eyes. Your customer's perception of your company's product quality and service after the sale is important. The customer's perceptions are reality.[b]

ENDLESS CHAIN REFERRALS

The endless chain approach to obtaining referrals is easy to use because it fits naturally into most sales presentations. A salesperson selling long-term health insurance might say, "Miss Remano, whom do you know who might be interested in our insurance plan?" This open-ended question gives the person the freedom to recommend several prospects and is less likely to be answered with a no response. Be sure to use your reference's name when you contact the new prospect—"Mary Remano suggested that I call you. . . ."

REFERRAL LETTERS AND CARDS

The referral letter method is a variation of the endless chain technique. In addition to requesting the names of prospects the salesperson asks the customer to prepare a note or letter of introduction that can be delivered to the potential customer. The correspondence is an actual testimonial prepared by a satisfied customer. Some companies use a referral card to introduce the salesperson. The preprinted card features a place for your customer to sign the new prospect's name and his own name.

Using an existing customer as an intermediary has several advantages. The amount of time spent on prospecting can be reduced, and the referral will make it easier to get an appointment. In addition, the views of a satisfied customer will often have a great deal of impact on the prospect. Needless to say, salespeople who are viewed as product experts, who are recognized as problem solvers and partners, are more likely to be the beneficiaries of referrals.

FRIENDS AND FAMILY MEMBERS

A person who is new in the field of selling often uses friends and family members as sources of information about potential customers. It is only natural to contact people we know. In many cases these people have contacts with a wide range of potential buyers.

DIRECTORIES

Directories can help salespeople search out new prospects and determine their buying potential. A list of some of the more popular national directories is provided here.

Middle Market Directory lists 14,000 firms worth between $500,000 and $1 million (available from Dun & Bradstreet).

Directory of Corporate Affiliations profiles about 4,000 leading U.S. companies along with their subsidiaries, divisions, and affiliates (available from Macmillan Directory Division).

Standard & Poor's Corporation Records Service provides details on more than 11,000 companies (available from Standard and Poor's).

Thomas Register of American Manufacturers provides a listing of 60,000 manufacturers by product classifications, addresses, and capital ratings (available from Thomas Publishing Company).

Polk City Directory provides detailed information on the citizens of a specific community. Polk, in business for over 125 years, publishes about 1,100 directories covering 6,500 communities in the United States and Canada. It can usually be obtained from the city government or chamber of commerce.

These are just a few of the better known directories. There are hundreds of additional directories covering business and industrial firms on the regional, state, and local levels. Some directories are free, while others must be purchased at a nominal fee. One of the most useful free sources of information is the telephone directory. Most telephone directories have a classified (yellow pages) section that groups businesses and professions by category.

If you are involved in the sale of products in the international market, a valuable resource is the world traders data reports published by U.S. and Foreign Commercial Service (US & FCS), which has district offices located in several cities throughout the nation. If you want to know more about a prospective customer or agent in a foreign country, US & FCS will provide a complete profile, including background information within the local business community, payment history, creditworthiness, and overall reliability and suitability as a trade contact.[9]

TRADE PUBLICATIONS

Trade publications provide a status report on every major industry. If you are a sales representative employed by Super Valu Stores, Fleming Companies Incorporated, Sysco Corporation, or one of the other huge food wholesaling houses that supplies supermarkets, then you will benefit from a monthly review of *Progressive Grocer* magazine. Each month this trade publication reports on trends in the retail food industry, new products, problems, innovations, and related information. Trade journals such as *Women's Wear Daily*, *Home Furnishings*, *Hardware Retailer*, *Modern Tire Dealer*, and *Progressive Architecture* are examples of publications that might help salespeople identify prospects.

TRADE SHOWS

A trade show is a large exhibit of products that are, in most cases, common to one industry, such as electronics or office equipment. The prospects walk into the booth or exhibit and talk with those who represent the exhibitor. In some cases, sales personnel invite existing customers and prospects to attend trade shows so they will have an opportunity to demonstrate their newest products.

Research studies conducted by the Trade Show Bureau (TSB) indicate that it is much easier to identify good prospects and actually close sales at a trade

The *Thomas Register of American Manufacturers* is one source of prospects for salespeople.

Thomas Register of American Manufacturers
Order Now And Get All Of This...

The most complete listings of North American manufacturers available with 1.5 million listings...
- 149,000 companies
- 50,000 product and service headings
- 1,700 company catalogs
- 105,000 brand and trade names
- 98,000 supplier ads for vendor comparisons

Over 50,000 pages of facts and figures organized to help you find the information you need in seconds. Who makes it? ...Who's closest? ...Who do I contact to order? ...Who do I contact to sell? ...What's their phone number and address?
You'll find the answers you need in Thomas Register — fast.

To Order Call 212–290–7277 or Fax 212–290–7365

show. TSB found that fewer sales calls are needed to close a sale if the prospect was qualified at a trade show.[10] Some marketers use special qualifying methods at trade shows. Brian Jeffrey, president of Jeffrey & Jeffrey Associates in Ontario, Canada, prepares a list of seven questions that will quickly qualify or disqualify prospects at a trade show.[11]

TELEMARKETING

Telemarketing is the practice of marketing goods and services through telephone contact. It has become an integral part of many modern sales and marketing campaigns. One use of telemarketing is to identify prospects. A financial services company used telemarketing to identify prospects for its customized equipment leasing packages. Leads were given to salespeople for consideration. Telemarketing can also be used to quickly and inexpensively qualify prospects for follow-up. Some marketers use the telephone to verify sales leads generated by direct mail, advertisements, or some other method.

DIRECT RESPONSE ADVERTISING

Many advertisements invite the reader to send for a free booklet or brochure that provides detailed information about the product or service. In the category of business-to-business marketing, advertising has the greatest inquiry-generating power.[12] Some firms distribute postage-free response cards (also known as bingo cards) to potential buyers. Recipients are encouraged to complete and mail the cards if they desire additional information. In some cases the name of the person making the inquiry is given to a local sales representative for further action.

The response card of the future will be more likely to have a toll-free telephone number instead of a return mail address. Callers with Touch-Tone phones will go through a series of voice prompts similar to a voice mail system. The caller will simply request that the document be mailed or faxed. Callers who have fax machines will be able to obtain the requested document in seconds.[13]

WEB SITE

Over 20,000 companies and business people have established web sites on the World Wide Web. A **Web site** is a collection of Web pages maintained by a single person or organization. It is accessible to anyone with a computer and a modem. Harris Simkovitz, an independent financial-products broker in Cherry Hill, New Jersey, decided to use a Web site to reach prospects. He designed a single Web page that features his picture, his biographical information, and his financial-planning philosophy. If this modest effort proves to be successful, he can later change the Web page content or add additional Web pages.[14] Many large firms, such as Century 21, maintain Web sites that feature twenty to thirty Web pages.

An up-to-date customer database can enhance prospecting.

COMPUTERIZED DATABASE

With the aid of electronic data processing it is often possible to match product features with the needs of potential customers quickly and accurately. In many situations a firm will develop its own computerized database. In other cases it is more economical to purchase the database from a company that specializes in collection of such information. There are lists (databases) for almost every conceivable prospect category. For example, lists are available for boat enthusiasts, computer industry professionals, and subscribers to many of the nations' magazines.

With the aid of a personal computer (PC), salespeople can develop their own detailed customer files. The newer PCs provide expanded storage capacity at a lower price than in the past. This means that salespeople can accumulate a great deal of information about individual customers and use this information to personalize the selling process.[15] For example, a PC can help an independent insurance agent maintain a comprehensive record of each policyholder. As the status of each client changes (marriage, the birth of children, etc.), the record can easily be updated. With the aid of an up-to-date database the agent can quickly identify prospects for the various existing and new policy options.

COLD CALLING

With some products, cold call prospecting is an effective approach to prospect identification. In **cold calling** the salesperson selects a group of people who may or may not be actual prospects and then calls (phone or personal visit) on each one. For example, the sales representative for a wholesale medical supply firm might call on every hospital in a given community, assuming that each one is a potential customer. Many new salespeople must rely on the cold call method because they are less likely to get appointments through referrals.[16] It takes time to develop a group of established customers who are willing to give referrals.

Cold calls are often used by new companies that are attempting to win acceptance of new products or services. Adolf Miera, owner of Chemical Milling International, used the cold call approach to introduce a process for reducing the thickness of aluminum sheets that are used in construction of commercial and military aircraft. To introduce his service, Miera used classic door-to-door selling. His first sales calls were not successful, but he finally obtained the first order that helped establish his company in the aircraft industry.[17]

NETWORKING

In simple terms, *networking* is the art of making and using contacts. **Networking** is people meeting people and profiting from the connections.[18] A growing number of consultants in the field of personal selling are recommending networking as an important source of prospects. Although networking has become one of the premier prospecting methods of the past decade, many salespeople are reluctant to seek referrals in this manner. In addition, many salespeople do not use effective networking practices. Skilled networkers suggest the following guidelines for identifying good referrals:

1. *Meet as many people as you can.* Networking can take place on an airplane, at a Rotary Club meeting, at a trade show, or at a reception.

CD Rom Technology can enhance development of a prospect database.

2. *When you meet someone, tell the person what you do.* Give your name and describe your position in a way that explains what you do and invites conversations. Instead of saying, "I am in stocks and bonds," say, "I am a financial counselor who helps people make investment decisions."

3. *Do not do business while networking.* It is usually not practical to conduct business while networking. Make a date to call or meet with the new contact later.

4. *Offer your business card.* The business card is especially useful when the contact attempts to tell others about your products or services.

5. *Edit your contacts and follow up.* You cannot be involved with all your contacts, so separate the productive from the nonproductive. Send a short letter to contacts you deem productive and include business cards, brochures—anything that increases visibility.[19]

dress, and account number they record the person's sizes, style preferences, hobbies and interests, birthday, previous items purchased, and any other appropriate information. With this information available, each customer becomes a "prospect" for future purchases. Sales personnel often call their customers when new products arrive.

Harvey Mackay, chief executive officer of Mackay Envelope Corporation, instructs his salespeople to develop a sixty-six–question customer profile. The form is divided into categories such as education, family, business background, special interests, and lifestyle. In the process of collecting and analyzing this information, the salesperson gets to know the customer better than competing salespeople do. Harvey Mackay describes the benefits of developing a customer profile:

> *If selling were just a matter of determining who's got the low bid, then the world wouldn't need salespeople. It could all be done on computers. The "Mackay 66" is designed to convert you from an adversary to a colleague of the people you're dealing with and to help you make sales.*[25]

He says that the sixty-six–item customer profile helps the salesperson systematize information in a way that will make it more useful and accessible.

This ad reminds us that it is important to be able to recall personal information about the customer.

> # Knowing a customer loves fishing landed me my biggest order.
>
> "I read a hilarious article about a guy who caught a giant catfish, and thought it would be great to send to a customer. I turned on Sharkware, typed in "fishing," and up popped the name of a customer who I haven't spoken to in months, who is a big fisherman. I clicked on his name and Sharkware dialed his number. We talked fishing, weather, then he said, "While you're on the phone..." It was my biggest order of the year. That's why I use Sharkware to manage my contacts, to-do list, calendar, phone calls -- both business and personal. But I shouldn't give away any more secrets."

Automating Prospect Information

In recent years we have seen growing use of information technology to improve the productivity of the sales force and the sales support personnel. The typical computer system also improves service to customers.

Hewlett-Packard was the first major corporation to automate its sales force.[26] Like many other companies, Hewlett-Packard discovered that being the least-cost producer (positioning your product with a price strategy) is not the best way to be competitive. With computerization, a company is in a stronger position to keep up to date on the customer's business and offer value-added service.

When it comes to organizing prospect information, the salesperson has two choices. Some salespeople record prospect information on blank file cards (4×6 is the most popular) or on preprinted file cards that have space for specific kinds of information, or they record information in loose-leaf notebooks. These systems are adequate for salespeople who deal with a small number of prospects and do not get involved in complex sales. The use of some type of computerized system is more appropriate for salespeople who deal with large numbers of prospects, frequently get involved in complex sales, and must continually network with management and members of the sales support team. Regardless of the system used, most salespeople need to collect and organize two

Prospect information, such as knowledge of family members, can help turn a prospect into a customer.

A friend's daughter's birthday gave me a reason to celebrate.

"I almost forgot there is more to a career than sitting behind a desk. Lucky for me, Sharkware never forgets. I turned the computer on one morning and a reminder appeared -- send a birthday card to the daughter of a friend. (He gave me a cigar the day she was born.) When my friend called to say thanks, he gave me a lead that turned into a new job. And since my company was talking about cutbacks, the way I look at it, Sharkware saved my life. That's why I use it to manage my life-- contacts, to-do list, calendar, phone calls; Sharkware takes care of it all. Bet I even remember my anniversary this year."

SHARKWARE™
Harvey Mackay's System for Success

© 1993 CogniTech Corporation. Sharkware is a registered trademark of CogniTech Corp..

Most salespeople who are now using contact management software wonder how they ever got along without it.

kinds of prospect information: information about the prospect as an individual and information about the prospect as a business representative.

THE PROSPECT AS AN INDIVIDUAL

The foundation for a sales philosophy that emphasizes the building of partnerships is the belief that we should always treat the other person as an individual. Each prospect is a one-of-a-kind person with a number of unique characteristics. The only possible way we can treat the prospect as an individual is to learn as much as possible about the person. The starting point is to learn the correct spelling and pronunciation of the prospect's name. Then acquire information about the person's educational background, work experience, special interests, hobbies, and family status. Interview industry people or employees at the company to acquire personal information.[27]

In Chapter 16 you will be introduced to the concept of communication-style bias and the benefits derived from an understanding of communication styles. You will also learn how to overcome communication-style bias and build strong selling relationships with style flexing. If at all possible, acquire information concerning the prospect's communication style before the sales call. Business associates or close friends of the prospect can supply this helpful information. (Communication styles are identified for each prospect in the sales automation case study.)

A lasting business partnership is based in large part on a strong personal relationship. The personal relationship grows when the salesperson takes time to acquire specific information about the other person. Dale Carnegie, a pioneer in the field of human relations training and author of *How to Win Friends and Influence People*, recognized the importance of taking a personal interest in others. He said, "You can make more friends in two months by becoming interested in other people than you can in two years by trying to get other people interested in you."

THE PROSPECT AS A BUSINESS REPRESENTATIVE

In addition to personal information about the prospect it is important to collect certain business-related facts. This is especially important when the prospect is associated with a business. At the outset determine if the prospect is authorized to purchase your product or service. Salespeople must also be concerned about the prospect's ability to buy. A potential buyer's credit rating is easy to check in most cases.

Before calling on the prospect it pays to review various aspects of the company operation. What does the company manufacture or sell? How long has the firm been in business? Is the firm a leader in the field? Does the firm have expansion plans? Each company has its own unique culture.

Most established firms have been doing business with one or more other suppliers. When possible, find out who the company buys from and why. It always helps to know in advance who the competition is. Salespeople who take time to study personal and business facts will be in a stronger position to meet the prospect's needs. They will also close more sales.

DEVELOPING A PROSPECTING AND SALES FORECASTING PLAN

A major barrier to prospecting is time. There never seems to be enough time for a salesperson to do everything that needs to be done. In many situations, less than half of the work week is devoted to actual sales calls. The remainder of the time is spent identifying and screening prospects, travel, paperwork, planning, sales meetings, and servicing accounts. Time devoted to prospecting often means that less time is available for actual selling. Given a choice, salespeople would rather spend their time with established customers. Attrition, of course, will gradually reduce the number of persons in this category, and prospecting will be necessary for survival.

Prospecting activities can be approached in a more orderly fashion with the aid of a plan. It is difficult to prescribe one plan that will fit all selling situations; however, most situations require the following similar types of decisions:

1. *Prepare a list of prospects.* You will recall that the prospect base includes current customers and potential customers. The process of enlarging the prospect base to include potential customers will vary from one industry to another. In the food service distribution industry, salespeople often start with a territorial audit.[28] This involves the collection and analysis of information about every food service operator (restaurants, hotels, colleges, etc.) in a given territory. Important information such as the name of the operation, name of owner or manager, type of menu, and so forth is recorded on a card or entered into a personal computer. Some salespeople in this industry pinpoint each operator on a map of the territory. When the audit is

complete, the salesperson analyzes the information on each food service operator and selects those who should be contacted.

A salesperson who sells hotel and convention services could use a variation of the territorial audit. The list of prospects might include local businesses, educational institutions, civic groups, and other organizations who need banquet or conference services.

2. *Forecast the potential sales volume that might be generated by each new account for each product.* A **sales forecast** outlines expected sales for a specific product or service to a specific target group over a specific period of time.[29] With a sales forecast the salesperson is able to set goals, establish a sales budget, and allocate resources with greater accuracy.

Total sales volume will decline if new accounts generate less volume than those that were lost. Some salespeople represent several product lines and must therefore try to estimate the sales potential of each. It is generally best to devote the largest amount of selling time to products that give you the greatest sales volume.

3. *Anticipate prospect calls when planning the sales route; a systematic routing plan saves time and reduces travel expenses.* The procedure used to determine which customers and prospects will be visited during a certain period of time is called **routing.** Consider calls on prospective customers in developing your route plan. This approach helps minimize the cost of developing new accounts.

A plan helps give prospect identification greater purpose and direction. It also helps reduce the cost of developing new customers. Without a plan, salespeople tend to give prospecting too little attention.

In most cases, an appointment will save time and money.

SECURE THE INTERVIEW

The use of scheduled appointments will vary from one industry to another. Some buyers will set aside time for sales calls and do not expect the sales representative to schedule an appointment. In other cases, the prospect may not meet with a salesperson who drops in unannounced. An appointment provides benefits to both the prospect and the salesperson. The prospect knows about the sales call in advance and can therefore make the necessary advance preparation. The buyer will be in a better position to give attention to the sales presentation.

When you make an appointment by telephone, use the following practices:

1. Plan in advance what you will say. It helps to prepare a written script to use as a guide during the first few seconds of the conversation.

2. Politely identify yourself and the company you represent. Set yourself apart from other callers by using a friendly tone and impeccable phone manners. This approach will help you avoid being shut out by a wary gatekeeper (secretary or receptionist).

3. State the purpose of your call and explain how the prospect can benefit from a meeting. In some cases it is helpful to use a powerful benefits statement that will get the prospect's attention and whet the person's appetite for more information. Present only enough information to stimulate interest.

4. Show respect for the prospect's time by telling the person how much time the appointment will take. Emphasize that you know her time is valuable.

5. Confirm the appointment with a brief note or letter with the date, time, and place of your appointment. Enclose your business card and any printed information that may be of interest to the prospect.[30]

You should anticipate resistance from some prospects. After all, most decision makers are very busy. Be persistent and persuasive if you genuinely believe a meeting with the prospect will be mutually beneficial.

SUMMARY

Prospect identification has been called the lifeblood of selling. A continuous supply of new customers must be found to replace those lost for various reasons. *Prospecting* is the systematic process of locating potential customers.

Analysis of both your product and your existing customers can help to identify, locate, and even profile your prospects. Important sources of new customers include referrals (both endless chain referrals, and referral letters and cards), friends and acquaintances, directories, trade publications, trade shows, telemarketing, direct response advertising, Web site, computer databases, cold calling, educational seminars, networking, and prospecting by nonsale employees.

These prospecting techniques produce a list of names that must be evaluated using criteria developed by each salesperson. The process of prospect evaluation is called *qualifying*. Basic questions that can be used to qualify a prospect include, is the person already buying from you, is the person a former customer, is the person a user of your product, and is the person currently buying from a competitor? An estimate of the amount of sales that could be generated from this prospect, and the prospect's credit rating should also be determined.

Information about both customers and prospects should be recorded systematically, whether on a special form, in a notebook, on cards, or in a computerized database. Information that is important to include about customers as individuals includes the correct name, age and experience, education, family status, special interests and hobbies, and communication style. Information that is important to include about customers as representatives of their business include the authority to buy, the business' ability to pay, the company operations, and the company buying practices.

Development of a prospecting and sales forecasting plan requires preparing a list of prospects, creating a forecast of potential sales volume from each new account, and anticipating prospect calls when planning a sales route. Then securing the interview can enable you to convert a prospect to a customer.

➤ KEY TERMS

Prospecting	*Cold Calling*
Prospect	*Networking*
Prospect Base	*Target Market*
Referral	*Qualifying*
Telemarketing	*Sales Forecast*
Web Site	*Routing*

➤ REVIEW QUESTIONS

1. What three qualifications must an individual have to become a prospect?
2. Why is an understanding of customer attrition important to salespeople? What percentage of a firm's customers are lost each year?
3. What is a *target market?* How does it apply to prospecting?
4. List the major sources of prospects.
5. Explain how the endless chain referral prospecting method works.
6. Describe five practices that can be used to make appointments by telephone.
7. What are the major arguments for scheduling an appointment with a prospect?
8. What is *networking?* How might a real estate salesperson use networking to identify prospects?
9. After the prospect list has been compiled, what is the next step?
10. What is *routing?* How does this relate to the prospecting plan?

➤ APPLICATION EXERCISES

1. You are a sales representative for the Xerox Corporation. Assuming Xerox has just designed a new, less expensive, and better quality copying machine, make a list of fifteen prospects you would plan to call. From the material in

this chapter, identify the sources you would use in developing your prospect list.

2. You are in the process of interviewing for a sales position with the Connecticut General Insurance Company. In addition to filling out an application form and taking an aptitude test, one of the items the agency manager requests of you is to develop a list of prospects with whom you are acquainted. He informs you that this list will be the prospects you will be working with during the first few weeks of employment. The agency manager recommends that you list at least fifty names. Prepare a list of ten acquaintances you have that would qualify as prospects.

3. Sales automation software is most commonly used in the prospecting phase of selling. New product releases are continually being developed that provide additional features and benefits to salespeople. The software used in this book is marketed by Symantec, a leader in the field. Access the Symantec web page and research the latest version of ACT! Click on and examine the latest demonstration copy of this number-one-selling sales automation software.

WWW

4. Locating companies to work for is a form of prospecting. Assuming you are interested in changing careers, develop a list of ten companies for which you would like to work. Assign each company a priority according to your interest, from the most desirable (1) to the least (10). Organize your list in six columns showing the company name, telephone number, address, person in charge of hiring, prospect information, and priority. What sources did you use to get this information?

➤ SALES AUTOMATION CASE STUDY

ACT! REVIEWING THE PROSPECT DATABASE

Becky Kemley is the sales manager in the Dallas, Texas office of Cadalyst Resources. Her company sells computer-aided design (CAD) products and services to architects, engineers, and corporate space planners. The productivity of these professionals and the critical mission of their companies can be considerably enhanced by selecting and using the correct CAD system. Becky's company is called a value-added reseller (VAR) because its people help customers maximize the value of the products bought through Cadalyst.

Becky's sales and technical support people may spend several months in the sales process (sales cycle). Salespeople telephone and call on prospects to determine if they qualify for Cadalyst's attention. Time is taken to study the customer's needs (needs discovery). The expert opinion of Cadalyst's technical people is incorporated into a sales proposal that is presented to the customer. The presentation may be made to a number of decision makers in the customer firm. The final decision to purchase may follow weeks of consideration within the firm and negotiations with Cadalyst.

Once a decision is made by a customer to buy from Cadalyst, Becky's people begin the process of acquiring, assembling, and installing the CAD system; and then follow through with appropriate training, integration, and support services.

Becky's company must carefully prospect for customers. Cadalyst may invest a significant amount of time helping a customer choose the right combination of products and services. This means that only the most serious prospects should be cultivated. Further, Becky's people must ascertain that if the investment of time is made in a customer, the customer will follow through with purchases from Cadalyst.

Becky is responsible for assuring that prospect information is collected and used effectively. The CAD salespeople use the ACT! Contact Management software to manage their prospect information. The system, which is identical to the software included with this textbook, allows salespeople to document and manage their sales efforts with each customer.

Becky has just hired you to sell for Cadalyst beginning December 1. Becky has given you the files of Mark David, a salesperson who has just been promoted to Cadalyst's corporate headquarters. Becky has asked you to review the status of Mark's twenty prospect accounts (which are included on the enclosed software disk). Mark's customers have been notified that Mark is leaving and that a new salesperson, you, will be contacting them. Becky wants you to review each prospect's record. You are to meet with Becky next Monday and be prepared to answer the following questions.

Access the ACT! software following the instructions in Appendix 2.

Questions

1. Which contact can you ignore immediately *as a prospect* for making a potential purchase?

2. Referring only to the *date close* category, which four prospects would you call immediately?

3. Referring only to the *dollar amount* of sales forecasted category, which four accounts would you call first? Does the likelihood of closing percentage category have any influence on decisions concerning which prospects to call first? Why?

4. According to information on the Contact Screens and Notes Windows, which prospecting method did Mark David appear to use the most? Give examples.

➤ CASE PROBLEM

Bill Coleman, general manager for ACT! contact software from Symantec Corporation, says, "Once you have customer, maintaining the relationship is a lot cheaper than finding a new customer." A growing number of salespeople are using ACT! software or one of its competitors to improve service to customers. Shannon O'Connell, sales representative for 800-SOFTWARE Incorporated (one of the nations largest resellers of microcomputer products), is giving her customers added value with ACT! contact software. Like most other salespeople, she is trying to cope with expanded duties, faster work pace, and customers with high expectations. ACT! software helps her in the following ways:

➤ **Customer profile.** Complete information on each customer is available on screen at the touch of a key. In addition to name, phone number, and address, she has a complete record of all past contacts. The profile also includes important personal as well as business information about the customer.

> **Organization and planning.** It is no longer necessary for Shannon to prepare a written "to do" list or a planning calendar. All this information can easily be entered into her portable computer. In the morning she simply clicks her Day At A Glance command and she is reminded of scheduled appointments, follow-up phone calls that need to be made, and other activities. If she needs to make a call at 2:00 P.M., she can press the Set Alarm button, which serves the same purpose as an alarm clock.

> **Correspondence.** ACT! software features a built-in word processor that makes it easy to prepare memos, letters, and reports. To send a standard follow-up letter to a customer, she simply brings up the letter from storage, enters the customer's name, and presses the appropriate key. The word processor automatically prints the inside address and mailing label. With ACT! software you can even send and receive E-mail. Most salespeople are responsible for numerous reports. The ACT! software can be used to generate a wide range of reports with a minimum of effort. It features thirty predefined reports for use in a wide range of sales and sales support areas.

David Florence, a sales representative with Motorola-EMBARC, makes over 100 phone calls each day. He appreciates the ACT! feature that permits automatic telephone dialing. He simply identifies the customer's name and presses a key.

QUESTIONS

1. If your goal is to maintain long-term partnerships with each of your customers, what features of the ACT! contact software will be most helpful?

2. Let us assume you are selling copy machines in a city with a population of 100,000 people. Your territory includes the entire city. What features of the ACT! software would you use most frequently?

3. Some salespeople who could benefit from use of ACT! software or a competing product continue to use a Rolodex or note cards to keep a record of the customers they call on. What are some barriers to adoption of this type of technology?

4. Examine the first ACT! Contact Screen presented in Appendix 2.
   a. What is Bradley Able's position within the company?
   b. What is the "date expected" for the sale to close?
   c. What is the forecasted dollar amount of this potential sale?

Part V

Developing a Presentation Strategy

The chapters included in Part V review the basic principles used in the strategic/consultative sales presentation. This information will be used as you prepare presentation objectives, develop a presentation plan, and identify ways to provide outstanding service after the sale.

To play any game well, you first have to learn the rules, or principles of the game. And second, you have to forget about them. That is, you have to learn to play without thinking about the rules. This is true whether the game is chess or golf or selling. Shortcuts won't work.

AL RIES AND JACK TROUT
MARKETING WARFARE

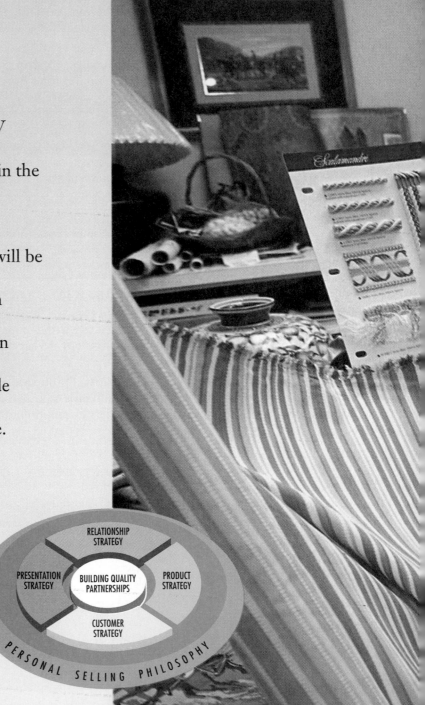

Approaching the Customer

LEARNING OBJECTIVES

When you finish reading this chapter, you should be able to

1. Describe the three prescriptions that are included in the presentation strategy

2. Describe the role of objectives in developing the presale presentation plan

3. Discuss the basic steps of the preapproach

4. Explain the merits of a planned presentation strategy

5. Describe the nature of team versus one-person presentation strategies

6. Describe group versus individual presentation strategies

7. Explain the purpose of informative, persuasive, and reminder presentations

8. Explain how to effectively approach the customer

9. Describe five ways to convert the prospect's attention and arouse interest

A pharmaceutical company that manufactures and distributes "miracle" drugs to health professionals really does not need a sales force, right? After all, if you are selling life-saving medical products you do not need to worry about sales efforts, right? The truth is, salespeople have played a key role in the success of Amgen, a relatively new pharmaceutical company that until recently had nothing to sell. Only after the Federal Drug Administration (FDA) approved a small number of drugs did Amgen evolve from a research and development lab to a manufacturer to a marketer. A breakthrough by the Amgen research and development laboratory set the stage for the new company direction. The new drugs had to be manufactured and sold to the medical community.

One of the first salespeople hired was Deborah Karish. She soon found that one of her greatest challenges was winning acceptance of her company, which was new to members of the medical community. Prospects were accustomed to buying products from well-established pharmaceutical companies. During a typical sales call Deborah is selling her company, her products, and herself. Health care professionals need ample assurances that she is well qualified to give sound professional advice concerning the use of complex medical products.[1]

As noted in Chapter 2, there are a wide range of career options in the field of personal selling. How do you know if you have selected the most suitable sales position? If the position provides you with the new energy needed each day to be a true consultant to your customers, then you have probably made the right choice. Shelly Jones, a partner with the consulting firm Korn/Ferry International, says that future sales positions will require the ". . . sophisticated skills of a business consultant, including the ability to spot opportunities in a changing marketplace." He also says, "The selling function will be less pitching product and more integrating your product into the business equation of your client, understanding the business environment in which your client operates."[2] This chapter provides you with the information needed to assume the role of consultant when approaching the customer.

Developing the Presentation Strategy

The presentation strategy combines elements of the relationship, product, and customer strategies. Each of the other three strategies must be developed before a salesperson can develop an effective presentation strategy.

The **presentation strategy** is a well-conceived plan that includes three prescriptions: (1) establishing objectives for the sales presentation, (2) developing the presale presentation plan needed to meet these objectives, and (3) renewing one's commitment to providing outstanding customer service (Fig. 9.1, Strategic/Consultative Selling Model).

The first prescription reminds us that we need to establish one or more objectives for each sales call. High-performance salespeople like Deborah Karish understand that it is often possible to accomplish several things during a single call. A common objective of sales calls is to collect information about the prospect's needs. Another common objective is to build relationships with those who will make the buying decision. In banking, for example, a major purchase may be influenced by two or three persons.

A carefully prepared presentation plan ensures that salespeople will be well organized during the sales presentation and prepared to achieve their objectives. A six-step presentation plan is introduced later in this chapter.

Establishment of objectives for the sales presentation and preparation of the presale presentation plan must be guided by a strong desire to offer outstanding customer service. Achieving excellence is the result of careful needs analysis, correct product selection, clear presentations, informative demonstrations, win-win negotiations, and flawless service after the sale. Salespeople who are committed to doing their best in each of these areas will be richly rewarded.

A PRESENTATION STRATEGY ADDS VALUE

The importance of planning and preparation was recognized in a national survey of 1,500 sales managers and sales representatives. When they were asked to rank fourteen personal selling skills in order of importance to their *long-term success*, precall planning was ranked as most important.[3]

How does pre-call planning add value? A well-planned presentation adds value because it is based on carefully developed sales call objectives and a presentation plan needed to meet these objectives. Good planning ensures that the presentation will be customized to meet the needs of the prospect.

FIGURE 9.1   The Strategic/Consultative Selling Model provides the foundation for a successful consultative-style presentation strategy.

Strategic/Consultative Selling Model*	
Strategic step	Prescription
DEVELOP A PERSONAL SELLING PHILOSOPHY	☑ ADOPT MARKETING CONCEPT ☑ VALUE PERSONAL SELLING ☑ BECOME A PROBLEM SOLVER/PARTNER
DEVELOP A RELATIONSHIP STRATEGY	☑ ADOPT DOUBLE–WIN PHILOSOPHY ☑ PROJECT PROFESSIONAL IMAGE ☑ MAINTAIN HIGH ETHICAL STANDARDS
DEVELOP A PRODUCT STRATEGY	☑ BECOME A PRODUCT EXPERT ☑ ADOPT FEATURE/BENEFIT PROCESS ☑ POSITION PRODUCT
DEVELOP A CUSTOMER STRATEGY	☑ UNDERSTAND BUYER BEHAVIOR ☑ DISCOVER CUSTOMER NEEDS ☑ DEVELOP PROSPECT BASE
DEVELOP A PRESENTATION STRATEGY	☑ PREPARE OBJECTIVES ☑ DEVELOP PRESENTATION PLAN ☑ PROVIDE OUTSTANDING SERVICE
* Strategic/consultative selling evolved in response to increased competition, more complex products, increased emphasis on customer needs, and growing importance of long-term relationships.	

Planning the Preapproach

Preparation for the actual sales presentation is a two-part process. Part one is referred to as the **preapproach.** The preapproach involves preparing presale objectives and developing a presale presentation plan. Part two is called the **approach** and involves making a favorable first impression, securing the prospect's attention, and developing the prospect's interest in the product (Fig. 9.2). The preapproach and approach, when handled correctly, establish a foundation for an effective sales presentation.

The preapproach should be viewed as a key step in preparing for each sales presentation. Professional salespeople complete the preapproach for every presentation whether it involves a new account or an established customer.[4] The preapproach includes the first two prescriptions for developing a presentation strategy: establishing objectives and creating a presale presentation plan.

ESTABLISHING PRESENTATION OBJECTIVES

Martin Jacknis, president of Results Marketing Incorporated, says that every salesperson should establish multiple objectives for each sales call. He states that salespeople often limit their potential by closing their minds to a wide range of possibilities.[5] For example, a salesperson might view obtaining the or-

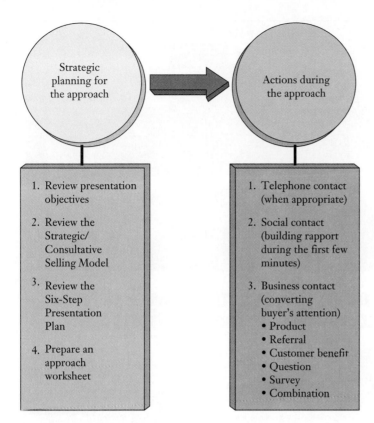

FIGURE 9.2   Preparing for the presentation involves planning for the activities that will occur before meeting the prospect and for the first few minutes of actual contact with the prospect.

der as the only important objective. We know that most sales are not closed during the first contact with the customer, so why not establish other objectives? Here are some additional objectives that might be established during the preapproach:

1. Obtain personal and business information to update the customer's file.
2. Provide sales literature for the prospect to review.
3. Conduct a needs assessment to determine if your product is suitable. (A second call may not be necessary.)
4. Make an appointment for the next sales call.
5. Secure a list of referrals.
6. Provide postsale service.

Setting multiple objectives helps reduce the fear of failure that salespeople often feel during the preapproach stage. It can be a confidence-raising experience. Achieving one or more objectives will engender a feeling of accomplishment. Once you have an appointment with the prospect and the presentation objectives have been established, consider sending a fax that outlines the agenda for the meeting. The fax will confirm the appointment and clarify the topics to be discussed.[6]

FACTORS INFLUENCING PRESENTATION OBJECTIVES
There are a number of factors affecting the objectives that you select for a sales presentation. Will the presentation be made to one person or a group? How fa-

Extensive strategic planning is required for salespeople who use computer graphics tied into a desktop projection system such as this one from Proxima.

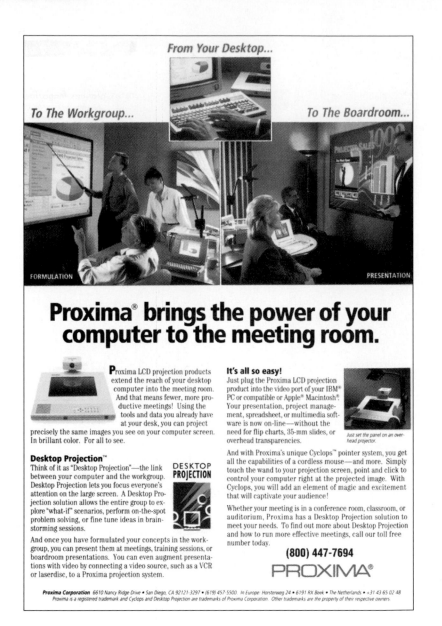

miliar is the prospect with the product? How much time will you need to spend with the prospect? Answers to these and other questions help the salesperson establish appropriate objectives.

Multicall sales presentations The use of **multicall sales presentations** will also affect the objectives that are established. Many companies that have adopted the need-satisfaction approach to personal selling use multiple sales calls. The purpose of the first call is to collect and analyze certain basic information that is used to develop a specific proposal. Once the proposal is prepared, the salesperson makes a second appointment to present it. In many cases additional calls will be needed to close the sale. The complexity of products has led to longer sales cycles in many industries.

Multicall sales presentations have become more common in the retail field. A growing number of clothing stores and independent tailors are now making office and home sales calls to sell suits for men and women. Sales personnel employed by Tom James Company, a firm that sells individually tailored suits, use a three-call plan. During the first home or office visit, the client reviews designs, picks out the fabric from a sample board of one-inch swatches, and gets measured. The suit is fitted during a second call and delivered during the third call.[7] Each of these calls may require different objectives.

TEAM VERSUS ONE-PERSON PRESENTATION OBJECTIVES

In today's ever-changing business environment, teamwork has surfaced as a major development. Presale planning and the actual sales presentation often require two or more people.[8] Team selling is ideally suited to organizations that sell complex, or customized products and services that require direct communication between customers and technical experts. In some situations the involvement of technical experts can shorten the selling cycle.[9] The team approach often results in more precise need identification, improved selection of the product, and more informative sales presentations. To achieve greater customization, Burlington Menswear, a New York-based clothing manufacturer, uses teams on most sales calls. Salespeople are teamed with a representative from a support area such as research and development, operations planning, or styling. These specialists often improve the need identification process and the identification of solutions to the customer's buying problem.[10] Complex problems often require pooled expertise.

A variation of the team approach to selling is used by some marketers. Salespeople are trained to seek the assistance of another salesperson or actually turn the customer over to another salesperson when problems surface. The other salesperson may bring to the selling situation greater ability to identify the customer's needs or select the appropriate product. Salespeople who have well-prepared presale objectives know when to seek assistance from another professional.

Some presentation strategies involve a team approach. The sales team might include a technical specialist or a senior company executive.

SELLING TO A BUYING TEAM

As products become more complex, we often see an increase in the number of decision makers involved in selling situations. The decision makers may be members of a well-trained buying team, a buying committee assembled for a one-time purchase, or a board of directors.

Sales representatives for Emergency One, Incorporated, a company that manufactures fire engines valued at $225,000 each, are accustomed to group selling presentations.[11] The group may include firefighters, the fire chief, and city officials who must approve such major purchases. Salespeople employed by IMR Records Management, Incorporated, a Middletown, Pennsylvania firm offering a variety of records management services, frequently make group sales presentations. The typical group might include a "techie" who knows a great deal about computers, department managers who ask tough questions about benefits to the company, and the CEO who may only want to talk price.[12]

As in any type of selling situation, the salesperson should attempt to determine the various buying influences. When possible, the role of each decision maker, the amount of influence he exerts, and each decision maker's needs should be determined before or during the presentation. Careful observation during the presentation can reveal who will use the product, who controls the finances, and who will provide the expertise necessary to make the correct buying decision. When you make a group selling presentation, make sure all parties feel involved. Any member of the group who feels ignored could prevent you from closing the sale. Be sure to direct questions and comments to all potential decision makers in the group.

INFORMATIVE, PERSUASIVE, AND REMINDER PRESENTATION OBJECTIVES

When preparing presale presentation objectives, it is important to make a decision concerning the overall purpose of the presentation. The major purpose

Well-prepared presale objectives will help salespeople address the needs of each person in a group selling situation.

may be to inform, persuade, or remind. The sale of highly technical products and services often begins with an informative sales presentation. The customer needs to be familiar with the product before making a buying decision. In another situation, where the customer's needs have been carefully identified and your product is obviously suited to these needs, a persuasive presentation would be appropriate. In the case of repeat customers, it is often necessary to remind them of the products and services you offer.

INFORMATIVE PRESENTATION

The objective of a presentation that involves a new or unique product is generally to inform customers of its features and explain how these features will benefit the customer. Typically, people will not purchase a product or service until they become familiar with its application. Informative presentations are usually more prevalent when the product is being first introduced to the market. A **detail salesperson** (introduced in Chapter 2) usually spends a great deal of time informing customers of new products and changes in existing products.

PERSUASIVE PRESENTATION

Some degree of persuasion is common to nearly all sales presentations. **Persuasion**—the act of presenting product appeals so as to influence the prospect's beliefs, attitudes, or behavior—is a strategy designed to encourage the buyer to make a buying decision. Persuasion can be integrated into every phase of the sales presentation. A friendly greeting and a firm handshake at the time of initial customer contact represent a relationship-oriented form of persuasion. An enthusiastic sales demonstration is another type of persuasion common in sales. Additional forms of persuasion include converting features to buyer benefits, repeating feature-benefit statements, and asking for the sale. Persuasive strategies are designed to elicit a positive response from the prospect. It is never a good idea, however, to apply too much persuasion in an attempt to sell a product or service. These actions can perpetuate the stereotype of the pushy, unprofessional salesperson.

REMINDER PRESENTATION

In some selling situations, the primary objective of the sales call will be to remind the prospect of products and services offered by the company. Without this occasional reminder the prospect may forget information that is beneficial. Computer salespeople might periodically remind customers about special services (training classes, service contracts, and customized programming, for example) available from the company they represent. An occasional reminder can prevent the competition from capturing the business.

Consideration of whether the overall presentation objective should be to inform, persuade, or remind will have a significant influence on your presale presentation plan and your efforts to provide outstanding service.

The time available to prepare presale objectives and create presale presentations will vary depending on the complexity of the product, the customer's knowledge of the product, and other factors. The successful outcome of a complex sale is usually dependent on the time and effort invested in preparation.

In some selling situations, the saleperson is given little time to prepare for the sales presentation. This is the case in some retail and service situations where customers arrive unannounced.

Developing the Six-Step Presentation Plan

Once you have established objectives for the sales presentation, the next step (prescription) involves developing the presentation plan. This plan helps you achieve your objectives.

Today, with increased time constraints, fierce competition, and rising travel costs, the opportunity for a face-to-face meeting with customers may occur less frequently. The few minutes you have with your customers may be your only opportunity to win their business,[13] meaning that careful planning is more critical than ever. Ken Daniels, team leader at AT&T Global Information Solutions, says, "Plan each sales call before you make it so you don't get sidetracked."[14]

In preparation for development of the presentation strategy, it is helpful to review the three broad strategic areas that have been described in previous chapters: relationship strategy; product strategy; and customer strategy. Why is this review so critical? It is because today's dynamic sales presentations require consideration of the simultaneous influences of the relationship, product, and customer strategies. A careful review of these three areas sets the stage for flexible presentations that meet the needs of the customer.

PLANNING THE PRESENTATION

Once you have sufficient background information, you are ready to develop a "customized" presale presentation plan. The plan is developed after a careful review of the **six-step presentation plan** (Fig. 9.3). This planning aid is a tentative list of activities that will take place during the sales interview. This presale activity will further strengthen your self-confidence and help avoid confusion in the presence of the prospect. In selling, a basic presale presentation plan makes good sense because an erratic sales presentation is apt to confuse the prospect.

CUSTOMIZING THE PRESENTATION

Preparing a customized sales presentation can take a great deal of time and energy. Nevertheless, this attention to detail will give you added confidence and help you avoid delivering unconvincing hit-or-miss sales talks.

A well-planned sales presentation is a logical and orderly outline that features the salesperson's own thoughts from one step to the next. The presentation is usually divided into six main parts (see Fig. 9.3).

1. *Approach*. Preparation for the approach involves making decisions concerning effective ways to make a favorable first impression during the initial contact, securing the prospect's attention, and developing the prospect's interest in the product. The approach should set the stage for an effective sales presentation.

2. *Presentation*. The presentation is one of the most critical parts of the selling process. If the salesperson is unable to discover the prospect's buying needs, select a product solution, and present the product in a convincing manner, the sale may be lost. Chapter 10 covers all aspects of the sales presentation.

3. *Demonstration*. An effective sales demonstration helps verify parts of the sales presentation. Demonstrations are important because they provide the customer with a better understanding of product benefits. The demonstration, like all other phases of the presentation, must be carefully planned. Chapter 11 is devoted exclusively to this topic.

The Six-Step Presentation Plan	
Step One: APPROACH	☐ Review Strategic/Consultative Selling Model. ☐ Initiate customer contact.
Step Two: PRESENTATION	☐ Determine prospect needs. ☐ Select product or service. ☐ Initiate sales presentation.
Step Three: DEMONSTRATION	☐ Decide what to demonstrate. ☐ Select selling tools. ☐ Initiate demonstration.
Step Four: NEGOTIATION	☐ Anticipate sales resistance. ☐ Plan negotiating methods. ☐ Initiate double-win negotiations.
Step Five: CLOSE	☐ Plan appropriate closing methods. ☐ Recognize closing clues. ☐ Initiate closing methods.
Step Six: SERVICING THE SALE	☐ Suggestion selling. ☐ Follow through. ☐ Follow-up calls.
Service, retail, wholesale, and manufacturer selling.	

FIGURE 9.3   The Six-Step Presentation Plan. A presale plan is a logical and an orderly outline that features a salesperson's thoughts from one step to the next in the presentation. Each step in this plan will be explained in Chapters 9 to 14.

4. *Negotiation.* Buyer resistance is a natural part of the selling/buying process. An objection, however, does present a barrier to closing the sale. For this reason, all salespeople should become skillful at negotiating resistance. Chapter 12 covers this topic.

5. *Close.* As the sales presentation progresses, there may be several opportunities to close the sale. Salespeople must learn to spot closing clues. Chapter 13 provides suggestions on how to close sales.

6. *Servicing the sale.* The importance of developing a long-term relationship with the prospect was noted earlier in this chapter. This rapport is often the outgrowth of postsale service. Learning to service the sale is an important aspect of selling. Chapter 14 deals with this topic.

In some cases you can assess the value of something by determining how long it has existed. A truly valuable idea or concept is timeless. The six parts of the presale presentation plan checklist have been discussed in the sales training literature for several decades; therefore they might be described as fundamentals of personal selling. These steps are basic elements of almost every sale and frequently occur in the same sequence. Of course, some sales are made without an objection, and some customers buy before the salesperson attempts to close.

The sales presentation should be a model of good two-way communication.

Although these six selling *basics* are part of nearly every seminar, workshop, and course devoted to sales training, the emphasis given each will vary depending on the nature of the selling situation.

BUILDING RELATIONSHIPS IN A DIVERSE WORLD

SELLING ACROSS CULTURES

The growth of international trade is creating some communication problems for salespeople. More firms are opening branch offices abroad or entering into joint ventures with foreign corporations than ever before. Yet all too often Americans going overseas have little knowledge of the language and culture of the host country. There are many subtle communication traps awaiting the unwary. For example, if you are visiting with a prospect in Mexico, you should always inquire about the person's spouse and family. In Saudi Arabia, you should not inquire about a client's family. In Latin America, people are often late for scheduled meetings. In Sweden, you should try to be prompt to the second.

A buyer for Marks & Spencer's, one of England's major department store chains, reminds us that communication style may be an issue in some cultures. He says, "If you want to sell to the British, write a nice, clear, nonexaggerating letter explaining the simple facts of your business, and ask for an appointment to come over and see me. I will be busy, but British buyers, unlike American buyers, will see you. I will give you half an hour to persuade me, and if you are flamboyant, I will reject most of what you say."

Many organizations are beginning to realize they must prepare their foreign-based employees for the diverse aspects of the new culture in which they will be living and working. For example, American females should be prepared to cope with far more male chauvinism than they would encounter back home. Men and women alike learn that aggressiveness may be counterproductive in some countries. In Japan, for example, people who wait and listen in a conversation earn respect.

How about business cards? Business cards are very important in most foreign countries, and it is common courtesy to have your card printed in English as well as in the local language.[a]

The Approach

After a great deal of preparation it is time to communicate with the prospect, either by face-to-face contact or by telephone. We refer to the initial contact with the customer as the *approach*. All the effort you have put into developing relationship, product, and customer strategies can now be applied to the presentation strategy. If the approach is effective, you will be given the opportunity to make the sales presentation. If, however, the approach is not effective, the chance to present your sales story may be lost. You can be the best-prepared salesperson in the business, but without a good approach there may be little chance for a sale.

The approach has three important objectives. First, you want to build rapport with the prospect. Second, you want to capture the person's full attention. Never begin your sales story if the prospect seems preoccupied and is not paying attention. Third, you want to generate interest in the product you are selling.

In some selling situations the first contact with the customer is a telephone call. The call is made to schedule a meeting or in some cases conduct the sales presentation. The more traditional sales call starts with the social contact and is followed by the business contact. The telephone contact, social contact, and business contact are discussed in this section.

THE TELEPHONE CONTACT

A telephone call provides a quick and inexpensive method of scheduling an interview. Several interviews can be arranged in a short period of time. Unlike a letter, a telephone call provides an opportunity for immediate two-way communication. In the retail field the telephone is often used to inform customers of new merchandise arrivals and special events such as a sale or fashion show.

Some salespeople use the telephone exclusively to establish and maintain contact with the customer. As noted in Chapter 2, inside salespeople (employed by wholesalers) rely almost totally on the telephone for sales. **Telesales,** not to be confused with telemarketing, includes many of the same elements as traditional sales: gathering customer information, determining needs, prescribing solutions, negotiating objections, and closing sales. Telesales is not scripted, a practice widely used in telemarketing. In some situations, telesales is as freewheeling and unpredictable as a face-to-face sales call. IBM is one of several companies that is expanding the telesales concept to sell to customers in North America and throughout the world.[15]

In Chapter 3 we examined some of the factors that influence the meaning we attach to an oral message from another person. With the aid of this information we can see that communication via telephone is challenging. The person who receives the call cannot see our facial expression, gestures, or posture, and therefore must rely totally on the sound of our voice and the words used. The telephone caller has a definite handicap.

The telephone has some additional limitations. A salesperson accustomed to meeting prospects in person may find telephone contact impersonal. Some salespeople try to avoid using the telephone because they believe it is too easy for the prospect to say no. It should be noted that these drawbacks are more imagined than real. With proper training a salesperson can use the telephone effectively to schedule interviews.

The telephone contact can set the stage for the social and business contact. The first few seconds of the call are crucial to the image you project.

The telephone can be a source of negative or positive first impressions. Nancy Friedman, the person who developed the popular Telephone Doctor training videos, says that most customers view telephone courtesy as a critical factor in their decision to purchase goods and services.[16] The first fifteen seconds of every phone call are crucial to your image.[17] To improve your telephone voice, follow these tips:

Be pleasant. *Build a pleasant business image with a "voice with a smile." Pleasantness is contagious.*

Be expressive. *Vary your tone of voice to add color and vitality to what you say. Talk at a moderate rate, neither too fast nor too slow.*

Be distinct. *Speak clearly and distinctly. Talk directly into the transmitter.*

Once you have the prospect on the line, clarify the purpose of the visit so the prospect knows what to expect. Also, get agreement on the amount of time needed for the visit and determine if anyone else needs to be present during the sales call. If others will be involved in making the buying decision, be sure they can be available for the meeting.[18]

THE SOCIAL CONTACT

According to many image consultants, "First impressions are lasting impressions." This statement is essentially true, and some profitable business relationships never crystallize because some trait or characteristic of the salesperson repels the prospective customer. Mark McCormack, author of *What They Don't Teach You at the Harvard Business School*, notes:

In any new business situation there is a kind of mutual sizing up that goes on between the players. Each is trying subtly to exert his or her influence over the other. Whoever is better equipped to control the impressions being formed will walk away accomplishing the most, certainly in the short term and most likely in the long term as well.[19]

BUILDING RELATIONSHIPS THROUGH TECHNOLOGY

PLANNING PERSONAL VISITS

Personally visiting prospects and customers helps build strong relationships, yet traveling is expensive and time consuming. A salesperson is challenged to plan visits that will optimize the investment represented by each trip. Automated access to prospect records helps salespeople quickly identify all the accounts in a given geographic area.

Automation empowers salespeople to rapidly review and compare an area's prospects on the basis of: position in sales cycle, potential size of account or purchase, likelihood of sale, and the contribution that the visit could make to information gathering and relationship building. A well-managed database will provide salespeople with appropriate business and social topics to discuss when calling selected prospects for an appointment. Many software programs will even automatically dial the phone. (See Sales Automation Application Exercise on p. 213 for more information.)

Sales personnel have only a few minutes to create a positive first impression. Dr. Leonard Zunin, coauthor of *Contact: The First Four Minutes*, describes what he calls the "four-minute barrier." In this short period of time a relationship can be established or denied. He notes that most people are unaware of the meaning and ramifications of those first four minutes.

Research conducted by Drs. Brad and Velma Lashbrook, members of the Wilson Learning Corporation staff, sheds some light on the "do's and don't's" of that period of first contact. Working with 605 salespeople, the Lashbrooks tested the idea that "a certain degree of social penetration (interpersonal comfort) is necessary for a buyer-seller relationship to develop to the degree that the two parties can engage in a decision-making process."[20] At the end of the data-gathering period the researchers stated that three factors were viewed as important by buyers involved in their study.

1. *Competence.* The salesperson is technically qualified to help solve a buying problem.

2. *Propriety.* The salesperson is the "right" kind of person to be working with. "This person is enough like me to understand and deal with my problem."

3. *Trustworthiness.* The salesperson can be trusted. "This person really wants to help me solve my problem."

The qualities of propriety and trustworthiness are intangibles that can best be developed in a sales setting that is free of "aversive" factors. An **aversive factor** is a mannerism, gesture, style of dress, breach of etiquette, or conversational topic that is offensive to the customer.

DEVELOPING CONVERSATION

The brief, general conversation during the social contact should hold the prospect's attention and establish a relaxed and friendly atmosphere for the business contact that is to follow. As mentioned in Chapter 3, there are three areas of conversation that should be considered in developing a social contact:

1. *Comments on here and now observations.* These comments may include general observations about the victory of a local athletic team or specific comments about awards on display in the prospect's office.

2. *Compliments.* Most customers will react positively to sincere compliments. Personal items in the prospect's office, achievements, or efficient operation of the prospect's business provide examples of things that can be praised.

3. *Search for mutual acquaintances or interests.* The discovering of mutual friends or interests can serve as the foundation for a strong social contact.

Communication on a personal basis is often the first step in discovering a common language that will improve communication between the salesperson and the prospect. How much time should be devoted to the social contact? There is no easy answer to this question. The length of the conversation will depend on the type of product or service sold, how busy the prospect appears to be, and your awareness of topics of mutual interest.

THE BUSINESS CONTACT

Converting the prospect's attention from the social contact to the business proposal is an important part of the approach. When you convert and hold your prospect's attention, you have fulfilled an important step in the selling process. Furthermore, without success in the beginning, the door has been closed on completing the remaining steps of the sale.

BUILDING QUALITY PARTNERSHIPS

RECOMMENDED READING

Some of the most influential books published during the past fifty years have stressed the importance of relationships in the business world. Some of these books have had a lasting influence on our culture. Pulitzer Prize-winning literature critic Jonathan Yardley selected the book entitled *How to Win Friends and Influence People* to appear on a list of ten books that he thought contributed most to American culture. This book has achieved sales of over 20 million copies since it was published in 1936. The author, Dale Carnegie, developed the following six rules for building relationships:

Rule 1: Become genuinely interested in other people.

Rule 2: Smile.

Rule 3: Remember that a man's name is to him the sweetest and most important sound in any language.

Rule 4: Be a good listener. Encourage others to talk about themselves.

Rule 5: Talk in terms of the other man's interest.

Rule 6: Make the other person feel important— and do it sincerely.

Although millions of people have read Dale Carnegie's book and thousands of people have completed the popular Dale Carnegie course, some of these people fail to understand the true meaning of his advice. You cannot pretend to be interested in the other person or fake attentive listening. Stephen Covey, author of the best-selling book entitled *The Seven Habits of Highly Effective People* says that the ability to build effective, long-term relationships is based on character strength, not quick-fix techniques. He says that you can easily pick up quick, easy techniques that may work in short-term situations, but if you do not possess deep integrity and fundamental character strength, human relationship failure will replace short-term success. Covey says that outward attitude and behavior changes do very little good in the long run unless they are based on solid principles governing human effectiveness. These principles include service (making a contribution), integrity and honesty (which serve as a foundation of trust), human dignity (every person has worth), and fairness.[b]

Some salespeople use a carefully planned opening statement or a question to convert the customer's attention to the sales presentation. A statement or question that focuses on the prospect's dominant buying motive is, of course, more likely to achieve the desired results. Buyers must like what they see and hear and must be made to feel that it will be worthwhile to hear more.

Throughout the years, salespeople have identified and used a number of effective ways to capture the prospect's attention and arouse interest in the presentation. Five of the most common will be explained in the following material:

Product demonstration approach

Referral approach

Customer benefit approach

Question approach

Survey approach

We also discuss combining two or more of these approaches.

PRODUCT DEMONSTRATION APPROACH
This straightforward method of getting the prospect's attention is used by sales representatives who sell copy machines, photographic equipment, automobiles, construction equipment, office furniture, and many other products. If the actual product cannot be demonstrated, salespeople can use appropriate audiovisual technology such as computer-generated graphics, slides, and videotapes. Trish Ormsby, a sales representative for Wells Fargo Alarm Services, uses her portable computer to create a visual image of security systems that meet the customer's security needs.[21]

REFERRAL APPROACH
Research indicates that another person will be far more impressed with your good points if these points are presented by a third party rather than by you.

The survey approach can be used to capture the prospect's attention.

The referral approach is quite effective because a third party (a satisfied customer) believes the prospect will benefit from your product. This type of opening statement has universal appeal among salespeople from nearly every field.

When you use the referral approach, your opening statement should include a direct reference to the third party. Here is an example: "Mrs. Follett, my name is Kurt Wheeler, and I represent the Cross Printing Company. We specialize in printing all types of business forms. Mr. Ameno—buyer for Raybale Products, Incorporated—is a regular customer of ours, and he suggested I mention his name to you."

CUSTOMER BENEFIT APPROACH

One of the most effective ways to gain a prospect's attention is to immediately point out one benefit of purchasing your product. Start with the most important issue (or problem) facing the client.[22] When using this approach, the most important buyer benefit is included in the initial statement. For example, the salesperson selling a Minolta Maxxum 5000i camera might open with this statement:

The Maxxum 5000i's autofocus system gives you the flexibility to shoot panoramic landscapes, striking portraits, and fast-moving sports action. With this system, your pictures always come out in precise focus.

Here is another example taken from the office copy machine field:

This new office copy machine can save your office staff valuable time each day. It will copy work nearly twice as fast as any other machine on the market.

The key to achieving success with the customer benefit approach is advance preparation. You must know a great deal about your prospect to pinpoint the buyer benefit, which should be emphasized in your opening statement.

QUESTION APPROACH

The question approach has two positive features. First, a question will almost always trigger prospect involvement. Very few people will avoid answering a direct question. Second, a question gets the prospect thinking about a problem that the salesperson is prepared to solve.

Molly Hoover, a sales training consultant, conducts training classes for sales managers and car dealers who want to better understand the subtleties of selling to the new woman car buyer. She suggests an approach that includes a few basic questions such as:

"Is the vehicle for business or pleasure?"

"Will you be buying within the next week or so?"[23]

These opening questions are not difficult to answer, yet they get the customer mentally involved. Some of the best opening questions are carefully phrased to arouse attention. The authors of *The Sales Question Book* offer some good examples:

"Are you aware that we just added three new services to our payroll and accounting package? Could I tell you about them?"

"We are now offering all our customers a special service that used to be reserved for our largest accounts. Would you be interested in hearing about it?"[24]

Once you ask the question, listen carefully to the response. If the answer is yes, proceed with an enthusiastic presentation of your product. If the answer is no, then you may have to gracefully try another approach or thank the prospect for her time and depart.

SURVEY APPROACH

Robert Hewitt, a Monterey, California financial planner, has new clients fill out a detailed questionnaire before the first appointment. This procedure is part of his customer strategy. He studies the completed questionnaire and other documents before making any effort to find a solution to any of the customer's financial planning needs. The survey (data collection) is an important part of the problem-solving philosophy of selling. It is often used in selling office machines, business security systems, insurance, and other products where the need cannot be established without careful study.

The survey approach offers many advantages. It is generally a nonthreatening way to open a sales call. You are simply asking permission to acquire information that can be used to determine the buyer's need for your product. Because the survey is tailor-made for a specific business, the buyer is given individual treatment. Finally, the survey approach helps avoid an early discussion of price. Price cannot be discussed until the survey is completed.

The product, referral, customer benefit, question, and survey approaches offer the salesperson a variety of ways to set the stage for the presentation strategy. With experience, salespeople learn to select the most effective approach for each selling situation. Table 9.1 provides examples of how these approaches can be applied in real-world situations.

COMBINATION APPROACHES

A hallmark of consultative-style selling is flexibility. Therefore a combination of approaches sometimes provides the best avenue to need identification. Sales personnel who have adopted the consultative style will, of course, use the question and survey approaches most frequently. Some selling situations, however, require that one of the other approaches be used, either alone or in combination with the question and survey approaches (Fig. 9.4). Here is an example of how a salesperson might use a referral and question approach combination.

Salesperson: Carl Hamilton at Simmons Modern Furniture suggested that I visit with you about our new line of compact furniture designed for today's smaller homes. He believes this line might complement the furniture you currently feature.

Customer: Yes, Carl called me yesterday and mentioned your name and company.

Salesperson: Before showing you our product lines, I would like to ask you some questions about your current product mix. First, what do you currently carry in the area of bedroom furniture?

TABLE 9.1 BUSINESS CONTACT WORKSHEET

This illustrates how to prepare effective real-world approaches that capture the customer's attention.

METHOD OF APPROACH	WHAT WILL YOU SAY?
1. Product	1a. *(Retail clothing)* "We have just received a shipment of new fall sweaters from Braemar International."
	1b. *(Business forms manufacturer)* "Our plant has just purchased a $300,000 Harris Graphics composer, Mr. Reichart; I would like to show you a copy of your sales invoice with your logo printed on it."
2. Customer benefit	2. *(Real estate)* "Mr. and Mrs. Stuart, my company lists and sells more homes than any other company in the area where your home is located. Our past performance would lead me to believe we can sell your home within two weeks."
3. Referral	3. *(Food wholesaler)* "Paula Doeman, procurement manager for Mercy Medical Center, suggested that I provide you with information about our computerized 'Order It' system."
4. Question	4. *(Hotel convention services)* "Mrs. McClaughin, will your 1995 Annual Franchisee Meeting be held in April?"
5. Survey	5a. *(Custom-designed computer software)* "Mr. Vasquez, I would like the opportunity to learn about your accounts receivable and accounts payable procedures. We may be able to develop a customized program that will significantly improve your cash flow."
	5b. *(Retail menswear)* "May I ask you a few questions about your wardrobe? The information will help me better understand your clothing needs."

Note that the combination approach complements the marketing concept. It can be used to maximize customer satisfaction and obtain repeat business. In addition, the combination approach can be used in all four types of selling—service, retail, wholesale, and manufacturing.

FIGURE 9.4 Combination approaches provide a smooth transition to the need discovery part of the consultative-style presentation.

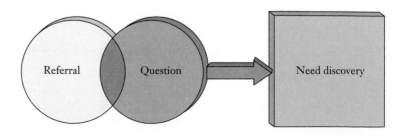

COPING WITH SALES CALL RELUCTANCE

The transition from the preapproach to the approach is sometimes blocked by sales call reluctance. Fear of making the initial contact with the prospect is a problem for rookies and veterans, and people in every selling field. Research conducted by Behavioral Sciences Research Press, Incorporated, reveals that about 40 percent of all salespeople will, at some point, experience call reluctance. For new salespeople, the problem can be career threatening.[25] Sales call reluctance may stem from concern about interrupting or intruding on the prospect, or it may stem from fear of saying the wrong thing or concern about not being able to respond effectively to the person who quickly begins asking questions. Sales call reluctance may surface because the salesperson fears rejection. Regardless of the reasons for sales call reluctance, you can learn to deal with it. Here are some suggestions:

> Be optimistic about the outcome of the initial contact. It is better to antici-pate success than to anticipate failure. Martin Seligman, professor of psy-chology at the University of Pennsylvania and author of the best-selling book *Learned Optimism*, says that success in selling requires a healthy dose of optimism.[26] The anticipation of failure is a major barrier to making the initial contact.

> Practice your approach before making the initial contact. A well-rehearsed effort to make the initial contact will increase your self-confidence and re-duce the possibility that you may handle the situation badly.

> Recognize that it is normal to feel anxious about the initial contact. Even the most experienced salespeople experience some degree of sales call re-luctance.

> Accept the fact that some attempts to approach the prospect will meet with rejection. Do not dwell on the rejection. Get busy and make contact with another prospect.

SUMMARY

As one sales consultant noted, "Organization multiplies the value of anything to which it is applied." This is especially true of precall planning. The well-pre-pared salesperson approaches the sales call with an attitude of confidence and expectancy.

Developing a presentation strategy involves preparing presale objectives, developing a presale presentation plan, and providing outstanding customer service. The presentation strategy combines elements of the relationship, prod-uct, and customer strategies.

Preparation for the sales presentation is a two-part process. Part one is re-ferred to as the *preapproach* and involves preparing presale objectives and devel-oping a presale presentation plan. Part two is called the *approach* and involves making a good first impression, securing the prospect's attention, and develop-ing the prospect's interest in the product.

Over the years, salespeople have identified several ways to convert the prospect's attention and arouse interest in the presentation. Some of the most common ways include the product demonstration approach, referral approach, customer benefit approach, question approach, and survey approach. This chapter also includes information on how to cope with sales call reluctance.

➤ KEY TERMS

Presentation Strategy

Preapproach

Approach

Multicall Sales Presentations

Detail Salesperson

Persuasion

Six-Step Presentation Plan

Telesales

Aversive Factor

➤ REVIEW QUESTIONS

1. What is the purpose of the preapproach? What are the two prescriptions included in the preapproach?

2. Explain the role of objectives in developing the presale presentation plan.

3. Why should salespeople establish multiple-objective sales presentations? List four possible objectives that could be achieved during a sales presentation.

4. Describe some common applications of telesales.

5. Describe the major purpose of the informative, persuasive, and reminder sales presentations.

6. What are the major objectives of the approach?

7. Review the Building Quality Partnerships box on p. 206. Why do you think Dale Carnegie's book *How to Win Friends and Influence People* appeared on the list of books that contributed most to American culture?

8. What are three ways to improve your telephone voice?

9. What methods can the salesperson use to convert the prospect's attention to the sales presentation?

10. Discuss why combination approaches are considered an important consultative-selling practice. Provide one example of a combination approach.

➤ APPLICATION EXERCISES

1. Assume that you are a salesperson who calls on retailers. For some time you have been attempting to get an appointment with one of the best retailers in the city to carry your line. You have an appointment to see the head buyer in one and one half hours. You are sitting in your office. It will take you about thirty minutes to drive to your appointment. Outline what you should be doing between now and the time you leave to meet your prospect.

2. Tom Nelson has just graduated from Aspen College with a major in marketing. He has three years of experience in the retail grocery business and has decided he would like to go to work as a salesperson for the district office of Procter and Gamble. Tom has decided to telephone and set up an appointment for an interview. Write out exactly what Tom should *plan* to say during his telephone call.

3. Concepts from Dale Carnegie's *How to Win Friends and Influence People* are referenced in this chapter. Access the Dale Carnegie home page on the Internet and examine the courses offered. Click on the "Sales Advantage Course" and read the description. Note the books that are used with this course. Is enthusiasm and remembering names an important part of the Approach?

➤ **S A L E S   A U T O M A T I O N   A P P L I C A T I O N   E X E R C I S E**

ACT! PLANNING PERSONAL VISITS

Sales software allows trip planners to examine the status of prospects in the geographic area to be visited. Assume that a salesperson using the ACT! demo wishes to visit the city of Bedford, Texas. The software permits a fast field search capability to sort and select the files of prospects in that city. By pressing at the Main Menu the key sequence, L E L C Bedford Enter, the user will see in the lower right corner of the screen 1 of 3. This new group of three means that there are three prospects in Bedford. To examine these files, the user may choose R C Enter Enter G. This will print Contact Screens 1 and 2 and the Notes Window of the Bedford group.

➤ **C A S E   P R O B L E M**

When Deborah Karish wakes up in the morning, she does not have to worry about a long commute to work. Her office is in her home. As an Amgen pharmaceutical sales representative, Deborah spends most of her day visiting hospitals, medical clinics, and doctors' offices. She spends a large part of each day serving as a consultant to doctors, head nurses, pharmacists, and others who need information and advice about the complex medical products available from her company. As might be expected, she also spends a considerable amount of time conducting informative presentations designed to achieve a variety of objectives. In some situations she is introducing a new product and in other cases she is providing up-to-date information on an existing product. Some of her presentations are given to individual health care professionals, and others are given to a group. Each of these presentations must be carefully planned.

Amgen began as a research and development laboratory. After developing a few breakthrough drugs and getting approval from the Federal Drug Administration (FDA) to sell them, a decision was made to create a manufacturing facility and initiate a nationwide marketing program. Although Amgen had discovered what might be described as "miracle" drugs, management knew that a sales force would be needed to win acceptance of the new products. Doctors are very cautious when it comes to prescribing a new drug to their patients. They demand accurate information concerning principal uses of the drug, dosage forms and strengths, dose instructions, and possible side effects.

Deborah uses informative and reminder presentations almost daily in her work. Informative presentations are given to doctors who are in a position to prescribe her products. The verbal presentation is often supplemented with audiovisual aids and printed materials. Reprints of articles from leading medical journals are often used to explain the success of her products in treating patients. These articles give added credibility to her presentations. Some of her informative presentations are designed to give customers updates on the prescription drugs she sells. Reminder presentations are frequently given to pharmacists who must maintain an inventory of her products. She has found that it is necessary to periodically remind pharmacists of product delivery procedures and policies, and special services available from Amgen. She knows that without an occasional reminder, a customer can forget information that is beneficial.

In some cases a careful needs analysis is needed to determine if her products can solve a specific medical problem. Every patient is different, so generalizations concerning the use of her products can be dangerous. When doctors talk about their patients, Deborah must listen carefully and take good notes. In some cases she must get additional information from company support staff. If a customer needs immediate help with a problem, she gives the person a toll-free 800 number to call for expert advice. This line is an important part of the Amgen customer service program.

Deborah's career in pharmaceutical sales has required continuous learning. In the beginning she had to learn the meaning of dozens of medical terms and become familiar with a large number of medical problems. If a doctor asks, "What is the bioavailability of Neutogen?" she must know the meaning of the medical term and be knowledgeable about this Amgen product.

Deborah also spends time learning about the people with whom she works. She recently said, "If I get along with the people I work with it makes my job a lot easier." When meeting someone for the first time, she takes time to assess his communication style and then adjusts her own style to meet his needs. She points out that in some cases the competition offers a similar product at a similar price. In these situations a good relationship with the customer can influence the purchase decision.

QUESTIONS

1. If you become a pharmaceutical sales representative, how important is it to adopt the three prescriptions for a presentation strategy? Explain.

2. Deborah Karish spends a great deal of time giving individual and group presentations. Why is it essential that she be well prepared for each presentation? Why would a *"canned"* presentation, one that is memorized and delivered almost word for word, be inappropriate in her type of selling?

3. Salespeople are encouraged to establish multiple-objective sales presentations. What are some objectives that Deborah Karish might achieve during a sales presentation to doctors who are not currently using her products?

4. What are some special challenges faced by Deborah Karish when she makes a group presentation? How might she enhance her group presentations?

5. Put yourself in the position of a pharmaceutical sales representative. Can you envision a situation when you might combine the elements of an informative, persuasive, and reminder presentation? Explain.

➤ S A L E S   A U T O M A T I O N   C A S E   S T U D Y

ACT! THE APPROACH

Becky Kemley, your sales manager at Cadalyst Resources, has notified Mark David's former prospects, by letter, that you will be calling on them soon. She wants to meet with you tomorrow to discuss your preapproach to your new prospects. Please review the prospect accounts that are included on the software disk enclosed with this textbook (see Chapter 8 Case Study).

Access the ACT! software following the instructions in Appendix 2.

Questions

1. Becky wants you to call on Robert Kelly. Describe what your call objectives will be with Mr. Kelly.

2. Describe a possible topic of your social contact with Mr. Kelly and how you would convert that to a buying contact.

3. Becky has given you a reprint of a new article about using CAD in warehouse automation. Which of your prospects might have a strong interest in this kind of article? How would you use this article to make an approach to that prospect?

PARTNERSHIP SELLING: A ROLE PLAY/SIMULATION (see Appendix 3, p. 421)

Developing a Relationship Strategy

Read *employment memorandum 2*, which announces your promotion to account executive. (In your new position, you will be assigned by your instructor to one of the two major account categories in the convention center market. You will be assigned to either the *association accounts market* or the *corporate accounts market*. Association accounts includes customers who have the responsibility for planning meetings for the association or group they are a member of, or are employed by. Corporate accounts includes customers who have responsibility for planning meetings for the company they represent. You will remain in the account category for the rest of the role plays.)

Note the challenges you will have in your new position. Each of these challenges will be represented in the future *sales memoranda* you will be receiving from your sales manager.

Read *sales memorandum 1* for the account category you are assigned. (Note that the "A" means association and your customer is Erin Adkins, and "B" means corporate and your customer is Leigh Combs.) Follow the instructions in the sales memorandum and strategically prepare to approach your new customer. Your call objectives will be to establish a relationship (social contact), share an appealing benefit, and find out if your customer is planning any future conventions (business contact).

You will be asked to assume the role of a customer in the account category that you are not assigned as a salesperson. Your instructor will provide you with detailed instructions for correctly assuming this role.

CHAPTER 10

Creating the Consultative Sales Presentation

LEARNING OBJECTIVES

When you finish reading this chapter, you should be able to

1. Describe the characteristics of the consultative sales presentation

2. Explain how to determine the prospect's needs

3. Discuss the use of questions to determine needs

4. Select products that match customer needs

5. List and describe three types of need-satisfaction presentation strategies

6. Present general guidelines for developing effective presentations

When Dave Tripp, sales representative for Harper Collins Publishers, won the "Sales Rep of the Year" award, his loyal customers were not surprised. To maximize service to his thirty retail and wholesale accounts in the Wisconsin and Minnesota area, he uses the consultative-selling approach exclusively. He takes pride in his ability to look through the bookseller's eyes and answer the question, "What can I do to bring more customers into this store?" Carol Erdahl, co-owner of The Red Balloon Bookshop, says, "It's his job to present what's new, but he's always looking out for us, suggesting things to promote the books."[1]

Tripp sees himself as a partner in the management of each bookstore. Drawing on his knowledge of what types of books sell well at each store, he works with buyers to predict demand for new releases. He also understands the value of building a relationship with store employees. He is on a first-name basis with salespeople at each store. He gets acquainted with their reading preferences and makes sure they get advanced copies of books in their favorite genres (science fiction, how-to, poetry, etc.).

Tripp's service to his customers is really the manifestation of such qualities as product knowledge (he needs to keep on top of a list of more than 16,000 books), dependability, and service after the sale.[2]

A growing number of salespeople, like David Tripp, have adopted the consultative sales presentation (Fig. 10.1). They support the selling philosophy expressed by Suzanne Vilardi, area sales manager of Swift Transportation:

> Be a consultant, a partner, an extension of your client's business. Be a friend, a problem solver. Balance your client's best interests with those of your own and your company.[3]

Figure 10.2 features key concepts related to creating the consultative-style sales presentation. This approach can be used effectively in the four major employment settings: service, retail, wholesale, and manufacturing. It results in increased customer satisfaction, more sales, fewer cancellations and returns, more repeat business, and more referrals.

The Consultative Sales Presentation

The sales presentation tells us a great deal about the degree of professionalism possessed by the salesperson and the company that the salesperson represents. David People, author of *Presentations Plus*, says, "The quality of your presenta-

The Six–Step Presentation Plan	
Step One: APPROACH	☑ Review Strategic/Consultative 　 Selling Model. ☑ Initiate customer contact.
Step Two: PRESENTATION	☐ Determine prospect needs. ☐ Select product or service. ☐ Initiate sales presentation.
Step Three: DEMONSTRATION	☐ Decide what to demonstrate. ☐ Select selling tools. ☐ Initiate demonstration.
Step Four: NEGOTIATION	☐ Anticipate sales resistance. ☐ Plan negotiating methods. ☐ Initiate double–win negotiations.
Step Five: CLOSE	☐ Plan appropriate closing methods. ☐ Recognize closing clues. ☐ Initiate closing methods.
Step Six: SERVICING THE SALE	☐ Suggestion selling. ☐ Follow through. ☐ Follow-up calls.
Service, retail, wholesale, and manufacturer selling.	

FIGURE 10.1   Creating the Sales Presentation

FIGURE 10.2 Salespeople who truly represent value to their customers plan ahead strategically for the actions taken during the presentation.

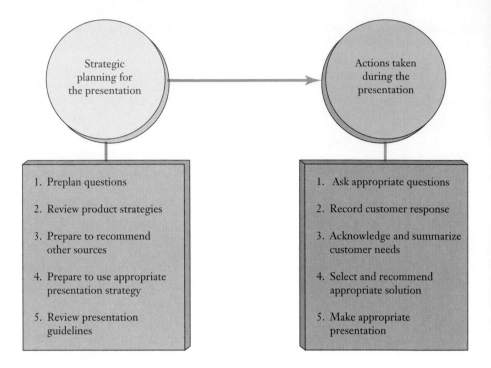

Strategic planning for the presentation

1. Preplan questions

2. Review product strategies

3. Prepare to recommend other sources

4. Prepare to use appropriate presentation strategy

5. Review presentation guidelines

Actions taken during the presentation

1. Ask appropriate questions

2. Record customer response

3. Acknowledge and summarize customer needs

4. Select and recommend appropriate solution

5. Make appropriate presentation

tion is a mirror image of the quality of your company, your product, your service, and your people."[4] To be most effective, the salesperson should think of the presentation as a four-part process. The Consultative Sales Presentation Guide (Fig. 10.3) features the four parts.

PART ONE—NEED DISCOVERY

A review of the behaviors displayed by high-performance salespeople helps us understand the importance of precise need discovery. They have learned how to skillfully diagnose and solve the customer's problems better than their competitors. This problem-solving capability translates into more repeat business and referrals, and fewer order cancellations and returns.

Unless the selling situation requires mere order taking (customers know exactly what they want), need discovery is a standard part of the sales presentation. It begins during the approach, when the salesperson uses questions or a survey during the initial contact with the customer. If neither of these two methods is used during the approach, need discovery begins immediately after the approach.

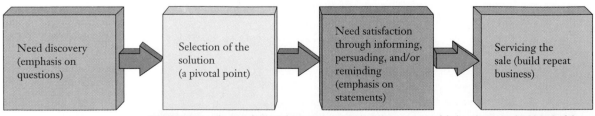

Need discovery (emphasis on questions)

Selection of the solution (a pivotal point)

Need satisfaction through informing, persuading, and/or reminding (emphasis on statements)

Servicing the sale (build repeat business)

FIGURE 10.3 The Consultative Sales Presentation Guide. To be most successful, the salesperson should think of the sales presentation as a four-part process.

The pace, scope, depth, and time allocated to inquiry depend on a variety of factors. Some of these include the sophistication of the product, the selling price, the customer's knowledge of the product, the product applications, and, of course, the time available for dialogue between the salesperson and the prospect. Each selling situation is different, so a standard set of guidelines for need discovery is not practical. Additional information on need discovery is presented later in the chapter.

PART TWO — SELECTION OF THE PRODUCT

The emphasis in marketing today is on determining customer needs and then creating or selecting custom-fitted solutions to satisfy these needs. Therefore an important function of the salesperson is product selection and recommendation. The salesperson must choose the product or service that will provide maximum satisfaction. When making this decision, the salesperson must be aware of all product options, including those offered by the competition. A John Deere farm equipment salesperson can, for example, offer a farmer a seed planter that features an almost endless combination of features. Some farmers want four-row planters; others want a twenty-four–row planter. Some use the planter to apply liquid fertilizer; others want a planter to apply dry fertilizer. A farmer can order a planter from Deere according to more than a million permutations.[5]

Salespeople who have the ability to diagnose a need accurately and select the correct product to fill this need usually experience a high degree of personal satisfaction and career success. These skills also make it possible to close more sales. Buyer resistance is less likely to surface when the correct product is prescribed.

PART THREE — NEED SATISFACTION THROUGH INFORMING, PERSUADING, OR REMINDING

The third part of the consultative sales presentation consists of communicating to the customer, both verbally and nonverbally, the satisfaction that the product or service will provide. The salesperson places less emphasis on the use of questions and begins making statements. These statements are organized into a presentation strategy that informs, persuades, or reminds the customer of the most suitable product or service. Later in this chapter, and in several of the remaining chapters, we discuss specific strategies to use during this phase of the sales presentation.

PART FOUR — SERVICING THE SALE

Servicing the sale is a major dimension of the selling process. These activities, which occur after closing the sale, ensure maximum customer satisfaction and set the stage for a long-term relationship with the customer. Service activities include suggestion selling, making credit arrangements, following through on assurances and promises, and dealing effectively with complaints. This topic is covered in detail in Chapter 14.

In those cases where a sale is normally closed during a single sales call, the salesperson should be prepared to go through all four parts of the Consultative Sales Presentation Guide. However, when a salesperson uses a multicall ap-

The sales presentation can inform, remind, or persuade.

proach, preparation for all the parts is usually not practical. The person selling life insurance or investments, for example, will almost always use a multicall sales presentation. Need discovery (part one) is the focus of the first call.

Need Discovery

A lawyer does not give the client advice until the legal problem has been carefully studied and confirmed. A doctor does not prescribe medication until the patient's symptoms have been identified. In like manner, the salesperson should not recommend purchase of a product without a thorough need identification.

Your best bet is to adopt the style used so successfully by most counselors. You start with the assumption that the client's problem is not known. The only way to determine and confirm the problem is to get the other person talking. You must obtain information to properly clarify the need. The counselor style requires that you be more concerned about the customer's welfare than closing the sale. This is consistent with the trend we discussed previously. The emphasis in selling is shifting from the product to the customer.

The counselor style often creates need awareness. Many customers do not realize that they actually have a need for your product or service. Even when they are aware of their need, they may not realize that an actual solution to their problem exists.

Need discovery begins with precall preparation when the salesperson is acquiring background information on the prospect. It continues once the salesperson and the customer are engaged in a real dialogue. Through the process of need discovery the salesperson establishes two-way communication by asking appropriate questions and listening carefully to the customer's responses. These responses will usually provide clues concerning the customer's dominant buying motive (Fig. 10.4).

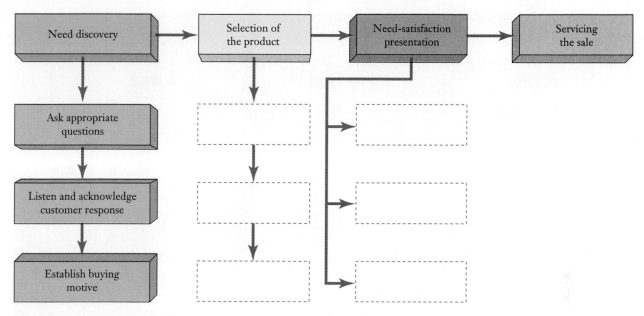

FIGURE 10.4   Three Dimensions of Need Discovery

ASKING QUESTIONS

Questions provide one of the most effective ways to involve the prospect. Appropriate questions reduce tension and build trust in a selling situation because they communicate interest in the other person's welfare. A sales presentation devoid of questions closes the door on meaningful two-way communication.

The art and science of using questions were discussed by Socrates more than 2,300 years ago. He noted, among other things, that questions tend to make people think. Kevin Daley, CEO of Communispond, describes the benefits of the Socratic approach: "The customer opens up and gives lots of useful information. A high level of trust is established, and the customer owns the decisions made."[6] In any selling situation we want the prospect to be actively thinking, sharing thoughts, and asking questions. Julie C. Wang, CEO of Wang Associates Health Communications, a New York City public relations company, warns us not to use a presentation that is too structured. She says, "Unless clients are interacting with you, you don't have any idea what issues are on their minds."[7] Until the person begins to talk freely, the salesperson will have difficulty discovering dominant buying motives and perceptions. A well-planned sales presentation will include a variety of preplanned questions (Table 10.1). We will describe the four most common types of questions used in the field of personal selling.

INFORMATION-GATHERING QUESTIONS

Linda Richardson, an adjunct personal selling professor at the Wharton Graduate School, has developed a corporate sales training program called Dialogue Selling. She says that the first step in the partnership-building process is to ask general questions that help you acquire important information about the prospect.[8] At the beginning of most sales presentations, there is a need to col-

TABLE 10.1 TYPES OF QUESTIONS USED IN CONJUNCTION WITH CONSULTATIVE SELLING

TYPE OF QUESTION	DEFINITION	WHEN USED	EXAMPLES
Information-gathering questions	*General questions designed to get the prospect to disclose certain types of basic information*	*Usually at the beginning of a sale*	*"How many miles per year do you drive your company car?" (auto leasing)*
Probing questions	*More specific questions designed to uncover and clarify the prospect's perceptions and opinions*	*When you feel the need to obtain more specific information that is needed to fully understand the problem and prescribe a solution*	*"What type of image do you want your advertising to project to current and potential customers?" (newspaper advertising)*
Confirmation questions	*Designed to find whether or not your message is understood by the prospect*	*After each important item of information is presented*	*"Do you see the merits of purchasing a copy machine with the document enlargement feature?" (office copy machine)*
Summary confirmation questions	*Designed to clarify your understanding of the prospect's needs and buying conditions*	*Usually used after several items of information have been presented*	*"I would like to summarize what you have told me thus far. You want a four-bedroom home with a basement and a two-car garage." (real estate)*

lect certain basic information such as: Why the prospect is considering a purchase (need); what product configuration is desired (product); what suppliers the prospect is considering (source); how much the prospect is planning to spend (price); and when the purchase will be made (time). **Information-gathering questions** are designed to elicit such information (see Table 10.1).

In most cases the information-gathering question is easy to answer. These questions help us acquire facts about the prospect that may reveal the person's need for the product or service. Questions of this type also help build rapport

A good salesperson and a good doctor have one thing in common. They encourage questions. *(Reprinted with special permission of King Features Syndicate.)*

with the customer. Here are some information-gathering questions that are used in selected selling fields.

"What price range did you have in mind?" (real estate)

"Do most of the packages you mail exceed twenty pounds?" (air freight)

"How many people will attend your meeting?" (hotel conference facilities)

Many salespeople use preplanned information-gathering questions. These questions are sometimes listed on a form or checklist. If the company does not provide a preprinted form or checklist, a worksheet (Table 10.2) can be easily developed. It is common practice to get the customer's permission before asking the first question. You might simply ask, "Do you mind if I get your answers to a few questions?"

PROBING QUESTIONS

Throughout the sales presentation the salesperson should make every effort to clarify the prospects' perceptions and opinions. Some will have a limited vocabulary for describing their problems; they know a problem exists but have difficulty expressing their views. High-performance salespeople realize that there is a common tendency for people to speak in generalities.[9]

Probing questions help you to uncover and clarify the prospect's perceptions and opinions (see Table 10.1). These questions encourage customers to give you more details about their problems. The more time customers invest in

---

TABLE 10.2 NEED DISCOVERY WORKSHEET

Preplanned questions (sometimes used with preprinted forms) are increasingly being used in service, retail, wholesale, and manufacturer selling. Salespeople who use the consultative approach frequently record answers to their questions and use this information to correctly select and recommend solutions that build repeat business and referrals. (Questions taken from **Shearson Lehman Brothers Selling Skills Training Program.**)

PREPLANNED QUESTIONS TO DISCOVER BUYING MOTIVES	CUSTOMER RESPONSE
1. *"Tell me a little bit about your investment portfolio."*	
2. *"What is the history of your family income?"*	
3. *"What are your major concerns when managing your financial affairs?"*	
4. *"What are your current investment objectives?"*	
5. *"What do you expect from your financial services consultants?"*	
6.	
7.	
8.	
9.	
10.	

talking to you about their problems, the greater your chance of seeing the total picture.

Although probing techniques will vary from one selling situation to another, there is a general format you should observe. Your probing should begin on a general basis and gradually narrow to the specifics that will ultimately give you the information needed to fully understand the problem and prescribe a solution.[10] Here are two examples of general probing questions:

"How do you feel about using a computer to keep your expense records?"

"What kinds of solutions have you already considered?"

These general probing questions are not threatening, and they give prospects a chance to talk about a problem or issue from their point of view. These questions also keep the focus of the sales presentation on the customer's agenda. General probing questions establish a rapport that is hard to achieve in any other way.

As the sales presentation progresses, you will need to use more specific probing questions that uncover the clues you need to custom fit your product or service to the prospect's needs. The following probing questions are more specific and more focused:

"What will be the consequences if you choose to do nothing about your current record-keeping problems?"

"Would a 20 percent reduction in turnaround time improve your profit picture?"

The best sales presentations are characterized by active dialogue. As the presentation progresses, the customer becomes more open and shares perceptions, ideas, and feelings freely. A series of good probing questions will stimulate the

This real estate salesperson, with the help of a computerized database of homes, is using probing and confirmation questions to clarify the needs of the customer.

BUILDING QUALITY PARTNERSHIPS

SOLVING CUSTOMER PROBLEMS USING A MULTIPLE QUESTION APPROACH

Neil Rackham conducted studies of 35,000 sales calls and from this research developed the material for his book entitled *Spin Selling*. The book describes strategies for making large-ticket sales and is based on a close examination of successful salespeople. SPIN is an acronym for situation, problem, implication, and need-payoff. Rackham recommends the multiple question approach which involves using four types of questions in a specific sequence.

Situation questions. These questions are used to collect facts and background information about the customer's existing situation. Some examples of situation questions include: How long have you held this position? How many people do you currently employ? Do you usually purchase or lease your equipment? These questions help you acquire information that may be needed later in the sales presentation.

Problem questions. These questions help the salesperson uncover specific problems, difficulties, or dissatisfactions. The salesperson is searching for areas where her product or service can solve existing problems. Examples of problem questions are:

Does your Canon copy machine make copies fast enough for you? Are you happy with your current lease plan? If the salesperson discovers a problem area, he uses implication questions.

Implication questions. These questions encourage the customer to think about the consequences of the problem. The objective of implication questions is to get the customer to understand the true dimensions of the problem area. If the customer who owns the Canon copy machine complains about delays caused by slow operation of the machine, the salesperson might ask this implication question: "Does the slow operation of the machine have a negative impact on office productivity? How do you think a faster copy machine would improve office productivity?" The reply might be, "It would reduce payroll because less operator time would be required."

Need-payoff questions. These questions build up the value or usefulness of a proposed solution in the customer's mind. Need-payoff questions focus on the solution rather than the problem. Here is an example: "Would restricted phone lines provide the cost savings you desire?"[a]

prospect to discover things that he had not considered before. Too many rapid fire probing questions may be threatening to your customer and should be avoided.

CONFIRMATION QUESTIONS

As a ship moves from one port to another, the captain and crew must continuously check instruments to be certain they stay on course. In a selling situation you must, from time to time, use confirmation questions to avoid the same problem. Is your language too technical? Is the prospect listening to you? Are you on target in terms of the person's needs and interests? Does the prospect agree with what you are saying? **Confirmation questions** are used throughout the presentation to determine if the message is correctly understood by the prospect (see Table 10.1). Many confirmation questions are simple and to the point.

"Do you agree with the findings?"

"If I understand you correctly, you want the Dolby 'C' noise reduction feature, is that correct?"

"Will this location appeal to your business partner?"

"Would you like me to explain how the security system is activated?"

Confirmation questions not only maintain the prospect's attention but also they clear up misunderstandings. In an ideal situation, the salesperson is getting feedback from the prospect throughout the presentation.

SUMMARY CONFIRMATION QUESTIONS

The length of a sales presentation can vary from a few minutes to an hour or more, depending on the nature of the product, the customer's knowledge of the product, and other factors. As the sales call progresses, the amount of information available to the salesperson and the customer increases. In most cases, the customer's buying conditions surface. **Buying conditions** are those qualifications that must be available or fulfilled before the sale can be closed. The customer may buy only if the product is available in a certain color or can be delivered by a certain date. In some selling situations, product installation or service after the sale are considered important buying conditions by the customer. In a complex sale, several buying conditions may surface. The salesperson has the responsibility of clarifying and confirming each condition.

One of the best ways to clarify and confirm buying conditions is with **summary-confirmation questions** (see Table 10.1). To illustrate, let us consider a situation where Tammy Harris, sales manager at a major hotel, has interviewed a prospect who wants to schedule a large awards banquet. After a series of information-gathering, probing, and confirmation questions, Tammy feels confident she has collected enough information to prepare a proposal. However, to be sure that she has all the facts and has clarified all important buying conditions, she asks the following summary confirmation questions:

> "Let me summarize the major items you have mentioned. You need a room that will comfortably seat sixty persons and ten of these persons will be seated at the head table?"

If the customer responds in the affirmative, Tammy continues with another summary confirmation question:

> "You want chicken served as the main course, and the price per person for the entire meal cannot exceed $15?"

Once all the buying conditions are confirmed, Tammy can prepare a proposal that reflects the specific needs of the customer, which results in a win-win situation. The salesperson wins because the proposal will be custom fitted to meet the customer's requirements. The chances of closing the sale improve. Also, the customer wins because she had the opportunity to clarify buying conditions and will now be able to review a specific proposal.

ELIMINATE UNNECESSARY QUESTIONS

It is important to avoid the use of unnecessary questions during a sales call. Salespeople need to acquire as much information as possible about the prospect before the first meeting. This preliminary information gathering is especially important when the prospect is a corporate buyer. These buyers expect the salesperson to be well informed about their operation and not waste time asking a large number of basic information-gathering questions. A growing number of corporate buyers want to establish a long-term partnership with suppliers. They assume that potential partners will conduct a careful study of their company before the first sales call.

BUILDING RELATIONSHIPS THROUGH TECHNOLOGY

PRESENTATION PLANNING WITH ACT! HARDCOPY

Salespeople regularly review the status of their prospects' files in their automated database. In some cases, this is done on the computer screen. In other situations, a printed copy of the database can enhance the process.

Salespeople review their files to ascertain at what phase each prospect is in the sales cycle. Then they will decide which action to take to help move the prospect to the next phase. Sales managers can be helpful with this process, especially for new salespeople. Managers can help salespeople evaluate the available information and suggest strategies designed to move to the next phase.

Even experienced salespeople count on their sales managers to help plan presentations. Managers can help salespeople evaluate their prospects' needs, select the best solution, and plan a presentation most likely to succeed. (See Sales Automation Application Exercise on p. 243 for more information.)

LISTENING, AND ACKNOWLEDGING THE CUSTOMER'S RESPONSE

Stephen Covey, the noted author and consultant, says that most salespeople sell products, not solutions. To correct this situation he encourages us, "Seek first to understand, then to be understood."[11] To understand the customer, we must listen closely and acknowledge every response.

The listening efficiency rate for most people is about 25 percent. This means they miss about 75 percent of the messages spoken by other people. Do salespeople do any better in this vital area of person-to-person communications? Research conducted by Communispond Incorporated, a New York-based consulting firm, indicates that the answer is probably no. A survey of 432 buyers at small as well as large companies found that salespeople talk too much and listen too little. Only 28 percent of the buyers said that they were impressed by salespeople who "really listen."[12]

With a little self-determination, most salespeople can improve their listening skills. One salesperson, aware of this limitation, decided he needed a constant reminder to listen more and talk less. His solution was to put a series of small signs that said *listen* in places where he would see them every day. He placed one on his bathroom mirror. He taped another sign inside his attaché case so he would see it just before each sales presentation. He even put a small listen sign on the rearview mirror of his car.

DEVELOPING ACTIVE LISTENING SKILLS

What does listening really mean? Dr. Frank Cancelliere, founder of Listening Dynamics, defines listening as "the active process of receiving and understanding what the other person is saying from their point of view."[13] He says that all too frequently, hearing is confused with listening.

The late Carl Rogers stated that through active listening we can understand what people mean when they speak and what they are feeling. **Active listening** is the process of sending back to the person what you as a listener think the individual meant, both in terms of content and in terms of feelings. It involves taking into consideration both verbal and nonverbal signals.[14] This ap-

In many selling situations note taking will demonstrate a high level of professionalism.

proach to listening enables the salesperson to check on the accuracy of what the customer said and what the customer meant. When the listener gives feedback to the speaker, the speaker has the opportunity to confirm or amend the listener's perceptions. Active listening involves four techniques that can be easily learned.

Encourage talking Let the prospects know you are listening and you want them to continue talking. This can be done by voicing such phrases as "I see," "good point," "uh-huh," and "go on." These short *prompts* or *cues* indicate that you understand the person's message and you want him to keep talking.[15]

Take notes Although note taking is not necessary in every sales presentation, it is important in complex sales where the information obtained from the customer is critical to the development of a good proposal. It is important that you capture your customer's major points. Make sure your notes are brief and to the point.[16] Lauren Arethas, eastern regional manager for *Interiors* magazine, says that a note pad and pen represent her most important sales tools. She says that when customers see her taking notes, their posture changes from a defensive, "Here comes the sales pitch," to a welcoming, "My needs are important."[17]

Paraphrase the customer's meaning with a confirmation question This involves stating in your own words what you think the person meant. This technique not only helps ensure understanding but also is an effective customer relations strategy. The customer will feel good knowing that not only are you listening to what has been said but also you are making an effort to ensure accuracy.

Express an understanding of the customer's feelings and perceptions In addition to paraphrasing the content, echo the feelings you felt were expressed or implied. It is important that we check on our perception of the customer's feelings. This step is especially helpful if the person is experiencing negative emotions such as doubt or frustration. When we describe our perception of the customer's feelings, that person is given the opportunity to elaborate on these feelings.

Obtain feedback We can ask questions to ensure our own understanding of the customer's thoughts and perceptions and to secure additional relevant

Sales Force Automation. Custom-fitted product selections and sales proposals can be matched immediately with complex customer needs by Xerox salespeople who use this TI-74 laptop computer.

information which can be described as **feedback.** Questions help us clarify misunderstanding.

Active listening is not easy. Gerry Mitchell, chairman of the Dana Corporation, described listening as "tough and grinding work." Like learning to give a speech, learning to listen takes practice. Many salespeople are enrolling in seminars and workshops designed to develop listening skills.

ESTABLISHING BUYING MOTIVES

The primary goal of questioning, listening, and acknowledging is to uncover prospect needs and establish buying motives. Our efforts to discover prospect needs will be more effective if we focus our questioning on determining the prospect's primary reasons for buying. When a customer has a definite need, it is usually supported by specific buying motives.

Selection of the Product

The second part of the consultative-style sales presentation consists of selecting or creating a solution that satisfies the prospect's buying motives. After identifying the buying motives the salesperson carefully reviews the available product options. At this point the salesperson is searching for a specific solution to satisfy the prospect's buying motives. Once the solution has been selected, the salesperson makes a recommendation to the prospect (Fig. 10.5).

If the sale involves several needs and the satisfaction of multiple buying motives, selection of the solution may take several days or even weeks, and involve the preparation of a detailed sales proposal. A company considering the purchase of automated office equipment would likely present this type of challenge to the salesperson. The problem needs careful analysis before a solution can be identified.

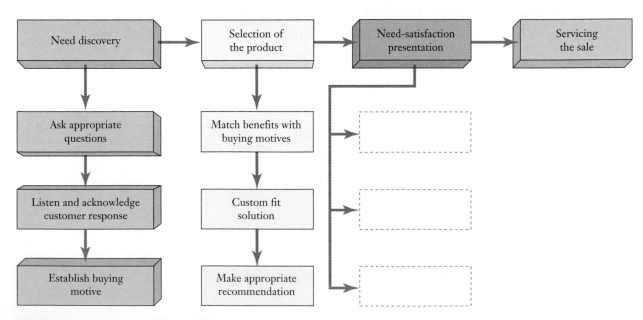

FIGURE 10.5 Three Dimensions of Product Selection

MATCH SPECIFIC BENEFITS WITH BUYING MOTIVES

As we noted in Chapter 6, products and services represent problem-solving tools. People buy products when they perceive that they fulfill a need. We also noted that today's more demanding customers seek a cluster of satisfactions that arise from the product itself, from the company that makes or distributes the product, and from the salesperson who sells and services the product (see Fig. 6.1). Each of these clusters may add value to the sale. Once the customer's needs and buying motives are firmly established, the salesperson can determine which specific benefits to emphasize. The emphasis here is on *specific* rather than *general* benefits. Research indicates that the success of a sales call is related to the number of different needs discovered and the specific benefits highlighted in response to those needs.

Vicki Lynn Cusick attempts to custom-fit her product solutions to meet the unique needs of each customer. Her average sale includes 31 items selected from the 5,000 products she represents.

CUSTOM FIT A SOLUTION

Most salespeople bring to the sale a variety of products or services. Vicki Lynn Cusick, a top salesperson for Atlantic Food Services, Incorporated, a Manassas, Virginia food distributor, can offer customers a mix of more than 5,000 items. A typical order from the restaurants she visits includes thirty-one different items.[18] Circuit City, a large retailer of electronics, offers customers a wide range of audio and visual entertainment options. The customer who wants to purchase a sound system, for example, can choose from many combinations of receivers, speakers, and so on.

MAKE APPROPRIATE RECOMMENDATIONS

The recommendation strategies available to salespeople are similar to those used by a doctor who must recommend a solution to a patient's medical problem. In the medical field, three possibilities for providing patient satisfaction exist. In situations in which the patient easily understands the medical problem and the appropriate treatment, the doctor can make a recommendation, and the patient can proceed immediately toward a cure. If the patient does not easily understand the medical problem or solution, the doctor may need to discuss

cathy®   **by Cathy Guisewite**

thoroughly with the patient the benefits of the recommended treatment. If the medical problem is within a medical specialty area, the doctor may recommend a trained specialist to provide the treatment. In consultative selling the salesperson has these same three counseling alternatives available to provide satisfaction to prospects.

RECOMMEND PRODUCT—CUSTOMER BUYS IMMEDIATELY

The selection and recommendation of products to meet customer needs may occur at the beginning of the sales interview, such as in the product approach; during the interview, just after the need discovery; or near the end, when suggestion selling occurs. At any of these three times, presentation of products that are well matched to the prospect's needs may result in an immediate purchase.

Immediate purchases often result when the customer is well aware of her need and the product that will fulfill the need, when product benefits are easily understood, and when the products being offered are well selected by the salesperson.

RECOMMEND PRODUCT—SALESPERSON MAKES NEED-SATISFACTION PRESENTATION

This alternative requires a full presentation of product benefits including demonstrations and handling of any objections before the sale is closed. In this situation the customer may not be totally aware of a buying problem, and the solution may not be easily understood or apparent. Because of this, the salesperson will need to make an in-depth presentation to define the problem and communicate a solution to the customer.

RECOMMEND ANOTHER SOURCE

Earlier in this book we indicated that professional salespeople may recommend that a prospect buy a product or service from another source, maybe even a competitor. If, after a careful needs assessment, the salesperson concludes that the products represented will not satisfy the customer's needs, the consultative salesperson will recommend another source.

Need Satisfaction—Selecting a Presentation Strategy

Decisions concerning which presentation strategy to emphasize have become more complex. This is due to several factors discussed in previous chapters: longer sales cycles, multiple buying influences, emphasis on repeat sales and referrals, greater emphasis on custom fitting of products, and building of long-term partnerships. The result is a need for a broader range of presentation strategies. Today, the need-satisfaction strategy involves assessing the customer's needs; selecting the product; and deciding whether to use an informative, persuasive, or reminder presentation (Fig. 10.6).

INFORMATIVE PRESENTATION STRATEGY

To be informative, a message must be clearly understood by the customer. Of course, clarity is important in any presentation, but it needs special attention in a presentation whose primary purpose is to inform. The **informative presen-**

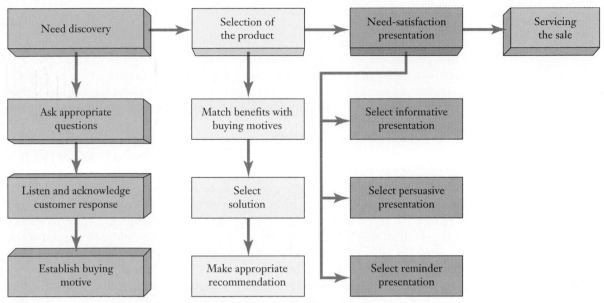

FIGURE 10.6   The Three Strategies to Use in Developing an Effective Need-Satisfaction Presentation

tation emphasizes factual information often taken from technical reports, company-prepared sales literature, or written testimonials from persons who have used the product. This type of presentation is commonly used to introduce new products and services. This strategy emphasizes clarity, simplicity, and directness.[19]

A variety of factors motivate sales personnel to adopt the informative presentation. Some have discovered that this strategy works best when you sell highly complex products that have to be custom fitted to unique needs. In addition, if the product's price is quite high, a factual presentation, devoid of emotion, may be the best approach. Some salespeople simply think that it is not appropriate to use persuasion during the sales presentation. They believe that a product should stand on its own merits and persuasion should not be necessary to sell it.

Within every major industry, new products are appearing at a rapid rate. In the grocery industry, for example, annual new product introductions number in the thousands. Many of these products are introduced to wholesalers and retailers through informative sales presentations. Sales personnel representing Procter and Gamble, Nabisco, General Mills, and many other companies deliver informative sales presentations on a regular basis.

PERSUASIVE PRESENTATION STRATEGY

Many salespeople believe that when a real need for their product exists, the stage is set for a persuasive presentation. The major goal of the **persuasive presentation** strategy is to influence the prospect's beliefs, attitudes, or behavior and to encourage buyer action. As one sales training consultant noted, "Persuasive selling is the ability to persuade someone to do what you want them to do . . . because they want to do it." He further stated that one of the most gratifying things we can do is persuade other people to our way of thinking when we genuinely care about their welfare and know that the product will provide them with significant satisfaction.[20]

Persuasion is commonly used in all professions. Medical doctors routinely use persuasion to influence patient behavior. In fact, doctors involved in the growing field of preventive medicine rely heavily on persuasion to encourage patients to adopt certain health practices. Teachers use persuasion to encourage students to complete assignments. Lawyers use persuasion to influence clients' feelings and opinions.

In the field of personal selling, persuasion is an acceptable strategy once a need has been identified and a suitable product has been selected. When it is clear that the buyer will benefit from ownership of the product or service, an enthusiastic and persuasive sales presentation is usually appropriate.

The persuasive presentation strategy requires a high level of training and experience to be effective, because a poorly planned and delivered persuasive presentation may raise the prospect's anxiety level. Be especially careful when calling on repeat customers or when making a multicall presentation. If you rely totally on the persuasive presentation in these situations, prospects may think they are being pushed into a purchase. The persuasive presentation, when handled properly, does not trigger fear or distrust.

REMINDER PRESENTATION STRATEGY

Studies show that awareness of a company's products and services declines as promotion is stopped. This problem represents one of the reasons many companies employ missionary salespeople to maintain an ongoing awareness and familiarity with their product lines. Other types of salespeople also use this presentation strategy. Route salespeople rely heavily on **reminder presentations** (sometimes called *reinforcement presentations*) to maintain their market share. They know that if they do not make frequent calls and remind customers of their products, the competition will likely capture some customers. The 12,800 Frito-Lay salespeople are in a strong position to use the reminder presentation strategy because they use handheld computers to manage orders. It only takes a minute or two to review a programmed product list in the presence of a customer.[21]

The reminder presentation also has many applications at the retail level. Sales personnel working with repeat customers are in a good position to remind them of products or services offered in their own department or another department located in some other area of the store.

Reminder presentations assume that in most cases the prospect understands at least the basic product features and buyer benefits. Salespeople using this strategy understand the value of repetition. They know that many of their recommendations will not be accepted until the second, third, or fourth time.

In some cases the reminder presentation will focus on factors other than a specific product or service. The presentation may include information that will indirectly influence the sale. When Nabisco sales representatives discuss their established products, they can point out that a large percentage of all cookies purchased by consumers are Nabisco products. Nabisco's cookies are delivered directly to supermarkets and other outlets by route salespeople who must negotiate every inch of scarce shelf space.[22]

Guidelines for Developing a Persuasive Presentation Strategy

There are many ways to incorporate persuasion into a sales presentation. In this section we review a series of guidelines that should be followed during preparation of a persuasive presentation.

PLACE SPECIAL EMPHASIS ON THE RELATIONSHIP

Throughout this book we have emphasized the importance of the relationship strategy in selling. Good rapport between the salesperson and the prospect is a necessary foundation for the use of a persuasive sales presentation. Robert Cialdini, an Arizona State University faculty member who specializes in persuasion research, says that people prefer to comply with requests or suggestions from people they know and like.[23] People seldom purchase products from salespeople they dislike or distrust.

Never presume a personal relationship with a buyer that does not exist. Sid Brown, a purchasing manager at James River Corporation, is one of many buyers who is irritated by a salesperson who "doesn't know me and acts like they've known me for years." He believes that a professional relationship needs to develop before a salesperson can project a high degree of sincerity.[24]

SELL BENEFITS AND OBTAIN CUSTOMER REACTIONS

People do not buy things, they buy what the things will do for them. They do not buy an auto battery, they buy a sure start on a cold morning. Office managers do not buy laser printers, they buy better looking letters and reports. Every product or service offers the customer certain benefits. The benefit might be greater comfort, security, feeling of confidence, or economy.

Some salespeople make the mistake of emphasizing only product features. They fail to translate these features into buyer benefits. If you are selling Allstate insurance, for example, you should become familiar with the service features. One feature is well-trained employees and the convenient location of Allstate offices across the nation. The benefit to customers is greater peace of mind in knowing that they will receive good service at a nearby location.

After you state the feature and convert it into a buyer benefit, obtain a reaction from the customer. You should always check to see if you are on the right track and your prospect is following the logic of your presentation. The reactions can be triggered by a simple confirming question. Here are some examples:

Feature	Benefit	Confirming question
Commercial-size package	Money saved	"You are interested in saving money, are you not?"
Automatic climate control system for automobile	Temperature in car not varying after initial setting	Would you like the luxury of setting the temperature and then not worrying about it?"

The feature-benefit-reaction (FBR) approach is used by many high-performance salespeople. Involving the customer with a confirmation question helps you maintain two-way communication with the customer.

MINIMIZE THE NEGATIVE IMPACT OF CHANGE

As we noted earlier, salespeople are constantly threatening the status quo. They sell people the new, the different, and the untried. In nearly all selling situations the customer is being asked to consider change of some sort, and in some cases it is only natural for the person to resist change.

Whenever possible, we should try to help the customer view change in a positive and realistic way. Change is more acceptable to people who understand the benefits of it and do not see it as a threat to their security. The prospect must be given realistic expectations about the products they are buying.[25] If the salesperson creates unrealistic expectations by exaggerating buyer benefits, long-term problems will likely surface. The credibility of the salesperson and the company he represents may suffer.

PLACE THE STRONGEST APPEAL AT THE BEGINNING OR END

Research indicates that appeals made at the beginning or end of a presentation are more effective than those given in the middle. A strong appeal at the beginning of a presentation, of course, will get the prospect's attention and possibly develop interest. Made near the end of the presentation, the appeal sets the stage for closing the sale.

USE A PERSUASIVE VOCABULARY

When developing a persuasive presentation, use words that will get the prospect's attention and build interest in your proposal. Several years ago a group of Yale University scholars published a list of the twelve most persuasive words in the English language: you, money, save, new, results, health, easy, safety, love, discovery, proven, and guarantee. Several of these words are appropriate for sales presentations. The word *partnership* has become one of the most persuasive words in the 1990s so far. It is a word that sends out the message, "I am looking out for your welfare." The salesperson who says, "I want to become a long-term partner with my customers" and means it will get the prospect's attention.

USE METAPHORS AND STORIES

Metaphors, sometimes referred to as *figurative language*, are highly persuasive sales tools. Metaphors are words or phrases that suggest pictorial relationships between objects or ideas. With the aid of metaphors you can paint vivid, visual pictures for prospects that will command their attention and keep their interest. The success of the metaphor rests on finding common ground (shared or well-known experiences) so that your message gets a free boost from a fact already known or believed to be true.[26] A salesperson presenting the expensive Wheel Horse garden tractor said, "This is the Mercedez-Benz of garden tractors," to emphasize the quality of this high-ticket product.

Donald J. Moine, noted speaker and sales trainer, says that stories will not only help you sell more products but also they will help you enrich relationships with your customers.[27] Not only does a good story focus the customer's attention, it can effectively communicate the value of a product or a service.

General Guidelines for Creating Effective Presentations

There are many ways to make all three need-satisfaction presentation strategies more interesting and more valuable. A more effective presentation can be developed using the following general guidelines. Each of these guidelines will be discussed in more detail in Chapters 11 to 14.

ENHANCE THE PRESENTATION STRATEGY WITH AN EFFECTIVE DEMONSTRATION

The need-satisfaction presentation can be strengthened if the salesperson pre-plans effective demonstrations that clarify the product features and benefits. When possible, demonstrations should also highlight the features and benefits that will satisfy the customer's buying motives and develop understanding of how the product performs.

Many salespeople encounter doubt or skepticism during the sales presentation. The prospect often wants some kind of assurance or proof. We must be prepared to substantiate our claims with factual information. This information can be provided in several ways. The following list of proof strategies is explained in detail in Chapter 11.

The product itself	Reprints
Models	Portfolios
Photos and illustrations	Graphs, charts, and test results
Samples	Guarantees and warranties
Testimonials and case histories	Audiovisual aids

Sales Force Automation. Salespeople can enhance their presentation strategy with proof device produced on computer software packages such as the popular Microsoft® PowerPoint®.

PREPLAN METHODS FOR NEGOTIATING AND CLOSING THE SALE

It is a good idea to assume that customers want to make the most efficient use of the time they spend purchasing goods and services. To make your presentation as concise and to the point as possible, you should preplan methods for negotiating misunderstandings or resistance that often surface during the presentation. You need to bring some degree of urgency to the selling environment by presenting focused solutions.[28] In most cases the focus of the negotiation will be on one of the following areas:

➢ *Need* awareness is vague or nonexistent.

➢ *Price* does not equal perceived value.

➢ The buyer is satisfied with present *source*.

➢ The *product* does not meet the buyer's perceived requirement.

Methods used to negotiate buyer resistance in each of these areas are introduced in Chapter 12.

It is also important to preplan closing and confirming the sale. This planning should include a review of closing clues that may surface during the sales presentation and methods of closing the sale. These and other topics are discussed in Chapter 13.

PLAN FOR THE DYNAMIC NATURE OF SELLING

The sales presentation is a dynamic activity. From the moment the salesperson and the customer meet, the sales presentation is being altered and fine-tuned to reflect the new information available. During a typical presentation the salesperson will ask numerous questions, discuss several product features, and de-

The dynamic nature of selling requires that the salesperson be prepared to respond to a wide variety of questions from the customer.

scribe the appropriate product benefits. The customer is also asking questions and, in many cases, voicing concerns. The successful sales presentation is a good model of two-way communication. Because of the dynamic nature of the sales presentation, the salesperson must be prepared to apply several different selling skills to meet the variety of buyer responses. Figure 10.7 illustrates how

Consultative selling skills	Parts of the Sales Presentation			
	Need discovery	Selecting solution	Need–satisfaction presentation	Servicing the sale
Questioning skills	• As a question approach • To find needs and buying motives • To probe for buying motives • To confirm needs and buying motives	• To confirm selection	• To confirm benefits • To confirm mutual understanding	• To make suggestions • To confirm delivery and installations • To handle complaints • To build goodwill • To secure credit arrangements
Presenting benefits	• As a benefit approach • To discover potential benefits	• To match up with buying motives	• To present and summarize features effectively	• To make suggestions • To use credit as a close
Demonstrating skills	• As a product approach • To clarify need	• To clarify selection	• To strengthen product claims	• When making effective suggestions
Negotiating skills	• To overcome initial resistance to sales interview • To overcome need objection	• To overcome product objection	• To overcome source, price, and time objection	• In handling complaints • To overcome financing objection
Closing skills	• When customer has made buying decision	• When buyer immediately recognizes solutions	• Whenever buyer presents closing signals	• After suggestion • To secure repeats and referrals

FIGURE 10.7   The Selling Dynamics Matrix. Salespeople can select from a variety of skills throughout the sales presentation.

the various selling skills can be applied during all parts of the sales presentation. For example, a salesperson must be prepared to use questioning skills when discovering needs, selecting a solution, conducting the need-satisfaction presentation, and servicing the sale. In creating effective presentations the salesperson should be prepared to meet a wide range of buyer responses with effective questions, benefit statements, demonstrations, negotiating methods, and closing methods.

KEEP YOUR PRESENTATION SIMPLE AND CONCISE

Numerous surveys have found that customers like sales presentations that are concise and free of unnecessary complexity. When the salesperson gives clients too much information or discusses topics that do not deal with their individual needs, they simply stop paying attention.[29]

The best way to achieve conciseness is to preplan your sales call. Think ahead of time about what you are going to say and do. Anticipate questions and objections the prospect may voice, and be prepared with accurate information and concise answers.

It is not always easy to determine the amount of detail to include in the sales presentation. A good rule of thumb is to tailor the presentation to meet the prospect's needs. Several years ago the KISS principle was introduced to the field of selling. This popular acronym stands for "keep it simple and straightforward." In other words, never make your sales presentation more complex than it needs to be.

SUMMARIZE THE PRESENTATION

Although a sales presentation may last only thirty minutes, the salesperson will have the opportunity to cover a great deal of information. Most people talk at a speed of about 125 words per minute. In a short time span of just fifteen minutes, the customer may be bombarded with approximately 1,900 words. For this reason the salesperson should summarize the presentation. The most effective summary statements emphasize benefits, not features. The *summary-of-benefits close* is discussed in detail in Chapter 13.

USE TIME WISELY

In many selling situations there is a certain amount of time pressure. Rarely does a salesperson have an unlimited amount of time to spend with the customer. Some buyers schedule their appointments at fifteen- or thirty-minute intervals.

Figure 10.8 illustrates an ideal breakdown of time allocation between the salesperson and the prospect during all three parts of the sales presentation. In terms of involvement the prospect assumes a greater role during the need-discovery stage. This is logical because the customer is usually in the best position to explain needs. As the salesperson begins the product selection process, the prospect's involvement decreases. During the need-satisfaction stage the salesperson is doing most of the talking, but note that the prospect is never excluded totally.

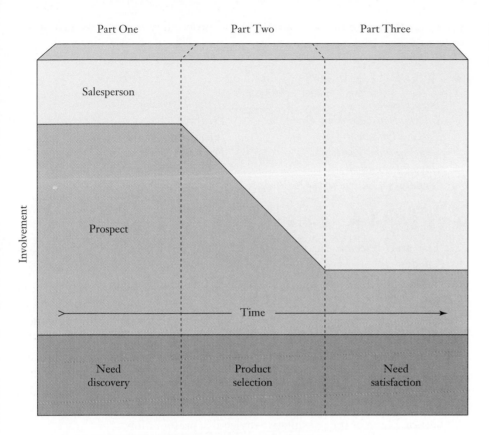

FIGURE 10.8 Time Used by Salesperson and Customer during Each Part of the Consultative Sales Presentation

SUMMARY

A well-planned and well-executed presentation strategy is an important key to success in personal selling. To be most effective, the presentation should be viewed as a three-part process: *need discovery*, selection of the product, and need satisfaction through informing, persuading, or reminding.

The most effective sales presentation is characterized by two-way communication. It should be a dialogue between the salesperson and the prospect, whose involvement should be encouraged with information-gathering, probing, confirmation, and *summary-confirmation questions*. Beware of assuming things about the prospect, and be sure the language of your presentation is clearly understood. Listen attentively as the prospect responds to your questions or volunteers information.

After making a good first impression during the approach the salesperson begins the presentation. The salesperson's ability to emphasize will be tested during this part of the sale, because this is where the prospect's buying motives are established. The salesperson's ability to verbalize product benefits will also be tested during this part of the sale.

Once you have selected a product or service that matches the customer's needs, you must decide which presentation strategy to emphasize. Need satisfaction can be achieved through informing, persuading, or reminding. The salesperson will, of course, use a combination of these presentation strategies in some cases. An effective presentation is an important part of the sales call and will often determine the ease or difficulty of proceeding through the rest of the steps to a successful sale.

➤ **KEY TERMS**

Need Discovery
Information-Gathering Questions
Probing Questions
Confirmation Questions
Buying Conditions
Summary-Confirmation Questions

Active Listening
Feedback
Informative Presentation
Persuasive Presentation
Reminder Presentations

➤ **REVIEW QUESTIONS**

1. List and describe the four parts of the Consultative Sales Presentation Guide.

2. List and describe the four types of questions commonly used in the selling field.

3. Define the term *buying conditions*. What are some common buying conditions?

4. What is the listening efficiency rate of most people? Describe the process of active listening, and explain how it will improve the listening efficiency rate.

5. Discuss the major factors that should be considered during the product selection phase of the consultative-style sales presentation.

6. Distinguish between the three types of need-satisfaction presentations: informative, persuasive, and reminder.

7. What are the guidelines to be followed when developing a persuasive sales presentation?

8. What are some advantages of using the feature-benefit-reaction (FBR) approach?

9. Discuss those factors that contribute to the dynamic nature of selling? What skills are used by salespeople to cope with the dynamic nature of personal selling?

10. Read the opening vignette that begins on p. 216 and then evaluate Dave Tripp's practice of building a close relationship with salespeople who work in the bookstores he visits. Does this practice represent appropriate use of Tripp's limited time? Explain.

➤ **APPLICATION EXERCISES**

1. Assume that you are a salesperson working in each of the following kinds of selling careers, and assume further that the prospect has given you no indication of what she is looking for. Identify the kinds of questions you will use to find your prospect's specific needs.

   a. Personal computer
   b. Carpet
   c. Financial planning

2. You are a department manager and have called a meeting with the five staff members in your department. The purpose of your meeting is to inform your staff of a new procedure your company has adopted. It is important that you develop understanding and support. What steps can you take to enhance communication with the group?

3. Pick a job that you would really like to have and for which you are qualified. Assume you are going to be interviewed for this job tomorrow afternoon. You really want this position and therefore want to be persuasive in presenting your qualifications. List facts about your qualifications concerning where you have worked previously, how much education you have, and what hobbies and activities you have been involved in. Use the feature-benefits worksheet in Chapter 5 (Table 5.1) as a guide to convert these employee facts to employer benefits in the form of selling statements.

4. The explosion of product options and the complex needs of today's customer make the salesperson's task of product selection more challenging. On the Internet, access Cincom Systems Inc., a leading international supplier of information technology. From their home page click on the general listing of "Products." From this list examine functions available with the "Sales Automation—CONTROL:Acquire" product. Carefully study the Acquire Sales Configurator and the Acquire Bid Management descriptions.

➤ SALES AUTOMATION APPLICATION EXERCISE

PRESENTATION PLANNING WITH ACT! HARDCOPY

Sales managers regularly help salespeople review the status of their accounts. These account review meetings often involve examining all the information available on the salespeople's most promising prospects. The sales manager and salesperson will each have a copy of all information currently available for the accounts. This requires a printout of data stored in the database. Print the information contained in Contact Screens 1 and 2 and the Notes Window for all contacts, press at the Main Menu the key sequence, L E R C Enter Enter A. Approximately forty pages of information will be printed.

➤ CASE PROBLEM

Annette Peterson is a real estate salesperson for Modern Homes, Incorporated. A young couple, John and Beth Reems, was referred to Annette by the sales manager. John and Beth are being transferred into the city due to John's job as manager of a local men's clothing store. Beth had been a computer systems analyst in a department store and will be looking for a similar position after the move.

Annette had no opportunity to visit with John and Beth until they arrived in the city today. The sales manager set up an appointment for them to meet at the office at 1:00 P.M. Following their arrival the following sales presentation occurred:

Annette: Good afternoon, Mr. and Mrs. Reems. My name is Annette Peterson.

John: Good afternoon. I am John Reems and this is my wife, Beth.

Beth: Good afternoon, Mrs. Peterson, we were looking forward to meeting you.

Annette: Please call me Annette. And how was your flight?

John: Oh, we had a lovely flight and got a wonderful view of the city as we circled for landing.

Beth: I enjoyed the flight also, and am looking forward to seeing the city and driving around to view the homes for sale. Our flight back leaves at 8:30 P.M. so we are not going to have a lot of time. Our looking is going to have to move rather quickly.

Annette: My sales manager told me you would have a limited time, so I've prepared an agenda for us to follow this afternoon. I have four homes that I selected from our computerized database. I picked up the keys for all four of them so we can drive out and take a look. Before we get going, though, I would like to show you a picture of each home and tell you a little about it. I am sure you will find all four of them very appealing.

John and Beth: Oh!

Annette: Here is the first one. It is priced at $146,000, has 2,000 square feet, and is a two-story. This house has two bathrooms and is located on a 65 by 135 foot lot. It was built in 1975 and has Andersen windows.

John and Beth: Uh-huh! (Beth looks for a pencil in her purse.)

Annette: Now here is a picture of the second house. I do not like this one as well as the first, but I thought maybe you would like to see it. This home was built in 1987 and is priced at $140,000. The taxes are $3,000 a year. It has 1,600 square feet and has U.S. Steel siding on it. It also has an attached 22 by 24 foot garage. The lot is 80 by 140 feet. It is a ranch-style home.

John and Beth: We do like ranch-style homes.

Annette: This picture is the third home that I chose. I really like this one. It is a split-level, priced at $138,900. The taxes are—oh, I'm sorry, the taxes do not seem to be listed for this one. I am sure we can find out what they are, however, if you are interested.

John: Well, we really are not interested in split-level homes. There are too many stairs to climb. By the way, how far are these homes from the store?

Annette: Well, most customers I have worked with do not concern themselves with how far, but rather how long it will take them to get to work. You will find that the city has an excellent system of streets with rapid uncongested traveling. The homes I am going to show you are all located in a suburb called Arbor Oaks. It would take you about 20 minutes to get from there to your store.

John: I see. (John looks at his watch to see what time it is.)

Annette: Here is the fourth home I picked out (showing a picture of the fourth home). This one is also a two-story and has a 24 by 24 foot garage. The price is $139,000 and it has an assumable mortgage of $80,500 with a 10 percent loan. The home is located on a cul-de-sac, with a 90 by 160 foot lot. I went through this house last week and remember that it has oak wainscoting in the family room and also vinyl siding. It has a high-efficiency furnace, air conditioner, and Maytag appliances.

QUESTIONS

1. Describe what you think John and Beth's impressions are of Annette.

2. Evaluate the strengths of Annette Peterson's presentation strategy.

3. Evaluate the weaknesses of this presentation strategy.

4. Assume you are the real estate salesperson in this case problem; then write out an outline that you would follow in giving your sales presentation.

5. Assuming that Annette Peterson follows the same pattern in the demonstration and close that she has already established in the presentation thus far, is she likely to close the sale? Why or why not?

6. Select five features brought out by Annette and convert them to buyer benefits. Use the forms presented in Chapter 5 (Tables 5.1 and 5.2).

➤ SALES AUTOMATION CASE STUDY

PRESENTATION PLANNING

Becky Kemley, your sales manager at Cadalyst Resources, wants to meet with you this afternoon to discuss the status of your prospect accounts (see Chapter 8 Case Study). It is common for prospects to have several contacts with Cadalyst before ordering a CAD system. These multicall contacts, or sales cycle phases, usually include getting acquainted and prequalifying, needs discovery, presentation, and finally closing. Becky wants to know what phase each account is in and, particularly, which accounts may be ready for a presentation. Using the software instructions in the Chapter 8 Case Study, review each of your accounts.

Access the ACT! software following the instructions in Appendix 2.

Questions

1. Which five accounts have already had a need discovery? Which two accounts are scheduled for a need discovery? Which six accounts are likely to buy but have not yet had a need discovery?

2. Which two accounts have had a need discovery and now need a product solution configured?

3. Which three accounts do not now have CAD and appear to be ready for your sales presentation?

4. For those accounts listed next that are ready for your sales presentation, which strategy would you use for each: informative, persuasive, or reminder?
   a. Able Profit Machines
   b. Big Tex Auto Sales
   c. International Studios
   d. Lakeside Clinic

5. Which accounts appear to be planning to buy without a need discovery or product configuration/proposal? What risks does this pose?

PARTNERSHIP SELLING: ROLE PLAY/SIMULATION (see Appendix 3, p. 421)

Understanding Your Customer's Buying Strategy
Read *sales memorandum 2 ("A" or "B" depending on the account category you were assigned in Chapter 9)*. Your customer has called you back because you made such a good approach in call 1 and wants to visit with you about a convention recently assigned. In this call you are to use the information gathered in sales call 1 to reestablish a good relationship, discover your customer's convention needs, and set an appointment to reurn and make a presentation.

Follow the instructions carefully and prepare information-gathering questions prior to your appointment. Keep your information-gathering questions general and attempt to get your customer to openly share information. Use probing questions later during the appointment to gain more insight. Be careful about doing too much of the talking. In the need discovery, your customer should do most of the talking, with you taking notes and using them to ask confirmation and summary-confirmation questions to check the accuracy of your perceptions concerning what the customer wants. After this meeting you will be asked to prepare a sales proposal from the information you have gathered.

Your instructor may again ask you to assume the role of a customer in the account category that you are not assigned to as a salesperson. If so, you will receive detailed customer instructions that you should follow closely. This will provide you with an opportunity to experience the strategic/consultative/partnering style of selling from a customer's perspective.

Custom Fitting the Sales Demonstration

LEARNING OBJECTIVES

When you finish reading this chapter, you should be able to

1. Discuss the important advantages of the sales demonstration

2. Explain the guidelines to be followed when planning a sales demonstration

3. Complete a demonstration worksheet

4. Develop selling tools that can strengthen your sales presentation

5. Discuss how to use audiovisual presentations effectively

Mitchell Weinstock walks confidently into a client's office; plugs his Macintosh Quadra into a conference room television; and then watches as the screen bursts into life with color, moving images, and sound. The presentation begins with a short message from Michael Mc-Connell, company president:

Hello, I'm Michael Mc-Connell, and I'd like to introduce you to SuperMac. First, I'll present a little of our company's history, then I'll turn the presentation back over to Mitchell.

On this day Weinstock, a sales representative for SuperMac Technology Incorporated, of Sunnyvale, California, is courting Health Net with a customized computer-generated presentation. SuperMac is in the graphic presentation business, so it makes sense to use a product demonstration that features attention-getting graphics. Company officials say that visual sales demonstrations have been the key to obtaining new accounts.[1]

The Sales Demonstration

With the increase in look-alike products and greater competition, salespeople are finding it more difficult to differentiate their products in the marketplace. In view of this challenge, the sales demonstration has become a more important communication tool. A well-planned **demonstration** adds sensory appeal to the product (Fig. 11.1). It attracts the customer's attention, stimulates interest, and creates desire. It is usually not possible to make this type of impression with words alone. The popularity of many products, from microwave ovens to microcomputers, has been credited to effective product demonstrations (Fig. 11.2).

A product demonstration contributes in a positive way to the selling/buying process. Both the customer and the salesperson benefit. The prospect can evaluate the product or service more effectively. The salesperson finds it easier to show what the product will do and how it will fit the customer's needs.

FIGURE 11.1 Conducting the Sales Demonstration

The Six–Step Presentation Plan	
Step One: APPROACH	☑ Review Strategic/Consultative Selling Model. ☑ Initiate customer contact.
Step Two: PRESENTATION	☑ Determine prospect needs. ☑ Select product or service. ☑ Initiate sales presentation.
Step Three: DEMONSTRATION	☐ Decide what to demonstrate. ☐ Select selling tools. ☐ Initiate demonstration.
Step Four: NEGOTIATION	☐ Anticipate sales resistance. ☐ Plan negotiating methods. ☐ Initiate double–win negotiations.
Step Five: CLOSE	☐ Plan appropriate closing methods. ☐ Recognize closing clues. ☐ Initiate closing methods.
Step Six: SERVICING THE SALE	☐ Suggestion selling. ☐ Follow through. ☐ Follow-up calls.
Service, retail, wholesale, and manufacturer selling.	

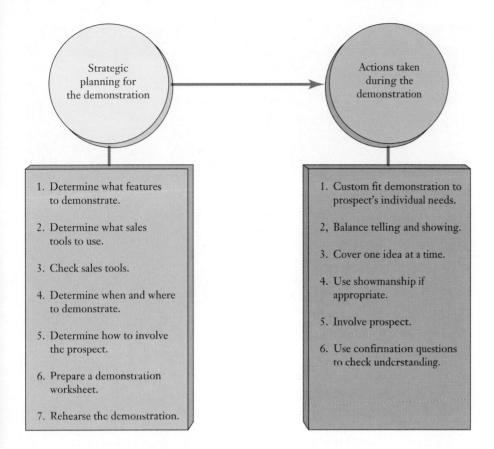

FIGURE 11.2   Poorly conducted demonstrations usually result from a lack of strategic planning and preparation.

Strategic planning for the demonstration

1. Determine what features to demonstrate.

2. Determine what sales tools to use.

3. Check sales tools.

4. Determine when and where to demonstrate.

5. Determine how to involve the prospect.

6. Prepare a demonstration worksheet.

7. Rehearse the demonstration.

Actions taken during the demonstration

1. Custom fit demonstration to prospect's individual needs.

2. Balance telling and showing.

3. Cover one idea at a time.

4. Use showmanship if appropriate.

5. Involve prospect.

6. Use confirmation questions to check understanding.

The Importance of the Sales Demonstration

The selling power of a demonstration can be seen daily on television. When a major corporation spends $150,000 for a thirty-second network time slot, naturally every effort is made to attract and hold the customer's attention. A commercial featuring the Land Rover Discovery shows the vehicle climbing a steep, rock-covered hillside. Sure enough, it makes it to the top. Goodyear Tire and Rubber Company wants to demonstrate the durability of its tires. The television commercial features an automobile driving over broken glass, railroad tracks, and rough streets. We see that the tires can take this punishment. Demonstration is the focal point of many television commercials. Salespeople can also use the demonstration to advantage. Some of the benefits that can add value to the sale are discussed here.

IMPROVED COMMUNICATION

In the previous chapter we noted the limitation of the verbal presentation; words provide only part of the meaning attached to messages that flow between the salesperson and the prospect. When we try to explain something with words alone, people frequently do not understand our messages.

Why is communication via the spoken word alone so difficult? One major reason is that we are visually oriented from birth. We grow up surrounded by the influence of movies, television, commercial advertising, road signs, and all

Strategic selling today involves customizing a product demonstration to each customer's unique set of buying conditions.

kinds of visual stimulation. People are accustomed to learning new things through the sense of sight or through a combination of seeing and hearing.

Many sales representatives recognize the limitations of the spoken word. When talking to prospects about the economic benefits of delivering training programs with a satellite system, a salesperson used a table (Table 11.1) to illustrate savings. With the aid of this table, prospects can visualize the economic benefits of the satellite delivery system compared to a competing system using high-bandwidth terrestrial lines.

IMPROVED RETENTION

In many selling situations the buyer does not make an immediate buying decision. The decision to buy may be made several days or weeks after the presentation. Therefore retention of information is important.

TABLE 11.1 HOW MUCH CAN A SATELLITE SYSTEM SAVE YOU?				
TYPE OF SYSTEM	**PER PERSON COST 20 SITES**	**PER PERSON COST 30 SITES**	**PER PERSON COST 40 SITES**	**PER PERSON COST 50 SITES**
Satellite delivery system	*$7.80*	*$7.20*	*$6.60*	*$6.00*
High-bandwidth terrestrial lines	*$7.10*	*$7.40*	*$7.70*	*$8.00*

These cost estimates are based on current satellite broadcast rates and rates for use of terrestrial lines. The per person cost is based on an audience size of 25 trainees at each site.

When we rely on verbal messages alone to communicate, retention of information will be minimal. A number of studies provide evidence to support this important point. Research conducted at Harvard and Columbia Universities found that audiovisuals improve retention from 14 to 38 percent over presentations with no visuals.[2]

PROOF OF BUYER BENEFITS

A well-planned and well-executed sales demonstration is one of the most convincing forms of proof. This is especially true if your product has dramatic points of superiority.

Salespeople representing Epson, Apple, IBM, and other computer manufacturers can offer the customer a wide range of printers costing up to $4,000. What is the real difference between a $300 dot matrix printer and a $3,000 laser printer? The laser equipment will print a neater and more attractive letter or report. The most effective way to provide proof of this buyer benefit is to show the customer material that has been printed on both printers. By letting the prospect compare the examples, the salesperson is converting product features to a buyer benefit. Nido Qubein, author of *Professional Selling Techniques*, says, "Don't expect your clients to accept at face value everything you say. Be prepared to prove by tests, findings, and performance records every claim you make."[3]

FEELING OF OWNERSHIP

Many effective sales demonstrations give the prospect a temporary feeling of ownership. This pleasant feeling builds desire to own the product. Let us consider the person who enters a men's clothing store and tries on a Hart Shaffner and Marx suit. During the few moments the customer is wearing the suit a feeling of pride is apt to develop. If the suit fits well and looks good, desire to own it will probably build.

Successful automobile salespeople encourage prospects to go for a demonstration ride. The new car almost always seems superior to the buyer's older model. New tires grip the road better. The car is usually free of squeaks and rattles. The steering is firm and precise. Finally, there is that indescribable smell that is found only in a new car. How could any buyer not feel pride of ownership? Without a demonstration ride, of course, the opportunity to build this desire would be lost.

Many firms offer prospects an opportunity to enjoy products on a trial basis. This is done to give people a chance to assess the merits of the product in their own home or business. One firm selling stereo systems offered potential customers a no-obligation–ten-day home trial. Nearly 90 percent of the people who participated decided to keep the equipment at the end of the trial period.

OTHER BENEFITS

Most salespeople gain added self-confidence when they incorporate an effective demonstration into the sales presentation. This is especially true of new salespeople who have not polished their verbal sales story. It is reassuring to know that it will not be necessary to rely completely on verbal skills.

When the demonstration involves the use of visuals, time may be saved. Research conducted at the Wharton Business School and the University of

---

BUILDING RELATIONSHIPS IN A DIVERSE WORLD

SELLING IN JAPAN

By almost any standard, Sunumu Nakamura is an outstanding salesperson. As a Prudential Japan, Ltd. insurance agent (called life planner in Japan) he has earned over $350,000 during a single year. According to Nakamura, success in selling comes from enthusiasm for learning, strong commitment to serving the customer, and hard work. He explains why he works about sixty hours every week: "If you want to succeed, you have to work harder and smarter." While the typical Prudential agent in Japan makes twelve calls per week, Nakamura's goal is to visit four clients every day, five days a week. He really does not view the long hours as a burden. He does not see helping customers purchase insurance as work. He says, "I feel it is a privilege to help my customers."

Nakamura uses a notebook computer to help customers see the advantages of certain insurance investments. However, he is careful to avoid information overload. He often uses simple pencil and paper diagrams to demonstrate the benefits of various insurance policies.[a]

Minnesota indicates that using visuals to complement a verbal presentation can reduce the amount of time required to present a concept by up to 40 percent.[4]

Planning Effective Demonstrations

Larry Newman, president of American Aircraft, an Albuquerque-based aircraft company, likes to conduct sales demonstrations in the sky. He sells the two-seat Falcon-XP, an airplane sold in kit form that requires 100 hours of assembly. Newman takes sales prospects to an altitude of 1,000 feet, letting the prospect experience the spectacular view. During the first few minutes of the flight he remains silent; then he explains the controls and lets the person fly the plane for a while. The presentation ends with Newman gliding the small craft to the ground.

In addition to being an outstanding salesperson, Newman has the distinction of being the first person to cross both the Atlantic and Pacific oceans in a balloon. He states that there is a challenge in ballooning that "you can't experience any other way, because if you fail, failure is ultimate."[5] He makes a comparison between ballooning and selling. Both take careful planning.[6]

An effective sales demonstration is the result of both planning and practice. Planning gives the salesperson a chance to review all of the important details that should be considered in advance of the actual demonstration. Practice (or rehearsal) provides an opportunity for a trial run to uncover areas that need additional polish. During the planning stage it helps to review a series of guidelines that have helped salespeople over the years to develop effective demonstrations.

USE CUSTOM-FITTED DEMONSTRATIONS

In nonmanipulative selling, each presentation is custom tailored because individual client problems and priorities are unique.[7] In other words, every aspect of the sales presentation, including the demonstration, should relate to the needs or problems mutually identified by the prospect and the salesperson.

It is possible to develop a sales demonstration so structured and so mechanical that the prospect feels like a number. We must try to avoid what some veteran marketing people refer to as the *depersonalization* of the selling/buying process. If the demonstration is overly structured, it cannot be personalized to meet specific customer wants and needs.

Columbus Show Case, maker of retail display cases for supermarkets, has successfully used custom-fitted demonstrations for the past decade. Several times each year a sales team made up of a salesperson, a marketing representative, and a technician visit supermarket headquarters throughout the United States and Mexico. Demonstrations take place in nearby hotels. Carl Aschinger, CEO of the Ohio-based company, says, "We target exactly who we want to meet. It could be the head buyer or merchandisers or the vice presidents of construction." About 40 percent of the sales calls result in a sale.[8]

COVER ONE IDEA AT A TIME

Pace the demonstration so that the customer does not become confused. Offer one idea at a time, and be sure the customer understands each point before moving on. This practice is especially important if the primary purpose of your sales presentation is to inform. When you neglect this practice, there is the danger that the customer's concentration will remain fixed on a previous point. Some demonstrations are ruined by a salesperson who moves too rapidly from one point to another. A good rule of thumb is to use a confirmation question to get agreement on each key point before moving on to the next. This approach will make closing easier because you have secured agreement on key points throughout the demonstration. Make the customer a part of every step.

Clarity is an essential ingredient of the sales demonstration. In fact, a major purpose of the demonstration is to clarify what the salesperson says. Avoid a highly complicated demonstration, which may confuse the potential buyer.

CHOOSE THE RIGHT SETTING

The location of the sales demonstration can make a difference. Some companies routinely rent space at a hotel, motel, or conference center so that the demonstration can be conducted in a controlled environment free of noise and other interruptions.

A firm selling modern log homes frequently conducts an open house at the site of a newly completed house. Potential customers are invited by letter or personal contact to tour the home at appointed times. After touring the home, prospects view a twenty-minute video that explains how the homes are constructed. Pictures of other homes built by the company are also shown.

Many salespeople visit the prospect's office and talk to the person across the desk. David Peoples, author of *Selling to the Top*, believes there is a better setting for the presentation. He suggests a one-on-one–stand-up presentation in a conference room that ensures privacy. This approach puts the customer on a pedestal and gives the person a feeling of being very special.[9]

CHECK SALES TOOLS

Be sure to check every item to be used in conjunction with the sales demonstration. If you are using audiovisual equipment, be certain that it is in good working condition. When using a projector, always carry an extension cord and a

---

LOWE'S HIRED A DECORATOR SO YOU WILL NOT HAVE TO

Decorating is more than cans of paint, rolls of wallpaper, and pieces of paneling. Lowe's Companies, Incorporated, one of America's largest home center retail companies, recognized that most of us need help decorating the rooms in our home. The company hired Don Sewell, a nationally known interior designer, to develop a series of home fashion panels. Don Sewell is an innovative designer with more than twenty years of experience. Each panel has actual samples of flooring, wallcovering, countertops, paint, and the like. These panels are on display in Lowe's Home Decor Centers. A salesperson can help customers achieve the look they want by using the panels to *demonstrate* the many designer options.

---

spare bulb. If you are selling real estate, the most critical aspect of preparing for the demonstration is becoming familiar with the property. Never show a home you have not seen.[10]

APPEAL TO ALL SENSES

Rolls-Royce has determined that smell sells in the highly competitive luxury car market. The British car company put the aroma of its leather upholstery on a scent strip in *Architectural Digest* so the 3 million readers would know what an automobile costing nearly $200,000 smells like.

In conducting a sales demonstration it is a good idea to appeal to all appropriate senses. When more than one sense is involved, retention is increased.[11] Each of the five senses—sight, hearing, smell, touch, and taste—represents an avenue by which the salesperson can attract the prospect's attention and build desire.

Although sight is considered the most powerful attention-attracting sense, it may not be the most important motivating force in every selling situation. In the field of cosmetics, for example, smell is often a significant factor. Smell is linked to the part of the brain associated with emotion, so it can have a great effect on behavior.[12] When presenting a food product, the taste and aroma may be critical.

Try to reach the prospect through as many senses as possible. Gary Eberle, owner of Eberle Winery located in San Luis Obispo County, California, understands this fundamental of personal selling. He spends several months each year selling his wines to retailers and restaurant owners. This hardworking entrepreneur says, "Ten months of the year I sell wine for a living, so I can play with my hobby for the other two months, which is making wine."[13] The sales presentation for a quality wine usually highlights four areas:

Consumer demand. The wine's sales potential is described in realistic terms.

Marketing strategies. Suggested ways to merchandise the wine are discussed.

Bouquet. The distinctive fragrance of the wine is introduced.

Taste. A sample of the wine is given to the prospect in a quality wineglass.

Comprehension and retention can be enhanced with visual images.

Note that a sales presentation featuring these appeals will reach the prospect through four of the five senses. Collectively, these appeals develop a strong motivating force. When you involve more than one sense, the sales presentation is more informative and more persuasive.

BALANCE TELLING, SHOWING, AND INVOLVEMENT

Some of the most effective sales demonstrations combine telling, showing, and involvement of the prospect. To plan an effective demonstration, consider developing a demonstration worksheet. Simply divide a sheet of paper into three columns. Head the first column, "Feature to be demonstrated." Head the second column, "What I will say." Head the third column, "What I or the customer will do." List the major features you plan to demonstrate in proper sequence in the first column. In the second column, describe what you will say about the feature, converting the feature to a customer benefit. In the third column, describe what you (or the customer) will do at the time this benefit is discussed. A sample demonstration worksheet appears in Figure 11.3.

In some cases involvement simply means placing the item in the customer's hands. A customer who holds something has symbolically taken possession of the item. This is often the first step toward purchasing what is being offered. A prospect who participates in a demonstration receives the strongest possible form of proof. Al Gunther, president of Summit Sports, has adopted this fundamental of personal selling in demonstration mountaineering equipment. In some cases, clients are involved in mountainside expeditions where they can put his products to the test. "That way, you can really learn about the products," he says. "Together you find features that would not be noticeable without actual field use."[14]

The most effective demonstrations include telling, showing, and involvement.

Prospects can be involved in many demonstrations. Two retail examples follow:

Furniture: To prove comfort or quality, have the buyer sit in a chair, lie on a mattress, or feel the highly polished finish of a coffee table.

Clothing: Have the customer try it on to highlight style, fit, and comfort features. This involvement is especially important in the sale of quality garments.

If it is not possible for the prospect to participate in the demonstration or handle the product, place sales literature, pictures, or brochures in the person's

Demonstration Worksheet		
Feature to Be Demonstrated	**What I Will Say (Include Benefit)**	**What I or the Customer Will Do**
Special computer circuit board to accelerate drawing graphics on a color monitor screen.	"This monitor is large enough to display multiple windows. You can easily compare several graphics."	Have the customer bring up several windows using computer keyboard.
Meeting room setup at a hotel and conference center.	"This setup will provide three feet of elbow space for each participant. For long meetings, the added space provides more comfort."	Give the customer a tour of the room and invite her to sit in a chair at one of the conference tables.

FIGURE 11.3   The demonstration worksheet enables the salesperson to strategically plan and then rehearse demonstrations that strengthen the presentation.

hands. After the sales call these items will remind the prospect of not only who called but why.[15]

USE SHOWMANSHIP

Showmanship can be defined as an interesting and appealing way of communicating an idea to others. Showmanship is especially important if the primary purpose of your presentation is to persuade. It can do a lot to improve the effectiveness of a sales demonstration. Showmanship in selling need not be equated with sensational or bizarre events. It may be a subtle act, such as carefully placing a fine diamond on a piece of black velvet before showing the jewel to the customer, or drawing attractive color graphics on a computer monitor.

Jim Gauerke often uses showmanship when he demonstrates the Fyrepel fire-entry suit developed for people involved in fighting fires. To demonstrate the lifesaving features of his product, he has donned the suit and walked between two wide, fiery pits of combusting JP4 jet engine fuel. Gauerke treads his way through the inferno, unscathed, for up to four minutes. This demonstration has helped close many sales.[16]

In simple terms, showmanship is the act of presenting product features in a manner that will gain attention and increase desire. It is never a substitute for thorough preparation and knowledge of your company, your product, and the prospect. Effective showmanship is never based on deceit or trickery. It should not be gaudy or insincere. When showmanship detracts from the image of the product or the salesperson it is counterproductive.

REHEARSE THE DEMONSTRATION

While you are actually putting on the demonstration, you will need to be concentrating on a variety of things. The movements you make and the multitude of things you do should be so familiar to you that each response is nearly automatic. To achieve this level of skill, you will need to rehearse the demonstration.

Rehearse both what you are going to say and what you are going to do. Merrie Spaeth, consultant and author of *Marketplace Communication*, says, ". . . if you don't rehearse, the best-conceived idea can go wrong."[17] Say the words aloud exactly as if the prospect were present. It is surprising how often a concept that seems quite clear as you think it over becomes hopelessly mixed up when you try to discuss it with a customer. Rehearsal is the best way to avoid this embarrassing situation. Whenever possible, have your presentation/demonstration videotaped before you give it. This is perhaps the best way to perfect what you will say and do.

The Use of Sales Tools

Nearly every sales organization provides its staff with sales tools or proof devices of one kind or another. Many of these, when used correctly, augment the sales effort. If the company does not provide these items, the creative salesperson secures or develops sales tools independently. In addition to audiovisual presentations, sales personnel can utilize a wide range of other selling aids. Creative marketing people are continually developing new types of sales tools. The following section summarizes some of the most common tools creative salespeople employ.

THE PRODUCT ITSELF

Without a doubt the best-selling aid is often the product itself. When Steve Jobs (the founder of Apple Computer) introduced Next Computer System, the first product offered by his company, Next Incorporated, he did it with flair. The setting for his product demonstration was the 3,000-seat Davies Symphony Hall in San Francisco. Jobs, known for his dramatic product introductions, stood alone on stage with just the computer and a vase of flowers. His product demonstration received rave reviews from the large audience.[18]

When demonstrating the actual product, be sure it is typical in terms of appearance and operation. Try to avoid a situation in which it becomes necessary to apologize for appearance, construction, or performance. Of course, you should be able to demonstrate the product skillfully.

MODELS

In some cases it is not practical to demonstrate the product itself because it is too big or immobile. It is easier to demonstrate a small-scale model or cross section of the original equipment. A working model, like the actual product, can give the prospect a clear picture of how a piece of equipment operates.

Cross sections (a portion or cutaway) can be used to reveal hidden product features. One manufacturer of air filters uses a cutaway model to illustrate how the product is constructed. A manufacturer of commercial ice-making machines used a cutaway model to illustrate the layers of insulation.

PHOTOS AND ILLUSTRATIONS

The old proverb, "One picture is worth a thousand words," can be put into practical application by a creative salesperson. A great deal of information can be given to the prospect with the aid of photos and illustrations. Consider these creative uses of photos:

> ➤ The salespeople at Domain's home-furnishing stores know that people who shop for furniture usually visit several stores and compare products. Before potential customers leave the store, they are given a Polaroid snapshot of the furniture they are considering. The salesperson writes his name on the back of the photo.[19]

> ➤ A Michigan-based restaurant equipment salesperson takes pictures of newly installed products. These photos are then used during sales presentations to new prospects. Prospects are often interested in seeing the actual equipment installation.[20]

> ➤ Chris Roberts, area manager for Downing Displays, a manufacturer of trade show displays, says that the photo presentation book is the most important item he takes on a first sales call. He says, "Because what we sell is very visual, it's important for the client to *see* the displays."[21]

Some salespeople organize photographs in a presentation album or a portfolio. Either option provides the flexibility needed by salespeople.

PORTFOLIO

A **portfolio** is a portable case or loose-leaf binder containing a wide variety of sales-supporting materials. The portfolio is used to add visual life to the sales message and to prove claims. A person who sells advertising might develop a

Photos can often be used to clarify verbal messages.

portfolio including the following items:

Successful advertisements used in conjunction with previous campaigns

Selected illustrations that can be incorporated into advertisements

A selection of testimonial letters

One or more case histories of specific clients who have used the media with success

The portfolio has been used as a sales aid by people who sell interior design services, insurance, real estate, securities, and convention services. It is a flexible sales aid that can be revised at any time to meet the needs of each customer.

REPRINTS

Leading magazines and journals sometimes feature articles that directly or indirectly support the salesperson's product. A reprint of the article can be a forceful selling aid. It is also an inexpensive selling tool. When *Car and Driver* published a very positive article on the New Mercedes-Benz SLK 2-door roadster, reprints quickly appeared in dealer showrooms. Pharmaceutical sales representatives often use reprints from journals that report on research in the field of medicine. In many cases the prospect will be far more impressed with the good points of your product if they are presented by a third party rather than you. A reprint from a respected journal can be very persuasive.

GRAPHS AND TEST RESULTS

A graph is a diagram used to illustrate change of some variable such as payroll, sales, or products manufactured. For example, a graph might be used to illustrate the increase in fuel costs over a ten-year period. In the field of selling, both line and bar graphs have been used successfully.

Although graphs are usually quite descriptive, the layperson may misunderstand them. It is best to interpret the graph for the prospect. Do not move too fast because the full impact of the message may be lost. Be totally familiar with the graph so that you can work with it confidently.

Test results from a reliable agency can often be convincing. To illustrate, let us look at a comparison of a top-quality acrylic paint and an ordinary latex paint.[22]

> Homeowner A hires a contractor to paint his 3,500-square foot home with ordinary latex paint. The cost of the paint is $15 per gallon for twenty gallons, or $300. Labor costs $2,000. Total cost is $2,300 for a job that will last perhaps four years. Cost per year of service is $575.

> Homeowner B hires the same contractor to paint an identical home with top-quality acrylic latex paint. Cost of the paint is $20 per gallon for twenty gallons, or $400. Labor costs $2,000. Total cost is $2,400 for a job that will last perhaps ten years. Cost per year of service is $240.

This type of factual information, prepared by the Rohm and Haas Paint Quality Institute, can be helpful when you are attempting to sell a product that may appear to be expensive in the customer's mind.

SAMPLES

Samples provide an effective way to demonstrate a product. Some samples are small amounts of the product that the prospect can use. In the food industry, for example, samples are often used to introduce new food items.

When Armor All protectant was first introduced, it was considered a revolutionary product. The manufacturer claimed it would protect from rot anything made of vinyl, plastic, rubber, leather, or wood. To build consumer demand for the product, samples were given to potential customers entering auto supply firms. In this case, samples provided a direct appeal to potential buyers.

COMPUTERS

As noted previously, a growing number of companies have started equipping salespeople with small, portable computers weighing only a few pounds. With the aid of these small computers a salesperson can compute financial options on the spot and close sales that might otherwise be lost. Salespeople using computers to send electronic messages or to get information from the corporate mainframe, spend less time in the office and more time on the road.

Duracell converted its 200-member sales force to laptop computers and quickly realized big gains in communication between field sales representatives and other key people in the company. Salespeople indicate that report filing is easier and faster. DuPont has equipped thousands of its field salespeople with laptops and easy-to-use software. The results have been quicker preparation of proposals and better sales presentations.[23]

Personal computers have played an important role in increasing sales force productivity. Salespeople have instant access to customer data, so it is often easier to customize the sales presentation. Many salespeople report that PC-based presentations, using graphics software, are very effective. Today's personal computer can produce striking visuals and attractive printed material that can be

A growing number of salespeople are using portable computers in conjunction with sales presentations.

given to the customer for future reference. A salesperson can present sophisticated products on the notebook computer using simple presentation modules.[24]

AUDIOVISUAL TECHNOLOGY

A large number of companies have started providing their salespeople with audiovisual aids such as videotapes, filmstrips, 35-mm slides, and computer-based presentations. There are several reasons audiovisual presentations have become more commonplace. First, there have been major advances in the development of hardware. The equipment is more reliable, more compact, and easier to operate. Next, the software is better. Many of today's videos, software packages, and transparencies feature professional actors, top-notch photography, and attractive graphics.

BUILDING QUALITY PARTNERSHIPS

FOUR MINUTES—SIX SLIDES

It took several years for Pilot Air Freight, a small freight-forwarding company, to get the attention of GTE, the giant electronics company. After nearly three years and more than 100 sales calls on GTE plants and offices around the country, the Pilot sales team was invited to make a formal sales presentation to GTE's traffic council, a twenty-five member body that approves or rejects supplier's proposals. Pilot Air Freight was one of twelve suppliers invited to make a presentation. Each supplier was given only four minutes to discuss her proposal and to show just six 35-mm slides. After answering some questions and making minor adjustments in their proposal, the sales team went home with their fingers crossed. A few days later the Pilot sales team learned that they had won a three-year contract. The sales calls helped Pilot Air Freight representatives build a relationship with GTE personnel. This investment of time and effort established the foundation for the new partnership.[b]

Many companies find that audiovisual presentations, although expensive to produce, can be a good investment. These presentations often reveal product uses, values, features, and benefits in an interesting manner that encourages the prospect to listen and ask questions. When GTE began selling its new digital Airfone system to various airlines, the sales staff used a multimedia program that included video, sound, animation and other high-tech wizardry. The sales team needed a powerful visual presentation that would deliver a wealth of technical information in an entertaining manner.[25]

When an audiovisual presentation fails to live up to expectations, some companies find that salespeople are not using the materials correctly. Most salespeople are not audiovisual experts and need training. On the next page are some suggestions on how to use audiovisual presentations to achieve maximum impact.

Computer-based presentations can be enhanced with the use of an LCD projection panelbook.

PANELBOOK. IT FITS NICELY IN TIGHT BUDGETS, TOO.

Portable LCD projection panels. Starting at just $3299.

You're probably as tight on money as you are on space.

That's why we developed the new PanelBook™ 450. Uniquely crafted to project presentations side-by-side from notebook computers, PanelBooks are up to 40 percent smaller than most panels.

And the PanelBook 450 has a price to match. That's because it utilizes In Focus Systems' innovative new TSTN[2] technology, giving its 16.7 million colors outstanding

saturation and contrast. Plus a response time fast enough for QuickTime™ and Video for Windows.™

As the market leader in LCD projection, we offer the broadest choice of LCD projection solutions available. So call us today. We've got a PanelBook to fit any budget.

CALL 1-800-294-6400 FOR A FREE GUIDE TO GIVING EFFECTIVE PRESENTATIONS. Not to mention any briefcase.

In Focus®
S Y S T E M S

NP4513 ©1993 In Focus Systems, Inc. 7770 SW Mohawk Street, Tualatin, Oregon 97062. Phone (503) 692-4968. Fax (503) 692-4476. In Europe: Planetenweg 91, NL-2132 HL, Hoofddorp, The Netherlands. Phone 31 (0) 2503 23200. Fax 31 (0) 2503 24388. In Focus Systems and TSTN are registered trademarks, and PanelBook is a trademark of In Focus Systems, Inc. All other products are trademarks of their holders.

1. Be sure the prospect knows the purpose of the presentation. Preview the material and describe a few highlights. Always try to build interest in advance of the audiovisual presentation.

2. Be prepared to stop the presentation to clarify a point or to allow the prospect to ask questions. Do not permit the audiovisual presentation to become a barrier to good two-way communication.

3. At the conclusion of the audiovisual presentation, review key points, and allow the prospect an opportunity to ask questions.

Finally, realize that the audiovisual presentation cannot do the selling for you. (If it could, you could send it to the prospect in the mail.) No matter how exotic the sales tool, you are still the central figure in the selling situation.

BOUND PAPER PRESENTATIONS

Although many salespeople are using some type of audiovisual presentation in conjunction with the sales demonstration, paper is still widely used. According to a recent Sales & Marketing Management/Simmons research study of 69,000 sales managers, bound paper presentations are the most popular medium.[26] With the aid of computer-generated graphics, it is easy to print attractive graphs, charts, and other proof information. Product guarantees and warranties are sometimes included in a bound paper presentation. Some markcters use guarantees and warranties to differentiate their products from competing products. Customer testimonials represent another common element of bound paper presentations. Proof letters describing tangible benefits of the product can enhance credibility. These letters make a difference because they feature the unbiased opinions of people who are in the same decision-making position.[27] Prospects like bound paper presentations because the document is readily available for future reference.

SUMMARY

In selling, the prospect is moving from a known quantity (the money in hand or an obligation for future payment) to something of an unknown quantity (amount of satisfaction to be gained from the potential purchase). With most people this produces anxiety and insecurity. The professional salesperson reduces prospect anxiety and insecurity by supplying proof of product performance. The objective of the *demonstration* part of the sale is to supply this proof.

People perceive impressions through the five senses. In the presentation the salesperson communicates verbally to the prospect primarily through the sense of sound. In the demonstration the salesperson broadens communication strategy to include as many of the other senses as possible. Generally, the more senses we appeal to, the more believable our sales appeal becomes.

In the demonstration the senses of sound and sight are combined when we tell the prospect about a product benefit and show the product, or a visual presentation of the product, at the same time. When we ask the prospect to personally operate the product or examine a sales tool, we simultaneously introduce a third sense—the sense of touch. If appropriate, the salesperson should also appeal to the senses of taste and smell.

Nearly every marketing-driven organization provides its salespeople with a variety of sales tools to use in the demonstration. A partial list of these tools includes the product itself, models, photos, reprints, *portfolios*, graphs, charts, computer printouts, samples, test results, testimonials, case histories, guarantees, and audiovisual presentations.

➤ KEY TERMS

Demonstration
Showmanship
Portfolio

➤ REVIEW QUESTIONS

1. List the benefits of using a sales demonstration during the presentation of a product or service.
2. What effect does showing (appealing to the sense of sight) have on retention when combined with an oral presentation?
3. Discuss the advantages of using the demonstration worksheet.
4. Explain why a salesperson should organize the sales presentation so that it appeals to as many of the five senses as possible.
5. List the guidelines to follow in planning an effective demonstration.
6. What is showmanship? Give an example.
7. Develop a list of the sales tools that the salesperson should consider when planning a sales demonstration.
8. Explain how magazines and trade journals can be used to assist the salesperson in a persuasive sales presentation.
9. Explain why audiovisual presentations are becoming more popular as a means of support for sales demonstrations.
10. What are some of the common sales functions performed by small, portable computers?

➤ APPLICATION EXERCISES

1. In many selling situations it is difficult, if not impossible, to demonstrate the product itself. List means other than the product itself that can be used to demonstrate the product features and benefits.
2. Automobile salespeople almost always go for a demonstration drive with a prospective car buyer. Evaluate the following three methods of demonstrating the car:
   a. Customer takes the demonstration ride alone.
   b. Customer and salesperson take demonstration ride together, with the customer driving.
   c. Customer and salesperson take demonstration ride together, with the salesperson driving the first part of the demonstration and the customer driving during the second part of the ride.
3. Assume that you are a salesperson engaged in selling the following products. List the senses you would appeal to, and tell how you would accom-

plish this in your sales presentation. Indicate the selling statements you would use in your demonstration.

   a. Coat
   b. Computer
   c. Life insurance
   d. Business security system

4. Develop a list of sales tools you could use in a job interview situation. What tools could you use to demonstrate your skills and capabilities?

5. As noted in this chapter, demonstration software is becoming increasingly popular. Real estate products are often showcased on the Web. Access the Iowa Realty home page on the Web. Assume you are a real estate salesperson and you have a client who wants to purchase a $250,000 to $300,000 home in the suburb of West Des Moines. On the home page click on "Des Moines." On the next screen fill in price range and click on "West Des Moines." Examine the properties matching your request. From this list, click on the home you personally like best and examine that information.

➤ CASE PROBLEM

Jack Alber is a manufacturer's sales representative for the Mayflower Appliance Company. Jack recently graduated from college with a major in marketing and went to work for Mayflower shortly thereafter. Mayflower manufactures and markets a line of small home appliances. As a sales representative, Jack calls on wholesalers and retailers that distribute small electrical appliances. Recently, Mayflower introduced in limited test markets a new line of small food processors. The company selected the name Orkan Food Processor for its new product line. After careful analysis of consumer, retailer, and wholesaler reactions in the test markets, Mayflower made several product improvements. Mayflower planned a full-scale introduction of the improved Orkan food processor for autumn. The promotion was planned to coincide with the important gift-buying season from October to December.

To accomplish the sales goal of 1 million units during the first year, Mayflower began its distribution promotion in June. In a national sales meeting, all sales representatives, including Jack Alber, were introduced to the new product line. The sales representatives were informed that the sales promotion for the Orkan Food Processor would be the biggest in the company's history. Included in the sales promotion program were the following:

1. A million-dollar advertising campaign including the Oprah Winfrey Show

2. Sales banners and window stickers for retailers, to develop point-of-purchase promotions

3. A package that featured four-color printed pictures of the Orkan Food Processor and shelf signs

4. A sales kit for each of the sales representatives that included the following: (a) the Orkan Food Processor itself; (b) the package; (c) sales banners, newspaper advertising slicks, and catalog specification sheets; and (d) a notebook computer and CD-ROM presentation software

The multimedia presentation contained a sales message from Mayflower's vice president of sales that outlined test market results, projected profit potential of the Orkan Food Processor, comments from consumers and retailers, and film clips of Oprah Winfrey making commercials for Orkan. The multimedia presentation was designed to be shown to retailers and wholesalers who were prospective dealers and distributors for the Orkan Food Processor.

This was the first time Jack had come into contact with audiovisual equipment in a sales presentation. Jack was a persuasive communicator and felt his best presentation was based on one-to-one communication with the prospect. Jack felt reluctant about trying to integrate multimedia into his presentation, even though he felt it was well prepared. Jack thought that it would be awkward to carry in, set up, and plug in the equipment and that he would lose the personal touch he had been so successful with in the past. As Jack flew home from the sales meeting, he decided he would try to introduce the new product line in his territory without using the multimedia presentation.

QUESTIONS

1. Based on Jack's strong personal selling skills, do you agree or disagree with his decision not to use the multimedia presentation. Why?

2. Describe how you would organize the presentation without the use of the multimedia presentation. Indicate where you would use each of the sales tools.

3. Describe how you would organize the presentation with the use of the multimedia presentation.

4. Describe how you could use showmanship in selling the Orkan Food Processor to (a) the wholesaler, (b) the retailer, and (c) the ultimate consumer.

5. Describe the senses you could appeal to in demonstrating the Orkan Food Processor. Explain how you would make each of these appeals.

6. How could you involve the prospect in demonstrating the Orkan Food Processor?

➤ SALES AUTOMATION CASE STUDY

CUSTOM FITTING THE DEMONSTRATIONS

Your Cadalyst Resources sales manager, Becky Kemley, has asked you to meet with her to discuss demonstrations. She wants you to tell her if any of your accounts needs a demonstration and, if so, what type of demonstration. Please review Mark David's former prospect accounts (see Chapter 8 Case Study).

Access the ACT! software following the instructions in Appendix 2.

Questions

1. Which two accounts need a demonstration of the speed, power, and strong presentation capabilities of the recommended CAD product configuration?

2. Which account needs to be shown that the recommended CAD product configuration will meet the account's specifications?

3. Which account with many sites will need a demonstration of Cadalyst's ability to put together a complex solution?

4. Which account seeking a low price needs a testimonial of Cadalyst's value-added ability to help customers maximize the power of their CAD?

5. Which account needs a demonstration of Cadalyst's financial stability?

PARTNERSHIP SELLING: A ROLE PLAY/SIMULATION (see Appendix 3, p. 421)

Developing a Sales Presentation Strategy — The Demonstration

Read sales memorandum 3 ("A" or "B" depending on the category you were assigned in sales call 1). In this role play your call objectives are to make a persuasive presentation, negotiate any customer concerns, and close and service the sale.

At this time you should complete item 1 of the presentation plan and prepare and price a product solution. This will include completing the sales proposal form. Also you should obtain a three-ring binder with pockets in the front and back for the development of a portfolio presentation. In this binder you should prepare your presentation and demonstration, following the instructions in items 2a, 2b, 2c, and 2d under the presentation plan. The presentation and demonstration materials (use the product strategy materials, i.e., photos, price lists, menus, awards, etc., provided to you with employment memorandum 1) should be placed in the three-ring binder as a part of your portfolio presentation. You may want to select a person as your customer and rehearse the use of these materials.

CHAPTER 12

Negotiating Buyer Resistance

LEARNING OBJECTIVES

When you finish reading this chapter, you should be able to

1. Describe common types of buyer resistance

2. Outline general strategies for negotiating buyer resistance

3. Discuss specific methods of negotiating buyer resistance

4. Describe ways to deal effectively with buyers who are trained in negotiating

The Stouffer Esmeralda Resort located in Palm Springs, California is a world-class hotel that offers the guest almost everything except a view of the ocean. The resort is located in the desert. Business meeting planners, representing groups from 50 to 500 persons, frequently seek what is called a *water destination*, a meeting site near a lake or ocean. Sherry Binger, sales manager at the Esmeralda Resort, has a ready response when customers raise concerns about a land-based location. She describes the exquisite swimming pools offered by the Esmeralda and the Oasis water park that can be used for water games. A wave machine is used at the water park to simulate ocean waves. She also describes the other recreation facilities that include a golf course, tennis courts, and a health spa. Of course some forms of buyer resistance are not communicated openly to Sherry and other members of the sales staff. She must often work hard to identify the resistance, clarify it, and then overcome it.[1]

Negotiating Buyer Resistance and Problems

Today salespeople like Sherry Binger and her prospects are more likely to negotiate problems from a position of strength (Fig. 12.1). The person who makes the buying decision is not only better educated in most cases, but also better prepared to make a decision.

NEGOTIATION—PART OF THE WIN-WIN RELATIONSHIP STRATEGY

Some of the traditional personal selling textbooks discussed how we should "handle" buyer objections. The message communicated to the reader was that personal selling is a "we versus they" process. Somebody wins, and somebody loses. The *win-win* solution, where both sides win, was not offered as an option.

Too often we were led to believe that buying problems or objections needed to be handled with some type of manipulation. Ron Willingham, author of *Integrity Selling*, notes the important difference between negotiation and manipulation:

> We don't view negotiation as manipulation. We don't see it as outtalking, outsmarting, or outmaneuvering people. We don't view it as combat or as an adver-

FIGURE 12.1   Negotiating Customer Concerns and Objections

The Six–Step Presentation Plan	
Step One: APPROACH	☑ Review Strategic/Consultative Selling Model. ☑ Initiate customer contact.
Step Two: PRESENTATION	☑ Determine prospect needs. ☑ Select product or service. ☑ Initiate sales presentation.
Step Three: DEMONSTRATION	☑ Decide what to demonstrate. ☑ Select selling tools. ☑ Initiate demonstration.
Step Four: NEGOTIATION	☐ Anticipate sales resistance. ☐ Plan negotiating methods. ☐ Initiate double-win negotiations.
Step Five: CLOSE	☐ Plan appropriate closing methods. ☐ Recognize closing clues. ☐ Initiate closing methods.
Step Six: SERVICING THE SALE	☐ Suggestion selling. ☐ Follow through. ☐ Follow-up calls.
Service, retail, wholesale, and manufacturer selling.	

Double-win salespeople have learned to anticipate certain objections and prepare with a well-planned and well-executed presentation.

sary relationship. Instead we view negotiating as a win-win activity—where seller and buyer sit down together and attempt to work out the best solution for both sides.[2]

In negotiations there are only two possible outcomes: win-win and lose-lose. The win-lose scenario is a deception. When the salesperson wins and the customer loses, it is a double loss. If the customer wins and the salesperson loses, it is also a double loss.[3] When the salesperson makes too many concessions and feels like a loser, service after the sale is likely to suffer. In fact, the salesperson may avoid dealing with the customer in the future. Win-win negotiations result in mutual respect, stronger relationships, and greater loyalty on the part of the salesperson and the customer.

What is **negotiation?** One definition is "working to reach an agreement that is mutually satisfactory to both buyer and seller." Another is "the way to reach a common understanding of the essential elements of a transaction."[4] As we noted in Chapter 1, the salesperson increasingly serves as a consultant or resource and provides solutions to buyers' problems. The consultant seeks to establish and maintain long-term relationships with customers. The ability to negotiate problems or objections is a necessary skill for all salespeople who adopt the consultative approach to personal selling. Figure 12.2 outlines the steps a salesperson can take to anticipate and negotiate problems.

It is important to keep in mind that negotiations often take place throughout the sales process—not just at the closing stage. Early negotiations may involve the meeting location, who will attend the sales presentation, or the amount of time available for the first meeting. Salespeople sometimes make early concessions to improve the relationship. This approach may set a costly precedent for later in the sale.[5] Some concessions can have a negative influence

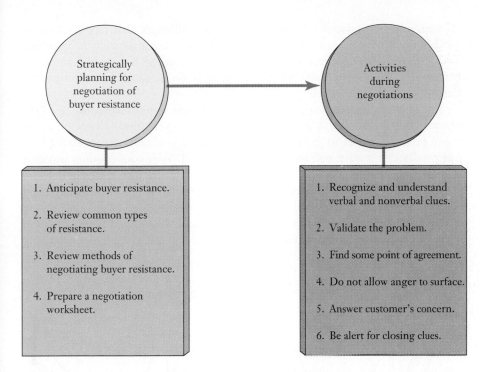

FIGURE 12.2   Today salespeople must be prepared to anticipate and negotiate buyer resistance and problems.

on the sales presentation. If, for example, you need forty minutes for an effective product demonstration, do not agree to a twenty-minute meeting.

Common Types of Buyer Resistance

Salespeople learn that patterns of buyer resistance exist, and they can therefore anticipate that certain concerns will arise during the sales call. With this information it is possible to be better prepared for each meeting with a customer. The great majority of buyer objections fall into five categories: need, product, source, price, and time.

RESISTANCE RELATED TO NEED FOR THE PRODUCT

If you have done your homework satisfactorily, then the prospect you call on probably has a need for your product or service. You can still expect, however, that the initial response may be, "I do not need your product." This might be a conditioned response that arises nearly every time the prospect meets with a sales representative. It may also be a cover-up for the real reason for not buying, which might be lack of funds, lack of time to examine your proposal carefully, or some other reason.

In some selling situations you can anticipate with great accuracy that the resistance will surface. Take, for example, the person selling a new type of office dictation equipment. This equipment is very advanced in terms of design and makes most existing equipment obsolete. Although the equipment offers the buyer many special features, resistance may still arise. Potential customers who already own dictation equipment are apt to say, "We are happy with our current system." Potential customers who do not own dictation equipment may say, "We can get along well without this equipment." In both cases the salesperson has encountered indifference related to need.

Sincere need resistance is one of the great challenges that face a salesperson. Think about it for a moment. Why would any customer want to purchase a product that does not seem to provide any real benefits? Unless we can create need awareness in the prospect's mind, there is no possible way to close the sale.

If you are calling on business prospects, the best way to overcome need resistance is to prove that your product is a good investment. Every privately owned business hopes to make a profit. Therefore you must demonstrate how your product or service will contribute to that goal. Will your product increase sales volume? Will it reduce operating expenses? If the owner of a hardware store says, "I already carry a line of high-quality tools," point out how a second line of less expensive tools will appeal to another large segment of the buying public. With the addition of the new line the store will be in a better position to compete with other stores (discount merchandise stores and supermarkets) that sell inexpensive tools.

Sometimes skepticism arises because the prospect is searching for more proof. © *April 1987 (Reprinted by permission of Sales & Marketing Management.)*

In some selling situations you must help the prospect solve a problem before you have any chance of closing the sale. Suppose the prospect says, "I am already overstocked." If you call on wholesalers or retailers, expect to hear this objection quite frequently. Often the prospect is unwilling to buy additional merchandise until older stock is sold. If there is no demand for the older merchandise, then a real problem exists. In this situation your best bet is to offer the buyer one or more solutions to the problem. Here are some tactics:

1. Suggest that the prospect hold a special sale to dispose of the unsold merchandise. It may even be necessary to sell the stock at a loss to recover at least part of the original investment. Closeouts can be painful, but it may be the best option.

2. Ask the prospect to accept a trial offer on a guaranteed sale or consignment basis. This option will allow the customer to acquire new merchandise without an initial cash investment and will open the door for your product.

3. If company policy permits, consider negotiating the purchase of the prospect's inventory. Give the customer a credit against a minimum opening order.

The key to negotiating need resistance in many cases is creative problem solving. Work closely with the prospect to overcome the barrier that prevents closing the sale.

RESISTANCE TO THE PRODUCT

In some cases the product itself becomes the focal point of buyer resistance. When this happens, try to discover specific reasons why the prospect has doubts about your product. Often you will find that one of the following factors has influenced the buyer's attitude:

1. The product is not well established. This is a common form of buyer resistance if you are selling a new or relatively new product. People do not like to take risks. They need plenty of assurance that the product is dependable. Use laboratory test results, third-party testimonials from satisfied users, or an effective demonstration to illustrate the product's strong points.

2. The product will not be popular. If the product is for resale, discuss sales results at other firms. Discuss the success other firms have had with your product. Also, discuss any efforts your company has taken to increase demand. For example, show the prospect sample advertisements that have appeared in the newspaper or commercials that have appeared on television.

3. Friends or acquaintances did not like the product. It is not easy to handle this form of buyer resistance. After all, you cannot say, "Your friend is all wet—our product is the best on the market!" Move cautiously to acquire more information. Use questions to pinpoint the problem, and clarify any misinformation that the person may have concerning your product.

4. The present product is satisfactory. Change does not come easily to many people. Purchasing a new product may mean adopting new procedures or retraining employees. In the prospect's mind the advantages do not outweigh the disadvantages, so buyer resistance surfaces. To overcome this resistance, we must build a greater amount of desire in the prospect's mind.

Concentrate on superior benefits that give your product a major advantage over the existing product.

RESISTANCE RELATED TO SOURCE

One of the hardest problems for a salesperson to overcome is the source objection. This is especially true if prospects feel genuine loyalty to their present supplier. We should not be surprised to hear a prospect say, "I have been buying from the Ralston Company for years, and their people have always treated me right." After all, the Ralston Company sales staff has no doubt taken great care to develop close ties with this prospect.

When dealing with the loyalty problem, it is usually best to avoid direct criticism of the competing firm. Negative comments are apt to backfire because they damage your professional image. It is best to keep the sales presentation focused on the customer's problems and your solutions.

There are positive ways to cope with the loyalty objection. Here are some suggestions:

1. Work harder to identify problems your company can solve with its products or services. With the help of good questions, you may be able to understand the prospect's problems better than your competitors.[6]

2. Point out that the business may profit from the addition of a second line. You do not expect the person to drop the present supplier, but you do want the person to try your product.

3. Point out the superior benefits of your product. Here you hope the logic of your presentation will overcome the emotional ties that may exist between the prospect and the present supplier.

4. Encourage the prospect to place a trial order, and then evaluate the merits of your product. Again, you are not asking the person to quit the present supplier.

5. Point out that the prospect's first obligation is to the business. As owner or manager, the person should continually be searching for ways to maintain or increase profits.

Source concerns can also be directed toward your company. For reasons that may be difficult to uncover, the prospect simply may not want to do business with your firm. Try to get the person to be specific about problems with your company. You must deal decisively with perceptions that are not accurate.

RESISTANCE RELATED TO PRICE

There are two important points to keep in mind concerning price resistance. It is one of the most *common forms* of buyer resistance in the field of selling. Therefore you must learn to negotiate skillfully in this problem area. The price objection is also one of the most common excuses. When people say, "Your price is too high," they probably mean, "You have not sold me yet."

Although price may not be the real barrier to closing the sale, do not overlook its importance. It is a major concern for many people. The professional buyer has no other choice than to search for the best possible buy. The typical prospect is also value conscious. It is important to keep in mind that in almost every selling situation getting the order depends on the right combination of price and quality.[7]

BUILDING QUALITY PARTNERSHIPS

THE WAY TO DEAL AT SATURN

The typical price negotiations that take place between a customer and the salesperson at an automobile dealership do not seem to provide the foundation for a strong partnership. About 68 percent of the consumers who participated in a recent survey said yes when responding to the statement, "I dread negotiations." The survey was conducted by J. D. Power & Associates, the company best known for its customer satisfaction research. Doris Ehlers, the J. D. Power account executive who conducted the study, said that dealers who skip the haggling are busier and better liked than traditional dealers. Most of the dealers who have adopted the no-dicker, one price approach say that their sales have increased since adopting the system.

General Motors conducted its own survey of car buyers and found that most dislike haggling over the price. The GM research also discovered that auto salespeople spend 25 percent of their time showing the car to customers and 75 percent of their time negotiating. When General Motors introduced the Saturn, a decision was made to change the role of the salesperson. The sticker price at Saturn dealers is fixed and there are no sales commissions. Pressure selling tactics are discouraged and outstanding customer service is encouraged. Don Hudler, Saturn's vice president of service and marketing, says, "We adopted some different role models, such as Nordstrom department stores."[a]

COPING WITH BUYERS WHO ARE TRAINED IN NEGOTIATION

In recent years, we have seen an increase in the number of training programs developed for professional buyers. One such course is Fundamentals of Purchasing for the Newly Appointed Buyer, offered by the American Management Association. Enrollees learn how to negotiate with salespeople. Some salespeople are also returning to the classroom to learn negotiation skills. Acclivus Corporation, a Dallas-based training company, offers the Acclivus Sales Negotiation course for salespeople who work in the business-to-business selling arena.

Professional buyers often learn to use specific tactics in dealing with salespeople. Homer Smith, author of *Selling through Negotiation*, provides these examples:

Budget limitation tactic[8] The buyer may say, "We like your proposal, but our budget for the convention is only $8,500." Is the buyer telling the truth, or is, the person testing your price? The best approach here is to take the budget limitation seriously and use appropriate negotiation strategies. One strategy is to reduce the price by eliminating some items. In the case of a fleet truck sale the salesperson might say, "We can deliver the trucks without radios and thus meet your budget figure. Would you be willing to purchase trucks without radios?"

Take-it-or-leave-it tactic[9] How do you respond to a buyer who says, "My final offer is $3,300, take it or leave it"? A price concession is, of course, one option. However, this will likely reduce profits for the company and lower your commission. An alternative strategy is to confidently review the superior benefits of your product and make another closing attempt. Appealing to the other person's sense of fairness may also move the discussion forward. If the final offer is totally without merit, consider calling a halt to the negotiation to allow the other party to back down from his position without losing face.[10]

Let us split the difference tactic[11] In some cases the salesperson may find this price concession acceptable. If the buyer's suggestion is not acceptable, then the salesperson might make a counteroffer.

These tactics represent only a sample of those used by professional buyers. To prepare for these and other tactics, salespeople need to plan their negotiating strategies in advance and have clear goals. To avoid falling prey to negotiating tricks, study all relevant information related to the sale and decide in advance on the terms you will (and will not) accept.[12]

NEGOTIATING PRICE WITH A LOW-PRICE STRATEGY

As noted in Chapter 6, some marketers have positioned their products with a price strategy. The goal is to earn a small profit margin on a large sales volume. Many of these companies have empowered their salespeople to use various low-price strategies such as quantity discounts, trade discounts, seasonal discounts, and promotional discounts. Some salespeople are given permission to match the price of any competitor. As noted in Chapter 6, one of the consequences of using low-price tactics may be lower commissions and lower profits.

HOW TO DEAL WITH PRICE RESISTANCE

As we have noted, price resistance is common, so we must prepare for it. There are some important "dos and don'ts" to keep in mind when the price concern surfaces.

Do add value with a cluster of satisfactions As noted in Chapter 6, a growing number of customers are seeking a cluster of satisfactions that includes a good product, a salesperson who is truly a partner, and a company that will stand behind its products (see Fig. 6.1). Many business firms are at a competitive disadvantage when the price alone is considered. When you look beyond price, however, it may become obvious that your company offers more value for the dollar.

Stephen Smith, senior account manager for Bell Atlantic, says that price is like the tip of the iceberg—it is often the only thing the customer sees. Salespeople need to direct the customer's attention to the value-added features that make up the bulk of the iceberg that is below the surface (Figure 12.3).[13] Do not forget to sell yourself as a high-value element of the sales proposal. Emphasize your commitment to customer service after the sale.

Do not make price the focal point of your sales presentation Price is not the most important thing that you are selling. If it were truly important, your company probably would not need you. A clerk could take the order over the telephone.

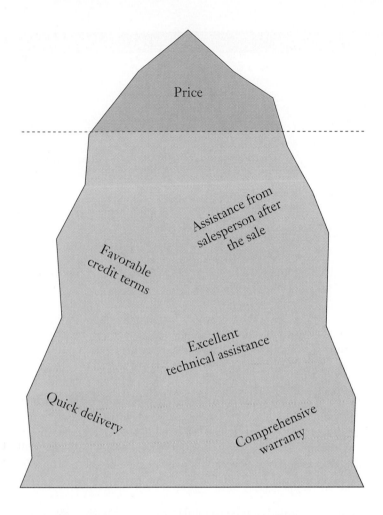

FIGURE 12.3 A sales proposal is sometimes like an iceberg. The customer sees the tip of the iceberg (price) but does not see the value-added features below the surface.

You may need to discuss price, but do not bring it up too early. The best time to deal with price is after you have reviewed product features and discussed buyer benefits.

Do not apologize for the price When you do mention price, do so in a confident and straightforward manner. Do not have even a hint of apology in your voice. Convey to the prospect that you believe your price is fair and make every effort to relate price to value. Many people fear paying too much for a product or service (Fig. 12.4). If your company has adopted a value-added strategy, point this fact out to the prospect. Then discuss how you and your company add value.

Do point out the relationship between price and quality In our highly competitive, free enterprise economy there are forces at work that tend to promote fair pricing. The highest quality can never be obtained at the lowest price. Quality comes from that Latin word *qualitas*, meaning, "What is the worth?" When you sell quality, price will more likely be secondary in the prospect's mind. Always point out the value-added features that create the

FIGURE 12.4 Price and value should balance in the prospect's mind.

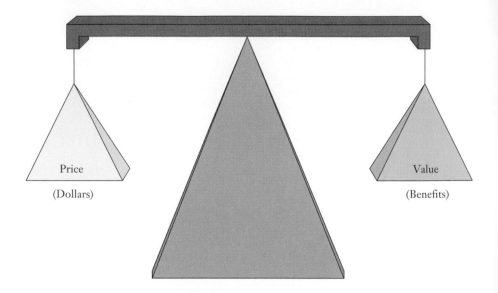

Price
(Dollars)

Value
(Benefits)

difference in price. Keep in mind that cheap products are built down to a price rather than up to a standard.[14] If you believe in your product and understand its unique features, price resistance will not bother you.

Do explain the difference between price and cost Price represents the initial amount the buyer pays for the product. Cost represents the amount the buyer pays for a product as it is used over a period of time. In Chapter 11 we discussed the results of a study conducted by the Rohm and Haas Paint Quality Institute. The cost per year when painting a home with ordinary latex paint was $575 compared to $240 for the same paint job using quality acrylic latex.

The price/cost comparison is particularly relevant with a product or service that lasts a long time or is particularly reliable. If one product requires servicing once a year, and a lower priced competing product requires servicing three times a year, the extra service calls must be part of the price/cost equation. In

Randall Murphy, President of Acclivus Corporation, explains the steps in a successful negotiation to a group of salespeople enrolled in his popular sales negotiation seminar. Courtesy Acclivus Corporation.

It's unwise to pay too much. But it's worse to pay too little.
    When you pay too much, you lose a little money, that is all.
    When you pay too little you sometimes lose everything, because the thing you bought was incapable of doing the thing it was bought to do.
    The common law of business balances prohibits paying a little and getting a lot. It can't be done.
    If you deal with the lowest bidder, it is well to add something for the risk you run.

John Ruskin

this case the product with the lower initial cost may *cost* more because of the two extra service calls.[15]

Do not make concessions too quickly   Give away concessions methodically and reluctantly, and always try to get something in return. A concession given too freely can diminish the value of your product. Also, giving a concession too easily may send the signal you are negotiating from a position of weakness.[16]

RESISTANCE RELATED TO TIME

If a prospect says, "I want time to think it over," you may be encountering resistance related to time. Resistance related to time is often referred to as the **stall.** D. Forbes Ley, author of *The Best Seller*, states that a stall signals conflict. He says, "The conflict is the agony of indecision between the desire to have your product versus feelings of uncertainty and anxiety."[17] A stall usually means the customer does not yet perceive the benefits of buying now. In most cases the stall indicates that the prospect has both positive and negative feelings about your product. Consider using questions to determine the negative feelings: "Is it my company that concerns you?" "Do you have any concerns about our warranty program?" "Does anyone else need to approve this purchase?"

It is all right to be persuasive if the prospect can truly benefit from buying now. If the price will soon rise, or if the item will not be available in the future, then you should provide this information. You must, however, present this information sincerely and accurately. It is never proper to distort the truth in the hope of getting the order.

General Strategies for Negotiating Buyer Resistance

The successful negotiation of buyer resistance is based in large part on understanding human behavior. This knowledge, coupled with a good measure of common sense, will help us overcome most forms of buyer resistance. It is also helpful to be aware of general methods for negotiating buyer resistance.

ANTICIPATE BUYER RESISTANCE

Many salespeople such as Sherry Binger, at Stouffer's Esmeralda Resort, have learned to anticipate certain problems and forestall them with a well-planned and well-executed presentation. Although buyer resistance is by no means insurmountable, it is a good idea to take preventative measures whenever possible. By anticipating problems we can approach the prospect with greater confidence and often save valuable time.

Salespeople frequently anticipate buyer resistance and plan ways to deal with it.

KNOW THE VALUE OF WHAT YOU ARE OFFERING

It is important that we know what is of real value to the customer, and not consider value only in terms of dollars.[18] The real value of what you are offering may be a value-added intangible such as superior product knowledge, good credit terms, or prompt delivery. An important aspect of the negotiation process is discovering what is of utmost importance to the buyer. Some salespeople make the mistake of offering a lower price the moment buyer resistance surfaces. In the customer's mind, price may be of secondary importance compared with the quality of service after the sale. As noted previously, do not be in a hurry to make price concessions.

PREPARE FOR NEGOTIATIONS

It helps to classify possible resistance with the aid of a negotiations worksheet. To illustrate how this form works, let us review an example from the food industry. Mary Turner is a salesperson for Durkee Famous Foods. She represents more than 350 products. Mary calls on supermarkets daily and offers assistance in the areas of ordering and merchandising. Recently, her company decided to offer retail food stores an allowance of $1 per case of olives if the store purchased fifteen or more cases. Prior to talking with her customers about this offer, Mary sat down and developed a negotiations worksheet, shown in Fig. 12.5. We cannot anticipate every possible problem, but it is possible to identify the most common problems that are likely to arise. The negotiations worksheet can be a useful tool.

UNDERSTAND THE PROBLEM

We have already noted that the prospect occasionally misunderstands the salesperson. It is just as easy for the salesperson to misunderstand the prospect. Therefore an important step in dealing with a problem is to make sure you un-

Negotiations Worksheet		
Customer's objection	Type of objection	Possible response
"Fifteen cases of olives will take up valuable space in my receiving room. It is already crowded."	Product	Direct denial: "You will not have to face that problem. With the aid of our merchandising plan you can display ten cases immediately on the sales floor. Only five cases will become reserve stock. You should move all fifteen cases in about two weeks."
"This is a poor time of the year to buy a large order of olives. People are not buying olives at this time."	Time	Indirect denial: "I agree that it has been a problem in the past, but consumer attitudes seem to be changing. We have found that olives sell well all year long if displayed properly. More people are using olives in the preparation of omelets, pizza, and other dishes. Of course, most relish trays feature olives. We will supply you with point-of-purchase material that suggests new ways to use this high-profit item."
"I would rather not tie up my money in a large order."	Price	Superior benefit: "As you know, olives represent a high-profit item. The average margin is 26 percent. With the addition of our $1.00 per case allowance the margin will rise to about 30 percent. This order will give you a good return on your investment."

FIGURE 12.5   Before the presentation it is important to prepare a negotiations worksheet.

derstand it. Be certain that both you and the prospect are clear on the true nature of what needs to be negotiated. When the prospect begins talking, listen carefully without interrupting, even when you think you know what the prospect is going to say. It is only common courtesy to give people the opportunity to express their point of view. With probing questions, you can fine-tune your understanding of the problem.

VALIDATE THE PROBLEM
When the prospect finishes talking, it is a good practice to validate the problem, using a confirmation question. This helps to isolate the true problem and reduce the chance of misunderstanding. The confirmation question might sound like this: "I think I understand your concern. You feel the warranty does not provide you with sufficient protection. Is this correct?" By taking time to

PART V DEVELOPING A PRESENTATION STRATEGY

ask this question you accomplish two important things. First, you are giving personal attention to the problem, which will please the customer. Second, you gain time to think about the best possible response.

As part of their customer strategy, salespeople must learn to distinguish between genuine problems and excuses. If the customer says, "I cannot afford your product," the statement might reflect the person's genuine belief that the price is too high, but it might also be used because the customer does not yet really think she has a need for your product.

A prospect may believe that a competing product is a better value. Instead of trying to justify this belief, the prospect raises a simple price or time objection. There is no precise method to separate excuses from genuine problems. Your experience and knowledge of the facts of the situation will be extremely useful. Tactful questions can also be helpful.

FIND SOME POINT OF AGREEMENT

Negotiating buying problems is a little like the art of diplomacy. It helps to know what points of agreement exist. This saves time and helps establish a closer bond between you and the prospect. At some point during the presentation, you might summarize by using a confirmation question: "Let us see if I fully understand your position. You think our product is well constructed and will provide the reliability you are looking for. Also, you believe our price is fair. Am I correct on these two points?"

Once all the areas of agreement have been identified, there may be surprisingly few points of disagreement. The prospect suddenly sees that the advantages of ownership far outweigh the disadvantages. Now that the air is cleared, both the salesperson and the customer can give their full attention to any remaining points of disagreement.

DO NOT DESTROY YOUR RELATIONSHIP STRATEGY WITH ANGER

In most situations the relationship between the salesperson and the prospect contains the seeds of conflict and disagreement. Conflict can arise when the salesperson and prospect fail to agree on need, price, credit terms, or other factors. When the customer becomes impatient or angry, the salesperson must be careful not to fuel this emotion. Most people's natural response when under attack is to defend themselves or to counterattack. Both of these tactics will usually fuel an upward spiral of heated disagreement.[19] If you want to earn the customer's trust and respect, avoid becoming defensive and argumentative. Ask questions and keep the customer talking so you learn more about the true nature of the problem. Also, listen to what the customer is saying. Listening without defending helps to defuse any anger.[20]

Specific Methods of Negotiating Buyer Resistance

There are seven specific methods of negotiating buyer resistance. In analyzing each problem we should try to determine which method will be most effective. In most cases we will use a combination of the following methods to negotiate buyer resistance.

BUILDING RELATIONSHIPS IN A DIVERSE WORLD

NEGOTIATING ACROSS CULTURES

Negotiations in the international area will vary from one country to another because of cultural differences. German buyers are more apt to look you in the eye and tell you what they do not like about your product. Japanese buyers, on the other hand, do not want to embarrass you and therefore will bury their concerns beneath several layers of courtesy. In China, now the largest market in the world for American products, negotiations are more straightforward. People who have been doing business in China for many years suggest a very direct approach to negotiations. However, do not become antagonistic. Do get involved in native business rituals which are intended to create a friendly atmosphere.

Americans are often impatient and most Chinese know this. It is best not to arrive at the negotiating table with a specific timetable. A major outcome of negotiations with the Chinese is to develop a relationship and a commitment to work together. This takes time.

When we enter into negotiations in foreign countries, it is important to understand and accommodate the customer's culture. You may not get every detail exactly right, but you will win respect by trying.[b]

DIRECT DENIAL

Direct denial involves refuting the opinion or belief of a prospect. The direct denial of a problem is considered a high-risk method of negotiating buyer resistance. Therefore you should use it with care. People do not like to be told they are wrong. Even when the facts prove the prospect is wrong, resentment can build if we fail to handle the situation properly.

When a prospect offers buyer resistance that is not valid, we sometimes have no option other than to openly disagree. If the person is misinformed, we must provide accurate information. For example, if the customer questions the product's quality, meet the concern head-on with whatever proof seems appropriate. It is almost never proper to ignore misinformation. High-performance salespeople counter inaccurate responses from the prospect promptly and directly.

The manner in which you state the denial is of major importance. Use a win-win approach. Be firm and sincere in stating your beliefs, but do not be offensive. Above all, do not patronize the prospect. A "know-it-all" attitude can be irritating.

INDIRECT DENIAL

Sometimes the prospect's concern is completely valid, or at least accurate to a large degree. This method is referred to as the **indirect denial.** The best approach is to bend a little and acknowledge that the prospect is at least partially correct. After all, if you offered a product that is objection proof, you would likely have no competitors. Every product has a shortcoming or limitation.[21] The success of this method is based in part on the need most people have to feel that their views are worthwhile. For this reason the indirect denial method is the most widely used. Here is an exchange that features the use of this approach. The salesperson is a key account sales representative for Pacific Bell Directory.[22]

Salesperson: The total cost of placing your six- by eight-inch ad in the yellow pages of five different Pacific Bell directories is $32,000.

Prospect: As a builder I want to reach people who are planning to build a home. I am afraid my ad will be lost among the hundreds of ads featured in your directories.

Salesperson: Yes, I agree the yellow pages in our directories do feature hundreds of ads, but the section for general contractors features less than thirty ads. Our design staff can prepare an ad that will be highly visible and will set your company apart from ads placed by other contractors.

Note that the salesperson used the words, "Yes, I agree . . ." to reduce the impact of denial. The prospect is less likely to feel his point of view has been totally disproved.

FEEL — FELT — FOUND

Successful salespeople are sensitive to clues that indicate the client feels something is wrong. One way to empathize with the client's objection is to use the "feel—felt—found" strategy. Here is how it works. Assume the customer is concerned about the complexity of the microcomputer, and says, "I do not think I can ever learn how to operate that thing." Your response might be, "I understand how you *feel*, Mr. Pearson. Many of my customers *felt* the same way, until they started using the PC-120 and *found* it quite easy to master."[23]

QUESTIONS

Another effective way to negotiate buyer resistance is to convert the problem into a question. Let us say that a prospect wants to trade used office equipment for new equipment but objects to the low trade-in allowance. The salesperson responds in this way: "Do you not feel that our trade-in allowance, which is slightly lower than what you expected, will be more than offset by the extra service and dependability of our company?"

Suppose a prospect interested in purchasing four new tires objects to the price, which is about $20 higher per set than the price of a competing firm. The salesperson uses a question to minimize the price difference: "Do you not feel that the convenience of our nationwide dealer network more than offsets the small price difference?" In this example the question is designed to encourage the tire buyer to weigh the disadvantage of a slightly higher price against the advantage of a national system of dealers who can provide convenient service. Questions often motivate the prospect to think in more depth about the salesperson's offer. Prior to a sales presentation, make a list of the objections you expect to hear from the prospect, and next to each one list the questions you can use to minimize it.

Linda Richardson, author of *Stop Telling, Start Selling*, suggests that we should ask questions and then listen with a "third ear." She encourages salespeople to listen for words that need more definition and then ask more questions if additional clarification is needed.[24]

THE SUPERIOR BENEFIT

Sometimes the customer raises a problem that cannot be answered with a denial. For example: "Your copy machine does not feature an automatic document feed mechanism. This means that our employees will have to spend more time at the machine." You should acknowledge the valid objection and then discuss one or more superior benefits: "We have not included the automatic

The product demonstration is one of the most convincing ways to overcome buyer resistance.

feature because it is less reliable than the manual approach. As you know, downtime is not only costly but also inconvenient." A **superior benefit** is a benefit that will, in most cases, outweigh the customer's specific concern.

DEMONSTRATION

If you are familiar with your product as well as that of your competition, this method of negotiating buyer resistance is easy to use. You know the competitive advantages of your product and can discuss these features with confidence.

The product demonstration is one of the most convincing ways to overcome buyer skepticism. With the aid of an effective demonstration you can overcome specific concerns.

Sometimes a second demonstration is needed to overcome buyer skepticism. This demonstration will provide additional proof. High-achieving sales personnel know when and how to use proof to overcome buyer resistance.

BUILDING RELATIONSHIPS THROUGH TECHNOLOGY

AUTOMATED SORTING AND PRODUCTIVITY

The notes of a busy salesperson can soon become extensive. Paper notes make it difficult if not impossible to cross reference important information within those notes.

An automated notes system gives salespeople immediate access to records containing needed words or phrases. This offers users many advantages, including a method of quickly finding information about people whose names may have been recorded in the notes. (See Sales Automation Application Exercise on p. 289 for more information.)

TRIAL OFFER

A **trial offer** involves giving the prospect an opportunity to try the product without making a purchase commitment. The trial offer (especially with new products) is popular with customers because they can get fully acquainted with your product without making a major commitment. Assume that a buyer for a large restaurant chain says, "I am sure you have a good cooking oil, but we are happy with our present brand. We have had no complaints from our managers." In response to this comment you might say, "I can understand your reluctance to try our product. However, I do believe our oil is the finest on the market. With your permission I would like to ship you thirty gallons of our oil at no cost. You can use our product at selected restaurants and evaluate the results. If our oil does not provide you with superior results, you are under no obligation to place an order."

In the case of office equipment the customer may be given the opportunity to use the product on a trial basis. An office manager might respond to the salesperson who sells dictation equipment in this manner: "I would not feel comfortable talking to a machine." In response to this issue a salesperson might say, "I can understand how you feel. How about using one of our demonstration models for a few days?"

THIRD-PARTY TESTIMONY

Studies indicate that the favorable testimony of a neutral third party can be an effective method of responding to buyer resistance.[25] Let us assume that the owner of a small business states that she can get along without a personal computer. The salesperson might respond in this manner: "Many small business owners think the way you do. However, once they use a personal computer, they find it to be an invaluable aid. Mark Williams, owner of Williams Hardware, says that his PC saves him several hours a week. Plus, he has improved the accuracy of his record keeping." Third-party testimony provides a positive way to solve certain types of buying problems. The positive experiences of a neutral third party will almost never trigger an argument with the prospect.

COMBINATION METHODS

As noted previously, consultative-style selling is characterized by flexibility. A combination of methods sometimes proves to be the best way to deal with buyer resistance. For example, an indirect denial might be followed by a question: "The cost of our business security system is a little higher than the competition. The price I have quoted reflects the high-quality materials used to develop our system. Would you not feel better entrusting your security needs to a firm with more than 25 years of experience in the business security field?" In this situation the salesperson might also consider combining the indirect denial with an offer to arrange a demonstration of the security system.

SUMMARY

Sales resistance is natural and should be welcomed as an opportunity to learn more about how to satisfy the prospect's needs. Buyers' concerns often provide salespeople with precisely the information they need to close a sale.

Resistance may arise from a variety of reasons, some related to the content or manner of the presentation strategy and others related to the prospect's own concerns. Whatever the reasons, the salesperson should *negotiate* sales resistance with the proper attitude, never making too much or too little of the prospect's resistance.

General strategies for negotiating buyer resistance include anticipating it, knowing the value of what you are offering, preparing for negotiations, understanding the problem, validating the problem, finding some point of agreement, and avoiding anger.

The best strategy for negotiating sales resistance is to anticipate it and pre-plan methods to answer the prospect's concerns. If a salesperson uses a negotiations worksheet, then it will be much easier to deal with buyer resistance.

We discussed the various types of problems likely to surface during the sales presentation. Most objections can be placed in one of five categories: need, product, source, price, and time.

Specific methods and combinations of methods of negotiating resistance will vary depending on the particular combination of salesperson, product, and prospect. We have described several common methods, but you should remember that practice in applying them is essential and that there is room for a great deal of creative imagination in developing variations or additional methods. With careful preparation and practice, negotiating the most common types of buyer resistance should become a stimulating challenge to each salesperson's professional growth.

➤ KEY TERMS

Negotiation   *Indirect Denial*
Stall   *Superior Benefit*
Direct Denial   *Trial Offer*

➤ REVIEW QUESTIONS

1. Explain why a salesperson should welcome sales resistance.

2. List the common types of buyer resistance that might surface in a presentation.

3. How does the negotiations worksheet form help the salesperson prepare to negotiate sales resistance?

4. Explain the value of using a confirmation question as a general strategy for negotiating buyer resistance.

5. List seven general strategies for negotiating buyer resistance.

6. John Ruskin (see Sales Tip on p. 279) says that it is unwise to pay too much when making a purchase, but it is worse to pay too little. Do you agree or disagree with this statement? Explain.

7. What is usually the most common reason prospects give for not buying? How can salespeople deal effectively with this type of resistance?

8. Professional buyers often learn to use specific negotiation tactics in dealing with salespeople. List and describe two tactics that are commonly used today.

9. When a customer says, "I want time to think it over," what type of

resistance is the salesperson encountering? Suggest ways to overcome this type of buyer resistance.

10. What are some positive ways to cope with the loyalty objection?

➤ APPLICATION EXERCISES

1. During an interview with a prospective employer the interviewer raises the objection that you are not qualified for the job for which you are applying. On the basis of your observation you do not believe the interviewer fully understands the amount of experience you have or that you really have the ability to perform the job requirements. Write how you would overcome the objection the interviewer has raised.

2. Your negotiation of sales resistance can be compared in part with how you manage interpersonal conflicts. In learning how to deal with conflicts constructively the first step is to become aware of your present and past style of managing conflict. Think back over the interpersonal conflicts you may have been involved in during the past few years. These conflicts may be with customers, friends, parents, spouse, teachers, boss, or subordinates. In the space provided, list the five major conflicts you can remember and how you resolved them.

Conflict   Resolution of Conflict
1.
2.
3.
4.
5.

Analyze your basic style of conflict management from these five examples. Do you tend to back away from conflicts (the "flight method" of conflict resolution), or do you look for conflict and stand your ground no matter what happens (the "fight method" of conflict resolution)? Would salespeople who have a flight style of handling objections close many sales? How about the salesperson who has a fight style? Which style would the salesperson who always used the direct denial method of negotiating tend to possess—flight or fight? Is the indirect denial a fight, a flight, or a somewhere in between style? Explain.

3. Assume you have decided to sell your own home. During an open house a prospect, whom you are showing through the house, begins to criticize every major selling point about your home.

   a. You have taken excellent care of your home, believe it to be a good home, and have done a lot of special projects to make it more enjoyable. What will be your emotional reaction to this prospect's criticisms? Should you express this emotional reaction?

   b. Underneath this surface criticism you think this prospect is really interested in buying your home. How would you negotiate the sales resistance he is showing?

4. Acclivus Corporation is a leading supplier of sales training programs. As noted in this chapter, one of their most popular programs is the "Acclivus

Sales Negotiation System." Access the Acclivus home page on the Internet, and click on the "What We Offer" screen. Study the information on the Negotiation training program. Also, click on the Advertising screen and study Acclivus' "R3evolution" concept. What is this concept? Click on the "Success Stories" screen and examine what organizations say about the negotiations training they have received.

➤ SALES AUTOMATION APPLICATION EXERCISE

ACT! AUTOMATED SORTING

One of the people on the Cadalyst Resources technical team, Linda, helped evaluate some prospects' CAD needs. If you are planning to meet with Linda, you might wish to have those records available for discussion. By using ACT! software, access all records containing the name Linda by pressing L E L K Linda Enter. After searching and sorting, ACT! will display five records. An examination of the records will show that Linda did assist on four accounts. The fifth record identifies Linda as the spouse of that prospect.

➤ CASE PROBLEM

Each year public and private organizations send thousands of employees to meetings held at hotels, motels, convention centers, conference centers, and resorts. These meetings represent a multimillion dollar business in the United States. Some of the largest providers of meeting space and related services are catering to clients in new and exciting ways. The Stouffer Esmeralda Resort hotel (introduced at the beginning of this chapter) provides a good example of such a destination. The goal of this hotel is to provide guests with an experience they will talk about the rest of their lives. The hotel offers 560 deluxe guest rooms, several suites, soundproof meeting rooms with state-of-the-art audiovisual technology, and continuous break service that will accommodate any agenda. Lavish customized meal events are a specialty of the Esmeralda Resort. Guests enjoy use of a championship golf course; tennis courts; swimming pools; and a fitness center complete with whirlpools, saunas, weight room, and acrobic classes. Several restaurants and lounges are available to guests.

In an ideal situation Sherry Binger, sales manager, likes to guide prospects on a site inspection of her property. This tour, in some ways, fulfills the function of a sales demonstration. Throughout the tour she describes special amenities and services offered by the hotel. She also uses this time to get better acquainted with the needs of the prospect. Once the tour is completed she will escort the prospect back to her office and complete the needs assessment. Next, she will prepare a detailed sales proposal. In most cases the proposal will be presented to the prospect at a second meeting. The proposal needs to contain accurate and complete facts because when signed, it becomes a legally enforceable sales contract.

Rarely will the sales proposal be accepted without modification. Professional meeting planners are experienced negotiators and will press hard for concessions. Some have completed training programs developed for professional buyers. The concessions requested may include a lower guest room rate, lower meal costs, complimentary suites, or a complimentary event such as a wine and cheese reception or a theme party:

Of course some buyer resistance is not easily identified. Sherry Binger says that she follows three steps in dealing with buyer resistance:

1. Locate the resistance. Some prospects are reluctant to accept a sales proposal, but the reason may be unclear. Sherry has discovered in some cases that small groups are concerned about the sheer size of the Esmeralda. They wonder if a small group will receive the same personalized attention given to a large group. Once this perception is uncovered, Sherry knows how to deal with it.

2. Clarify the resistance. If a prospect says, "I like your facilities, but your prices are a little high," then the salesperson must clarify the meaning of this objection. Is the prospect seeking a major price concession or a small price concession?

3. Overcome the objection. Sherry says, "You must be prepared for negotiations and know the value of what you are offering." The resort must earn a profit, so concessions can only be made after careful consideration of the bottom line.

Sherry has discovered that the best way to negotiate buyer resistance is to make sure both the prospect and the resort feel like winners once the negotiations are finalized. If either party feels like a loser, a long-term partnership will not be possible.

QUESTIONS

1. If you were selling convention services for a hotel located in a large city, what types of buyer resistance would you expect from a new prospect?

2. Let us assume that you are representing the Stouffer Esmeralda Resort Hotel and you are meeting with a new prospect in her office. She is a busy meeting planner who does not want to visit your property until she has a meeting with you. What are some tools that you might use during the sales presentation? What proof devices might you use to support your claims?

3. If you meet with a professional buyer who is trained in negotiation, what tactics can you expect the person to use? How would you respond to each of these tactics?

➤ SALES AUTOMATION CASE STUDY

NEGOTIATIONS

Becky Kemley (see Chapter 8 Case Study) has asked you to review Mark David's former prospect account. She wants you to look for accounts in which you might anticipate objections to things within a presentation.

Access the ACT! software following the instructions in Appendix 2.

Questions

1. Which account might voice a time objection and say, "We want to put off our decision for now," and how would you propose dealing with this objection?

2. Which account might try to get you to agree to a lower price and how would you respond?

3. Which account might you anticipate would use the phrase "we want to shop around for a good solid supplier." What would be your response?

PARTNERSHIP SELLING: A ROLE PLAY/SIMULATION (see Appendix 3, p. 421)

Developing a Presentation Strategy—Negotiating

Refer to *sales memorandum 3* and strategically plan to anticipate and negotiate any objections and/or concerns your customer may have to your presentation. You should prepare a negotiations worksheet to organize this part of your presentation.

The instructions for item 2e directs you to prepare negotiations for the time, price, source, and product objections. You will note that your price is approximately $200 more than your customer budgeted for this meeting. You will have to be very effective in negotiating a value added strategy because your convention center is not a low price supplier (see Chapter 6 on value added product strategies).

During the presentation you should use proof devices from the product strategy materials provided in *employment memorandum 1* to negotiate concerns you anticipate. You may also want to use a calculator to negotiate any financial arrangements such as savings on parking, airport transportation, etc. Place these materials in the front pocket of your three-ring binder (portfolio) so you can easily access them during your presentation. You may want to secure another person to be your customer, instructing them to voice the objections you have anticipated, and then you respond with your negotiation strategies. This experience will provide you with the opportunity to rehearse your negotiation strategies.

Closing and Confirming the Sale

LEARNING OBJECTIVES

When you finish reading this chapter, you should be able to

1. Describe the proper attitude to display toward closing the sale

2. List and discuss selected guidelines for closing the sale

3. Explain how to recognize closing clues

4. Discuss selected methods of closing the sale

5. Explain what to do when the buyer says yes and what to do when the buyer says no

Dana Bengtson, sales representative for Ryder Commercial Leasing & Services, understands the importance of patience in selling. It took him two years to convince Burris Foods, a Delaware-based food distributor, to replace its in-house truck fleet with leased trucks from Ryder. Soon after his first contact he arranged for efficiency studies of Burris's existing transportation system. With this information he was able to demonstrate the cost advantages of leasing. Although he seemed to be moving toward a close, Burris officials let it be known that they did not want to continue talks about leasing, at least for the time being. Bengtson realized it was time to slow down negotiations and be patient. In his words, it was time to "do nothing." Later Bengtson resumed his closing efforts. He sent Burris officials' articles on long-term vehicle leasing and information on the food distribution business. He restructured his proposal to make it more appealing. After six more months of hard work, he was rewarded with a seven-year lease agreement worth $3 million annually to Ryder. Dana Bengtson closed this sale because he knew when to speed up and when to slow down negotiations.[1]

Developing an Attitude Toward Closing the Sale

The excitement and personal satisfaction Dana Bengtson feels after closing a sale are common among both new and experienced salespeople. When the prospect says yes, the salesperson receives both a personal and an economic reward. The amount of personal satisfaction received on closing the sale depends on the salesperson's attitude toward the product. Salespeople who believe strongly in their product enjoy converting prospects to customers. They also look forward to a continuing partnership with the new customer.

Closing the sale is less difficult if everything is handled properly throughout the sales presentation. A strategically prepared salesperson approaches the close with confidence (Fig. 13.1). Closing is usually more difficult when some aspect of the sales presentation has not been handled properly. Maybe a negative first impression still lingers in the prospect's mind. Perhaps the sales demonstration did not go smoothly. Maybe sales resistance was not negotiated effectively. These and other factors can serve as barriers to closing the sale.

Some sales are lost because the salesperson attempts to close too early or too late. Sometimes, salespeople try to close before the prospect is ready to

The Six–Step Presentation Plan	
Step One: APPROACH	☑ Review Strategic/Consultative Selling Model. ☑ Initiate customer contact.
Step Two: PRESENTATION	☑ Determine prospect needs. ☑ Select product or service. ☑ Initiate sales presentation.
Step Three: DEMONSTRATION	☑ Decide what to demonstrate. ☑ Select selling tools. ☑ Initiate demonstration.
Step Four: NEGOTIATION	☑ Anticipate sales resistance. ☑ Plan negotiating methods. ☑ Initiate double–win negotiations.
Step Five: CLOSE	☐ Plan appropriate closing methods. ☐ Recognize closing clues. ☐ Initiate closing methods.
Step Six: SERVICING THE SALE	☐ Suggestion selling. ☐ Follow through. ☐ Follow-up calls.
Service, retail, wholesale, and manufacturer selling.	

FIGURE 13.1 Effective closing methods require careful planning.

A strategically prepared salesperson approaches the close with confidence.

buy. An early closing attempt may be interpreted as "pressure" selling. We must take care to avoid giving the prospect a feeling of anxiety about being sold something.

It is also possible to close too late by ignoring obvious closing clues. Sometimes, salespeople keep on talking long after buyers have decided to make the purchase. When this happens, customer attitudes sometimes change, and the sales are lost.

Another barrier to closing the sale is the early "retreat." When the buyer says no, the salesperson may give up too soon. These and other barriers are discussed in this chapter.

LOOKING AT CLOSING FROM THE PROSPECT'S POINT OF VIEW

Closing the sale will no doubt be easier if you look at this aspect of selling from the prospect's point of view. Recognize the concerns that may surface in the person's mind.

Do I really need this product?

Does this product measure up to the competition?

Should I postpone buying?

Will this supplier stand behind the product?

What will my friends think if I buy this item?

These are genuine concerns that could prevent the buyer from saying yes to your proposal. It is best to anticipate these concerns and develop an effective sales presentation that will eliminate them.

DETERMINATION IS THE KEY

Joe Batten, author of the popular sales training film, *Ask for the Order and Get It*, believes that determination is a major key to success in personal selling. He describes determination as a firm, unyielding stand never to let a sale you have worked to make go unasked for. Determination prevents you from taking a quick no for an answer. Determination keeps you from mistaking a customer's doubt for refusal, recognizing that the word no may mean "no for now," or "no based on what I currently know."[a]

CLOSING THE SALE IS A PROCESS

Closing should be viewed as part of the selling process—the logical outcome of a well-planned presentation strategy. There is a building process that begins with an interesting approach and need discovery. It continues with effective product selection and presentation of benefits that build desire for the product. After a well-planned demonstration and after dealing with sales resistance, it is time to ask for the sale.

The image of a salesperson who makes a quick pitch, writes up an order, and disappears has faded into history. In the new economy the customer realizes the need for a partner, someone to be there when needed, to consistently advise and to help solve problems on a continuing basis.[2]

THE TIMIDITY FACTOR

Vince Peters, director of sales training and development for Wyeth-Ayerst International, a large pharmaceutical company, says that some salespeople are overly polite and hesitant to ask for the sale: "They don't want to seem pushy or overly assertive."[3] The point is that you should view the relationship between buyer and seller as a partnership where both benefit. It means that in some cases you must take the initiative and assert yourself. The salesperson who confidently asks for the sale after the customer says no is displaying the boldness that is often needed in personal selling.

Guidelines for Closing the Sale

A number of factors increase the odds that you will close the sale (Fig. 13.2). These guidelines for closing the sale have universal application in the field of selling.

FOCUS ON DOMINANT BUYING MOTIVES

Most salespeople incorporate the outstanding benefits of their product into the sales presentation. This is only natural. However, be alert to the *one* benefit that generates the most excitement. The buying motive that is of greatest interest deserves the greatest emphasis. Vince Peters tells his 8,000 Wyeth-Ayerst salespeople that the key to closing ". . . is to find out exactly what a prospect is looking for."[4]

FIGURE 13.2 The presentation strategy should include reviewing these guidelines for closing and confirming the sale.

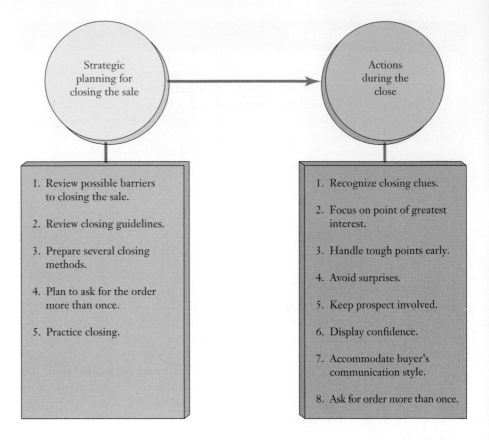

Strategic planning for closing the sale → Actions during the close

1. Review possible barriers to closing the sale.

2. Review closing guidelines.

3. Prepare several closing methods.

4. Plan to ask for the order more than once.

5. Practice closing.

1. Recognize closing clues.

2. Focus on point of greatest interest.

3. Handle tough points early.

4. Avoid surprises.

5. Keep prospect involved.

6. Display confidence.

7. Accommodate buyer's communication style.

8. Ask for order more than once.

Zig Ziglar, author of *Secrets of Closing the Sale*, reminds us that when closing it is important to give prospects a reason to buy, or some information so that they can act in their own best interests. He says, "This helps you move closing from being *selfish* on your part to being *helpful* to the prospect."[5] To apply this premise, focus your close on the point of greatest interest, and give the prospect a reason for buying.

NEGOTIATING THE TOUGH POINTS BEFORE ATTEMPTING THE CLOSE

Many products have what might be thought of as an Achilles' heel. In other words, the product is vulnerable in one or more areas. Negotiate a win-win solution to the tough points before you attempt to close the sale. Such factors can lose the sale if you ignore them. The close should be a positive phase of the sales presentation. This is not the time to deal with a controversial issue or problem.

In the case of Maytag washing machines, Hickey-Freeman–hand-tailored suits, Lexus automobiles, or Ritz-Carlton conference facilities, the Achilles' heel may be price. Each of these products may seem expensive in comparison with competing ones. People who sell them find ways to establish the value of their product before attempting the close.

This Little Charlies Pizza ad focuses on one of the dominant customer buying motives in the food service industry. Focusing on dominant buying motives helps close sales.

AVOID SURPRISES AT THE CLOSE

Some salespeople make the mistake of waiting until the close to reveal information that may come as a surprise to the prospect. For example, the salesperson quotes a price but is not specific concerning what the price includes. Let us assume that the price of a central air-conditioning unit is $1,800. The prospect believes that the price is competitive in relation to similar units on the market and is ready to sign the order form. Then the salesperson mentions casually that the installation charge is an extra $225. The prospect had assumed that the $1,800 fee included installation. Suddenly, the extra fee looms as a major obstacle to closing the sale.

The surprise might come in the form of an accessory that costs extra, terms of the warranty, customer service limitations, or some other issue. Do not let a last-minute surprise damage the relationship and threaten the completion of a sale.

DO NOT ISOLATE THE PROSPECT DURING THE SALE

Adults are self-directing people. They are most comfortable when they have a voice in matters that influence their lives. Do not forget this important point at the time you attempt to close. Involve the customer in the close if at all possible.

You can achieve involvement with questions. You might summarize points of agreement with carefully phrased confirmation-type questions. Here are some examples:

> "Ms. Hansen, you seem to agree that this model combines good looks with durability. Is that right?"

> "Mr. Walker, you do agree that your current electric bills are too high. Is that right?"

You might also let the prospect summarize the positive aspects of your product. This might be done by using the following types of questions:

> "What features of our product do you like best?"

> "What aspects of our customer service program do you find most appealing?"

Sometimes it is possible to involve the prospect in some type of "doing" activity such as a demonstration. For example, a salesperson selling carpet might hand the prospect a sample case and ask the person to pick out her favorite color. The prospect might be asked to hold the sales proposal as the salesperson explains the details.

DISPLAY A HIGH DEGREE OF SELF-CONFIDENCE AT THE CLOSE

Do you believe in your product? Do you believe in your company? Have you identified a genuine need? If you can answer yes to each of these questions, then there is no need to display timidity. Look the prospect in the eye, and ask for the order. Do not be apologetic at this important point in the sales presentation. Cavett Robert, noted sales consultant, once said, "The prospect is persuaded more by the depth of your conviction than he is by the height of your logic."[6] A display of self-confidence during the close is very important.

ASK FOR THE ORDER MORE THAN ONCE

Too often, salespeople make the mistake of asking for the order just once. If the prospect says no, they give up. A survey on closing attempts found that almost 50 percent of all salespeople asked for the order once and then gave up if the prospect said no.[7] Another 20 percent attempted to close two times and then gave up. Some of the most productive salespeople asked for the order three, four, or even five times. A surprising number of yes responses come on the fourth or fifth attempt. Of course not all of these closing attempts necessarily came during one call.

BUILDING QUALITY PARTNERSHIPS

AN INSPIRING EXAMPLE

Ben Feldman was an unlikely candidate to earn the title "Greatest Life-Insurance Salesperson in History." He talked softly, hesitantly and had a deceptively sleepy appearance. He was so shy that he once insisted on standing behind a screen when he spoke to an audience of fellow insurance salespeople. This quiet demeanor seemed to appeal to most customers because he closed thousands of sales. He joined New York Life Insurance Company in the early 1940s and soon started making his mark. In the 1950s he became the first agent to write a million dollars in new business a month. In the 1960s he was the first salesperson to write a million a week. When he was in his prime, Feldman's income approached $5 million a year.

He sold life insurance by talking about life, not death. He focused his attention on owners of small industrial corporations. Feldman appealed to their need to protect their assets with large amounts of life insurance. He would show prospects his "tax book," a loose-leaf binder that contained the financial histories of people whose businesses or property had to be sold because they died without enough life insurance to pay estate taxes. Taped inside were a $1,000 bill and a few pennies. He would point to the pennies and say, "For these you can get this"—the bill. This sales tool helped him close many sales.

In 1993, New York Life marked Ben Feldman's 50th year with the company by proclaiming "Feldman's February." The company initiated a national competition in which agents were encouraged to sell their best to honor Feldman. The winner of the Feldman February competition was Ben Feldman. Working the phones as he recovered from a health problem he recorded sales of over $15 million.[b]

The founder of National Retail Workshops, a company specializing in retail sales training, states that for every 100 retail sales presentations, 20 percent of the customers simply say, "I'll take it," and buy the product without a closing attempt. In 20 percent of the situations the salesperson makes a closing attempt. In 60 percent of the presentations, no attempt is made to close the sale.

Many customers will think more highly of you if you have the courage to ask for the order. Do not be timid. If you beat around the bush, they may begin to question your commitment to the product. If you are fearful of asking for the order, or ask once and give up, you will never achieve success in personal selling.

RECOGNIZE CLOSING CLUES

As the sales presentation progresses, you need to be alert to closing clues (sometimes called buying signals). A **closing clue** is an indication, either verbal or nonverbal, that the prospect is preparing to make a buying decision. It is a form of feedback, which is so important in selling. When you detect a closing clue, it may be time to attempt a close.

Many closing clues are quite subtle and may be missed if you are not alert. This is especially true in the case of nonverbal buying signals. If you pay careful attention—with your eyes and your ears—many prospects will tell you how to close the sale. As we have noted earlier in this text, one of the most important personality traits salespeople need is empathy, the ability to sense what the other person is feeling. In this section we will review some of the most common verbal and nonverbal clues.

VERBAL CLUES

Closing clues come in many forms. Spoken words (verbal clues) are usually the easiest to perceive. These clues can be divided into three categories: (1) questions, (2) recognitions, and (3) requirements.

Questions One of the least subtle buying signals is the question. You might attempt a trial close after responding to one of the following questions:

"Do you have a credit plan to cover this purchase?"

"What type of warranty do you provide?"

"How soon can our company get delivery?"

Recognitions A recognition is any positive statement concerning your product or some factor related to the sale, such as credit terms or delivery date. Some examples follow:

"We like the quality control system you have recommended."

"I have always wanted to own a boat like this."

"Your delivery schedule fits our plans."

Requirements Sometimes, customers outline a condition that must be met before they will buy. If you are able to meet this requirement, it may be a good time to try a trial close. Here are some requirements that the prospect might voice:

"We will need shipment within two weeks."

"Our staff will need to be trained in how to use this equipment."

"All our equipment must be certified by the plant safety officer."

In some cases, verbal buying clues will not jump out at you. Important buying signals may be interwoven into normal conversation. Listen closely whenever the prospect is talking.

NONVERBAL CLUES

Nonverbal buying clues will be even more difficult to detect. Once detected, this type of signal is not easy to interpret. Nevertheless, you should be alert to body movement, facial expression, and tone of voice. Here are some actions that suggest that the prospect may be prepared to purchase the product:[8]

The prospect's facial expression changes. Suddenly, the person's eyes widen, and genuine interest is clear in the facial expression.

The prospect begins showing agreement by nodding.

The prospect leans forward and appears to be intent on hearing your message.

The prospect begins to examine the product or study the sales literature intently.

When you observe or sense one of these nonverbal buying clues, do not hesitate to ask for the order. Keep in mind that the modern approach to selling holds that there may be several opportunities to close throughout the sales presentation. Important buying signals may surface at any time. Do not miss them.

Methods of Closing the Sale

There is no *best* closing method. Your best bet is to preplan several closing methods and use the ones that seem appropriate (Fig. 13.3). Given the complex nature of many sales, it is often a good idea to be prepared to use a combination of closing methods. Do keep in mind that your goal is not only to close the sale, but also to develop a long-term partnership. A win-win closing strategy results in repeat business and the opportunity to obtain referrals.

Closing Worksheet		
Closing clue (prospect)	Closing method	Closing statement (salesperson)
"Our staff will need to be trained in the use of this equipment."	**Negotiating-the-single problem close**	"We will send our technical staff to your company as soon as the product arrives. They will spend two days with your staff showing them the entire operational program. In addition, they will be on call for any questions or service during the following six weeks."
"That sounds fine."	**Direct appeal close**	"Good, may I get your signature on this order form?"
"What kind of financing do you offer?"	**Limited choice close**	"We have two financing methods available: ninety-day open credit or two-year–long-term financing. Which of these do you prefer?"
"Well, we don't have large amounts of cash available at this time."	**Assumption close**	"Based on your cash position, I would recommend you consider our lease-purchase plan. This plan allows you to pay a very small initial amount at this time and keep the cash you now have for your everyday business expenses. I will be happy to write up your order on the lease-purchase plan."

FIGURE 13.3   Preparing for the close requires the preplanning of several closing methods. Research indicates that in many selling situations several closing attempts will be necessary.

TRIAL CLOSE

Charles B. Roth, noted sales consultant, once said, "Start your presentation on a closing action, continue it on a closing action, and end it on a closing action." This may be overdoing it a little, but Mr. Roth does make an important point. You should not postpone attempts to close until your sales presentation is completed.

A **trial close,** also known as a *minor point close,* is a closing attempt made at an opportune time during the sales presentation to encourage the customer to reveal readiness or unwillingness to buy. When you are reasonably sure that the prospect is about to make a decision but is being held back by natural caution, the trial close may be appropriate. It is a good way to test the buyer's attitude toward the actual purchase. A trial close is often presented in the form of a probing or confirmation question. Here are some examples:

"We can arrange an August first shipment. Would this date be satisfactory?"

"Which do you prefer, the dark green or the blue finish?"

"Would you rather begin this plan on July first or July fifteenth?"

"Do you want one of our staff members to supervise the installation?"

"Will a $250 down payment be possible at this time?"

Some salespeople use the trial close more than once during the sales presentation. After the salesperson presents a feature, converts that feature to a buyer benefit, and confirms the prospect's agreement that the benefit is important, it would be appropriate to use a trial close.[9]

In broader terms, it would be appropriate to attempt a trial close after steps two, three, or four of the six-step presentation plan (Fig. 13.4).

SUMMARY-OF-BENEFITS CLOSE

Let us assume that you have discussed and demonstrated the major benefits of your product and you detect considerable buyer interest. However, you have covered a great deal of material. There is a chance that the prospect will not be able to put the entire picture together without your help. At this point you should summarize the most important buyer benefits. Your goal in the **summary-of-benefits close** is to reemphasize the benefits that will help bring about a favorable decision.

Let us see how this closing method works in the hospitality industry. Terry Hall, sales manager of the Emory Hotel, recently called on Mr. Ray Busch, director of marketing for a large corporation. Near the end of the sales presentation, Terry summarized the major benefits in this manner: "Mr. Busch, we can provide you with a conference room that will seat 200 people comfortably and four smaller rooms for the workshops you have planned. Our staff will serve a noon lunch, and the cost will be less than $9 per person. Finally, we will see that each of your employees receives a pad of paper, a pen, and a copy of the conference program. Should I go ahead and reserve these facilities for November 24?" In the process of reviewing all the important points you provide the buyer with a positive picture of the proposal.

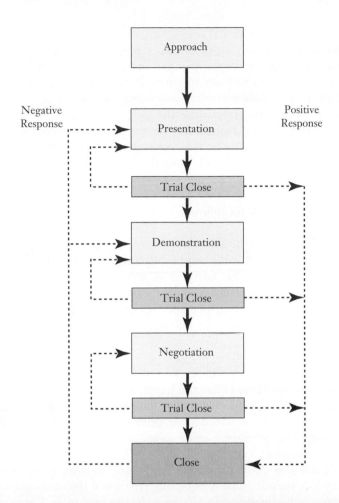

FIGURE 13.4 The trial close should be attempted at an opportune time during the sales presentation. It is appropriate to initiate a trial close after steps two, three, or four of the six-step presentation plan.

When you are making a group sales presentation, closing the sale may offer a greater challenge.

ASSUMPTION CLOSE

The **assumption close** assumes the customer is going to buy.[10] This closing approach comes near the end of the planned presentation. If you have identified a genuine need, presented your solutions in terms of buyer benefits, presented an effective sales demonstration, and negotiated buyer resistance satisfactorily, it may be natural to assume the person is ready to buy. In the assumption close you actually assume that the prospect has already bought the product and then ask one or more questions about a minor point. Here are some examples:

> Do you want this purchase added to your charge account?"

> "Will next Friday be OK for delivery, or will you need it sooner?"

In place of asking a question the salesperson may start doing something such as writing up the order. The order might be completed and handed to the prospect along with a pen. The salesperson says. "Can I get your signature here?" or some similar statement. This must be done with a positive mental attitude. You are confident that the prospect is ready to buy and you are only bringing the selling-buying process to a close.

SPECIAL CONCESSION CLOSE

The **special concession close** offers the buyer something extra for acting immediately. A special inducement is offered if the prospect will agree to sign the order. The concession may be part of a low-price strategy such as a sale price, a quantity discount, a more liberal credit plan, or an added feature that the prospect did not anticipate.

You should use this closing approach with care, because some customers are skeptical of concessions. This is especially true when the concession comes after the salesperson has made what appears to be the final offer. Let us assume that a customer is interested in buying a certain piano. The salesperson says in a firm voice, "The price is $5,800." The customer says, "The price seems awfully high." After a few minutes of discussion the customer seems to be losing interest in the purchase. The salesperson says, "I think that price is firm, but let me check with the boss." A few minutes later the salesperson returns and says, "You are in luck. We can cut the price by $400."

What will be the impact of the $400 price concession? It may be the factor that motivates the buyer to say yes. On the other hand, it may have a negative influence on the person's attitude. Here are some thoughts that might surface in the prospect's mind:

> I wonder why the salesperson had to discuss the price with the boss.

> Why was the lower price not quoted in the first place?

> Maybe if I start to leave, the salesperson will lower the price again.

> If she is willing to lower the price, maybe there is something wrong with the product.

If the $5,400 figure provides the store with an adequate profit margin, it may be best to quote this price in the first place. It is difficult to establish specific guidelines for every selling situation, but a good rule of thumb is to avoid "gimmicks." Today's better educated buyer is not fooled easily.

NEGOTIATING THE SINGLE-PROBLEM CLOSE

After a complete sales presentation, you may find that a single problem surfaces and stands in the way of closing the sale. This problem often surfaces when a trial close is used. For example, the industrial buyer seems generally interested in your rust preventative but wants one-week delivery. Your delivery plan requires two weeks. The young couple seems interested in the home design you propose, but wants to wait six months before the start of construction. The single problem may be price, delivery terms, credit terms, or some other factor.

The first rule of thumb is never to lose patience with the prospect. The problem may seem insignificant from your point of view, but it may be quite important to the buyer. Clarify the customer's position concerning the problem. Try to determine if the objection is the only factor preventing the purchase. The conversation might go like this:

Salesperson: Let us see if I understand your position, Dr. Lopez. You agree that the Acucan intra-oral video camera will improve the dental care given your patients. However, you want to delay the purchase for ninety days because you have already hit the limit in terms of income tax write-offs for the year. Is this the major reason for delaying the purchase?

Prospect: Yes. The capital improvement tax deduction limit is $17,500. I have already taken write-offs on equipment purchases up to this amount.

Salesperson: If you would like to take delivery of the Acucam within the next two weeks, I can arrange a lease payment plan. During the remaining three months of this year you would make monthly payments of $250. On January 1, you would make one payment of $8,250, which is the balance owed on the principal. This amount will be a write-off on next year's taxes.[11]

If the product or service is right for the prospect, then a single problem should not prevent you from closing the sale. Help the customer weigh the many advantages of the product. This might be done by reviewing two or three of the product's superior points.

LIMITED CHOICE CLOSE

In many selling situations it is a good idea to provide the prospect with a choice. This is one way to qualify the customer. In the **limited choice close,** allow the person to examine several different options, and try to assess the degree of interest in each one. As you near the point where a close seems appropriate, remove some of the options. This will reduce confusion and indecision.

You often see the limited choice technique used in office equipment sales. If a small business owner wants to purchase a copy machine, most vendors will offer several models for consideration. Let us assume that the prospect has examined four models and seems to be uncertain about which one would be the best choice. The salesperson might determine which copier is least appealing and eliminate it as an option. Now the prospect can choose between three

Instantaneous information can be very helpful in closing the sale. RAM's Wireless Data Networks can provide this type of assistance.

copiers. If the prospect seems to favor one copier, it would be appropriate to ask for the order.

When using the limited choice close, follow these simple steps:

1. Cease showing new products when it appears that the prospect has been given ample selection.

2. Remove products that the prospect does not seem genuinely interested in and concentrate on the options the prospect seems to be interested in.

DIRECT APPEAL CLOSE

The **direct appeal close** has the advantages of clarity and simplicity. This close involves simply asking for the order in a straightforward manner. It is the most direct closing approach, and many buyers find it attractive. Realistically, most customers expect salespeople to ask for the sale.

The direct appeal should not, of course, come too early. It should not be used until the prospect has displayed a definite interest in the product or service. The salesperson must also gain the prospect's respect before initiating this appeal. Once you make the direct appeal, stop talking. Raymond Slesinski, Digital Equipment sales trainer, tells his trainees, "After asking a closing question, do not speak, even if the prospect doesn't answer quickly." His advice is to give the prospect time to think about your offer.[12]

To illustrate the application of this closing method, let us observe Colleen White as she attempts to close a sale in the office of a buyer for a large department store. Colleen represents a firm that manufactures a wide range of leather clothing and accessories. Near the end of her planned presentation she senses that the prospect is quite interested in her products but seems reluctant to make a decision. This is how she handles the close: "Ms. Taylor, I have reviewed our complete line. You agree that your customers like this type of merchandise. If we send the order in today, you will have the merchandise in time for the pre-Christmas buying season. With your help I would like to prepare the first order." Notice this direct appeal close was strengthened by the addition of an important benefit—delivery in time for the pre-Christmas buying season.

Practice Closing

Your success in selling will depend in large part on learning how to make these seven closing methods work for you. You will not master these approaches in a few weeks, but you can speed up the learning process with preparation and practice. Practice in front of a video recorder, and then sit back and observe your performance. The video monitor provides excellent feedback. Unlike comments from other salespeople or your sales manager, this feedback is totally objective. Use the closing worksheet (see Fig. 13.3) to prepare for practice sessions. You need to learn these methods so well that you can use them without consciously thinking about them.

One of the most important outcomes of practice is increased self-confidence. Think about Larry Wilson's views on the importance of confidence: "Fear of failure and fear of rejection are the most significant barriers to success and fulfillment in selling."[13]

Confirming the Sale When the Buyer Says Yes

Congratulations! You have closed the sale and have established the beginning of what you hope will be a long and satisfying relationship with the customer. Before preparing to leave, be sure that all details related to the purchase agreement are completed. Check everything with the buyer, and then ask for a signature if necessary.

Once the sale has been closed, it is important to take a few moments to reassure the customer. This is the **confirmation step** in closing the sale. Before you leave, reassure the customer by pointing out that he has made the correct decision, and describe the satisfaction that will come with ownership of the product. The reason for doing this is to resell the buyer. You are congratulating the person for making a wise decision. Once the sale is closed, the customer may be required to justify the purchase to others. Your words of reassurance will be helpful.

When the customer says yes, take a few moments to express appreciation and congratulate the person for making a wise decision.

Before leaving, thank the customer for the order. This is very important. Everyone likes to think that a purchase is appreciated. No one should believe that a purchase is taken for granted. Even a small order deserves words of appreciation. In many cases a follow-up–thank-you letter is appropriate.

In several previous chapters we said that a satisfied customer is one of the best sources of new prospects. Never hesitate to ask, "Do you know anyone else who might benefit from owning this product?" or a similar question. Some customers may even agree to write an introductory letter on your behalf.

After you complete the sale, you should do everything possible to make sure the customer receives maximum satisfaction from the purchase. This may require a detailed explanation of how to operate and maintain the product. Some sales representatives make it a practice to be present when the product is delivered. They want to make sure the customer does not have any problems with the new product. How to "service" a sale properly is described fully in Chapter 14.

WHAT TO DO WHEN THE BUYER SAYS NO

High-performance salespeople recognize that they cannot close every sale. They recognize hopeless selling situations and avoid doing or saying something that will jeopardize the relationship they have established with the prospect. The proper response may set the stage for a future sale.

Never treat a lost sale as a defeat. When you adopt the win-win relationship strategy, there is never a winner and a loser. When the sales interview is over, both the customer and the salesperson should feel like winners. A strong display of disappointment or resentment is likely to close the door to future sales.

Faced with the possibility of a failed presentation strategy, some salespeople abandon their relationship and customer strategies and turn to selling methods that are unethical, illegal, or both. Sometimes, sales representatives will imply that if the prospect postpones signing the order, the item may not be available. If in fact the company has a large surplus of these products, the salesperson has been dishonest. Another unethical practice is suggesting that the price will increase sharply soon, when in all likelihood the price will not change. If the customer finds out later that your information was not correct, you are likely to lose the opportunity for repeat business.

In some selling situations it is proper to reopen the presentation. If you are preparing to leave and think of an effective approach to closing the sale, do not hesitate to use it. You might recall an important point that was overlooked earlier. For example, you might want to review a testimonial from a satisfied customer. A third-party opinion might reopen the door and set the stage for the close.

PREPARE THE PROSPECT FOR CONTACT WITH THE COMPETITION

Some prospects refuse to buy because they want to take a close look at the competing products. This response is not unusual in the field of selling. You should do everything possible to help the customer make an intelligent comparison.

It is always a good practice to review your product's strong points one more time. Give special emphasis to areas in which your product has a superior advantage over the competition. To illustrate, let us assume you are selling a commercial quality facsimile machine designed for high-volume users. The prospect seems to like your product but insists on looking at a competing product before making a buying decision. At this point you should review the exclusive features of your product and encourage the customer to remember these points when making a comparison. Make it easy for the person to buy your product at some future date.

BUILDING RELATIONSHIPS IN A DIVERSE WORLD

TEAM SELLING INCREASES BUSINESS

Hewlett-Packard, a leader in the field of information systems, has achieved success by responding to the unique needs of a diverse client group. Customers represent financial services, oil and gas exploration, retail, utilities, and many other industries. Once an industry is targeted, a selling team is organized to build an information database of good prospects. One team member is designated the "silver fox," a business development manager responsible for building strong relationships with the key decision makers. This person will collect information concerning the prospect's needs and determine the next course of action. A promising prospect will be invited to Hewlett-Packard's corporate offices for a full-day presentation on how the company can address the prospect's needs.

Customer responsiveness at Hewlett-Packard has improved as a result of sales force automation (SFA). After the company incorporated SFA in its selling, sales representatives are spending 27 percent more frontline time with customers; response-time availability is up by 50 percent; and customer satisfaction has improved significantly. With the aid of electronic communications, the company has sharply improved lead follow-up.[c]

BUILDING RELATIONSHIPS THROUGH TECHNOLOGY

ADDING AND DELETING PROSPECTS

 Prospect and customer databases are continually changing. Promotions, transfers, mergers, and many other events cause additions and deletions to a salesperson's automated data. Most software makes this an easy process and warns users against the inadvertent removal of an account.

Smart salespeople use the power of the computer to track more than just the immediate decision makers in a customer's organization. Most sales experts advise salespeople to develop as many relationships as possible within accounts because, among other reasons, information gathering is strongly enhanced. (See Sales Automation Application Exercise on p. 312 for more information.)

ANALYZE LOST SALES

When you experience a no-sale call, try to benefit from the experience. A lost sale can be a good learning experience. Take a good, objective look at your presentation, and try to identify any weaknesses. Were you able to arouse genuine interest early? Did you ask well thought out questions? Was the sales demonstration handled properly? Were you able to deal effectively with buyer resistance? If you do pinpoint a weakness, consider how to avoid this problem in the future. When you experience a no-sale call, salvage as much as possible from the experience. If you anticipate a return call, do record any new information you have learned about the prospect. This might include personal information, company information, or purchase priorities. Callbacks frequently yield good results, so avoid the temptation to give up after a single call on a prospect.

It often helps to discuss a lost sale with your sales manager, a fellow salesperson, or someone else who understands the selling-buying process. Your goal is to find out why you could not close the sale.

Do not spend *too much* time analyzing lost sales. Jack Falvey, author and sales consultant says that we get no's for many unknown or subjective reasons, so a time-consuming study of every no-sale call may not be cost effective. He cautions salespeople to avoid dwelling on rejection and to keep moving forward.[14] Learning how to deal with no's is an important key to success in selling.

Longer Selling Cycles

Longer selling cycles have become a fact of life in recent years. One reason for this change is that more people are involved in purchasing some products. The purchase of highly technical products such as computers, security equipment, and robotics may involve persons from many areas of the organization. In some cases the buyer has more options than in the past. Larry Wilson describes the phenomenon of longer sales cycles in the field of personal selling:

> *When I started Wilson Learning, it normally took us thirty to sixty days to close a sale with a major client. After five years, it was ninety days. The current sales force is working on sales cycles of six months to a year.*[15]

Customers who have more options than in the past are likely to take more time to make a buying decision. This is especially true in the case of expensive products. People are less likely to purchase an expensive product on the spur of the moment. How should salespeople respond to longer selling cycles? Larry Wilson says that working in a long-term, multidecision sales cycle requires a different set of abilities:

> *It will take strategic planning, patience and the ability to develop long-term personal relationships to succeed in the new game. New rules require new skills.*[16]

SUMMARY

Closing the sale is usually not difficult if everything is handled properly throughout the sales presentation. When the sales presentation is well organized and well delivered, the close is part of the process that results in a sale.

The salesperson must be alert to *closing clues* from the prospect. These clues fall into two categories: verbal and nonverbal. Verbal clues are the easiest to recognize, but they may be subtle as well. Here again it is important to be an attentive listener. The recognition of nonverbal clues is more difficult, but practice in careful observation will help in detecting them.

Several closing methods may be necessary to get the prospect to make a buying decision; therefore it is wise for the salesperson to preplan several closes. These closing methods should be chosen from the list provided in this chapter and then customized to fit the product and the type of buyer with whom the salesperson is dealing.

The professional salesperson is not discouraged or offended if the sale is not closed. Every effort should be made to be of further assistance to the prospect—the sale might be closed on another call. Even if the sale is lost, the experience may be valuable if analyzed to learn from it.

➤ **KEY TERMS**

Closing Clue	*Special Concession Close*
Trial Close	*Limited Choice Close*
Summary-of-Benefits Close	*Direct Appeal Close*
Assumption Close	*Confirmation Step*

➤ **REVIEW QUESTIONS**

1. List some aspects of the sales presentation that can make closing and confirming the sale difficult to achieve.

2. Explain the timidity factor problem in closing the sale.

3. What guidelines should a salesperson follow for closing the sale?

4. Why is it important to look at closing from the prospect's point of view?

5. What three verbal clues can the prospect use to indicate that it is time to close the sale? What nonverbal clues should the salesperson be alert to?

6. Explain how the limited choice close might be used in the sale of men's and women's suits.

7. Is there a best method to use in closing the sale? Explain.

8. What is meant by a trial close? When should a salesperson attempt a trial close?

9. Explain the summary-of-benefits close.

10. What confirming steps should a salesperson follow when the customer says yes? What should be done when the customer says no?

> ## APPLICATION EXERCISES

1. Which of the following statements, often made by prospects, would you interpret as buying signals?

    a. "How much would the payments be?"
    b. "Tell me about your service department."
    c. "The company already has an older model that seems good enough."
    d. "We do not have enough cash flow right now."
    e. "How much would you allow me for my old model?"
    f. "I do not need one."
    g. "How does that switch work?"
    h. "When would I have to pay for it?"

2. If the prospect is ready to buy before you have presented all your selling points, should you make an effort to complete your sales presentation? Explain your answer.

3. You are an accountant who owns and operates an accounting service. You have been contacted by the president of an advertising agency about the possibility of your auditing her business on a regular basis. The president has indicated that she investigated other accounting firms and thinks they price their services too high. With the knowledge you have about the other firms you know you are in a strong competitive position. Also, you realize her account would be profitable for your firm. You really would like to capture this account. How will you close the deal? List and describe two closing methods you might use in this situation.

4. Ryder Commercial Leasing and Services is the topic of the opening material in this chapter. Access this company's web site at http://www.ryder.com/ and view the information provided. Examine articles in the company news section, and determine if any of this information would be helpful in closing the sale. Examine the business services section. Does it appear that Ryder is able to partner with their potential customers?

> ## SALES AUTOMATION APPLICATION EXERCISE

ACT! ADDING AND DELETING PROSPECTS

Adding and deleting contact screens is easy with ACT! as it is with most contact management software. Access the ACT! software following the instructions in Appendix 2. Create a Contact Screen for B. H. Rivera by pressing the following keys: Ins (insert key) D Graphic Forms DownArrow B. H. Rivera DownArrow 3195556194 DownArrow DownArrow DownArrow President DownArrow DownArrow DownArrow 2134 Martin Luther King DownArrow DownArrow DownArrow Atlanta DownArrow GA DownArrow 61740. Now press the DownArrow until the cursor is in the

ID/Status field and enter Prospect. Pressing F10 will then save the Contact Screen. The ACT! software in this book is a demonstration version which limits the number of contacts to 25. The full version of ACT! has no such limit. Do not enter more than 25 contacts into the demonstration version.

Pressing Del (delete key) will remove a contact. A warning screen will be displayed. This screen warns that all deletions will be permanent and asks whether you wish to delete the contact displayed on the screen or a group of contacts. Caution is advised when deleting or using the delete function.

➤ C A S E   P R O B L E M

Ruan and Clark Distributing is a respected wholesale-broker of building products, including a quality line of carpeting. Three years ago, Bob Thompson graduated from college and accepted a sales position with Ruan and Clark as the representative for the carpet line.

During the past six months, Bob has been calling on Woodside Building and Supply Company, one of the firms in his territory. Woodside already carries carpet lines from several of Bob's competitors. Woodside dominates its trading area in several product lines, including carpet. Bob has called on the buyer, Jim Cooney, four times; however, he has not been able to close the sale. Recently, Ruan and Clark took a new line of carpet that Bob felt offered his dealers an excellent buy.

In calling Woodside for the fifth time, Bob decided to use the new product line to try to close the sale. The following sales presentation took place:

Bob: Hello, Jim. It's good to see you.

Jim: (In a warm, friendly tone of voice) Good to see you again, Bob, but I'll tell you right up front I don't have a budget to buy additional goods! I would like to find out what you have, but even if you *gave* me a roll of carpet, I wouldn't be able to find a place here to store it.

Bob: I'm sorry to hear that, because we have just added another product line that we think is going to revolutionize the carpet industry. (Bob shows Jim a sample of the new line—a toast color with alternating rows of cut and uncut yarn.) Our carpet mill took the popular traditional candy stripe, built it up to a higher quality, and changed its styling to appeal to more of your customers. In short, with this new toast-colored, ten-year-guaranteed carpet you will no longer have to compete with your competitors on the same product. This will give your salespeople a strong competitive advantage in their sales presentation. Our sales forecasting indicates that within twelve months this new product will take over 25 percent of the traditional market.

Jim: Bob, this is an appealing line.

Bob: (Handing the sample to Jim) Because of our mill's innovation in construction you get a much better feel in the surface yarns, don't you?

Jim: Yes, it does feel good.

Bob: This construction feature, along with the improved rubber backing, will give your customers a better quality piece of goods. In addition, Jim, the mill has been able to hold the price on these goods to a competitive level. What do you think of it?

Jim: (Inspecting the goods a second time) I like it, Bob, but as I said before . . .

Bob: (Breaking in and focusing in on the space problem) Jim. I can appreciate your space problem, but I am in a position to ship you as little as one roll now, so you can get into the market immediately and find out how well this product is suited for your situation.

Jim: (Showing more interest) Well, I would like to try it, but I just cannot see how I can do it today.

Bob: That is too bad, Jim, because we are running this new line at a special introductory price. The regular price on these goods is $4.89 a yard, but we are introducing it at $3.99. (Bob feels he now has Jim wanting the goods; however, he thinks Jim may want to put the sale off until later.)

Jim: That is a good price, Bob, but I am just . . .

Bob: (Interrupting Jim) Also, we will pay the freight at $3.99, which will save you an additional 15 percent. (Bob really wants to open the Woodside account because of the high sales Woodside will experience and the future profitability his company will achieve. Under any other circumstances he would never have offered to pay the freight at this price.)

Jim: (In a quiet voice) That sure sounds like something I should take advantage of.

QUESTIONS

1. Based on the information given, do you think this sale can be closed?
2. Assume you are Bob. After Jim's last comment, which close would you use next? Why?
3. What appeared to be the major obstacle to closing this sale?
4. Did Jim give any closing clues? Identify them.
5. Did Bob use any trial closes? Identify them.
6. What did you like and what did you dislike about the way Bob attempted to close this sale?

➤ SALES AUTOMATION CASE STUDY

FORECASTING THE CLOSE

You are interested in discovering what your commissions may be for the next few months, just from Mark David's former accounts (see Chapter 8 Case Study). To do this, you will review the information on each Contact Screen. There are four fields on the first page of the Contact Screen from which you can forecast your expected sales: CAD Needed:, Likelihood:, Dollar Amount:, and Date Close:. When Mark worked with these accounts, he entered the data that are in each of these fields. In the CAD Needed field, he entered the number of CAD stations he thought the account might order. In the Likelihood field, he estimated the percentage of possibility that the account might place an order (0.80 means 80%). The Dollar Amount field refers to how much Mark thought the account would spend and the month Mark felt they would order is in the Date Close field (01/31 means January).

You can estimate each month's likely sales by multiplying the Dollar Amount field number times the Likelihood field percentage number. An 80% chance of a $100,000 sale is a forecast of $80,000 in sales. If the Date Close field for several accounts is 12/31, you can calculate the sales for that month (December) by totaling the forecasts for each account. For an estimate of your commission income, multiply each month's forecast by 10%.

Mark did not show that any of his forecasted sales were 100%. He recognized that he might not close these sales, not for the total amount anticipated (Dollar Amount), or not during the month projected. Mark knew that these prospects would not close themselves; he would have to take certain steps to increase the possibility that the prospect would place an order. To collect your commissions, you have to discover the steps most likely to close these sales.

Access the ACT! software following the instructions in Appendix 2.

Questions

1. What would your commission income be for all Mark's accounts if you closed them as Mark forecasted?

2. What kind of special concession might be necessary to close the sale with Quality Builders?

3. What kind of close may be necessary to get an order from Computerized Labs?

4. What kind of close would be appropriate for the Lakeside Clinic?

PARTNERSHIP SELLING: A ROLE PLAY/SIMULATION (see Appendix 3, p. 421)

Developing a Presentation Strategy—Closing the Sale
Refer to sales memorandum 3 and strategically plan to close the sale with your customer. To consider the sale closed you will need to secure the signature of your customer on the sales proposal form. This will guarantee your customer the accommodations listed on the form. These accommodations may change depending on the final number of people attending your customer's convention. This is an important point to keep in mind when closing the sale; however, you still must get the signature to guarantee the accommodations.

Follow the instructions carefully, and prepare a closing worksheet listing at least four closes using the methods outlined in this chapter. Two of these methods should include the summary of the benefits, and the direct appeal. Remember it is not the policy of your convention center to cut prices, so your methods should include value-added strategies.

Use proof devices to make your closes more convincing and place them in the front pocket of your three-ring binder/portfolio for easy access during your presentation. You may want to secure another person to be your customer, and practice the closing strategies you have developed.

Servicing the Sale

Never underestimate the power of indifference. This time-proven fundamental has universal support in the business community, yet many sales and marketing professionals still do things that give the customer an "emotional" slap in the face. Aurora Pucciarello, CEO of Dallas-based Max Distribution, describes how a valued customer was lost due to indifference. Near the end of a lucrative three-year contract, the client indicated a desire to renew it. All she and her sales staff had to do was complete a basic proposal. "We were told to just fill out the same numbers as before. We thought great, we've got them in our pocket." The proposal was filed away and forgotten. Later a phone call from the client let Pucciarello know she had missed the proposal deadline and lost the business. This client accounted for 10 percent of her total sales. She cried that day.[1]

The Importance of Customer Service

A growing number of organizations are giving increased attention to customer service (Figure 14.1). Financial institutions, public utilities, airlines, retail stores, restaurants, manufacturers, and wholesalers face the problem of gaining and retaining the patronage of clients and customers. Building partnerships with customers has been given a high priority by the majority of America's most successful enterprises. These companies realize that keeping a customer happy is a good strategy. To regain a lost customer can be five to six times more expensive than keeping a current customer satisfied.[2]

Tony Allessandra, a well-known sales trainer and consultant, says that there are three possible outcomes when a customer does business with an organization.[3]

The moment of truth. In these selling situations the customer's expectations were met. Nothing happened to disappoint the customer, nor did the salesperson do anything to surpass the customer's expectations. The customer is apt to have somewhat neutral feelings about his relationship with

The Six–Step Presentation Plan	
Step One: APPROACH	☑ Review Strategic/Consultative Selling Model. ☑ Initiate customer contact.
Step Two: PRESENTATION	☑ Determine prospect needs. ☑ Select product or service. ☑ Initiate sales presentation.
Step Three: DEMONSTRATION	☑ Decide what to demonstrate. ☑ Select selling tools. ☑ Initiate demonstration.
Step Four: NEGOTIATION	☑ Anticipate sales resistance. ☑ Plan negotiating methods. ☑ Initiate double–win negotiations.
Step Five: CLOSE	☑ Plan appropriate closing methods. ☑ Recognize closing clues. ☑ Initiate closing methods.
Step Six: SERVICING THE SALE	☐ Suggestion selling. ☐ Follow through. ☐ Follow-up calls.
Service, retail, wholesale, and manufacturer selling.	

FIGURE 14.1   Servicing the sale involves three steps: suggestion selling, follow-through, and follow-up calls.

Many companies such as SeaFest/JAC know that customer service is an excellent way to achieve a competitive advantage in a highly competitive market.

the salesperson. The moment of truth will usually not build customer loyalty.

The moment of misery. This is the outcome of a selling situation where the customer's expectations were not met. The customer may feel a sense of disappointment or even anger. Many customers who experience the moment of misery will share their feelings with others and often make a decision to "fire" the salesperson.

The moment of magic. This is the outcome of a sale where the customer received more than she expected. The salesperson surpassed the customer's expectations by going the extra mile and providing a level of service that added value to the customer/salesperson relationship. This extra effort is likely to establish a foundation for increased customer loyalty. William Toller, CEO of Witco Chemical Company, says that the key to the loyalty-centered approach to customer relationships is developing and managing a "customer value package." He believes that service quality is one major element of that package.[4]

CUSTOMER SERVICE AS THE QUALITY EDGE

Customer service can be defined as those activities that enhance or facilitate the role and use of the product. In good times and bad, quality customer service builds profits by attracting new accounts and keeping old ones active. The point of view that "service pays" is accepted by successful firms that have adopted the marketing concept and seek to establish long-term partnerships with customers.

Many companies are finding that customer service is an excellent way to achieve a competitive advantage in a highly competitive market. Alan Raedels, professor of business administration at Portland State University, notes that as more companies compete with the same products at basically the same price, then the next major battlefield is likely to be service.[5] Nordstrom is a good example of a company that competes successfully with a value-added strategy that focuses on excellence in service. As Nordstrom has evolved into a specialty department store, top management has maintained a consistent service philosophy.

BUILDING QUALITY PARTNERSHIPS

DEBBIE MCKINNEY PUTS SERVICE FIRST

Debbie McKinney is one of those rare persons who has an avocation that complements her career. On weekends she is busy caring for her horses and attending horse shows. During the week she is involved in the sale of medical products used in the care and healing of horses. As a sales representative for Schering-Plough, a leading producer of pharmaceuticals used in veterinary medicine, she provides assistance to distributors, veterinarians, and research personnel at medical centers. These professionals view her as a source of the newest research and development findings in selected areas of veterinary science.

On many occasions she has delivered antibiotics or painkillers to an account that has run out of medication in the middle of an animal's therapy and does not have the luxury of waiting for a new shipment to arrive. These efforts can sometimes help save an animal's life. In her sales territory the "patient" may be a $1 million racehorse or a child's pet pony. On other occasions she has added value to her sales by serving as a marketing or financial advisor to her clients. Excellent service, which has become the hallmark of her personal selling career, has been generously rewarded. She has established a long-term partnership with many of her customers, and the result has been a considerable amount of repeat business. She is a member of the company's Distinguished Sales Representative Club and has been the number one sales representative in the Eastern Region of the United States.[a]

Debbie McKinney

APPEALING TO POWERFUL MOTIVATORS

A well-planned customer service program appeals to two powerful motivators. One is *recognition*. Most of us respond positively to positive forms of recognition. By the same token we respond negatively to a display of indifference by another person or organization. Thus the salesperson who sends customers a handwritten thank-you note after the sale or calls them to determine if they are pleased with the purchase is communicating a powerful message: "We value your business and want you to be a satisfied customer." This form of customer service builds customer loyalty and repeat business.

The second powerful motivator is the *need for security*. Many customers today complain about a feeling of helplessness after the sale. Sometimes the product is not installed properly. In some cases the product does not perform as expected. These quality-related problems produce feelings of insecurity. The value-added sales organization that develops a reputation for quality service after the sale will have a real advantage in the marketplace.

Building Long-Term Partnerships with Customer Service

Customers remember people like Debbie McKinney, mentioned earlier, who come through with service when they need it. Of course they remember who does not. One of the most talked about books of the past decade, *In Search of Excellence*, reports that the excellent companies in America are more driven by their "close-to-the-customer" orientation than by technology or by a desire to be low-cost producers.[6]

A sales organization that can develop a reputation for servicing each sale will be sought out by customers who want a long-term partner to help them with their buying needs. Satisfied customers represent an "auxiliary" sales force—a group of people who will recommend customer-driven organizations to others. If customers are pleased with the service that they receive after the sale, be assured that they will tell other people. Word-of-mouth advertising is a powerful force in marketing.

THE IMPORTANCE OF LIFETIME CUSTOMERS

Most companies find that repeat business is essential if the firm is to earn a satisfactory level of profit. The amount of profit earned on the first sale or maybe even on the first few sales may cover only the direct and indirect expenses associated with developing the account. To illustrate, let us look at the experience of Harold Mason, sales representative for an institutional food supply company. He sells food products to schools, colleges, hospitals, and large restaurants.

When construction began recently on a new hospital in his sales territory, he made a courtesy call to the administrator. The hospital would not open for several weeks, but he wanted to introduce his company. While having lunch with the administrator, he learned the name of the new purchasing agent who would join the administration staff soon.

Two weeks later, Mr. Mason called on the purchasing agent and introduced his complete food line. One week later he returned to the hospital and closed the sale. Here is a summary of the expenses incurred during the first three calls:

Travel	**$88.50**
Meals	45.50
Lodging	140.30
Sales literature	10.90
Samples	8.70
Communications (phone calls, letters, etc.)	14.25
Total expenses	**$308.15**

The first order sent to the hospital provided the company with a profit margin of $74. Two weeks later, Mr. Mason obtained a second order. This was a slightly larger order, and the company earned a profit margin of $83. So far the company has received $157 in profits, slightly over half the cost of developing the account. Only after the third order has been delivered will the expenses be covered in full. This example illustrates the importance of repeat business. Hotels, retail stores, and other businesses face the same problem. Every organization must recover overhead expenses to make a profit.

RESPONDING TO INCREASED POSTSALE CUSTOMER EXPECTATIONS

When John J. Creedon, CEO of Metropolitan Life Insurance Company, was asked how his company competed for sales, he responded: "By trying to exceed your customer's expectations of good service."[7] In other words, make sure customers experience those "moments of magic."

People buy expectations, not things, according to Ted Levitt, author of *The Marketing Imagination*. They buy the expectations of benefits you promised. Once the customer buys your product, expectations increase. Levitt points out that after the sale is closed, the buyer's attitude changes.

> *The fact of buying changes the buyer. He expects the seller to remember the purchase as having been a favor bestowed on him by the buyer, not as something earned by the seller. Hence it is wrong to assume that to have gained an account gives you an advantage by virtue of having gotten "a foot in the door." The opposite is increasingly the case. If the buyer views the sale as a favor conferred by him*

The sale merely consummates the courtship. Then the marriage begins. How good the marriage is depends on how well the relationship is managed by the seller.

Ted Levitt, editor, Harvard Business Review

SALES TIPS

on the seller, then he in effect debits the seller's account. The seller owes him one. The seller is in the position of having to rebuild his relationship from a deficit position.[8]

Increased customer expectations, after the sale is closed, require a strategic plan for servicing the sale. Certain aspects of the relationship, product, and customer strategies can have a positive influence on the customer's heightened expectations.

How do we respond to a customer who has increased expectations? First, we should take the steps required to strengthen a relationship. Some examples follow:

> Initiate phone calls to thank the customer and find out if she is pleased with the product. Do not limit your customer contact to scheduled callbacks.

> Accept responsibility for problems; never shift the blame to others.

> Always tell customers what you *can* do for them rather than tell them what you *cannot* do for them.

These are only a few of the relationship-building strategies available to sales personnel. With just a little imagination you can develop a series of postsale activities that will meet the customer's increased expectations.

Second, we should reexamine our product strategy. In some cases we can enhance customer satisfaction by suggesting related products or services. If the product is expensive, we can follow through and offer assistance in making credit arrangements. If the product is complex, we can make suggestions con-

A follow-up phone call to thank the customer and find out if he or she is pleased with the product will strengthen the relationship after the sale.

cerning use and maintenance. Each of these forms of assistance may add value to the sale.

Customer Service Methods

Sales & Marketing Management magazine states that customer service encompasses all activities that enhance or facilitate the sale and use of one's product or service. The skills required to service a sale are different from those required prior to the sale (Fig. 14.2). High-performance sales personnel do not abdicate responsibility for delivery, installation, warranty interpretation, or other customer service responsibilities. They continue to maintain a client relationship with suggestion selling, follow-through on promises, and follow-up activities.

ADDING VALUE WITH SUGGESTION SELLING

Suggestion selling is an important form of customer service. This is the process of suggesting merchandise or services that are related to the main item sold to the customer. The suggestion is made when, in the salesperson's judgment, the added item will provide the customer with additional satisfaction.

The salesperson who is genuinely interested in helping customers solve their problems can enhance the relationship with suggestion selling. Some of the best ways to engage in suggestion selling follow.

Suggest related items In some cases there are related products or services that will add to the customer's satisfaction. To illustrate, let us look at the sale of town houses. Many real estate firms offer the customer a basic

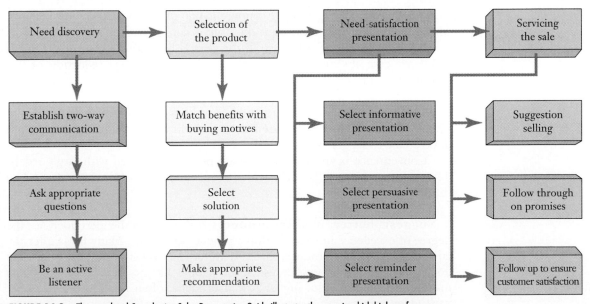

FIGURE 14.2 The completed Consultative Sales Presentation Guide illustrates the ways in which high-performance salespeople use value-added strategies to service the sale and build repeat business and referrals.

dwelling plus a choice of options. The option list might include a fireplace, a screened patio, or an outdoor gas grill.

Selling related merchandise at an auto agency is quite common. Most customers can choose from a long list of options including special trim, upscale stereo systems, antilock braking system, and a host of other items.

Suggestion selling is no less important when selling services. For example, a travel agent has many opportunities to use suggestion selling. Let us assume that a customer purchases a two-week vacation in Germany. The agent can offer to book hotel reservations or schedule a guided tour. Another related product would be a rental car.

Sometimes a new product is simply not "right" without related merchandise. A new business suit may not look right without a new shirt and tie. An executive training program held at a fine hotel can be enhanced with a refreshment break featuring a variety of soft drinks, fresh coffee, and freshly baked pastries. That new stereo receiver may not sound right until it is matched with a set of quality speakers.

Suggest new items New products and services are being introduced at a record pace. Some are brand-new features, while others are variations of existing items. Many buyers need help in keeping up with new product introductions. In most cases the salesperson who has already established a relationship with the customer is in the best position to introduce new products. Frank Smith, successful direct sales representative for Institutional Food House, a distributor based in South Carolina, mentions new items when making routine sales calls on his accounts. His goal is to introduce two or three new items during each visit. He also holds new product presentations once a month.[9]

Suggest a larger quantity The customer can benefit in several ways from buying a larger quantity. Economy is one of the most common benefits. Many companies offer a discount on large orders. A grocer may be offered a ten-case shipment at $9.90 a case. If the person buys fifteen cases, the price is $0.60 per case cheaper. In the retail food business a price reduction of this amount is significant.

Sometimes a large order is a good hedge against rising prices. The prices of oil, sugar, paper, antifreeze, and other products have also increased in recent years. When a salesperson is sure that prices will rise in the near future, it is a good policy to suggest a larger quantity.

Convenience is another value-added benefit associated with large orders. The customer is saved the inconvenience of running out of the item at a critical time.

Suggest better quality products Quality can be described as the degree of excellence inherent within a product or service. Many firms offer the customer a choice of products that vary in terms of quality and price. This is a good marketing strategy because most people like to have a choice when making a purchase. Also, higher priced products often provide the customer with added value.

The effort to sell better quality goods is known as *trading up* in the field of selling. It is an important selling method that often benefits the customer. The higher priced item may be the best buy when such factors as durability, comfort, or trade-in value are considered.

HOW AND WHEN TO USE SUGGESTION SELLING

Customers will view suggestion selling as a form of value-added service when it is presented correctly. There is a right way and a wrong way to make suggestions. Here are some guidelines to follow (Fig. 14.3).

1. *Plan for suggestion selling during the preapproach step.* Before meeting with the customer, develop a suggestion selling plan that includes your objectives for this important dimension of selling. This may involve writing down a list of items that you might suggest after you close the sale.[10] Suggestion selling is easier when you are prepared.

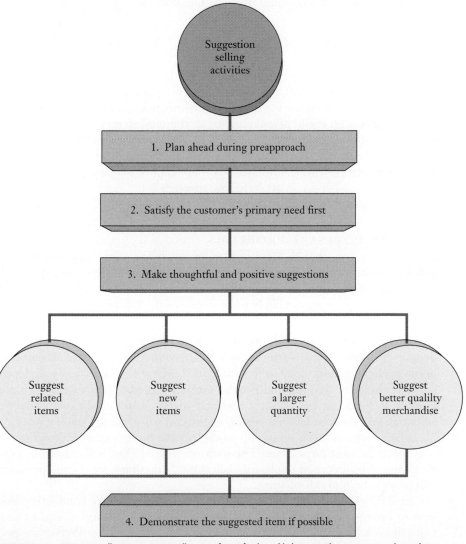

FIGURE 14.3 Customers will view suggestion selling as a form of value-added service when it is presented according to this suggested selling guide.

2. *Make suggestions after you have first satisfied the customer's primary need.* If you make suggestions too early, the customer may become confused or fail to give your proposal full attention.

3. *Make your suggestion thoughtful and positive.* "We just received a new order of silk ties that would go well with your new shirt. Let me show you the collection." Avoid questions like, "Can we ship anything else?" This question invites a negative response.

4. *Show the suggested item if at all possible, or use sales tools to build interest.* If you have suggested a shirt to go with a new suit, allow the customer to see it next to the suit. In industrial selling, show the customer a sample, or at least a picture if the actual product is not available.

Suggestion selling is a means of providing value-added service. When you use it correctly, customers will thank you for your thoughtfulness and extra service. It is also a proven sales-building strategy. Use it often.

FOLLOWING THROUGH ON ASSURANCES AND PROMISES

A major key to an effective customer service strategy is follow-through on assurances and promises that were part of the sales presentation. Did your sales presentation include claims for superior performance; promises of speedy delivery; assistance with credit arrangements; guaranteed factory assistance with installation, training, and service?

Most sales presentations are made up of claims and promises that the company can fulfill. However, fulfillment of these claims will depend to a large degree on after-sale action. Postsale follow-through is the key to holding that customer you worked so hard to develop.

COMMON POSTSALE PROBLEMS

Every salesperson should become familiar with the most common postsale problem areas. Identify the leading problem areas in your company, and be aware of possible solutions. Many studies indicated that customer-related problems after the sale are most likely to be in one of the following areas:

Making credit arrangements Credit has become a common way to finance purchases. This is true of industrial products, real estate, automobiles, home appliances, and many other products. Closing the sale often will depend on your ability to develop and present attractive credit plans to the customer. Even if you do not get directly involved in the firm's credit and collection activities, you must be familiar with how the company handles these matters.

Several agencies can supply up-to-date credit information. A credit bureau is available in most large cities. The national firm of Dun & Bradstreet, Incorporated, publishes credit books for each state. Sometimes, local bank personnel will provide helpful information.

Making credit decisions gets a lot tougher when you are conducting business in foreign countries. Overseas transactions can be complex, and in some cases there is little recourse if a customer does not pay. Doron Weissman, president of Overseas Brokers, a freight forwarder and export brokerage firm in Great Neck, New York, says, "When I sell my services, I automatically qualify

Salespeople often assist with credit arrangements and provide counsel to prospective customers.

the account to make sure they're financially able to meet my demands. If not, I move on."[11]

Late deliveries A late delivery can be a problem for both the supplier and the customer. To illustrate, let us assume that the supplier is a manufacturer of small appliances and the customer is a department store chain. A late delivery may mean lost sales due to out-of-stock conditions, cancellation of the order by the department store, or loss of future sales.

The causes of late delivery may be beyond your control. It is not your fault if the plant closes because of labor trouble or weather conditions. It is your responsibility, however, to keep the customer informed of any delays. You can also take steps to prevent a delay. Check to be sure your order was processed correctly. Follow up to see if the order was shipped on time.

BUILDING RELATIONSHIPS IN A DIVERSE WORLD

THE YODOBASHI CAMERA STORE, TOKYO

Customers in Japan expect to receive excellent customer service before, during, and after the sale. A good example of outstanding customer service can be observed during a visit to the Yodobashi Camera store in Tokyo. The store is laid out and staffed in a way that makes shopping truly enjoyable. Cameras are displayed on over 1,000 feet of counter space, and customers are encouraged (not pressured) to try out every camera sold by the store. Salespeople stand behind the counter, smiling and bowing politely as customers walk by. An American visiting the store discovers that the sales staff speak perfect English and possess a great deal of knowledge about each camera. He buys a zoom lens and receives his credit card receipt with a smile and a small gift box. The salesperson says, "This is a small gift for you as a way of saying thank you for shopping with us."

Japanese department stores have a strong client base of regular customers. Mitsukoshi, a popular department store in Tokyo, has found that about half its sales come from regular customers. The store maintains computerized lists with personal data about its customers. Some observers say that the computer reports are of little value because salespeople take pride in their ability to memorize personal data about each of their customers. Most say they can anticipate the customer's needs.[b]

Improper installation Buyer satisfaction is often related to proper installation of the product. This is true of consumer products such as automatic dishwashers, central air-conditioning, solar heating systems, and carpeting. It is also true of industrial products such as electronic data processing equipment and air quality control systems. Some salespeople believe it is to their advantage to supervise product installation. They are then able to spot installation problems. Others make it a practice to follow up on the installation to be sure no problems exist.

<table>
<tr>
<td>**SALES TIPS**</td>
<td>**Creating the Lifetime Customer**
When we build a plant or purchase a computer—when we acquire just about any new asset—by accounting conventions, it begins to depreciate on day one. But there is one asset that can *appreciate* over the years. That asset is the well-served customer, who becomes the most significant sustainer of the business, the lifetime customer.[c]

Tom Peters</td>
</tr>
</table>

Need for customer training to use or care for product For certain industries it is essential that users be well skilled in how to use the new product. This is true of office dictation equipment, electronic cash registers, farm implements, and a host of other products. Technology has become so complex that many suppliers must provide training as part of the follow-up to ensure customer satisfaction. Most organizations that sell microcomputers and other types of electronic equipment for office use now schedule training classes to ensure that customers can properly use and care for the products. These companies believe that users must be skilled in handling their equipment.

Price changes Price changes need not be a serious problem if they are handled correctly. The salesperson is responsible for maintaining an up-to-date price list. As your company issues price changes, record them accurately. Customers expect you to quote the correct price the first time.

PREVENTING POSTSALE PROBLEMS

There are ways to prevent postsale problems. The key is conscientious follow-up to be sure everything has been handled properly. Get to know the people who operate your shipping department. They are responsible for getting the right merchandise shipped on time, and it is important that they understand your customers' needs.

Become acquainted with people in the credit department. Be sure that they maintain a good, businesslike relationship with your customers. This is a delicate area; even small mistakes (a "pay now" notice sent too early, for example) can cause hurt feelings.

Some organizations ask customers to evaluate their postsale activities. Union Pacific sends out over 200 customer satisfaction surveys every month. Customers are asked to grade Union Pacific's performance on a scale of one to five (five is the top mark) in areas such as delivery and billing. If a customer responds to any survey item with a three or below, the account manager must develop an action plan to solve the problem.[12] Unfortunately, most companies do not use proactive methods to uncover customer complaints. Most wait for contact from the unhappy customer.[13]

Customer Follow-Up Methods

Customer follow-up methods usually have two major objectives. One is to express appreciation for the purchase and thus enhance the relationship established during the sales presentation. You no doubt thanked the customer at the time the sale was closed, but it would not hurt to say thank-you again a few days later. The second purpose of the follow-up is to determine if the customer is satisfied with the purchase. Both of these methods will strengthen the buyer-seller relationship.

In survey after survey, poor service and lack of follow-up after the sale are given as primary reasons people stop buying from us. Most customers are sensitive to indifferent treatment by the sales representative. With this fact in mind you should approach follow-up in a systematic and businesslike way. There are four follow-up methods.

PERSONAL VISIT

This is usually the most costly follow-up method, but it may produce the best results. It is the only strategy that allows face-to-face, two-way communication. When you take time to make a personal visit, the customer knows that you really care.

Use the personal follow-up to keep the customer informed of new developments, new products, or new applications. This information may pave the way for additional sales. When you do make a personal visit, do not stay too long. Accomplish the purpose of your visit as quickly as possible, and then excuse yourself.

TELEPHONE

The telephone provides a quick and efficient way to follow up a sale. A salesperson can easily make ten or twelve phone calls in a single hour, and the cost will be minimal. If you plan to send a thank-you card or letter, follow it up with a thank-you call. The personal appeal of the phone call will increase the effectiveness of the written correspondence. The telephone call has one major advantage over written correspondence. It allows for a two-way exchange of information. Once an account is well established, you may be able to obtain repeat sales by telephone.

BUILDING RELATIONSHIPS THROUGH TECHNOLOGY

ISLANDS OF INFORMATION

Companies often use many different software programs that contain information about customers. The firm will have customer purchase and payment history in its accounting system. Customer service problems may be recorded in the service department's software. A help desk program may be used by people in customer support.

The company's salespeople may be using one software program to manage their contacts with customer personnel, another program to prepare quotes, and yet another for correspondence with customers. To reduce these "islands" of customer information, more companies are finding ways to merge this information or to acquire software that performs more than one of these functions.

LETTER OR CARD

Written correspondence is an inexpensive and convenient form of customer follow-up. Letters and cards can be used to thank the customer for the order and promise continued service.[14] Some companies encourage their salespeople to use a formal letter typed on company stationery. Other companies have designed special thank-you cards, which are signed and sent routinely after a sale is closed. The salesperson may enclose a business card. These thank-you cards do have one major limitation: They are mass produced and therefore lack the personal touch so important to customer satisfaction.

CALL REPORT

The **call report** is a form that serves as a communications link with persons who can assist with customer service. The format varies, but generally it is a simple form with only four or five spaces. The sample call report form that appears here is used by a company that installs security systems at banks and other financial institutions.

A form like this is one solution to the problem of communication between the company personnel and the customer. It is a method of follow-through that triggers the desired action. It is simple, yet businesslike.

Follow-up programs can be as creative or ingenious as you wish according to Nancy Friedman, president of a national telephone training company. She suggests you customize your follow-up program to meet the needs of your customer.[15] You can use these four methods independently or in combination. Your main consideration should be some type of appropriate follow-up that (1) tells customers you appreciate their business and (2) determines if they are satisfied with the purchase.

Your Relationship Strategy Should Encompass All Key People

Some salespeople do a great job of communicating with the prospect but ignore other key people involved in the sale. To illustrate how serious this problem can be, let us look at the approach used by Jill Bisignano, a sales represen-

---

THE CALL REPORT

Date: October 26, 199—
To: Walt Higgins, service engineer
From: Diane Ray, sales representative

Action Promised: Visit the First National Bank of Middleberg within the next week to check on installation of our security system.

Assistance Needed: System B-420 was installed at the First National Bank of Middleberg on October 24. As per our agreement, you should make a follow-up call to check the installation of the system and provide bank personnel with a Form 82 certification checklist. The form should be given to Mr. Kurt Heller, president.
Copies to: Mr. Kurt Heller

tative for a major restaurant supply firm. Jill had called on Bellino's Italian Restaurant for several years. Although she was always very friendly to Nick Bellino, she treated the other employees with nearly total indifference. One day she called on Nick and was surprised to learn that he was retiring and had decided to sell his restaurant to two longtime employees.

As you might expect, it did not take the new owners long to find another supplier. Jill lost a large account because she failed to develop a good personal relationship with other key employees. It pays to be nice to everyone.

Here is a partial list of people in your company and in the prospect's company who can influence both initial and repeat sales.

1. *Receptionist.* Some salespeople simply do not use common sense when dealing with the receptionist. This person has daily contact with your customer and may schedule most or all calls. To repeatedly forget this individual's name or display indifference in other ways may cost you dearly. Display a friendly but businesslike attitude toward this person. Do not be patronizing or aloof.

2. *Technical Personnel.* Some products must be cleaned, lubricated, or adjusted on a regular basis. Take time to get acquainted with the people who perform these duties. Answer their questions, share technical information with them if necessary, and show appreciation for the work they are doing.

3. *Stock Clerks or Receiving Clerks.* People working in the receiving room are often responsible for pricing incoming merchandise and making sure that these items are stored properly. They may also be responsible for stock rotation and processing damage claims.

4. *Management Personnel.* Although you may be working closely with someone at the departmental level, do not forget the person who has the final authority and responsibility for this area. Spend time with management personnel occasionally and be alert to any concerns they may have.

This is not a complete list of the people you may need to depend on for support. There may well be other key people who influence sales. Always look beyond the customer to see who else might have a vested interest in the sale.

Solving the Customer's Problem

In recent years we have learned more about the impact of customer complaints. Research indicates that unhappy customers often do not initiate a verbal or written complaint. This means that postsale problems are not likely to come to the attention of salespeople or other personnel within the organization. We also know that unhappy customers do share their negative experiences with other people. A double loss occurs when the customer stops buying our products and takes steps to discourage other people from buying our products. When complaints do surface, we should view the problem as an opportunity to strengthen the business relationship. To achieve this goal, follow these suggestions.

1. *Give customers every opportunity to disclose their feelings.* Companies noted for outstanding customer service rely heavily on telephone systems—like toll-free "hotlines" to ensure easy access. At Federal Express, Cadillac Division

of General Motors, and IBM, to name a few companies, specially trained advisors answer the calls and offer assistance.[15] When customers do complain, by telephone or in person, encourage them to express all their anger and frustration. Do not interrupt. Do not become defensive. Do not make any judgments until you have heard all the facts as the customer sees them.[16] If they stop talking, try to get them to talk some more. Most of us feel better once we have had the opportunity to express our concerns fully.

2. *As the customer is talking, listen carefully and attentively.* You will need accurate information to solve the problem. One of the biggest barriers to effective listening is emotion. Do not become angry, and do not get into an argument.

3. *Keep in mind that it does not really matter whether a complaint is real or perceived.* If the customer is upset, you should be polite and sympathetic. Do not yield to the temptation to say, "You do not really have a problem." Remember, problems exist when customers perceive they exist.[17]

4. *Do not alibi.* Avoid the temptation to blame the shipping department, the installation crew, or anyone else associated with your company. Never tear down the company you work for. The problem has been placed in your hands, and you must accept responsibility for handling it. "Passing the buck" will only leave the customer with a feeling of helplessness.

5. *Politely share with the customer your point of view concerning the problem's cause.* At least explain what you think happened. The customer deserves an explanation.

6. *Decide what action must be taken to remedy the problem.* If you have not been empowered to solve the problem and must check with someone else, do it quickly. There should never be a long delay in dealing with a customer's complaint.

The value of customer complaints can emerge in two forms. First, complaints can be a source of important information that may be difficult to obtain by other means. Second, customer complaints provide unique opportunities for companies to *prove* their commitment to service. Loyalty builds in the customer's mind if you do a good job of solving her problem.[18]

Improving Customer Service through Self-Evaluation

Self-evaluation is one key to improving customer service. Most of us grow and develop by learning to review our work in an objective manner. Of course your sales manager will evaluate your performance from time to time, but this review is no replacement for honest self-appraisal.

On a regular basis, every salesperson should honestly try to answer the questions that follow. This self-appraisal exercise will help pinpoint areas that need strengthening. If the answers are "sometimes" or "once in a while," then you may be neglecting your customers.

Do I maintain a written record of customer assurances and promises?

Do I use a call report to follow up on assurances and promises?

Do I maintain a written record of each customer's unique personal characteristics?

Do I follow up each sale to determine the customer's perception of the purchase?

Do I show my appreciation for purchases at the close of every sale?

Do I maintain communication and rapport with key persons who work closely with the customer?

Do I keep the customer informed of new developments?

Do I handle the customer complaints quickly and efficiently?

Any salesperson who can answer yes to all these questions has a customer service program to be proud of. Excellent service after the sale continues to be the best way to achieve a competitive edge in sales.

SUMMARY

Servicing the sale is a major dimension of the selling process, with the objectives of providing maximum customer satisfaction and establishing a long-term relationship. Good service ensures that the product will meet the customer's needs, and also satisfies the needs for security and recognition discussed in Chapter 7 (see Maslow's hierarchy of needs). A reputation for good service is helpful in attracting new accounts and keeping old ones.

The *customer service* strategy is made up of three activities: adding value with *suggestion selling*, following through on assurances and promises, and using appropriate follow-up strategies. These activities create a positive impression of the salesperson and the company, which results in increased patronage buying.

A salesperson depends on the support of many other people in servicing a sale. Maintaining good relationships with support staff members who help service your accounts is well worth the time and energy required. Regular and objective self-evaluation is also a valuable practice. Efficient performance of the functions involved in customer service is important to ensure continuing customer satisfaction and should be a matter of professional pride.

➤ KEY TERMS

Customer Service
Suggestion Selling
Call Report

➤ REVIEW QUESTIONS

1. What two powerful motivators can a salesperson appeal to with a well-planned customer service program? Explain the significance of each one.
2. Define customer service. List the activities associated with this phase of personal selling.
3. Explain how suggestion selling fits into the definition of customer service.
4. Explain some of the reasons customer service is considered a profit stimulator.
5. List and describe four guidelines to follow when using suggestion selling.

6. How does credit become a part of servicing the sale?

7. The Sales Tips box on p. 328 describes the value of the lifetime customer. Is it realistic to believe that people will become lifetime customers in our very competitive marketplace?

8. List and describe four customation follow-up methods.

9. What types of customer service problems might be prevented with the use of a call report?

10. List five self-evaluation questions a salesperson should regularly review to improve customer service.

➤ APPLICATION EXERCISES

1. You are a salesperson working in the paint department at a Home Depot store. A customer has just purchased fifteen gallons of house paint. Assume that your store carries everything in the painting line, and list as many items as you can think of that could be used for suggestion selling. Explain how your suggestions of these items could be a service to the customer.

2. You work as a wholesale salesperson for a plumbing supply company. One of your customers, a contractor, has an open line of credit with your company for $10,000 worth of products. He is currently at his limit; however, he is not overdue. He just received word that he has been awarded a $40,000 plumbing contract at the local airport. The contract requires that he supply $9,000 worth of plumbing products. Your customer does not have the cash to pay for the additional products. He informs you that unless you can provide him with some type of financing, he may lose the contract. He says that he can pay you when he finishes his next job in sixty days. Explain what you will do.

3. You have just interviewed for a job that you really would like to have. You have heard it is a good idea to follow up an interview with a thank-you note or letter and an indication of your enthusiasm for the position. Select the strategy you will use for your follow-up, and explain why you chose it.

4. Using your search engine, examine the Internet for information on customer satisfaction. Type in "customer satisfaction"+selling. Are you surprised by the number of queries on this subject? Examine some of the queries related to what customers have said about specific company customer service programs.

WWW

➤ SALES AUTOMATION CASE STUDY

ACT! SERVICING THE SALE

You have taken over a number of accounts of another salesperson, Mark David. Most of these accounts are prospects, they have not yet purchased from Cadalyst. Two accounts did purchase CAD systems from Mark, Ms. Karen Murray of Murray D'Zines, and Ms. Judith Albright, owner of Picadilly studio. You now want to be sure that these sales are well serviced.

Access the ACT! software following the instructions in Appendix 2.

Questions

1. Whom should you speak with, within Cadalyst, before following through and contacting each of the customers? What would you need to discover?

2. What will be your follow-up strategy for each customer?

3. Does the fact that these customers initiated their orders (they were not sold the products, they bought them) influence your follow-up strategy?

4. Might other customers or prospects be affected by your service activities? How will this influence your activities? Could customer service be your competitive edge?

5. Do you see any suggestion selling opportunities with these two accounts? Which suggestion selling methods should you consider?

➤ CASE PROBLEM

If you spend time visiting highly successful companies such as Federal Express, Southwest Airlines, or Motorola, you learn about a series of rituals, stories, and heroes that express the organizations' "corporate culture." Often the heroes you hear about are employees who provided some form of customer service that was "beyond the call of duty." Ginger Trumfio, assistant editor of *Sales & Marketing Management*, says that keeping customers happy and coming back requires more than smiles and thank-yous. She believes that building customer loyalty requires outrageous service:

> . . . in today's business climate salespeople need to do more than follow up on promises, meet deadlines, and create win-win situations to keep clients happy — and coming back. Salespeople need to be outrageous, shocking, even death-defying.

Outrageous? Shocking? Death-defying? Does good customer service really require this much effort? Trumfio contacted several sales forces to find examples of outrageous service. Three examples follow.

Example one: The industry standard for morning express air carrier deliveries had been 10:30 A.M. Xerox Corporation had a critical need to get emergency parts to its technicians much earlier. Airborne Express carefully studied Xerox's needs and developed a plan to guarantee delivery times across the United States ranging from 8:00 to 9:30 A.M. Airborne has taken several steps to track Xerox packages throughout the process of delivery. For example, the scanner of every driver has been coded to beep and read "Xerox" when there is a Xerox package to be delivered. Once drivers realize they have an urgent package, the load plan is prioritized to make that delivery first.

Example two: Tony Heineman, account executive at KTUL Channel 8 in Tulsa, Oklahoma, describes a telephone conversation he had with the media buyer for a local company. He immediately detected that she was in a bad mood, so he asked her what was wrong. She explained that nearly every media representative in town had called that day to inquire about the details of a large media buy her company was about to make. Heineman sensed that something else might be bothering the buyer and asked,

"What's *really* wrong?" He discovered that she was concerned about car repairs that she needed but could not afford. He said, without hesitation, "Don't move, I'm on my way." Heineman jumped in his car and drove to his client's office. He picked up her car and took it to a friend who is a mechanic at a local dealer. The mechanic agreed to repair the car at no charge. The next day he returned the car to his client who was both happy and relieved.

Example three: David Lubelkin, president of Industrial Edge USA, an apartment house supply company in Orange, New Jersey, gave outrageous service during a winter snowstorm. On a cold January day, after a major snowstorm, he received a call from a desperate customer who needed sixty pounds of rock salt to be delivered to a property located 100 miles away. Predictions of sleet and icy rain threatened to bring traffic to a halt. Knowing that his delivery trucks were already on the road and not due back until late in the day, Lubelkin promised to deliver the salt needed by the customer. He quickly met with company CEO Stephen Weitraub and a decision was made to rent a truck for the delivery. The trip, normally a one and a half hour drive turned into a four and a half hour crawl at an average speed of 20 miles per hour. After dropping off the salt, the return trip took even longer. It was 10:00 P.M. when they finally returned to the office.[19]

QUESTIONS

1. Do you agree that outrageous service is needed to build customer loyalty? Explain.

2. Is there a downside to outrageous service after the sale? Reflect on the three preceding examples as you answer this question.

3. How might these acts of outrageous service influence the organization's "corporate culture"?

4. Would you consider following through on assurances and promises, and customer follow-up to be examples of outrageous customer service? Explain.

PARTNERSHIP SELLING: A ROLE PLAY/SIMULATION (see Appendix 3, p. 421)

Developing a Presentation Strategy-Servicing the Sale

Refer to sales memorandum 3, and strategically plan to service the sale with your customer. After closing the sale (getting the customer's signature) there are several steps to add value and build customer confidence and satisfaction. These steps are important to providing total quality customer service and should provide for repeat sales and a list of referred customers.

Following the instructions in item 2g of your presentation plan you need to schedule a future appointment to telephone or personally call and confirm the number of people attending the convention, and final room and menu needs (see convention center policies). Also, during this conversation you may suggest beverages for breaks, audio-visual needs, and any other items that will make this an outstanding convention for your customer.

You should have your calendar available to suggest and write down dates and times for this future contact. Any special materials such as a calendar can be placed in the back pocket of your portfolio. You may want to secure another person to be your customer and practice the customer service strategies you have prepared.

At this point you should be strategically prepared to make the presentation outlined in sales memorandum 3 to your customer. Your instructor will provide you with further instructions.

Part VI

Management of Self and Others

Personal selling requires a great deal of self-discipline and self-direction. Chapter 15 examines the four dimensions of self-management. Chapter 16 introduces communication style bias and explains how to build strong relationships with style flexing. The final chapter examines the fundamentals of sales force management.

By knowing our own communication style, we get to know ourselves better. And we get along with others better as we develop the ability to recognize — and respond to — their styles.

PAUL MOK AND DUDLEY LYNCH

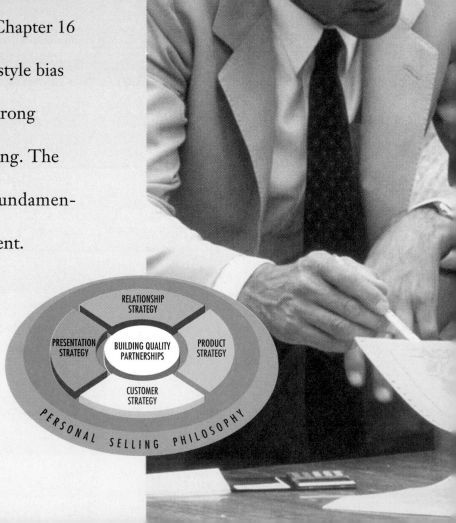

Management of Self: The Key to Greater Sales Productivity

Julio Melara, born to Honduran immigrant parents, made work the centerpiece of his life at an early age. Throughout high school he cut grass, worked as a busboy, delivered newspapers, and sold newspaper subscriptions. While attending college he worked as a courier with *New Orleans City Business*, a local business newspaper. By age 23 he was top producer and head of national sales. Later he left the newspaper and went into radio advertising sales. By age 28, Melara broke all sales records at WWL and became the radio's first million-dollar producer. He is a self-motivated person who says that he has learned a great deal from such books as *The Power of Positive Thinking* by Norman Vincent Peale. He is also someone who believes in management of self. Goal setting is the central theme of Melara's sales philosophy. He believes that written goals (personal and professional) facilitate growth and success.[1]

A salesperson is much like the individual who owns and operates a business. The successful sales representative, like the successful entrepreneur, depends on good self-management. Both of them must keep their own records, use self-discipline in scheduling their time, and analyze their own performance.

High-performance salespeople and successful entrepreneurs have one more characteristic in common. They realize that all development is really self-development.[2]

Management of Self—A Four-Dimensional Process

What makes a salesperson successful? Some people believe the most important factor is hard work. This is only partly true. Some people work hard but do not accomplish much. They lack purpose and direction. This lack of organization results in wasted time and energy.

In this chapter we approach management of self as a four-dimensional process consisting of the following components:

1. *Time management.* There are only about 250 business days per year. Within each day there is only so much time to devote to selling. Selling hours are extremely valuable. You must learn how to conserve this precious resource.

2. *Territory management.* A sales territory is a group of customers and prospective customers assigned to a single salesperson. Every territory is unique. Some territories consist of one or two counties, while others encompass several states. The number of accounts within each territory will also vary. Today, territory management is becoming less of an art and more of a science.

3. *Records management.* Every salesperson must maintain a certain number of records. These records help to "systematize" data collection and storage. A wise salesperson never relies on memory. Some of the most common records include planning calendars, prospect forms, call reports, summary reports, and expense reports.

4. *Stress management.* A certain amount of stress comes with many selling positions. Some salespeople have learned how to take stressful situations in stride. Others allow stress to trigger anger and frustration. Learning to cope with various stressors that surface in the daily life of a salesperson is an important part of the self-management process.

Time Management

A salesperson can increase sales volume in two major ways. One is to improve selling effectiveness, and the other is to spend more time in face-to-face selling situations. The latter objective can best be achieved through improved time and territory management.

Improving the management of both time and territory is a high-priority concern in the field of selling. These two closely related functions represent major challenges for salespeople.

Let us first look closely at the area of time management. There is definitely a close relationship between sales volume and number of customer contacts made by the salesperson. You have to make calls to get results.

SALES TIPS	Inner peace is having serenity, balance, and harmony in our lives achieved through the appropriate control of events.
	Hyrum W. Smith, president, Franklin Quest Company

TIME-CONSUMING ACTIVITIES

Some salespeople who have kept careful records of how they spend their time each day are surprised to learn how little is spent in face-to-face selling situations. The major time-consuming activities in personal selling are travel, time spent waiting to see a customer, completion of sales records, casual conversation, time spent on customer follow-through and follow-up, and time spent in face-to-face selling. Salespeople need to carefully examine each of these activities and determine whether too much or too little time is spent in any area. One way to assess time use is to keep a time log. This involves recording, at the end of every hour, the activities in which they were engaged during that time.[3] At the end of the week, add up the number of minutes spent on the various activities and ask yourself, "Is this the best use of my time?"

Once you have tabulated the results of your time log, it should be easy to identify the "time wasters." Pick one or two of the most wasteful areas, and then make plans to correct the problem. Set realistic goals that can be achieved. Keep in mind that wasting time is usually a habit. To manage your time more effectively, you will need to form new habits.

TIME MANAGEMENT METHODS

Sound time management methods can pave the way to greater sales productivity. The starting point is forming a new attitude toward time conservation. You must view time as a scarce resource not to be wasted. The timesaving strategies presented here are not new, nor are they unique. They are being used by time-conscious people in all walks of life.

A BRIEFCASE FULL OF TO DOS

Fighting traffic to get to a client's office was tough enough for the president and chief salesman of a building-restoration firm, but what *really* bugged him was driving to and from his own office several times a day.

To control his time, the executive put together a travel/paperwork briefcase. The idea is simple: Outfit a hard-sided briefcase with the supplies needed to set up a productive office anywhere you park your car.

In the briefcase are

- A notebook to record sales calls, client addresses, and phone numbers
- Correspondence to be answered, phone messages to be returned, and paperwork to be completed
- Cellophane tape, stapler, and other stationery supplies

Whenever he has time between appointments, the executive pulls into a parking lot, calls the office on his car phone, and takes care of business.[a]

DEVELOP A SERIES OF PERSONAL GOALS

According to Alan Lakein, author of *How to Get Control of Your Time and Your Life*, the most important aspect of time management is knowing what your goals are. He is referring to all goals—career goals, family goals, and life goals. People who cannot or will not sit down and write out exactly what they want from life will lack direction. They often move from one task to another without finishing what they set out to do.

The goal-setting process, as noted in Chapter 3, requires that you be clear about what you want to accomplish. If your goal is too general or vague, progress toward achieving that goal will be difficult to observe. Goals such as "I want to be a success" or "I desire good health" are much too general. Goals should also reflect the values that govern your life. For example, if one of your governing values is "I love my family" then you may commit yourself to spending quality time with family members.

Goals have a great deal of psychological value to people in selling. Sales goals, for example, can serve as a strong motivational force. To illustrate, let us assume that Mary Paulson, sales representative for a cosmetic manufacturer, decides to increase her sales by 15 percent over the previous year. She now has a specific goal to aim for. She will receive a feeling of personal satisfaction and increased economic rewards if she achieves her goal. Goal statements, according to Alan Lakein, help bring your future into the present by giving you a clearer view of what your ideal future looks like.

PREPARE A DAILY "TO DO" LIST

Every salesperson needs a daily plan (Fig. 15.1). Start each day by thinking about what you hope to accomplish. Then write down the activities. Putting your thoughts on paper forces you to clarify your thinking. Moff D. Warren,

Most people who achieve success in selling have a strong work ethic. They are "self-starters" who are committed to more than the eight-hour day or the forty-hour week.

© 1998 Dean Vietor from The Cartoon Bank. All rights reserved.

"I'll have to take a rain-check. Things are piling up here."

FIGURE 15.1 A daily list of activities can help us set priorities and save time.

	Date _____
DAILY TO DO LIST	

Priority	Items to do
3 ←	— *Call Houston Motors to check on installation of copy machine.*
2 ←	— *Call Price Optical to make an appointment for product demonstration.*
4 ←	— *Attend Chamber of Commerce at 3:00 P.M.*
1 ←	— *Call Simmons Furniture and deal with customer complaint.*

Notes for tomorrow:

president of Intellective Innovations, says, "If you write down exactly what needs to be done, not only does it make you psychologically ready for the day, it also helps you think broadly as you develop strategies for your business."[4] It is much easier to coordinate activities written in black and white than to try to carry them around in your head.

Now you should rank these activities from most important to least important. Make sure that daily activities are related to attaining the goals you have established. Begin each day with the highest priority task. Resist the urge to relegate the tasks you dislike to the bottom of the list.[5]

Preparing a daily "to do" list should become a habit. Try not to let busy-work crowd planning out of your schedule. After all, preparation of a to do list will usually require only five to ten minutes. This small investment of time will pay big dividends.

MAINTAIN A PLANNING CALENDAR

Ideally, a salesperson needs a single place to record daily appointments (personal and business), deadlines, and tasks. Unfortunately, many salespeople write daily tasks on any slip of paper they can find—backs of envelopes, three-by-five cards, napkins, or Post-it notes. Hyrum W. Smith, CEO of Franklin Quest, the company that created the popular Franklin Time Management System, calls these pieces of paper "floaters."

They just float around until you either follow through on them or lose them. It's a terribly disorganized method for someone who wants to gain greater control of his or her life.[6]

The use of floaters often leads to the loss of critical information, missed appointments, and lack of focus. Select a planning calendar design (the Franklin Day Planner is one option) that will bring efficiency to your daily planning efforts. You should be able to determine at a glance what is coming up in the days and weeks ahead (Fig. 15.2).

Some salespeople are using electronic pocket organizers to store hundreds of names, addresses, and phone numbers. These organizers can be used to keep track of appointments and serve as a perpetual calendar. You simply key in a birthday or anniversary, and a gentle beep will jog your memory on the appropriate date. The electronic organizer can also be used to keep track of appointments.[7]

ORGANIZE YOUR SELLING TOOLS

You can save valuable time by finding ways to organize sales literature, business cards, order blanks, samples, and other items needed during a sales call. You may waste time on a callback because some item was not available during your first call. You may even lose a sale because you forgot or misplaced a key selling tool.

If you have a great deal of paperwork, invest in one or more file cabinets. Some salespeople purchase small, lightweight cardboard file boxes to keep their materials organized. These boxes can easily be placed in your car trunk and moved from one sales call to another. The orderly arrangement of selling tools is just one more method of time conservation.

The key to regular use of the four timesaving techniques described previously is *commitment*. Unless you are convinced that efficient time management is important, you will probably find it difficult to adopt these new habits. A salesperson who fully accepts the "time is money" philosophy will use these techniques routinely.

SAVING TIME WITH TELEPHONES, FACSIMILE (FAX) MACHINES, AND ELECTRONIC DATA INTERCHANGE

As the cost of a sales call increases, more and more salespeople are asking the question, "Is this trip necessary?" In many situations a telephone call can replace a personal visit. The telephone call may be especially useful in dealing with accounts that are marginal in terms of profitability. Some customers actually prefer telephone contact for certain types of business transactions. Here are some situations in which the phone call is appropriate:

Call the customer in advance to make an appointment. You will save time, and the customer will know when to expect you.

Use the telephone to keep the customer informed. A phone call provides instant communication with customers at a low cost.

Build customer goodwill with a follow-up phone call. Make it a practice to call customers to thank them for buying your product and determine if the customer is satisfied with the purchase.

June '99

SUNDAY	MONDAY	TUESDAY	WEDNESDAY	THURSDAY	FRIDAY	SATURDAY
		1 10:30 Wheat First Securities 12:00 Lunch with Roy Williams 3:00 Farrell's Service Center	**2** 9:00 Demonstration at Charter Federal 11:00 Demo at Mills, Inc. 3:30 Meet with Helen Sisson	**3** 9:00 Austin & Son Storage 10:30 Demo at CMP Sporting Goods 1:00 Attend Computer Trade Show	**4** 9:00 Sales Meeting at Imperial Motor Lodge 1:30 Demo at Omega Homes	**5** 10:00 Take Dana to soccer game
6	**7** 8:00 to 12:00 Sales Training 1:30 Meet with M.I.S. staff at Mission College	**8** 9:30 Park Realty 11:00 White Tire Service 2:00 Demo at Ritter Seafood	**9** 9:00 Demonstration at Ross accounting services 11:00 Prospecting 2:30 Meet with technical support staff	**10** 8:30 Meet with Helen Hunt 12:00 Lunch with Tim 1:00 Demo at Collins Wholesale 4:00 Parent-Teacher conference	**11** 9:00 Demo at National Bank 1:00 to 5:00 Update sales records	**12** 9:00 10-K run (starts at YMCA building)
13	**14**	**15**	**16**	**17**	**18**	**19**

NOTES

	MAY 1999						
S	M	T	W	T	F	S	
						1	
2	3	4	5	6	7	8	
9	10	11	12	13	14	15	
16	17	18	19	20	21	22	
23/30	24/31	25	26	27	28	29	

	JULY 1999						
S	M	T	W	T	F	S	
				1	2	3	
4	5	6	7	8	9	10	
11	12	13	14	15	16	17	
18	19	20	21	22	23	24	
25	26	27	28	29	30	31	

FIGURE 15.2 Monthly Planning Calendar Sample. Shown is the first twelve days of a monthly planning calendar for a computer service sales representative

The cellular car telephone has become a convenient and time-saving sales tool.

Use the telephone to deal with customer problems. With the aid of the telephone you can provide personalized service in a hurry.

Voice mail automated telephone systems are now being used by companies of all sizes. These systems not only answer the phone and take messages but also provide information-retrieval systems that are accessible by telephone. This technology is especially useful for salespeople who need to exchange information with others.[8] For many salespeople the cellular car telephone has become a convenient and timesaving sales tool. A pager can also be used to facilitate communication with customers and the main office.

The fax machine takes telecommunication a step further. With the aid of a fax machine, salespeople can send and receive documents in seconds, using

BUILDING RELATIONSHIPS THROUGH TECHNOLOGY

FAX AND ACT!—INSTANTANEOUS CONFIRMATIONS

Close-up and personal information sharing creates a core on which successful relationships may be built and sustained. Friends have long supplemented their personal visits with letters, telegrams, and telephone calls.

Contemporary technology offers new ways to enhance and extend relationship-rich communica-

tions. Enlightened salespeople use the fax and computer modem as fast, thus effective, methods to give information to their customers. The automated fax can be particularly useful to quickly convey and amplify temporary thoughts such as the confirmation, affirmation, or verification follow-up. (See Sales Automation Application Exercise on p. 360 for more information.)

standard public or cellular telephone lines. Detailed designs, charts, and graphs can be transmitted across the nation or around the world.

Electronic Data Interchange (EDI) provides a fast and efficient way of exchanging common documents such as purchase orders, invoices, sales reports, and fund transfers. EDI is meeting the needs of companies that no longer want to transfer information on paper. In today's fast-paced world, if you only do business on paper, some firms will not buy your products. Most Fortune 500 companies are using EDI today.[9]

With the aid of a fax machine, salespeople can send and receive documents in seconds.

Territory Management

Many marketing organizations have found it helpful to break down the total market into manageable units called sales territories. A **territory** is the geographic area where prospects and customers reside. Although some firms have developed territories solely on the basis of geographic considerations, a more common approach is to establish a territory on the basis of classes of customers. Each account is classified according to sales potential. Regardless of how the sales territory is established, it is essentially a specific number of present and potential accounts that can be called on conveniently.

WHAT DOES TERRITORY MANAGEMENT INVOLVE?

To appreciate fully the many facets of territory management, it will be helpful to examine a typical selling situation. Put yourself in the shoes of a salesperson who has just accepted a position with a firm that manufactures a line of high-quality tools. You are responsible for a territory that covers six counties. The territory includes eighty-eight auto supply firms that carry your line of tools. It also includes thirty-eight stores that do not carry your tools. On the basis of

---

BUILDING RELATIONSHIPS IN A DIVERSE WORLD

MINORITY-OWNED BROKERAGE SETS HIGH STANDARDS

E. G. Bowman Company Incorporated, the first and largest minority-owned brokerage firm on Wall Street, recently celebrated four decades of service. The company was founded by Ernesta Procope who got her start selling $25 auto and home insurance policies to the residents of Brooklyn's Bedford-Stuyvesant section. One year after founding the company, Ernesta married John Procope, and they have worked successfully as a husband and wife management team.

E. G. Bowman offers a wide range of services and products spanning the insurance map. Although the Procopes have seen yearly premiums rise to $35 million, success has not come easy. John Procope says, "It's still tough for us to get appointments with major corporations—and still tough for us to write insurance with black companies." To achieve success, says John Procope, ". . . we have to run three times as fast to get the business." The Procopes say that the secret to success is setting customer service standards that are higher than the competition. Once the new client comes on board, the Procopes make sure the customer gets lots of personal attention. Today the company's hard-won clients include Pepsico, IBM, Apple Bank, and RJR Nabisco.[b]

this limited information, how would you carry out your selling duties? To answer this question, it will be necessary to follow these steps:

STEP 1: CLASSIFY ALL CUSTOMERS

Each account should be classified according to potential sales volume. This effort will require answers to two questions: What is the dollar amount of the firm's current purchases? What amount of additional sales might be developed with greater selling effort? Store A may be purchasing $3,000 worth of tools each year, but potential sales for this firm amount to $5,000. Store B currently purchases $2,000 worth of tools a year, and potential sales amount to $2,500. In this example, store A clearly deserves more time than store B.

It is important to realize that a small number of accounts may provide a majority of the sales volume. Many companies get 75 to 80 percent of their sales volume from 20 to 25 percent of their total number of customers. The problem lies in accurately identifying which accounts and prospects fall into the top 20 to 25 percent category. Once this information is available, you can develop customer classification data that can be used to establish the frequency of calls.

All classifications should be updated from time to time to ensure that customers are being called on frequently enough. The typical sales territory is constantly changing, and account classification information can become outdated. Classification of customers requires intimate knowledge of their operation.

STEP 2: DEVELOP A ROUTING AND SCHEDULING PLAN

Many salespeople have found that travel is one of their most time-consuming nonselling activities. A great deal of time can also be wasted just waiting to see a customer. The primary objective of a sales routing and scheduling plan is to increase actual selling by reducing time spent traveling between accounts and time spent waiting to see customers.

If a salesperson called only on established accounts and spent the same amount of time with each customer, routing and scheduling would not be difficult. In most cases, however, you need to consider other variables. For example, you may be expected to develop new accounts on a regular basis. In this case, you must adjust your schedule to accommodate calls on prospects. Another variable involves customer service. Some salespeople devote considerable time to adjusting warranty claims, solving customer problems, and paying goodwill visits.

There are no precise rules to observe in establishing a sales routing and scheduling plan, but the following guiding principles apply to nearly all selling situations:

1. Obtain or create a map of your territory, and mark the location of present accounts with pins or marking pen. Each account might be color coded according to sales potential. This will give you a picture of the entire territory. Some companies are using mapping software to create a territory picture that can be viewed on the computer screen at any moment during the day. Today's competitive pressures place sales territories under constant scrutiny and review.[10] With the aid of mapping software, sales people can perform rapid analyses of sales opportunities in a geographic area.

With the aid of mapping software salespeople can perform rapid analysis of sales opportunities in Europe.

2. If your territory is quite large, consider organizing it into smaller subdivisions. You can then plan work in terms of several trading areas that make up the entire territory.

3. Develop a routing plan for a specific period of time. This might be a one- or two-week period. Once the plan is firm, notify customers by telephone or letter of your anticipated arrival time.

4. Develop a schedule that accommodates your customers' needs. Some customers appreciate getting calls on a certain day of the week or at a certain hour of the day. Try to schedule your calls in accordance with their wishes.

5. Think ahead, and establish one or more tentative calls in case you have some extra time. If your sales calls take less time than expected or if there is an unexpected cancellation, you need optional calls to fill in the void.

6. Decide how frequently to call on the basis of sales potential. Give the greatest attention to the most profitable customers.

SALES CALL PLANS

You can use information from the routing and scheduling plan to develop a **sales call plan.** This proposal is a weekly action plan, usually initiated by the sales manager. Its primary purpose is to ensure efficient and effective account coverage.

The form most sales managers use is similar to Figure 15.3. One section of the form is used to record planned calls. A parallel section is for completed calls. Additional space is provided for the names of firms called on.

The sales manager usually presents the sales call plan to individual members of the sales staff. The plan's success will depend on how realistic the goals are in the eyes of the sales staff, how persuasive the sales manager is, and what type of training accompanies the plan's introduction. It is not unusual for members of the sales force to respond with comments such as, "My territory is different," "Do not put me in a procedural straitjacket," or "My territory cannot be organized." The sales manager must not only present the plan in a convincing manner but also provide training that will help each salesperson implement the plan successfully.

Records Management

Although some salespeople complain that paperwork is too time consuming and reduces the amount of time available for actual selling, others recognize that accurate, up-to-date records actually save time. Their work is better organized, and quick accessibility to information often makes it possible to close more sales and improve customer service.

A good record-keeping system gives salespeople useful information with which to check their own progress. For instance, an examination of sales call plans at the end of the day provides a review of who was called on and what was accomplished. The company also benefits from complete and accurate records. Reports from the field help management make important decisions. A company with a large sales force operating throughout a wide geographic area relies heavily on information sent to the home office.

FIGURE 15.3   Sales Call Plan

Sales Call Plan

Salesperson _____   For week ending _____

Territory _____   Days worked _____

_____

Planned Calls	**Total Completed Calls**
Number of planned calls _____	Number of calls only _____
Number of planned presentations _____	Number of presentations _____
Number of planned telephone calls _____	Number of telephone calls _____

Account Category Planning

Number of orders _____

A. Account calls _____   Total miles traveled _____

B. Account calls _____   A. Account calls _____

C. Account calls _____   B. Account calls _____

         C. Account calls _____

Companies called on	Address	Date	Customer rating	Comments about call

COMMON RECORDS KEPT BY SALESPEOPLE

A good policy is never to require a record that is not absolutely necessary. The only records worth keeping are those that provide positive benefits to the customer, the salesperson, or the personnel who work in sales-supporting areas of the company. Each record should be brief, easy to complete, and free of requests for useless detail. Where possible the format should provide for the use of check marks as a substitute for written responses. Completing sales record forms should not be a major burden.

What records should you keep? The answer to this question will vary depending on the type of selling position. Some of the most common records salespeople keep are described in this section.

A good record keeping system gives sales-people useful information wihich can be used to enhance service to customers.

CUSTOMER AND PROSPECT CARD FILES

Most salespeople find it helpful to keep records of customers and prospects. Each of these cards has space for name, address, and phone number. Other information recorded might be the buyer's personal characteristics, the names of people who might influence the purchase, or appropriate times to make calls. Of course, many salespeople have replaced their card files with computerized record systems.

CALL REPORTS

The call report (also called activity report) is a variation of the sales call plan described earlier in this chapter. It is used to record information about the people you have called on and about what took place. The call report is one of the most basic records used in the field of selling. It provides a summary of what happened during the call and an indication of what future action is required. The call report (daily and weekly) featured in Figure 15.4 is typical of those used in the field.

We are seeing less emphasis on call reports that require only numbers (calls made each day, number of proposals written, etc.). Companies that emphasize consultative selling are requesting more personal information on the customer (information that will expand the customer profile) and more information on the customers short- and long-range buying plans.[11]

EXPENSE RECORDS

Both your company and the government agencies that monitor business expenses will require a record of selling expenses. These usually include such items as meals, lodging, travel, and in some cases entertainment expenses. Some expense records must be accompanied by receipts.

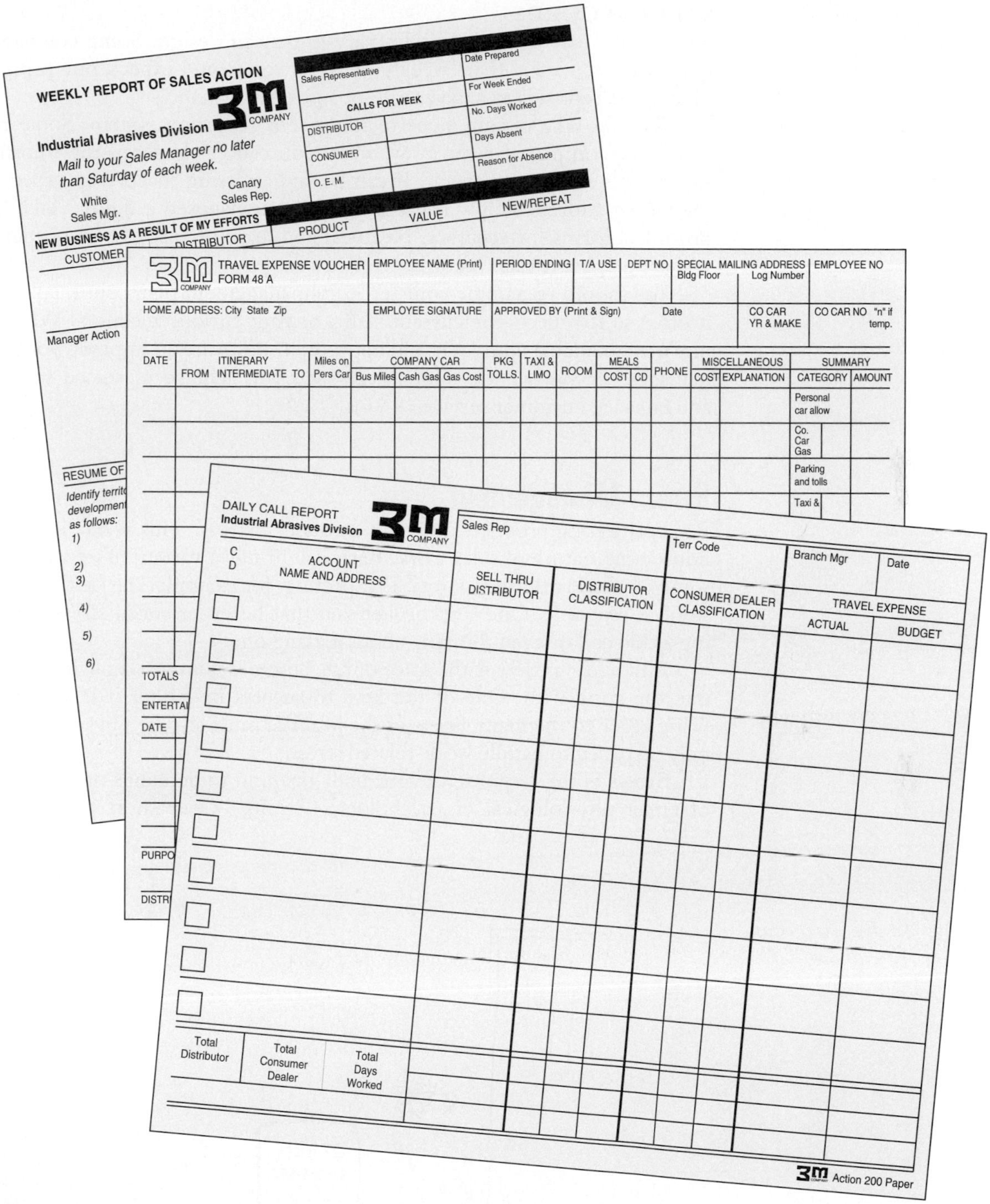

FIGURE 15.4   Call report, expense voucher, and weekly sales report. These are three of the most common records kept by 3M salespeople.

SALES RECORDS

The records used to report sales vary greatly in design. Some companies require daily reports, others weekly ones. As you would expect, one primary use of the sales report is to analyze salespeople's performance.

You can take certain steps to improve a reporting system. Some records should be completed right away, while you can easily recall the information. Accuracy is always important. It can be embarrassing to have an order sent to the wrong address simply because you have transposed a figure. Take time to proofread forms for accuracy. Neatness and legibility are also important when you are preparing sales records.

You should reexamine your territory management plan continually. Update it often so it reflects the current status of your various accounts. When possible, use a portable computer and appropriate software to improve your records management system. Computers can help you achieve increased selling time and enhance customer service.

Stress Management

Personal selling produces a certain amount of stress. This is due in part to the nonroutine nature of sales work. Each day brings a variety of new experiences, some of which will cause stress. Prospecting, for example, can be threatening to some salespeople. One stockbroker said that he experienced stress when making a cold call or even thinking about making one.[12]

Although "variety is the spice of life," there is a limit to how much diversity one can cope with. One of the keys to success in selling is learning how to bring order to the many facets of the job. We must also be physically and mentally prepared to handle work-related stress.

Stress is the response of your body or mind to demands on it, in the form of either physiological or psychological strain.[13] Over short periods of time,

© 1984 M. Twohy; American Management Associations.

stress is usually not a serious problem. In fact, some stress is beneficial. Stress in our life becomes a serious problem when we are unable to respond to stressors without creating excessive wear and tear on the body. Regardless of your physical condition, too much stress can harm and even kill you if left unchecked.[14]

Stress might be caused by trying to figure out ways to meet a sales quota or schedule travel throughout a sales territory. Missed appointments, presentations before large groups, and lack of feedback concerning your performance can also create stress. Ironically, some of the timesaving tools used by salespeople (fax machines, car phones and electronic mail) make it difficult for them to escape the pressures of their job.[15] Many salespeople feel they are "on call" twenty-four hours a day.

The term **technostress** is used to describe a disease caused by an inability to cope with various technologies in a healthy manner. The person who suffers from technostress has an unreasonable desire to constantly upgrade and improve technology, and feels uncomfortable when she does not have access to her machines. Being organized to the point of obsessiveness is another characteristic of technostress.[16]

Physical signs of stress overload might take the form of pounding of the heart, chronic fatigue with no apparent physical cause, diarrhea and cramping, trembling and nervous tics, and chest pains with no apparent physical cause. Psychological symptoms include undue anxiety, depression, abrupt changes in mood, paranoia, and reduced interest in personal relationships.[17] There are a number of ways to reduce stress in your life. Three stress management strategies are discussed here.

MAINTAIN AN OPTIMISTIC OUTLOOK

Researchers evaluated the coping strategies of 101 salespeople from three companies. They found that those who face job-related stress with an optimistic outlook fared better than those with a pessimistic attitude. The research team found that optimists used "problem-focused" coping strategies, while pessimists used "emotion-focused" techniques. The optimistic salespeople most frequently focused on various ways to solve the problem. Pessimists were more likely to try avoiding the problem and direct their feelings toward other people.[18]

PRACTICE HEALTHY EMOTIONAL EXPRESSION

When stress occurs, you may undergo physiological and psychological changes. The heartbeat quickens, the blood pressure rises, and tension builds. To relieve the pressure, you may choose a *fight* or *flight* response. Fighting the problem may mean unleashing an avalanche of harsh words or ignoring the other person. These reactions, of course, are not recommended. This behavior may damage relationships with team members, customers, or customer support personnel.

Flight is the act of running away from the problem. Rather than face the issue squarely, you decide to turn your back on it. The flight response is usually not satisfactory; the problem will seldom go away by itself.

When you are confronted with stress, there is a third option. You can accept the stress-producing condition and vow not to let it cause massive tension. Accept the problem as a "fact of life," and avoid overreaction. This is the mature approach to coping with stress. It means making a conscious effort not to let problems get you down.

MAINTAIN A HEALTHY LIFESTYLE

An effective exercise program—jogging, tennis, golf, racquetball, walking, or some other favorite exercise—can "burn off" the harmful chemicals that build up in your bloodstream after a prolonged period of stress. Salespeople at Owens Corning in Toledo, Ohio formed a Sales Wellness Advisory Team (SWAT). The team organized a health screening for Owen's 600 salespeople and instituted an incentive program that rewarded those who reached exercise goals.[19] The food you eat can play a critical role in helping you manage stress. Health experts agree that the typical American diet—high in saturated fats, refined sugar, additives, caffeine, and even too much protein—is the wrong menu for coping with stress. Leisure time can also provide you with the opportunity to relax and get rid of work-related stress. Mike McGinnity, director of sales and marketing at the Excelsior Hotel in Little Rock, Arkansas, encourages his salespeople to take full advantage of vacation. He helps them organize their work load so they are able to fully enjoy their vacation.[20]

One additional way to handle stress is to come to work rested and relaxed. Dr. Louis E. Kopolow, an expert in the field of stress management, says, "The

Exercise is an excellent way to moderate stress.

An Action Plan to Reduce Stress

1. Take 15 minutes.

2. Make two columns on a piece of paper. Write "Work" at the top of one, "Personal" at the top of the other. Write down all the things that are driving you crazy.

3. Underline the most important things on the lists.

4. Separate them into "chronic" and "acute."

5. For each one, ask yourself: What do I need to do to reduce the stress arising from this factor *right now?* Some answers could be as simple as "Get a good night's sleep."

6. Take action.[c]

SALES TIPS

best strategy for avoiding stress is to learn how to relax."[21] Fatigue will reduce your tolerance for dealing with stressful situations. How much sleep do you need each night? The number of hours of sleep required for good health varies greatly from person to person, but eight hours seems to be about average. The critical test is if you feel rested in the morning and prepared to deal with the day's activities.

In many respects, salespeople must possess the same self-discipline as a professional athlete. Sales work can be physically demanding. Lack of proper rest, poor eating habits, excessive drinking, and failure to exercise properly can reduce one's ability to deal with stress and strain.

BUILDING QUALITY PARTNERSHIPS

FOUR MODERATORS OF STRESS

The stress-related tension that surfaces in our lives can be a barrier to effective interpersonal relations. The psychological problems that can result from too much stress are anxiety, depression, instability, and reduced interest in personal relationships. The authors of *The One-Minute Manager Gets Fit* have identified four moderators of stress. When these four are in good working order, they can help prevent stress from turning into strain.

1. *Autonomy* is a sense we get on weekends of being able to do what we want. Autonomy can also be working independently or having the necessary skills and qualifications to be able to move from one job to another.

2. *Connectedness* relates to the ties we have with those around us. People with a high sense of connectedness feel they have strong, positive relationships in all areas—at home, at work, and in the community.

3. *Perspective* has to do with the meaning of life—the direction, the purpose, the passion that you feel for what you are doing. It keeps you from letting little things get you down. Because you are looking at the big picture, normal strains of daily life do not get blown out of proportion.

4. *Tone* is your energy level, your physical well-being and appearance, and how you feel about your body. By having better tone a person can definitely improve self-esteem and, in doing so, help moderate stress.[d]

SUMMARY

In this chapter we described management of self as a four-dimensional process. It involves time management, *territory* management, records management, and management of *stress*.

All salespeople can learn more about their products and improve their selling skills. However, there is no way to expand time. Our only option is to find ways to improve time and territory management. The four timesaving techniques discussed in this chapter should be used by every salesperson. When used on a regular basis, they will set the stage for more face-to-face selling time.

The first step in territory management is classification of all customers according to potential sales volume. You normally should spend the most time with accounts that have the greatest sales potential. The second step requires developing of a routing and scheduling plan. This plan should reduce time spent traveling between accounts. In some cases you can substitute telephone calls for personal calls.

A good record-keeping system provides many advantages. Accurate, up-to-date records can actually save time because work is better organized. The company also benefits because sales reports provide an important communication link with members of the sales force. Computers will assume an expanded role in record keeping in the years ahead.

There is a certain amount of stress associated with sales work. This is due in part to the nonroutine nature of personal selling. Salespeople must learn to cope with the factors that upset their equilibrium. Three stress management strategies were discussed.

➤ KEY TERMS

Territory   *Stress*
Sales Call Plan   *Technostress*

➤ REVIEW QUESTIONS

1. Describe how a salesperson is much like the individual who owns and operates a business.

2. Management of self has been described as a four-dimensional process. Describe each dimension.

3. What are the two major ways a salesperson can increase sales volume?

4. How can a salesperson use a time log to improve time management?

5. List four techniques the salesperson should use to make better use of valuable selling time.

6. Effective territory management involves two major steps. What are they?

7. What is a sales call plan? Explain how it is used.

8. Describe the most common records kept by salespeople.

9. What is the definition of stress? What are some indicators of stress?

10. The Building Quality Partnerships box on p. 357 describes four modera-

tors of stress. Which of these four moderators do you think is most important for persons employed in the sales field? Explain.

➤ **APPLICATION EXERCISES**

1. The key to successful time management lies in thinking and planning ahead. You must become conscious of yourself and decide what you want from your time. You can manage your time only when you have a clear picture of what is going on within and around you. To assess the quality of your working time, it might be helpful to keep a careful record for a certain amount of time showing exactly how you have used your day. Over this period of time, write down everything you have done and how long it took. Next you can appraise your use of time and decide whether or not your time was put to good use. Some pertinent questions you might ask yourself in appraising your use of time are suggested by the following "time analysis questions":

   a. What items am I spending too much time on?
   b. What items am I spending too little time on?
   c. What items offer the most important opportunities for saving time?
   d. What am I doing that does not need to be done at all?
   e. How can I avoid overusing the time of others?
   f. What are some other suggestions?

2. Deciding on a goal can be the most crucial decision of your life. It is more damaging not to have a goal than it is not to reach a goal. It is generally agreed that the major cause of failure is the lack of a well-defined purpose. A successful life results not from chance, but from a succession of successful days. Prepare a list for the following categories:

   Career goals
   1.
   2.
   3.

   Family goals
   1.
   2.
   3.

   Educational goals
   1.
   2.
   3.

   Interpersonal relationship goals
   1.
   2.
   3.

3. Interview someone you know who uses a planning calendar. What kind is it—pocket, desk, or some other type? How long has the person been using it? How important is the calendar to daily, weekly, monthly, and yearly planning? Has the person ever considered discontinuing its use? What are

the person's suggestions for someone who does not use one? Write your answer.

WWW

4. Time management is an important part of a successful salesperson's job. Using your search engine, examine the Internet for information on time management. Type in "time management" +selling. Examine the training products and services available on this topic.

➤ SALES AUTOMATION APPLICATION EXERCISE

ACT! FAX CORRESPONDENCE

The client who promptly receives a faxed note is more likely to remember and honor a commitment. Quickly confirming an agreement reached by telephone is easy for ACT!. At any Contact Screen, press the keys W F E. This displays the fax cover sheet which, by itself, may be used to convey a short confirmation message. Press the DownArrow key twice to position the cursor at Subject and enter I look forward to lunch with you Friday noon at Jimmy's and press F10. Press P D Enter Enter N and the fax cover will be sent to your printer. If your computer is running fax software, you could send the fax cover note directly to your client's fax machine.

➤ CASE PROBLEM

Julio Melara, introduced at the beginning of this chapter, has achieved success in three different sales and marketing positions in the fields of radio broadcasting and publishing. At age thirty-one he holds the position of executive vice president of the $10 million New Orleans Publishing Group and publisher of *New Orleans Magazine.* He is convinced that success comes to those who have the right attitude and the will to win. Now that he has proved himself in two very competitive fields, Melara is ready to share the beliefs and success principles that made a difference in his own career. His success formula is made of five elements.

1. You have to believe you can achieve your dreams and desires. He likes to quote a verse from the book of Proverbs that says, "As a man thinketh, so he is." Put another way, "If you believe, you will achieve." Salespeople tend to behave in a way that supports their own ideas of how successful or unsuccessful they will be. Those who have serious doubts about their capabilities tend to reduce their efforts or give up altogether when faced with major challenges.

2. Put all your goals in writing. A written goal, reviewed daily, is much more likely to be achieved. Melara says that a written goal keeps the vision in front of you. Many salespeople avoid setting goals because they do not understand the importance of this self-improvement method. As we make and keep commitments to ourselves, we begin to establish a greater sense of self-confidence and self-control. For many salespeople, goals become an integral part of their plan to break old habits or form new ones.

3. Get all the education and information that you can. Melara is fond of saying, "You'll never earn more unless you learn more." In recent years, most

salespeople have had to develop expertise in the area of computer technology. Knowledge of the customer's business is not an option if you want to build a strong partnership. Developing expertise in appropriate areas can result in increased self-confidence.

4. **Commit to excellence in everything that you do.** There is an interconnection among the many areas of work and family. Melara believes that salespeople must fulfill both work and family responsibilities. Many sales and marketing organizations have found that family problems are linked to employee problems such as tardiness, absenteeism, and low productivity. Of course, problems at work often have a negative influence on one's personal life.

5. **Protect your enthusiasm.** Melara says, "Watch the friends you hang out with, the people you associate with, and the television programs you watch." Enthusiasm for work and work-related activities is often fragile. The negative views of a co-worker or a friend can erode our enthusiasm. One of the best defenses against loss of enthusiasm is to maintain positive expectations about the future.

QUESTIONS

1. Which of these elements will make the most important contribution to a career in personal selling? Explain.

2. Reflect on your own approach to accomplishing tasks and select two of Melara's elements you would find easy to adopt. Then select two elements that you would find difficult to adopt. Explain your choices.

3. How might goal setting be used in conjunction with time management?

4. How might a commitment to excellence improve the processes of territory management and records management?

5. Do you agree or disagree that the people you associate with can influence your enthusiasm?

Communication Styles: Managing the Relationship Process

LEARNING OBJECTIVES

When you finish reading this chapter, you should be able to

1. Discuss communication-style bias and how it influences the relationship process

2. Explain the benefits derived from an understanding of communication styles

3. Identify the two major dimensions of the communication-style model

4. Name the four major communication styles in the communication-style model

5. Learn how to identify your preferred communication style and that of your customer

6. Learn to overcome communication-style bias and build strong selling relationships with style flexing

Fortune magazine once described Lee Iacocca as the most popular business figure in America. He has been on the cover of *Time, Parade, Life, Business Week, Newsweek, Fortune,* and numerous other publications. He also has authored *Iacocca,* an autobiography that became one of the best-selling books in the history of publishing. Although he retired as CEO for Chrysler Corporation several years ago, he continues to be a prominent public figure.

Organizations are still willing to pay him $60,000 for a thirty-minute speech.[1] Lee Iacocca's high visibility throughout America is due in part to his communication style. You might remember the television commercials that featured Iacocca. In a blunt and authoritative voice he declared: "If you can find a better car—buy it." He definitely projects the image of someone who is "in charge."

Communication Styles—An Introduction to Managing Selling Relationships

Almost everyone has had the pleasant experience of meeting someone for the first time and developing instant mutual rapport. There seems to be something about some people that makes you like them instantaneously—a basis for understanding that is difficult to explain. On the other hand, we can all recall meeting people who "turn us off" almost immediately. Why do these things happen during the initial contact? To answer this question, we must understand a unique form of bias that can surface in almost any social or business setting. The information presented in this chapter can help you reduce tension and increase trust in all types of business relationships.

COMMUNICATION-STYLE BIAS

Bias in various forms is quite common in our society. In fact, local, state, and national governments have passed many laws to curb blatant forms of racial, age, and sex bias. We also observe some degree of regional bias when people from various parts of the country meet.

The most frequently occurring form of bias is not commonly understood in our society. What has been labeled **communication-style bias** is a state of mind that almost every one of us experiences from time to time, but we usually find it difficult to explain the symptoms. Communication-style bias develops when we have contact with another person whose communication style is different from our own. For example, a purchasing agent was overheard saying, "I do not know what it is, but I just do not like that sales representative." The agent was no doubt experiencing communication-style bias but could not easily describe the feeling.

Have you ever wondered why it is so difficult to talk with some people and so easy to talk with others? It is often a matter of communication style. Your communication style is the "you" that is on display every day—the outer pattern of behavior that others see. If your style is very different from the other person's, it may be difficult for the two of you to develop rapport. All of us have had the experience of saying or doing something that was perfectly acceptable to a friend or coworker and being surprised when the same behavior irritated someone else. However, aside from admitting that this happens, most of us are unable to draw meaningful conclusions from these experiences to help us perform more effectively with people in the future.[2]

In recent years, thousands of salespeople have learned to manage their selling relationships more effectively through the study of communication styles. David Merrill and Roger Reid, authors of *Personal Styles and Effective Performance*, report that more than 100,000 people have completed the Interpersonal Discovery Workshop designed to improve communication-style awareness. Those enrolling have been predominantly in sales and management positions. This practical theory of human behavior, based on research by the Swiss psy-

---

By knowing our own communication style, we get to know ourselves better. And we get along with others better as we develop the ability to recognize—and respond to—their styles.[a]

From Paul Mok and Dudley Lynch, "Easy New Way to Get Your Way"

SALES TIPS

choanalyst Carl Jung and others, helps them achieve improved sales productivity. The psychology of behavior patterns is a practical blend of concepts taken from the fields of psychology, communication, and sociology.

COMMUNICATION-STYLE PRINCIPLES

The theory of behavioral- or communication-style bias is based on a number of underlying principles. A review of these principles will be beneficial before we examine specific styles.

1. *Individual differences exist and are important.* It is quite obvious that we all differ in terms of physical characteristics such as height, shoe size, facial features, and body build, but the most interesting differences are those patterns of behavior that are unique to each of us. Each of us displays an individual combination of nonverbal characteristics. Voice patterns, eye movement, facial expression, and posture are some of the components of our communication style. Additional characteristics are discussed later in this chapter.

2. *Individual style differences tend to be stable.* Our communication style is based on a combination of hereditary and environmental factors. Our style is somewhat original at the time of birth; it takes on additional individuality during the first three to five years of life. By the time we enter elementary school, the teacher should be able to identify our communication style. This style remains fairly constant throughout life.

3. *There is a finite number of styles.* Most people display one of several clusters of similar behaviors, and this allows us to identify a small number of behavioral categories. By combining a series of descriptors we can develop a single "label" that will describe a person's most preferred communication style.

4. *Everyone makes judgments about people based on communication style.* As noted in Chapter 3, when people meet you for the first time, they form an imme-

Group sales presentations can be very challenging because in most cases you are attempting to relate to several different communication styles.

diate and distinct impression of you. This impression tends to influence the actions of other people.[3]

The ability to identify another person's communication style, and to know how and when to adapt your own preferred style to it, can afford you a crucial advantage in dealing with people. The ability to "speak the other person's language" is an important relationship-management skill.[4]

IMPROVING YOUR RELATIONSHIP-MANAGEMENT SKILLS

Anyone who is considering a career in selling will benefit greatly from the study of communication styles. These concepts provide a practical method of classifying people according to behavioral style and give the salesperson a distinct advantage in the marketplace. A salesperson who understands communication-style classification methods and learns how to apply them can avoid common mistakes that threaten interpersonal relations with customers. Awareness of these methods greatly reduces the possibility of tension arising during the sales call. Tony Alessandra and Michael O'Connor, authors of *People Smart*, state, "If we don't think first of the other person, we run the risk of unintentionally imposing a tension-filled win-lose or lose-lose relationship on them."[5]

A major goal of this chapter is to help you better understand your own most preferred communication style. Another important goal is to help you develop greater understanding and appreciation for styles that are different from

---

BUILDING QUALITY PARTNERSHIPS

LIFO DEVELOPS NEW GOLDEN RULE

Communication style principles and practices serve as the foundation for High Performance Selling, a sales training program offered by Stuart Atkins Incorporated (SAi), a California-based training company. This training program is a version of LIFO Training which has been completed by 2 million people in over 10,000 organizations. LIFO training invites self-examination and promotes self-development. At the beginning of the High Performance Selling program enrollees complete the LIFO Survey. This self-scoring instrument helps each participant identify her most preferred communication style and her least preferred communication style. There are four basic styles or ways of seeing problems, people, and situations. The most preferred style represents the person's primary selling strengths. These are the factors that contribute the most to one's success in selling. Our least preferred style represents a source of untapped strengths that can be used to increase sales.

The High Performance Selling program re-minds us that often we are selling products and services to a person who has a different preferred style than our own. If we always rely on our major selling strengths (most preferred style) we will not achieve our full potential. This is especially true if the customer's most preferred style is our least preferred style. Salespeople often overuse their favorite selling strengths to the point of unproductive excess.

High Performance Selling provides an emphatic reminder that customers have communication style preferences. If we can identify the customers' most preferred style, we can adjust our approach to meet their needs. Most of us have been taught to use the Golden Rule, which means, "Do unto others as you would have them do unto you." In recognition of the fact that not everybody wants to be sold the same way, the creators of High Performance Selling developed a new golden rule for salespeople: Do unto others as they want to be done unto.[b]

FIGURE 16.1 The first step in determining your most preferred communication style is to identify where you are on the dominance continuum.

Low _____ High

your own. You will learn how to manage your selling relationships more effectively by learning how to flex your style in a variety of selling situations.

Communication-Style Model

This section introduces you to the four basic communication styles. One of these will surface as your most preferred style. The communication-style model that defines these styles is based on two important dimensions of human behavior: dominance and sociability. We look at the dominance continuum first.

DOMINANCE CONTINUUM

Dominance can be defined as the tendency to control or prevail over others.[6] Dominant people tend to be quite competitive. They also tend to offer opinions readily and be decisive and determined. Each of us falls somewhere on the dominance continuum illustrated by Figure 16.1.

A person classified as being high in dominance is generally a "take charge" type of person who makes a position clear to others. A person classified as being low in dominance is usually more reserved, unassertive, and easygoing. Dominance has been recognized as a universal behavioral characteristic. David W. Johnson developed the Interpersonal Pattern Exercise to help people achieve greater interpersonal effectiveness. He believes that people fall into two dominance categories:

1. *Low dominance:* These people have a tendency to be quite cooperative and eager to assist others. They tend to be low in assertiveness.

2. *High dominance:* These people tend to give advice freely and frequently initiate demands. They are more aggressive in dealing with others.[7]

The first step in determining your most preferred communication style is to identify where you fall on the dominance continuum. Do you tend to rank low or high on this scale? To answer this question, complete the Dominance Indicator form in Table 16.1. Rate yourself on each scale by placing a check mark on the continuum at the point that represents how you perceive yourself. If most of your check marks fall to the right of center, you are someone who is high in dominance. If most of your check marks fall to the left of center, you are someone who is low in dominance. Is there any best place to be on the dominance continuum? The answer is no. Successful salespeople can be found at all points along the continuum.

High

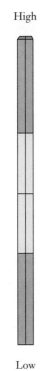

Low

FIGURE 16.2 The second step in determining your most preferred communication style is to identify where you are on the sociability continuum.

SOCIABILITY CONTINUUM

Sociability reflects the amount of control we exert over our emotional expressiveness.[8] People who are high in sociability tend to express their feelings freely, while people who are low in this dimension tend to control their feelings. Each of us falls somewhere on the sociability continuum illustrated in Figure 16.2.

TABLE 16.1 DOMINANCE INDICATOR

Rate yourself on each scale by placing a check mark on the continuum at the point that represents how you perceive yourself.

I PERCEIVE MYSELF AS SOMEWHAT

Cooperative	+———+———+———+———+	Competitive
Submissive	+———+———+———+———+	Authoritarian
Accommodating	+———+———+———+———+	Domineering
Hesitant	+———+———+———+———+	Decisive
Reserved	+———+———+———+———+	Outgoing
Compromising	+———+———+———+———+	Insistent
Cautious	+———+———+———+———+	Risk-taking
Patient	+———+———+———+———+	Hurried
Complacent	+———+———+———+———+	Influential
Quiet	+———+———+———+———+	Talkative
Shy	+———+———+———+———+	Bold
Supportive	+———+———+———+———+	Demanding
Relaxed	+———+———+———+———+	Tense
Restrained	+———+———+———+———+	Assertive

Sociability is also a universal behavioral characteristic. It can be defined as the tendency to seek and enjoy interaction with others. Charles Margerison, author of *How to Assess Your Managerial Style*, says that high sociability is an indication of a person's preference to interact with other people. He says that low sociability is an indicator of a person's desire to work in an environment where the person has more time alone instead of having to make conversation with others.[9] The person who is classified as being low in the area of sociability is more reserved and formal in social relationships.

The second step in determining your most preferred communication style is to identify where you fall on the sociability continuum. To answer this question, complete the Sociability Indicator form shown in Table 16.2. Rate yourself on each scale by placing a check mark on the continuum at the point that represents how you perceive yourself. If most of your check marks fall to the right of center, you are someone who is high in sociability. If most of your

TABLE 16.2 SOCIABILITY INDICATOR

Rate yourself on each scale by placing a check mark on the continuum at the point that represents how you perceive yourself.

I PERCEIVE MYSELF AS SOMEWHAT

Disciplined	—+—————+—————+—————+—+	Easygoing
Controlled	—+—————+—————+—————+—+	Expressive
Serious	—+—————+—————+—————+—+	Lighthearted
Methodical	—+—————+—————+—————+—+	Unstructured
Calculating	—+—————+—————+—————+—+	Spontaneous
Guarded	—+—————+—————+—————+—+	Open
Stalwart	—+—————+—————+—————+—+	Humorous
Aloof	—+—————+—————+—————+—+	Friendly
Formal	—+—————+—————+—————+—+	Casual
Reserved	—+—————+—————+—————+—+	Attention-seeking
Cautious	—+—————+—————+—————+—+	Carefree
Conforming	—+—————+—————+—————+—+	Unconventional
Reticent	—+—————+—————+—————+—+	Dramatic
Restrained	—+—————+—————+—————+—+	Impulsive

check marks fall to the left of center, you are someone who is low in sociability. Keep in mind that there is no best place to be. Successful salespeople can be found at all points along this continuum.

With the aid of the dominance and sociability continuums we are now prepared to discuss a relatively simple communication-style classification plan that has practical application in the field of selling. We will describe the four basic styles: Emotive, Director, Reflective, and Supportive.

FOUR STYLES OF COMMUNICATION

By combining the two dimensions of human behavior, dominance and sociability, we can form a partial outline of the communication-style model (Fig. 16.3). Dominance is represented by the horizontal axis, and sociability is represented by the vertical axis. Once the two dimensions of human behavior are combined, the framework for communication-style classification is established.

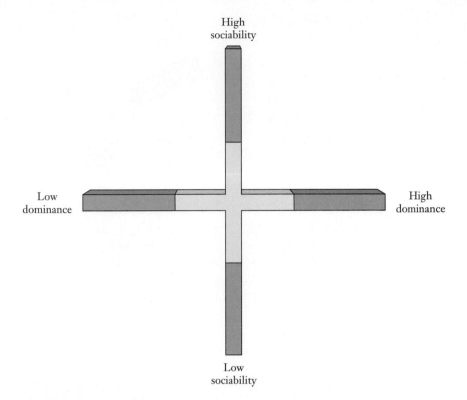

High
sociability

Low
dominance

High
dominance

Low
sociability

FIGURE 16.3   When the dominance and sociability dimensions of human behavior are combined, the framework for communication-style classification is established.

THE EMOTIVE STYLE

The upper right-hand quadrant of Figure 16.4 defines a style that combines high sociability and high dominance. We will call this the **Emotive style.** Emotive people like Jesse Jackson and Jay Leno usually stand out in a crowd. They are expressive and willing to spend time maintaining and enjoying a large number of relationships.[10] Oprah Winfrey, the well-known television personality, and talk show host David Letterman provide excellent models of the Emotive communication style. Sandra Bullock provides still another example. They are outspoken, enthusiastic, and stimulating. Larry King, popular talk show host, and Bill Clinton also project the Emotive communication style. The Emotive person wants to create a social relationship quickly and usually feels more comfortable in an informal atmosphere. Some of the verbal and nonverbal clues that identify the Emotive person follow:

1. *Appears quite active.* This person gives the appearance of being busy. A person who combines high dominance and high sociability is often restless. The Emotive person is likely to express feelings with vigorous movements of the hands and a rapid speech pattern.

2. *Takes the social initiative in most cases.* When two people meet for the first time, the Emotive person will be more apt to initiate and maintain the conversation as well as to initiate the handshake. Emotives rate high in both directness and openness.

3. *Likes to encourage informality.* The Emotive person will move to a "first name" basis as soon as possible (too soon in some cases). Even the way this person sits in a chair will communicate a preference for a relaxed, informal social setting.

FIGURE 16.4 The Emotive style combines high sociability and high dominance.

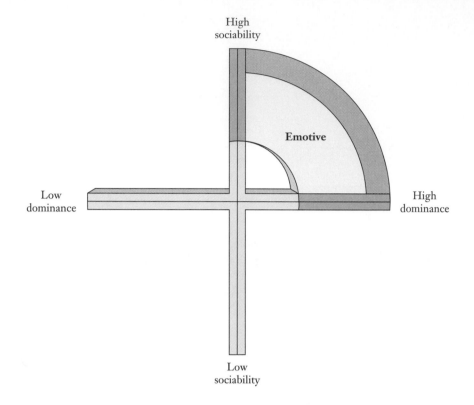

4. *Expresses emotional opinions.* Emotive people generally do not hide their feelings. They often express opinions dramatically and impulsively.

THE DIRECTOR STYLE

The lower right-hand quadrant defines a style that combines high dominance and low sociability. We will call this the **Director style** (Fig. 16.5).

To understand the nature of people who display the Director communication style, picture in your mind's eye the director of a Hollywood film. The

Emotive people like Jesse Jackson are enthusiastic, outspoken, and stimulating.

KEY WORDS FOR THE EMOTIVE STYLE

Sociable	Unstructured
Spontaneous	Excitable
Zestful	Personable
Stimulating	Persuasive
Emotional	Dynamic

person you see is giving orders in a loud voice and is generally in charge of every facet of the operation. Everyone on the set knows this person is in charge. Although the common stereotyped image of the Hollywood film director is probably exaggerated, this example will be helpful as you attempt to become familiar with the Director style.

Lee Iacocca, Sam Donaldson (television commentator), and Bob Dole project the Director style. The late Vince Lombardi, successful coach of the Green Bay Packers for many years, and Barbara Walters, television commentator, typify this communication style. These people have been described as frank, demanding, aggressive, and determined.

In the field of selling you will encounter a number of customers who are Directors. How can you identify these people? What verbal and nonverbal

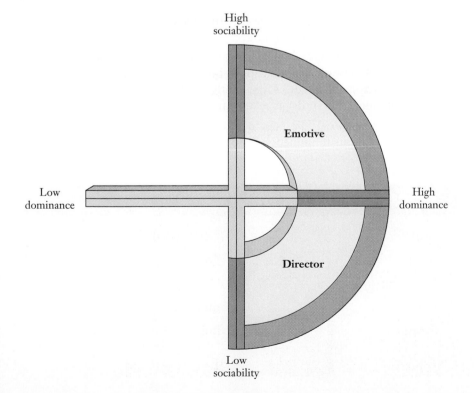

FIGURE 16.5   The Director style combines high dominance and low sociability.

Bob Dole is known for his frank, demanding, and aggressive communication style.

clues can we observe? A few of the behaviors displayed by Directors follow:

1. *Appears to be quite busy.* The Director generally does not like to waste time and wants to get right to the point. General Norman Schwarzkopf and Judge Joseph Wapner of the "People's Court" television show display this behavior.

2. *May give the impression of not listening.* In most cases the Director feels more comfortable talking than listening.

3. *Displays a serious attitude.* A person who is low in sociability usually communicates a lack of warmth and is apt to be quite businesslike and impersonal. Mike Wallace, one of the stars on the popular "60 Minutes" television show, seldom smiles or displays warmth.

4. *Voices strong opinions.* The person who is high on the Dominance continuum usually wants to influence the other person's point of view.

KEY WORDS FOR THE DIRECTOR STYLE

Aggressive	Determined
Intense	Frank
Requiring	Opinionated
Pushy	Impatient
Serious	Bold

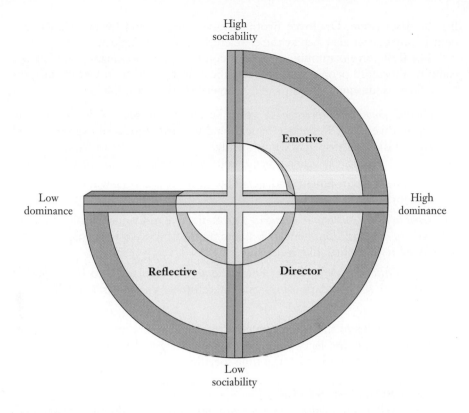

The Director may rely on a loud tone of voice or firm gesturing with the hands to drive home a point.

THE REFLECTIVE STYLE

The lower left-hand quadrant of the communication-style model features a combination of low dominance and low sociability (Fig. 16.6). People who regularly display this behavior are classified as having the **Reflective style.**

The Reflective person tends to examine all the facts carefully before arriving at a decision. Like a cautious scientist, this individual wants to gather all available information and weigh it carefully before taking a position. The reflective type is usually a stickler for detail.[11] The late physicist, Albert Einstein,

Persons with the Reflective style, such as former president Jimmy Carter, tend to control their emotions and examine all the facts when making a decision.

KEY WORDS FOR THE REFLECTIVE STYLE	
Precise	Scientific
Deliberate	Preoccupied
Questioning	Serious
Disciplined	Industrious
Aloof	Stuffy

fits the description. Dr. Joyce Brothers, psychologist, and former U.S. President Jimmy Carter also display the characteristics of the Reflective type.

The Reflective communication style combines low dominance and low sociability; therefore people with this classification tend to be reserved and cautious. Some additional behaviors that characterize this style follow:

1. *Controls emotional expression.* It would be unusual to see a Reflective person cry at a wedding. Reflective people tend to curb emotional expression and are less likely to display warmth openly.

2. *Displays a preference for orderliness.* The Reflective person enjoys a highly structured environment and generally feels frustration when confronted with unexpected events.

3. *Tends to express measured opinions.* The Reflective individual usually does not express dramatic opinions. This communication style is characterized by disciplined, businesslike actions.

4. *Seems difficult to get to know.* The Reflective person tends to be somewhat formal in social relationships and therefore is viewed as aloof by many people.

In a selling situation the Reflective customer does not want to move too fast. This person wants the facts presented in an orderly and unemotional manner and does not want to waste a lot of time socializing.

THE SUPPORTIVE STYLE

The upper left-hand quadrant shows a combination of low dominance and high sociability (Fig. 16.7). This communication style is called the **Supportive style** because these people find it easy to listen and usually do not express their views in a forceful manner. Former U.S. President Gerald Ford and entertainers John Denver, Kevin Costner, Mary Tyler Moore, Patrick Duffy, and Neil Armstrong (Apollo 11 crew member) display the characteristics of the Supportive style.

Low visibility generally characterizes the lifestyle of Supportive people. They complete their tasks in a quiet, unassuming manner and seldom draw attention to what they have accomplished. In terms of assertiveness, persons with the Supportive style rank quite low. Someone who ranks high on the dominance continuum is likely to view the Supportive individual as being too easygoing. In some cases, Supportive people are too agreeable; they often do not

KEY WORDS FOR THE SUPPORTIVE STYLE	
Lighthearted	Patient
Reserved	Sensitive
Passive	Relaxed
Warm	Compliant
Docile	Softhearted

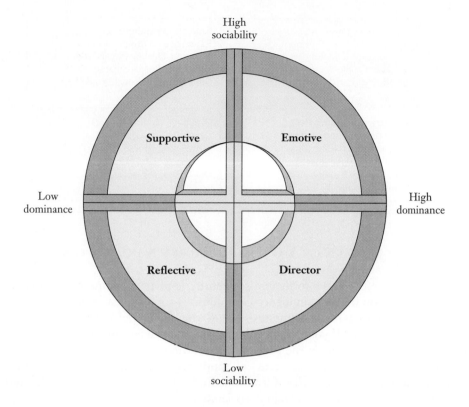

FIGURE 16.7 The Supportive style combines low dominance and high sociability.

state their opinions because they want to avoid conflict. This behavior may be viewed as a sign of weakness by the Director, who seldom avoids taking a position. Other behaviors that commonly characterize the Supportive person follow:

1. *Gives the appearance of being quiet and reserved.* People with the Supportive behavioral style can easily display their feelings, but not in the assertive manner common to the Emotive individual.

2. *Listens attentively to other people.* In selling, good listening skills can be a real asset. This talent comes naturally to the Supportive person.

3. *Tends to avoid the use of power.* Whereas the Director may rely on power to accomplish tasks, the Supportive person is more likely to rely on friendly persuasion.

4. *Makes decisions in a thoughtful and deliberate manner.* The Supportive person usually takes longer to make a decision.

POPULARITY OF THE FOUR-STYLE MODEL

We are endlessly fascinated by ourselves, and this helps explain the growing popularity of the four-style model presented in this chapter. To satisfy this insatiable appetite for information many training and development companies offer training programs that present the four social or communication styles. Figure 16.8 features the approximate equivalents of the four styles presented in this chapter.

FIGURE 16.8 The four basic communication styles have been used in a wide range of training programs. For comparison purposes the approximate equivalents to the four communication styles discussed in this chapter are listed.

Supportive (Manning/Reece) Amiable (Wilson Learning) Supportive-Giving (Stuart Atkins Inc.) Relater (People Smarts) Steadiness (Personal Profile System)	Emotive (Manning/Reece) Expressive (Wilson Learning) Adapting-Dealing (Stuart Atkins Inc.) Socializer (People Smarts) Influencing (Personal Profile System)
Reflective (Manning/Reece) Analytical (Wilson Learning) Conserving-Holding (Stuart Atkins Inc.) Thinker (People Smarts) Cautiousness/Compliance (Personal Profile System)	Director (Manning/Reece) Driver (Wilson Learning) Controlling-Taking (Stuart Atkins Inc.) Director (People Smarts) Dominance (Personal Profile System)

DETERMINING YOUR COMMUNICATION STYLE

You now have enough information to identify your own communication style. If your location on the dominance continuum is right of center and your position on the sociability continuum is below the center mark, you fall into the Director quadrant. If your location on the dominance continuum is left of center and your position on the sociability continuum is above the center mark, then your most preferred style is Supportive. Likewise, low dominance matched with low sociability forms the Reflective communication style, and high dominance matched with high sociability forms the Emotive style.

Of course, all of us display some characteristics of the Emotive, Director, Reflective, and Supportive communication styles. However, one of the four styles is usually predominant and readily detectable.[12]

Some people who study the communication-style model for the first time may initially experience feelings of frustration. They find it hard to believe that one's behavioral style tends to remain quite uniform throughout life. People often say, "I am a different person each day!" It is certainly true that we sometimes feel different from day to day, but our most preferred style remains stable.

The Supportive person might say, "I sometimes get very upset and tell people what I am thinking. I can be a Director when I want to be!" There is no argument here. Just because you have a preferred communication style does not mean you will never display the behavioral characteristics of another style. Some people use different styles in different contexts and in different relationships.[13] Reflective people sometimes display Emotive behavior, and Emotive people sometimes display Reflective behavior. We are saying that each person has one most preferred and habitually used communication style.

Managing Communication-Style Bias

The most important reason for our discussion of communication styles is this: Communication-style bias is a barrier to success in selling. This form of bias is a common problem in sales work simply because salespeople deal with people from all four quadrants. You cannot select potential customers on the basis of their communication style. You must be able to develop rapport with people

People with the Supportive communication style are usually quiet and unassuming.

from each of the four quadrants. William J. Stanton, author of *Fundamentals of Marketing*, said, "Salespeople probably need more tact, diplomacy, and social poise than other employees in an organization."[14]

HOW COMMUNICATION-STYLE BIAS DEVELOPS

To illustrate how communication-style bias develops in a sales situation, let us observe a sales call involving two people with different communication styles. Mary Wheeler entered the office of Dick Harrington with a feeling of optimism. She was sure that her product would save Mr. Harrington's company several hundred dollars a year. She had done her homework and was 99 percent certain that the sale would be closed. Thirty minutes after meeting Mr. Harrington she was walking out of his office without the order. What went wrong?

Mary Wheeler is an "all business" type who is Director in terms of communication style. Her sales calls are typically fast paced and focused. She entered the office of Mr. Harrington, a new prospect, and immediately began to talk business. Mr. Harrington interrupted to ask if she wanted coffee. She declined the offer and continued her sales presentation. Mr. Harrington asked Mary if she enjoyed selling. After a quick glance at her watch, she responded by saying that selling was a rewarding career and then quickly returned to her sales presentation.

Mr. Harrington's communication style is Supportive. He feels uncomfortable doing business with strangers and likes slow-paced interactions with people. He felt tension when Mary failed to establish a social relationship. She should have spent a few minutes socializing with Mr. Harrington after entering his office. The "all business" approach she used would be more appropriate for the Director or Reflective communication style.

One of the most important steps in mastering the sales process is for the salesperson to adapt his selling behavior to the customer's communication style. Communication is *always* the responsibility of the salesperson. This is not a responsibility that can be shared.[15]

DEVELOPING STYLE FLEXIBILITY

When people are introduced to communication styles for the first time, they often label individual styles as being "more favorable" or "less favorable" for selling careers. The truth is, there is no one best place to be on the communication-style model because there are no best types of personality.[16] Successful salespeople come from all four quadrants. What these high achievers have in common is style flexibility.

MATURE AND IMMATURE BEHAVIOR

There is a mature and an immature side to each behavioral style. Let us examine the Emotive style to illustrate this point. People with this style are open, personable individuals who seem genuinely friendly. The natural enthusiasm displayed by the mature Emotive is refreshing. On the other hand, an Emotive person may be too talkative and too emotional and may lack the ability to listen to others; this is the immature side of the Emotive communication style.

You will recall that we used the words *industrious* and *precise* to describe the Reflective style. These are words that apply to the mature side of the Reflective person. We also used the words *aloof* and *stuffy.* These words describe the immature side of the Reflective.

The good news is that we all have the potential for developing the mature side of our communication style. Our most preferred communication style does not change, but matures as we mature.

STRENGTH/WEAKNESS PARADOX

It is a fact of life that your greatest strength can become your greatest weakness. If your most preferred style is Reflective, people will likely respect your well-disciplined approach to life as one of your strengths. However, this strength can become a weakness if it is exaggerated. The Reflective person can be too serious, too questioning, and too inflexible.

People with the Director style are open and frank. They express their true feelings in a direct manner. In most cases we appreciate candor, but we do not like to be around people who are too straightforward or too blunt in expressing their views. When people come across as *opinionated*, they tend to antagonize others. We should avoid pushing our strengths to the point of unproductive excess.[17]

To illustrate how strengths become weaknesses in excess, let us add more detail to our communication-style model. Note that it now features three zones that radiate out from the center (Fig. 16.9). These dimensions might be thought of as intensity zones.

FIGURE 16.9 The completed communication-style model provides important insights needed to manage the relationship process in selling.

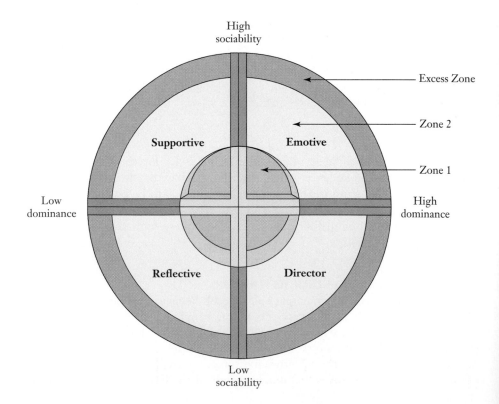

Zone one People who fall within this zone display their unique behavioral characteristics with less intensity than those in zone two. The Emotive person, for example, is moderately high on the dominance continuum and moderately low on the sociability continuum. As you might expect, zone one communication styles are more difficult to identify because there is less intensity in both dimensions (dominance and sociability).

Zone two Persons who fall within this zone display their unique behavioral characteristics with greater intensity than persons in zone one. The zone two Reflective person falls within the lowest quartile of the dominance continuum and the lowest quartile of the sociability continuum.

The boundary line that separates zone one and zone two should not be seen as a permanent barrier restricting change in intensity. Under certain circumstances we should abandon our most preferred style temporarily. A deliberate move from zone one to zone two, or vice versa, is called style flexing.

Excess zone The excess zone is characterized by a high degree of intensity and rigidity. When people allow themselves to drift into this zone, they become very inflexible, which is often interpreted by others as a form of bias toward their style. In addition, the strengths of the inflexible person become weaknesses. Extreme intensity in any quadrant is bound to threaten interpersonal relations.

We are apt to move into the excess zone and exaggerate our style characteristics under stressful conditions. Stress tends to bring out the worst in many people. Here are some of the behaviors that salespeople and customers may display when they are in the excess zone.

The excess zone is characterized by a high degree of intensity and rigidity. We are more apt to move into the excess zone under very stressful conditions.

Emotive style	Expresses highly emotional opinions Stops listening to the other person Tries too hard to promote own point of view Becomes outspoken to the point of being offensive Uses exaggerated gestures and facial expressions to make a point
Director style	Gets impatient with the other person Becomes dictatorial and bossy Will not admit being wrong Becomes extremely competitive Is cold and unfeeling when dealing with people
Reflective style	Becomes stiff and formal during social relationships Is unwilling to make a decision Avoids displaying any type of emotion Displays a strong dislike for change Is overly interested in detail
Supportive style	Agrees with everyone Is unable to take a strong stand Becomes overly anxious to win approval of others Tries to comfort everyone Constantly seeks reassurance

Developing Communication-Style Flexibility

Style flexing is the deliberate attempt to adjust one's communication style to accommodate the needs of the other person. Doing what is appropriate is the essence of style flexing.[18] You are attempting to communicate with the other person on her own "channel." In a selling situation you should try to determine the customer's most preferred style as quickly as possible, and flex your own accordingly. Style sensitivity and flexing are not developed overnight, of course. It takes practice.

The clues that can help you identify the person's communication style are everywhere. Listen closely to the customer's tone of voice. A Supportive person will sound warm and friendly. The Reflective customer's voice is more likely to be cautious and deliberate. Pay particular attention to gestures. The Emotive individual will use his hands to communicate thoughts and ideas. The Director also uses gestures to communicate but is more controlled and less spontaneous. The Reflective person will appear more relaxed, less intense. The Emotive individual is an open, impulsive communicator, while the Reflective person is quite cautious. The Supportive type will be personal and friendly, while the Reflective person may seem difficult to get to know. To avoid relationship tension, consider the following suggestions for each of the four styles.

SELLING TO EMOTIVES

If you are attempting to sell products to an Emotive person, keep in mind the need to move at a pace that will hold the attention of the prospect. Be enthusiastic, and avoid an approach that is too stiff and formal. Take time to establish goodwill and build relationships. Do not place too much emphasis on the facts and details. To deal effectively with Emotive people, plan actions that will provide support for their opinions, ideas, and dreams.[19] Plan to ask questions concerning their opinions and ideas, but be prepared to help them get "back on track" if they move too far away from the topic. Maintain good eye contact, and above all, be a good listener.

SELLING TO DIRECTORS

The key to relating to Directors is to keep the relationship as businesslike as possible. Developing a strong personal relationship is not a high priority for Directors. In other words, friendship is not usually a condition for a good working relationship. Your goal is to be as efficient, time disciplined, and well organized as possible; and to provide appropriate facts, figures, and success probabilities. Most Directors are goal-oriented people, so try to identify their primary objectives and then determine ways to support and help with these objectives. Early in the sales presentation, ask specific questions and carefully note responses. Look for specific points you can respond to when it is time to present your proposals.

BUILDING RELATIONSHIPS IN A DIVERSE WORLD

VERSATILITY IS KEY

One way to increase sales and enjoy selling more is to reduce the tension between you and the prospect. Personal selling is almost never a tension-free activity, but there are effective ways to control the tension that is likely to surface during the selling process. Dr. David Merrill, one of the early pioneers in development of communication style instruments and training programs, uses the term *versatility* to describe our ability to control the tension we create in others. He believes it is important to understand your preferred communication style, but you must also be willing to control personal behavior patterns and adapt to the people with whom you have contact. In jobs such as selling, which require a high degree of interpersonal effectiveness, versatility can be the key to success.

Roger Wenschlag, author of *The Versatile Sales-person*, defines versatility as, "The degree to which a salesperson is perceived as developing and maintaining buyer comfort throughout the sales process." This does not mean you must become "another person" and display behaviors that make you uncomfortable. However, you should be able to temporarily adjust your behavior to fit the buyer's style. Versatility displayed by the salesperson sends the message, "I care about the relationship."

Versatility has another benefit according to Tony Alessandra, author of *People Smarts*. He notes that this quality enables you to interact more productively with difficult people.

The wonderful thing about versatility is that it can be learned. We can learn to control what we say and do to make others more comfortable.[c]

SELLING TO REFLECTIVES

The Reflective person will respond in a positive way to a thoughtful, well-organized approach. Arrive at meetings on time and be well prepared. In most cases it will not be necessary to spend a great deal of time building a social relationship. Reflective people appreciate a no-nonsense, businesslike approach to personal selling. Use specific questions that show clear direction. Once you have information concerning the prospect's needs, present your proposal in a slow, deliberate way. Provide as much documentation as possible. Do not be in too big a hurry to close the sale. Never pressure the Reflective person to make quick decisions.

SELLING TO SUPPORTIVES

Take time to build a social relationship with the Supportive person. Spend time learning about the things that are important in this individual's life—family, hobbies, and major interests. Listen carefully to personal opinions and feelings. Supportive individuals like to conduct business with sales personnel who are professional but friendly. Therefore, study their feelings and emotional needs as well as their technical and business needs. Throughout the presentation, provide personal assurances and support for their views. If you disagree with a Supportive person, curb the desire to disagree too assertively; Supportive people dislike interpersonal conflict. Give them the time to comprehend your proposal. Patience is important.

As you develop your communication-style identification skills and become more adept at style flexing, you will be better able to manage the relationship process. With these skills you should be able to open more accounts, sell more to established customers, and more effectively meet the pressures of competition. Most important, your customers will view you as a person better able to understand and meet their needs.

A WORD OF CAUTION

It is tempting to put a label on someone and then assume the label tells you everything you need to know about that person. If you want to build an effective partnering type relationship with a prospect, you must acquire additional information about that person. Stuart Atkins, a respected authority on communication styles and author of *The Name of Your Game* says that it requires real effort to look beyond the label and to experience the whole person as a dynamic process.[20] You must also be careful not to let the label you place on yourself become the justification for your own inflexible behavior. Try not to let the label justify or reinforce why you are unable or unwilling to communicate effectively with others.[21]

SUMMARY

The primary objective of this chapter is to introduce *communication-style bias* and examine the implications of this concept for salespeople. Many sales are lost because salespeople fail to develop a relationship with the prospect. Communication-style bias contributes to this problem. Every salesperson who is willing to develop style sensitivity and engage in appropriate *style flexing* can minimize one of the most common barriers to success in selling.

The communication-style model is based on two continuums that assess two major aspects of human behavior: *dominance* and *sociability*. By combining them as horizontal and vertical continuums we create quadrants that define four styles of communication. We have called these the *Emotive, Director, Reflective*, and *Supportive styles*. With practice in observation you should be able to increase your sensitivity to other people's styles. Practice in self-awareness and self-control will give you the ability to flex your own style and help others to feel at ease.

➤ K E Y   T E R M S

Communication-Style Bias	*Director Style*
Dominance	*Reflective Style*
Sociability	*Supportive Style*
Emotive Style	*Style Flexing*

➤ R E V I E W   Q U E S T I O N S

1. What is the most prominent form of bias in our society? Explain.

2. Describe the four major principles that support communication-style theory.

3. What are the benefits to the salesperson who understands communication style?

4. What two dimensions of human behavior are used to identify communication style?

5. Describe the person who tends to be high in sociability.

6. What are the four communication styles? Develop a description of each of the styles.

7. What is the reaction of most people who study communication styles for the first time? Why does this reaction surface?

8. What is the major reason for introducing communication styles in a textbook on selling?

9. Explain the statement, "Your greatest strength can become your greatest weakness."

10. The Building Relationships in a Diverse World box on p. 381 suggests that we should try to control what we say and do to make others more comfortable. Is it realistic to expect salespeople to follow this advice? Explain your answer.

➤ A P P L I C A T I O N   E X E R C I S E S

1. Oprah Winfrey has been referred to as one of America's best talk show hosts.

   a. On the dominance continuum, mark where you think her television personality belongs.

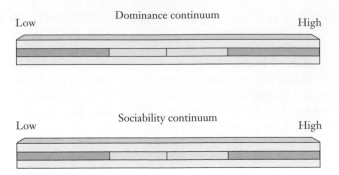

Dominance continuum

Low ... High

Sociability continuum

Low ... High

b. On the sociability continuum, mark where you believe her television personality belongs.

c. Using the two continuums to form the communication style model, what is Oprah Winfrey's television communication style? Does Oprah Winfrey possess style flexibility? Explain this in terms of (i) the different styles of guests on her program and (ii) her apparent popularity with millions of people.

d. Describe Oprah Winfrey's personality using statements and terms from this chapter.

e. Have you ever observed Oprah Winfrey slipping into her excess zone? Explain.

2. Many salespeople, after being introduced to communication-style psychology, attempt to categorize each of their customers. They report that their relationships become mutually more enjoyable and productive. Select five people whom you know quite well (supervisor, subordinate, customer, teacher, friend, or members of your family). Using the two behavioral continuums in this chapter, determine these people's communication styles. Using your own descriptive terminology in conjunction with terminology in Chapter 16, develop a descriptive behavioral profile of each of these people. Explain how this information will improve your relationship with each of these people.

3. Self-awareness is important in personal selling. As we get to know ourselves, we can identify barriers to acceptance by others. Once you have identified your most preferred communication style, you have taken a big step in the direction of self-awareness. If you have not yet determined your most preferred communication style, take a few minutes to complete the Dominance Indicator form (Table 16.1) and the Sociability Indicator form (Table 16.2). Follow the instructions provided on pages 366 to 368.

4. Myers-Briggs Personality Types and Jungian Personality Types are two very popular descriptions of the material in this chapter. Using your search engine, access the Internet sites that refer to these concepts. Type in "jungian"+personality profiles to access the Jungian personality types. To access the Myers-Briggs types, type in "Myers-Briggs"+personality profiles. Does the number of queries indicate anything about the validity and popularity of these theories? Examine specific queries about both of these theories. Do you see the relationship between these two theories and the material in this chapter?

WWW

➤ CASE PROBLEM

Ray Perkins has been employed at Grant Real Estate for almost two years. Prior to receiving his real estate license he was a property manager with a large real estate agency in another community. During his first year with Grant, he was assigned to the residential property division and sold properties totaling $825,000. He then requested and received a transfer to the commercial division.

Three months ago, Ray obtained a commercial listing that consisted of twenty-six acres of land near a growing residential neighborhood. The land is zoned commercial and appears to be ideally suited for a medium-sized shopping center. Ray prepared a detailed prospectus and sent it to Harold Maynard, president of Mondale Growth Corporation, a firm specializing in development of shopping centers. One week later he received a letter from Mr. Maynard requesting more information. Shortly after receiving Ray's response, Mr. Maynard called to set up an appointment to inspect the property. A time and date were finalized, and Ray agreed to meet his plane and conduct a tour of the property.

Ray is a quiet, amiable person who displays the Supportive communication style. Friends say that they like to spend time with him because he is a good listener.

QUESTIONS

1. If Mr. Maynard displays the characteristics of the Director communication style, how should Ray conduct himself during the meeting? Be specific as you describe those behaviors that would be admired by Mr. Maynard.

2. If Mr. Maynard wants to build rapport with Ray Perkins, what behavior should he display?

3. It is not a good idea to put a label on someone and then assume the label tells us everything about the person. As Ray attempts to build rapport with Mr. Maynard, what other personal characteristics should he try to identify?

Some sales managers work hard to maintain a competitive spirit among members of their sales force. Marga McNally, vice president of sales for WRC-TV, an NBC-owned station in Washington, DC, takes a different approach. She works hard to build a sense of team effort and shared accomplishment among her eleven salespeople. McNally's management style emphasizes brainstorming and teamwork. She says, "I want salespeople who will be competitive going out the door and collaborative when they come back in the door." McNally wants her salespeople to share winning sales strategies, critique each other, and help work out what is best for the customer. She believes the best way to build a partnership with customers is to discover solutions that are right for the customer and not just right for her TV station. This is accomplished by listening without any preconceived notions. "We take a pad and pencil with us on customer calls rather than a canned presentation. Then we come back and brainstorm together on how to respond."[1]

Career Opportunities in Sales Management

Salespeople frequently have the opportunity to advance to a management position. The first promotion for many is to the position of sales manager. Those who achieve success at this level may advance to management positions that offer even greater challenge and increased economic rewards.

The sales manager is one of the key persons in any marketing organization. This person has primary responsibility for developing sales force objectives and seeing that they are achieved. A major responsibility of the sales manager is to provide the training and coaching that will permit salespersons to achieve their full potential. The productivity of a sales force depends primarily on how it is trained, organized, automated, and managed.

Sales Management Functions

The **sales manager** is responsible, in most cases, for development of sales strategies to meet sales goals, possessing knowledge of various markets, supervising the activities of salespeople, conducting sales force training, and evaluating sales efforts.[2] The sales manager's duties will vary somewhat from one marketing organization to another. To illustrate, let us examine the duties assigned to two different sales managers.

Karen Carlson is a district sales manager for a large cosmetic manufacturer. She supervises twelve cosmetic sales representatives. Although she does not recruit and hire sales representatives, she has total responsibility for their training and supervision. She assumes a major role in customer relations. Ms. Carlson is also responsible for setting and administering sales quotas and budgets. She works closely with the marketing director, who is responsible for establishing sales territories.

Ken Overland is a sales manager for a Midwest firm that manufactures livestock-feeding equipment. He is responsible for supervising the firm's entire sales force, which includes eight people. In this capacity he assumes a wide range of duties. Mr. Overland is solely responsible for recruiting, hiring, training, and supervising every salesperson. He measures the performance of each sales force member and makes all decisions in the area of compensation. He sets up all sales territories and establishes sales quotas and budgets. Mr. Overland is also responsible for coordinating the firm's advertising program.

Although sales managers are primarily involved with the supervision of the sales force, they often assume a wide range of additional duties. Most are involved in establishing sales quotas and developing the firm's sales revenue or income budget.

At the beginning of each fiscal year, most marketing organizations must establish a sales forecast. Sales managers are often involved in both short- and long-range forecasting. They also assume responsibility for seeing that the goals are achieved.

Today's sales managers are very much involved in the role of "helper." In fact, providing the sales staff with sales support services is one of their most important duties. Sales managers maintain a steady flow of information to salespeople and also provide a variety of selling tools and aids. Successful sales managers also help salespeople cope with the rapid change and uncertainty that permeates today's business environment.[3]

Besides supervising the sales force, sales managers are often involved in establishing sales quotas, developing long- and short-term forecasts, and seeing that goals are achieved.

Qualities of a Good Sales Manager

Sales managers can have a dramatic influence on the salespeople they supervise. Depending on the leadership qualities adopted, sales managers can have an advantageous, neutral, or even detrimental effect on the performance of sales subordinates.[4]

Effective leadership has been discussed in hundreds of books and articles. A careful review of this material indicates that most successful supervisory-management personnel have certain behaviors in common. Writers of this material agree that there are two important dimensions of effective leadership.[5] We shall label these dimensions *structure* and *consideration*.

STRUCTURE

Sales managers who display **structure** clearly define their own duties and those of the sales staff. They assume an active role in directing their subordinates' work. Policies and procedures are clearly defined, and subordinates know what is expected of them. Salespeople also know how well they are doing because the structured supervisor evaluates their productivity and provides feedback. Members of the sales force usually appreciate the predictable nature of the highly structured sales manager. The following behaviors provide evidence of structure:

An effective sales manager provides regular feedback. All employees want to know "where they stand" with the manager.

1. *Planning takes place on a regular basis.* The effective sales manager thinks ahead and decides what to do in the future. Strategic planning is the process of determining the company's current position in the market; determining where you want to be and when; and making decisions on how to secure the position you want.[6] Strategic planning gives meaning and direction to the sales force.

2. *Policies and procedures are clearly defined.* In addition, they are communicated to every member of the sales force as part of the orientation and training program. Each employee is kept up to date should policies and procedures be revised.

3. *Decisions are made promptly and firmly.* An effective sales manager is willing and able to make decisions in a timely way. An ineffective manager often postpones important decisions, hoping the problem will go away. Of course, most decisions cannot be made until all the facts are available. A good sales manager keeps the lines of communication open and involves subordinates in making the truly important decisions.

4. *Performance of salespeople is appraised regularly.* All employees want to know "where they stand" with the manager. An effective sales manager provides regular feedback. When a salesperson is not performing up to established standards, the sales manager takes immediate action.

Although structure is an important aspect of sales management, too much structure can sometimes create problems. In an effort to become better organized and more systematized, some sales organizations have developed detailed policies and procedures that rob salespeople of time and energy. Filling out endless reports and forms, for example, can cause unnecessary frustration and may reduce productivity.[7]

CONSIDERATION

A sales manager who displays the dimension of **consideration** is more likely to have relationships with salespeople that are characterized by mutual trust, respect for salespeople's ideas, and consideration for their feelings. A climate of good two-way communication usually exists between the manager and the employee. The sales manager who possesses consideration also acknowledges salespeople's accomplishments and regularly recognizes work well done. The following behaviors provide evidence of consideration:

1. *Regular and efficient communication receives a high priority.* Whenever possible the effective manager engages in face-to-face communication with salespeople. They do not rely entirely on memos, letters, or sales reports for information sharing, but arrange face-to-face meetings. The effective sales manager is a good listener and creates an atmosphere of cooperation and understanding. Members of the sales staff feel free to discuss their problems and concerns openly.

2. *Each salesperson is treated as an individual.* The sales manager takes a personal interest in each member of the sales force. No one is treated like a "number." The interest is genuine, not artificial. The effective sales manager does not endanger effectiveness by showing favoritism to anyone.

3. *Good performance is rewarded often.* Positive reinforcement is one of the strongest morale-building factors in the work environment.

Ken Blanchard, co-author of *The One Minute Manager,* says, "The key to developing people will always be to concentrate on catching them doing something right instead of blaming them for doing something wrong."[8] Recognition for a job well done is always appreciated. Successful sales managers have learned how to praise performance in a variety of ways. In addition to providing structure and consideration, effective sales managers always set a good example. They show a good example in such areas as product knowledge, customer relations, promptness, dress and grooming, and other important elements. A good "role model" is extremely important because members of the sales staff learn many things through observation. A sales manager who is late for appointments, fails to keep the staff informed, manages time poorly, and fails to maintain honest relations with customers hardly qualifies for a leadership role.

Finally, a true leader possesses a great deal of self-control. A manager who is subject to emotional tantrums, moodiness, or inconsistency in interpersonal relations will not be an effective leader.

Recruitment and Selection of Salespeople

Careful recruitment and selection of salespeople is very important. This is one of the most significant tasks sales managers perform. When they hire the wrong person, several problems may arise.

SALES TIPS

It's easier to think in stereotypes than it is to analyze people in depth; and an astounding number of people, including an unfortunate number of sales managers, have embraced the concept of the "born salesman."[a]

From James G. Carr, "Attractive or Effective"

If the new salesperson is not a top producer, the business must absorb the cost of low productivity.

If the new employee is not able to provide good service, regular customers may be lost. Established customers represent one of the firm's most valuable assets.

If the new employee quits after a few months or must be fired, the business will suffer an economic loss. The money invested in salary, benefits, travel expenses, and training can be significant. It can cost anywhere from $10,000 to $100,000 a year in terms of training, salary and benefits, and lost productivity when the wrong person is hired.[9]

Positive reinforcement is one of the strongest ways to build morale. Effective managers reward their subordinates for good performance.

Successful salespeople are often difficult to identify. The selection of sales personnel today is, however, more of a "science" and less of an "art." Sales managers no longer need rely on "gut feelings." The ability to identify sales aptitude accurately can be acquired. Many progressive sales organizations recognize the need to help sales managers develop the interviewing skills necessary to make profitable hiring decisions. It is impossible to avoid occasionally hiring a poor performer, but sales managers can improve their average by using some established recruitment and selection guidelines.

DETERMINE ACTUAL JOB REQUIREMENTS

To decide what type of applicant is needed, the manager should first outline the duties the person will perform. The sales manager must have a clear picture of the job requirements before beginning the recruitment process.

Some sales managers make every effort to discover the success factors that contribute to the achievements of their high-performance salespeople. Success factors are the skills, knowledge, abilities, and behaviors considered critical for successful performance.[10] This information may be collected by use of interviews with salespeople or customers, by observing the salesperson during sales calls, or by some other method.

After a careful study of the duties the salesperson will perform and identification of the success factors, a job description should be prepared. A job description is an explanation of what the salesperson will do and under what conditions the work will be performed. It is a good idea to spell out in as much detail as possible the abilities and qualities that the applicant needs to be successful. This can be accomplished by answering a few basic questions about the position.

1. Will the person be developing new sales territory or assuming responsibility for an established territory?

2. Is the product or service well established, or is it new to the marketplace?

3. Will the salesperson work under the sales manager's close supervision or independently?

4. What amount of travel is required? What is the likelihood of eventual transfer?

Once the job description is prepared, the foundation has been established to determine the type of person to be hired. There is no substitute for knowing what the job requires.

SEARCH OUT APPLICANTS FROM SEVERAL SOURCES

To identify the best possible person, it is usually best to seek applicants from more than one source. As a rule of thumb, try to interview three or more applicants for each opening. Some suggested sources of new employees follow.

1. *Candidates within the company.* One of the first places to look is within your own company. Is there someone in accounting, engineering, customer service, or some other area who aspires to a sales position? These people have the advantage of being thoroughly familiar with the company's product offering, policies, operations, and what it takes to please the customer.[11]

2. *College and university students.* Many business firms are turning to college and university campuses to recruit salespeople. Placement offices are usually cooperative and often publicize openings.

3. *Trade and newspaper advertisements.* A carefully prepared newspaper advertisement will often attract well-qualified job applicants. A well-written ad should describe the job requirements *and* spell out the opportunities. All information should be accurate. The ad should "sell" the position, but it should not exaggerate its benefits.

4. *Employment agencies and listings.* Nearly 2,000 public employment offices are located throughout the United States. These offices will recruit applicants and screen them according to your specifications. There is no charge for this service. There are also many private employment agencies. These firms specialize in matching applicants to the job and usually do some initial screening for employers. A fee is assessed for the services these agencies provide.

5. *Internet.* Many companies are using the Internet to recruit for sales positions. The largest Internet recruiting site is the Online Career Center, a nonprofit recruitment and human resources database that posts job listings.

BUILDING RELATIONSHIPS IN A DIVERSE WORLD

KNOW YOUR CUSTOMERS

"Katherine Barchetti is perhaps the best independent retailer I've ever seen," said Robert Sprague, a retail consultant. She may also be the best salesperson in Pittsburgh. Barchetti operates K. Barchetti Shops, a 3,500 square-foot men's store and 1,500 square-foot women's store. These upscale retail stores meet the buying needs of a very small but discriminating market niche. Her customers are willing to pay $1,395 for an Italian suit and $350 for a pair of dress shoes. She visits the New York market frequently to buy items for her customers that are not available at other Pittsburgh stores.

Barchetti understands that personalized service to her customers builds loyalty. She makes every effort to know what her customers want and need. She knows about 500 customers on a first name basis and maintains a database of about 28,000 clients. She understands the importance of maintaining a record of each customer's sizes, styles, and buying habits. If a customer likes Ferragamo men's shoes or Hugo Boss suits, Barchetti is probably aware of these preferences.[b]

SELECT THE BEST-QUALIFIED APPLICANT

Once you have identified qualified applicants, the next step is to select the best person. This is becoming more difficult as products become more complex, customers become more sophisticated, and competitors become more aggressive. Selecting the best-qualified applicant will never be easy, but there are some qualifications and characteristics that all sales managers should look for. One of the most important qualities is a high level of interest and enthusiasm for the job and high degree of self-motivation. Salespeople have to be self-starters. Barry Farber, president of Farber Training Systems, says that he would hire a salesperson without experience or knowledge of the industry who is willing to give 110 percent versus someone who has experience and is highly skilled, but who is not motivated.[12]

Some sales managers use a performance test to identify the self-motivated person. Alan Gold of The Office Place, an office supply and equipment dealer in Anchorage, Alaska, conducts one interview to make a general assessment of the candidate. If the person seems to have potential, he sets a date for a second interview. He gives the candidate a product ID number and tells the person to be prepared to make a presentation on that product at their next meeting. The candidate's motivational level is measured by the efforts made to obtain enough information about the product and the company to prepare a good presentation.[13]

Reliability is another quality to search for. Do not hesitate to check references to determine police records, problems at previous jobs, or pattern of instability. The applicant for a sales position must be able to earn your complete trust.

One of the greatest challenges is hiring salespeople who can develop a close, trusting, long-term relationship with customers. As we have noted previously, the manner in which salespeople establish, build, and maintain relationships is no longer an incidental aspect of personal selling. Mike Mitchell, vice president of human resources for Tiffany & Company, says, "We look for people who feel a great sense of purpose in serving our customers. You can train people to be consultative in their approach to the point that they master the mechanics of the sales process, but you can't teach someone to care."[14]

Experts in the field of employment testing say that psychological tests can be helpful as an element of the hiring process. Psychological assessments can provide objective information about a candidate's skills and abilities.[15] However, test results should always be used *in conjunction* with information obtained from interviewing the candidate and the findings of reference checks.

Orientation and Training

Once you have selected the best-qualified salesperson, two things should be done to ensure that this person becomes a productive member of your staff. First, give the new employee a thorough orientation to your business operation. Provide the orientation *before* the person begins working. This will include a review of your company's history, philosophy of doing business, mission statement, business policies, compensation plan, and other important information.

Orientation of new salespeople is one of the many duties performed by a sales manager. It's important that salespeople receive this early assistance.

Second, initiate a training program that will help the person achieve success. Sales training that is carefully planned and executed can make a major contribution to the performance of every salesperson. Study results indicate that salespeople have a more positive view about their job situation, greater commitment, and improved performance when their sales managers clarify their job role, how to execute their tasks, and how their needs will be satisfied with successful job performance.[16]

Even salespeople with great potential are handicapped when the company fails to provide adequate training. Keep in mind that in the absence of formal training, employees will develop their own approaches to performing tasks.

Many sales managers believe that new salespeople (those with no prior sales experience) need special attention during the orientation and training period. One expert said, "They must be managed differently, compensated differently, and they must be gradually converted to the ranks of experienced sales professionals. It is often an eighteen-month process."[17]

The size of the firm should not dictate the scope of the training program. Even the smallest marketing organization should have a formal sales training program. This program should have three dimensions:

1. Knowledge of the product line, company marketing strategies, territory information, and related areas

2. Attitude toward the company, the company's products and services, and the customers to be served

3. Skill in applying personal selling principles and practices—the "doing" part of the sales training program

An important part of the sales training program is foundation level instruction. This aspect of sales training focuses on the *basics*. If salespeople are to plan and execute a sales call successfully, they must first master certain fundamental selling skills—the skills that form the foundation for everything salespeople do in

WINNING THROUGH TEAMWORK

There is no shortage of motivational speakers who can fire up your sales force. One of the most popular speakers these days is Pat Riley, the successful coach who has guided the Los Angeles Lakers to four National Basketball Association championships and now coaches the New York Knicks. Hundreds of Fortune 500 companies have paid $25,000 to have him inspire their sales and marketing personnel. He likes to discuss with audiences the ideas presented in his book entitled *The Winner Within: A Life Plan for Team Players.* Drawing on his experience on the basketball court, Riley talks about the universal importance of cooperation and teamwork. The sales manager who wants to get the best performance from a sales force must understand one important principle of human behavior:

> It all has to start with trust. A good manager is tough, compassionate, and deals with the truth each day. People working for that kind of leader will recognize those qualities and allow themselves to be infiltrated with a team concept.

Riley tells his audiences that success does not happen without dedication, goals, and ability to work together. He also believes that all salespersons should be rewarded for their effort. Riley encourages sales managers to develop effective competition plans.[c]

their careers. The steps that make up the Six-Step Presentation Plan (approach, presentation, demonstration, negotiation, close, and servicing the sale) represent fundamental selling skills (see Fig. 14.1).

Sales Force Motivation

It is helpful to note the difference between internal and external motivation. An **internal motivation** is an intrinsic reward that occurs when a duty or task is performed. If a salesperson enjoys calling on customers and solving their problems, this activity is in itself rewarding, and the salesperson is likely to be self-motivated.[18] Internal motivation is likely to be triggered when sales positions provide an opportunity for achievement and individual growth. **External motivation** is an action taken by another person that involves rewards or other forms of reinforcement that cause the worker to behave in ways to ensure receipt of the award.[19] A cash bonus given to salespeople who achieve a sales goal provides an example of external motivation. Experts on motivation agree that organizations should attempt to provide a mix of external rewards and internal satisfaction.

A basic contention among too many sales managers has been that sales productivity can be improved by staging more elaborate sales contests, giving more expensive recognition awards, or picking truly exotic meeting locations. This point of view ignores the merits of internal motivation. One of the foremost critics of external rewards is Alfie Kohn, author of *No Contest: The Case against Competition* and *Punished by Rewards: The Trouble with Gold Stars, Incentive Plans, A's and Other Bribes.* Kohn states that a reward system that forces people to compete for awards or recognition may undermine cooperation and teamwork. In addition, he says that reward plans often create a situation where some salespeople are winners and some are losers. Kohn further declares, "For each person who wins, there are many others who carry with them the feeling of having lost."[20]

In many cases, intrinsic motivators (achievement, challenge, responsibility, advancement, growth, enjoyment of work itself, and involvement) have a longer term effect on employee attitudes than extrinsic motivators (contests, prizes, quotas, and money). A salesperson who is intrinsically satisfied in the job will work willingly at high-performance levels.

Although criticisms of external rewards have a great deal of merit, the fact remains that large numbers of organizations continue to achieve positive results with carefully developed incentive programs. It is possible to design programs that will have long-range benefits for both the organization and the individual employee. Kirby Bonds, the San Francisco regional sales manager for Avis Rent-A-Car's corporate sales division, has used sales contests to identify new accounts, build business within existing accounts, and generate endorsement letters from satisfied customers. Bonds keeps contest time frames short so more of his salespeople have an opportunity to win.[21]

Because people bring different interests, drives, and values to the workplace, they react differently to attempts at motivation. When possible, motivation strategies should reflect the needs of the sales force. Sales managers need to discover the individual differences between salespeople. What are their current and future aspirations? What rewards do they want from their jobs?

Experts on motivation agree that organizations should provide salespeople with a mix of external rewards and internal satisfaction. The Achievement Award featured in this advertisement is an example of an external reward.

Is there a good match between what matters most to them and the work they are doing? Are there any conflicts between the salesperson's job and family life?

Some sales managers are discovering that simply asking salespeople for their opinions and then following up on their suggestions, where appropriate, are excellent ways to motivate them. Effective communication seems to be an underutilized form of motivation. Salespeople should work in an atmosphere that encourages open, free, two-way communication.[22]

Many sales managers have discovered the value of communicating positive expectations to their salespeople. They recognize that most people can be greatly influenced by the expectations of others. Goethe gave sales managers some good advice when he said, "If you treat a man as he is, he will remain as he is; if you treat him as if he were what he could be, he will become what he could be." With the aid of effective supervision practices and job enrichment it is possible to release the motivation within each salesperson.

Compensation Plans

Compensation plans for salespeople combine direct monetary payments (salary and commissions); and indirect monetary payments such as paid vacations, pensions, and insurance plans. Compensation practices vary greatly throughout the field of selling. Furthermore, sales managers are constantly searching for the "perfect" sales force compensation plan. Of course, the perfect plan does not exist. Each plan must be chosen to suit the specific type of selling job, the objectives of the firm's marketing program, and the type of customer served.

We are beginning to see some trends in the area of sales force compensation. A growing number of companies are linking sales pay to customer satis-

Recognition for success in sales can be an effective form of external motivation.

faction. The consulting firm of Hewitt Associates says that 27 percent of companies use some measure of customer service in the sales-incentive programs.[23] Many companies are following the lead of DuPont, Digital Equipment, Data General, and Tandem Computers in developing teams made up of sales representatives, engineers, and technicians. In response to this trend we are seeing the use of team compensation plans.[24] Needless to say, selecting a fair method of compensation for team members is a dilemma for many companies. Team development and outcomes may suffer if equitable compensation plans are not developed.[25]

In the field of selling there are five basic compensation plans. Here is a description of each:

Straight commission plan. *The only direct monetary compensation comes from sales. No sales, no income. Salespeople under this plan are very conscious of their sales. Lack of job security can be a strong inducement to produce results. However, these people may also concentrate more on immediate sales than on long-term customer development.*

Commission plan with a draw provision or guaranteed salary. *This plan has about the same impact on salespeople as the straight commission plan. However, it gives them more financial security.*

Commission with a draw or guaranteed salary plus a bonus. *This plan offers more direct financial security than the first two plans. Therefore salespeople may adhere more to the company's objectives. The bonus may be based on sales or profits.*

Fixed salary plus bonus. *Salespeople functioning under this compensation plan tend to be more company centered and to have a fairly high degree of financial security if their salary is competitive. The bonus incentive helps motivate people under this plan.*

Straight salary. *Salespeople who work under this compensation plan are usually more company centered and have financial security.*

According to *Dartnell's 29th Sales Force Compensation Survey 1996–1997*, over 75 percent of the companies participating in the survey used some form of compensation plan that combined base salary and incentive.[26] The salary plus bonus and salary plus commission plans are both quite popular.

As might be expected, many companies are experimenting with some variation of these basic plans. In some situations, salespeople are rewarded for achieving a specific objective such as developing new accounts or improving the quality of customer service. Awards in the form of cash or points that can be used to "purchase" prizes can be used. Award programs can be styled to suit a variety of sales objectives:

Specific product movement. *Bonus points can be given for the sale of certain items during specified "push" selling periods.*

Percentage sales increase. *Sales levels can be established with points that are given only when those levels are reached.*

Establish new accounts. *A block of points can be awarded for opening a new account or for introducing new products through the existing outlets.*

Increase sales activity. *For each salesperson, points can be awarded based on the number of calls.*[27]

There is no easy way to develop an effective compensation plan. There are, however, some important guidelines for your efforts to develop a good plan. First, be sure that your sales and marketing objectives are defined in detail. The plan should complement these goals. If sales and marketing objectives are in conflict with the compensation plan, problems will surely arise.

Second, the compensation plan should be field tested before full implementation. Several questions should be answered: Will the new plan be easy to administer? How does the proposed plan differ in terms of payout compared with the existing plan?

Third, explain the compensation plan carefully to the sales force. Misunderstanding may generate distrust of the plan. Keep in mind that some salespeople may see change as a threat.

Fourth, change the compensation plan when conditions in the marketplace warrant change. One reason for the poor showing of many plans is that firms fail to revise their plan as the business grows and market conditions change.[28]

Assessing Sales Force Productivity

As the cost of maintaining a sales force increases, sales managers must give more attention to measuring productivity. The goal is to analyze the profitability of each salesperson's sales volume. This task is complicated because sales territories, customers, and business conditions vary.

The problem of measuring sales force productivity is more complicated than might appear at first glance. In most cases, sales volume alone will not tell you how much profit or loss you are making on the sales of each member of the sales force. A small manufacturer was losing money until he analyzed the profitability of sales generated by each person. He found that one salesperson created a loss on almost every order. This salesperson was concentrating on a market that had become so competitive that she had to reduce the markup to make sales.

Some sales managers view the frequency of calls as an indicator of success. This information is only helpful when compared to the profit earned on each account. The number of calls made on an account should bear some relationship to the sales and profit potential of that account. In some cases it is possible to maintain small accounts without frequent personal calls.

To compare a salesperson's current productivity with the past can also be misleading. Changes in products, prices, competition, and assignments make comparisons with the past unfair—sometimes to the salesperson, sometimes to the company. It is better to measure cumulative quarterly, semiannual, or annual results in relation to established goals.

Some sales managers use performance evaluation criteria that communicate to the sales force which elements of their jobs are most important and how they are doing in each area. Evaluating salespeople involves defining the bases on which they will be evaluated, developing performance standards to determine the acceptable level of performance desired on each base, monitoring actual performance, and giving salespeople feedback on their performance.[29]

Sales force automation programs such as Commander Profit help the sales manager assess key sales force productivity measurements.

Some of the most common criteria for assessing the productivity of salespeople are listed as follows:

Quantitative Criteria

Sales volume in dollars

Sales volume compared to previous year's sales

Sales volume by product or product line

Number of new accounts opened

Amount of new account sales

Net profit dollars

Number of customer calls

Qualitative Criteria

Attitude

Product knowledge

Communication skills

Personal appearance

Customer goodwill generated

Selling skills

Initiative

In most cases it is best to emphasize assessment criteria that can be expressed in numbers (quantitative). The preceding quantitative items are especially significant when accompanied by target dates. For example, you might assess the number of new accounts opened during a six-month period. Of course, a sales manager should not ignore the other criteria listed here. The other items can affect a salesperson's productivity, and you do have to make judgments in these areas.

SUMMARY

Many capable salespeople have advanced to the position of *sales manager.* This job involves such diverse duties as recruiting, selecting, training, and supervising salespeople. Some sales managers are concerned solely with the management of salespeople; others have responsibility for additional marketing functions such as advertising and market research.

The sales manager is part of the management team and therefore must be concerned with leadership. An effective sales manager is an effective leader. Although the qualities of effective leaders are subject to debate, most research tells us that such people display two dimensions: *structure* and *consideration.*

Many sales managers are involved directly or indirectly in recruiting and selecting salespeople. This is an important responsibility, because mistakes can be costly. A portion of the company's profit picture and the firm's image will be influenced positively or negatively by each member of the sales force.

Training and motivating salespeople are almost daily concerns of the sales manager. Training should always be viewed as an investment in human resources. Training helps members of the sales force reach their fullest potential.

We discussed the difference between *internal* and *external motivation.* In many cases intrinsic motivators (achievement, challenge, responsibility, involvement, and enjoyment of work itself) have a longer term effect on employee attitudes than extrinsic motivators (contests, prizes, and money). Sales managers need to discover the individual differences between salespeople to select the most effective motivation strategies.

The most common *compensation plans* were discussed. Compensation plans should be field tested before full implementation.

Assessing sales force productivity is a major responsibility of the sales manager. Sales managers use both quantitative and qualitative criteria.

➤ KEY TERMS

Sales Manager	*Internal Motivation*
Structure	*External Motivation*
Consideration	*Compensation Plans*

➤ REVIEW QUESTIONS

1. What is the sales manager's primary responsibility?

2. Are all sales managers' duties the same? Explain.

3. What are the two main leadership qualities displayed by most successful sales managers? Define and explain each of these qualities.

4. Is a large amount of self-control important as a personal quality for sales managers? Explain.

5. What is a job description? Explain the importance of job descriptions in selecting salespeople.

6. What are four sources of recruiting new salespeople?

7. What should sales managers look for in selecting new sales salespeople? Describe at least three important qualities.

8. What are some common criticisms of external rewards?

9. List and describe the five basic compensation plans for salespeople.

10. What are the *best* criteria for measuring a salesperson's performance? List additional criteria that should be considered in evaluating individual performance.

➤ APPLICATION EXERCISES

1. Assume that you are a manager of a wholesale electrical supply business. Sales have increased to a level where you need to hire another salesperson. What sources will you use in recruiting a good professional salesperson? What criteria will you use in selecting the person you hire?

2. Carefully analyze the following types of selling positions:

   a. A territory selling position for a national manufacturer that requires the salesperson to provide customer service to a large number of accounts plus open up several new accounts each month

   b. A retail sales position in the cosmetics department of a department store

   c. An automobile salesperson who sells and leases new and used cars

   d. A real estate salesperson who sells residential real estate

   Assuming that each of the preceding positions is full time, identify the type of compensation plan you think is best for each. Supply an explanation for each of your answers.

3. Schedule an appointment with two sales managers. Interview each of them, using the following questions as a guide:

   a. What are your functions as a sales manager?

   b. How do the functions of a sales manager differ from those of a sales-person?

   c. What criteria do you use in selecting salespeople?

   d. What kinds of training programs do you have for new salespeople?

   e. What method of compensation do you use for your salespeople?

   f. How do you evaluate the performance of your salespeople?

   g. What personal qualities are important for becoming a sales manager?

Write the answers to these questions. Summarize the similarities and differences of the sales managers' responses.

4. The Internet lists many sources of training in the field of sales management. Using your search engine, type in "sales management." How many queries did you come up with? Examine one or more of the training programs and list the topics that are covered. Compare this list of topics with the material presented in this chapter.

➤ **C A S E   P R O B L E M**

One of the more interesting developments in sales force management is the use of customer feedback to improve the performance of salespeople. Most of these programs are relatively new and go by a variety of names such as *360 degree feedback, customer-conscious compensation,* and *customer satisfaction rewards.* Organizations that have adopted this assessment strategy believe salespeople will benefit from feedback collected from the customers they serve. Also, information collected can be used by the company to improve customer service.

    The use of customer-driven evaluation programs is on the increase because of the rising regard for the role of sales at many companies. Tom Mott, a consultant with Hewitt Associates, says, "Salespeople who were volume pushers are now becoming the manager of their company's relationship with the customer." Mott points out that customer feedback is likely to reflect on the performance of the salesperson and the performance of the company. If problems surface in either area, customer dissatisfaction may surface.

    Data collection methodology is not uniform at this point. Some companies use telephone surveys while others use mailed questionnaires. IBM has experimented with a series of in-person meetings that bring together corporate customers, their IBM sales representatives, and the salesperson's boss.

    Some salespeople have not welcomed the use of customer evaluations. Maryann Cirenza, senior account executive at Teleport Communications Group (TCG) of New York, said that she felt betrayed when she saw the questionnaire the company was sending to her customers. One of the questions asked, "Does your sales rep know your industry?" Cirenza said, "I thought the company was checking up on me." Later her anger subsided when she learned the survey was not simply a monitoring system but a trial run for a new compensation plan. After field testing the surveys, TCG used customer feedback to set bonuses. Cirenza was actually rewarded for good customer service by earning a bonus of about 20 percent of her base pay. Greg Buseman, a Chicago-based IBM salesman, believes the shift to compensation through customer feedback has improved personal selling at his company. He now spends more time understanding the customer's business and learning to be a problem solver for his clients.[30]

QUESTIONS

1. Should the customer be given a major voice in determining how salespeople are performing? Explain.

2. Should sales force compensation be linked to customer feedback? What are the advantages and disadvantages of this approach?

3. Assume you are a sales manager preparing to develop and implement a customer feedback system. How might you gain support for this system from members of your salespeople? What data collection method would you use?

4. Research indicates that customers rank "understanding of our business" as an important criterion used to evaluate salespeople. Why is this criterion ranked so high?

Finding Employment: A Personalized Marketing Approach

The principles of strategic/consultative selling can be used to prepare a personalized marketing campaign to secure a high-paying, professional career position. In Chapter 1 we identify the marketing concept. This concept states that a good marketing program begins with research. After finding out the "what, where, when, why, and how much" during research, the marketing mix is developed (Fig. A.1). In designing a marketing mix, the elements of product, place, promotion, and pricing are coordinated to satisfy the need uncovered during the research phase. The following material will relate each of these five steps to the development of a personal marketing program for securing a job.

Research Phase

During the research phase of the personal marketing program, the emphasis is on need discovery: (1) what type of career the individual is seeking, (2) what the market (in which that position exists) is looking for in applicants, and (3) what the market is willing to pay (Fig. A.2). This information is the starting point for the development of the rest of the personal marketing plan. Securing this basic information is fundamental to the personal marketing program. Job seeking without this important first step is a waste of time. Many job seekers do not

FIGURE A.1 The Employment Marketing Mix

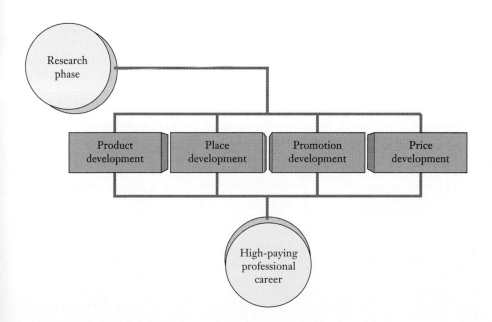

405

FIGURE A.2 Research Conducted before Designing a Job Marketing Mix

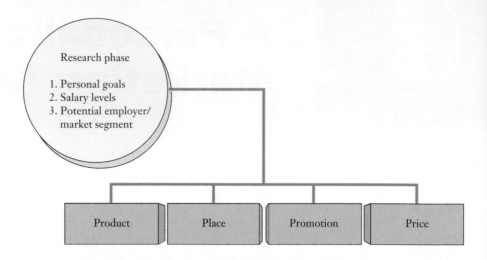

start with this first step and consequently fail to find a rewarding career position.

Deciding what you want to do in a career consists of setting goals. In setting career goals a positive, realistic, and flexible attitude must prevail. A decision should be made on a long-term (five-year) career goal based on the premise that everything will go right for the next five years. This requires a positive, realistic attitude. An intermediate-term (two- to three-year) goal that will lead to the five-year goal should also be determined. With this information a short-term career goal (from one month to one year, depending on circumstances) should be decided on that will lead to the intermediate-term goal and subsequently to the long-term goal.

Realistic salary goals should also be researched and established for each of these time segments (Fig. A.3). This information is extremely important because most interviewers will ask about goals during the interview.

The next step in the research process is to determine in which industries (market segments) the career opportunities exist that complement the goals you have set. This is called market segmentation. A preliminary list of twenty or more companies should be prepared. Later this list will be turned into a prospect list.

The final step in the research process is to determine what qualities or benefits that the particular market segment wants in the people it selects for employees. In determining the hiring motives (see Chapter 7 on buying motives), does the market look for quantitative backgrounds, such as a minimum number

FIGURE A.3 Setting Position and Salary Goals

of years of education or a minimum number of years of experience? Does it look for qualitative background, such as a positive attitude (see Chapter 3), a professional image (see Chapter 3), or a certain communication style (see Chapter 16)? During this stage it is important to find out which of these benefits or combination of benefits the potential employer (market segment) is looking for, because the design of the marketing mix will be based on these findings.

Product Development

After the research phase of the personal marketing program is complete, the next phase is the development of the marketing mix. This begins with a product development program—securing the proper amount and kind of education and job experience, fostering an appropriate appearance (packaging) and attitude, and promoting positive leadership abilities (Fig. A.4).

It is important to take each of these areas of development and convert it into a benefit that will help the prospective employer or market segment achieve its objectives. For example, being elected an officer of a social or professional organization (fact) usually means that the individual has a high-energy level, tends to get along well with people, and is respected by peers (benefits). These are all important benefits that will help a prospective employer meet quotas and profit objectives (see Chapter 6).

Place Development

The second step in the personal marketing mix consists of developing a sophisticated prospect base (see Chapter 8). The prospect base is made up of potential employers who offer career positions corresponding to the career goals set in the research phase. This prospect list should include the company name, address, telephone number, names and titles of individuals to be contacted con-

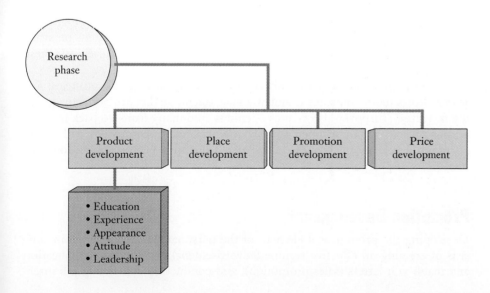

FIGURE A.4 Product Development Activities Associated with Finding Employment

FIGURE A.5   Place Development
through Using a Prospect List

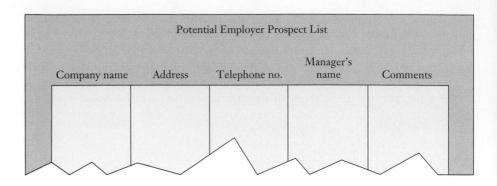

Potential Employer Prospect List

Company name	Address	Telephone no.	Manager's name	Comments

cerning employment, and other background information on the company (Fig. A.5). The number of prospects will depend on the desired size of the market to be contacted. Job seekers using direct mail marketing programs may contact up to 200 prospects, while telephone and direct contact personal marketing programs will begin with about twenty potential employers.

SOURCE OF POTENTIAL EMPLOYERS

The easiest source of potential employers to add to the prospect list is probably the classified section of the newspaper; however, "seldom does anything good come easy," and the newspaper is generally not the best source of prospective employers. In many cases either the best positions advertised in the newspaper are informally filled before they are advertised or the competition for them is extremely keen. It is not uncommon for a company to receive 100 to 150 résumés for jobs offering competitive salaries. In other cases, companies mass merchandise jobs that are unattractive and difficult to fill. While newspapers should not be overlooked in developing a prospect list, it is wise to use them with caution.

Research findings reported by the U.S. Department of Labor indicate that fewer than a third of job seekers relied on classified advertising. Most job seekers contacted the prospective employer directly.

The most effective prospective-employer lists are developed with the aid of directories, referrals, friends, acquaintances, and cold canvassing (Fig. A.6). Specialized employment agencies also provide computerized printouts on available openings. (See Chapter 8 for detailed description of each of these methods.)

Do not include in your list only companies with existing job vacancies. Research shows that companies frequently have openings that are not actively being recruited. Turnover also creates openings, and many firms go back into applicant files to fill these openings. In addition, many companies will create openings, especially for trainees, when a well-qualified person applies for a career-oriented position.

Promotion Development

Developing the promotional element of the personal marketing program consists of creating an effective résumé (advertisement), writing good application and thank-you letters (sales promotion), and conducting convincing job inter-

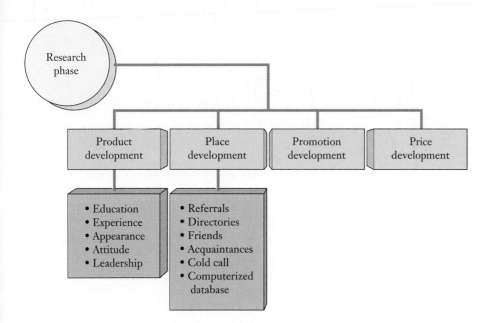

FIGURE A.6   Sources for Developing a Prospective Employer List

views (sales presentation) (Fig. A.7). The rules for developing each of these promotional concepts are much different at the professional-career level than at part-time and entry levels. They also tend to be different for acquiring a position in the private business sector than in public employment. The following promotional principles relate mainly to the professional-career level in private business, although many also apply to securing entry level, part-time, or public employment positions.

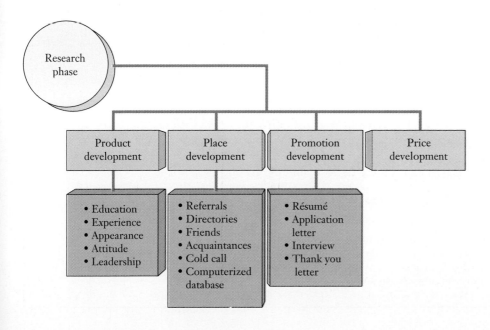

FIGURE A.7   Promotional Elements Used to Market Yourself

CYNTHIA ELIZABETH SMITH

Current Address	**Permanent Address**
1305 34th Street	617 Hail Street
Des Moines, Iowa 50311	Rockport, Illinois 60202
(515) 277–4753	(312) 246–3872

Objectives: To secure a growth-oriented position in merchandising or management at the retail or wholesale level

Primary Skills: Have acquired background skills in selling, buying computers, and management at Drake through classroom work and On the Job Training

Possess progressive work experience in retail, from a small specialty store to a large department store

Have the ability to understand and apply creative design concepts through my previous classroom experience

Have the ability to work effectively and harmoniously with a wide range of people

Have the ability to rapidly learn new techniques and concepts

Summary: Twenty-one-year-old college graduate with a degree in marketing; enjoy working with people; willing to work hard to achieve success in chosen career

WORK EXPERIENCE

1997–Present Von Maurs, Des Moines, Iowa

Started in a Retail Management Trainee position; duties and responsibilities include Professional Selling, Visual Merchandising, Buying and Inventory; exposure to a broad variety of management and supervisory philosophies

1997 Mark Henri Ltd., Des Moines, Iowa

Started as a fashion consultant for a small women's specialty store, which is an affiliate of Seiferts; learned basic store procedures, selling and display techniques; worked part-time during the summer while attending college

1997 Temporary Manpower, Chicago, Illinois

Temporary office service, which consisted of working as a librarian for an accounting firm, Author Young and Company; also as a receptionist for Loyola Law School; worked during the summer while attending evening classes

1994–96 Evanston Park District, Glen Ellyn, Illinois

Park District Counselor; taught safety to young children, instructed crafts, and coached a girl's softball team; also worked as a receptionist at the main office

1994 Maloney's Restaurant, Lombard, Illinois

Hostess at a restaurant; seated customers, cleaned tables, and ran the register; worked during the summer

EDUCATION

Drake University, Des Moines, Iowa

Graduated with a B.S.B.A. in Marketing and an emphasis in Art and Design; major areas of study include Selling, Sales and Promotion, Marketing, Marketing Management, Accounting, Economics, Basic Computer Language, and Consumer Behavior; earned a G.P.A. of 3.3

Completed an internship study program at Von Maurs, at Valley West Mall in Des Moines, Iowa; major emphasis included learning different store procedures

Graduated from Glenbard West High School, in Glen Ellyn, Illinois

ORGANIZATIONS, ACTIVITIES, and INTERESTS

College:

Member of Kappa Kappa Gamma Social Sorority

Vice President and Charter Member of Marketing Club—attended a large number of personal and professional development seminars

Greek Week representative

Panhellenic Representative

Director of house Variety Show

Registrar of Kappa Kappa Gamma

Little Sister of Sigma Alpha Epsilon

Intramural Football

Honors and Awards:

Alpha Lambda Delta Freshman Honor Society

Dean's list for three semesters

Creating a good résumé should be thought of as creating an advertisement. It should be a professional, business-oriented selling aid that stands out even though it is part of a pile of twenty or more résumés. It should attract attention and interest, as a good advertisement does when a reader is looking through a magazine and stops to study one of the ads. The résumé should be long enough (one to four pages, depending on depth of background) and well-written, supplying benefits so that it gets the prospective interviewer to desire and take action to set up a personal interview. The letter of application and thank-you letter should also take the interviewer's mind through the mental steps in the buying process—attention, interest, desire, conviction, and action (see Chapter 7).

THE INTERVIEW

The interview should be viewed as a strategic/consultative sales presentation (see Chapters 9 to 14). The applicant should be well prepared with preapproach information such as determination of goals, answers to challenging questions (negotiating objections), clear understanding of personal qualities and benefits, and knowledge of the interviewer and the company. When meeting the interviewer, a good first impression (good social contact) must be made. Transition from social contact to need discovery (finding out precisely what the company is looking for in an applicant) should be preplanned with well-chosen questions. Effective listening will result in productive two-way communication that maintains positive impressions. Effective listening also helps determine which parts of the interviewee's background (benefits) should be stressed. If for some reason the interviewer has not seen the résumé, the interviewee should offer it at this point to demonstrate the selling points made so far. Closing questions should be preplanned by the interviewee. These might include questions such as, "When do you plan to fill this position?" or "May I call you back on Friday?" Courtesy closing statements such as, "Thank you very much for an informative interview" or "I appreciate the time you spent with me, and I enjoyed our visit very much" should be preplanned.

Price Development

Price development involves salary negotiations. Adequate preinterviewing preparation is important for effective salary negotiations (Fig. A.8). The following guidelines should be followed during salary negotiations:

1. Determine the amount of money you will want to make during the first year of employment. Convert this to a range with a difference of $3,000 to $5,000 (*example:* $25,000 to $30,000).

2. Try to find out what salary range the position pays before the interview.

3. Plan to state that while starting salary is important, it is more important to know what can be made during the first year, given an excellent review.

4. As a general rule, if possible, postpone salary discussions until a job offer is made. This maintains a better bargaining position.

FIGURE A.8 The Complete Marketing Program Used to Find a High-Paying Professional Career

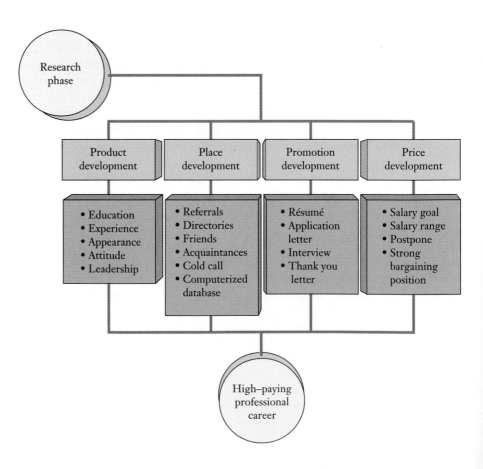

5. Position yourself in a strong bargaining position with a good personal marketing program.

   a. Have goals well thought out and be able to articulate them clearly.

   b. Have outstanding references.

   c. Have outstanding written materials that show achievement and accomplishment.

   d. Possess good knowledge of industry, company, product personnel, and salary ranges.

   e. Be currently employed with no sense of urgency to leave.

   f. Sell credentials first and discuss salary second.

   g. Indicate your knowledge of how to get a job.

   h. Become effective in face-to-face selling situations.

SUMMARY

From the employer's viewpoint the decision to purchase the personal marketing package of a career-oriented job seeker is a major one. An employee who stays with a company five to seven years (a statistical average) will be paid $200,000 to $350,000 in salary (five to seven years times an average annual salary of $40,000). The $200,000 to $350,000 salary plus the cost of benefits is the price the employer is paying for the marketing package. When you make an analogy between the price of a human resource and the purchase of a piece of equipment, it becomes apparent that this is a large purchase. Therefore a company is going to carefully examine all dimensions of the purchase.

A job seeker with knowledge of the job-changing process realizes the dollar value of the purchase an employer is making and designs a professional personal marketing program with this in mind. The personal marketing program emphasizes a high-quality professional approach to identifying the right product, positioning it in the right places with the right quality and quantity of promotion, and the right price.

Software for Sales Automation Applications

The software that you will use for the Sales Force Automation Case Study is available on the Internet. You will copy (download) the software from the Internet onto a (floppy) diskette. Previous users will find that the software is the same as that found in earlier editions, only the method of distribution has changed.

The software that you will download onto your diskette is a special compressed version. This software needs to be loaded (installed) onto the hard disk drive of a computer before you can use it. Once it is installed in a computer, the ACT! demonstration program will begin and you can start using the Case Study data that is included with it. The original copy of the compressed software stays on the diskette so that you can reuse it (or copy it). Following are instructions for both downloading and running the software.

Downloading from the World Wide Web and Installing the Sales Automation Case Study Software

Computer System Requirements

To download the Sales Automation Case Study software, you need to use a computer system that has Web browser software and a modem, or other connection to the Internet. You will need access to the Internet's World Wide Web, which is available through Internet service providers. You will also need one formatted, IBM-compatible, 1.44 megabyte diskette.

To install from the diskette and run the software, your computer must be IBM-compatible with at least 2.5 megabytes of storage available on your hard disk.

Finding the Selling-Today Web Page

The software is located on the Selling-Today Web page. You can find this page by entering in this address:

http://www.Selling-Today.com
(Please note the hyphen between Selling and Today)

When the Selling-Today Web page opens, you will find instructions on downloading the Sales Automation Case Study software. The software consists of a demonstration copy of ACT! along with the data you will need. Please read the instructions found on the Selling-Today Web page.

Downloading the Files

Downloading means that you will save (copy) files (software) from the Web onto a diskette in your computer. At the time of this printing the software consists of three separate files, which means that you will download three times. Beacuse the Web allows periodic improvements to be made, the procedure that you should follow may differ slightly from these instructions. It is important to read the instructions found on the Web page.

To save (not open) each of the files, point with your mouse as directed by the Web page instructions and click with your **right** mouse button. This will bring up a menu of choices. Choose "Save Target <u>A</u>s" if you are using Microsoft's Internet Explorer or "<u>S</u>ave Link As" if your are using a Netscape browser. If you are using another browser, consult its users guide for instructions. After selecting to save a file, the computer will display a "Save As" dialog box. This window will display your saving options. Using your mouse, select the menu button (often a down arrow) found next to the Save In field. This will display a list of places to save the file, including 3½ Floppy (A:). On most computers, the diskette drive is drive A:. Making this selection will save the file to the diskette. Confirm that a formatted, IBM-compatible, 1.44 megabyte diskette is in your diskette drive and choose the Save button. The software will begin to download.

The time it will take to download a file will vary, depending on the file's size and the capacity of your Internet connection. Many browsers will show a window that displays a progressive update of the progress of your download. Your computer's diskette drive light may also be on or flashing. When the update window closes and drive turns off, please select the next file, until all files are downloaded. It might take as much as 30 minutes to finish downloading all files.

Installing the ActDemo.exe Program

After the software has been downloaded, you will need to install it. Switch to DOS (or a DOS window) and select your diskette drive (usually A:\>). Choose the hard disk drive that you want to use (usually C:\>). If you want to use drive C:, type **Install C:\Demo** and press Enter. This will create a "Demo" subdirectory on your hard disk drive, automatically copy the files to that subdirectory, and run the program. This may take several minutes, and the screen may be blank for a while.

When the installation is finished, the Case Study software will begin to run and this introduction screen will be displayed.

Thank you for your interest in ACT!
ACT! is available through your local computer software dealer.

Symantec Corporation
10201 Torre Avenue
Cupertino, CA 95014-2132
(800) 441-7234

After reading the information on the introduction screen, press any key and the opening ACT! screen will appear:

```
┌─────────────────────────────────────┐
│   Automated Contact Tracking         │
│     U.S.A. Version 2.01              │
│     Copyright 1986, 1990             │
│   Contact Software International      │
├─────────────────────────────────────┤
│       Press any key to begin         │
└─────────────────────────────────────┘
```

Press any key and the Contact Screen is displayed:

```
 File  Edit  Schedule  Clear  Write  Lookup  Phone  View  Report
╭───────────────────────────────────────────────────╮
│ Name:  Able Profit Machines, Inc.    Addrs:  5000 N. Cooper Blvd │
│ Contact:  Mr. Bradley J. Able             :  Suite 200           │
│ Phone:  416-555-1000  X:   CC:            :                      │
│  Title:  President                  City:  Waco                  │
│   See:  Sharon                     State:  TX                    │
│  Dear:  Brad                         ZIP:  78332                 │
│  Call:    /  /  : am Re:                                         │
│Meeting:   /  /  : am Re:                                         │
│  To-Do:   /  /  : am Re:                                         │
│       Last Results:  Needs Discovery                            │
│        Status/Id:  Prospect       Referred by:  Colleen Landers │
│        Firm Size:  500.00 people  CAD Needed:      10.00        │
│      CAD in Use:  None              Likelihood:     0.70        │
│     CAD Stations:              Dollar Amount:  250,000.00       │
│    ACCOUNT CODE:  Engineering                                  │
│     Date Expected:  1/31/                                       │
│   Spouse's Name:  Peggy                                         │
│ C:\DEMO                                     Name 1 of 20        │
╰───────────────────────────────────────────────────╯
 F1 = Help Fri 27-Nov 3:06 pm
```

◄ **CONTACT SCREEN**

This software is "menu driven," which means that you can operate the program by selecting from lists of choices. The main menu is displayed at the top of the Contact Screen. Secondary or "window" menus appear when you make menu selections. Please press the F1 function key for an explanation of any menu entry.

Experimenting with the combination of menus and help screens will allow you to quickly learn how to operate this software.

Searching for Information (To be used with Chapters 8-14, the Sales Automation Case Studies)

To search for the answers to the Case Problem questions, proceed to the first Contact Screen.

Select **V**iew by highlighting the word View on the main menu or typing the letter V. The **V**iew window will appear over your Contact Screen:

```
┌─────────────────────────────────────────┐
│ View                                     │
├─────────────────────────────────────────┤
│ List                               F8    │
│ Contact Screen 2                   F6    │
│ Activities                    Alt + F9   │
│                                          │
│ History                     Shift + F9   │
│                                          │
│ Notes                              F9    │
│ Reference Library           Shift + F3   │
│                                          │
│ Totals                       Ctrl + F9   │
├─────────────────────────────────────────┤
│ Expenses                    Shift + F2   │
├─────────────────────────────────────────┤
│ System Status                            │
└─────────────────────────────────────────┘
```
◄ **VIEW WINDOW**

From the View menu, choose the letter **N** for **N**otes. Notes taken by the previous salesperson for this account will appear in the Notes window.

File   **E**dit   **S**chedule   **C**lear   **W**rite   **L**ookup   **P**hone   **V**iew   **R**eport

```
┌──────────────────────────────────────────────────────────────────┐
│   Name:  Able Profit Machines, Inc.    Addrs:  5000  N.  Cooper  Blvd│
│ Contact: Mr. Bradley J. Able              :  Suite 200            │
│  Phone:  416-555-1000  X:  CC:            :                       │
│   Title: President                     City: Waco                 │
│    See:  Sharon                       State: TX                   │
│   Dear:  Brad                           ZIP: 78332                │
│ ---L------T------T------T------T------T------T------T------R      │
│ 11/29                                                             │
│                                                                   │
│ 11/10 Joe and I met. Joe's report on the needs discovery shows how the│
│ 10 CAD stations they need can be phased in with staggered training so │
│ there's no disruption in production. Phasing in over 18 months will spread│
│ the cost over three annual budgets, too.                          │
│                                                                   │
│ 11/09 Nice meeting this morning. Joe and I spent most of the time with│
│ Bill Franklin. Bill's son, Jim, is a junior in engineering at State U. Jim is in-│
│ terested in part-time computer-related work. I will mention this to our presi-│
│ dent, maybe we could help Jim. Bill's chief CAD concern is work interrup-│
│ tions. Talked a moment about Sam Pearlman. I mentioned Sam's sister,│
│ Peggy, and Bill seemed impressed that I knew Peggy is married to Brad.│
│ He laughed when I said Joanna was busy.                           │
│                                                                   │
│ 11/09 Will meet. I need Joe, our technical specialist to team with me on│
│ this one—too technical for me. Thanked Brad for referrals he provided.│
│                                                                   │
│ 11/02 Good guy. Very cooperative. Supportive. Has big production facil-│
│ ity. Builds vending machines—sold over the globe. Large engineering│
│ dept. Bill Franklin is Chief Engineer but Mr. Able "Call me Brad" wants to│
│ stay on top of the CAD decision process. Brad may be reluctant to budget│
│ for entire CAD needs at one time. "He has a boss too, you know," his│
│ board of directors. Sounds like he wants to negotiate a lower price.│
│     Brad suggested we call on Sam Pearlman at 213-555-4545 and    │
│ Joanna Barkley over in Savannah, at Computer Products.            │
└──────────────────────────────────────────────────────────────────┘
```
◄ **CONTACT SCREEN**

◄ **NOTES WINDOW**

While in the notes window, press the PgDn key and you will notice that the earliest notes (see dates) are at the bottom. When you are finished reviewing these notes, press the Escape (Esc) key. This will close the Notes Window and return you to the Contact Screen.

SOFTWARE FOR SALES AUTOMATION APPLICATIONS **419**

By pressing the PgDn key while in the Contact Screen, you will bring up the next customer record. Notice that at the bottom right of the screen is the record number. It tells you the number of contacts in your database and which one is being displayed now—Name **2 of** ( ). Records are sorted by the Name field. By pressing the PgUp key, you will transfer back to the first contact. Check the record number to verify. Pressing the End key will take you to the end of the current list of contacts; the Home key will return you to record number 1.

Press the PgDn key to return to Contact 2. By pressing the **V**iew and **N**otes keys, you will be able to review the sales notes for this Contact. Press Escape and PgDn to move to the next Contact Screen, and so on, until you have reviewed the notes on each of the Contact Screens. You should now be prepared to answer the questions posed in the Case Studies.

Software Status

The information that is included with the demonstration software is all of the information you will need for the Case Studies in this book. The program on your hard disk drive can be run as many times as you need for your assignments. After completing the Sales Automation Case Study, you may choose to leave the demonstration software on your hard disk drive or you may remove it. If you need another copy of the software, you may re-install it from your diskette or download it again from the Selling-Today Web page.

Partnership Selling: A Role Play/Simulation for *Selling Today*

TABLE OF CONTENTS

Introduction

Salespeople today are working hard to become more effective in such important areas as person-to-person communications, needs analysis, interpersonal relations, and decision making. This role play/simulation will help you develop these critical selling skills. You will assume the role of a new sales trainee employed by the Park Inn International Convention Center.

PART I:

Developing a Sales-Oriented Product Strategy will challenge you to acquire the necessary product information needed to be an effective sales representative for the Park Inn (see Chapters 5 and 6). Your sales manager, T. J. McKee, will describe your new trainee position in an employment memorandum. Your instructions will include the study of materials featured on the following pages, viewing a video that describes the convention facilities and services provided by a competitor, and role playing the request made in a T. J. McKee customer service/sales memorandum.

PART II:

Developing a Relationship Strategy, another employment memorandum, will inform you of a promotion to an account executive position. A sales memorandum will inform you of your assignment to accounts in a specific market segment. Part II also involves a role play on the development of a relationship with a new customer in your market segment (see Chapters 3 and 9). Your call objective will be to acquire background information on your new customer, who may have a need for your services.

PART III:

Understanding Your Customer's Buying Strategy involves a needs analysis role play (see Chapters 7 and 10). You will again meet with the customer who has indicated an interest in scheduling a business conference at your convention center. During this meeting you will acquire information to complete Part IV, which involves preparation for the sales presentation.

PART IV:

Developing a Presentation Strategy will involve preparation of a sales proposal and a *portfolio* presentation (see Chapters 10–14). This section also involves a third role play with the customer. During the role play you will reestablish your relationship with the customer, present your proposal, negotiate customer concerns, and attempt to close and service the sale.

Throughout completion of the role play/simulation, you will be guided by the employment and sales memoranda (from the sales manager) and instructions and additional forms provided by your instructor.

As you complete this simulation activity, note that the principles and practices you are learning to use have application in nearly all personal selling situations.

General Instructions for Role Playing

OVERVIEW

The primary goal of a simulation in personal selling should be to strike a balance between just enough detail to focus on the process of selling and not so much as to drown in an ocean of facts. Either too much detail or too little detail can develop anxiety in role play participants. *Partnership Selling* is designed to minimize anxiety by including only the facts needed to focus on learning the processes involved in high-performance selling.

Some anxiety will occur, however, because you are asked to perform under pressure (in terms of building relationships, securing strategic information, changing people's thinking, and getting them to take action). Learning to perform in an environment full of genuine, but nonthreatening pressure, affords you the opportunity to practice your selling skills so you will be prepared for real-world selling anxiety.

The following suggestions for role playing will help you develop the ability to perform under stress.

INSTRUCTIONS FOR SALESPERSON ROLE PLAYS

1. Be well prepared with product knowledge.

2. Read information for each role play ahead of time.

3. Follow specific instructions carefully.

4. Attempt to sense both the context and the facts of the situation presented.

5. Conduct a mental rehearsal. See yourself successfully conducting and completing the role play.

6. Be prepared to take notes during the role play.

7. After the role play, take note of your feelings and mentally put them into the context of what just occurred.

8. Be prepared to discuss your reaction to what occurred during the role play.

INSTRUCTIONS FOR CUSTOMER ROLE PLAYS

1. Read the instructions carefully. Be sure to note both the role play instructions and the information you are about to share.

2. Attempt to sense both the context of the buying situation and the individual facts presented in the instructions.

3. Let the salesperson initiate greetings, conversations, and concluding actions. React appropriately.

4. Supply only the customer information presented in the background description.

5. Supply customer information in a positive manner.

6. Do not attempt to throw the salesperson off track.

PART ONE: DEVELOPING A SALES-ORIENTED PRODUCT STRATEGY

PARK INN
INTERNATIONAL™
EMPLOYMENT MEMORANDUM 1

To: New Convention Sales Center Trainees
From: T. J. McKee, Sales Manager
Re: Your New Sales Training Program—"Developing a Product Selling Strategy"

I am extremely happy that you accepted our offer to join the Sales and Marketing Department. Enclosed is a copy of your new position description (see p. 428). Your first assignment as a trainee will be to learn about our product and what we have recently done to provide *total quality* customer service. *To apply what you are learning, I would like you to follow up on a customer service request I recently received. (See memo p. 457.)* You will use the following product information to complete the assignment:

AN AWARD-WINNING UPDATE (See pp. 430–449)

We have recently completed a *$2.8 million investment in our convention center.* This customer service investment included renovating all guest rooms and suites, lobby and front desk area, meeting rooms, restaurant and lounge, and enclosure of the swimming pool. Enclosed is a copy of the "Regional Architect's Award" which our facility won. We are the only facility in the Metro Area to have been presented with this award.

MEETING AND BANQUET ROOMS (See pp. 447–449)

The Park Inn offers convention planners just over *8,000 square feet of award-winning meeting space* in attractive, newly renovated meeting and banquet rooms. Our Central Park East and West rooms are conveniently located on the lobby level of the hotel. Each of these rooms can accommodate 180 people in a theater-style setting or 80 in a classroom-style setting. They also have a divider wall which can be retracted and, with the combined rooms, can accommodate up to 370 people.

    The Top of the Park provides a spectacular view of the city through windows that surround that ballroom. This unique room, located on the top floor, can accommodate 225 classroom style, 350 banquet style, or 450 people theater style. Also located in the Top of the Park is a revolving platform area which slowly moves, giving guests a 360 degree panoramic view of the city. The Parkview Room, which is also located on the top floor of the hotel, can accommodate 150 people theater style and 80 people classroom style.

    In addition for *groups booking forty rooms or more, we provide one luxurious suite **free**.* This suite features a meeting room, bedroom, wet bar with refrigerator, and jacuzzi.

    Be sure your clients understand that our meeting rooms *need to be reserved.* The first organization to sign a sales proposal for a specific date has the designated rooms guaranteed.

GUEST ROOM DECOR AND RATES (See pp. 441 and 451)

Our recent renovation included complete redecoration of all 250 of our large and spacious guest rooms. This includes all new furniture, wallcoverings, drapes, bedspreads, and carpets. Our interior designer succeeded in creating a comfortable, attractive, restful atmosphere. *Seventy of our rooms are designated nonsmoking.*

(continued)

ROOM RATES *(continued)*

	REGULAR RATES	*GROUP RATES*	*SAVINGS*
Single	$78	$68	$10
Double	$88	$78	$10
Triple	$96	$86	$10
Quad	$104	$94	$10

A comparison of competitive room, parking, and transportation rates are presented on p. 451.

BANQUET MEALS (See pp. 435–439)

Our executive chef, Ricardo Guido, recently won the *National Restaurant Association's "Outstanding Chef of the Year" Award*. His winning entry consisted of the three chicken entrees featured on the enclosed menus. Ricardo served as Executive Chef at the five-star rated Williamsburg Inn in Williamsburg, Virginia before we convinced him to join us six months ago. He personally oversees all our food and beverage operations. Ricardo, in my opinion, is one of the outstanding chefs in the country. His expertise and commitment to total quality customer service will help develop long-term relationships with our customers.

The enclosed dinner selections are only suggestions. We will design a special menu for your clients if they wish. A 16% gratuity or service charge is added to all group meal functions.

HOTEL/MOTEL AND SALES TAXES

All room rates are subject to the *local hotel/motel room tax, which is an additional 8%. In addition, all billings must have a 4% sales tax added. (The sales tax is not added to the hotel/motel tax and does not apply to gratuities.)*

LOCATION, TRANSPORTATION, AND PARKING (See map on p. 433)

We are located in a dynamic growing metropolitan area of over 400,000 people. With *convenient access, just off of Interstate 237 at the downtown exits*, we are within a block of the nationally recognized climate controlled sky-walk system. This five-mile system is connected to theaters, excellent shopping, the civic center, the metropolitan convention center, and a large selection of ethnic and fast-food restaurants. Our location offers guests the privacy they deserve during their meetings, yet is close enough to downtown to enjoy all the excitement.

Free courtesy van transportation (also known as limousine service) is provided for our overnight guests to and from the airport, as well as anywhere in the downtown area. This service saves our guests who arrive by plane from *$8.00 to $10.00 each way.*

Guests who will be driving to the hotel will find over *300 parking spaces* available to them at *no charge.* Unlike other downtown properties, our free parking saves guests up to *$6.00 per day* in parking fees. For security purposes, we have closed-circuit camera systems in the parking lot and underground parking areas.

VALUE-ADDED GUEST SERVICES AND AMENITIES

Our convention center owners have invested heavily in the facility to provide our clients with *total quality service,* unmatched by our competition. Additional value-added services and amenities include:

- A large *indoor pool, sundeck, sauna, whirlpool, and Nautilus exercise room* in an attractive tropical atmosphere (see p. 445)
- "Cafe in the Park" featuring 24-hour continental cuisine seven days a week
- "Pub in the Park" where friendly people meet, featuring *free hors d'oeuvres* Monday through Friday, 5 to 7 P.M.
- Cable television with *free in-room movies*
- A.V. rental of most equipment in-house, at a nominal fee (see p. 453)
- Photocopying and FAX services available and a Quickcopy printer located across the street from the hotel
- *Free coffee and donuts or rolls* in the lobby each morning from 6 to 8 A.M.
- A team of *well-trained, dedicated, and friendly associates* providing total quality front desk, food, and guest services

SALES LITERATURE (See pp. 430–446)

Included in your product training materials are photos, references, letters, room schedules, sales proposals, and other information that you will use in your written proposals and verbal sales presentations. When you move into outside sales, you should use these tools to create effective sales portfolios.

TOTAL QUALITY COMMITMENT

Our convention center is committed to *total quality customer service. Our Partnership Style of Customer Service and Selling* is an extension of our total quality process. The Total Quality Customer Glossary provides definitions of terms that describe our total quality process (see p. 429).

The Hotel and Convention center industry is mature and well established. Our sales and customer service plan is to *establish strong relationships, focus on solving customer problems, provide total quality customer service, and become a long-term hotel and convention center partner with our clients.* By utilizing this type of selling and customer service, your compensation and our sales revenue will both increase substantially.

Enclosures
TJM:ESS

PARK INN
I N T E R N A T I O N A L™

POSITION DESCRIPTION — CONVENTION CENTER ACCOUNT EXECUTIVE

COMPANY DESCRIPTION

The Park Inn Convention Center is a total quality, full-service equal opportunity employment convention center that has recently made large investments in the physical facility, the food and beverage department, and sales department. Company culture includes an effective and enthusiastic team approach to creating *total quality* value-added solutions for customers in a very competitive industry. The primary sales promotion tool is *Partnership Selling* with extensive marketing support in the form of photos, reference letters, team selling, etc. The company goal is to increase revenues 20 percent in the coming year by providing outstanding customer service.

SUCCESSFUL ACCOUNT EXECUTIVE WILL

1. Acquire necessary convention center company, product, industry, and competitive information through company training program
2. Be committed to a total quality customer service process
3. Develop a list of potential prospects in the assigned target market
4. Develop long-term total quality selling relationships that focus on solving the meeting planner's convention center needs
5. Achieve a sales volume of $700,000 to $800,000 annually

WORKING RELATIONSHIPS

Reports to: Sales Manager
Works with: Internal Support Team including Food Service, Housekeeping and Operations, Customer Service and Front Desk; External Relationships including customers, professional associations, and industry personnel

SPECIFIC REQUIREMENTS

1. Must project a positive and professional sales image
2. Must be able to establish and maintain long-term relationships
3. Must be goal oriented with a plan for self-improvement
4. Must be flexible to deal effectively with a wide range of customers
5. Must be good at asking questions and listening effectively
6. Must be accurate and creative in developing customer solutions
7. Must be clear and persuasive in communicating and negotiating solutions
8. Must be good at closing the sale
9. Must follow through on promises and assurances
10. Must have math skills necessary for figuring sales proposals

SPECIFIC REWARDS

1. Attractive compensation package that includes base salary, a commission of 10 percent of sales, bonuses, and an attractive fringe benefit package
2. Pride in working for an organization that practices total quality management in employee relations and customer service
3. Extensive sales and educational support
4. Opportunity for growth and advancement

EOE/AA/TQM

TOTAL QUALITY CUSTOMER SERVICE GLOSSARY

DIRFT—DO IT RIGHT THE FIRST TIME means being prepared, asking the right questions, selecting the right solutions, and making effective presentations. This creates repeats and referrals.

QIP—QUALITY IMPROVEMENT PROCESS means always striving to better serve our customers resulting in high-quality, long-term relationships.

TQM—TOTAL QUALITY MANAGEMENT means the commitment to support and empower people to deliver legendary customer service.

QIT—QUALITY IMPROVEMENT TEAM means a team approach to deliver outstanding customer service.

COQ—COST OF QUALITY means the ultimate lowering of cost by providing outstanding service the first time, so as to build a list of repeat and referred customers.

PONC—PRICE OF NONCONFORMANCE means the high cost of not meeting high standards. This results in correcting problems and losing customers. PONC also causes longer sales cycles and higher sales costs.

POC—PRICE OF CONFORMANCE means the lower costs of providing outstanding customer service, and achieving a list of repeat or referral customers.

WIIFM—WHAT IS IN IT FOR ME means the psychic and monetary rewards in the form of personal enjoyment, higher salaries, commissions, or bonuses caused by delivering outstanding customer service.

QES—QUALITY EDUCATION SYSTEMS means internal and external educational activities designed to improve the quality of customer service.

YOU—THE MOST IMPORTANT PART OF QUALITY means the on-going program of self-improvement that results in outstanding customer service, and personal and financial growth.

THE ALL NEW PARK INN
(With an award winning
2.8 million dollar renovation)

REGIONAL ARCHITECTS ASSOCIATION

"EXCELLENCE IN RENOVATION DESIGN"

PRESENTED TO:

Park Inn International

WITH SPECIAL RECOGNITION FOR CREATING AN OUTSTANDING CONVENTION ENVIRONMENT.

PRESENTED ON THE ELEVENTH DAY OF MARCH, 199_.

Allen Rogge
CHAIRPERSON, DESIGN SELECTION COMMITTEE

Patricia Bennett
PRESIDENT, REGIONAL ARCHITECTS ASSOCIATION

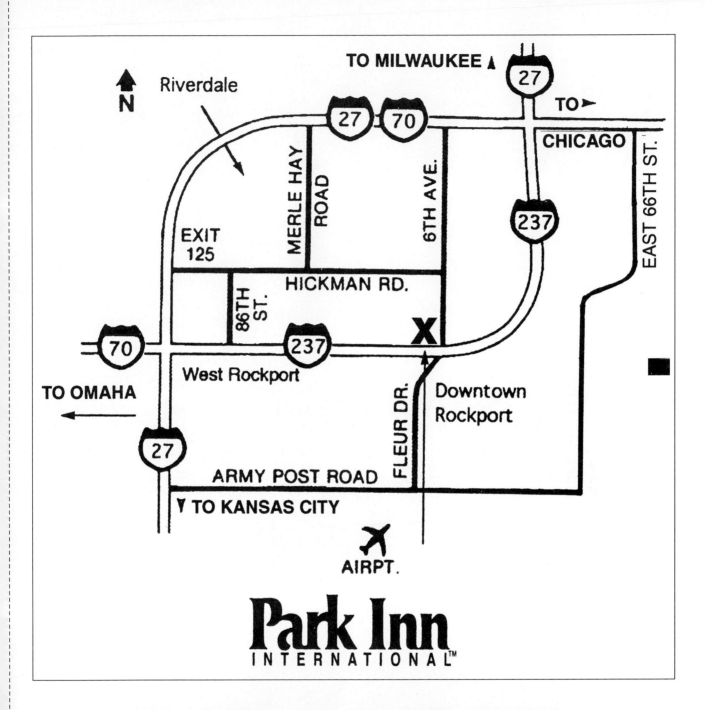

CONVENIENT, EASY TO FIND LOCATION WITH "FREE" PARKING

Conveniently located at 1237 and 6th Ave.
Just 8 miles from Rockport International Airport

OUTSTANDING FOOD SERVICE
**Personally Supervised by Award-Winning
"Executive Chef of the Year"
Ricardo Guido**

NATIONAL RESTAURANT ASSOCIATION

EXECUTIVE CHEF OF THE YEAR

AWARDED TO:

Ricardo Guido

PRESENTED ON THE ELEVENTH DAY OF APRIL, 199-.

Ella Reed

CONFERENCE CHAIRPERSON

Patricia Reed

PRESIDENT, NATIONAL RESTAURANT ASSOCIATION

LITHO IN U.S.A.

MENU SELECTIONS

All selections include tossed greens with choice of dressing, choice of potato (baked, oven browned, au gratin, or mashed), rice or buttered noodles, rolls with butter, coffee, decaffeinated coffee, tea, or iced tea.

ENTREES

CHICKEN WELLINGTON—Boneless breast of chicken topped with a mushroom mixture, wrapped in puff pastry shell and baked to a golden brown $10.95

CHICKEN BREAST TERIYAKI—Marinated boneless breast of chicken grilled and topped with our *special* teriyaki sauce $10.95

CHICKEN BREAST NEW ORLEANS—Baked boneless breast of chicken, garnished with peppers, mushrooms, onions, and Monterey Jack cheese $10.95

ROASTED TURKEY WITH STUFFING—Slices of roasted turkey with savory stuffing and a rich turkey gravy and cranberry sauce $10.95

BROILED CHOPPED SIRLOIN—Lean ground chuck broiled to perfection and served with a rich mushroom sauce $10.95

ROASTED PRIME RIB OF BEEF, AU JUS—A thick slice of juicy prime rib served with au jus and creamy horseradish sauce $15.95

BROILED NEW YORK STRIP STEAK—Center cut New York strip steak broiled to perfection, topped with our own seasoned herb butter $16.50

BROILED FILET MIGNON—A steak from the center cut tenderloin, broiled and served with a rich red wine sauce $17.50

SLICED PORK LOIN WITH MUSTARD SAUCE—Boneless loin of pork oven roasted and sliced, served with a mustard sauce $11.95

GRILLED PORK CHOP—A thick cut of pork grilled to juicy perfection $12.95

BROILED ORANGE ROUGHY—A filet of orange roughy broiled and covered with basil-lemon sauce $12.95

BROILED HALIBUT STEAK—Tender flaky halibut cut into steaks and broiled in lemon-butter served with fresh lemon slices $13.95

Prices do not include 16% service charge or Sales Tax.

ATTRACTIVE, COMFORTABLE GUEST ROOMS
(All new furnishings and HBO in every room)

LUXURIOUS TWO-ROOM SUITES
(Features meeting/living room, bedroom, wet bar with refrigerator and Jacuzzi)

A TROPICAL PARADISE

For relaxation after a day's work—
attractive pool, sauna, whirlpool, sundeck,
and Nautilus fitness center

BRIGHT, COMFORTABLE, AND STRATEGICALLY ARRANGED MEETING ROOMS

Everything you need for outstanding meetings

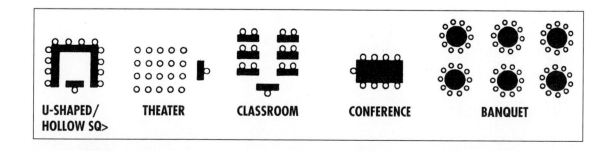

U-SHAPED/ HOLLOW SQ>   THEATER   CLASSROOM   CONFERENCE   BANQUET

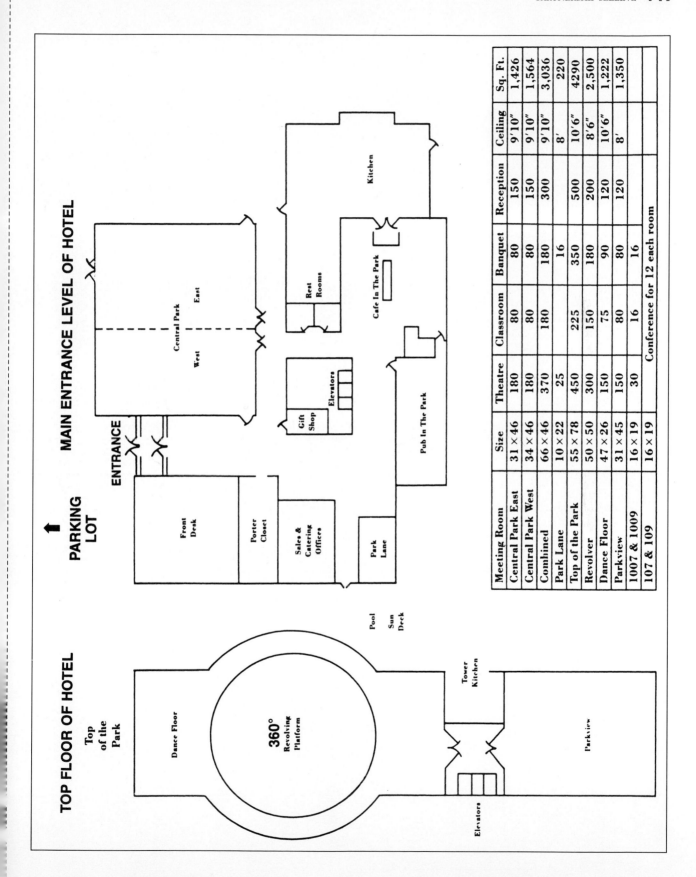

MAIN ENTRANCE LEVEL OF HOTEL

PARKING LOT

ENTRANCE

Front Desk

Porter Closet

Sales & Catering Offices

Park Lane

Central Park

West   East

Gift Shop

Elevators

Rest Rooms

Cafe In The Park

Pub In The Park

Kitchen

TOP FLOOR OF HOTEL

Top of the Park

Dance Floor

360° Revolving Platform

Pool

Sun Deck

Tower Kitchen

Elevators

Parkview

Meeting Room	Size	Theatre	Classroom	Banquet	Reception	Ceiling	Sq. Ft.
Central Park East	31 × 46	180	80	80	150	9'10"	1,426
Central Park West	34 × 46	180	80	80	150	9'10"	1,564
Combined	66 × 46	370	180	180	300	9'10"	3,036
Park Lane	10 × 22	25		16		8'	220
Top of the Park	55 × 78	450	225	350	500	10'6"	4290
Revolver	50 × 50	300	150	180	200	8'6"	2,500
Dance Floor	47 × 26	150	75	90	120	10'6"	1,222
Parkview	31 × 45	150	80	80	120	8'	1,350
1007 & 1009	16 × 19	30	16	16			
107 & 109	16 × 19		Conference for 12 each room				

METRO AREA COMPETITIVE SURVEY

QUOTED GROUP RATES (IN DOLLARS) FOR HOTEL/MOTEL GUEST ROOMS

HOTEL/MOTEL	SINGLE	DOUBLE	DAILY PARKING	AIRPORT TRANS.
Park Inn	**68**	**78**	**Free**	**Free**
Marriott	70	80	6	10 each way
Sheraton	75	95	6	12 each way
Hilton	70	90	7	9 each way
Embassy	72	93	6	8 each way
Guest Quarters	74	94	Free	8 each way
Carlton	65	85	8	3 each way
Saboe	65	75	Free	12 each way
Chesterfield	60	70	Free	13 each way
Best Western	55	60	Free	15 each way
Days Inn	50	55	Free	12 each way
Sunset Inn	45	n/a	Free	12 each way

RENTAL RATES

DAILY EQUIPMENT RATES

25-Inch Monitor and VCR	$100.00
Cassette Deck	$ 25.00
Handheld Microphone (additional)	$ 15.00
6- or 8-Foot Tripod Screen	$ 20.00
9 × 12 Foot Fast Fold Screen	$ 45.00
Lavalier Microphone	$ 20.00
Pentium Personal Computer	$125.00
Prop Easels	$ 6.00
Flipchart and Markers	$ 15.00
Projection Cart	$ 10.00
35-mm Projector with Remote	$ 35.00
Overhead Projector	$ 35.00
16-mm Projector	$ 25.00
6-Foot Tables with Tablecloth and Skirting	$ 10.00
Extension Cords for 110 Volt	$ 10.00
3 × 5 Foot Grease Boards	$ 10.00

MEETING ROOM RATES

SQUARE FEET	MEETING ROOM	4 HOURS	8 HOURS	24 HOURS
4,290	**Top of the Park**	**$400**	**$600**	**$900**
1,426	**Central Park East**	**$150**	**$200**	**$300**
1,564	**Central Park West**	**$160**	**$200**	**$300**
3,036	**Combined Central Park**	**$300**	**$400**	**$500**
220	**Park Lane**	**$ 25**	**$ 40**	**$ 60**
2,500	**Revolver**	**$300**	**$500**	**$700**
1,222	**Dance Floor**	**$100**	**$175**	**$275**
1,350	**Park View**	**$110**	**$185**	**$300**
304	**1,007 and 1,009**	**$ 40**	**$ 60**	**$ 80**
304	**107 and 109**	**$ 40**	**$ 60**	**$ 80**

- Meeting room rental charges based on set changes at 12:00 noon, 5:00 P.M., or 10:00 P.M.
- For groups of 20 or more who are reserving 20 or more guest rooms or scheduling 20 or more banquet meals, rental rates will be waived for rooms up to 1,600 square feet for up to 8 hours of use per day.
- For groups of 50 or more who are reserving 50 or more guest rooms or scheduling 50 or more banquet meals, rental rates will be waived for all rooms for up to 24 hours of use.

THE PRINCIPAL COMPANY

1900 Grand Avenue
Rockport, IL 50322

December 15, 199_

Carroll Parez, General Manager
The Park Inn
555 West Side Street
Rockport, IL 50310

Dear Carroll:

On behalf of our employees I thank you and your associates for the wonderful time we had at the Park Inn during our convention last month. Enclosed is a check for $22,991.23 to pay the invoice for the meeting costs.

The hospitality that we received during our time there was unparalleled. The friendliness and dedication of the staff simply made our time so enjoyable we hated to leave.

The Chicken New Orleans was superb. Our *heartfelt thanks to Chef Ricardo Guido* for creating the best meals we have ever had at a convention.

Without reservation I will direct anyone looking for convention space to your award-winning property. The group who gave you the award certainly knew what was important to convention planners. You may count on us to return in the future.

Sincerely,

Reggie Regan

Reggie Regan, Vice President
Field Sales Division

Enclosures:
Schedule for our next eight convention dates
Check
Service Evaluation

ss

REFERENCES

COMPANY/ADDRESS	TELEPHONE NO.	DATE OF BOOKING
Association of Business and Industry 2425 Hubbell Mr. James Warner (Director)	265–8181	July 1–2
Acme Supply Company 2531 Dean Linn Compiano (Training Manager)	265–9831	July 14
Rotary International 1230 Executive Towers Mr. Roger Shannon (Executive Director)	792–4616	July 28–29
Archway Cookie Company Boone Industrial Park Mr. Bill Sorenson (Sales Manager)	432–4084	August 9
West College 4821 College Parkway Toni Bush (Athletic Director)	283–4142	September 9–11
Travelers Insurance Company 1452 29th Mr. Richard Wiese (Training Manager)	223–7500	November 14
Meredith Corporation 1716 Locust Mrs. Carol Rains (Public Relations)	284–2654	November 23–24
Pioneer Hi-Bred Incorporated 5700 Merle Highway Mrs. Sheri Sitterly (Administrative Services)	272–3660	December 12–13

CONVENTION CENTER POLICIES AND GENERAL INFORMATION

FOOD AND BEVERAGE

- No food or beverage (alcoholic or otherwise) shall be brought into a public meeting place.
- All bars close in accordance with state law. All state laws applicable to drinking age will be strictly enforced. IDs are required. Bartenders have the right to refuse service.

- A 16% gratuity or service charge and applicable sales tax will be added to all food and beverage purchases. Any group requesting a tax exemption must submit their Certificate of Exemption prior to the event.
- There is a $25 setup fee for each meal function of 25 persons or less.

GUARANTEES

- The Convention Center will require your menus and meeting room requirements no later than two weeks before your meeting or food function.
- Convention Center facilities are guaranteed on a "first confirmed, first served" basis.

- A meal guarantee is required 48 hours prior to your function. This guarantee is the minimum your group will be charged for the function. If no guarantee is received by the catering office, we will then consider your last number of attendees as the guarantee. We will be prepared to serve 5% over your guaranteed number.

BANQUET AND MEETING ROOMS

- As other groups may be utilizing the same room prior to or following your function, please adhere to the times agreed on. Should your time schedule change, please contact the Catering Office, and every effort will be made to accommodate you.

- Function rooms are assigned by the room number of people anticipated. If attendance drops or increases, please contact the Catering Office to ensure proper assignment of rooms.

AUDIO VISUAL SERVICES

- A wide selection of audio visual equipment and services is available on a rental basis.

PARK INN
I N T E R N A T I O N A L™

CUSTOMER SERVICE/SALES MEMORANDUM 1

To: **Convention Sales Trainee**
From: **T. J. McKee, Sales Manager**
Re: **Assistance with a Customer Request**

A new prospect called and requested that we immediately submit a proposal for a planned Rockport meeting. Please review the profile in our automated database (printed as follows).

CONTACT REPORT

Name: Graphic Forms	Address: 2134 Martin Luther King	
Contact: B. H. Rivera	:	◄ **CONTACT**
Phone: 314–619–4879	:	**SCREEN**
Title: President	City: Atlanta	
Sec:	State: GA	
Dear: B. H. Rivera	ZIP: 61740	

(McKee) Visited with B. H. Rivera on the phone. Seemed very interested. Nice emotive person. Has a son, Matt, attending West College. Also knew Toni Bush of West, who is an excellent account of ours. B. H. wants a proposal ASAP to cover the following buying conditions:

1. Ten single guest rooms for two nights—Friday and Saturday
2. A meeting room for 20 people, classroom style, Friday and Saturday from 2 to 6 P.M.
3. Dinner for 20, banquet style, at 6 P.M. each night
   Friday: Grilled Pork Chops
   Saturday: Broiled Orange Roughy
4. A swimming pool

◄ **NOTES WINDOW**

Complete the following customer service/sales assignment using the material in your product sales training program (pp. 425–456) and the forms on the next three pages. (See Chapters 5 and 6 on Developing a Product Strategy.)

1. *Complete the strategic planning form (p. 458).*
   This is an internal form which we prepare to custom fit our product for each customer's unique needs. In the first column, write what the customer needs. Complete the form by matching proof devices and feature-benefit statements in the remaining columns. This information will be used to complete your sales proposal and sales statements in the remaining columns. This information will be used to complete your sales proposal and sales letter.

2. *Complete the sales proposal worksheet (p. 459)*
   Our sales proposal needs to contain accurate and complete facts because when signed, it becomes a legally enforceable sales contract. All the product and pricing guidelines have been supplied in your sales training materials. You should sign your name with your new job title "Account Executive" in the lower left-hand corner of the form.

3. *Write a sales letter (p. 460).*
   Prepare a letter that custom fits and positions the benefits that will appeal to B. H. Rivera. Be sure to list any sales literature you will be sending under the Enclosure section of your letter. (Use business letter format on p. 454.)

Make file copies of everything you prepare so our food and beverage, housekeeping, and accounting departments will have them available.

We should send or fax the proposal, cover letter, and sales literature by tomorrow afternoon.

Thank you.

Enclosures

STRATEGIC SALES PLANNING FORM A

MATCHING BUYING CONDITIONS WITH PROOF DEVICES AND FEATURE BENEFITS

Buying Condition *You indicated you wanted . . .*	Proof Device *Here is . . .*	Feature *which has (have) . . .*	Benefit *which means to you . . .*	Confirmation Question *What do you think?*
____ (number) guest rooms	A picture of one of our guest rooms (see p. 441)	Just been remodeled	Your people will enjoy clean, comfortable, spacious, and attractive surroundings	Is that what you had in mind?

Instructions—Strategic Planning Form A

Step 1   Write all four of the customer's buying conditions in the first column.

Step 2   For each buying condition (see Chapters 5 and 6 on Developing a Product Strategy)

     a. Write a description and the page number (from your product strategy unit) of the specific proof devices you will include in your letter or use in a presentation.

     b. Write the product feature you will describe.

     c. Write the customer benefits you will describe about the feature.

     d. Write the confirming question you will ask to make sure this is the benefit your customer wants.

PARK INN
INTERNATIONAL™

SALES PROPOSAL

Customer Name: _____ Title: _____

Organization Name: _____ Telephone: _____

Address: _____

Date(s) of Meetings: _____

Kind of Meetings: _____

Buying Conditions (Needs): _____

_____

_____

A. Meal Functions Needed

	Time	Description	Quantity	Price	Total
Meal 1 Meal 2 Other		(Beverages, set up fees, etc.)			

Total _____

Sales Tax _____

Service Charge _____

Total Meal Cost _____

B. Meeting and Banquet Rooms and Equipment Needed (describe time, date, and cost)

Total _____

Sales Tax _____

Total Meeting/Banquet Rooms and Equipment Charges _____

C. Guest Rooms Needed

Number of Rooms Needed	Description (dates, locations, special conditions)	Group Rate Per Room	Total Cost

Total _____

Room Tax _____

Sales Tax _____

D. Total Customer Costs (from above)

Total Guest Room Charges _____

A. $_____ plus B. $_____ plus C. $_____ equals **Total Charges** $_____

_____   _____
Authorized Signature   Date   Customer Signature   Date

_____   _____
Title   Title

PARK INN
INTERNATIONAL™

555 West Side Street, Rockport, IL 50322
618-225-0925   Fax 618-225-9386

PARK INN
INTERNATIONAL™
EMPLOYMENT MEMORANDUM 2

To: New Convention Center Account Executives
From: T. J. McKee, Sales Manager
Re: Your New Sales Assignment

Congratulations on successfully completing your training program, and receiving your new appointment. You will find three challenges as you partner with your accounts.

Your *first challenge will be establishing relationships* with your customers. This will require that you do strategic planning before you can call on your client for the first time. Make sure your initial meetings focus on subjects of interest to your customer.

Your *second major challenge will be to gain a complete and accurate understanding of your customer's needs*. You should prepare to ask good questions, take detailed and accurate notes, and confirm your customer's and your own understanding of their need. This process is a part of our total quality management program which strives to provide total quality customer service.

Your *third challenge as an account executive will be to make good presentations*. Our industry, as most others these days, is competitive and is characterized by many look-alike products and some price cutting. Always *organize and deliver good presentations* that focus on (1) providing solutions to immediate and long-term customer needs, (2) negotiating double-win solutions to customer concerns, and (3) closing sales that keep our facility full. This approach will give you a competitive edge and help you maintain high-quality, long-term profitable relationships.

Effectively meeting these challenges will also require that you have a program of *self-improvement*. This will enhance your career as an account executive.

Attached you will find a memorandum on an account I would like you to develop. Please follow the instructions included, and provide me with appropriate feedback on your progress. I look forward to working with you on this account.

P. S. I want to compliment you on your excellent work on the B. H. Rivera account. B. H. called while you were attending a training meeting and said that your proposal and letter looked very good. Their organization was impressed with our facility, the apparent quality of our food, and your letter. Their organization will be scheduling a total of *eleven more meetings* at our convention center during the next twelve months if everything works the way you describe it. Each of these sales will be reflected in your *commission checks*. Great work.

PARK INN
INTERNATIONAL™

SALES MEMORANDUM 1A

To: **Association Account Sales**
From: **T. J. McKee, Sales Manager**
Re: **Developing the Erin Adkins YWCA Account (Call 1, Establishing a Relationship Strategy)**

My sales assistant has called Erin Adkins, chairperson of the YWCA Physical Fitness Week program (see following contact report), and set up an appointment for you on Monday at 1:00 P.M. in Erin's office. During your first sales call with Erin, your call objectives will be to (1) Establish a strong relationship, (2) Share an appealing benefit of our property to create customer interest, (3) Find out if your customer is planning any conventions in the future.

As we discussed during your training class, using Erin Adkins' prospect information presented below and the sales tools in your product strategy materials, your presentation plan should be to (see Chapters 3 and 9)

1. Use compliments, comments on observations, or search for mutual acquaintances to determine which topics Erin wants to talk about (Erin will only want to talk about three of these topics). This should set the stage for a good relationship.
2. Take notes on the topics of interest to Erin so we can add them to our customer information data bank for future calls. (Erin will share three new items of information on each topic of interest, if you acknowledge interest.)
3. Show and describe an appealing and unique benefit of our facility so we will be considered for Erin's future convention needs. (Consider using the Architect's Award, p. 431.)
4. Discuss any conventions Erin may be planning.

Name: YWCA	Address: 16 Ruan Center
Contact: Erin Adkins	:
Phone: 515-555-3740	:
Title: Chairperson, Physical Fitness Programs	City: Rockport
Sec:	State: IL
Dear: Erin	ZIP: 50322

◄ **CONTACT SCREEN**

(McKee) Toni Bush, the Athletic Director of West College, supplied the following information about Erin Adkins:
1. Toni and Erin have a close relationship.
2. Erin just designed and built a new home.
3. Erin appears in local TV advertising about the YWCA.
Toni reports that in Erin's office you will observe the following:
4. An autographed picture of the Chicago Bulls basketball team
5. A Schwinn Air-dyne Fitness Cycle

◄ **NOTES WINDOW**

Comments, Compliments, and Questions	**Notes on New Items of Interest to Customer**
(Toni Bush suggested you mention his name.)	1. (Example) Toni Bush is my cousin 2. 3.
	1. 2. 3.
	1. 2. 3.

PARK INN
INTERNATIONAL™

SALES MEMORANDUM 1B

To: **Corporate Account Sales**
From: **T. J. McKee, Sales Manager**
Re: **Developing the Leigh Combs, Epic Design Systems Account (Call 1, Establishing a Relationship Strategy)**

My sales assistant has called Epic Design Systems (see following contact report) and set up an appointment for you on Monday at 1:00 P.M. in Leigh's office. During your first sales call with Leigh, your call objectives will be to (1) Establish a strong relationship, (2) Share an appealing benefit of our property to create customer interest, (3) Find out if your customer is planning any conventions in the future.

As we discussed during your training class, using Leigh Comb's prospect information presented below and the sales tools in your product strategy materials, your presentation plan should be to (see Chapters 3 and 9)

1. Use compliments, comments on observations, or search for mutual acquaintances to determine which topics Leigh wants to talk about (Leigh will only want to talk about three of these topics). This should set the stage for a good relationship.
2. Take notes on the topics of interest to Leigh so we can add them to our customer information data bank for future calls. (Leigh will share three new items of information on each topic of interest, if you verbally or nonverbally acknowledge interest.)
3. Show and describe an appealing and unique benefit of our facility so we will be considered for Leigh's future convention needs. (Consider using the Executive Chef's Award, p. 437.)
4. Discuss any conventions Leigh may be planning.

Name: Epic Design Systems	Address: 2401 West Towers
Contact: Leigh Combs	: Suite 200
Phone: 416-555-1000 X: CC:	:
Title: Customer Service Manager	City: West Rockport
Sec: Rhiannon	State: IL
Dear: Leigh	ZIP: 50265

◄ **CONTACT SCREEN**

(McKee) Linn Compiano, the Training Manager at Acme Supply Company, provided the following information about Leigh Combs:
1. Leigh has been on vacation.
2. Leigh is Linn Compiano's cousin.
Linn reports that in Leigh's office you will observe the following:
3. A large picture of Napoleon Bonaparte
4. A degree from our state university
5. An extra-large bookcase containing many business books

◄ **NOTES WINDOW**

Comments, Compliments, and Questions	Notes on New Items of Interest to Customer
(Linn Compiano mentioned that Leigh Combs just returned from a very enjoyable vacation.)	1. (Example) Spent one week in California 2. 3.
	1. 2. 3.
	1. 2. 3.

PRESALE PLAN WORKSHEET

SALES CALL 1 — ESTABLISHING A RELATIONSHIP

Name:_____

Your appointment for your first call is scheduled for (1) _____ at (2) _____

P.M. Your appointment was set up by (3) _____. On entering your prospect's office, you

will need to (4) _____ yourself, (5) _____ hands, and explain your

(6) _____ objectives. Your next step will be to make a (7) _____,

(8) _____, or do a search for mutual acquaintances or interests. When your customer opens

up and shares new information, you are instructed to (9) _____ _____ and

take (10) _____. If you are successful in getting your customer to talk about things in which

(s)he is interested, you should receive (11) _____ new pieces of relationship information.

At the appropriate time during your call you will convert attention from the (12) _____

to showing a (13) _____ device and presenting a (14) _____

_____, to interest your customer in your convention center. In completing your call

(15) _____ you are asked to (16) _____ _____ if your cus-

tomer is planning any future (17) _____. If you have not received a total of

(18) _____ new pieces of relationship information, you should go back and talk about things

of interest to your customer. The (19) _____ screen on the contact report provides factual

information about your prospect while the (20) _____ _____ contains

information that reflects your customer's interests. Erin Adkins is involved with the (21)

_____. Erin also knows (22) _____ _____

of West College. Leigh Combs is a (23) _____ _____ manager

and has just returned from (24) _____. There are at least two important items to (25)

_____ in both Erin's and Leigh's office.

ASSESSMENT FORM 1
RELATIONSHIP STRATEGY

Salesperson's Name:_____

Date:_____

Assessment Item	Excellent		Average		Poor	Did Not Do
1. Conducted good verbal introductions (shared full name, title, and company name)	10	9	8	7	6	0
2. Made good nonverbal introduction (good entrance, carriage, handshake, and seating posture)	10	9	8	7	6	0
3. Communicated call objectives (shared why salesperson was calling)	10	9	8	7	6	0
4. Verbalized effective comments and compliments (sincerely made comments and compliments on five relationship topics)	10	9	8	7	6	0
5. Kept conversation focused on customer topics (acknowledged new information provided by customer)	10	9	8	7	6	0
6. Took effective nondistractive notes (was organized and prepared to take notes)	10	9	8	7	6	0
7. Attractively showed material on convention center (was well prepared with a proof device)	10	9	8	7	6	0
8. Made effective benefit statement (made a benefit statement that appealed to customer)	10	9	8	7	6	0
9. Effectively inquired about convention needs (asked good questions about future needs)	10	9	8	7	6	0
10. Effectively thanked customer (communicated appreciation, said thank-you, indicated interest in prospect future business)	10	9	8	7	6	0

Relationship Presentation:_____

Total Points

Your Name:_____

***Return this form to salesperson and discuss
your reaction to this presentation!***

PART THREE: UNDERSTANDING YOUR CUSTOMER'S BUYING STRATEGY

PARK INN
INTERNATIONAL™

SALES MEMORANDUM 2A

To: **Association Account Salesperson**
From: **T. J. McKee, Sales Manager**
Re: **Erin Adkins Account—phone call from customer**
         (Call 2, Discovering a Customer's Buying Strategy)

Erin Adkins from the YWCA, whom you called on recently, left a message for you to stop in about a program they are planning. Congratulations on making that first call so effectively. Apparently, you established a good relationship.

As we discussed in your training program, your *call objectives* should be to

1. Reestablish your relationship
2. Discover Erin's buying conditions (the what, why, who, when, and what price needs), so we can custom fit a program for them
3. Set up an appointment to present your solution

Also, as we discussed, your *presentation plan* for this call should include (see Chapters 7 and 10)

1. In advance of your meeting, prepare general *information-gathering questions* to get your customer talking and to achieve your call objectives. (Use our form that follows.)
2. Later in your meeting, use *probing and confirmation questions* to clarify and confirm Erin's and your own perception of each buying condition.
3. During your sales meeting, write down each of Erin's buying conditions. (Use our form that follows.)
4. To end your first meeting, use your notes to construct a *summary-confirmation question* to clarify and confirm all six of Erin's buying conditions.
5. Schedule an appointment to make your presentation.

Good luck!

INFORMATION-GATHERING QUESTIONS	NOTES ON BUYING CONDITIONS
(Example: Can you share with me what you had in mind?)	(Example: Needs a small meeting room)
	1.
	2.
	3.
	4.
	5.
	6.

PARK INN
I N T E R N A T I O N A L™

SALES MEMORANDUM 2B

To: Corporate Account Salesperson
From: T. J. McKee, Sales Manager
Re: Leigh Combs Account—phone call from customer
(Call 2, Discovering a Customer's Buying Strategy)

Leigh Combs from Epic Design Systems, whom you called on recently, left a message for you to stop in about a program they are planning. Congratulations on making that first call so effectively. Apparently, you established a good relationship.

As we discussed in your training program, your *call objectives* should be to

1. Reestablish your relationship
2. Discover Leigh's buying conditions (the what, why, who, when, and what price needs), so we can custom fit a program for them
3. Set up an appointment to present your solution

Also, as we discussed, your *presentation plan* for this call should include (see Chapters 7 and 10)

1. In advance of your meeting, prepare general *information-gathering questions* designed to get your customer talking and to achieve your call objectives. (Use our form below.)
2. Later in your meeting, use *probing and confirmation questions* to clarify and confirm Leigh's and your own perceptions of each buying condition.
3. During your sales meeting, write down each of Leigh's buying conditions. (Use our form below.)
4. To end your first meeting, use your notes to construct a *summary-confirmation question* to clarify and confirm all six of Leigh's buying conditions.
5. Schedule an appointment to make your presentation.

INFORMATION-GATHERING QUESTIONS	NOTES ON BUYING CONDITIONS
(Example: Can you share with me what you had in mind?)	(Example: Needs a small meeting room)
	1.
	2.
	3.
	4.
	5.
	6.

PRESALE PLAN WORKSHEET

SALES CALL 2 — DISCOVERING A CUSTOMER STRATEGY

Name:_____

In call 2, your first objective is to (1) _____ _____ _____. To do this you should plan

to visit about (2) _____ information you acquired in call (3) _____.

Because your (4) _____ requested this meeting, you probably do not have to state your

(5) _____ _____ at the beginning of the call. The reason this meeting

was requested is because you apparently did a good job of (6) _____ _____ _____ the

_____ in call 1. In discovering your customer's needs (buying conditions) "what" refers

to services your customer needs and (7) _____ _____ refers to the

budget that your customer has. (8) _____ refers to the people coming, and

(9) _____ refers to the reason for the meeting. To secure general information you

should use (10) _____-_____ questions, and to get the details you should

use (11) _____ questions. (12) _____ questions check your

customer's and (13) _____ - _____ perceptions. (14)

_____-_____ questions are used to summarize and check a list of things the

customer needs. Active listening requires that you (15) _____ _____ so you have

a record to work from in custom fitting a solution. You will also use your (16) _____

to construct your (17) _____-_____ question. When you have re-

ceived (18) _____ buying conditions from your customer you will be prepared to set up an

(19) _____ to come back and make a (20) _____. Your second call

objective is to (21) _____, and your third call objective is to schedule an (22)

_____. Erin Adkins is in the (23) _____ accounts market, and Leigh

Combs is in the (24) _____ accounts market.

CUSTOMER STRATEGY

Salesperson's Name:_____

Date:_____

Assessment Item	Excellent		Average		Poor		Did Not Do
1. Effectively reestablished relationship (made enthusiastic comments about information from first meeting)	10	9	8	7	6		0
2. Communicated positive body language (entrance, carriage, handshake, and seating)	10	9	8	7	6		0
3. Communicated positive verbal language (used positive words, showed enthusiasm with well-modulated voice)	10	9	8	7	6		0
4. Used customer's name effectively (used name at least three times)	10	9	8	7	6		0
5. Asked quality information-gathering questions (seemed prepared, questions were general and open ended)	10	9	8	7	6		0
6. Asked quality probing questions (followed up to secure all details)	10	9	8	7	6		0
7. Verified custom needs with good confirmation questions (wanted to be correct in interpreting customer needs)	10	9	8	7	6		0
8. Appeared to take effective notes (was organized and nondistracting, used notes in confirming needs)	10	9	8	7	6		0
9. Effectively set up next appointment (requested another meeting; suggested and wrote down date, time, and place)	10	9	8	7	6		0
10. Effectively thanked customer (communicated appreciation, said thank you, indicated enthusiasm for next meeting)	10	9	8	7	6		0

Discovering Customer Needs Presentation:_____

Total Points

Return this form to salesperson and discuss your reaction to this presentation!

Your Name:_____

PART FOUR: DEVELOPING A SALES PRESENTATION STRATEGY

PARK INN
I N T E R N A T I O N A L™

SALES MEMORANDUM 3A

To: **Association Account Sales**
From: **T. J. McKee, Sales Manager**
Re: **Your recent meeting on the Erin Adkins Account**
        (Call 3, Developing a Presentation Strategy)

Congratulations on doing such a thorough job of discovering Erin's buying conditions. I found that your list of buying conditions includes the kind of customer information important to increasing our sales and partnering with our clients. I would like to see a copy of Erin's proposal when you complete it.

Reviewing what we discussed during your training, your next call objectives are

1. Make a persuasive sales presentation that custom fits your proposal to Erin's needs
2. Negotiate any concerns Erin may have
3. Close and confirm the sale
4. Build repeat and referral business

Also, as we discussed, your *presentation plan* for this call should be to

1. Prepare and price a product solution that meets Erin's needs. *Complete the Sales Proposal Worksheet* (p. 475).
2. Before your sales call, prepare a *portfolio* presentation (see model on p. 474) that follows these guidelines.
   a. Review the relationship information, and prepare for those topics you will discuss.
   b. Prepare a summary-confirmation question that verifies the buying conditions secured in your second call (see Chapter 10).
   c. Select sales tools (proof devices), and create feature/benefit selling statements that appeal to Erin's buying conditions (see Chapter 11).
   d. Plan confirmation questions that verify Erin's acceptance of your solution to each buying condition. *Complete Strategic Planning Form A2* (p. 478) for items b, c, and d.
   e. Prepare to negotiate the time, price, source, and product objections. *Complete Strategic Planning Form B* (p. 479) (see Chapter 12).
   f. Prepare at least four closing methods in addition to the summary of benefits. *Complete Strategic Planning Form C* (p. 480) (see Chapter 13).
   g. Plan methods to service the sale. Follow up by scheduling an appointment between now and the convention date (telephone call or personal visit) to follow through on guarantees concerning rooms and meals, suggestions about audio visual needs, and any possible changes in the convention schedule. *Complete Strategic Planning Form D* (p. 481) (see Chapter 14).
3. During the sales call reestablish the relationship, and using your portfolio presentation
   a. Confirm all of Erin's previous buying conditions
   b. Match a proof device and feature/benefit selling statement with each buying condition
   c. Confirm Erin's acceptance to each of your proposed benefit statements
   d. Negotiate any sales resistance
   e. Close the sale
   f. Service the sale to get repeats and referrals

Good luck!

PARK INN
INTERNATIONAL™

SALES MEMORANDUM 3B

To: **Corporate Account Sales**
From: **T. J. McKee, Sales Manager**
Re: **Your recent meeting on the Leigh Combs Account**
(Call 3, Developing a Presentation Strategy)

Congratulations on doing such a thorough job of discovering Leigh's buying conditions. I found that your list of buying conditions includes the kind of customer information important to increasing our sales and partnering with our clients. I would like to see a copy of Leigh's proposal when you complete it.

Reviewing what we discussed during your training, your next *call objectives* are

1. Make a persuasive sales presentation that custom fits your proposal to Leigh's needs
2. Negotiate any concerns Leigh may have
3. Close and confirm the sale
4. Build repeat and referral business

Also, as we discussed, your *presentation plan* for this call should be to

1. Prepare and price a product solution that meets Leigh's needs. *Complete the Sales Proposal Worksheet* (p. 475).
2. Before your sales call, prepare a *portfolio* presentation (see model on p. 474) that follows these guidelines:
   a. Review the relationship information, and prepare for those topics you will discuss.
   b. Prepare a summary-confirmation question that verifies the buying conditions secured in your second call (see Chapter 10).
   c. Select sales tools (proof devices), and create feature/benefit selling statements that appeal to Leigh's buying conditions (see Chapter 11).
   d. Plan confirmation questions that verify Leigh's acceptance of your solution to each buying condition. *Complete Strategic Planning Form A2* (p. 478) for items b, c, and d.
   e. Prepare to negotiate the time, price, source, and product objections. *Complete Strategic Planning Form B* (p. 479) (see Chapter 12).
   f. Prepare at least four closing methods in addition to the summary-of-benefits close. *Complete Strategic Planning Form C* (p. 480) (see Chapter 13).
   g. Plan methods to service the sale. Follow up by scheduling an appointment between now and the convention date (telephone call or personal visit) to follow through on guarantees concerning rooms and meals, suggestions about audio visual needs, and any possible changes in the convention schedule. *Complete Strategic Planning Form D* (p. 481) (see Chapter 14).
3. During the sales call reestablish the relationship, and using your portfolio presentation
   a. Confirm all of Leigh's previous buying conditions
   b. Match a proof device and feature/benefit selling statement with each buying condition
   c. Confirm Leigh's acceptance to each of your proposed benefit statements
   d. Negotiate any sales resistance
   e. Close the sale
   f. Service the sale to get repeats and referrals

Good luck!

PRESALE PLAN WORKSHEET
SALES CALL 3 — DEVELOPING A PRESENTATION

Name:_____

In opening your third sales call, your first activity should be to (1) _____ the relationship. To do this you will comment on topics discussed in call number (2) _____. After this step, you will make a (3) _____ type presentation. The first page in your presentation will be a (4) _____ of items discovered in call (5) _____. To present this you will use a (6) _____ _____ question. If your customer (7) _____ you will return to the (8) _____ (9) _____ condition, repeat it, and show a (10) _____ _____ from your (11) _____ strategy materials. In describing what you have shown, you will make one or more (12) _____ statements, and then you will use a (13) _____ _____ to see if your customer agrees and likes your solution. If your customer disagrees with any of your (14) _____ statements or raises a concern, you have an (15) _____ to overcome or (16) _____. If your customer agrees you will proceed on through all (17) _____ buying conditions. After you have successfully gone through all the buying instructions, you are instructed to summarize the (18) _____ and (19) _____ the sale. Prior to the customer signing your sales proposal, you will need to overcome the (20) _____ concerns. After addressing each concern you should try to (21) _____ the sale. Overcoming these concerns is best accomplished by you (22) _____ them and preparing ahead of time. After closing you will (23) _____ _____ _____ by scheduling an (24) _____ to follow up on meeting details, such as (25) _____ concerning rooms and meals.

ASSESSMENT FORM 3

PRESENTATION STRATEGY

Salesperson's Name:_____
Date:_____

Assessment Item	Excellent	Average		Poor	Did Not Do
1. Reestablished a good relationship (talked sincerely and enthusiastically about topics of interest to customer) Comments:	10	9	8	7	6	0
2. Confirmed needs from previous meeting Comments:	10	9	8	7	6	0
3. Made solution sound appealing (used nontechnical, customer-oriented benefit statements) Comments:	10	9	8	7	6	0
4. Used proof devices to prove sales appeals (made product sound appealing) Comments:	10	9	8	7	6	0
5. Verified customer's understanding of solution Comments:	10	9	8	7	6	0
6. Negotiated price objection (established high value to price impression) Comments:	10	9	8	7	6	0
7. Negotiated time objection (Created need to sign now using empathy) Comments:	10	9	8	7	6	0
8. Negotiated source objection (knew the competition well) Comments:	10	9	8	7	6	0
9. Asked for the order, closed sale (attempted to close after each objection) Comments:	10	9	8	7	6	0
10. Serviced the sale (established relationship that would result in referrals or repeat sales opportunities) Comments:	10	9	8	7	6	0

Overall quality of sales portfolio and proof devices

Comments:

	25	20	15	0	5	0

Presentation Points
_____

Total Points
_____

Return this form to salesperson and discuss your reaction to this presentation!

Your Name:_____

PORTFOLIO PRESENTATION MODEL

Three-ring binder with pockets recommended

PAGE 1 Summary of Customer's Buying Conditions 1. 2. 3. 4. 5. 6. (confirmation question)	**PAGE 2** Buying Condition 1	**PAGE 3** Proof Devices (could be more than one) (state benefits, ask confirmation question)	**PAGE 4** Buying Condition 2
PAGE 5 Proof Devices (state benefits, ask confirmation question)	**PAGE 6** Buying Condition 3	**PAGE 7** Proof Devices (state benefits, ask confirmation question)	**PAGE 8** Buying Condition 4
PAGE 9 Proof Devices (state benefits, ask confirmation question)	**PAGE 10** Buying Condition 5	**PAGE 11** Proof Devices (state benefits, ask confirmation question)	**PAGE 12** Buying Condition 6
PAGE 13 Proof Devices (state benefits, ask confirmation question)	**PAGE 14** Summary of Benefits 1. 2. 3. 4. 5. 6. (trial close)	**FRONT POCKET MATERIALS** Additional value-added pages as needed to over- come sales resistance and close the sale	**BACK POCKET MATERIALS** Additional value-added pages as needed to service the sale

PARK INN
INTERNATIONAL™

SALES PROPOSAL

Customer Name: _____ Title: _____

Organization Name: _____ Telephone: _____

Address: _____

Date(s) of Meetings: _____

Kind of Meetings: _____

Buying Conditions (Needs): _____
_____
_____

A. Meal Functions Needed

	Time	Description	Quantity	Price	Total
Meal 1					
Meal 2					
Other		(Beverages, setup fees, etc.)			

Total _____

Sales Tax _____

Service Charge _____

Total Meal Cost _____

B. Meeting and Banquet Rooms and Equipment Needed
(Describe time, date, and cost)

Total _____

Sales Tax _____

Total Meeting/Banquet Rooms and Equipment Charges _____

C. Guest Rooms Needed

Number of Rooms Needed	Description (dates, locations, special conditions)	Group Rate Per Room	Total Cost

Total _____

Room Tax _____

Sales Tax _____

Total Guest Room Charges _____

D. Total Customer Costs (from above)

A. $_____ plus B. $_____ plus C. $_____ equals **Total Charges** $ _____

_____   _____   _____   _____
Authorized Signature   Date   Customer Signature   Date

_____   _____
Title   Title

PARK INN
INTERNATIONAL™

555 West Side Street, Rockport, IL 50322
618-225-0925   Fax 618-225-9386

MEETING AND BANQUET ROOM SCHEDULE OF EVENTS

1ST THURSDAY OF NEXT MONTH

Central Park East
>   Open—Expect confirmation tomorrow

Central Park West
>   Open—Expect confirmation tomorrow

Park Lane
>   10:00 A.M. C of C Membership Committee
>   2:00 P.M. County Central Planning Committee

Top of the Park
>   Open—Expect confirmation tomorrow

Revolver
>   Open

Dance Floor
>   7:00 P.M. IBM Dinner and Dance

Parkview
>   Open—Expect confirmation tomorrow

1007 and 1009
>   11:00 A.M. Advertising Prof's Luncheon
>   7:00 P.M. IBM Communication Seminar

107 and 109
>   10:00 A.M.—Expect confirmation tomorrow

ATTENTION: Phone 225-0925, ext. 8512
immediately to confirm reservations.

STRATEGIC SALES PLANNING FORM A2

MATCHING BUYING CONDITIONS WITH PROOF DEVICES AND FEATURE/BENEFITS

BUYING CONDITION *You indicated you wanted . . .*	PROOF DEVICE *Here is . . .*	FEATURE *which has (have) . . .*	BENEFIT *which means to you . . .*	CONFIRMATION QUESTION *What do you think?*
1. ___ (number) guest rooms	A picture of one of our guest rooms (see p. 441)	Just been remodeled	Your people will enjoy clean, comfortable, spacious, and attractive surroundings	Is that what you had in mind?
2.				
3.				
4.				
5.				
6.				

Optional Role Play 3-A Instructions (see Chapters 10 and 11)

Step 1 Prepare your presentation plan by completing the above form.

Step 2 Organize your presentation plan by placing the above information on $8\frac{1}{2}'' \times 11''$ sheets of paper according to the portfolio presentation plan on page 474. Select proof devices from the product strategy materials presented on pages 425–456 and the completed proposal on page 475.

Step 3 Using the portfolio materials you have prepared, pair off with another student who will play the role of your customer. Review your customer's buying conditions, present your solutions with benefit statements, prove your sales appeals with demonstrations, secure your customer's reactions and summarize the benefits presented. Discuss your customer's reactions to your presentation. This exercise will help you prepare for call 3.

STRATEGIC PLANNING FORM B

ANTICIPATING AND NEGOTIATING SALES RESISTANCE WORKSHEET

PART I	ANTICIPATING SALES RESISTANCE	PART II	NEGOTIATING SALES RESISTANCE
Type	What Customer Might Say	Methods*	What You Will Say (Include Proof Devices you will use)
Time	"I would like to take a day to think over your proposal."	Indirect denial	"I understand, but . . . ." (Show p. 477, Schedule of Events.)
Price	"That price is way over my budget."		
Source	"I'm going to check with the Marriott."		
Product	"I'm concerned about the size of your meeting rooms."		

Optional Role Play 3-B Instructions

Using the preceding material you have prepared, pair off with another student who will play the role of your customer. Provide your customer with the material in Part I and instruct her to raise sales resistance in any order she chooses. Playing the role of the salesperson, you will respond with the material you prepared in Part II. Continue the dialogue until all the types of sales resistance have been successfully negotiated. Discuss with your customer her reaction to your methods of successfully negotiating the different types of sales resistance. This exercise will help you prepare for Sales Call 3.

*Method of Negotiating Sales Resistance: (see Chapter 12)

- Direct Denial
- Indirect Denial
- Question
- Third Party
- Superior Benefit
- Demonstration
- Trial Offer
- Feel, Felt, Found

STRATEGIC PLANNING FORM C

CLOSING AND CONFIRMING THE SALE WORKSHEET

PART I	PART II	
Verbal and Nonverbal Closing Clues	Method of Closing*	What You Will Say (Include proof devices you will use)
Agreement with each benefit	Summary of the benefits and direct appeal	"Let me review what we have talked about . . . . May I get your signature?" (Use p. 475, Sales Proposal.)
Agreement after an objection to price, time, or source	Assumption	
Appears enthusiastic and impatient	Trial close and assumption	
Agreement with all benefits but will not under any circumstances go over budget	Special concession	
Agreement with all benefits except closing today	Negotiate the single problem	

Optional Role Play 3-C Instructions

Using the preceding material you have prepared, pair off with another student who will play the role of your customer. Provide your customer with the appropriate closing clues from Part I and instruct him to provide verbal or non-verbal closing clues in any order he chooses. Playing the role of the salesperson, you will respond with the material you prepared in Part II. Continue the dialogue until you have responded to all the anticipated closing clues. Discuss with your customer his reaction to your methods of successfully closing and confirming the sale. This exercise will help you prepare for Sales Call 3.

*Method of Closing the Sale (see Chapter 13)

- Trial Close
- Summary of the Benefits
- Assumption
- Special Concession
- Negotiate the Single Problem
- Limited Choice
- Direct Appeal

STRATEGIC PLANNING FORM D

SERVICING THE SALE WORKSHEET

PART I	PART II
What You Will Do to Add Value to the Sale	What You Will Say or Write to Add Value to the Sale
1. Schedule appointments to confirm rooms and final counts on meals. Dates Time 1_____ 1_____ 2_____ 2_____	"I would like to call to confirm . . . ." (Show p. 456, Convention Center Policies, and write date and time on your calendar.)
2. Make suggestions during next meeting about audio visual equipment, beverages for breaks, etc.	
3. Provide personal assurances concerning your continuing efforts to make the meeting an outstanding success.	
4. Prepare thank-you letter concerning call 3.	

Optional Role Play 3-D Instructions

Using the preceding material you have prepared, pair off with another student who will play the role of your customer. Using the topics identified in Part I, verbally present what you have prepared in Part II on this form. Discuss with your customer her reaction to your methods of servicing the sale. This exercise will help you prepare for Sales Call 3.

Method of Servicing the Sale (see Chapter 14)

- Suggestion Selling
- Follow through on Promises and Obligations
- Follow up to ensure Customer Satisfaction

END NOTES

CHAPTER 1

1. *The Sales Engine: At the Heart of Economic Development* (Pasadena, CA: Intelecom).
2. Interview with Zak Mandour, May 13, 1996.
3. Gail E. Schares, "Colgate-Palmolive Is Really Cleaning up in Poland," *Business Week*, March 15, 1993, pp. 54–56.
4. Roger Brooksbank, "The New Model of Personal Selling: Micromarketing," *Journal of Personal Selling & Sales Management*, Spring 1995, pp. 61–66.
5. Thomas A. Stewart, "After All You've Done For Your Customers, Why Are They Still Not Happy?" *Fortune*, December 11, 1995, p. 179.
6. Jaclyn Fierman, "Americans Can't Get No Satisfaction," *Fortune*, December 11, 1995, p. 187.
7. Robert Frank, "Frito-Lay Devours Snack-Food Business," *Wall Street Journal*, October 27, 1995, p. B-1.
8. William D. Perreault and E. Jerome McCarthy, *Basic Marketing: A Managerial Approach*, 12th ed. (Homewood, IL: Irwin, 1996), p. 45.
9. William J. Stanton, B. J. Walker, and M. J. Etzell, *Fundamentals of Marketing*, 10th ed. (New York: McGraw-Hill, 1994), p. 464.
10. Dennis Fox, "Ringing up Prospects," *Sales & Marketing Management*, March 1993, pp. 75–77.
11. Larry Wilson, *Changing the Game— The New Way to Sell* (New York: Simon & Schuster, 1987), p. 126.
12. Allan J. Magrath, "The Preeminence of Selling," *Sales & Marketing Management*, January 1990, p. 16.
13. Leslie Agnello-Dean, "Converting Salespeople to Consultant/Advisors," *Sales & Marketing Training*, March–April 1990, p. 18.
14. William M. Pride and O. C. Ferrell, *Marketing*, 10th ed. (Boston: Houghton Mifflin, 1997), p. 518.
15. Robert B. Miller and Stephen E. Heiman, *Strategic Selling* (New York: Warren Books, 1985), p. 26.
16. "Menu Analysis: Key to the Sale," *Institutional Distribution*, May 15, 1990, pp. 122–124.
17. Fiona Gibb, "The New Sales Basics," *Sales & Marketing Management*, April 1995, p. 81.
18. John O'Toole, "Get Inside Your Clients Skin," *Selling*, May 1995, p. 77.
19. Francy Blackwood, "Equal, But Not Separate," *Selling*, June 1996, pp. 74–75. "Books & Videos," *Training*, February 1996, p. 62.
20. John Heinrich, "Relationship Selling," *Personal Selling Power*, May–June 1995, p. 32.
21. Arthur Andersen Retailing Issues Letter, November 1992, p. 4.
22. "Replacing Suppliers with Partners," *Inside PR*, October 1990, p. 10.
23. Thayer C. Taylor, "Electronics in Sales: Best Is Yet to Come," *Sales & Marketing Management*, July 1994, p. 40.
24. C. D. Peterson, "The Owner's Edge," *Success*, May 1990, p. 12.

SOURCES FOR BOXED FEATURES

a. "Salesmen in the Middle Kingdom," *U.S. News and World Report*, January 11, 1988. Joseph Kahn, "P & G Viewed China as a National Market and Is Conquering It," *Wall Street Journal*, September 12, 1995, pp. A-1 and A-7. Karl Schoenberger, "Motorola Bets Big on China," *Fortune*, May 27, 1996, pp. 116 and 118.

b. Harvey B. Mackay, "Humanize Your Selling Strategy," *Harvard Business Review*, March–April 1988, p. 36. "Mutual Fund Investors Have 7,607 Choices," *The San Jose Mercury News*, May 7, 1995, p. 50.

c. Ralph W. Clark and Alice Darnell Lattal, "The Ethics of Sales: Finding an Appropriate Balance," *Business Horizons*, July–August 1993, p. 66.

CHAPTER 2

1. Charles Butler, "Why the Bad Rap?" *Sales and Marketing Management*, June 1996, p. 64.
2. *Statistical Abstract of the United States*, 1995, 115th ed. (Washington, DC: U.S. Department of Commerce, 1995), p. 412.
3. Gerhard Gschwandtner, "Street Smart" *Personal Selling Power*, January–February 1993, p. 29.
4. William Keenan Jr., "Sales Compensation 1996–1997," Supplement to *Selling*, February 1997.
5. "1995 Industry Report," *Training*, October 1995, p. 38.
6. "Sales Serves as Road to Managerial Success for Women," *Sales & Marketing Management*, May 1993, p. 14. "A Show of Force," *Selling*, January–February 1995, p. 15.
7. Barry L. Reece and Rhonda Brandt, *Effective Human Relations in Organizations* (Boston: Houghton Mifflin, 1996), p. 412.
8. "Big Deal Worth the Price," *Selling*, July–August 1996, p. 14.
9. Francy Blackwood, "5 Hot Fields," *Selling*, July–August 1995, p. 49.
10. Ibid., pp. 54–56.
11. Leonard Berry, "Stores with a Future," *Retailing Issues Letter*, March 1995, p. 2.
12. Robert Kreitner, Barry L. Reece, and James P. O'Grady, *Business*, 2nd ed. (Boston: Houghton Mifflin, 1990), p. 376.

13. "Telemarketing Rings in New Business Era," *Advertising Age*, January 27, 1986, p. 52.
14. Francy Blackwood, "Selling With vs. Selling To," *Selling*, December 1995, pp. 28–29.
15. Linda Corman, "Look Who's Selling Now," *Selling*, July–August 1996, pp. 46–53.
16. Ibid., p. 53.
17. Malcolm Fleschner, "The Little Pickup That Could," *Personal Selling Power*, April 1993, pp. 28–29.
18. "Hidden Sellers," *Success*, May 1993, p. 23.
19. James Koch, "Portrait of the CEO as Salesman," *Inc.*, March 1988, p. 45.
20. Bill Kelley, "Training: 'Just Plain Lousy' or 'Too Important to Ignore'?" *Sales & Marketing Management*, March 1993, p. 68.
21. "Professionalism in Selling," *Personal Selling Power*, January–February 1993, p. 21.
22. "Ticket to Ride," *Personal Selling Power*, May–June 1992, p. 42.
23. News Release issued by Certified Marketing Services, Inc. September 6, 1996.

SOURCES FOR BOXED FEATURES

a. "Women in Sales: A New Area of Catalyst Research," *Catalyst Perspective*, New York, NY, February 1993, p. 1. Malcolm Fleschner, "Closing the Gender Gap," *Personal Selling Power*, November–December 1993, p. 31. "Professionalism in Selling," *Personal Selling Power*, January–February 1993, p. 22. Sue Shellenbarger, "Sales Offers Women Fairer Pay, but Bias Lingers," *Wall Street Journal*, January 24, 1995, p. B-1.

b. "Professionalism in Selling," *Personal Selling Power*, January–February 1993, p. 22. *Profiles in Customer Loyalty*, Learning International, Stamford, CT, 1989, p. 22.

CHAPTER 3

1. *Sales Talk: Communication Styles* (Pasadena, CA: Intelecom).
2. John Grossman, "Homework, and

Attention to Detail," *Selling*, May 1994, p. 72.

3. Daniel Goleman, *Emotional Intelligence* (New York: Bantam Books, 1995), p. 39.

4. L. B. Gschwandtner and Gerhard Gschwandtner, "Balancing Act," *Selling Power*, June 1996, p. 24.

5. Ibid.

6. Nancy S. Wood, "The Secret to Lasting Rapport," *Personal Selling Power*, March 1993, p. 52.

7. Denis Waitley, *Empires of the Mind* (New York: William Morrow, 1995), p. 3.

8. Jonathan J. Ward, "Foolish Inconsistency," *Sales & Marketing Management*, March 1993, p. 32.

9. J. D. Power and Associates, *Fact Sheet* (Los Angeles, CA: 1993).

10. "Partnering: The Heart of Selling Today" (Des Moines, IA: American Media Incorporated, 1990).

11. Larry Wilson, "Selling in the 90s" (Chicago: Nightingale Conant, 1988), p. 35.

12. Madelyn Callahan, "Teaching the Sales Relationship," *Training and Development*, December 1992, p. 35.

13. Maxwell Maltz, *Psycho-Cybernetics* (Englewood Cliffs, NJ: Prentice-Hall, 1960), p. 2.

14. "The Keys to Good Selling," *Sales & Marketing Management*, January 1990, p. 32.

15. Barry L. Reece and Rhonda Brandt, *Effective Human Relations in Organizations* 6th ed. (Boston: Houghton Mifflin 1996), pp. 110–111.

16. Denis Waitley, *The Double Win* (Old Tappan, NJ: Fleming H. Revell Company, 1985), p. 31.

17. Robert B. Miller and Stephen E. Heiman, *Strategic Selling* (New York: Warner Books, 1985), p. 60.

18. "The Strength of Character," *Royal Bank Letter* (Royal Bank of Canada, May–June 1988), p. 1.

19. Jan Gelman, "How to Make a Great First Impression," Selling, July–August, 1995, p. 60.

20. Ginger Trumfio, "More than Words," *Sales & Marketing Management*, April 1994, p. 55.

21. "Get to the Truth of the Message," *The Pryor Report*, Vol. VI, No. 1A, p. 7.

22. Susan Bixler, *The Professional Image* (New York: Putnam Publishing Group, 1984), p. 216.

23. "Handshaking Tips," National Association for Professional Saleswomen, June 1983, p. 4.

24. Adapted from Leonard Zunin, *Contact: The First Four Minutes* (New York: Nash Publishing, Ballantine Books, 1972), p. 109.

25. "Name That Customer," *Personal Selling Power*, January–February 1993, p. 48.

26. Janet G. Elsea, *The Four-Minute Sell* (New York: Simon & Schuster, 1984), p. 34.

27. Rich Wilkins, "Serve and Ye Shall Get," *Personal Selling Power*, March 1993, p. 40.

28. Leonard Zunin, *Contact: The First Four Minutes* (New York: Nash Publishing, Ballantine Books, 1972), p. 109.

29. John T. Molloy, *Dress for Success* (New York: Peter H. Wyden, 1975); *The Woman's Dress for Success Book* (Chicago: Follett Publishing, 1977); and *Live for Success* (New York: Morrow, 1981).

30. Anne M. Phaneuf, "Decoding Dress Codes," *Sales & Marketing Management*, September 1995, p. 139.

31. Susan Bixler, *Professional Presence* (New York: G. P. Putnams' Sons, 1991), p. 141.

32. Kathleen A. Bishop, "The Silent Signals," *Training and Development Journal*, June 1985, p. 36.

33. Paul Galanti, "Talking Motivates—Communication Makes Things Happen," *Personal Selling Power*, November–December 1995, p. 88.

34. "Giving Great Presentations," *Success*, May 1990, p. 30.

35. "When in Japan," *Sales & Marketing Management*, June 1990, p. 38.

36. "Sales-Related Book Picked in Top Ten for Shaping America's Culture," *Des Moines Register*, April 3, 1985, p. 3.

37. Barry L. Reece and Rhonda Brandt, *Effective Human Relations in Organiza-*

tions, 6th ed. (Boston: Houghton Mifflin, 1996), pp. 485–486.

38. L. B. Gschwandtner, "Mary Lou Retton," *Personal Selling Power*, 15th Anniversary Issue, 1995, p. 99.

39. Shad Helmstetter, *What to Say When You Talk to Yourself* (New York: Pocket Books, 1982), p. 72.

SOURCES FOR BOXED FEATURES

a. Anthony Alessander, "Qualities That Make a Top DSR," *Institutional Distribution*, August 1988, p. 40.

b. Robert McGarvey and Scott Smith, "Etiquette 101," *Training*, September 1993, p. 51; Ann C. Humphries, "Errors Steal Power from Power Lunch," *San Jose Mercury News*, November 4, 1990, p. 2.

c. Janet G. Elsea, *The Four-Minute Sell* (New York: Simon & Schuster, 1984), p. 9.

d. "Portrait of a Broker at the Top of His Form," *Success*, September 1986, p. 51; Don Wallace, "Update on Hansberger," *Success*, May 1990, p. 50.

CHAPTER 4

1. Leslie Scism, "Some Agents 'Churn' Life-Insurance Policies, Hurt Their Customers," *Wall Street Journal*, January 3, 1995, p. 1.

2. "Can Art Ryan Move 'The Rock'?" *Business Week*, August 5, 1996, p. 70.

3. Stephen R. Covey, *The 7 Habits of Highly Effective People* (New York: Simon & Schuster, 1989), p. 18.

4. "Values Added," *Inc.*, January 1986, p. 3.

5. Betsy Weisendanger, "Doing the Right Thing," *Sales & Marketing Management*, March 1991, p. 83.

6. Robert Levering, Milton Maskowitz, and Michael Katz, *The 100 Best Selling Companies to Work for in America* (New York: New American Library, 1985), p. 206.

7. Ibid., 1985, p. 310.

8. Ibid., p. 326.

9. Dawn Anfuso, "Soul-Searching Sustains Values at Lotus Development," *Personnel Journal*, June 1994, pp. 54–61.

10. Robert Nylera, "Scruples in the Real World," *Selling*, May 1995, pp. 75–76.

11. Dawn Marie Driscoll, "Don't Confuse Legal and Ethical Standards," *Business Week*, July–August 1996, p. 44.

12. Julia Lawlor, "Stepping Over the Line," *Sales & Marketing Management*, October, 1995, pp. 90–101.

13. Bob Cox, "Good Ethics Mean Good Business during Hard Times," *Des Moines Register*, April 19, 1993, p. B-21.

14. Dawn Marie Driscoll, "Don't Confuse Legal and Ethical Standards," *Business Week*, July–August 1996, p. 44.

15. George Kegley, "Broker With a Difference: A. G. Edwards, Chairman," *Roanoke Times & World-News*, April 13, 1990, p. B-6.

16. Leslie Scism, "Prudential Management Knew of Abuses by Its Agents, Regulators Report Says," *Wall Street Journal*, July 9, 1996, p. B-6.

17. Thomas J. Peters and Robert H. Waterman, Jr., *In Search of Excellence* (New York: Harper & Row, 1982), p. 6.

18. "Rivalries, Law Policies Take a Toll on Ethics," *Wall Street Journal*, March 22, 1990, p. B-1.

19. "Business's Big Morality Play," *Dun's Review*, August 1980, p. 56.

20. Dena Bunis, "Sex in Business: Scandal Generates Concerns," *Roanoke Times & World News*, August 12, 1990, p. D-9.

21. Fiona Gibb, "To Give or Not to Give," *Sales & Marketing Management*, September 1994, pp. 136–139.

22. Linda Corman, "The 13 Sins of Selling," *Selling*, September 1994, p. 77.

23. Steven Sack, "Watch the Words," *Sales & Marketing Management*, July 1, 1985, p. 56.

24. Ibid.

25. Rob Zeiger, "Sex, Sales & Stereotypes," *Sales & Marketing Management*, July 1995, pp. 52 and 53.

26. Carol Wheeler, "Getting the Edge on Ethics," *Executive Female*, May–June 1996, p. 47.

27. "What Is the Best Advice on Selling You Have Ever Been Given?" *Sales & Marketing Management*, February 1990, p. 9.

28. Gerhard Gschwandtner, "Lies and Deception in Selling," *Personal Selling Power*, 15th Anniversary Issue, 1995, p. 62.

SOURCES FOR BOXED FEATURES

a. "The Greatest Capitalist in History," *Fortune*, August 31, 1987, p. 31; Jeffrey P. Davidson, "Integrity: The Primary Sales Tool," *Personal Selling Power*, November–December 1986, p. 22.

b. Urban C. Lehner, "Native Intelligence," *Wall Street Journal*, December 10, 1993, p. R-16; John Bussey and James McGregor, "What, Why and How," *Wall Street Journal*, December 10, 1993, p. R-19.

c. Robert Mager, *Developing Attitude toward Learning* (Belmont, CA: Lear Siegler/Fearon Publishers, 1968), p. 61.

d. "Putting First Things First," *Inc.*, December 1987, p. 168.

e. "Managing Values," *Inc.*, September 1987, p. 10.

CHAPTER 5

1. *In Position: Product Selling Strategies* (Pasadena, CA: Intelecom).

2. "Software Gives Reps a Hand," *Sales and Management Technology*, March 1996, p. 6.

3. Susan Caminiti, "What the Scanner Knows about You," *Fortune*, December 3, 1990, p. 51.

4. "Rubbermaid—Breaking All the Molds," *Sales & Marketing Management*, August 1992, p. 42.

5. "Mutual Fund Investors Have 7,607 Choices," *San Jose Mercury News*, May 7, 1995, p. 50.

6. John Naisbitt, *Megatrends* (New York: Warner Books, 1982), p. 24.

7. Lawrence Edelman and Jane Fitz Simon, "Sales Force Tarnishes Digital," *San Jose Mercury News*, October 15, 1989, p. E1.

8. "97 Ways to Sell More in '96," *Selling*, January–February 1996, p. 53.

9. Interview with Michael Wright, MBNA American Bank N.A., Newark, DE, Spring 1992.

10. Tom Peters, *Thriving on Chaos* (New York: Alfred A. Knopf, 1988), p. 159.

11. "TQM: Forging Ahead or Falling Behind," *Human Resources Focus*, July 1993, p. 24.

12. Interview with Michael Wright, MBNA American Bank N.A., Newark, DE, Spring 1992.

13. Interview with Michelle A. Reece, The Certified Medical Representatives Institute, Inc., Roanoke, VA, July 19, 1996.

14. James X. Mullen, "In (Name Here) We Trust," *Selling*, October 1995, p. 79.

15. "Name That Brand," *Fortune*, July 4, 1988, p. 11.

16. Robert Levering and Milton Moskowitz, *The 100 Best Companies to Work for in America* (New York: New American Library, 1993), p. 373.

17. Ibid., p. 343.

18. "A New Chain of Command," *Personal Selling Power*, January–February 1995, p. 58.

19. "Grassroots Problem Solving," *Inc.*, March 1996, p. 92.

20. "From Xerox," *Personal Selling Power*, April 1993, p. 12.

21. "Plant Tours," *Agency Sales Magazine*, June 1996, p. 31.

22. Alan Test, "The Scoop on the Competition," *Personal Selling Power*, November–December 1995, p. 38.

23. "Best Advice," *Sales & Marketing Management*, January 1990, p. 34.

24. "Software Aids for Sales Reps," *Success*, May 1990, p. 29.

25. Andy Cohen, "Long-Distance Learning," *Sales & Marketing Management*, June 1996, p. 55.

26. Interview conducted with Joseph Vadala, May 20, 1993.

27. "Group Selling," *Success*, May 1990, p. 29.

SOURCES FOR BOXED FEATURES

a. Bernard Smith, "Product Training Series Not Just for Sales Reps,"

NPTA Management News, November 1993, p. 27.

b. Edwin McDowell, "Ritz-Carlton's Keys to Good Service," *New York Times*, March 31, 1993, p. D-1; Jennifer Walsh, "The Pursuit of a Benchmark: How Nissan/Infiniti Developed Its Service Standard," *Multinational Business*, The Economist Intelligence Unit, New York, NY, Winter 1992–93, pp. 24–25; "Ritz-Carlton Hotel Company Receives ASTD Corporate Award," *American Society for Training and Development*, Alexandria, VA, May 10, 1993, pp. 1–3.

CHAPTER 6

1. Andy Cohen, "Starting Over," *Sales & Marketing Management*, September 1995, pp. 40–41.
2. Joanna J. Johnson, "A New Perspective on Marketing," *Construction Dimensions Magazine*, April 1990, p. 13.
3. Teri Lammers, "The Open-Book Travel Analysis," *Inc.*, July 1992, p. 95.
4. Tom Peters, *Thriving on Chaos* (New York: Alfred A. Knopf, 1988), pp. 89–91.
5. Edward O. Welles, "Virtual Realities," *Inc.*, August 1993, pp. 50–58.
6. Carl K. Clayton, "Sell Quality, Service, Your Company, Yourself," *Personal Selling Power*, January–February 1990, p. 47.
7. Francy Blackwood, "Building a Record," *Selling*, April 1996, p. 22.
8. William M. Pride and O. C. Ferrell, *Marketing*, 10th ed. (Boston: Houghton Mifflin, 1997) p. 217.
9. "Product Positioning," *Agency Sales Magazine*, June 1990, p. 59.
10. Ellen Goodman, "Have Consumers Grown Weary of Too Much Choice?" *Roanoke Times & World-News*, October 15, 1987, p. 17.
11. J. Thomas Russell and W. Ronald Lane, *Kleppner's Advertising Procedure* (Englewood Cliffs, NJ: Prentice-Hall, 1996), pp. 46–47.
12. Lawrence Ladin, "Selling Innovation: Tips for Commercial Success," *Wall Street Journal*, March 20, 1995, p. A-14.
13. "Sales Support Is Northwestern's No. 1 Policy," *Sales & Marketing Management*, June 1987, p. 66.
14. Michael D. Mondello, "Naming Your Price," *Inc.*, July 1992, p. 82.
15. Michael Treacy, "You Need a Value Discipline—But Which One?" *Fortune*, April 17, 1995, p. 195.
16. Albert D. Bates, "Pricing for Profit," *Retailing Issues Letter*, Vol. II, No. 8, September 1990, p. 2.
17. Stephanie Anderson Forest, "Chipping away at Frito-Lay," *Business Week*, July 22, 1991, p. 26.
18. Thomas Petzinger, Jr., "This Former Salesman Treats Development Like a Sacred Cow," *Wall Street Journal*, September 29, 1995, p. B-1.
19. "Assistance Galore," *Fortune*, February 1, 1998, p. 14.
20. Malcolm Fleschner and Charles Lee Browne, "Value Sells," *Selling Power*, March 1996, pp. 48–52.
21. Adopted from a model described in "Marketing Success through Differentiation—of Anything," *Harvard Business Review*, January–February, 1980.
22. Tom Peters, *Thriving on Chaos*, (New York: Alfred A. Knopf, 1988), p. 92.
23. Joanna Johnson, "A New Perspective on Marketing," *Construction Dimensions*, April 1990, p. 14.
24. Ted Levitt, *Marketing Imagination* (New York: Free Press, 1983), p. 80.
25. Ibid., p. 81.
26. Tom Peters, *Thriving on Chaos*, (New York: Alfred A. Knopf, 1988), p. 92.
27. Madalyn Callahan, "Tending the Sales Relationship," *Training and Development*, December 1992, p. 32.
28. Larry Wilson, *Changing the Game: The New Way to Sell* (New York: Simon & Schuster, 1987), p. 200.
29. Ibid., p. 201.
30. Ted Levitt, *Marketing Imagination* (New York: Free Press, 1983), p. 84.
31. Francy Blackwood, "The Concept That Sells," *Selling*, March 1995, pp. 34–36.

32. Malcolm Fleschner, "8 Hidden Benefits of High-Tech Presentations," *Personal Selling Power,* April 1993, p. 30.

33. John Fellows, "A Decent Proposal," *Personal Selling Power,* November–December 1995, p. 56.

34. Adapted from John Fellows, "A Decent Proposal."

SOURCES FOR BOXED FEATURES

a. Adapted from discussion in Leonard L. Berry, A. Parasuraman, and Valerie A. Zeithaml, "The Service-Quality Puzzle," *Business Horizons,* September–October 1988, pp. 35–43; Robert Kreitner, *Management,* 5th ed. (Boston: Houghton Mifflin, 1992), pp. 613–614.

b. Susan Moffat, "Japan's New Personalized Production," *Fortune,* October 22, 1990, p. 132.

CASE CREDITS

Francy Blackwood, "The Concept That Sells," *Selling,* March 1995, pp. 34–36; *Systems Furniture Overview,* Steelcase Incorporated, November 1995, pp. 48–50.

CHAPTER 7

1. Christopher Power, "Flops," *Business Week,* August 16, 1993, p. 76.

2. *Step by Step: The Buying Process* (Pasadena, CA: Intelecom).

3. Dick Schaaf and Tom Cothran, "Sales Training in the Era of the Customer," *Sales Training,* February 1988, p. 4.

4. "Six Selling Rules," *Training and Development Journal,* March 1988, p. 40.

5. Michael Hammer and James Champy, *Reengineering the Corporation: A Manifest for Business Revolution* (New York: Harper Business, 1993) p. 18.

6. Tom Peters and Nancy Austin, *A Passion for Excellence* (New York: Random House, 1985), p. 71.

7. Stanley Brown, "This is no Psyche Job," *Sales & Marketing Management,* March 1995, p. 32.

8. "Belonging Satisfies Basic Human Need," *Menninger Letter,* August 1995, p. 6.

9. Amy Dunkin, "Buoying Women Investors," *Business Week,* February 27, 1995, p. 126.

10. Ibid.

11. "The Sales Pyramid," *Everybody Sells Supplement to Success,* May 1992, p. 27.

12. William M. Pride and O. C. Ferrell, *Marketing,* 10th ed. (Boston: Houghton Mifflin, 1997), pp. 143–148.

13. William F. Schoell and Joseph P. Guillinan, *Marketing* (Boston: Allyn & Bacon, 1992), p. 164.

14. "Met Life Targets the Rich," *Des Moines Register,* June 5, 1993, p. 10.

15. Donella H. Meadows, "We Are, to Our Harm, What We Watch," *Roanoke Times & World-News,* October 16, 1994, p. G-3.

16. Metta Spencer, *Foundations of Modern Sociology* (Englewood Cliffs, NJ: Prentice-Hall, 1976), p. 64.

17. William J. Stanton and Charles Futtrell, *Fundamentals of Marketing,* 8th ed. (New York: McGraw-Hill, 1987), p. 114.

18. Christopher Knowlton, "Customers: A Tougher Sell," *Fortune,* September 26, 1988, p. 66.

19. Phil Kline, "Dominant Buying Motive is the Result of Strong Emotions," *Marketing News,* May 24, 1993, p. 4.

20. James Georges, "The Not-So-Stupid Americans," *Training,* July 1994, p. 90.

21. Phil Kline, "Dominant Buying Motive is the Result of Strong Emotions," *Marketing News,* May 24, 1993, p. 4.

22. "A Selling Guide to Bentonville," *Selling,* April 1994, p. 70.

23. Edith Cohen, "A View from the Other Side," *Sales & Marketing Management,* June 1990, p. 108.

24. Bill Sharfman, "The Power of Information and Quality," *Autoweek,* February 1996, p. 97.

25. Martin Everett and Betsy Wiesendanger, "Marketing by Design," *Sales & Marketing Management,* March 1992, p. 26.

26. E. Jerome McCarthy, *Basic Marketing* (Homewood, IL: Irwin Publishing, 1981), pp. 472–474.

27. Lyda Lawrence, "Phase Change: Larry Wilson on Selling in a Brave New World," *Sales Training*, February 1988, pp. 16–17.

28. William M. DeMarco and Michael D. Maginn, *Sales Competing Research Report* (Boston, MA: Forum Corporation, 1982), p. 25.

29. "Consultative Selling," *Training*, May 1988, p. 80.

30. Ibid.

31. Tom Peters and Nancy Austin, *A Passion for Excellence*, (New York: Random House, 1985), p. 45.

SOURCES FOR BOXED FEATURES

a. From an interview conducted by Paul Lienert, "John Rock—Oldsmobile's Future: Rock Solid," *Automobile*, March 1993, pp. 96–103; Mark Vaughn, "It's No Ciera, Madre," *Autoweek*, August 5, 1996, pp. 16–17.

b. Patricia 'cia' Rodemann, "Selling to the New Demographics," *Wall Paper*, February 1996, pp. 22–25; Barry L. Reece and Rhonda Brandt, *Effective Human Relations in Organizations* (Boston: Houghton Mifflin, 1996), pp. 397–399; Marlene L. Rossman, *Multicultural Marketing* (New York: AMCOM), 1994.

CHAPTER 8

1. ACT! Demonstration video, Symantec Corporation, Cupertino, CA, 1994; Stephen H. Wildstrom, "Can Your Rolodex Do This," *Business Week*, May 27, 1996, p. 18.

2. Gerhard Gschwandtner, "Thoughts to Sell By," *Personal Selling Power*, 15th Anniversary Issue, 1995, p. 122.

3. Dorothy Leeds, "Where Are the Real Decision Makers?" *Personal Selling Power*, March 1993, p. 62.

4. "Customer Relations: Covering the Bases," *Inc.* October 1987, p. 140.

5. Gerhard Gschwandtner, "The Funnel Concept," *Personal Selling Power*, May–June 1993, p. 22.

6. Gerhard Gschwandtner, "The Funnel Concept," p. 23.

7. "Eliminate Cold Calling to Heat up Sales," *Sales & Marketing Management*, August 1995, p. 31.

8. Roger Pell, "It's a Fact . . . Qualified Referrals Bring More Sales to Your Company," *Personal Selling Power*, January–February 1990, p. 30.

9. "Export Help," *Inc.*, August 1988, p. 103.

10. Donald J. Moine, "Boothmanship," *Personal Selling Power*, May–June 1986, p. 22.

11. "How Significant Are Trade Shows to Your Marketing Efforts?" *Sales & Marketing Management*, August 1992, p. 22.

12. "Advertising Scores High in Lead Generation," *Sales & Marketing Management*, April 1994, p. 25.

13. "Response Cards Enter the Electronic Age," *Sales & Marketing Management*, April 1990, p. 27.

14. Jan Gelman, "What Are You Waiting For?" *Selling*, July–August 1996, pp. 32–39.

15. "PCs Make Selling More Personal," *Sales and Marketing Digest*, October 1987, p. 98.

16. Alan Test, "Cold Calls Are Hot," *Agency Sales Magazine*, September 1995, p. 28.

17. Norman Sklarewitz, "Tiny Chemical Milling Wins Them with the Basics," *Sales & Marketing Management*, February 1990, pp. 58–59.

18. Anne Baber and Lynne Waymon, "No-Nonsense Networking," *Your Company*, Summer 1993, p. 34.

19. Michele Marchetti, "Do You Have the Knack for Networking?" *Sales & Marketing Management*, January 1996, p. 30.

20. "May I Present My Card?" *Personal Selling Power*, January–February 1993, p. 48.

21. "Hitting It Out of the Ballpark," *Inc.*, February 1996, p. 93.

22. "A Company of Lead Generators," *Inc.*, September 1987, p. 111.

23. William F. Schoell and Joseph P. Guiltinan, *Marketing* (Boston: Allyn & Bacon 1992), p. 29.

24. Tracy Emerick, "The Trouble with Leads," *Sales & Marketing Management*, December 1992, p. 58.

25. Harvey Mackay, *Swim with the Sharks* (New York: William Morrow, 1988), pp. 43, 44.

26. Thayer C. Taylor, "From Practitioner to Preacher," *Sales & Marketing Management*, February 1990, p. 86.

27. Geoffrey Brewer, "Selling to Senior Executives," *Sales & Marketing Management*, July 1996, p. 43.

28. "Prospecting Is Where the Gold Is," *Institutional Distribution*, May 15, 1990, pp. 70–72.

29. Joel R. Evans and Barry Berman, *Marketing*, 2nd ed. (New York: Macmillan, 1985), p. 235.

30. John Fellows, "Your Foot in the Door," *Selling Power*, March 1996, pp. 64, 65.

SOURCES FOR BOXED FEATURES

a. Interview with Mike Muhney, co-founder of Contact Software International, producer of ACT! contact software; Stephen H. Wildstrom, "Can Your Rolodex Do This?" *Business Week*, May 27, 1996, p. 18.

b. Peter B. Stark, "Maintaining Partnerships," *Personal Selling Power*, October 1994, p. 51.

CHAPTER 9

1. *Going the Distance: The Consultative Sales Presentation* (Pasadena, CA: Intelecom).

2. Francy Blackwood, "From Salesperson to Consultant: The Race Will Go to Those with Vision," *Selling*, July–August 1995, p. 55.

3. Regina Eisman, "Justifying Your Incentive Program," *Sales & Marketing Management*, April 1993, p. 52.

4. "6 Steps to Take Before You Sell," *Institutional Distribution*, May 15, 1990, p. 18.

5. I. Martin Jacknis, "Multiple Choice," *Inc.*, December 1987, p. 184.

6. "Set the Agenda," *Personal Selling Power*, May–June, 1995, p. 79.

7. David Greising, "The Newest Wrinkle in Buying Suits," *Business Week*, April 16, 1990, p. 96.

8. Dawn R. Detter-Schmelz and Rosemary Ramsey, "A Conceptualization of the Functions and Roles of Formalized Selling and Buying Teams," *Journal of Personal Selling & Sales Management*, Spring 1995, pp. 47, 48.

9. Cathy Hyatt Hills, "Making the Team," *Sales & Marketing Management*, February 1992, p. 54.

10. Charles Butler, "Why the Bad Rap?" *Sales & Marketing Management*, June 1996, p. 66.

11. Douglas Kott, "Pumping Iron," *Road and Track*, July 1989, pp. 60–70.

12. Malcolm Fleshner, "8 Hidden Benefits of High Tech Presentations," *Personal Selling Power*, April 1993, pp. 31, 32.

13. James E. Lukaszewski and Paul Ridgeway, "To Put Your Best Foot Forward, Start by Taking These 21 Simple Steps," *Sales & Marketing Management*, June 1990, p. 84.

14. "97 Ways to Sell More in '96," *Selling*, January–February 1996, p. 50.

15. Francy Blackwood, "Did You Sell $5 Million Last Year?" *Selling*, October 1995, pp. 44–53.

16. Michele Marchetti, "Dial 'R' for Rudeness," *Sales & Marketing Management*, December 1995, p. 33.

17. John H. Melchinger, "Get the Most from Your Telemarketing Voice," *Personal Selling Power*, November–December 1990, p. 25.

18. Dennis Fox, "Ringing up Prospects," *Sales & Marketing Management*, March 1993, p. 77.

19. Mark McCormack, *What They Don't Teach You at the Harvard Business School* (New York: Bantam Books, 1984), p. 26.

20. "Teach Trainees to Make a Good First Impression," *Training/HRD*, May 1980, p. 6.

21. Melissa Campanelli, "Sound the Alarm," *Sales & Marketing Management*, December 1994, pp. 20–25.

22. James E. Lukaszewski and P. Ridgeway, "To Put Your Best Foot Forward, Start by Taking These 21 Simple Steps," *Sales & Marketing Management*, June 1990, p. 84.

23. Abner Littel, "Selling to Women Revs up Car Sales," *Personal Sell-*

ing Power, July–August, 1990, p. 50.

24. "Six Great Upselling Questions," *Personal Selling Power*, April 1993, p. 44.

25. "Confront Call Reluctance," *Personal Selling Power*, September 1995, p. 46.

26. Alan Farnham, "Are You Smart Enough to Keep Your Job?" *Fortune*, January 15, 1996, pp. 34–42.

SOURCES FOR BOXED FEATURES

a. Barry L. Reece and Rhonda Brandt, *Effective Human Relations in Organizations*, 6th ed. (Boston: Houghton Mifflin, 1996), pp. 54–56; Charlene Marmer Solomon, "Global Operations Demand That HR Rethink Diversity," *Personnel Journal*, July 1994, p. 44; Lennie Copeland and Lewis Griggs, *Going International* (New York: Random House, 1985), p. 54.

b. *Des Moines Register*, April 3, 1985, p. 3; Stephen R. Covey, *The 7 Habits of Highly Effective People* (New York: Simon & Schuster, 1989), p. 22; Ibid., p. 34.

C H A P T E R 1 0

1. Betty Wiesendanger, "Reading His Customers Right," *Selling*, September 1996, p. 60.

2. Ibid., pp. 60–62.

3. "97 Ways to Sell More in '96," *Selling*, January–February 1996, p. 50.

4. David Peoples, *Presentations Plus* (New York: John Wiley & Sons, 1988), p. 4.

5. Thomas Petzinger, Jr., "At Deere They Know a Mad Scientist May Be a Firm's Biggest Asset," *Wall Street Journal*, July 14, 1995, p. B-1.

6. Kevin Daley, "Socrates on a Sales Call," *Marketing News*, May 6, 1996, p. 4.

7. Patricia M. Carey, "In Sales Presentations, Practice Makes Perfect," *Your Company*, Summer 1992, p. 7.

8. Gail Gabriell, "Dialogue Selling," *Success*, May 1993, p. 34.

9. Dorothy Leeds, "The Art of Asking Questions," *Training and Development*, January 1993, p. 58.

10. "How to Ask the Right Questions," *Agency Sales Magazine*, June 1990, p. 64.

11. "Getting into the Habit," *Sales & Marketing Management*, May 1996, p. 68.

12. Arthur Bragg, "Put Your Program to the Test," *Sales & Marketing Management*, February 1990, p. 10.

13. Frank Cancelliere, *Creative Listening* (audiotape) (San Francisco: New Dimensions Foundation, 1987).

14. Joseph A. DeVito, *The Interpersonal Communication Book*, 4th ed. (New York: Harper & Row, 1986), p. 52.

15. Charles Surasky, "Five Minutes to Better Listening," *Personal Selling Power*, January–February 1993, p. 68.

16. Robert A. Lupe, Jr., "Improving Your Listening Ability," *Supervisory Management*, June 1992, p. 7.

17. Ginger Trumfio, "Ready! Set! Sell!" *Sales & Marketing Management*, February 1994, p. 84.

18. "Vicki Lynn Cusick: Pioneer Moves to the Top of the Heap," *Institutional Distribution*, August 1988, p. 105.

19. Jeanne Ferguson and Maria Miller, *You're Speaking: Who's Listening?* (Chicago: Scientific Research Associates, 1980), p. 119.

20. Art Bauer, "Persuading and Selling, What Does It Take?" (*American Media Eagle*, special sales edition) (Des Moines, Iowa: American Media, June 1982), p. 2.

21. Robert Frank, "Frito-Lay Devours Snack-Food Business," *Wall Street Journal*, October 27, 1995, p. B-1.

22. Bill Saporito, "The Tough Cookie at RJR Nabisco," *Fortune*, July 18, 1988, p. 33.

23. Janny Scott, "Gotcha! Americans Are Finding It Harder and Harder to Escape the Weapons of Persuasion," *Roanoke Times & World News*, August 8, 1993, p. A-1.

24. Linda Corman, "The 13 Sins of Selling," *Selling*, September 1994, p. 76.

25. Richard Whitely, "Do Selling and Quality Mix?" *Sales & Marketing Management*, October 1993, p. 70.

26. "A Place for NLP," *Training*, December 1984, p. 20.

27. Donald J. Moine, with Linda Seard, "Whatever You Sell: Sell It with a Story," *Personal Selling Power*, January–February 1989, p. 130.

28. "97 Ways to Sell More in '96," *Selling*, p. 52.

29. Michele Marchetti, "That's the Craziest Thing I Ever Heard," *Sales & Marketing Management*, November 1995, p. 77.

SOURCES FOR BOXED FEATURES

a. Neil Rackham, *Spin Selling* (New York: McGraw-Hill, 1988), pp. 67–89.

CHAPTER 11

1. Dennis James, "Show and Tell—Presentations That Work," *Success*, May 1993, p. 44.

2. Bert Decker, *You've Got to be Believed to Be Heard* (New York: St. Martins Press), 1992, p. 33.

3. Nido Qubein, *Professional Selling Techniques* (New York: Berkley, 1983), p. 101.

4. Joseph Cillo, "The Power of Imagery and Graphics," *Presentation Products Magazine*, March 1990, p. 76.

5. Adapted from Mark Thalenberg, "Salesmen in Dangerous Territory," *Sales & Marketing Management*, June 3, 1985, p. 52.

6. Ibid., p. 53.

7. Anthony Alessandra and Phil Wexler, "The Professionalization of Selling," *Sales & Marketing Training*, February 1988, p. 42.

8. Susan Greco, "Selling on the Road," *Inc.*, March 1995, p. 109.

9. David Peoples, *Selling to the Top* (New York: John Wiley & Sons, 1993), p. 197.

10. Tom Hopkins, "Demonstrating Property to Your Clients," *The Real Estate Professional*, January–February 1996, p. 70.

11. Valerie M. Chamberlain and Catherine S. Krals, *Vocational Education Journal*, February 1993, p. 55.

12. Jan Gelman, "Mixing Dollars and Scents," *Selling*, June 1995, p. 15.

13. Steve Heimoff, "Taking the Road Less Traveled," *Wine Spectator*, October 31, 1990, pp. 67–70; Jeff Morgan, "Geyser Peak's Turnaround," *Wine Spectator*, November 15, 1995, pp. 37–40.

14. Mark Thalenberg, "Salesmen in Dangerous Territory," *Sales & Marketing Management*, June 3, 1985, p. 53.

15. Jay Levenson, "Profile of a Good Salesperson," *Purchasing Management*, December 1983, p. 6.

16. Mark Thalenberg, "Salesmen in Dangerous Territory," *Sales & Marketing Management*, June 3, 1985, pp. 50–56.

17. Merrie Spaeth, "Prop up Your Speaking Skills," *Wall Street Journal*, July 1, 1996, p. A-14.

18. "Founder of Apple Shows What's Next," *Roanoke Times & World News*, October 13, 1988, p. B5.

19. "Seeing Is Believing," *Inc.*, July 1990, p. 95.

20. "Demonstrating with Flair," *Institutional Distribution*, May 15, 1990, p. 114.

21. Ginger Trumfio, "Ready! Set! Sell!" *Sales & Marketing Management*, February 1995, pp. 82–84.

22. "Good Paint Is Worth the Price," *Roanoke Times & World News*, March 25, 1990, p. 11.

23. "Smart Managers Use Technology to Sell Better," *Personal Selling Power*, April 1990, p. 45.

24. Melissa Campanelli and Thayer C. Taylor, "Meeting of the Minds," *Sales & Marketing Management*, December 1993, pp. 80–85.

25. Francy Blackwood, "Present Your Best Case," *Selling*, January–February 1995, pp. 26–28.

26. "The Presentation Paper Trail," *Sales & Marketing Management*, March 1995, p. 49.

27. Kristin Woods, "Mightier than the Sword," *Personal Selling Power*, October 1994, p. 48.

SOURCES FOR BOXED FEATURES

a. Gerhard Gschwandtner, "Day in the Life of a Japanese Insurance Agent: How This Sales Professional Earns over $350,000 a Year," *Personal Selling Power*, March 1992, pp. 46–50.

b. Martin Everett, "This Is the Ultimate in Selling," *Sales & Marketing Management*, August 1989, pp. 28–38.

CHAPTER 12

1. *Breaking through: Dealing with Buyer Resistance* (Pasadena, CA: Intelecom).
2. Ron Willingham, *Integrity Selling* (Garden City, NJ: Doubleday, 1987), p. 100.
3. Tom Reiley, "Step up Your Negotiating Success," *Personal Selling Power*, April 1990, p. 40.
4. Pat Paterson, "Break Down the Wall," *Institutional Distribution*, August 1988, p. 126.
5. Gregg Crawford, "Let's Negotiate," *Sales & Marketing Management*, November 1995, pp. 28–29.
6. "The Readers Forum," *Personal Selling Power*, January–February 1993, p. 12.
7. John O'Toole, "Inside the Mind of a Buyer," *Selling*, October 1994, p. 75.
8. Homer Smith, "How to Cope with Buyers Who Are Trained in Negotiation," *Personal Selling Power*, September 1988, p. 37.
9. Ibid.
10. Robert Adler, Benson Rosen, and Elliot Silverstein, "Thrust and Parry," *Training & Development*, March 1996, p. 47.
11. Homer Smith, "How to Cope with Buyers Who Are Trained in Negotiation," *Personal Selling Power*, September 1988, p. 37.
12. Robert Adler, Benson Rosen, and Elliot Silverstein, "Thrust and Parry," *Training & Development*, March 1996, p. 44.
13. Joseph Conlin, "Negotiating Their Way to the Top," *Sales & Marketing Management*, April 1996, p. 58.
14. Roland M. Sandell, "Five Sure-Fire Methods to Overcome Objections to Price," *American Salesman*, October 1976, p. 38.
15. Alan Test, "Answering the Price Objection," *Agency Sales Magazine*, April 1996, pp. 56–57.
16. Joseph Conlin, "Negotiating Their Way to the Top," *Sales & Marketing Management*, April 1996, p. 62.
17. D. Forbes Ley, "The Stall—A Decision Not to Make a Decision," *Selling Advantage* (Malvern, PA: Progressive Business Publications), 1995, pp. 1, 2.
18. Bill Voelkel, "Help Yourself Negotiate the Sale," *Sales & Marketing Management*, October 1987, p. 97.
19. Thomas C. Keiser, "Negotiating with a Customer You Can't Afford to Lose," *Harvard Business Review*, November–December 1988, p. 31.
20. Ibid.
21. Jeff Keller, "Objections? No Problem," *Selling Power*, September 1996, pp. 44–45.
22. Adapted from Nanci McCann, "Irate over Rates," *Selling*, July–August 1996, p. 25.
23. Tony Allessandra and Jim Catheart, "Turn Objections into Sales."
24. "Objections Become Opportunities," *Success*, May 1993, p. 33.
25. Richard V. Concilio, "Overcoming Sales Resistance," *Pace*, April 1988, p. 106.

SOURCES FOR BOXED FEATURES

a. "No-Dicker Car Dealers Gaining Popularity," *Marketing News*, September 28, 1992, p. 19; "Saturn Mission," *Success*, June 1993, p. 56.
b. Sarah Lubman, "Round and Round," *Wall Street Journal*, December 10, 1993, p. R-3; Urban C. Lehner, "Native Intelligence," *Wall Street Journal*, December 10, 1993, p. R-16; "Getting to Yes, Chinese Style," *Sales & Marketing Management*, July 1996, pp. 44, 45.

CHAPTER 13

1. Linda Corman, "The Slow and Steady Ryder Racer," *Selling*, January–February, 1996, pp. 56–58.
2. "How to Prosper in the New Economy," *Personal Selling Power*, January–February 1993, p. 52.
3. Andy Cohen, "Are Your Reps Afraid to Close?" *Sales & Marketing Management*, March 1996, p. 43.
4. Ibid., 43.

5. Zig Ziglar, *Secrets of Closing the Sale* (New York: Fleming H. Revelle, 1984), p. 51.

6. Ibid.

7. "How to Avoid Eleven Common Errors." *Institutional Distribution*, May 15, 1990, p. 94.

8. "The Closing Moment," *Personal Selling*, October 1995, p. 48.

9. Len D'Innocenzo, "How to Close a Sale," *Personal Selling Power*, March 1990, p. 23.

10. Kerry L. Johnson, *Sales Magic* (New York: William Morrow, 1994), pp. 192, 193.

11. Adopted from Nanci McCana, "Coming to Terms with Financing Issues," *Selling*, May 1995, pp. 25, 26.

12. "Salestalk," *Sales & Marketing Management*, May 1990, p. 116.

13. Larry Wilson, *Changing the Game: The New Way to Sell* (New York: Simon & Schuster, 1987), p. 104.

14. Jack Falvey, "Adventures in No-Man's Land," *Selling*, April 1996, pp. 83, 84.

15. Larry Wilson, *Changing the Game* (New York: Simon & Schuster, 1987), p. 56.

16. Ibid., p. 58.

SOURCES FOR BOXED FEATURES

a. *Training Guide: Ask for the Order and Get It* (Des Moines, IA: Creative Media Division, Batten Batten Hudson and Swab, 1977), p. 3.

b. Rick Hampson, "The Greatest Seller of Them All," *Roanoke Times & World-News*, November 26, 1993, p. A8; Gerald L. Manning and Barry L. Reece, *Selling Today* (Boston: Allyn and Bacon, 1984), pp. 64, 65 (personal interview with Ben Feldman).

c. Thayer C. Taylor, "Computers & Office Equipment," *Sales & Marketing Management*, September 1993, p. 59; Thayer C. Taylor, "From Practitioner to Preacher," *Sales & Marketing Management*, February, 1990, p. 86.

C H A P T E R   1 4

1. Susan Greco, "Five Ways to Blow a Sale," *Inc.*, September 1996, p. 101.

2. Jeff Rowe, "Many Still Undervalue the Fine Art of Customer Service," *Des Moines Register*, November 15, 1993, p. B-21.

3. "Relationships with Customers Must Be Job Number 1," *Food-Service Distributor*, July 1989, p. 74.

4. Joan O. Fredericks and James M. Salter, II, "Beyond Customer Satisfaction," *Management Review*, May 1995, pp. 29–32.

5. Steven Koepp, "Why Service Is so Bad," *Time*, February 2, 1987, p. 53.

6. Tom Peters and Robert Waterman, *In Search of Excellence* (New York: Harper & Row, 1982), p. 186.

7. "How to Keep Clients," *Success*, May 1989, p. 14.

8. Theodore Levitt, *The Marketing Imagination* (New York: Macmillan, 1983), p. 117, 118.

9. Adrienne Johnson, "Frank Smith Builds on His Past," *Institutional Distribution*, July 1988, p. 300.

10. "14 Routes to Longer Orders," *Institutional Distribution*, May 15, 1990, p. 116.

11. Sally J. Silberman, "An Eye for Finance," *Sales & Marketing Management*, April 1996, p. 26.

12. Andy Cohen, "Engineering Satisfied Customers," *Sales & Marketing Management*, October 1995, p. 56.

13. "How Do You Get Customer Feedback?" *Inc.*, January 1993, p. 31.

14. Nancy Friedman, "Follow-up or Foul-up: Service after the Sale," *Agency Sales Magazine*, October 1992, pp. 21–22.

15. "Customer Care—Phone Feedback," *Inc.*, June 1993, p. 30.

16. Bradley E. Wesner, "From Complaint to Opportunity," *Selling Power*, May 1996, p. 62.

17. Ibid.

18. Michael Abrams and Matthew Paese, "Wining and Dining the Whiners," *Sales & Marketing Management*, February 1993, p. 73.

19. Adopted from Ginger Trumfio, "Anything for a Client," *Sales & Marketing Management*, June 1994, pp. 102–105; Michael Traecy and Fred Wiersma, *Discipline of Market Leaders*,

(Reading, MA: Addison-Wesley 1995), pp. 144–152.

SOURCES FOR BOXED FEATURES

a. Based on interviews with Debbie McKinney.
b. Susan Bass, "Service: Changing Values," *Stores*, September 1990, p. 69.
c. Tom Peters, "Creating the Lifetime Customer," *Insight*, January, 1988, p. 29.

CHAPTER 15

1. Dana Ray, "The Secret of Success," *Personal Selling Power*, November–December 1995, pp. 80–83.
2. "Sales Agency Management #17," *Agency Sales Magazine*, September 1990, p. 56.
3. Barry J. Farber, "Not Enough Hours in the Day," *Sales & Marketing Management*, July 1995, pp. 28, 29.
4. "You Said It," *Sales & Marketing Management*, July 1990, p. 24.
5. Robert H. Tardiff, "Control Your Time," *Personal Selling Power*, May–June 1995, pp. 72, 73.
6. Hyrum W. Smith, *The 10 Natural Laws of Successful Time and Life Management* (New York: Warner Books, 1994), p. 108.
7. "Electronic Organizers: Godsends or Gimmicks," *Business Week*, February 19, 1990, p. 144.
8. "Voice-Mail: Helping to Increase Executive Efficiency," *Black Enterprise*, March 1990, p. 35.
9. Thomas J. Wall, "The ABCs of EDI," *SMT*, June 1996, pp. 30–32.
10. Richard Lewis, "Putting Sales on the Map," *Sales & Marketing Management*, August 1992, p. 79.
11. Nancy Arnott, "Brake out of the Grid!" *Sales & Marketing Management*, July 1994, pp. 68–75.
12. "Prospecting Threat Inventory," *Competitive Advantage*, July 1988, p. 7.
13. Shane R. Premeaux, R. Wayne Mondy, and Arthur Sharplin, "Stress and the First-Line Supervisor," *Supervisor Management*, July 1985, p. 36.
14. Ibid.
15. "Slow Down, You Move Too Fast," *Sales & Marketing Management*, June 1990, p. 29.
16. Veronica Fowler, "Technostress: New Disease of the 90s," *Des Moines Sunday Register*, December 6, 1992, pp. 1G and 2G.
17. Barry L. Reece and Rhonda Brandt, *Effective Human Relations in Organizations*, 6th ed. (Boston: Houghton Mifflin, 1996), p. 381.
18. "Optimism Slows Job Stress," *Menninger Letter*, May 1993, pp. 1, 2.
19. Sandra Lotz Fisher, "Stress—Will You Cope or Crack?" *Selling*, May 1996, p. 31.
20. Geoffrey Brewer, "Person-to-Person," *Sales & Marketing Management*, December 1995, p. 29.
21. Louis E. Kopolow, "Plain Talk About . . . Handling Stress," *Agency Sales Magazine*, August 1990, p. 59.

SOURCES FOR BOXED FEATURES

a. "A Briefcase Full of To-Dos," *Success*, March 1988, p. 3.
b. Shelly Branch, "A Premium Asset on Wall Street," *Black Enterprise*, December 1993, pp. 100–105.
c. Kenneth Blanchard, D. W. Edington, and Marjorie Blanchard, *The One-Minute Manager Gets Fit* (New York: William Morrow, 1986), pp. 25–28.
d. Sandra Lotz Fisher, "Stress—Will You Cope or Crack?" *Selling*, May 1996, p. 29.

CHAPTER 16

1. Alex Taylor, III, "How I Flunked Retirement," *Fortune*, June 24, 1996, p. 61.
2. David W. Merrill and Roger H. Reid, *Personal Styles and Effective Performance* (Radnor, PA: Chilton Book, 1981), p. 1.
3. The four principles discussed are drawn from Ron Zemke, "From Factor Analysis and Clinical Psychology: Better Ways to Help Train People," *Training*, August 1976, p. 12.
4. Robert M. Hecht, *Office Systems*, February 1990, p. 26.
5. Tony Alessandra and Michael J.

O'Connor, *People Smart* (LaJolla, CA: Keynote Publishing, 1990), p. 10.

6. The dominance factor was described in an early book by William M. Marston, *The Emotions of Normal People* (New York: Harcourt, 1928). Research conducted by Rolfe LaForge and Robert F. Suczek resulted in the development of the Interpersonal Checklist (ICL) that features a dominant-submissive scale. A person who receives a high score on the ICL tends to lead, persuade, and control others. The Interpersonal Identity Profile, developed by David W. Merrill and James W. Taylor, features a factor called "assertiveness." Persons classified as being high in assertiveness tend to have strong opinions, make quick decisions, and be directive when dealing with people. Persons classified as being low in assertiveness tend to voice moderate opinions, make thoughtful decisions, and be supportive when dealing with others.

7. David W. Johnson, *Reaching Out—Interpersonal Effectiveness and Self-Actualization*, 2nd ed. (Englewood Cliffs, NJ: Prentice-Hall, 1981), p. 44.

8. The research conducted by LaForge and Suczek resulted in identification of the hostile/loving continuum, which is similar to the sociability continuum. Their Interpersonal Checklist features this scale. L. L. Thurstone and T. G. Thurstone developed the Thurstone Temperament Schedule, which provides an assessment of a "sociable" factor. Persons with high scores in this area enjoy the company of others and make friends easily. The Interpersonal Identity Profile developed by Merrill and Taylor contains an objectivity continuum. A person with low objectivity is seen as attention seeking, involved with the feelings of others, informal, and casual in social relationships. A person who is high in objectivity appears to be somewhat indifferent toward the feelings of others. This person is formal in social relationships.

9. Charles Margerison, *How to Assess Your Managerial Style* (New York: AMACOM, A Division of American Management Association, 1979), p. 49.

10. Pierce J. Howard and Jane M. Howard, "Buddy, Can You Paradigm?" *Training & Development*, September 1995, p. 31.

11. Len D'innocenzo and Jack Cullen, "Chameleon Management," *Personal Selling Power*, January–February 1995, p. 61.

12. Rod Nichols, "How to Sell to Different Personality Types," *Personal Selling Power*, November–December 1992, p. 46.

13. Stuart Atkins, *How to Get the Most from Styles-Based Training* (Beverly Hills, CA: Stuart Atkins, 1996), p. 1.

14. William J. Stanton, *Fundamentals of Marketing* (New York: McGraw-Hill, 1984), p. 449.

15. John Emery, "Mastering Vital Steps," *Business Outlook*, November 3, 1986, p. 14.

16. Tony Alessandra and Michael J. O'Connor, *People Smart* (LaJolla, CA: Keynote Publishing, 1990), p. 15.

17. Stuart Atkins, *How to Get the Most from Styles-Based Training* (Beverly Hills, CA: Stuart Atkins, 1996), p. 3.

18. Robert Bolton and Dorothy Grover Bolton, *Social Style/Management Style* (New York: American Management Association, 1984), p. 54.

19. David W. Merrill and Roger H. Reid, *Personal Styles and Effective Performance* (Radnor, PA: Chilton Book, 1981), pp. 134, 135.

20. Stuart Atkins, *The Name of the Game* (Beverly Hills, CA: Ellis & Stewart, 1981), p. 51.

21. Chris Lee, "What's Your Style," *Training*, May 1991, p. 28.

SOURCES FOR BOXED FEATURES

a. Paul Mok and Dudley Lynch, "Easy New Way to Get Your Way," *Readers Digest*, November 1982, p. 73.

b. Stuart Atkins, *LIFO Personality Digest* (Beverly Hills, CA: Stuart Atkins, 1991), p. 126; *High Performance Selling* (Beverly Hills, CA: Stuart Atkins), pp. 1–10.

c. Roger Wenschlag, *The Versatile Sales-*

person (New York: John Wiley & Sons, 1989), pp. 165–171. Perry Pascarella, "To Motivate Others Try Versatility," *Industry Week*, May 1982. Rod Nichols, "How to Sell to Different Personality Types," *Personal Selling Power*, November–December 1992, pp. 46–47. David M. Merrill and Roger Reid, *Personal Styles and Effective Performance* (Radnor, PA: Chilton Book Company, 1981), p. 2; Tony Alessandra, *People Smarts* (San Diego, CA: (Pfeiffer & Company 1994), p. 55.

C H A P T E R   1 7

1. William Keenan, Jr., "These 10 Managers Show They Have What It Takes to Lead and Succeed," *Sales & Marketing Management*, August 1995, pp. 38, 39.
2. Phillip Gelman, "The Good Sales Manager," *Personal Selling Power*, January–February, 1993, p. 56.
3. Sally J. Silberman, "Troubling Transitions," *Sales & Marketing Management*, February 1996, pp. 20, 21.
4. Alan J. Dubinsky, Francis J. Yammarino, Marvin A. Jolson, and William D. Spangler, "Transformational Leadership: An Initial Investigation in Sales Management," *Journal of Personal Selling & Sales Management*, Spring 1995, pp. 17–29.
5. These dimensions are described in Edwin A. Fleischman, *Manual for Leadership Opinion Questionnaire* (Chicago: Science Research Associates, 1960), p. 3.
6. Phillip Gelman, "The Good Sales Manager," *Personal Selling Power*, January–February, 1993, p. 56.
7. Jack Falvey, "The Absolute Basics of Sales Force Management," *Sales & Marketing Management*, August 1990, p. 8.
8. Ken Blanchard, "3 Secrets of the One Minute Manager," *Personal Selling Power*, March 1993, p. 48.
9. Barry J. Farber, "On the Lookout," *Sales & Marketing Management*, October 1995, pp. 34, 35.
10. Richard J. Mirabile, "The Power of Job Analysis," *Training*, April 1990, p. 70.
11. Paul Tulenko, "The Key Role of Selling," *San Jose Mercury News*, August 23, 1992, PC-1.
12. William Keenan, Jr., "Who Has the Right Stuff?" *Sales & Marketing Management*, August 1993, p. 28.
13. Ibid., p. 28.
14. Gerhard Gschwandtner, "A Jewel of a Company," *Personal Selling Power*, March 1995, p. 17.
15. "Professionally Speaking," *Sales and Marketing Management*, February 1996, p. 27.
16. Alan J. Dubinsky, Francis J. Yammarino, Marvin A. Jolson, and William D. Spangler, "Transformational Leadership: An Initial Investigation in Sales Management," *Journal of Personal Selling & Sales Management*, Spring 1995, p. 27.
17. Jack Falvey, "The Care and Feeding of New Salespeople," *Sales & Marketing Management*, February 1990, p. 22.
18. Barry L. Reece and Rhonda Brandt, *Effective Human Relations in Organizations*, 6th ed. (Boston: Houghton Mifflin, 1996), p. 153.
19. Ibid., p. 153.
20. Alfie Kohn, "Why Incentive Plans Cannot Work," *Harvard Business Review*, September–October 1993, pp. 58, 59.
21. "Selling with Sales Contest," *Sales & Marketing Management*, June 1995, p. 35.
22. Stewart A. Washburn, "Fire up Your Sales Force," *Business Marketing*, July 1990, p. 52.
23. "Labor Letter," *Wall Street Journal*, March 29, 1994, p. 1.
24. Ibid.
25. Dawn R. Deeter-Schmelz and Rosemary Ramsey, "A Conceptualization of the Functions and Roles of Formalized Selling and Buying Teams," *Journal of Personal Selling & Sales Management*, Spring 1995, p. 58.
26. William Keenan Jr., "Sales Compensation 1996–1997." Supplement to *Selling*, February 1997.
27. "Point Incentive Sales Programs," *SBR Update*, Vol. I, No. 4.

28. Roger Ricklefs, "Enterprise," *Wall Street Journal*, March 6, 1990, p. B-1.
29. Donald W. Jackson, Jr., John L. Schlacter, and William G. Wolfe, "Examining the Bases Utilized for Evaluating Salespeople's Performance," *Journal of Personal Selling & Sales Management*, February 1995, p. 57.
30. Lisa Holton, "Look Who's in on Your Performance Review," *Selling*, January–February 1995, pp. 47–55; Barry L. Reece and Rhonda Brandt, *Effective Human Relations in Organizations* (Boston: Houghton Mifflin, 1996), p. 204; "Customer Ratings Are Misleading," *Selling*, November 1996, p. 1.

SOURCES FOR BOXED FEATURES

a. James G. Carr, "Attractive or Effective," *Pace*, September 1988, p. 24.
b. Wendy Bounds, "Tenacity Sells High Fashion to Pittsburgh," *Wall Street Journal*, December 23, 1993, p. B-1.
c. Kerry Rottenberger-Murtha, "How to Play above the Rim," *Sales & Marketing Management*, September 1993, pp. 28, 29.

GLOSSARY

A

active listening The process of sending back to the person what you as a listener think the individual meant, both in terms of content and in terms of feelings. It involves taking into consideration both verbal and nonverbal signals. **[227]**

approach The first contact with the prospect, either face-to-face or by telephone. The approach has three objectives: to build rapport with the prospect, to capture the person's full attention, and to generate interest in the product you are selling. **[194]**

assumption close After the salesperson identifies a genuine need, presents solutions in terms of buyer benefits, conducts an effective sales demonstration, and negotiates buyer resistance satisfactorily, the assumption that the prospect has already bought the product. The closing activity is based on the assumption that a buying decision has already been made. **[304]**

aversive factor A mannerism, gesture, style of dress, or breach of etiquette that is offensive to the customer. **[205]**

B

body language A form of nonverbal communication that has been defined as "messages without words" and "silent messages." **[57]**

bridge statement A translational phrase that connects a statement of features with a statement of benefits. This method permits customers to connect the features of your product to the benefits they will receive. **[110]**

buyer action theory The five mental steps—attention, interest, desire, conviction, and action—that lead to a buying decision. This is a widely accepted theory in selling, advertising, and display that explains how customers buy. **[156]**

buyer resolution theory A selling theory that recognizes a purchase will be made only after the prospect has made five buying decisions involving specific affirmative responses to the following items: need, product, source, price, and time. **[156]**

buying conditions Those circumstances that must be available or fulfilled before the sale can be closed. **[226]**

buying motives An aroused need, drive, or desire that initiates the sequence of events that may lead to a purchase. **[150]**

C

call reluctance The fear of making contact with the customer. **[211]**

caveat emptor A philosophy that states, "Let the buyer beware." The buyer is expected to examine the product and presentation carefully. Once the transaction is concluded, the business relationship ends for all practical purposes. **[75]**

character Your personal standards of behavior, including your honesty and integrity. Your character is based on your internal values and the resulting judgments you make about what is right and what is wrong. **[56]**

closing clue An indication, either verbal or nonverbal, that the prospect is preparing to make a buying decision. **[299]**

499

cold calling A method of prospecting in which the salesperson selects a group of people who may or may not be actual prospects and then calls on each one. [176]

communication-style bias A state of mind we often experience when we have contact with another person whose communication style is different from our own. [363]

compensation plans Pay plans for salespeople that combine direct monetary pay and indirect monetary payments such as paid vacations, pensions, and insurance plans. [397]

confirmation questions A type of question used throughout the sales presentation to find out if the message is getting through to the prospect. It checks both the prospect's level of understanding and the prospect's agreement with the presentation's claims. [225]

confirmation step Reassuring the customer after the sale has been closed, pointing out that he has made the correct decision. This may involve describing the satisfaction of owning the product. [307]

consideration Sales managers displaying consideration are more likely to have relationships with salespeople that are characterized by mutual trust, respect for the salesperson's ideas, and consideration for their feelings. [390]

consultative-style selling An approach to personal selling that is an extension of the marketing concept. Emphasis is placed on need identification, need satisfaction, and the building of a relationship that results in repeat business. [9]

culture The arts, beliefs, institutions, transmitted behavior patterns, and thoughts of a community or population. [147]

customer service All those activities enhancing or facilitating the sale and use of a product or service, including suggestion selling, delivery and installation, assistance with warranty or service contract, securing credit arrangements, and making postsale courtesy calls. [319]

customer strategy A carefully conceived plan that will result in maximum customer responsiveness. [15]

D

demonstration A sales and marketing technique that adds sensory appeal to the product. It attracts the customer's attention, stimulates interest, and creates desire. [248]

detail salesperson A salesperson representing a manufacturer, whose primary goal is to develop goodwill and stimulate demand for a product or product line. This person usually assists the customer by improving the customer's ability to sell the product. [36]

direct appeal close Involves simply asking for the order in a straightforward manner. It is the most direct closing approach. [306]

direct denial Involves refuting prospect's opinion or belief. The direct denial of a problem is considered a high-risk method of negotiating buyer resistance. [283]

Director style A communication style that displays the following characteristics: appears to be businesslike, displays a serious attitude, and voices strong opinions. [370]

dominance Reflects the tendency to influence or exert one's will over others in a relationship. Each of us falls somewhere on this continuum. [366]

double win The view that "if I help you win, I win too." [55]

E

emotional buying motives Those motives that prompt the prospect to act as a result of an appeal to some sentiment or passion. [150]

Emotive style A communication style that displays the following characteristics: appears to be quite active, takes the social initiative in most cases, likes to encourage informality, and expresses emotional opinions. [369]

entry-level sales representative Anyone who is learning about the company's products, services, and policies, as well as proven sales techniques, in preparation for a sales assignment. **[39]**

esteem needs The desire to feel worthy in the eyes of others, to develop a sense of personal worth and adequacy or a feeling of competence and importance. **[145]**

ethics Rules of conduct used to determine what is good or bad. They are moral principles or values concerned with what ought to be done—a person's adherence to honesty and fairness. **[73]**

expected product Everything that represents the customer's minimal expectations. **[130]**

external motivation Action (taken by another person) that involves rewards or other forms of reinforcement that cause the worker to behave in ways to ensure receipt of the reward. **[395]**

F

feedback Relevant information that helps the salesperson understand the prospect's thoughts and perceptions. Questions can be used to obtain feedback. **[230]**

field salesperson A salesperson employed by a manufacturer who handles well-established products that require a minimum of creative selling. The position usually does not require a high degree of technical knowledge. **[36]**

G

generic product Describes only the basic substantive product being sold. **[130]**

I

indirect denial Often used when the prospect's concern is completely valid, or at least accurate to a large degree. The salesperson bends a little and acknowledges that the prospect is at least partially correct. **[283]**

information-gathering questions Questions used to collect certain basic information from the prospect. These questions help the salesperson to acquire facts about the prospect that may reveal the person's need for the product or service. **[222]**

informative presentation Emphasizes factual information that is often taken from technical reports, company-prepared sales literature, or written testimonials from people who have used the product. **[232]**

inside salesperson A salesperson employed by a wholesaler who solicits orders over the telephone. In addition to extensive product knowledge, the inside salesperson must be skilled in customer relations, merchandising, and suggestion selling. **[35]**

intermediate sales representative A salesperson who has broad knowledge of the company's products and services and sells in a specifically assigned territory. She maintains contact with established customers and develops new prospects. **[29]**

internal motivation An intrinsic reward that occurs when a duty or task is performed. **[395]**

interpersonal intelligence The ability to discern and respond appropriately to the moods, motivations, temperaments, and desires of other people. **[49]**

interpersonal value Win-win relationship building with the customer that results from keeping that person's best interest always at the forefront. **[131]**

L

limited choice close The salesperson giving the prospect the opportunity to examine several different items and trying to assess the degree of interest in each one. **[305]**

M

marketing concept A belief that the business firm should dedicate all its policies, planning, and operation to the satisfaction of the customer; a belief that the final result of all business activity should be to earn a profit by satisfying the customer. **[5]**

marketing mix The combination of elements (product, promotion, place, and price) that creates continuing customer satisfaction for a business. **[8]**

multicall sales presentations A standard practice in some industries where products are complex and buying decisions are made by more than one person. The purpose of the first call is to collect and analyze certain basic information that is used to develop a specific proposal. **[196]**

N

need discovery The salesperson establishing two-way communication by asking appropriate questions and listening carefully to the customer's responses. **[220]**

need-satisfaction theory A selling theory that positions the salesperson as a consultant whose objective is to solve buying problems for customers. This theory is consistent with the marketing concept of discovering customer needs and then providing satisfaction, while at the same time making a profit. **[156]**

negotiation Working to reach an agreement that is mutually satisfactory to both buyer and seller. **[270]**

networking Networking is the practice of making and using contacts. It involves people meeting people and profiting from the connection. **[176]**

O

organizational culture A collection of beliefs, behaviors, and work patterns held in common by people employed by a specific firm. **[100]**

outside salesperson A salesperson, employed by a wholesaler, who must have knowledge of many products and be able to serve as a consultant to the customer on product or service applications. This position usually requires an in-depth understanding of the customer's operation. **[36]**

P

partnering A strategically developed, high-quality relationship that focuses on solving the customer's buying problem. **[51]**

patronage buying motives A motive that causes the prospect to buy a product from one particular company rather than another. Typical patronage buying motives include superior service, attractive decor, product selection, and competence of the salesperson. **[153]**

perception A process whereby we receive stimuli (information) through our five senses and then assign meaning to them. **[149]**

personal selling Involves person-to-person communication with a prospect. It is a process of developing relationships; discovering customer needs; matching appropriate products with these needs; and communicating benefits through informing, reminding, or persuading. **[4]**

personal selling philosophy Involves three things: full acceptance of the marketing concept, developing an appreciation for the expanding role of personal selling in our competitive national and international markets, and assuming the role of problem solver or partner in helping customers to make complex buying decisions. **[4]**

persuasion The act of presenting product appeals so as to influence the prospect's beliefs, attitudes, or behavior. **[199]**

persuasive presentation A sales strategy that influences the prospect's beliefs, attitudes, or behavior; and encourages buyer action. **[233]**

physiological needs Primary needs or physical needs, including the need for food, water, sleep, clothing, and shelter. **[143]**

portfolio A portable case or loose-leaf binder containing a wide variety of sales-supporting materials. It is used to add visual life to the sales message and to prove claims. **[258]**

potential product Refers to what may remain to be done, that is, what is possible. **[131]**

preapproach Activities that precede the actual sales call and set the stage for a personalized sales approach, tailored to the specific needs of the prospect. This involves the planning necessary for the actual meeting with a prospect. **[194]**

presentation strategy A well-conceived plan that includes three prescriptions: establishing objectives for the sales presentation; preparing the presale presentation plan needed to meet these objectives; and renewing one's commitment to providing outstanding customer service. **[16]**

probing questions Help the salesperson to uncover the prospect's perceptions or opinions. **[223]**

product One of the four P's of the marketing mix. The term product should be broadly interpreted to encompass services, ideas, and issues. **[4]**

product benefit A feature that provides the customer with personal advantage or gain. This usually answers the question, "How will the customer benefit from owning or using the product?" **[109]**

product buying motives Reasons that cause the prospect to buy one particular product brand or label over another. Typical product buying motives include brand preference, quality preference, price preference, and design or engineering preference. **[155]**

product configuration If the customer has complex buying needs, then the salesperson may have to bring together many different parts of the company's product mix in order to develop a custom-fitted solution. The product selection process is often referred to as product configuration. **[97]**

product development Testing, modifying, and retesting an idea for a product several times before offering it to the customer. **[95]**

product feature Anything that a customer can feel, see, taste, smell, or measure to answer the question, "What is it?" Features include technical facts about such aspects as craftsmanship, durability, design, and economy of operation. **[109]**

product life cycle Stages of a product from the time it is first introduced to the market until it is taken off the market, including the stages of introduction, growth, maturity, and decline. **[122]**

product positioning Refers to decisions, activities, and communication strategies that are directed toward trying to create and maintain a firm's intended product concept in the customer's mind. **[122]**

product strategy A well-conceived plan that emphasizes acquiring extensive product knowledge, learning to select and communicate appropriate product benefits that will appeal to the customer, and positioning the product. **[13]**

promotional allowance A price reduction given to a customer who participates in an advertising or sales support program. **[126]**

prospect Someone who has three basic qualifications. First, the person must have a need for the product or service. Second, the individual must be able to afford the purchase. Third, the person must be authorized to purchase the product. **[167]**

prospect base A list of current customers and potential customers. **[167]**

prospecting A systematic process of identifying potential customers. **[167]**

psychic income Consists of factors that provide psychological rewards; helps to satisfy these needs and motivates us to achieve higher levels of performance. **[30]**

Q

qualifying Examining the prospect list to identify the people who are most apt to buy a product. **[179]**

quality control The evaluation or testing of products against established standards. This has important sales appeal when used by the salesperson to convince a prospect of a product's quality. **[97]**

quantifying the solution The process of determining if a sales proposal adds value. Quantifying the solution is especially important in situations where the purchase represents a major buying decision. **[97]**

quantity discount A price reduction made to encourage a larger volume purchase than would otherwise be expected. **[126]**

R

rational buying motives Prompt the prospect to act because of an appeal to the prospect's reason or better judgment; include profit potential, quality, and availability of technical assistance. Generally these result from an objective review of available information. **[151]**

reciprocity A mutual exchange of benefits, as when a firm buys products from its own customers. **[80]**

reference group Two or more people who have well-established interpersonal communications and tend to influence the values, attitudes, and buying behaviors of one another. They act as a point of comparison and a source of information for a prospective buyer. **[147]**

referral A prospect who has been recommended by a current customer or by someone who is familiar with the product. **[171]**

Reflective style A communication style that displays the following characteristics: controls emotional expression, displays a preference for orderliness, tends to express measured opinions, and seems difficult to get to know. **[373]**

relationship selling Salespeople who have adopted relationship selling working hard to build and nourish long-term partnerships. They rely on a personal, customized approach to each customer. **[17]**

reminder presentation Sometimes called the reinforcement presentation. This assumes that the prospect has already been involved in an informative or persuasive presentation. The customer understands at least the basic product features and buyer benefits. **[234]**

retail salesperson Salesperson who is employed at the retail level to help prospects solve buying problems. This person is usually involved in selling higher priced, technical, and specialty retail products. **[35]**

role A set of characteristics and expected social behaviors based on the expectations of others. All the roles we assume may influence our buying behavior. **[146]**

routing The procedure used to determine which customers and prospects will be visited during a certain period of time. **[184]**

S

safety and security needs Needs that represent our desire to be free from danger. **[143]**

sales automation A term used to describe those technologies used to improve communications in a sales organization and improve customer responsiveness. These activities are used to improve the productivity of the sales force and the sales support personnel. **[20]**

sales call plan A plan developed with information taken from the routing and scheduling plan. The primary purpose of the plan is to ensure efficient and effective account coverage. **[350]**

sales engineer A person who must have detailed and precise technical knowledge and the ability to discuss the technical aspects of his products. He sometimes introduces new products that represent a breakthrough in technology. **[36]**

sales forecast Outlines expected sales for a specific product or service to a specific target group over a specific period of time. **[184]**

sales manager The person who is responsible for hiring, training, and directing sales personnel. **[82]**

satisfactions The positive benefits that customers seek when making a purchase. Satisfactions arise from the product itself, from the company that makes or distributes the product, and from the salesperson who sells and services the product. **[119]**

security needs These needs represent our desire to be free from danger and uncertainty. **[143]**

self-actualization The need for self-fulfillment; a full tapping of one's potential to meet a goal; the need to be everything one is capable of being. This is one of the needs in Maslow's hierarchy. **[145]**

self-image A set of ideas, attitudes, and feelings you have about yourself that influences the way you relate to others. **[53]**

self-talk An effort to override past negative mental programming by erasing or replacing it with conscious, positive new directions. It is one way to get rid of barriers to goal achievement. **[67]**

senior sales representative A salesperson at the highest nonsupervisory level of selling responsibility. She is completely familiar with the company's products, services, and policies; usually has years of experience; and is assigned to major accounts and territories. **[29]**

showmanship An interesting and attractive way of communicating an idea to others. Showmanship is especially important if the primary purpose of your presentation is to persuade. **[257]**

six-step presentation plan Preparation involving consideration of those activities that will take place during the sales presentation. **[200]**

sociability Reflects the amount of control one exerts over emotional expressiveness. People who are high in sociability tend to express their feelings freely, while people who are low on this continuum tend to control their feelings. **[366]**

social class A group of people who are similar in income, wealth, educational background, and occupational prestige. **[147]**

social influence Buyer behaviors influenced by the people around us. These are the forces that other people exert on buying behavior. **[146]**

social needs Needs that reflect a person's desire for affection, identification with a group, and approval from others. **[144]**

special concession close Offers the buyer something extra for acting immediately. **[304]**

stall Resistance related to time. A stall usually means the customer does not yet perceive the benefits of buying now. **[279]**

strategic market plan Takes into consideration all the major functional areas of the business that must be coordinated, such as production, promotion, finance, and personnel. **[11]**

stress The response of the body or mind to demands on it, in the form of either physiological or psychological strain. **[354]**

structure Sales managers clearly defining their own duties and those of the sales staff. They assume an active role in directing their subordinates. **[388]**

style flexing The deliberate attempt to adjust one's communication style to accommodate the needs of the other person. **[380]**

subculture Within many cultures the groups whose members share ideals and beliefs that differ from those held by the wider society of which they are a part. **[149]**

suggestion selling The process of suggesting merchandise or services that are related to the main item being sold to the customer. This is an important form of customer service. **[323]**

summary-confirmation questions Questions used to clarify and confirm buying conditions. **[226]**

summary-of-benefits close Involves summarizing the most important buyer benefits, reemphasizing the benefits that will help bring about a favorable decision. **[302]**

superior benefit A benefit that will, in most cases, outweigh the customer's specific concern. **[285]**

Supportive style A communication style that displays the following characteristics: appears quiet and reserved, listens attentively to other people, tends to avoid the use of power, and makes decisions in a thoughtful and deliberate manner. **[374]**

surface language A pattern of immediate impressions conveyed by appearance—clothing, hairstyle, etc. **[61]**

T

target marketing Involves prescreening all prospective buyers in a given community or territory on the basis of a variety of factors that indicate their willingness or ability to buy selected products. **[178]**

technostress This term is used to describe a disease caused by an inability to cope with various technologies in a healthy manner. **[355]**

telesales The process of using the telephone to acquire information about the customer, determine needs, suggest solutions, negotiate buyer resistance, close the sale, and service the sale. **[203]**

territory The geographic area where prospects and customers reside. **[348]**

time-period pricing Adjusting up or down during specific times to spur or acknowledge changes in demand. **[126]**

trial close A closing attempt made at an opportune time during the sales presentation to encourage the customer to reveal readiness or unwillingness to buy. **[302]**

trial offer Involves giving the prospect an opportunity to try the product without making a purchase commitment. **[286]**

U

unconscious expectations Certain views concerning appropriate dress. **[61]**

V

value-added concept Adding value to a product with a cluster of intangibles such as better trained salespeople, increased levels of courtesy, dependable product deliveries, better service after the sale, and innovations that truly improve the product's value in the customer's eyes. **[128]**

value-added product Product that exists when salespeople offer the customer more than they expect. **[130]**

W

wardrobe engineering Combining the elements of psychology, fashion, sociology, and art into clothing selection. **[61]**

Web site A collection of Web pages maintained by a single person or organization. It is accessible to anyone with a computer and a modem. **[175]**

written proposals A specific plan of action based on the facts, assumptions, and supporting documentation included in the sales presentation. Written proposals vary in terms of format and content. **[134]**

CREDITS

PHOTO CREDITS:

pp. 0-1: Jose Pelaez/The Stock Market. **p. 4:** Courtesy of Jaguar Corporation. **p. 6:** Blair Seitz/Photo Researchers, Inc. **p. 8:** Trozzo Photography. **p. 10:** Sepp Seitz/Woodfin Camp & Associates. **p. 12:** John Coletti/Allyn & Bacon. **p. 18:** John Coletti/Allyn & Bacon. **p. 29:** Bill Anderson/Monkmeyer. **p. 31:** SuperStock, Inc. **p. 32:** Page Chichester. **p. 33:** John Curtis/Offshoot. **p. 37:** Frank Siteman/Omni-Photo Communications, Inc. **p. 38:** Frank Siteman/Tony Stone Images. **pp. 46-47:** Romilly Lockyer/The Image Bank. **p. 49:** John Coletti/Allyn & Bacon. **p. 56:** Romilly Lockyer/The Image Bank. **p. 57:** SuperStock, Inc. **p. 59:** Courtesy of Telegraph Colour Library/FPG International. **p. 62:** John Coletti/Allyn & Bacon. **p. 66:** Michal Heron/Monkmeyer. **p. 79:** John Coletti/Allyn & Bacon. **p. 81:** Steve Gottlieb/FPG International. **p. 85:** Spencer Grant/Monkmeyer Press. **pp. 90-91:** Sam Sargent/Gamma-Liaison, Inc. **p. 94:** Jose L. Pelaez/The Stock Market. **p. 102:** Bill Bachman/Image Works. **p. 103:** Courtesy of Xerox. **105:** Tony Freeman/PhotoEdit. **p. 107:** Michael Rosenfield/Tony Stone Images. **p. 119:** Courtesy of Walden Paddlers, Inc. **p. 121:** Courtesy of The New England Company. **p. 124:** Courtesy of RYKO Manufacturing Co. **p. 127:** Courtesy of Mercedes-Benz of North America, Inc. **p. 128:** David Pollack/The Stock Market. **p. 130:** Bob Daemmrich/Stock, Boston. **pp. 138-139:** SuperStock, Inc. **p. 142:** Mike Kagen/Monkmeyer Press. **p. 148:** Copyright 1997 Goldmine Software Corporation. **p. 152:** Michal Heron/Monkmeyer Press. **p. 155:** James Pickerell/The Image Works. **p. 158:** John Coletti/Stock, Boston. **p. 175:** John Coletti/Allyn & Bacon. **p. 184:** John Coletti/Allyn & Bacon. **pp. 190-191:** Jeff Greenberg/Unicorn Stock Photos. **p. 197:** David Joel/Tony Stone Images. **p. 198:** John Coletti/Allyn & Bacon. **p. 202:** SuperStock, Inc. **p. 204:** Mike Malyszko/FPG International. **p. 207:** John Coletti/Allyn & Bacon. **p. 220:** Jose Pelaez/The Stock Market. **p. 224:** Jeffrey Shaw. **p. 228:** John Coletti/Allyn & Bacon. **p. 231:** Institutional Distribution Magazine. **p. 238:** Index Stock Photography, Inc. **p. 250:** Richard Pasley/Stock, Boston. **p. 255:** John Coletti/Allyn & Bacon. **p. 256:** Uniphoto Picture Agency. **p. 259:** Jeff Greenberg/Unicorn Stock Photos. **p. 261:** John Coletti/Allyn & Bacon. **p. 270:** Vincent Serbin/DeWys, Inc. **p. 278:** Courtesy Acclivus Corporation. **p. 280:** John Coletti/Allyn & Bacon. **p. 285:** Sam Sargent/Gamma-Liaison, Inc. **p. 294:** John Coletti/Allyn & Bacon. **p. 303:** John Coletti/Allyn & Bacon. **p. 308:** John Coletti/Allyn & Bacon. **p. 320:** Courtesy Schering Plough. **p. 322:** SuperStock, Inc. **p. 327:** SuperStock, Inc. **pp. 338-339:** Courtesy of Index Stock Photography, Inc. **p. 343:** Willie Hill, Jr./Image Works. **p. 347:** Michael Paras/Photographic Resources. **p. 348:** Jose L. Pelaez/The Stock Market. **p. 349:** Stephen Agricola/Stock, Boston. **p. 352:** Dana White/PhotoEdit. **p. 356:** SuperStock, Inc. **p. 364:** Jeff Greenberg/Peter Arnold, Inc. **p. 370:** Ira Wyman/Sygma. **p. 372:** Steven Starr/Stock, Boston. **p. 373:** Courtesy of The White House Photo Office. **p. 376:** Timothy A. Murphy/The Image Bank. **p. 379:** John Coletti/Allyn & Bacon. **p. 388:** Charles Gupton/Stock, Boston. **p. 389:** Michael Newman/PhotoEdit. **p. 391:** Jonathan Nourak/PhotoEdit. **p. 394:** John Coletti/Allyn & Bacon. **p. 397:** Jose L. Pelaez/The Stock Market. **p. 430:** Park Inn International. **p. 435:** Park Inn International. **p. 441:** Beth Manning. **p. 443:** Park Inn International. **p. 445:** Park Inn International. **p. 447:** Park Inn International.

NAME INDEX

NOTE: Boldface pages locate figures; italicized pages locate tables.

SUBJECT INDEX

NOTE: Boldface pages locate figures; italicized pages locate tables.